HABERDASHERS' ASKE'S
GIRLS

19.99

Frontispiece: Domenico Veneziano, *The Annunciation* (c. 1445)

God and the Universe

God and the Universe

Arthur Gibson

London and New York

First published 2000
by Routledge
11 New Fetter Lane, London EC4P 4EE

Simultaneously published in the USA and Canada
by Routledge
29 West 35th Street, New York, NY 10001

Routledge is an imprint of the Taylor & Francis Group

© 2000 Arthur Gibson

Typeset in Times by Taylor & Francis Books Ltd
Printed and bound in Great Britain by Biddles Ltd,
Guildford and King's Lynn

All rights reserved. No part of this book may be reprinted or
reproduced or utilised in any form or by any electronic,
mechanical, or other means, now known or hereafter
invented, including photocopying and recording, or in any
information storage or retrieval system, without permission in
writing from the publishers.

British Library Cataloguing in Publication Data
A catalogue record for this book is available from the British Library

Library of Congress Cataloging in Publication Data
A catalog record has been requested for this title

ISBN 0–415–23666–5

For Niamh O'Mahony

Contents

List of illustrations   xiii
Preface   xv
Acknowledgements   xix

PART I
Renaissance in language   1

Prologue   3
Poststructuralism and a renaissance future? 3
Simplicity, cosmology and Ockham's razor? 25
Ending poststructuralism? 30
Counter-intuitive Renaissance 38
Metaphoric cosmology 39
The scope of relevance? 42

1 The freedom to question   47
Calculated madness 47
The realism of metaphor 52
Past reality 54
Live metaphor 56
Eschatology and values 57

2 The expression of God in language   60
Imitation and meaning 60
God manifestation 65
Simulating subjects 68
Reproduction logic 70
Indeterminate theology 73
Theological names 75
The variable value of believing 79

x   Contents

Astronomical beliefs and intentions 82
Live metaphoric 'revelation'? 87

PART II
All in God's space–time?   95

3 Extending scientific languages   97
Being scientific? 97
Magnetic poles and monopoles 100
Monopoles in cosmology 103
Scientific dimensions of live-metaphor 107
Space–time 110
Counter-intuition 114
Strings of dimensions 117
Schizoid live-metaphor? 120
Cosmic strings 124
What is metal? 132
The double mirror 141
The cosmological constant 146
Counter-intuitive creativity 151

4 The beginning of the matter   164
Points about manifolds 164
Language about beginning 173
Observation and infinity 176
Observation and generality 180
Noting superstrings 185
Uniformity and matter 186
Supermassive black hole realism 190
Causal originality 195
Causality and indeterminacy 197

PART III
The cosmology of life   209

5 The beginning of life   211
Biology and entropy 211
The cosmology of devolution 214
Cancer and evolution 216

Contents xi

6 Prediction and the cosmology of God 223
Live metaphors of transcendence 223
Prediction 227
Social prediction 233
Virtual reality and foreknowledge 242
Logical prediction 255
History and imagining futures 258
Unique individualism 259
Knowledge of the future 264

PART IV
Cosmological ethics 269

7 God and ethical cosmology 271
Counter-intuitive speculation 271
Physical and ethical universes 273
The matter of narrative 276
Transforming the familiar 280
The empire of justice 285
Contradictory violence 291

8 The practice of legal cosmology 294
The experiment of legal cosmology 294
Contrary laws 295
→ *The economic end 299*
→ *The world of violence 301*
→ *Killing logic 305*

9 Eschatological cosmology 310
Allegorical apocalypse? 310
Catastrophe mathematics 313
Transforming the universe's end 315
The material universe as allegory 318

10 Creating conclusive beginnings 322

Notes 327
Bibliography 336
Name index 363
Subject index 369

Illustrations

Cover   N81 in the smaller Magellanic cloud

Plates

Frontispiece   Domenico Veneziano, *The Annunciation* (*c.* 1445)
1   Domenico Veneziano, *The Annunciation* (*c.* 1445)
2   Jean Corbechon, *Des Proprietez des Choses* (*c.* 1415)
3   Tibor Csernus, *Untitled* (1987)
4   Sample of the new generation cosmology from the Boomerang project

Figures

0.1	Hawking and Turok (1998) start the universe	6
0.2	Jodrell Bank neutron star pulses of PSR 1958	41
2.1	A fifth century BC Greek vase	67
2.2	Superliminal candidate quasar 3C263	85
3.1	A universal monopole	102
3.2	Quasars 1146+111 B and C	121
3.3	Spectra of double quasars	122
3.4	Problem chart for a cosmic string	131
3.5	1,500 atom metal image	133
3.6	A six-bond carbon	139
3.7	The sculpture 'Untitled' (1974) by Ruth Asawa	143
3.8	A Hawking key for starting the universe	147
3.9	A Wagner key for ending the universe	159
4.1	Hawking's transcendental astronaut	178
4.2	An overview of the primeval sky by Boomerang	188
4.3	Everett–Penrose branching worlds model of a universe	198
4.4	Penrose's options for Everett's universe	199
4.5	Close-up shot of the universe	207
6.1	History after the big bang à la Boomerang	252
9.1	Volcanic eruption on an Ionian moon	320

Preface

This book is written by a philosopher who also has a history of research in other subjects that began in, led to, or is motivated by, philosophy. John Milbank has been a significant bastion of encouragement and insight; Frank Madsen and Lyn Chase provided considerable support, as have many other friends. At Cambridge Bill Saslaw first introduced me to radio astronomy, later guiding my research, and enabling me to study and discuss his then forthcoming book, Saslaw (1985). Early on Fred Hoyle encouraged me, and Sir Bernard Lovell welcomed me for a three-year period to Jodrell Bank, to gain some experience in observational research issues. There he, Rod Davies and Andrew Lyne were helpful and encouraging. Since 1980 many Cambridge cosmologists, astronomers and their departments, with whom I have had periodic contact, have readily given assistance and offered facilities, especially Sir Martin Rees, and others at the Cambridge Astronomy Institute. Stephen Hawking, via his seminars, as well as individual staff over some years at DAMTP at Cambridge University, have been variously supportive, and discussion with John Polkinghorne was instructive. Peter Edwards educated me on what it is to be a metal. It was helpful to reflect on the evolution of consciousness with Sir Andrew Huxley, and mentality with Sir Martin Roth. Vivian Wyatt and later Gabby Dover guided me into some study and research on evolutionary genetics, debated with me, and the latter recommended that I send my analysis to *Nature*; I did the revision as the editor suggested, but prefer the piece to appear here in its present form (Chapter 5).

At Routledge I very much appreciate Roger Thorp's scholarly understanding, care and advice. I am grateful for discussion about music with Christopher Hogwood, John Deathridge, Sylvina Milstein, Xi-Lin Wang and Jonathan Miller; in helpful exchanges Edward Said bridged music and literature. In the latter subject I have had the advantage of earlier guidance and stimulus over many years from Sir Frank Kermode, and for a few years from George Steiner, as well as Raymond Williams. I have also enjoyed discussions with Malcolm Bowie, Mark Chinca, Marian Hobson, Tim Mathews, Jeremy Moule, Chris Prendergast, and Paul Julian Smith. Friendship, research, and collaboration for some sixteen years with David

Kelley in French literature, as well as later sharing with him that peculiarly valuable social occasion he called teaching, constitutes a special case of mutual debt; unfortunately his spirited death came before he could do battle with my latest round demurring from his ludic nihilism. As he said endearingly of Jean Tardieu, 'What a sod for leaving us like that'.

Episodic discussion with various philosophers, in some cases commencing from when I was a student, is appreciated – namely: Elizabeth Anscombe, Tom Baldwin, Jeremy Butterfield, Nick Denyer, Peter Geach, Ian Hacking, Jane Heal, Jean Khalfa, Jean-Francois Lyotard, John Marenbon, Nick Denyer, Karl Popper, Timothy Smiley, Gregory Vlastos and Bernard Williams. A debt is now dispatched by acknowledging conversations Piero Sraffa had with me when I was an undergraduate, and not least my appreciation of his humour, such as the time when he enquired: 'In what language shall I be mad this evening?' I think he spoke in French on that occasion.

My stay at Columbia Philosophy Department afforded valued exchanges with Arthur Danto, Isaac Levi and Sidney Morganbesser. Parts of this book were delivered as lectures at New York University, under the aegis of its Humanities Research Council, arranged by Ed Oakes. I was at home in NYU's Philosophy Department; there I enjoyed some discussion with all its members at various times, including Paul Boghossian and Roy Sorensen, as well as some of its former staff such as Colin McGinn. I was also welcomed to the NYU Law School by Ronnie Dworkin and Tom Nagel.

In April 1994 an invitation from the Director of the Princeton Institute for Advanced Study, occasioned by Lyn Chase, to join the Institute's international meeting of scientists and mathematicians to celebrate Freeman Dyson's work was a valued opportunity to exchange ideas there. In Washington, as guest of Antonin Scalia, and also James Rosenau, I profited from diverse discussions on law and international politics. In Cambridge Glanville Williams was a source of advice and stimulus, as also have been Sir Robbie Jennings, Eli Lauterpacht and Vaughan Lowe. Recently research with Jim Bergeron has taken me along new juridical pathways. The later sections of this book on law and ethics benefit from some practical engagement behind the scenes in a range of problematic international political and diplomatic contexts. Thanks are due to various non-academic colleagues in those spheres for invitations and enabling me to collaborate with them, often in difficult situations.

Dialogue on a variety of topics with distinguished friends from earlier years, such as Mark Morris, is warmly recalled. Courteous engagement has been enjoyed with all the staff at the Cambridge Divinity Faculty for a long period, with too little space here to mention them all, but among those no longer there I should include: Peter Baelz, Geoffrey Lampe, Donald MacKinnon, Henry Chadwick, John Milbank, Charlie Moule, Chris Rowland, and Rowan Williams. Occasional or periodic discussion with scholars and writers in subjects other than mine are valued; not least those with Pat Boyde, Noam Chomsky, Lord Dacre, G.R. Evans, Ilya Gersevitch, Sir Ernst

Gombrich, Roald Hoffmann, Malcolm Longair, Gerard Mace, Frank Madsen, Ed Oakes, a spread of Fellows at Trinity College Cambridge, Lucas Azzoug, the crowd at his philosophy café, and Kip Gresham.

When I was a student, Bernard Williams said to me that there were two sorts of atheist: Protestant or Roman Catholic. I suggest a third type to be feared above the conjunction of these two: one who disposes of 'Roman' from the latter, and recalls Oliver Cromwell in Ireland as the former: the Irish Catholic atheist, who will engage with the other side. Niamh O'Mahony, by whom the ideas in this book have been challenged and refined, exemplifies such a one.

It is a tribute to my contact with the above people to observe that what follows no doubt frequently disagrees with their views.

Arthur Gibson
Cambridge
ag205@cam.ac.uk
August 2000

Acknowledgements

Acknowledgements of permission for use of illustrations are as follows: Cover, Mohammad Heydari-Malayeri (Paris Observatory), Boomerang and NASA; Frontispiece and Plates 1 and 2, by permission of the Syndics of the Fitzwilliam Museum, Cambridge; Plate 3, Tibor Cernus, and for the assistance of Claude Bernard Gallery New York and Hossein Majidi (Digital Imaging Cambridge); Plate 4, Boomerang project team and NASA; Figure 0.1, S.W. Hawking, Neil Turok and Elsevier Journals; Figure 0.2, Andrew Lyne and Jodrell Bank Mullard Radio-Astronomy Laboratories; Figure 2.1: National Archaeological Museum of Athens; Figure 2.2: J.A. Zensus, D.H Hough, P.R. Porcast, *Nature*; Figure 3.1: John D. Barrow, Joseph Silk, Basic Books, Heinemann. Figures 3.2 and 3.4: E.L. Turner and *Nature*; Figure 3.4: A.A. Stark and Nature; Figure 3.5: Peter Edwards; Figure 3.6: Roald Hoffmann; Figure 3.7: Ruth Aswa and Oakland Museum of California; Figure 3.8 S.W. Hawking; Figure 4.1: courtesy of S.W. Hawking, *Modern Physics Letters* and World Scientific Publishing; Figure 4.2 Boomerang, NASA, NSF; Figures 4.3, 4.4: Sir Roger Penrose and Cambridge University Press; Figure 4.5: NASA, NSF, the Italian Space Agency, Italian Antarctic Research Programme; Figure 6.1: Boomerang, NASA, NSF; Figure 9.1 NASA.

My thanks and acknowledgment are also due to the Boomerang team, NASA, NSF, the Italian Space Agency, Italian Antarctic Research Programme, the University of Rome La Sapienza in Italy, the Particle Physics and Astronomy Research Council in the United Kingdom, the USA Department of Energy's National Energy Research Scientific Computing, Cobe projects; also Richard Sword, of the Cambridge Astronomy Institute, for his expertise with some of the astronomical plates.

I should like to thank the following University of Cambridge libraries and staff for their helpful assistance: especially David McKitterick, Librarian of the Wren Library Trinity College, and also its archivist Jonathan Smith; the University Library, Scientific Periodicals Library, Library of Department of Applied Mathematics and Theoretical Physics, Faculty of Philosophy, Astronomy Institute, New York University Library, and Dr Peta Dunstan of the Divinity Faculty.

Thanks are due to other colleagues at the University of Cambridge, and the University of Surrey Roehampton, not least also to those in Paris, the USA, including various remote links with Harvard, NASA and a number of other space agencies, all of whom have provided the occasion for courteous engagement and support. The University of Surrey Roehampton readily provided a research grant towards the cost of colour plates.

Finally, Mary Warren's outstanding judgement and expertise in copy-editing has been invaluable. At Routledge, Hywel Evans and Shankari Sanmuganathan have been helpful in editorial matters and Vicki Collier typeset the book.

Part I
Renaissance in language?

Prologue

Poststructuralism and a renaissance future?

Has culture got above itself?

Ours is a time of small things. That seems to be how the universe started. May we use such a beginning as a metaphor for the origin of a future cultural renaissance in the third millennium AD? This would require a big bang between now and then; yet perhaps the chaos conditions are about right.

Cosmology is the study of the relations between 'what there is' and generalisation. This involves understanding the relations between the material universe and transcendence. Transcendence is that which is left over when scientific explanation is not consistently exactly reducible to its physical subject. The sense of 'consistently exactly reducible' entails puzzles here. This assertion provokes the question of whether or not science's capabilities can in principle lead to proving that this gap between empiricism and transcendence will be closed by scientific progress. Such a conclusion could be interpreted so as to imply that the scientific closure will prove that there is no God; or imply that science will run into a materialist brick wall. On such views, beyond the barrier we would find that there is an empirical realm at variance with scientific assumptions of quantitatively measurable material, and that God exists, or does not exist, as a consequence of penetrating this unknown sphere. Or that science is irrelevant to higher questions. This book is especially written for those, atheist or theist, who query why we should pursue the question of God in relation to philosophy and cosmology. I argue that cosmology is counter-intuitive and irreducibly transcendental.

Analytical philosophy often embodies the familiar spirit that it is not a philosopher's job to come up with solutions – for example, a solution to the meaning of life. This book argues for a wind of change, and it proposes solutions. Philosophers such as Berlin (1979) illustrate how it is possible to coexist with analytical philosophy and find little space for it when answering philosophical questions. Both approaches are significant; each requires new directions discontinuous with both, while learning from them. We need to allow some counter-intuitive relations in our thinking about truth, and what the term 'God' might cover. These relations themselves are affected by the disputable identity of philosophy; so such discussion has a subplot battling with where the future of philosophy should go. Sure, this book will be a mere starting point, no doubt defective and provisional.

The term 'system' has been degraded by failures in its use prior to the emergence of modernism. But let us imagine some comparably universalised idea of philosophy, which avoids the pitfalls of 'system', embracing logic, creativity, science, and ethics, together with their relations.

One could assess competing philosophies and cultures, ever so slightly trimming them with qualifications which do not much change their direction or momentum; or, with apparent lack of caution, attempt something which might be regarded as audacious and ironic. The present book argues for the latter – a philosophy with a content addressing a range of universal questions. If, for example, a philosopher such as Bernard Williams (1985, 1995) wishes to argue that ethical theory should be constructed from the perspective of a first person human agent, presumably it would be valid to propose that a first person contrasting conception of an alien or of God could be sought and defended? Bernard Williams (1993a: 72) claims that religion is incurably unintelligible; it might be. Rather, the concern in the present book, in addition to the question of what philosophy could become in the future, is to enquire, what is it to develop an account of God that is not dependent on the foibles of religious people? It is a separate, interesting, question whether or not we deem the result a subset of science fiction, film theory or of transcendent philosophy.

Some analytical philosophers are understandably condemnatory about, for example, the lack of logical clarity and accuracy in non-formal cultural philosophies. Yet one can sympathise with the criticism, by some cultural specialists, that analytical philosophy has no significant answers about, or wisdom in universal questions. Analytical philosophy tends to presuppose that criticism of itself reaches this misunderstanding by equivocation over the identity of philosophy. Cultural philosophy might retort that such an allegation embodies a mythical isolation of form and content. To the extent to which one can generalise about a typical person outside of such subjects, both styles of philosophising are often impenetrable and lack a grasp of what humans want from philosophy. This book proposes neither agreeing with any or all of these policies, whilst seeking to avoid an insipid blend.

Is it possible to relate, utilise and transform some of the many competing philosophies, techniques, culture theories, distinct academic subjects, without resorting to mere studies of method, to produce a fresh philosophy? Dare one boldly theorise artistically to reform certain territories and boundaries claimed by formal philosophy, yet advance some of its distinctions, while harnessing features of literary philosophies to it? Could we redeploy insights in reductionist philosophies to oppose their reductionism? Can we avoid being reactionary when we appeal to counter-intuitive reformulations of past cultural concepts, while yet becoming more futurist than, say, what many writers label as post-structuralism? Can we include some astrophysical science in this admixture? To express the problems another way: how do you reach a new future if we are transfixed by the past and/or too regulated by present fashions?

Quite reasonably, Richard Rorty (1989, 1997, 1998) asserts that many previously fundamental personal and public questions about the meaning of life are redundant. For example, the question 'Does God exist?' seems anachronistic. Scientific culture has swept aside the past, and any attempt to take transcendentalism seriously is typically deemed reactionary. The present book embraces no such polarity, and attempts to offer a fresh approach. It explores the prospect of constructing a counter-intuitive realism, by means of which both ancient questions and post-structuralist insights sometimes align, not infrequently disappear or transform. Traditional lines of demarcation between the arts and the sciences are insecure. My view is that newer, deeper science supports the rejection of a formal system as a paradigm for scientific empirical knowledge, and that, in certain respects, knowledge gained through the arts is epistemologically as secure as experimentally grounded theory of knowledge in science. This book indirectly argues that as mechanistic models become redundant as sole frameworks for science, aesthetic qualitative identities seem to underlie a deeper appreciation of empirical functions.

For those who think that scientific precision is more exact than art, they should be challenged to expose imprecision in Mozart's chromatic harmony. Or explain away the internal limits to accuracy in mathematical knot theory related to quantum gravity (see Atiyah 1990 and Baez 1994). Or solve the hitherto ineradicable paradoxes generated by two-valued logic systems? I shall argue that these remarks do not confuse or conflate autonomous scientific and artistic languages in my cross-referencing and comparison of different subjects; nor do they presuppose a traditional grand metaphysical system. They press us to recognise the need for a cultural revolution.

Are we averse to the multiverse?

Fin-de-siècle occidental artistic and scientific modernisms tend to be dismissive of, or have reactionary confidence in, or are contrary about, our relations to the past in relation to what we should expect future knowledge to be. So what's new? Marian Hobson (1995), exposing neglected aspects of Diderot's use of analogy and illusion, shows us how Diderot's conception of 'digression' is fundamental to fresh scrutiny of what it is to be a 'connection' in, and between, different subjects, and how this pertains to analogy and virtual reality. This insight has fundamental ramifications for handling exploration of what it is for us to have knowledge. Diderot's grasp of a digression can be used as a mirror to reflect features of surprise in cosmology.

In the second half of the twentieth century AD, Augustine's idea of an

6 *Renaissance in language*

eternal universe lost out to interpretations of the big bang start to the universe at a finite time. Yet later work initiated by Andrei Linde developed a multiverse approach, refined by Martin Rees:[1] the prospect that there is an infinite ensemble of universes with laws different from ours; Rees does not rule out other alternatives, however. The notion of a multiverse is almost a ready-made symbol for the third millennium: infinite variety and the burgeoning of new futures; equally, however, the past could be like that, and not a reactionary singularity. This seems capable of ironic use.

Proposing a new anthropic perspective, Hawking and Turok (1998) disputed Linde's claim of a multiverse. They argue that the most likely scenario for the universe is a spatially infinite model in which the universe dissipates to infinity or recollapses without a multiverse future (see Figure 0.1). The changing scenarios presuppose, of course, a variety of constant factors and calculations. Yet depending on whether or not the Linde/Rees or the Hawking/Turok theory is adopted, the sense of what is a digression from a relevant analysis or of what the nature of the universe consists switches.

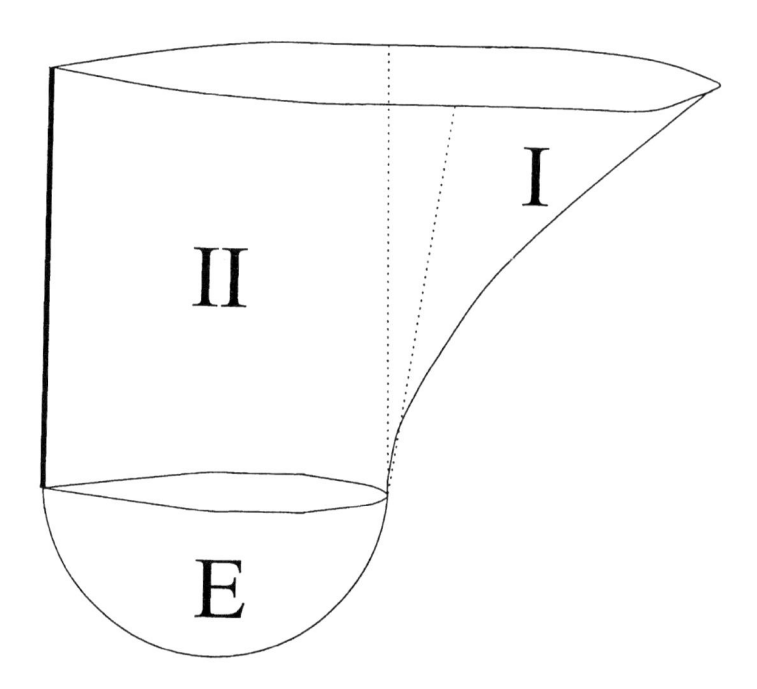

Figure 0.1 Hawking and Turok (1998) start the universe

Source: Stephen Hawking and Neil Turok, and Elsevier Journals

Note: The heavy line marks the singularity, with (II) a De Sitter like region emerging from the singularity into an open inflating universe comprising region (I). E is a half deformed four sphere.

How do such specific surprise switches associate with more general cultural patterns, and are these switches characteristic of general tendencies of the future to emerge from the present? Are we uniquely dislocated from the past's legacy, because of twentieth century science? Is the late twentieth century's malaise the upshot of an historically unparalleled modernism? What, then, are our future's conceptual prospects? Such questioning has justification both in humanities and sciences. One strand of this interrogation should have to do with making explicit our assumptions about relations. What is it to construct a relevant new relation between two, or more, known theories of states of affairs? A subset of such an enquiry is the challenge to give explicit attention to what it is to assess relations between irrelevance and relevance. Study of (ir)relevance, which as a noun (or some expression) in ordinary usage often incorrectly mimics completeness; it obviously should unpack into 'x is relevant to y with respect to such and such properties'. The misleading impression given by the noun's completeness, which seems to mirror ways in which we do not intuitively have a grasp of what it is to detect, at least in the most accurate form, non-obvious or counter-intuitive conditions of how concepts connect. Sometimes we foreclose on an incomplete explanation as if it were complete. Perhaps this is a condition to which culture is prone, especially when the *Zeitgeist* has corporate assurances that we need to look no further than the promoted fashions.

At times we seem to have a penchant for irrelevance in the sense of novelty, but often only so within the mores of a fashionable boundary; otherwise irrelevance is taken to be a proper prohibition on incorrect or improbable scenarios. Contiguous to this boundary, however, there is a genuine problem: aspects of the external and internal worlds are unexpected or counter-intuitive. The conjunction of our human tendencies to accede to the use of successful patterns, with some deeper unexpected facets of the cultural or scientific universes, might not be perceived or falsely construed. Sometimes the ways in which we would come to a grasp of how to discover such parameters is beyond us. For example, do we occupy a typical region of spacetime in this universe? This question is undecided, though it has a variety of competing anthropic and misanthropic supporters. At some distance from this sort of problem is our own perception of what is typical for the world.

Hanging out together

Consequently, maybe it is healthy, unfashionably, to unsettle ourselves. Conversely, what better traditional philosophy with which to start than Plato's? Well, think again.

Consider the strange case of Socrates. He was an untypical thinker, and Wittgenstein has some parallels with Socrates in this regard,[2] though these two philosophers were differently individualist. It is helpful to approach this issue biographically, with some authority. Shortly before his death, the leading classical philosopher Gregory Vlastos stated that, in 1953, though having spent a year at Princeton completing a state-of-the-art research book manuscript on Socrates, instead of sending it to the publisher in 1953, he binned it because: 'it was a lemon'. He told us that he did not realise until the 1980s the reasons why his instinct propelled him to do this. Vlastos stated that he did not, in 1953, know the fundamental identity and significance of Socrates's *strangeness*; nor, he confessed, was he aware of the importance of paradox to this ancient Greek philosopher; neither did he recognise that Socrates' irony was not deception; nor, Vlastos impresses on us, was he aware of the importance of Plato's later research on mathematics to his (Plato's) philosophy. Vlastos's (1991) subsequent book, *Socrates*, informs us of the foregoing biographical history.

Vlastos accordingly places 'strangeness' at the centre of his depiction of Socrates' philosophy. This 'strangeness' is a complex way of holding together ignorance, and a grasp of wisdom, within the limits of human experience. Vlastos's basic point is quoted by him from the Alcibiades' speech in Plato's *Symposium* (221D):

> Such is [Socrates'] strangeness that you will search and search among those living now and among men of the past, and never come close to what he is himself and to the things he says.

In Greek this term 'strangeness'[3] has a wide range that includes 'wild', 'outrageous' and 'bizarre' (the latter sense I return to below). In an only apparently contrary perception, however, Socrates (and Wittgenstein, for example) frequently achieve that which has the ring of truth – to those who have no appetite for scholastic, academic and analytical philosophy. This proportion of people increased enormously in the last thousand years with the onset of medieval 'systems'. It accelerated, in a different direction, to break all records in the twentieth century as witnessed by many trends in analytic and continental philosophies. We have academic philosophy, corporate education and dumbing-down trends in materialism to thank for this shrinkage from Plato's deeper diet. Unfortunately, due to our ignorance, and perhaps because of many academic institutions' unwillingness or commercial inability to facilitate the 'wild', 'strange' and 'original' in the above senses, we are not always clear on what the division of labour is between deep difficult thinking and mere technical abstraction. Obviously, it would be facile to copy a mannered form of such 'strangeness' – not unknown in followers of some philosophers. Counterfeits of such counter-intuition are to be avoided. It is the independence, the freedom, the originality of such thinking that comprises the wildness. The way forward is not to copy Plato as hero, however; but to note that he was a free-thinking philosopher, not an institutional academic.[4] In an era that confuses deep or high knowledge, at which a philosopher connives with corporate academic professionalism, the difference is a matter of elusive importance.

There are exceptions to this trend, of course, as we return here to relate this difference to the foregoing issue of philosophy's relation to the deep content of other subjects. Amartya Sen (1997) has done very significant philosophy with economics as its content. Not infrequently this economic content has made a contribution to change philosophy. A facet of his research ties up with two features of the foregoing, those of bizarreness and internal consistency. The above use of Socrates's 'bizarreness' strikes a helpful contrast with Amartya Sen's (1995: 19–31) no doubt accurate employment of the term. He identifies in our contemporary theory a failure to realise that: '*purely* internal consistency' entails a relation to external properties. Sen is considering the way that making a choice functions by having to presuppose motivations which entail external features:

> The bizarreness lies not in the simple fact that the claim under dispute is false, but that it could not possibly make sense unless the choices are taken to be statements in a way they cannot possibly be. Underlying the mistaken claim, there is a basic disorientation about the nature of choice acts as such.[5]
>
> (ibid.: 26)

Let us call Socrates' strangeness 'true strangeness, or bizarreness'. The opposed 'false bizarreness' is that topic about which Sen (1995) writes and helpfully depicts.

At the side of such true bizarreness, there are three other basic considerations. First, the use of, say, strangeness has to be placed in contexts of a recognition of the valuable improvements in the world as a consequence of attempts to implement the values of integrity, moderation, decency, liberty and equality.

Second – not so obvious – is the point that some elements of resistance to these qualities (unintended or purposive), as well as an array of blunted perceptions due to any manner of things (stress, indolence, indoctrination, lack of opportunity or attention), may not be corrected simply by an appeal to those qualities.

Third, in such contexts manifesting the second point, Socrates' strangeness, is what I classify as a property of counter-intuition. A necessary internal property of this type of counter-intuition is originality. Its functioning elements operate, for example, in dispositions, concepts, reasoning and creativity that alert us to the value of these qualities and others like them. This is not unlike the successful indirect and elegant proof in mathematics that achieves the solution of a problem that has no direct proof.

Exemplifying this in depth is the philosophical significance of the proof of Fermat's great last theorem:[6] the case of a strange counter-intuition whose properties furnish a standard solution of common-sense value. We might deem such counter-intuition as internal properties of the high knowledge itself, and/or an intrinsic feature of our perceptual involvement of the discovery process which excavates strange properties. It seems clear to me that many instances of such counter-intuition are internal to the state external to the perceiver. There are many other counterparts, I suggest, to such a proposal of which this is only an impressionist slice.

For instance, the articulation of the emotions, especially in relation to deep creativity, impinge on much unresolved moral philosophy, and philosophy of the mind, in the function of counter-intuitive states, i.e. 'strange' in the foregoing sense. Wollheim's (1999) profound work on the emotions might be the occasion to develop this perspective, in whose thesis the deep creative emotions are interactive and, one might add, in the American sense of the expression, 'have attitude'. The paradox is that for much of the significant creative outcome of such attitude (great art and high knowledge) the original, and originating, strangeness is at first a barely acceptable revolutionary matter, yet subsequently an object of common appreciation. The foregoing is also what good philosophy should be like.

Is a subject its own boss?

One problem is that a specialist within a subject will tend to expect any input from another subject as secondary or ornamental. But revolutions in science and the arts violate this assumption, as we shall see. Unexpected cross-connections between subjects are often the stuff of revolutionary transformation of a subject; obviously we should not regard this as a remit for universal novelty. The term 'system' for a philosophy, or as a formal basis for a science, is now inexact or an anachronistic infelicity. Past grand systems in culture and science proved internally and externally contrary. No new grand merger employing a mechanistic type of model is likely to succeed. Contrariwise, this does not bar a counter-intuitive universal theory engaging with multi-disciplinary construction, while preserving specialist insights in a group of subjects such as logic, ethics, aesthetic theory and cosmology.

It is now almost canonical to cite Nietzsche to support claims that any use of realism is degraded beyond respectable utility. This may be premature celebration. Even though one may not concur with all John Richardson (1996: 221–90) argues in his conclusion that Nietzsche was proposing an unexpected form of a correspondence theory of truth, the existence of this sort of specialist exposition of Nietzsche shows how little some postmodernist reductionists have attended to the nature of their fuel. So tanked up, they could blow up. To suppose, as many do, that the epistemological indeterminacy pervading many of the twentieth century options is the rule for all future alternatives, I argue, is a failure to understand our ignorance of the identity of the future(s), and of the counter-intuitive creative and scientific vision of what the future can offer.

Past, present and future relations impinge on this topic. We find difficulty in knowing when we perceive the past or mix the past with our reflections and hopes. We need our pasts and our futures to create our present. The past is no self-contained continuum, neither is the present, nor is the future, despite their temporal isolation from each other. Filled with relativities and fractures, culture mirrors partial precedents that recur in fragmentary forms. Perhaps at some deep level of typology the sun has seen nothing new under it, though technology and artistic originality nevertheless often have no past token precedent.

Is science romantic?

Even so, there are threats to a claim for a strongly unique twentieth-century modernism in science. Cunningham and Jardine (1990) have shown how Romanticist cultural notions pervade empirical science of the Romantic era. Another comparative task is assessment of the roles of cultural modernism in the emergence of nineteenth- and twentieth-century science, as well as its relations to Romanticism.

Ian Hacking (1995) has opened up quite fresh questions about our memory of the past in relation to science: new ways of forming and making questions are produced by new science and fresh conjectural knowledge. A new science can be like a semantic contagion which generates invented memories: a negative or positive contagion. It would be too much to generalise this over all science, not least since Hacking is writing of multiple personality and the sciences of memory. But as the most general of sciences, cosmology – together with some of the successful presuppositions of science in the twentieth century – has obliterated vast areas of our cultural history while recovering extensive regions of our astronomical past. How our memories and the status of future science stand in relation to such elimination is not obviously always accurate in memory or prediction. It would not be helpful to romanticise with an invented memory about the ancient past. Contrariwise, we should avoid the sycophantic humility of presenting ourselves as servants to a time of unique scientific competence for insight into the foundations of reality.

The claims for subtle, sometimes unacknowledged, formal and aesthetic interfaces between the arts and sciences are of course very ancient. For example, quadratic algebra's 'normal forms' appear in nineteenth-century BC Old Babylonian cuneiform, in which the ordinary lexical expressions are retained yet given a technical sense.[7] Here the distinction, of the form which we readily presuppose, between a formal mathematical language and a literary natural language, is highly questionable.

In third millennium AD arts and sciences, though they are remote from ancient culture, we, more readily than earlier twentieth-century empiricist scientists, apprehend an oblique interrelation between the languages of arts and sciences. In such ways the relations between arts and sciences are perplexing and timely for reassessment; so too are the ways in which we, often all too artificially, impose notions of individuation and segmentation on to 'movements' in history in connection with presupposing how the arts and the sciences contrast, distinctive though they obviously are at many levels. At this early juncture, then, I ask for you to suspend judgement, more than usually in what follows, of your presuppositions of relevance and discontinuity as we explore the possibility of new approaches to questions of transcendence and cosmology. Surprise and digression may indeed be excuses for irrelevance and novelty. Conversely, they may attend the retrieval of unexpected past connections and possible futures consequent on the frontiers of new research.

Is past continuity different from now?

We can benefit from the conceptual vertigo which reflection on unexpected cross-connections can bring. Although aspects of the mathematical physics of star collapse – black holes – was developed principally by Stephen Hawking in the 1970s,[8] the late eighteenth-century Abbé Laplace (1799) devised central features of black hole mathematics. Laplace predicted that certain old stars would have a gravity strong enough to prevent light escaping from them. He was using mathematics so refined that they are, in certain respects, co-extensive with Hawking's own work. For this reason Laplace's original paper was included as an appendix in Hawking and Ellis (1973). This example engages not only with the issue of the relation of modernism's origins to science, but also the larger issue of history's internal causal relations. Most people would think of black holes as canonical examples of late twentieth-century science, excluded by definition from the possible scope within eighteenth-century science. An instance such as Laplace's black hole mathematics is generally untypical of much technology: the latter has no relevant past, in the sense that there was no technology even provisionally to test for Laplace's claims – such as indirect observations of black holes. But we can articulate Laplace so as to question our assumptions of cultural discontinuity. His case may indirectly reflect other continuities that will serve to test our own sense of modernity, by which we judge what is the art of the possible future.

In relation to such waves of conceivable continuity, nevertheless, we can agree with Bernard Williams' (1993b: 2, 12, 166–67) view that we should not deny the otherness of the ancient world, or any other world temporally disconnected from our own. Yet Williams also states that the ancient Greeks were more modern than we have recently been encouraged to suppose, and he disagrees with Oscar Wilde's opinion: 'Whatever, in fact, is modern in our lives is due to the Greeks. Whatever is an anachronism is due to medievalism'. We can value an ironic reading of Wilde here, whilst avoiding the imperialism which he possibly was parodying. Williams (1997) has argued, in relation to what philosophy could become, that it will have both the feature of what is 'non-obvious' to us, and the activity of tracing features in the history of philosophy.

Is post-structuralism imperious?

As a contribution to a disinterested approach, I suggest that Rorty (1989: 6–7, 1997) is an example of an imperialist whose often valuable ironising can nevertheless be disconnected from his philosophy. He claims that, 'Truth cannot be out there – cannot exist independently of the human mind – because sentences cannot so exist or be out there'.

We need not prove that God exists to show that Rorty is relying on the sort of dogmatic stance of which he accuses old fashioned 'grand' metaphysicians. If God exists, God is at liberty, privately or publicly, to employ expressions of sense that have or have not a tautological relation to the truth/falsehood of our sentences, whether or not we know them. So for Rorty to use 'cannot', he simply falls into a modal fallacy. That he may presuppose that God does not exist does not, of course, warrant his 'cannot'; but only 'may not' or 'possibly not', since he has no empirical or deductive use of 'cannot' to sustain atheism, even if atheism were found to be true.

Rorty next states that,

> If we cease to attempt to make sense of the idea of such a non-human language ['of a being who had a language of his own'], we shall not be tempted to confuse the platitude that the world may cause us to be justified in believing a sentence true with the claim that the world splits itself up, on its own initiative, into sentence-shaped chunks called 'facts'.
>
> (1989: 5)

But this sort of dogmatism is merely an agnostic version of the sort of credal belief in God that he is opposing, and the collective 'we' obscures a large portion of humans who fail to comply with his hope for future worldviews.

Another presupposition of Rorty's (1989: 16) is that the prescription of scientific language as metaphor has forfeited claims that sentences can comply with certain 'facts'. Below I offer an approach to metaphor, termed 'live metaphor', which false-foots Rorty's sort of reductionism, and related attempts to drive a wedge between metaphor and truth, while I provide accommodation for a strong sense of the poetic force in creative and scientific languages. It will take a number of books to cover the ground envisaged for this project; this present book attempts to lay a preliminary multi-disciplinary foundation and overview. Rorty assumes that if one is to produce grand metaphysical schemes, then one is committed to a return to an ossified past. He has the advantage of manifesting the fashion of the post-structuralist age. I wish to argue that, with a twist of details, such oppositions disappear, and enable a more surprising, unexpected non-obvious future for some culture and philosophy.

Let's be avant-garde again?

Post-structuralists such as Rorty are not sufficiently avant-garde; but, like early modernists, they are still fleeing from an institutionalised past which, though we should demur from much of it, it contained, often subverted, elements of possible futures susceptible to conceptual liberty that can be readily combined with cultural needs for the twenty-first century.

We tend to use individual cases, understood or misinterpreted, as the basis for generalisation in which our experience of present and future are smoothed into a past continuum. Surface perception mimics continuity; and at times it obscures actual relations. When we conceptualise, we both interpret, and use already interpreted data. We quantise history into discrete parcels. There are indeed periods and movements, perceived as identities; but the oft-disputed edges of these identities are not marginal, and, properly exposed, question the identification of our parcelling up of history. The terms we employ to mark these identities have a peculiar coercion. For example, consider the identity and emergence of Romanticism in relation to changes in the perceived status of 'God' in the eighteenth and nineteenth centuries. We can trace the genesis of European Romanticism to Mme de Staël, emblazoned in her polemical manifesto *De l'Allemagne* that so enraged Napoleon.[9] She champions a God of Romantic love and global religion, appealing among others to Kant. Romanticism itself is regarded as the mother of modernism. Should we consider no one to be founder of the latter, or identify Chateaubriand, Baudelaire, or some other candidate(s)? If one chooses Baudelaire as founding father, what Jonathan Culler (1994) has termed his satanic verses in *Les Fleur du Mal* demolish the Romantic god of de Staël, though we may finally want to argue that Baudelaire is a Romantic realist modernist. Can we, and, if so, how can we, adjudicate and suture such movements, or fragments of them, together, to use them as premises to represent the past accurately in relation to our future choices? And how do such responses impinge on our capacity to employ these categories to apprehend other pasts?

A medievalist future philosophy?

Earlier epochs are susceptible to similar problematic collisions as the above types of puzzles and revisions. It has been thought that the future awaits a Dark Age; but this seems unwarrantedly reactionary in the light of good potentialities in the present world. The possible futures are not reverse patterns of the past, for example, by which a medieval modernism leads to a dark age. Prior to considering some grounds for a future renaissance, we should reflect on why a medieval new modernism is both informative and yet not sufficiently adroit a conception to blemish us with a route to a future Dark Age after post-structuralism. Although there are continuities in history, such patterns do not imply that the causal edges of the context in which they occur will also display a cyclic generative capability.

Some remarkable parallels have been shown between medieval and modern philosophy.[10] Geach (1972) reported that a good proportion of these parallels are not the product of conscious attempts by modern philosophers to learn from the past, but inadvertent by-products of attempts by them to expose the identity of a topic, reproducing an insight extant in the medieval period which had been lost or neglected. Stephen Nichols (1991) applies the term 'modernism' to phenomena in the medieval period (because, among other things, of the impact of Aristotle's ideas on motion to science and theology). There is obviously something important in this proposal, not least with the isolation of a significant role for individual authorship and personal interiority, contributing to a sort of twefth-century renaissance blossoming that enriches this notion[11]. The medieval world was not an island unto itself. Indeed, it is problematic relevantly to package the philosophy of history into the discrete quanta which some historians of ideas have presupposed for various epochs. Pasnau (1997) has argued that Cartesian dualism was not a substantial break from the medieval world in the way Rorty (1997: 293–4) supposes. He claims that there is a continuity between some of Aquinas' philosophy of mind and the twentieth century's, as does Geach (1971) in relation to Wittgenstein. Although we should reflect on Hacking's (1995) impish but interesting suggestion that facets of Wittgenstein's thought can be found in Descartes, yet the effect of such an alignment is to explode Cartesian dualism (as argued elsewhere in Gibson (1998a)) by producing a partial parallel with Wittgenstein and Aquinas on the issue of what consciousness is.

Certainly, there are many substantial changes in the history of ideas pertinent to the present study. The philosopher Norman Kretzmann (1997: 23; 1999) ironises some post-structuralist contemporary theology by observing, of the traditional idea of theology as the study of God, it to be one which 'Living theologians are of course familiar with the idea, and almost all of them would repudiate it as utterly obsolete'. Clearly, in this respect modernist and post-structuralist theology are not medieval, though a contrasting situation obtains for the later medieval uses of Pseudo-Dionysius (the citations of which are second only to Aristotle in Aquinas' *Summa theologiae*). And this might warn us to think of Aquinas not only as an Aristotelian.

Kretzmann's (1997: 23–24; cf. 1999: 7) fresh analysis of Aquinas' natural theology, based on *Summa contra gentiles*, refines the concepts of a top-down versus bottom-up approach to the possible links between philosophy and theology, in which they could be regarded as two species of the same genus, termed 'Grandest Unified Theory' (Kretzmann 1997: 22–25). In this perspective bottom-up theology is natural theology which employs philosophical methods. The present book is concerned with a counter-intuitive formulation of some issues in a top-down philosophy which is outside of Kretzmann's remit. Kretzmann (1997: 24) stated that the Grandest Unified Theory theology starts with the presuppositions of: (a) 'divinely revealed truths about the first principles and most fundamental principles of reality and of human nature and behaviour in particular', and (b) 'the conviction that God exists', and (c) 'with some conception of God's nature'[12]. Kretzmann here notes that this 'non-philosophical "revealed" theology', then, can be thought of as theology from the top down, though he quite properly claims that the history of theology and philosophy do not always entirely accord with this division of labour.

Outside of this priority, there is a neglected issue about (a). From within the viewpoint of philosophy, what would it be to present some criteria and presuppositions which are stipulative to be (a)? One could leave aside conceptions of (b) and (c) in this type of scrutiny of (a). Such an analysis of (a) might hold a similar position, if for many not the same interest, as what would it be to present some criteria and presuppositions which are stipulative for a non-intuitionistic logic foundation for mathematics. Or, for the doctrine that rhetorical syllogisms are founded upon probable or necessary consequences. Or, that the earliest astrophysical states of the universe concur in principle with a realist extensional logic. One may find, in examining such questions, that some data or claims external to the logic are relevant for illustration (as in Chapter 2 below). But the identity of the investigation, in the case of (a) is not theology; neither in the present book is it, loosely construed, philosophy of religion. The approach here is intended to be a philosophy. Where it diverts into fresh perspectives, this is to persuade readers about the capacity of philosophy and logic to deal with other subjects and their connections. It is not a strategy to confuse theology with philosophy.

The following formulation in which Kretzmann so accurately represents the history of the two cultures, are new schizoid goalposts which I wish to dispute, deconstruct and merge, if I may be allowed the live metaphor, into a sort of monopole:

> Philosophical theology is what was produced by most medieval theologians ... and what is being produced now by philosophers of religion. Technically and traditionally, philosophical theology is part of revealed theology rather than of philosophy. And it's only philosophical theology, never philosophy herself, that can and should be recognised under philosophy's old job description of *ancilla theologiae*, theology's maid-servant.
>
> (Kretzmann 1997: 25)

Nor is this to reduce theology to philosophy. Perhaps some aspects of these boundaries, as with the gendered dependencies here, are anachronisms best left unexhumed. No subject has the upper hand in universalization, least of all in philosophy. Although philosophy should not be a handmaid to theology, philosophy's boundaries should not be restricted by claims of autonomy in theology. Rather, some theology is best forgotten; yet this is not the same as agreeing with the theologians whose view of 'philosophy of religion' is so enfeebled that it is neither philosophy nor theology, but only a subject without an ontology distinct from any other subject such as lay appreciation of poetry.

Philosophers do and should make states of affairs explicit in any subject which presupposes a top-down set of presuppositions, not just theology. Perhaps this is most obvious in the philosophy of mathematics with Platonism (cf. Hartry Field (1989) versus Bob Hale (1994a)). Hawking and Turok's (1998) theory that the universe will probably always expand, presupposes, as does much cosmology, experimentally non-veridical top-down classes of presuppositions. Gathering such precedents, I wish to advance the proposal that there can be a philosophical top-down approach to transcendent metaphysical and theological issues, which thereby is itself philosophy in a proper sense of that term. The type of unphilosophical head start which is manifested in much of traditional theology, of which Kretzmann precisely writes, is not one that is adopted here. But this does not therefore commit one to a bottom-up philosopher's approach to the heavier issues of transcendence. It is rather puzzling to have to address what I take to be an incorrect opposition: a philosopher looks at transcendence in theology and is accordingly relocated by the fashion of culture into becoming a subset of theology. Conversely, natural theology is allowed to be philosophy. Apart from finding natural theology boring, it appears to me that philosophers would do well to be wary of this contrast, though it operates for some of the two cultures' territories. It will take the rest of the book to explain this. Suffice it here to maintain that Aquinas' use of philosophy to encourage examination of transcendent issues should not be pushed aside as a medieval dumbing-down of philosophy, and it can be linked to a Renaissance concern with new future philosophical explorations at the frontiers of philosophy, as well as its relations to other subjects.

Has the past a new future?

That there is no procession to universal knowledge in institutional attempts to evolve us into conformity is no proof that cultural relativity is the basis for truth. It is too bald simply to suggest that, since Nichols (1991) perceives modernism in medievalism, could not twentieth-century mod-ernism be placed in parallel with a fragment of the medieval world? It would be proportionately rash to assume that some future century will provide a post-structuralist Renaissance (on the grounds that some scholars apprehend the signs of a new medieval period at the beginning of the third millennium). Perhaps, however, some insight may be filtered in from this all too partial set of relations. There are ingredients which are, as it were, sideways on to this relation, and asymmetrical to renaissance characteristics. For example, just as the Renaissance emphasised the past at the expense of the contemporary, one could envisage the future as a means of informing the present's use of the past. At the end of the twentieth century many worldviews stressed the gross force of blind contingency, open futures, and the arbitrary play of languages. Might we not consider the prospect of a new future Renaissance, or a fresh global cultural synthesis, for the future radically to reconstrue the past, as a counter-intuitive outcome of our modernisms? No doubt there are other possibilities; yet supporting this view, we do not have to be classified as reactionary exponents of either history or the future. Malcolm Bowie (1993: 39, 109), suggests that, 'The future ... is not a matter of free speculative play ... The future in psychoanalysis is always bound to be approachable only by a retrospective and retroactive route ... those of the past – rediscovered, recreated'. Gibson (1997b) maintains that, if applied to past cultural foundational claims, such a perception will result in unpredicted insights.

Some 'postmodern' theologians have appealed to their conjectural interpretation of Derrida's deconstruction to 'modernise' the negative theology of John of the Cross and others. Rowan Williams (1992) has questioned the view that such equations and the interpretation of deconstruction have to lead to this sort of reductionism. If we identify a modernism, of relevant sorts, in the mediaeval world, we may recognise that the Renaissance was one of its consequences. Such alleged twentieth-century modernist parallels with the past, and their counter-charges, are suggestive of deep unresolved problems in our ignorance of cultural spacetimes in general. The Renaissance was not a unitary entity, and coincidence of it with one of our possible futures would have to allow for its esoteric and contrary identities.

This looking to the past opposes the apparent emphasis, if not every tendency, of nineteenth-century modernism. Conversely, Holland (1993: xi) has spoken of Baudelaire as someone blown irresistibly backwards into the future: he, the foundling father, looking aghast at the toxic waste which 'progress' hurls at his feet, subject to and oddly manifesting the cultural masochism and authoritarianism of his day. Baudelaire's schizophreniform[13] figures for demon deities and Satan in *Les Fleur du Mal* seem to reflect Baudelaire's own indeterminacy of consciousness, rather than merely mirror an atheist's determined ontology as to whether or not, or whenever, they could have transcendental ontologies. Some of these French nineteenth-century literary features attending the emergence of modernism reflect similar polemical combats in the mediaeval world. Baudelaire's unique synthesis of already ancient poetic archetypes, such as the 'forest' and 'familiar' motifs, for example, in his poems 'Correspondences' and 'Obsession', encounter and mediate as subplots debates in theology through, for example, Dante's *Inferno*, the Old Testament, and the Mesopotamian *Epic of Gilgamesh*.[14] Such continuities certainly subsume dislocations between their pasts and futures. Typical authors, exemplified by Baudelaire, display a high modernism in their Romanticising self-knowledge of spiritual bankruptcy and its concomitant disintegration, questioning an often all too ossified institutional culture.

Modernism and post-structuralism have to some extent encouraged relations between the arts and sciences. There has also been both a recognition and overstatement of contrasting modernism and post-structuralism, with the sciences depicted as the veridical vehicles for exposing the physical world. To speak of a 'physical world' already suppresses, as though it were fact, what is a fictional segmentation of the world: physical features should contribute, with other qualitative (aesthetic and other) realities, to constitute the world. Clearly we are not in a position to assume that physical science has exposed all physical functions relevant to ascertaining the scope and identity of its theories. An error of purported detail, when corrected, may lay bare a fundamental difference of cosmology.

Science is not an a conceptual island entire to itself. I shall argue that the humanities are part of the same empirical mainland. Just as we find disputes within science about its identities and scope, there are territorial conflicts within the humanities. This covers central domains, including the relation of theology to the arts and sciences. Within theology there are entrenched lines of demarcation about its own dominion. Karl Barth opposed the view that natural theology is independent of a theology of revelation, while appreciating common logical functions in the two.[15] Swinburne (1992: 219) highlights, from the standpoint of a traditional analytical philosophy of religion, some past damaging conflicts between theology and science, whilst affirming that the weighing of different kinds of evidence in science and theology is no different in principle though it varies in scale.

Is scientific cosmology metaphysics?

Current research in astrophysical cosmology tends to support these sorts of view. In a book remarkable for its title – *The Renaissance of General Relativity* – the cosmologist Dallaporta states:

> If one insists that 'true science' is rooted only in experiment ... one must admit then that, in respect of the totality of knowledge required for the understanding of the whole cosmos, its capacity of grasping 'reality' is clearly limited to that portion of the universe not too dissimilar from our own surroundings and that any attempt of speculative to pass over these limits is not truly 'scientific', but only 'metaphysics'.
>
> (Dallaporta 1993: 331)

Dallaporta goes on to argue that much of large-scale physics and cosmology cannot correctly be treated as truly scientific if rigorous definition is implemented, because much of cosmology does overpass this boundary. He maintains that the consequence of applying, for example, quantum-mechanical considerations to masses larger than the Planck mass 1 produces 'a consequence that has not to be taken literally' (Dallaporta 1993: 330). Therefore, much of the universe's early history, which is presented as science and related deep-structure aspects of local physics, is conceptually part of a discipline to whose standards they do not comply. Cosmology of the early universe is science, even though its conclusions need to be grounded in, or sometimes grounded by, astrophysics and observation – as shrewdly demonstrated by, for example, Martin Rees (1995, 1999). Dallaporta's point articulates the view that these spheres of science are metaphysics. His position is that some astrophysical science is metaphysical cosmology. From within a quantum-mechanical perspective, he claims that we cannot make inferences about cosmology when they are to be taken 'literally'. Whatever 'literally' means here (and Dallaporta seems to be thinking of a straightforward use of equations and observations that functionally describe physical states and events in a veridical way) 'literally' clearly leaves us with metaphoric conceptions and terms in such physics.

That there is metaphor in scientific cosmology, I shall argue, is evidence of, with suitable qualifications, signifying functions parallel with some live metaphor in the humanities, though we should allow for the many contrasts between the two subjects. This book maintains that such signifying functions can produce thought bridges involving the provision of inference relations between cosmology, metaphysics and theology. The succeeding chapters defend the view that many of the deep questions on both sides of these disciplines involve counter-intuitive thinking and empirical functions. When comparisons are made at fundamental levels, chronic bomb damage is observed in the sectarian walls between some empirical science and arts, which expose common underlying links. This is not to universalise relativism, nor is it to dismantle realism.

Was Einstein a renaissance figure?

Looking back to Einstein's work as a Classic,[16] as scientifically analogous with Kermode's formulation for the literary sphere, another apt live metaphor is that he was succeeded by the sort of 'mediaevalist' modernist focus of Heisenberg's quantum probability. Indeterminacy restored the mystery and incalculability to empirical observation. More recent developments retrieved and/or developed for scrutiny unexplored possibilities by a renaissance in general relativity and universal theories at the cosmological level. What could be more in the spirit of renaissance than the global TOE – 'the theory of everything'. Hawking (1993) and others, such as Everett (1973), restore a sort of ironic renaissance causality at the universal level.

Competing tendencies, and factors attempting to realise possible futures, pulse with varying strengths in any period. An example of this state of affairs concerns Einstein. There was, in principle, a series of direct routes, we now know, from Einstein's work to late twentieth-century cosmology – one which was neglected in his time, that did not necessarily have to pass through the dogma of physics in the intervening years, though it did. Einstein himself was responsible, Salam (1992: 6–7) suggests, for the non-publication and disappearance of Kaluza's 1919 paper (see Brian Greene (2000: 185–203) for further details) which proposes a spacetime with five dimensions. This is now crucial to superstring and the cosmological theory of everything (TOE). In such ways there are probably many hidden variables within established astrophysics and cosmology, and in their boundaries, which effectively metaphorise the functioning of the theories that operate in neglect of such hidden variables, in addition to the many recognised and disputed cases of metaphoric shift within scientific discourse,[17] which I reclassify below as a species of live metaphor.

It is interesting to have a significant figure poking his nose into another subject's business. Sir Bernard Lovell (1992), a leading founder of radio astronomy, offered a historian's judgement. He depicted the Renaissance as having a twisted relation to our own time in such a way that it still shocks – in particular, when we consider Galileo. We may impishly select 'flatness' as an illustration to exemplify changing cultural paradigms. Long ago there were those who believed in a flat earth. It is not merely mischievous to note in this context that the astronomer Martin Rees (1995: 45–51) asks the question, 'Is the universe flat?' We now experience a three-dimensional universe whose overall distribution has the conjectured observational character of flatness, related as a product to the question of the role of (as they are currently formulated) two-dimensional strings in its origin.

Is the universe tied in knots?

So? Let us be logically ironic. Within the mathematics of string theory – aimed at the universe's earliest history – Edward Witten (1989) claims that cosmologists are struggling to escape a parallel with the mediaeval flat world. With regard to higher symmetries in string theory, fundamental to the TOE, a route has yet to be worked out as to how fully to formulate string theory in more than two dimensions. Michael Atiyah (1988) formulated the challenge to construct a more than two-dimensional solution to this problem. Witten responded by finding a three-dimensional definition of the relevant mathematics of knots and strings that can be related to quantum gravity.[18] It is one thing to achieve some three-dimensional definitions, ostensibly progressing along the route to achieve an underlying unified framework. As Witten (1989: 38) remarks, 'To bring order to this chaos looks hopeless. But by stripping out of flatland and looking at things from the standpoint of three dimensions [he notes that Atiyah suggests four] one can find a more powerful viewpoint'. This is a most unexpected inversion: we think it obvious to conceive the foundations of cosmology in four or more (particularly ten) dimensions.

Why do two-dimensional analyses work so well? Are they merely an accidental by-product of whatever stage we are at in solving technical problems? Maybe it is more than that. Is an instinct for a two-dimensional form part of a live metaphor instinct arising from our experience of surfaces, or merely an accident of current formal restrictions in string theory? Even if, or when, the restriction to two-dimensions is overcome, perhaps it may still be arguable that the emergence at all of the string theory in two-dimensions reflects a feature of our conceptual nature or characteristics of the early and later universe's structural ontology, possibly by appealing to a Kantian notion of perception and ontology.[19]

Could there be some conceptual relation between string and knot two-dimensional media used in mathematical cosmology, and other two-dimensional media such as painting and literary writing? As Carter and Saito (1994) demonstrate, the motion picture has been a central resource in representing and studying knotted surfaces in string theory which are deployed to depict the equations of quantum gravity and related phenomena. Jeffrey Weeks (1985) explains how to visualise the early universe's geometry (manifolds) in two-dimensional surfaces. This preoccupation with the visual is internal to the natures of the conceptions and not merely ornamental and didactic. Rather as three-dimensional cornices on a ceiling may be a motif that can be interpreted to depict a property of musical language.[20]

The status of sense in language has been the source of massive controversy, as has the status of the thought which it represents. Part of this dispute is the way in which mathematical and linguistic senses, as domains of significance, are abstract and multi-dimensional in their diverse inter-relations. This abstract status has a puzzling yet obvious relation to the ontology it represents. Just as a proper name does not die when its bearer does, so mathematics is, in the relevant sense, independent of the ontologies it depicts. In standard scenarios of the universe's origin(s), this gap between equations and their three (or plus) dimensional ontologies seems to disappear. Before the time of the Planck era (10^{-43}s) the relevant physics are unknown, or, as Rees (1995) says, are so speculative as to have a short shelf life.

Can the universe throw dice?

Consequently, if I may seem to digress, should we not loosen up tendencies to inflexibility, or a too narrow focus in the way that we sometimes reflect on apparently unrelated items? We may not be inclined to think of connections between an element, for example, in pure mathematics and a feature of aesthetic experience in art. This inclination often articulates an understandable worry about our misuse of analogy in which misperception is obscured by a misleading superficial similarity between terms. In the context of abstract art and music, Mallarmé's most abstract poetry, *Un Coup de Dés*, scholars have exposed unexpected formal bases linking formal and aesthetic types of enterprise.[21] Here we have the reverse of misuse of analogy: the exposure of underlying formal patterns in two-dimensional creativity. I want to argue that this can be extended to scientific cosmological language and the use of abstract language in creative attempts to visualise counter-intuitive realism and transcendence.

It may be worth exploring a possible metaphoric relation between the semiotic realm and its possible capacity to mirror exotic ontology in the context of original creativity. On some approaches to God and creation there is an irreducible, analytically unbridgeable gap in the dislocation between a proposed God's ontology, and the created world. One cannot infer necessity from contingency. Expressed *that* way, clearly a modal fallacy is involved. But just as mathematicians straddle gaps between infinity and the infinitesimal, so we might profit from assessing how 'incongruent counterparts' function.[22] Can creator and created, on opposed sides of multi-dimensional spacetime, be interfaced? (Perhaps, in attempting to answer this type of question, we should envisage an unrealised scientific future to the sort of questioning and styles Pascal (1954: 112–30) aborted, whilst continuing through the barrier he would not transcend, expressed in *Pensee* 687, when terminating correspondence with Fermat on probability in 1654.)[23] I suggest that current developments in the arts and sciences require radically new styles of discourse and mixing of distinct subjects to produce solutions to questions of transcendence and cosmology.

Let us suppose that the two-dimensional string theory, applied to the creation of the spacetime that resulted in the big bang, has a natural expression in two dimensions (is physically accurate in four and, in principle, is expressible in even more). We could thus sketch a scenario in which the relations between the two speech-act dimensions and the two string dimensions facilitate a *rejection* of the claims that in principle a creative speech-act is 'mystical' and not ontological.

Does modernism reduce to subjectivity?

Employing his perception of William James's pragmatism, Richard Rorty (1997) takes it that a proper philosophy of religion shrinks to a philosophy of mind.

This ignores the rational criteria external to solely intentional assessment of a topic, to which, following Levi's (1997) analysis of pragmatist rationality, we are committed. Pragmatism is not its own rational god: it utilises logic external to itself. So it is not free to sell off whatever it whimsically deems redundant. Rorty wants to define realist transcendence as a category error; but it is itself a category error to suppose that this is a consequence of understanding pragmatism. Rorty (1989: 8) thinks of himself as auxiliary to the poet rather than the physicist. Rorty (ibid.: 16), I think rightly, concludes that 'our language' in science is the outcome of sheer contingencies, which press us to admit that scientific revolutions are metaphoric redescriptions. He includes the big bang as one of these metaphors. But he does not allow for a revolution which treats his own stylistics as revisable and redescribable so as to be deployed to the worldviews he opposes. The present book suggests that the philosopher and the cosmologist are midway between the poet and the physicist. Accordingly, the book develops a concept of counter-intuitive realism which is a union of many differing fragments of culture and science, whilst not proffering the faithful sum of the institutions that led to their production. In this I agree with Rorty (ibid.: 96) that one can step aside from what he calls the Plato–Kant canon, though surely we can do this *and* make some positive redescriptive use of the canon. Let us also ironise Rorty's use of the term to include the Bible in this canon. I place metaphor at the centre of science, though proposing a fresh idea of metaphor – live metaphor – claiming that we can combine the notion of scientific truth in the universe with imagining and calculating it.

Contrariwise, Pippin approaches the conclusion of his study of modernism by stating that

> modernity ... is itself irresistibly provoked by the growing, ever more plausible possibility that what has been taken to be absolute and transcendent was contingent and finite ... Or, the modern ethos is always as self-deflating as self-inflating. Again, as presented by Kant, this means that the central sensibility that results from such reading of the modern revolution is not so much a need for some new positive realisation of who or what we 'truly' are, as it is a great, pervasive eternal unease with anyone pretending to speak in the name of such a truth.
> (Pippin 1991: 65)

The picture is a familiar one, retailed as urgent insight. But are we here being blackmailed into a now anachronistic presumption about the seeming uniqueness and significance of (merely) our modernism? Surely 'Plausible possibility' and 'contingent' are modalities whose logics entail their own possible negation. Yet Pippin mischievously operates them as if they have no reverse drive. Such treatments neglect to allow that contingent propositions can be counter-intuitive. Consequently they can produce inferential surprises. We need to dig much deeper than this sort of modernist conceptual policy operating as absolute prohibition. In such claims as those Pippin makes, 'modernism' assumes the role of an imperialism inexorably banning unfashionable possibilities. It is not that I have a reactionary scenario to restore past paradigms. Rather, we are so extensively ignorant of the relations of present scientific culture to universal generalisation and the reductionism required by concepts of simplicity, as well as these to elements in past cultures, that we have no relevant veridical criteria for adopting the position of certainty the modernism of, say, Pippin (1991) or the nihilistic pragmatism Rorty (1998) demands. A way of countermanding this reductionism is to assess aspects of past and present notions of simplicity, together with some of its relations to cosmology. Catherine Pickstock's (1997) analysis concludes that the pluralist modernism of, for example, distinctions crafting virtual reality, has an originating point in the later medieval world with Duns Scotus. Clearly Duns Scotus would not have judged that such modernist features even contingently imply Rorty's reductionism.

Simplicity, cosmology and Ockham's razor

Is Ockham's razor too complicated?

Although I have no interest in supposing that the medieval world can instruct science in a post-structuralist world, mischievous lessons can result from aligning some of their partial and unpredictably misleading similarities. Gibson (1998b) characterised Ockham's philosophy of simplicity, according to which Ockham had at least six competing and some contrary versions for the doctrine which later generations were to reduce to that conceptual singularity – the posthumously named Ockham's razor. Some scientific contexts appear to contradict Ockham's razor by the presence of informative complexity in a new more productive theory that is more informative than previous simpler scenarios, as with fundamental physics and superstrings (cf. Gross 1989). Although scientists appeal to Ockham's razor, their use of it often explicitly conflicts with Ockham's own express claim that it should only be employed outside the scope of observation statements,[24] which complies well with his desire to press demonstrative science into admission of uncertainty.

Ockham was aiming at a reduction of individuation in ontology,[25] and he denied that some relational states between propositions have to be distinct.[26] Ockham's use of a complex subtraction procedure employing negation to achieve reduction of entities is also a negation of parsimony, since its strategy is, albeit temporarily, to acknowledge the functionality of complex propositions, whilst negating them to achieve their elimination. In this perspective Ockham presupposes holistic metaphysical conjecture as epistemology, couched as semantic method. In a sense, Ockham has chosen the least equable, and yet experimentally productive, elements of two opposed universes of discourse: ontology and holism, though in experimental science their admixture is used profitably. Yet, as Horst (1996: 365–70) argues in a perspective outside of Ockham's studies (that of computational philosophical psychology), this approach to simplicity is in danger of overstating and being misleading about materialism in relation to ontology and psychology.

Ockham's desire to characterise ontology as the function of parsimony internalises a tension between realism and epistemology. If one conceives that necessity in reason is a criterion of identity for restricting ontological plurality, then ontological contingencies may be justifiably censored. This consideration can cut against empirical productivity as much as it can semantics. Ockham's way of meeting this tension is to internalise a version of anti-realism into the epistemological programme. But this 'anti-realism' is precariously positioned in relation to the traditions which he controverts, in particular, if contrasted with twentieth-century opponents of realism. Ockham, subsequent to what appears to be an early position in which he agrees with Scotus, attacks Duns Scotus's strong realism, though concurring with Duns Scotus that real relations are mind-independent. His aim is commendable in his parsimonious wish to place limits on excessively strong claims about empiricism, and at a time when scientific mythology and ignorance falsely generalised local experience.

Ockham and modernism in physics

Goddu's (1990: 208–31) study on Ockham rightly argues that this tendency is in keeping with our contemporary physics. Goddu furnishes us with the example in quantum mechanics of the scope of Bell's Theorem as an example of how to relate Ockham's interest in simplicity and anti-realism to select aspects of current physics, though obviously there is no possibility of placing Ockham's concepts in overall parallel with modern physics (however it has a place in the explanation of the role of elementary as against complex laws: see Arecchi 1997: 67). Bell's theorem has an implication that, in universalising realist claims in science, we must relinquish claims on locality or determinism respecting universal claims for empiricism. Clearly, even in this perspective, Ockham is a far cry from Bell. Ockham was concerned to argue that positing additional entities is not in principle a strategy for resolving realist problems in favour of a strong realism, just as the proposal that there are hidden variables in quantum mechanics does not resolve the issue of action at a distance without a medium. It seem clear that his view was being opposed by William of Crathorn (cf. Tachau 1988: 255–74). Crathorn, concerned with the purported uncertainty involved in intuitive cognition, affirms that incomplete objects in a propositional context are complex, disputing Ockham's reductionism and epistemological certainty (cf. Pasnau 1997). Crathorn's comprehension of propositional complexity, in the context of incomplete objects, is an unexpected partial parallel with our modern concepts of the incompleteness of a logical predicate (to be attached to a subject term) and limits to experimental knowledge of quantum, which pulls against Ockham's two-name theory. But whilst disagreeing with Crathorn and others, Ockham was impelled by the razor(s) to admit incompleteness as a conceptual condition so as to meet the restrictions of ignorance and yet adequacy according to empirical reductionism.

Would Ockham's razor be better as cosmology?

The above scenario interpreting Bell by Goddu is only a local difficulty when contrasted with a newer cosmological problem which can be derived from this scenario when other considerations are brought to bear on Ockham's ontology and anti-realism. Ockham's concern to link parsimony and anti-realism, together with a sense of empirical modesty in science, perhaps has its most fundamental, yet extreme, instance in a new area of research in the astrophysical cosmology of the early universe. The most exotic instance of Ockham's razor would be a single equation functioning as 'the' universal for the whole universe as a singularity, or one theorem specifying its state at certain levels at any time. This raises fundamental problems, not only for Ockham, but also for astrophysical cosmology itself. In his later work, Ockham inclined to the intellectio theory of the universal, according to which a universal concept simply is the act of cognition itself (though he has variant versions of the theory (cf. Ockham's *Ordinatio* for his later view). For him a universal signifies particulars: in this case, of the origin of the universe; in current astrophysics, the universe was the only particular. Ockham's anti-realism is an important support here; one cannot observe either position or momentum in this scenario. Further, in the earliest primordial cosmology, general relativity does not yet exist; so Ockham's razor objection applies against treating motion as a separate reality between things.

The cosmologists' 'Theory of Everything' (TOE) is a conjecture; a thesis that some philosophers have said is impossible. Contrariwise, the researches of astrophysicists such as Rees (1995, 1997, 1999) support its tenability. Rees offers mathematical and empirical evidence in which he presents a résumé of physics and observational evidence to suggest a reduction to only four basic cosmic numbers, with a single curvature number underpinning them for inflationary models of the primordial big bang hypothesis. (Rees suggests that some suitable version of the big bang scenario has a one-in-ten chance of being correct.) This accords well with Ockham's desire to achieve an ascending generality over ontology as a function of reduction in entities.

As indicated above, there is a fresh fundamental puzzle within such interpretations for Ockham, and within our contemporary cosmology, as well as philosophy applied to it. As mentioned above, Dallaporta (1993) argues that domains of microphysics and observational astrophysics – from which the foregoing results are ultimately derived – are metaphysics. He asserts this view because the basis for the above TOE violates some foundations of standard physics; yet it is clear that he accepts standard astrophysics as science.

In many areas of observational cosmology, theories and their theoretical languages are pushed into mathematical metaphor, as is the language of observation and inference. This situation comprises a complex metaphoric extension of the variables thus used. Bell (1987) had already warned, before some of the later of these results were known to cosmology, that quantum mechanical equations at the foundations of microphysics had entered a metaphoric zone, which he deemed to be akin to 'literary' use of terms and literary criticism so unstable and extended are they from local general physics. No doubt he intended guarded use of this comparison; he evidently supposed there to be some systematic similarity, however. One of the variables employed in the cosmology which gives rise to the surprising inference and reduction of entities to a singularity is the Planck mass. It is a

28 *Renaissance in language*

fundamental constant in local physics and physicists do not regard its truth as open to question. Yet the states of affairs indicated in the foregoing, and quantum-mechanical considerations, have been employed to imply that there exist masses larger than the Planck mass, which are not taken to be possible in terrestrial physics by Dallaporta (1993: 330) – the 'consequence has not to be taken literally'. Nevertheless, it is a consequence of scientific research. This type of consequence is the current scientific evidence of a singularity, and singularity states of affairs, in which reductionism, numerical integration and observation yield a bare ontology that sustains an original paraphrase of Ockham's claim.

Can a formal language use poetic sense?

There is a significant problem of language here that can assist us to revive a neglected relation within medieval debate. 'Improper supposition' in Ockham's writing is a non-literal metaphorical use of a name, with proper supposition having a formal 'literal' identity which was exclusive of improper supposition. But it appears that we cannot properly keep them apart if we follow inferences in Ockham's philosophy. Such a situation partially mirrors our contemporary debates on the contrasts between 'literal' scientific formal language (as with mathematical functions) and metaphoric usage. The two arenas collapse into each other. That is to say, in the state of affairs in which one seems to be able to construct universalised statements and their inferences tied to empirical theory, literal and metaphoric expressions intermingle and inject each other. A stronger form of this is possible: necessarily, for one to be capable of manufacturing language which embodies universalisation and empirical relations – for example a (or the) singularity – then one has to employ metaphoric expressions in formal inferences. (I return to the relations between 'literal' and 'metaphoric' in Chapter 2, and in various later parts of the book.) So, let us resort, even merely for convenience, to the way of phrasing medieval distinctions which I suggest have post-structuralist and scientific analogues; cosmology has brought together separate areas of proper and improper supposition that Ockham and others kept apart. Yet Ockham unwittingly indirectly commits himself to this sort of eventuality by insisting on a parsimonious razor associated with empirically based anti-realism.

This is not the context in which to explore a number of extensive issues here: Ockham associates immateriality with the capacity for knowing concepts, while his anti-realism allows for experimenting with links between semantic theory and ontology. Is it too bold to allow a deconstructed Ockham a new theory fed by cosmology concerning creation? Ockham concludes a study on universals by stating: 'What primarily moves the intellect is not a universal but a singular. Therefore, the singular is primarily understood with a primacy of generation'.[27] But in the origin of our universe, consensus has it that the universal was the singular. This is also said to be true of the Theory of Everything.

Are consequences between simplicity and complexity counter-intuitive?

The foregoing cosmological state of affairs can be classed as an extreme case of Popper's (1972) conjectural knowledge in which Ockham's universalising aspirations over a reductionist ontology together with an anti-realist theory of knowledge have support. It may be that only in a counter-intuitive state of affairs can these aspects of Ockham be realised together. It would be a genetic fallacy to infer, from the prospect that Ockham's razor and anti-realism apply to a hypothesis directed at the beginning of the universe, that they hold true of it now. But I argue that a counter-intuitive version of Ockham's razor could be a policy for the theory of multiverse beginnings, without supposing that his principle(s) of parsimony is generally true. The relations of simplicity to complexity, in the light of counter-intuitive consequences, remain unexplored by Ockham and analytical philosophy.

Anti-realism is a highly contingent enterprise in relation to ontology. Casimer Lewy's (1976) view, for example, was that strict implication lies beyond the presuppositions of what various forms of entailment are. He argued that such presuppositions are strongly counter-intuitive. Lewy exposed how these difficulties also cover the whole sphere of what it is to be contingent propositions. Although Lewy employed the term 'counter-intuitive' to mark a central feature of these problems, yet he did not define it nor give it any attention, though his use of it to summarise the foregoing sort of difficulty advertises some of its properties. (So in drawing attention to the value of some of his analysis, I am not advocating his overall approach.) Ockham was grossly ignorant of this whole arena, and its relation to simplicity. If one adds to it the self-inhering complexity in any deep ontological issue in the cosmology of the universe which attract anti-realism, we may have to consider the prospect of a complex counter-intuitive realism to counter, or counter-intuitively combine with, Ockham's principle of parsimony.

The explanatory appeal of simplicity is that it allows testable generalisation to employ a controlled form of reductionism as a presupposition. But our ignorance of the universe and logic is such that it is not always clear that the conjunction of generalisation and reductionism matches the universe. Such simplicity has the property of suppressing complexity in its presupposition, since the universe and those properties encapsulated in generalisation are complex.

This is a counter-intuitive relation which uneasily mirrors some current observations. I do not wish to pursue this point much further here, save to illustrate the foregoing. Saunders *et al.* (1991) claim in their redshift survey to overturn some assumptions about density and distribution in the early universe, though their conclusions have been questioned. For example, the discovery of giant congregations of overdense galaxies, the Great Attractor, the Great Wall,[28] in contrast with massive high voids of space, seem to sit uneasily with the uniform distribution of the cosmic microwave background radiation. As Hu (2000) notes, the Boomerang observations, of over 14 billion light years away and conjecturally of some 300,000 years after the big bang, have highlighted this by reporting some major asymmetries in the early universe's plasma state before galaxies were formed. De Bernardis *et. al.* (2000) argue that the observational data are inconsistent with current models based on topological defects, and maintains that they are consistent with a subset of cold dark matter models of the universe. Longair (1994: 1–6, 376–77) regards this disparity as a fundamental problem, while exclaiming that the latter is a 'miracle that the dispersion ... relation remains constant [for infrared] out to redshifts of two and possibly beyond'. More generally, Polkinghorne (1994) suggests that complexity, in which the behaviour of the parts of complex systems is more than the sum of their parts, enables one to recognise the incompleteness of science yet envisage a means to infer a reality more subtle in which some domains are metaphysical.

It seems that some aspects of the foregoing cosmological, astronomical and astrophysical results are counter-intuitive. When they are contrasted, for example, with some fashionable philosophical, and a cultural over-confident abstraction of profiles ascribed to local experimental science, we have a number of deep problems. One of them, to be pursued in subsequent chapters, is the challenge of how to formulate what it is to be a correspondence between the universe (or part of it) and language we employ to depict it. Even refined versions of correspondence theory in philosophy have not taken account of such puzzling empirical states of affairs.

Ending poststructuralism?

Does the past correspond to the future?

Always occupying the present, we humans sometimes tend to be inconsistently bivalent toward the past and future, using the present to condemn the past or condone it, and to discover a new future which complies with either recipe. Alternatively, there could be the option of complex counter-intuitive correspondences.

It is common for some of the writers cited above, such as Rorty (1997), to presuppose a standardised notion of correspondence theory, which they then demolish or discount by often subtle appeal to a variety of alternative notions of language and pragmatism. Too readily do they turn this admixture into a self-evident deconstruction of the possibility of a fresh approach to a theory which articulates a concept of correspondence. It is worth adding here to the foregoing reference to John Richardson's (1996) exposition of Nietzsche as an unexpected protagonist of a counter-intuitive version of correspondence theory. Richardson shows that Nietzsche uses an unexpected sense of 'system' to structure his writings. Whether or not we fully agree with Richardson, it is still fairly clear that such a possibility removes the objection to theory of correspondence that has often been accepted. This opposes Rorty's (1997) alleged dissolution of transcendent philosophies, valuable though much of the work in his *Mirror of Nature* (1980) is.

If we, thus, merely provisionally, align Richardson's (1996) new idea of correspondence in Nietzsche with, for example, a philosophically refined presentation of the cosmologist Dallaporta's (1993) use of 'consequence' and the cosmology contiguous to it examined above (and to be discussed further below), we have a quite revolutionary basis for a scenario of a transcendent correspondence of scientific language to non-observational science. That is to say, Dallaporta argued that empirical science in exotic areas, of which some microphysics is also a corollary, goes well outside justified empirical calculations. This violates a standard realist notion of scientific correspondence of theory to experiment. Oddly, despite this, there is a veridical connection between observation in cosmology and theory, which generates confirmation of results in some terrestrial sciences, as subsequent chapters argue. So here we have a policy of counter-intuitive correspondence of cosmological science with a counter-intuitive realism, where 'counter-intuitive' here has the value of a deviation from correspondence of theory to experiment in the quantifiable realm of, for example, laboratory physics. The resultant prospects, for new correspondence theories, are not small potatoes.

It is salutary to observe in relation to the foregoing that scientists seem to be far more modest about their conceptual claims, which index their relations to an epoch's cultural identities, than are some post-structuralists who have already, effectively, instructed what future humanities and science will discover in their relations to the universe. But surely is not this judgement of mine, in mood if not content, a disguised form of the reactionary attitude against modernism? No; quite the reverse. It is a familiar psychoanalytical picture: the liberated victims of censorship unconsciously imitate the intolerance of the conceptual fathers they have, rightly, castigated.

We should distinguish between a person n_1 at t_1 holding a concept p (say, that there are absolute truths to be known about God), from n_1 at t_1 holding a concept q whose sense is an interpretation of concept p (say, that we must believe in a given version ϕ of p). Such relations should also be kept separate from the criteria, if they are accessible, to assess the external world's context ξ at t_1 in which '$(p \Leftrightarrow q) \rightarrow r$' is asserted as a piece of worldview, from which accordingly extrapolations r are made and perhaps causally coerced about p. The criteria of judgement, about the world context functions of ξ, tend in the later historical context φ (say, post-structuralism) to be confused or conflated with the criteria for exposing the possibility of p, by presupposing a suppressed premise, namely, the false consequence '$(p \Leftrightarrow q) \rightarrow r$'. This would be rather like concluding that possibly Newton's gravitational theory is false because of our view of his background assumptions about alchemy. That is to say, some people act as if, or claim to infer, from demolishing a version ϕ in q that p is impossible. For example, Rorty (1997) in effect does this regarding all theistic truth claims for all cultures at all times, as a function of our evolutionary progress. He seems to assign the sort of omniscience to himself which is a capacity internal to the God whom he has purported to show cannot exist. Rorty has suppressed the premise by banning p as impossible. Yet, since not even consciousness has yet been explained by evolution, it seems premature to take it that self-evidently we know the status and identity of a range of universal metaphysical states or their negation. Certainly, there is interaction between a believer and his culture, and some background assumptions in a cultural context eradicate the credibility of some epistemological claims; we should also allow for the ways in which progress of understanding in later cultures reveals a past conception p to have no correspondence in the actual world or to be wrong, whereas p was held to be true in a former culture. (For example, incredible as it is, that human child sacrifice is right, or that the earth is flat). But in conjunction with such recognition we should acknowledge that civilised culture has a record of privileging the arbitrary as though it were a decision procedure for discarding variant interpretations, using belief premises as functions in the service of an imperious sense of a culture's progress. In this respect, one may conclude that Rorty has a profile which is quite similar to his home country's (USA) foreign policy. Surely we need to be far more modest about our claims to know and supersede the mastery of possibility than is customary in post-structuralism? And to accept this, as argued here, is the contrary of championing the past as the criterion of truth.

A willingness to look afresh at the past as well as future possibilities has partly to do with the prospect, to be argued below, that some past and present collisions between humanities and science should now give way to the possibility of a partial integration of features in both subjects. But we should guard against overstating and attempt correctly to focus this sort of rapprochement.

One psychoanalytically revealing feature of human linguistic life is our propensity to name as singular what is irreducible to one phenomenon. Science and humanities pull against this characteristic by attempting universal generality. Yet some scientists interested in terrestrial matters find the lack of local laboratory proof in cosmology a distasteful sign of too easy generality, whilst much history of the humanities variously pitches between no generality and all universality. So there are internal disagreements in science and within the humanities, though there are areas of agreement. Although preserving a strong sense of individuation here, yet we should also look afresh at divisions which might be healed by transforming, as well as mapping the way aspects of the sciences and humanities share common properties.

Do we compose our consciousness?

In musical aesthetics Dahlhaus remarked:

> More rewarding than a search for precedents of modernity is a study of the initiatives and interrupted developments that have been left aside by the history that leads up to us.
>
> (Dahlhaus 1983: 100)

Now this may be overstatement (not least since it could be applied to modernism itself with profit). Yet it need not be a reactionary project; it could be a visionary, counter-intuitive means to future renaissance. We could apply here a distinction which Christine Brooke-Rose (1991, 1981) developed: the palimpsest novel – Pynchon's *Vineland* (1990), *Gravity's Rainbow* (1973) and Eco's *Name of the Rose* (1980) exemplify this distinction. We could take these types of enterprises as metaphors used to excavate neglected subjunctive counterfactual possibilities in history, as well as attempting to conceive the future by exploring ignored possibilities in our contemporary research in science and the arts. For Brooke-Rose, these novels map out possibilities unrealised in the history in which they are fictionally set. The point of the palimpsest novel is to construct new possible histories of the past for our future. Fundamental advances in science often stand as palimpsest rewritings of earlier veridical science. Chaos theory in cosmology is like a palimpsest reification of quantum theory, for example. A conjunction of the arts and sciences has palimpsest elements. The present book develops and employs elements from the philosophies of astrophysics, cosmology, philosophy, literary cultures and ethics to formulate an approach to constructing aspects of philosophical cosmology.

Implementation of the foregoing scenario requires to some degree an explicit sense of scientific metaphor and its relation to consciousness. Language-consciousness is a subordinate aspect of the larger question of consciousness, which is the still scientifically unexplained product of the origin of species. Sir Andrew Huxley (1982) has called this the most important unresolved problem concerning the origins of life. Although this situation only indirectly impacts on literary metaphor, it is worth noting that John Bayley (1961) has argued for the fundamental and problematic role of consciousness in Shakespeare. These tensions reflect dilemmas for the functions metaphor which I am challenging when offering the transformed counter-intuitive notion of mimesis presented below. The present priorities require a new perspective for language-consciousness. The exploration of its structure functioning at cosmological levels, obliquely yet fundamentally pivot on basic questions about the nature of creative thought in relation to its representation by use of language in the arts and sciences.

I propose that this language-consciousness generally, and as it pertains to religion, is manifestly one of live metaphor, or of personification of consciousness. As Paxson (1994: 165) shows, a personified text can be a metaphor for the consciousness it mediates. Language itself is a live metaphor for the thought processes. There is a frequently canvassed view about choices in reading a narrative between the realism in a text as opposed to the accurate reader's reality. This book attempts to break down or qualify this opposition at relevant junctures.

We can read either subjectively or objectively Ingmar Bergman's thesis 'a theatre's basis in reality is its audience'.[29] Following a live metaphor view, which is rather like a performance, a text's realism mirrors these possible worlds of realism in a text and the reader's psychological realism. The combination of these two options lead to a reading of what some of history's new possibilities are. Obviously this perspective should not be overstated; it is intended as a supplement to already distinguished work, though the use of detail can produce inferences which result in general differences. Salmon Rushdie's *The Satanic Verses* (1988) has been used by Christine Brooke-Rose to illustrate, somewhat untypically, the above type of reinterpretation of literary history and narratives about it. Some Islamic responses to the *Satanic Verses* portray how external non-textual social parameters dislodge what could have been another reading of it – free from the context composed by such readers. Many empirically impossible things happen in such novels; the foregoing Eco's *Name of the Rose* and Pynchon's *Vineland* fall into this category of inventing unexpected histories. Such novels can be treated as complex metaphors which evoke unrealised narrative possibilities, and at times ontological potential of the past. This could be a lesson for a modernist's inattention to the past.

A return to some former religious norms is to be avoided, of course; but the possibility of a future creative environment partly devolves on uptake from unused or misused fragments from history, as well as new compositions. The marvellous potential in the third millennium for fresh cultural experiment and insight could transform or expose elements of the ancient past, and yield a quite fresh framework for our possible futures. If this can be done in a palimpsest novel, can we not achieve it in a philosophy?

Could we personify a future realism?

Such a view could be founded on a realism developed from a suitable notion of language-consciousness. This approach could be a subset of a generalised thesis presupposing the reciprocity of the arts and the sciences at suitable creative levels, set in an interactive live metaphor for scientific languages. In this I am especially concerned with science that displays the highest level of empirical generality, that of astrophysical cosmology. I wish to argue that this is an appropriate case for receiving and testing claims about reciprocity between arts and sciences.

Within this perspective certain religious language could contain uses which mirror universalising tendencies in arts–sciences rapprochement. The employment of 'mirror' here is tricky, deriving from the foregoing appeal to the metaphor of dramaturgy. The concept of a mirroring between (inter)disciplinary structures has many precedents. Torrance's *Theological Science* (1969) and his (1999) study of time, with their original attention to some patristic and medieval philosophies of science, are cases in point.

In contrast, Malcolm Bowie's (1993) explicit nuanced and ironised formulation, as well as critical assessment, of Lacan's use of 'mirroring' is one of an array of approaches that can contribute to depict quantifiable value relations between transcendent language in psychoanalysis and French poetry; nor is this dependent on a Lacanian reading. Bowie's (1978) study of difficulty in Mallarmé, facilitates Dee Reynolds' (1995) exposure of mirror structures in symbolist transcendent language. In the last three works cited, the authors present matching relations between music, dance-drama, geometry and rhythmic form in connection with poetic transcendence. This is taken to be informative about the natures of mentality and beauty. I shall argue the same for divine cosmology in relation to transcendence.

Schulte-Sasse (1987: 12–14) has maintained that the theory of drama and representation pioneered by Szondi (1987) is defective because it absorbs some of Lukács's thesis that art has a mimetic structure. This judgement may be true with some traditional versions of mimesis, as with Auerbach (1968); but in this book I shall attempt to draw on and develop a multifarious form of mimesis which sidesteps this criticism, and suggest that abstract states in art can be mimetic of mental states. Szondi's theory, I propose, can benefit from being drawn into this new framework at the junctures where he pinpoints self-consciousness and its dialogue as central to mimesis.

In this perspective, the live (not dead) metaphoric visualisation of properties ascribable to the transcendental, the metaphysical and the divine, is a counter-intuitive use of mimesis which I shall argue has parallels with attempts to infer the identity of the early history of the universe from its later states. The above mix of visual, literary, mental, audio and conceptual relations have parallels with the philosophy of film, particularly in perspectives attracted through psychoanalytical studies. Later in the book I add an analysis of virtual reality mimesis to this mix, hoping to dispute the conflicts between intentionalist and anti-intentionalist opinions about meaning. Communication presupposes informative transmission and perception, though I do not underestimate the problems associated with codes of interpretation. An upshot of this position is that it is not enough to adopt notions of realism and language-consciousness, nor endless pluralistic models for them. One requires accounts of the two phenomena which are both generalised and specific to examples in associated humanities and scientific narratives.

Consider three widely separated cases where language-consciousness can emerge: music, pure mathematics and visual art – the latter two to be explored in more detail, and the former briefly, in this book.

We should not assume that the materials or disciplines are relevantly formulated for such a project. For example, music theory may herald some applications of logic to composition which might stimulate new reflections on the domain of logic and how logic might be extended to include aesthetic properties. Boretz's (1972) conversion of Goodman's theory of action to music may not be attractive to some on account of its nominalist origin, but it indicates a possible demarcation point for applying logic to music. More sophisticated research by Milstein (1992) on Schoenberg brings us closer to a suitable presentation of creative logical possibilities. Malcolm Bowie's (1978) and Scott's (1988) treatment of musicality in Mallarmé's poetry opens up the prospect of relating musical form to poetic metaphysics, linked to pictorial poetics, in which Mallarmé used symbolism reminiscent of theology.

These sorts of projects press for and answer the question: 'Is music a language?' 'Music has syntax' would be a helpful response to one part of this question. Music shares a relative-identity with language, at the level of a live metaphor, and this book thus defends the view that languages exhibit relative-identity relations, such as that used in John's Gospel and Aquinas's *Summa*.[30] It is worth considering a scenario in which music has linguistic syntax but no semantics, and that in place of semantics it has a signifying system to represent the values which correlate with emotions or tonal qualities. In this way, music may correlate with other languages, such as those in cosmology, though domains other than emotion, of course, would occupy the position which semantics holds in natural languages, as I attempt to show below.

Do music and mathematics share beauty?

Within a context of transcendence, this time-sharing project might be jump-started by assessing Polkinghorne's (1998) elegant dismantling of the whole prospect of *traditional* proofs in natural theology, whilst he wants the topic of proof to survive; that he is a distinguished mathematical physicist is worth noting. It is true that these traditional proofs are almost crudely mechanistic, and as 'proofs' inept in the light of current research work on logic. But in the same study Polkinghorne desires (as does, for example, the chemist Hoffmann (1990)) to recognise that there is beauty in various mathematical equations. Such a view seems to reflect a wish to classify this sort of beauty as a transcendent property. It is as yet unclear in the limits of our understanding to what extent this 'transcendent' notion is simply a departure from currently calculable properties in objective phenomena, or an aspect which mirrors a sense outside physical phenomena.

In Polkinghorne's desire to associate divinity in some sense with the natural world, he concurred with me that the following project attends to possible relations that should be explored. Why not transfer the claims of mathematical beauty over to the natural theology proofs area? And why not deem the natural theology proofs as rough misleading approximations, of what would constitute actual proofs, so we can proceed to attempt to construct the latter using some real mathematics and refined logic? Although this book will not implement this programme in detail, it will examine some problems which it leaves aside. Let us suppose that, just as with, say, Dalton's theory of the atom, only fragments of an early scientific theory survive (are invariant with respect to) a current scientific account of the atom. Consider placing this in parallel with 'proofs' in natural theology, though we have as yet no logically adequate natural theology, unlike atomic theory.

Asserting judgements of mathematical beauty is tantamount to admitting such formal aesthetic properties. Given the ways in which mathematical proofs have complex and sometimes approximating relations to the physical world, we should allow some such gap or indeterminacy with regard to natural theology. Within this gap is the problem of whether or not an aesthetic and mathematical properties pick out a single ontological feature, as in the case of using more than one description of a single intentional action. The breakdown of parallel here may coincide with the collapse of one's grasp of 'following a rule', especially in asymmetries between first and third persons (cf. Ebbs 1997). My aim is not polemical here; the purpose is merely to soften up unphilosophical dogmatism both in science and in religion. We know too little about the subjects to form the final judgements which the spirits of reactionary Christianity and of modernism have imposed.

Is intelligibility universal?

Within the above arena is a creative topic, which might be expressed as follows. If music is not a language, then language cannot express all that is fundamental in the universe. Music shares some properties with natural, scientific, and logical languages. I propose that musical language resembles or has an informative live metaphor relation to cosmological aesthetic language. Just as a symphonic score codes properties which are disclosed in its performance, so details of the universe's meaning are displayed in the unfolding cosmological observations; correctly understood at a number of levels, this involves the assignment of aesthetic properties to the universe.

One feature of this conjunction, to be explored in Chapters 3 and 4, is the use of pure mathematics to provide ontologies for the very early universe – as, for example, in Wada (1986). The familiar claim that mathematics contains beauty is apt here; the application of the Scrödinger equation to the big bang illustrates this type of beauty (cf. Boukricha 1985). We should, in agreement with Gombrich (1986: 119), be wary of imposing Platonic metaphysics on stylised beauty, whilst surely Penrose (1994a, 1990) is justified in suggesting that basic features of mathematics such as an algorithm mirror a transcendental order and beauty. But we should note concern that some aesthetics (overlaying the world of 'descriptive' science) may obscure experimental clarity.

At the centre of this issue, when theological concerns obtrude, is whether or not one can consistently regard God as a cosmological actor with the universe manifesting aesthetic properties which in some way mirror the projected creator. Mothersill (1984: 383) uses a Kantian approach in which expressions such as 'beautiful' function as a logical predicate of a proposition. Although I do not follow Kant, this appears an interesting move, yet it does not follow that one has thereby to presuppose a system of laws of taste. We need to formulate concepts of counter-intuition (see below) and what it would be to have laws which did not occupy a position in a system to expand on such logical predicates, however. Perhaps shifts of meaning in scientific revision of concepts betray the need for a different sort of perception of science from that which is sometimes proffered. Something which is akin to aesthetics? Can astronomy and astrophysics assist one to a realist Romantic future?

Counter-intuitive Renaissance?

Can we know what we expect?

The term 'counter-intuition' will be scrutinised later. For now, let us assume that 'counter-intuition' is a conclusion which follows from the negation of what a person skilled in standard art of conclusion-reaching would expect as its antecedent.[31] Counter-intuition may be a matter of surprise about what we expect, and/or the surprise of objective discovery, such as curved spacetime. Sometimes the goalposts of counter-intuition shift. But, as with, for example, Gödel's incompleteness theorems, our intuitions are genuinely falsified: we would have thought that proofs for the foundations of arithmetic can be completed. Concerning vast areas of complexity, where dispute is rife, perhaps there is only a little hope that the boundaries between counter-intuition and fantasy or science-fiction can be determined. Questions of transcendence are prone to fall into this class, and are infected by whatever spirit of the age is adopted to deem it that rationality supports a particular consensus on the 'nature' of reality.

This interacts with the formulation of movements down history. Could not a sort of new Renaissance multidisciplinary approach, radically linked to new developments in arts and science replace post-structuralism with a positive basis? This would require recognition of connections across separated subjects. We do not have a free warrant for generalised interdisciplinary synthesis; yet there is a need to investigate the possibility that multidiscipline specialities could cross-fertilise in a manner productive for the most general scientific account of the universe. Academia tends to exhaust the world of learning by reducing the variety of subjects to what faculties there are.

There is another subject needing to intercede: the set of connections between these subjects, which is itself the most general subject, the cement of the universe. In some suitably refined sense, this would be cosmological interpretation. Frequently these connections are counter-intuitive to many institutional or traditional ways of thinking within the confines of individual disciplines; and this could reflect why such links are not always recognised or positioned for what they are. The recent discovery that the foundations of arithmetic are random and unexpectedly complex in their randomness[32] manifests the idea that counter-intuitive foundations can subsume the familiar notions which they fracture. Consequently, the sort of criteria which concern language-consciousness and its content are often those that are counter-intuitive.

Is there a standpoint from outside of the universe?

Obviously there are dangers here. Imagination may dictate empirical structure; some history of the visual arts exemplifies this. For example, specific roles were accorded paintings in eighteenth- and twentieth-century England, with the roles of paintings in civic humanism, under the influence of, especially, Joshua Reynolds, and subsequently Hazlitt. These were inverted from public institutional to private aesthetic functions, informed as they were by theories competitively (dis)associating the political republic and the republic of taste.[33] It is the underlying general presuppositions of culture which determine the choice. This provides an analogy with cosmology: should it be seen on its own terms only, or does it require supplementing with external cement from other subjects? Indeed, does this way of posing the issue presuppose a prejudice in favour of autonomy in cosmology? Might not the deepest assessment of data within cosmology entail universals apparently external to it?

This thesis complements the view that, with respect to cosmology and issues in philosophy, some researches are reaching a stage for use in achieving a generalised conception of counter-intuitive creativity, in which a breakthrough quite discontinuous with the hitherto normative science versus arts oppositions is conceivable. The old systems twist and groan under the threshold pressure to describe new worlds; and there is a tendency to measure the worth of new contributions by appeal to normative constraints which are actually conjectural in status.

Metaphoric cosmology

How does science mess with metaphor?

Metaphor associates the old and the new. Some natural language metaphors in physics are misused in popularised employment ('charm' particles are not entranced) if their metaphoric senses have no significant empirical descriptive value.[34] But it does not follow from this that the mathematical and abstract physical representations of the phenomena do not themselves contribute some metaphoric feature in description. With regard to other metaphors, however, natural language terms can have a figurative sense, as with 'superstrings' which can be considered to have a live metaphoric descriptive sense (as I suggest below). Polkinghorne's (1991: 29–30) suggestion is that a relevant class of metaphors are 'shorthand', for example, for ellipsis or metonymy. Artistic metaphors can be employed in, and can be applied to, cosmology in such a way as to confer (to expose) religious explanatory power, reminiscent of aesthetical insight, on the physical universe. This will involve aligning discontinuous topics, creating dislocations, producing fractured sequences; in short, a series of ring systems and intercalations to bring into sight the possibilities of linking cosmology and philosophy/theology by treating other subjects as their cement.

The conjectural provisional status of much cosmology makes the significance of revision in theory in the light of new observations a significant matter for insisting that cosmology does not of itself hold the position of an experimental science, in the relevant sense. Cosmology manifests a special identity whose structure is susceptible to metaphysical explanation. Some might wish to argue that this reception of metaphysics is so much the worse for cosmology. Certainly astronomical sense is less quantifiable in its calculative experimental basis than is local physics, though the universe is a bigger place than the physics laboratory. Nevertheless local physics also manifests substantial discontinuities, such as transcendental terms (theorising about light, for example). It contains no final unification. Complete synthesis in the various branches of local physics has not been achieved, so cosmology and local physics share some comparable restrictions in which both edge forward, not only experimentally in different ways, but also by provisional hypotheses which integrate qualitative and quantitative data. This hybrid will at times be uneasy, certainly provisional, yet on occasions it manifests descriptive power which not only questions contemporary assumptions but encapsulates stronger versions of reality than previously supported.

Astronomy is constantly having to redress and transform observational theories, sometimes with metaphoric experimental and mathematical language, albeit adorned with relatively accurate quantitative measurements. Some of the early 1970s' Jodrell Bank neutron star pulses (see Figure 0.2) did not correctly expose some states of the binary and millisecond pulsars. The research at that stage (one might plausibly argue when later research is taken into account) amounted to a sort of misleading surface grammar such as Wittgenstein (1995a) suggested in his *Investigations*, or, for example, Anscombe's (1957) view that 'intending', though grammatically an act, is a mental state.

Can we observe metaphors?

Sometimes metaphors in science embody a provisional usage of empirical and mathematical description. In such occurrences, metaphor drops out of

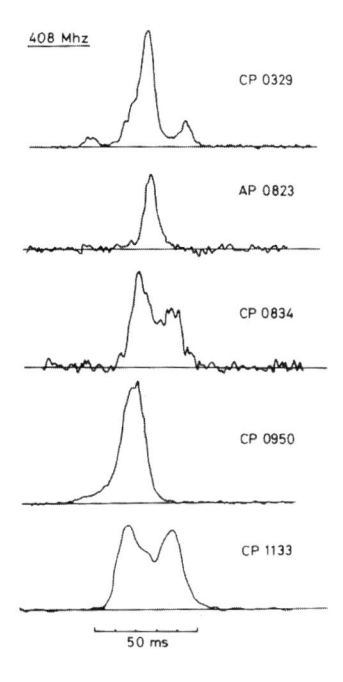

Figure 0.2 Jodrell Bank neutron star pulses of PSR 1958
Source: Andrew Lyne and Jodrell Bank Radio-Astronomy Laboratories

the equation as experimental insight is increased. Outside of the scope of this situation there appear to be types of usage in which an accurate account of a physical state of affairs is achieved by incorporating and retaining live metaphor. That is to say, subject to later qualification, it might crudely be stated ontological states of affairs precisely display live metaphoric functions. The present book will cite a variety of such uses to present an assessment of prospects; a brief discussion to introduce selected aspects is suitable for an introductory purpose here. At Jodrell Bank, Smith and Lyne (1987) generated a metaphoric jump for the language of pulsars in their research on the millisecond binary pulsar PSR 1913+16 – two pulsars, in a double pulsar set. The speed ~10-3 is appreciably near the velocity of light. Its companion pulsar has a bizarre orbit which almost caresses the surface of its twin. It seems that the one pulsar gave birth to the other by transferring mass from its surface, creating a highly abnormal gravitational field. (Chapter 4 below deals with the relevance of this pulsar type for general relativity.) It appears that this pulsar typifies a class of neutron stars which went through rebirth, and they leave the impression of being younger than they actually are. They seem to be white dwarfs which did not go through the trauma of a supernova explosion; this was quite the contrary of previously interpreted observations. Wolzyzan discovered that planets orbit pulsars by noticing irregularities in the reception of pulses,[35] partly as a result of noticing anomalies in some observations. It appears accurate to designate many of these anomalies and also description of some of the alternating states associated with pulsars as evidence of live metaphor within the observational and theoretical languages. The odd gravitational fields associated with the pulsars, and the exchange of mass, are a bewitched surface grammar which are easily perceived as if they obscure their actual history.

In this context the change from one pulsar paradigm to another provokes the use of a switch in frames of reference for metaphoric terms such as 'birth' and 'rebirth', which also reflect a metaphoric shift in the scope of pulsar conception. This type of illustration, specific though it is, depicts how astronomical hypothesis related to cosmology makes use of metaphors which not only carry the explanatory theme of a new breakthrough but also interlock with quantitative measurements.

The use of 'metaphor' here has to be carefully modified and qualified, reflected in the 'live metaphor' thesis to be advanced below. This has a relation to, but is in many ways is quite different from, Hesse's (1983) idea of scientific language as metaphor. Although prediction is a criterion of science, no one envisaged that pulsars (such as the binary ones) have the properties which they do. But, in contrast with some exotic affairs in the universe, these binary pulsars are somewhat low level cases of objects of counter-intuition of which there are almost infinitely higher level unexpected orders of counter-intuitive states deeper in the matter of the universe and early in its history, of which superstrings are an example (see Chapter 3). Just as the wave-particle theories of light are transcendental, so more exotic cosmological phenomena exhibit surprising transcendence by comparison with laboratory science.

Some scientists may contend that some day there will be a plain explanation of such topics which makes any transcendental opinion redundant. But it should be noticed that this conjecture is itself transcendental on two counts: first, it presupposes a principle of universal intelligibility; second, it metaphysically requires that the imagined scenario has properties which eliminate transcendence. With the emergence of quantum mechanics at the microphysical and cosmological scales, to say the least, it is not obvious that this view is correct. So it is a modest move, for the moment, to return to the present local context to position ourselves.

The scope of 'relevance'

What of unscientific contexts for cosmology?

The tendency to metaphorise in science is not a use of processes in historical or social vacuums. The mental activity mirrored in scientific discourses lives in conjunction, perhaps in contract, with the societies which craft the enterprise of science. Scientific objectivity and realism, as well as imagination, usually properly connive at reducing or removing the distorting influences of non-empirical, untheoretical external impacts on science. But sometimes such external experience is positive in its contribution to observation and theory building in science. For these, and other, reasons, it is worth while contrasting and observing some boundaries and characteristics of our cultures as they impinge on scientific creativity and perceptions of relevance to cosmology, including our apprehension of our place in present history.

The present might start anywhere: with the modern city built on sand, as seen through Apollinaire's poem, 'Zone':

> Tu marches vers Auteuil tu veux aller chez toi a pied
> Dormir parmi tes fetiches d'Oceanie et de Guinee
> Ils sont des Christ d'une autre croyance
> Ce sont des Christ inferieur des obscures esperances

> You walk back to Auteuil you want to walk home
> To sleep in the midst of your fetiches from Guinea and the South Sea Isles
> They are the Christs of another form and another faith
> These are the lesser Christs of obscure aspirations.

David Kelley offered an interpretation of Apollinaire's later poetry by proposing that there is a suggested resolution of

> how to find a poetic language capable of affirming without contradicting by the nature of that affirmation, the conditions of modern urban experience, one which can accommodate the sense of cultural fragmentation which is an important element in that experience – the 'heap of broken images' of which Eliot speaks in *The Waste Land* – without attempting to totalise it in a way which belies its nature, one which can replace the perspectives of European civilisation since the Renaissance without denying the significance of its cultural inheritance or residue, which can make out of what has been perceived as an artistic decadence, artistic rebirth.
>
> (Kelley 1985: 95–96)

Let us take this poetry as a token among other types of genres.

We are subject to peculiar tensions. If all the constraints are adhered to, how can there ever be change? If an element in the modern society is the heap of broken images, what would it be to contradict that heap? If we criticise the contemporary 'contradictions of Christianity', are we allowed to extirpate this 'Christianity' which is like this, and yet retain a 'poetic language capable of affirming without contradicting … the conditions of modern urban experience'; or is modernity to insist that Christians should not contradict the fact that they are contradictory; or perhaps this is the sense spoken by an *urbane* corpse? Is anything permissible? Do 'the conditions of modern experience' cover minority artists in urban society who might produce a fundamental change in artistic perception? If so, would not this innovatory conduct violate these conditions yet fulfil the sense of cultural fragmentation?

Could the Renaissance contribute to a future one?

Why leave the experiences of people in the Renaissance out of the urban experience of relevance to us? We may take note of Giddens' (1984) emphasis on the importance of historical context, yet accept a significant role for stretching the idea of time-geography over different epochs of history, rather than seeing each one in epoch-making fashion as contradictorily privileged because it is later than the last. And are there not places in the world where some of the Renaissance's pulses still provoke murmurs to life, especially if working classes of the Renaissance are deemed party to metropolitan society?

Could some counter-intutive use be made of select Renaissance views on religion to regain a transcendent God? If this is too anachronistic, might not you consider that eager early twentieth-century modernism too readily cast off *certain* fragments of the old mantle of nineteenth-century religion, not least since postmodernism may seem now to be nearing cyclic death? Might not even the people living in ancient biblical times have got the pulse of human experience well enough to inform modern humanity in ways unacceptable to postmodern man? This position is not a doxographic acceptance that past culture contains the answers to our questions or is continuous with modern life.

Yet, if we generalise the scope of modernity to range over previous preoccupation's with it, many cultural restrictions in 'taste' in the present may appear short-sighted, if not viciously circular. Why do we not include the Italian (or any other) Renaissance's 'nature' and its 'cultural fragmentation' in our *idea* of urban experience, and thereby avoid 'denying the significance of its cultural inheritance' for us? True, we shall hack away parts of it which are unsound or inimical – though the parameters between decadence and rebirth mimic each other, so we need to take care. Why should a temporal dislocation between ourselves and, for example, the Renaissance terminate all unfashionable spheres of transcendence, in select areas, for third-millennium society? True, there were many institutional monoliths which are best left dead; and such intolerance and persecution of the past are hopefully gone forever. But do such phenomena and the modern world entail the sort of conceptual discontinuity which postmodern religion permits?

Has science really discredited the transcendent religious past to the extent often supposed? Could a facet of this supposed bankruptcy be a modernist presumption? Just because metaphysical systems are unfashionable, it does not follow that there is no true one. If past French poetry be allowed one, why not God? Distinctive in style, Mallarmé's *Un coup de Dés*, with its metaphysical concern for contingency, perfect pattern, creativity, and our finite consciousness, offers a creative form which has yet to be fully explored in relation to philosophy. If it is argued that, as a work involving universals, 'Mallarmé's text literally negates the contingency of the world in order to create an absolute reality of the text in metaphysical terms' (Kelley 1985: 90), why not restore some perception of the Bible to this privileged modernist canon? Can we, in some suitably narrow sense, suture this literary source of Christianity to a cosmology?

Was Aristotle a biologist who got out of his depth?

Could an unexpected avant-garde emerge to champion the ancient past in a revolutionary way, and yet reinterpret that past in a manner which preserves some aspect of the ancient status, albeit transformed by technical insights, for Christian 'revelation'? Rorty asserts that: 'We should encourage people who are tempted to dismiss Aristotle as a biologist who got out of his depth, or Berkeley as an eccentric bishop, or Frege as an original logician with unjustified epistemological pretensions'.[36] No doubt if Aristotle attracts this attention, all the theologians who have contributed to forming the modern boundaries for God should be tolerant enough to encourage the extension of Rorty's judgement. Those who oppose Rorty's advice about Aristotle (and admire the latter's influence on modern philosophy and theology) could perhaps be encouraged similarly to treat parts of the Bible, or other disrupting ancient literature that was contemporary with Aristotle.

It follows from Rorty's ironising counter-intuitive propositions that his own estimation of himself and others in some ways will be incorrect. Who is this self-evident disposable Aristotle? Hardly the one attended to in current research on Aristotle's logic. Smiley (1998) has argued the importance of Aristotle's theory of implication for present research in logic and the relations of relevance logic. Aristotle's use of concepts of deduction in the *Prior Analytics*, the *Rhetoric*, the *Topics*, as well as to a lesser extent his extension of the logic terminology in his *Poetics* have value for our concerns. Gibson (2000c) maintains that Aristotle's explanation of predicative content, his cross-connection between logic, rhetoric and the enthymeme, in the perspective of Burnyeat's (1994) pioneering study on the latter topic, have significance for the sort of conception, developed in the present analysis, which links logic and creative language. That is to say, the use of deduction in natural language does not have to be the expression of a system. The enthymeme is a part of the rhetoric which Aristotle treated as a deductive device in natural language. We can use this as a basis for developing a fresh approach to the logic of creative language.[37]

What would happen if current research for third-millennium astrophysics, cosmology and philosophy were to paraphrase some ancient ideas? Might the result be, not ornamentation, not mere novel interest, but possibly a fresh, unexpected avant-garde of what traditionally might have been perceived of as a new allegorical or typological worldview? Particularly might not this be the case when some of the counter-intuitive technical insights of research in astrophysical cosmology are utilised to generate a discontinuity with some of the present unreal Christian cultural metropolises?

Terence Cave (1988), in a perspective of the history of French literary poetics and English fiction narratives from Shakespeare to Conrad, wishes to position 'recognition' as the moment for perceiving a hidden structure which is actually problematic, a precarious knowledge which can lapse to fraudulence. The recognition of solutions in theology and philosophy of religion to do with divining God in cosmology has perhaps had more than its fair share of such lapses. This present study argues that not only is there now need for synthesis of the basis for explaining what recognition of divinity in narrative is, but the book also proposes that a tentative look at recent research in various topics concerning cosmology provokes recognition of some uniquely new scenarios for deriving universal senses from the world and religious narratives.

1 The freedom to question

Calculated madness

Is originality unbalanced?

Hacking (1995) has introduced us to some of the ways by which multiple personality diagnosis sometimes mirrors the clinicians almost as much as it does patients. He shows how the intentional descriptions of symptoms, and even the prognosis, can be a medical invention induced by a semantic contagion composed and implemented not only by patients but by predisposed observers. We could adopt this as a complex live metaphor that fits some philosophical and scientific situations where we have a recalibrating of measurements, and shifts of consciousness, involving new approaches to cosmology. I intend it that summaries of this prospect to be a sort of aphoristic puzzle whose deciphering application is perplexing.

Foucault (1965) and Derrida (1982), though disagreeing on philosophy and method, stressed the importance of clinical metaphors in mental health as figures to test tradition and modernity. We may find Foucault's position unbalanced, while agreeing that: 'there are crises of reason in strange complicity with what the world calls crises of madness' (Derrida 1982: 63). Hacking's (1995) profound studies on this area show how little we have hitherto understood aspects of madness, and clinicians have not understood the full implication of their own methods of classifying some of these matters. Hacking (1998: 10) argues that the latter clinical conditions are even more extensively confused than Wittgenstein describes for natural language in ordinary uses. Let us allow that there might be a distinction between what might be called, no doubt oddly, mad falsehoods and mad truths. The latter are not those, for example, in which someone might have thought of a genius descending into a final uncreative madness. Rather, mad truths may simply be maddening truths for those whose traditions they violated or destroy.

To generalise this, one might argue that there are collective pulses of such oppositions: for example, when a society's family members practice human sacrifice of their young as a normal function of belief. Perhaps such a society is clinically insane in respect of such causal mental states. It may be difficult to suppose that such a judgement could be placed against a scientific society whose virtues include *experiment* and *rationality*. We should always recall, however, that it is temporally limited interpretations of carefully regulated versions of experiment and rationality which we are handling here. If we add to this scenario the role of the unconscious as a presupposition of these two qualities, then the issue is further complicated, and a logic of fuzzy functions is requisite to map our perceptions of our reasoning. If we underplay our own fuzziness, then we have our experiment and rationality wrong. Consequently, we might falsely label a true insight as a false mad one. Consider two examples. First, if a presupposition about the existence or non-existence of God falsely underscores our judgement (say, the existence of infinities structured into the way things are somewhere), then we will come unstuck at some stage of inference about the identity of mathematics. Second, if our perceptions of what is the logic state of our consciousness – that it is algorithmic, is wrong, and it turns out to be non-algorithmic, this could have severe consequences for the general confidence many have in our being rational animals.[1]

With this background we have a perspective into which to place Wittgenstein's own explicit comment on the use of craziness:

> Even to have expressed a false thought boldly and clearly is already to have gained a great deal. It's only by thinking even more crazily than philosophers do that you can solve their problems. Imagine someone watching a pendulum and thinking: God makes it move like that. Well, isn't God equally free to act in accordance with a calculation?
>
> (Wittgenstein 1980a: 75)

Of course, 'crazily' here is a sort of special use lifted from ordinary usage, and it is so employed in the present context.

Now Wittgenstein's reference to a 'pendulum' is no give-away remark, with only a proverbial sense. Wittgenstein's apparently general remark, I believe, also alludes to his assessment of Brouwer's pendulum.[2] Brouwer was a constructivist about the identity of mathematics (in contrast with, say, G.H. Hardy who argued for the roles of discovery and infinity in pure mathematics). Wittgenstein highly regarded Brouwer's finitism, though disputed aspects of it.[3] It is a controversial issue to interpret this state of affairs, not least with the way in which certain of Wittgenstein's views have been incompletely published.[4] Brouwer's pendulum number is a recursive notion, but it is not comparable in size to 0, from the domain of the reals.[5] Wittgenstein wanted to reject the approach, partly because it did not specify quantity in relation to 0.

Wittgenstein's (1978: 221) view was that irrational numbers are a process, not a result. So for Wittgenstein, Brouwer is both weakening logic and limiting empiricism, for is there not mathematics in which '*God* [is] equally free to act in accordance with a calculation?' I think that Wittgenstein here was, or ought to have been, tracking the ways in which constructive experience in mathematical calculations are transcended by certain insights and discoveries in mathematics. This state of affairs counter-intuitively displaces Brouwer's emphasis on constructive instinct.

Outside of the usual limits of calculations that show the mastery of an empirical technique there are arrays of calculations that exceed our ability to compute results, yet turn out to be unfalsifiable and apparently true. At the far end of these domains – for example, the strange and esoteric subject of random walks on infinite graphs and groups in pure mathematics[6] – there has been enormous success and precision with the construction of new equations that appear to be true, yet are not all empirically testable in the narrow ways for which Wittgenstein allowed in his constructivism. Nevertheless, in the above quotation, he wrote with apparent support for activities involving calculations that exhibit a certain special crazy sense of excess. The term 'God' in his remark appears to concede that analytically we have to allow, as a consequence of a mastery of mathematical truth, that there are transcendent mathematical functions which are counter-intuitive in ways that mirror God.

In a sad but quite clear-minded state, when Wittgenstein's old sparring-partner, Piero Sraffa, was in the initial stages of the illness that was to take away his memory (he knew that he already was having Alzheimer's disease periods of blankness), one evening he arrived for dinner at the Trinity High Table. Ironically, with quite self-conscious mischief, he interrogated himself by saying to those present:[7] 'in which language shall I be crazy this evening?' In later conversation, it seemed obvious that Sraffa was here recollecting and alluding to a discussion he had had with Wittgenstein, reflected in the latter's above quotation. Sraffa well knew that he was already embarked on a 'crazy' custom which he would repeatedly follow, tragically knowing that, at some later point, he would not know he had ever said it before. He knew that his joke circumscribed our normal mental incomplete states of grasping a concept when we think that we are in full control of what we know. Sraffa's idea was that we employ thought-bridges to transcend a subject, by moving to another, and that this is effective for insight into both. Some thought-bridges are assumed to be unstable because they are prohibited by the fictional limiting scopes traditionally imposed on subjects' identities, as well as confused forms of thought-bridges. What one might term a counter-intuitive true, logical, empirical crazy theory is sometimes barred from the canon of rational insight because we have incorrectly drawn the complex boundaries of understanding.

Yet, in following a rule, we follow only one fragment of its understanding, which we conflate with being the sense of the rule. In such ways we falsely localise universality and restrict sense. This imperialism, when applied to make claims that exclude, or presuppose the absence of, transcendence in language, goes beyond, and against, what our grasp of language authorises.

Obviously it does not follow from this that our language contains transcendent semantics. Rather that rule-following analysis does not exclude this possibility. But it does eventually follow that we are unclear about, and, in following, for example, Frege's analytical philosophy, we all too easily underestimate the mystery of language and its relations to the functions of its antecedents in consciousness. This type of view is consistent with Wittgenstein's later conception of language. As Marion has shown, Frege repeatedly used 'grasp' (*Fassen* and *Erfassen*) to portray how we procure meanings or concepts, yet Frege never explained what this involves, nor did he explain how we might individuate modes of presentation.[8] In contrast, Wittgenstein's (1974: 50) later writings argue that, for example, 'Rules do not follow an act of comprehension'. We may wish to qualify this to 'do not always', or 'do so partially', or 'do only on an interpretation which is not always a matter of entailment'; or we may wish to argue that the ways rules are implicitly assumed, or formally specified, are not finely tuned enough to specify the full range of senses required for our introspection of a statement's sense, or such like. But these options still leave us with the problem raised and fixed by Wittgenstein: grasping a concept is not itself the rule, or a rule; nor is it an internal property of the understanding of the rule. Namely, our interpretation of what it is to know language is a deconstruction of language. That this is a matter of implication in understanding logic, and not a philosophy external to analytic philosophy, should be a caution both to analytic philosophers and to those philosophers external to its realm. Our ignorance brings us together, whether it be a matter of logic or of speculative literary metaphysics.

It is relevant to the link between philosophy and scientific cosmology, to be developed in the present book, to mention that Marion's (1998) profound research exposes new strengths in, and continuities between, Wittgenstein's conception of language and of the foundations of mathematics. The ways in which Wittgenstein's published book on the foundations of mathematics was edited so as to miss out some of the intermediate paragraphs in his original manuscripts has obscured the merit and relevance of his views there to central aspects of his philosophies. Wittgenstein was not concerned with the search for new 'facts'. Rather, we should attend to the ways in which ignorance of grasping the sense of a concept, or grasping it crudely, leaves us ignorant of how to understand it. Generalised, this feature leads to the implication that we may be ignorant of how to understand the universe even though we may have knowledge of it. Consequently, turning this around, attention to the distinction between the grounds for knowledge and routes to understanding, and concentration on the latter, can yield fresh understanding. So we should not slip into using the knowledge that in Wittgenstein's view philosophy is not after new facts, falsely to infer that philosophy does not discover fresh understanding. This connects with Wittgenstein's view that mathematical equations and logic are not tautologies.[9]

Some may wish to dispute or push aside Wittgenstein's views. Without going through the full sequence of the foregoing from a variety of standpoints which still sustains the conclusion with others' recent researches, we might single out Timothy Williamson's (1998) profound analysis concerning the quite narrow windows of interpretation through which our introspection has to go to achieve an understanding of the relations between logical rules and our grasp of what we do or do not understand in propositional claims. Williamson argues that in our attempts to understand uses of language (for example, Davidson's 1984) we too readily slip into equivocations of sense in assessing expression of the form 'he understands the possibility of being mistaken'. It seems, consciousness is non-algorithmic. So if language maps consciousness appropriately, then our very freedom from being a Turing machine, opens us up to our being ignorant when we do not know it.

In the states of knowledgeable ignorance in which we all find ourselves – and for contexts where we think we know, we (which includes scientists) would do well to ponder: (a) people who are specialists in a given subject may be ignorant of its overall sense; and, (b) people who are not specialists may be free to grasp an understanding that has been missed by those in (a). Sure, this is not a recipe for using ignorance as a basis for understanding, nor to confuse the borderlands of ambiguity with the central content of concept. Rather, the *Zeitgeist* of a culture may (pre)dispose a privileging of a finite set interpretations on the basis of supposing, wrongly, that these are just, and only, what it is to be the rational and empirical potential of the way things are. The third millennium starts out in the knowledge that scientific theories work, and yet are not irreducibly true in their extant forms.[10] Although there have been massive gains in the discoveries of science, we should not place our culture in the superposition that forecloses conceptions outside of its grasp of knowledge. To deny this really would be scientific Romanticism after the manner of *Schadenfreude*.

Does originality have to collide with tradition?

Sometimes universalising discourse loses local anchorage:

> Through the Word addressed by God to us in Jesus Christ ... we are reminded that 'number' is not an independent mode of rationality but obtains only along with 'word', our other primary mode of rationality, and that they are conjoint forms of contingent order deriving from and pointing to the non-contingent, self-sufficient order beyond them in God. Thus an epistemological as well as ontological effect of the incarnation of the Word ... is to disclose and re-establish the all-important connection between number and word in our human interaction with the rest of creation.
>
> (Torrance 1981: 141)

Such a claim rides over a nest of growing problems. Yet these words of a dogmatic traditional theologian indirectly highlight the value of further exploration of (alleged) unexpected interrelatable topics. The quotation oddly connects with symbolist questions posed by aspects of Mallarmé's puzzle concerning number and randomness in *Un coup de dés*, which reflect the latter's presuppositions about Stoic logic and geometry. From these types of considerations it eventually follows that we need to propose that apparently conflicting viewpoints, bits of worldview, contrary perceptions – with ever so slight yet counter-intuitive adjustments – can be integrated into a complementary cosmology. It may be that this resolution will eventually unify the humanities and sciences, appropriately reconfigured. If this were to be true, the complex conjunction of disparate identities would converge over how to represent reality.

The realism of metaphor

Is realism naïve?

Hesse (1983) has deemed scientific cosmology to be myth, and drawn attention to parallels and contrasts between the truth claims of scientific cosmology in relation to religious doctrines of creation. Her position partly arises because she adopts aspects of Durkheim, a non-realist view of meaning, and she presents a notion of scientific language as metaphor which derives from Black's interaction thesis. This bundle of elements is said by Hesse to oppose a Newtonian approach to science customary in earlier pre-relativity perspectives: realism is assumed to be an underdetermined fiction. Conversely, relativity and quantum physics are presented as warrant for Hesse's anti-realism or critical realism, which she advances on the hopes of consensus and coherence. Whilst this position has many merits, and it acts as a corrective against some forms of realism, the following analysis will dispute part of it by offering a distinct thesis.

We would do well at this juncture to reserve for further attention Polkinghorne's (1990: 31) proposal that in religious discourse the role of symbol, as an apotheosis, rather than merely traditional metaphor, is forefronted in contrast with physics. I suggest live metaphor could bridge aspects of the gap between the two poles or emphases in certain contexts.

Complex spacetime relations cannot yet be depicted in a perfectly exact realist framework, partly due to alternate elastic and rigid geometry candidate theories. Some (live, not dead) metaphoric signification is thus required because neither elastic nor rigid models fit perfectly. This is characteristic of a group of domains in theories. The conjunction of these two examples implies neither realist nor non-realist conclusions about the matter. It entails realism and non-realism, or none of these options. This situation is unstable, and it is revisable. It is usual to recognise that there is literal as well as figurative language in science. My suggestion, to be developed below, is to advance the idea that scientific discourse uses live metaphor, which supports, what I wish to call, a counter-intuitive realist position. This results in some alignment with aspects of language outside of science.

Criticising Black's (1962) view that a metaphor is formed by two subjects, Soskice (1985) develops I.A. Richards (1936) concept of metaphor involving description cognition, networks of comparative expressions (contextual interactions), though she distances her view from his emotive theory of meaning, defending her idea that active metaphor 'suggests a community of relations' (1985: 95), itself a live metaphor. I wish to add that individual dead metaphors can be formed into a complex live metaphor. A photograph is a live metaphor which has quantifiable and true/false truth conditions. Here, live metaphor's function is to be a truth-conditional proposition with a realist ontology. We may generalise this to cover, for example, a geometric map of spacetime, whose truth-conditions are depicted by complex live metaphor. This is especially apt for new theories that have veridical support, since they typically are the product of metaphoric extensions supported by experiment and/or quantifiable measurement.

Given that metaphor participates in, and as a member of, a community of relations, we may, with suitable qualification, recognise metaphor at many or perhaps all levels or exchange – sentences, themes, narratives, subjects. Viewing a metaphoric relation between the arts (including theology) is thus apt. Cosmology is a complex live metaphor. General relativity and quantum physics are vastly important in present cosmology; Newtonian approaches are not solely dead metaphors, consigned, as Hesse may seem to assume, to history of science in cosmology. For example, Saslaw's research (1985) into the gravitational structure of galaxies, and their relation to the history of the universe, proceeds without relativistic or quantum theory, yet it is one of the most advance and refined treatments available. This is not to underestimate the applications of relativity and quantum theory to cosmology.

Is reality subject to inflation?

Goncharov and Linde injected a chaotic inflation into supergravity for the opening epoch of the universe (see Linde 1990). Rees (1995; 1999) interprets and extends Linde's conception to produce the idea of a multiverse, a near-infinite ensemble of universes. These extensions of language, using such terms as 'supergravity' and 'multiverse', illustrate the foregoing point about the use of metaphor. But it would be misleading to isolate the cases of Saslaw, and Goncharov and Linde, as though they respectively depict the history and present basic state of affairs. Yet such contrasts dispose of an all too neat ascription of realism to the past, and non-realism to the present, as alleged functions of the needs of cosmology, at the hands of philosophy of religion and of science. Realism and non-realism non-figurative and metaphoric, interconnect as complementary, if not consistent, fragments of scientific worldviews. Such a situation *may* pass close to Black's or Hesse's interaction view of metaphor, but it prevents this close encounter from being conflated with evidence for global non-realist theory as a requirement of current cosmology. According to Guth (1998), the correct model for the early universe is the inflationary scenario. On this view the universe accelerated exponentially after the 'big bang', into a flat disc-like expansion. This carried the Grand Unified Theory (GUT) state of the singularity into the deep structure of the universe.

In Hawking's (1983) Euclidean approach to the inflationary universe model, we see an unexpected utilisation of, and yet development from, Euclid. Such a scenario presupposes hitherto unsolved solutions in quantum gravity to problems of the emergence of time, its non-temporal relations, and whether or not 'reduction' in science is a singular notion supportable by primordial physics (see Butterfield and Isham 1999). This might caution against the package deal that Hesse offers. One could maintain that the reluctance to be non-realist at the universalised global level is partly a result of insights deriving from Hesse's own work. Beyond this, the following presents the view that metaphoricity does not entail a non-realist view of meaning or science. Since metaphor in such cosmology of the early universe is presented in the community of equations intended as pieces of history, one may consider such metaphor as a mirror, psychoanalytically speaking, and as an energetically creditable depiction, of the ontology. This is a highly unstable physical hypothesis in the nature of cosmology. Yet conceding readily that such metaphor will pitch and migrate unevenly, it may lead one to the inference that in proportion to the viability of the physics, and allowing for the gap between signifier and signified – limited in freedom by live not dead metaphor, live metaphor can have a referent external to its medium whose ontological criteria coincide non-trivially with the criteria presupposed in the metaphor: like a film recording of an event, though a 'virtual reality' simulation may be a more apt mapping term for this scenario.

Past reality

Are we idioms?

Rorty (1980) claims that we ossify ourselves into the contemporary worldview. This would be rather like being in an idiom such as 'kick the bucket'. The 'idiom' being that sense whose signifier's internal component words make no contribution to its sense, but only their conjunction. Our semantics even use idiom to speak of ontology, to break out of a postmodernist *cul de sac*. Our past dies on us, in Rorty's view, as with the 'literal' sense of 'kick' and 'bucket' in the idiom – sense is ossified.

Shohat and Stam (1994: 104) have demonstrated the distorting effect of one culture on others, not least in the eurocentric film that treats the 'Third World', itself a blemished designation, as spectacle, and not as realist subject. But might not this self-reflection, this awareness, contribute to a restoration of and continuity with elements of past consciousness if stimulated by a search for a community's future? Might not this sort of relation to the past be more akin to a live metaphor than to an idiom, as with the relation between the live metaphor of a person on a television, and the person. Could not a modern awareness of ancient insights enable a transformation and yet preservation of conceptual fragments of our past?

What does the primeval past signify? Is it *our* past in any informative sense? Do the first microseconds of this universe's origin hold information which can furnish (non-tautological) evidence about God for a cosmological proof? Would this sidestep fallacies alleged to be involved in principle in any discussion about inference from the world to God? What is the significance for theology of Everett's theory that the whole universe is a wave function?[11] Everett's view has been linked to Hawking's black hole theorem to construe the universe as a quantum object.[12] How does this pertain to issues of God's relation to the world? Does this provoke problems for eschatology? At one level eschatological discontinuity is analogous with Thom's model for catastrophe mathematics. Could this yield a formal framework for some eschatological discourse? Before tackling these questions we need some rather more modest queries and precedents.

What does a paraphrase preserve?

For example, if one abstracts some features from an ancient cosmology and paraphrases them into the logical distinctions of modern astrophysical or philosophical or theological cosmology, what status does the paraphrase hold for informing one about the ancient cosmology? One might interpret Aristotle's syllogistic metalogic in this way.[13] In this vein, Aristotle deployed elements of an outstanding compactness proof which articulates proof-theoretic techniques which were otherwise unknown until after Frege. So this confers on Aristotle an understanding of certain features of the post-Frege insights. Before someone claims that this is anachronistic, he should be cautioned: it could be a philosophical crime to assume that all modernist comprehension was unavailable to the ancient world; that would be an odd imperialism. This ironically reverses Rorty's (1998) ironic treatment of the biologist Aristotle, converting the Greek philosopher into a prescient mathematical logician. Perhaps some of Rorty's conceptions had already occurred to Aristotle, who had already been bored by the secular mysticism of some pre-Socratics.

We might equally raise the prospect of ironising logic. Sorensen (1998) beautifully exposes an equivocation in the most basic syllogism: 'All men are mortal; Socrates is a man; therefore Socrates is mortal', if the equivocation is run from the specific to the generic. We should wish to avoid trading on equivocation. But the territory outside of, for example, Rorty's packaging of analytical philosophy as an imperious domain awaits exploration. The extension of our grasp of logic and its generalisation leave open new domains for study. We might wish to avoid Rorty's reductionist pragmatism by being *logically* pragmatic ourselves. For example, notice that natural languages make heavy use of live metaphor, and the sense of extending semantics by further metaphorisation is akin to the ways in which logic is extended. This could be employed as a relative basis for admitting domains of logic as species of live metaphor, in the sense that extension of meaning can be paraphrased by logic. This impressionist scenario obviously requires much further work.[14]

Is it possible to transform some features of ancient theological narrative and relate them to modern science, outside of a conservative reactionary apologetic theology, and in a perspective of contemporary philosophy? For example, could logic and linguistics enable one to infer that the conjunction of the Bible and theology in this previous question yields continuity? And the wider question: does a given subject grammar require of any tradition that it has some structural continuity with another tradition in another language and its grammar, where one is a perception of the other? If so, how would the law of contradiction operate between these two traditions? Is some Christian theology universal semantics? This enormously elusive task would need to head the contrast between symbol and metaphor; I suggest criteria could eventually be found to guide attempts properly to interface these two domains.

Live metaphor

What is alive in metaphor?

Terminologies and their definitions come and go in general linguistics. 'Live metaphor' is no exception; yet the thesis attached to this term in the book is partly distinct and original. As suggested so far in the foregoing, here live metaphor marks a concept which is quite different from that aired by Ricoeur (1977), though the present book tackles some of the problems he raised, whilst echoing some unease with his thesis. J.L. Cohen's (1993) examination of metaphor basically concurs with, but is not exhaustively definitive of, the way live metaphor is conceived in the present work, though here the use of language is the resource for the distinction, rather than a system of rules for language typified by Cohen's approach; Cohen does not develop a 'live metaphor' distinction. Film is an example of a special species of live (not dead) metaphor. Live metaphor is distinct from the dead metaphor exemplified in a literary form by 'root of the problem': this will not inform us of the identity of (whatever people mean by) a 'literal' tree root, whereas conversely the photograph is a live metaphor which can facilitate identification of the referent of an image.[15]

What is an abstract live metaphor?

But does this type of illustration work for an abstract term such as 'if'?

Does live metaphor collapse as a device with which to map conditional terms? Is there no visual counterpart for conditionality? A first move in countering that objection is to position the psychogenesis of 'if': the mental source – the element in thought, which matches 'if'. 'If' represents a psychological presupposition. The logical conditional is a live metaphor for this presupposition. I suggest that scrutiny of issues connected with Mallarmé's most difficult poem *Un coup de dés* will be illuminating for this purpose. His use of the dynamics of spatiality, geometry and conditionality, as a series of devices to achieve a vision of union between abstraction, creativity and representation, offers a poetics of contingency that extends the notion of live metaphor into the bridge between symbol and metaphor.[16]

Later chapters advance the idea that there are different types of live metaphor, and it is hoped that discussion resolves some of the issues raised by Davies (1982) where he shows that distinct theories may be needed for distinct types of metaphor, though the scope of his scenario does not include live metaphor. Davies refers to Davidson's (1980: 252) dismissal of an informative comparison between a metaphor and a photograph.[17] Live metaphor does not fall under the scope of Davidson's. I will sustain the link between illustrative visualising medium and live (not dead) metaphor, seeking to show that this sort of relation can furnish us with a theory in which bivalent truth conditions operate.

My rationale is that there are certain styles of narrative which can be interpreted as true according to a matching sequence of logic. A generalised form of this is a matching sequence corresponding to a world under a given interpretation, enlarged in certain contexts to a universe, or a multiverse,[18] or the scope of what there is including transcendent states. This has parallels with Chihara's (1998) conception of transworld identity without possible worlds.[19] Clearly we have only a modest comprehension of the relations between logic and creative literature; yet I shall suppose that in principle, supported by the example of theistic narrative characterised below, there are logically true sequences in narrative displaying counter-intuitive mimesis which speak to divinity and cosmology and their conjunction.

Eschatology and values

Can we isolate the present from our pasts?

The ontological basis of live metaphor is that things are like one another, in relevant respects; obviously it is crucial to identify the disanalogies.

Eschatology is temporally directed to the future. Yet the future has a past. In spacetime it is quite easy to get lost and confuse time-points. This also applies to the application of causal concepts to time in the universe. We should be wary not to conflate causes with effects. In cosmological scenarios the end of history is sometimes the time-reverse of the beginning (whatever *that* means), though they are fundamentally distinct. We should avoid presupposing that the conditions which our existence satisfies are those of another spacetime prior to organic life. A basic problem for organic evolutionary theory is to explain in what sense the evolutionary environment, which is said to be the consequence of an environment that was not (by definition) evolutionary, is different in the former and latter cases. We cannot sustain a circular argument since the two environments are functionally distinct. Evolutionary culture is so nested into our perceptions that this shift tends to pass us by. But this distinction is fundamental to the possibility of life. A common way of treating it at the cosmological level, which smoothes away the sharpness of the problem that it constitutes, is to introduce anthropomorphism.

Is physical matter anthropomorphic?

This book's aim to harness some relations between arts and cosmology is not an unqualified scenario, and should be distanced from approaches which suppose that the existence of humanity somehow privileges anthropomorphism on scientific grounds. In their anthropic principle, Barrow and Tipler (1986) could be excessively comprehensive in their use of anthropomorphic culture in a merger (or wager) with cosmology. It seems strange that, on the one hand, early Christianity's attempt to represent God anthropomorphically should have been criticised, whilst, on the other hand, anthropomorphism in astrophysical cosmology should be promoted to a universalising property. Of course, the priority in the causal relation of direction from humans to God is reversed in the anthropic principle so as to embrace the concept that humans exist because the universe's conditions furnish the conditions for humans to exist. But since the premises for being human are not identical to the premises for being the universe, it is circular to infer universal anthropomorphism of the physical universe from the existence of humanity.

Even within theories of evolutionary biology there is a principle of excess evident in selection: many physical properties do not support life, and a collection of features in humanity are not functionally identical to the conditions for survival (stupidity, greed, false consciousness, to indicate merely a few). So the slack in physical reality leaves a gap both ways from materialism to humanity, and vice versa, that leaves the thesis of cosmological anthropomorphism unsupported.

Note that my conclusion is not that on grounds of chance humanity could not or did not appear by chance in an atheistic universe (though I believe this proposition to be false on other grounds). My argument amounts to the claim that the physical universe and randomness, chaos and distributions of probabilities, display a functional state of affairs from which it is false to infer that cosmological anthropomorphism follows from a description of a universe in which they function, since they furnish premises that require the negation of an anthropomorphism. Merely to suggest that, given sufficient time, anthropomorphism would surmount such 'improbabilities' and 'come to exist' is a misunderstanding of the empirical problem. Non-theistic anthropomorphism reads back from an existing subject to a time prior to its existence (not that this objection applies to all other non-anthropomorphic theses), and retrojects the existence as an effect of a randomising cause. But that move is the fallacy. There is no subject 'anthropomorphic entity', nor necessary *and* sufficient conditions in the scientifically conceived empirical states of affairs to infer its ontology. A slight illustration manifests the principle: the appearance of a smile on a human face, just because it exists, does not entail that the inorganic universe has a smile on it, nor that it caused the smile, even though the latter may in fact be a psychological response to the universe.

How could evolutionary anthropomorphism come to exist?

Nevertheless an aim of cosmology should be inclusive generality. If God (with the suitable properties of creativity) exists, it would follow that the physical universe's, or our region of spacetime, conditions could embody a functional pattern that yields humanity, since a non-random God could operate in this way. If such a situation obtains, and creative patterns have been distributed through different ontological and perceptual media, then a deep anthropomorphism could be true. This consequence would follow because of the additional conditions that divine creativity had implemented: the same type of pattern in physical and in the biological subjects manifesting anthropomorphism, not solely on empirical grounds of what physical properties the physical universe has.

Nevertheless, even if these premises were true, given what humanity there is on our planet, it would certainly be problematic to regard ideology and epistemology as irrelevant to criteria and conditions which mould cosmology and philosophy, as well as their possible future applications. (Later in this book, subsequent to examining a series of issues concerning philosophy of science and astrophysical cosmology and philosophical cosmology, the final part of the book considers presuppositions which are, it is argued, contingently and counter-intuitively embedded in such an anthropomorphism in relation to ethical ideology.) History and eschatology are subsets of anthropomorphic epistemology and metaphysics. Their retrojective and predictive conjectures are variously employed in cosmology, tense logic, social science and theology. We do indeed need exploration of anthropologies to explain what we are. And the complex roles of anthropomorphism directed at conceiving transcendent claims require of us an account of what it would be to supply the epistemological criteria for divine anthropomorphism, just in case there is such an ontological state. Central to anthropomorphism is language as a function of thought, whose human precondition – consciousness – still has to be explained by evolution theory; so we have little explanatory basis for a metaphysics of human mental anthropomorphism.

2 The expression of God in language

Imitation and meaning

Can ancient anthropomorphism be reborn?

Even if God exists, how could there be true description of God? Answers to this question are not infrequently imprisoned by its history. Opposed viewpoints forged in debate are prone to cast artificial yet influential limits for fresh possibilities. This point applies to both religious and scientific narratives.

There are many ways in which this chapter heading has been approached. The philosophical focus of the present book excludes a literary and linguistic treatment of the issue, though it is worth mentioning some samples of research among many which could be adapted as presuppositions for the purpose of this section. For example, Brooke (1985) and Young (1994) variously contribute to outline one basis for interrogating issues of typology and mimesis in connection with divine terminology. Rogerson's (1984) notion of a corporate personality (presumably without business overtones) is readily related to the concept of an intermediate agent going proxy for an identity. Gibson (1981; 2000c) offers considerations for applying logic to literary types.

Consider Genesis 1–2 as an ancient example of speaking about God. This is not to introduce a biblicist programme here; instead, to suggest that the start of a community's creative naming tradition is relevant for its literary identities. One may following Kripke's (1980) theory concerning naming origins to implement this, though it would not yield sufficient criteria for the subsequent symbolic and paranomastic uses of names. Corbechon's sublime fifteenth century depiction of biblical creation (see Plate 2) is all too readily taken to be a type of perception which adequately represents the sort of 'literal' sense in Genesis. Such literalism presumes knowledge of authorial intentions behind Genesis. It too lightly uses 'literal' and ignores the problem of explaining what literalism is, which for a linguist is already a deeply puzzling affair – even without theological complications. Conversely, an alternative way of taking Genesis, as a singular dead metaphor, is too easy. Particularly is this the case if, for example, gender typology is explored in relation to textual creativity. Renaissance studies in personification, or prosopeia, by Erasmus in *De copia*[1] have a concern to represent abstract virtues, as has Sherry (1550), while indiscriminately mixing myths and actual identities, drawing on medieval and Classical sources. Current personification poetics revives and transforms this tradition.[2] I introduce this as a facet of the scene being developed for the context here, as a tonal property for live the metaphor theory.[3]

Clearly we should avoid ways of reading Genesis that involve forming uncritical boundaries composed of incorrect contrasts between religious and scientific narrative creativity. In any interpretation the contrasts between religion and science will be massive. Obviously, technical insights in astronomy and mathematics have provoked withdrawal of hitherto influential Christian – and also atheistic attempts – to study questions about claims for God. But some critical assumptions strike inaccurate oppositions. As Newlands (1994: 148–51) contends, we should not amputate *Genesis* 1 by injecting *creatio ex nihilo*; rather, we have regard for its thematic use of *creatio per verbum*, with Augustine's point that God created *time* (*Confessions* 1982: 11, 12–31).[4] Time in spacetime also has its beginning with this universe. The narrative identity of Genesis 1–2 is not a disabling result of being composed long before scientific narrative; it is a cosmic poem. So we should consider how a poem can speak of history (such as Aristotle's *Poetics* delineates). And reflect on what is, presumably, the fundamental gap between the form of scientific cosmology now, and its style in a few hundred years.

Although it is beyond the scope of this cosmology book to apply live metaphor to Genesis creation, such a thesis is a profitable enterprise.[5] An aim of this book is to show that there are some common areas between religious and scientific languages regarding creative aspects of languages which are employed to address cosmological problems.

In an attempt to link scientific and theological languages, the current chapter will offer elements for a fresh approach to representing some categories of Bible language which (it is hoped) have other applications to theology and philosophy of language. Later chapters will combine this with an account of some aspects of scientific language cosmology. A disputable view of this project might be that two new theories about scientific and theological languages are needed only because the connection between God and science has no justification in standard uses of theological and cosmological languages. This objection would be unrealistic because there are no standard languages in theology, and astronomers confess the chronic contrary limitations of languages in cosmology (an issue to be discussed in Chapter 3). This is particularly the case when we start to delve into the depths of both subjects. It is often the limits of a particular language's vocabulary and its uses, even notation in mathematics, which have held up progress, as the history of both subjects attest. Obviously, by the way, it does not follow from aligning some logical patterns in two distinct subjects that one is committed to infer that the two subjects share qualitative or empirically grounded features. A cryptic summary of my view of logic and languages, which are to be linked to suitable concepts of God and cosmology, is that the two languages exhibit massive use of complex live metaphor. This view rests on the proposal offered in this book that a tenable explanation of the nature of meaning is by use of the idea of live metaphor.[6]

Can mimesis be avant-garde?

I suggest a counter-intuitive view of mimesis as a basis for explaining live metaphor. The above outline alludes to many intersecting disputes to which later chapters will explicitly come. Here we need to gather a small batch of them to introduce the topic of how to express God in language. On one view, description of a subject is a type of imitation – *mimesis*, a representation. When in *The Poetics* Aristotle wrote about imitation in the poetic arts, his theory of mimesis included representation of, not only concrete objects, but, abstract elements such as plots, character relations and values. These abstract features illustrate how his view can be extended to apply to representation in abstract art, since such art is partly a manifestation of abstract relations. The extension gives a precedent which can be applied to transcendental topics in theology: but we need to be careful about and wary of presupposing a particular concept of mimesis. I shall argue that Aristotle gave the wrong concept for the type of semantics in a divine cosmology.

Another problem is that many concepts of mimesis (often pseudo-Aristotelian), have been given a bad press in relation to many modern literary and aesthetic theories. Prendergast's (1986) research on mimesis and some French literary analysis, on one interpretation, propose a substantial revision of the opposition to mimesis among the avant-garde. He has demonstrated that the demolition of mimesis by some avant-garde movements was superficial; here Prendergast coyly employs such movements own distinctions to demonstrate that these do not recognise the deeper complexity and nature of mimesis. Prendergast has subverted this demolition of mimesis and argued that deeper versions of mimesis may resist deconstruction, while he nevertheless appreciates that standard uses of mimesis amount to a form of policing by institutions of thought. Mimesis is often a reflection of the way some traditions normatively represent what is arbitrary.

Prendergast introduces Kermode's (1979) use of the notion that narratives embody an 'internal probability system', by which narratives express and dispose to constrain their representation by readers. Kermode (1986a, b) further develops this notion of an internal probability system when writing of his principle of excess sense, by which there is always extra semantic potential ascribable to the senses of expressions beyond that exposed by traditional expectations. This internal probability system may seem to imply Aristotle's own employment of probability in his explanation of mimesis. Probability patterns readily bolster the position that mimesis is not concerned with truth but with probability and accident; not with determinable answers, yet with approximation and tragic representation.

Before commenting on how an aspect of Aristotelian studies relates to this issue, I note that the concept of live metaphor advanced in this book sidesteps the need to treat the choice of senses in narratives as probability functions, though this does not oppose the idea that there is excess sense and indeterminacy in a text with truth claims. For example, a narrative can be probabilistic, yet not inductive;[7] and probability may be paraphrased deductively.[8] Altieri's (1995) study of the relation between modernist poetry and painterly abstraction is one among a number of the alternative ways of looking at representational models of narrative. The depiction of abstraction in modernist poetry using relations with abstract painting concurs with a trend in the present study to use live metaphor to represent narrative. Popper's (1982) rejection of induction and introduction of a 'true or false' scenario for hypotheses can be drafted in as a component in a theory about the contents of narrative, and linked to live metaphor theory. The 'internal probability system' can then be regarded as a psychology of expectation operating in a possible decision theory about the choices available to interpreters of a narrative, rather than a property of the narrative itself.

This book replaces probability with the choice between truth or falsity. So here truth, I propose, is established as the central nerve for a counter-intuitive mimesis with which to represent the universals of life.

As Sternberg (1985) has noticed, Aristotle does not allow the movement from 'ignorance to knowledge' to become a universal principle of dramatic structure. This movement from 'ignorance to knowledge' can have a counter-intuitive pull against agnostic or secular metaphysics. Aristotle offers an intuitively plausible view of mimesis for agnostic culture; but aspects of it are not adequate for theism. Aristotle exposed some *syntax* of representation; yet in eliminating (as a universal) the principle 'ignorance to knowledge', Aristotle prevented mimesis from deriving its universalisable *sense*. If we can have knowledge of God, then our representing the movement from 'ignorance to knowledge' assumes an altogether more significant role than Aristotle assigns it. Prendergast airs the idea that mimesis is unstable because such mimetic representation hits a 'psychic nerve'. Prendergast's book is a point of departure for the prospects of a new territory, but does not survey it. I shall try to formulate a futurist map and show that this nerve is deeply counter-intuitive, especially when deployed to represent the universals which God's identity instantiates.

What is the status of mimesis?

Aristotle introduced 'possibility' and 'necessity' as alternatives to 'probability', as a standard for a concept of imitation. The present book offers a fresh approach to mimesis, while pursuing its prime divine objective, which nests itself into possibility and necessity. In this context, 'possibility' is not what is possibly true, but truth which has possible application contingent on the believer's choice. Consequently, this book will aim to incorporate values of truth into its options whilst eschewing probability as a restriction on the foundation of knowledge about God, though probability will be a domain reserved for representing human fallibility and choice. ('Will' as a parameter in structuring 'believing', along the lines of Helm (1994: 32–57), interacts as a disposition to influence the foregoing idea of probability and 'believing a concept to be there', however.)

The body of this book is not special pleading for a 'private language' and theory of mimesis for divinity which does not apply to aesthetic and literary topics that traditionally receive mimetic explanation. As already seen, one feature to ward off this spirit of privacy is the use of various disciplines.

It is part of the argument that research in, for example, aesthetics and cosmology, independently generates the concept of meaning deployed in divine cosmology. A core notion for this view is that live metaphor should revise and extend Aristotelian mimesis. (It may be a matter of taste as to whether you would classify the product so divergent from much Aristotelian mimesis that you would wish it to be renamed. My own view is that this may be so, but that Aristotle's own treatment, as far as we have it, leaves space for such a development, not least because he has overlaps with Plato's views and modifies them; so we would do well to give fresh attention here.) If one has to address the question of whether or not ancient anthropomorphism can be reborn, the query has to be dissolved and transformed. I argue that the criteria of identity presupposed in certain uses of transcendent anthropomorphic language in the ancient world can be paraphrased, with equivalence in truth claims, into live metaphor employing the explanation which accompanies live metaphor in the present book. It follows from such a formulation, upon careful interpretation, that a range of ancient infelicities limiting anthropomorphism are left out of the equation between ancient and modern uses. Live metaphor, we shall see, preserves and yet deletes certain properties in the function of being live metaphor, as does film. In other words, the identity of such conceptual metonymy metaphor is to go proxy for what is absent. What is absent from the equation is ancient literal anthropomorphism. What is present is a live metaphorised representation of what it is to be a transcendent phenomenon portrayed in language. Just as Goulder (1964) ascribed correspondence to such typological narrative, so this study claims that some biblical narrative displays it, in this philosophical analysis. What I would add to Goulder's (1964) and Brock's (1985) exposure in Near Eastern literature of typology in varying narratives is the idea that we are dealing with counter-intuitive correspondences and types which occupy a creatively exotic and thus unstable edge of a universe of discourse. In this respect, such linguistic phenomena have a counterpart position in cosmology.

Live metaphor, relevantly formulated for divinity and other spheres of originality, is a counter-intuitive idea which can also be a basis for the explanation of natural and formal language. The priority of divine subject expounds the idea of live metaphor in the context of language about God, and then returns in subsequent chapters, to live metaphor and its implications for scientific and ethical languages. The 'live metaphor' notion is not a single distinction but a multi-layered notion, drawing on the current study and other insights in metaphor theory – adjusting them into the present theme.

God manifestation

Have we allowed for original personification?

Let us attempt to outline a trajectory in a philosophy of language using theistic terms with which to address this question. We will try and take account not only of 'God' as a quality of other things but also as a unique creative (logically) individual predicative identity. We are not stuck with old nineteenth century anthropomorphic projections. Personification and live metaphor had been neglected as conceptions that sustain the representation of transcendent phenomena, both in astrophysics and in matters divine.[9] The following implements the various researches already cited, as a premise which presents a live metaphor approach to philosophy of language and philosophy of literature, though the following is presented in a self-contained form.

In the Bible, this identity is sometimes represented by anthropomorphised mediating agents or images of Christ. Trembath (1991: 65–66) stresses, as I do here, a criterion of revelation in terms of its reception by human subjects (the 'O' observer below), and yet to depict aspects of the perceived objective origins. The following examples show that it is possible to characterise ancient religious representation using logical techniques and aesthetic distinctions. A basis for the logical techniques is presented in Gibson (1981, 1997b, 2000a) within the framework of Near Eastern linguistics and philosophical logic; the aesthetic and literary component is devised in Gibson (1987, 2000a). Other scholars' insights are implemented for support and to show how the concepts can stand, to some degree, irrespective of my own particular viewpoints.

Such procedures engage with the logic of dramatic representation whereby an actor goes proxy for a character. This is a form of personification. In Plato, 'Socrates' is a 'personification' of Socrates, not unlike a biblical angel, or speech of Yahweh in which an agent is proxy for God. In Kierkegaard, the question of personification related to pseudomity is absolutely central, and problematic with reference to personal identity and the prospect of representing the authorial identity. That is to say, the issues of how humans beings communicate their actual identity are deeply vexing.

This was ignored or underestimated in castigation of notions that purport to depict God and a sense of a deity's identity.

This concurs with the theme of God as cosmic producer. The following pages exemplify how this dramatic logic, used with other tropes, encapsulates the representation of one individual by another individual depicting a live metaphorised reality. In keeping with this priority, the reader could regard the presence of biblical narrative in the following as metaphoric dramatic texts or records of dramatised performances. Clearly this figure of drama is only one of many and is not a narrow fixed focus: it will need supplementing and adapting in a variety of ways, and the figure of film as a live metaphor realism, introduced in the foregoing, will also embrace pictorialist poetics – a revised *ut pictura poesis*.

Hopefully the outcome is a foundation for a counter-intuitive version of mimesis which sidesteps some traditional problems. This version may resolve or clarify some difficulties about identity in Christology, but here it is principally deployed to pave the way for associating divinity with cosmology. As Jameson (1992) proposes, Mallarmé's *Un coup de dés* becomes coterminous with the composition and its medium. In applying this notion to film, Jameson enables us to construct filmic realism for issues of literary texts about divinity, and scientific metaphor. God and science, of course, are never the signifiers which depict them; yet the signifiers can succeed in producing a verisimilitude of relevant aspects of their ontologies relative to a basis that can be represented in a deduction.[10] So signs can trace transcendental issues.

Can one subject be another?

There will be divergence of view over which piece of theistic narrative to use in analysis as a typical sample. Perhaps here we could employ a text which influenced disparate traditions – the 'burning bush' narrative in Exodus 3, partly because Gibson (1981: 126–64) presents the logico-linguistics applicable to the present purpose, in which Exodus 3–4's deep structure contains logical criteria of identity. G.I. Davies (1992: 177–78) frames the context for us by demonstrating the thematic contrast between Exodus 3–4, and 1–2, in which unity and perceptual functions are central. It is worth noting the dramatic performance in Exodus 3–4.

Superficially there seem to be two divine subjects: the angel and Yahweh. But we have a scene in which God is said to be subject when the angel is stated to be speaking: 'the angel of the Lord appeared … God called unto him out of the midst of the bush' (Exodus 3:2–4). The angel is a medium for God. Here, as with the (albeit distinct) type of divine agents in Genesis 1: 26, speech-acts partly function to override the presence of text in order to simulate a consciousness of extra-narrative creative presence.

Such types of agency occur in the New Testament as well. Acts 7: 30–32 reproduces and alludes to Exodus 3 (although the name 'Yahweh' is here

Figure 2.1 A fifth century BC Greek vase

Source: National Archaeological Museum of Athens

Note: This fifth century BC Greek vase illustrates a mimetic use of human images to represent divinity. Some Christianity derives continuity from earlier Classical Greek motifs: its depiction of wings is similar to those in Veneziano's 1106 *Annunciation*. The identities of 'angels' in the Bible seem fundamentally distinct to such motifs.

replaced by 'the Lord'). Within John's Gospel we have the rarefied theme of Christ calling Jews 'gods', quoting Psalm 82: 6 – 'Know ye not that ye are gods?' Here the theistic term 'gods' (identical in syntax in the Psalm's Hebrew to the term used of Yahweh) is identified with human agents, though irony and parody are afoot in the narrative. This agency use of words for God has a firm basis, not only in the Bible but also in theological narratives such as the Dead Sea Scrolls. In the Melchizedeq Scroll we have the same type of use of 'god' for a person.[11] In 1 John 1 this sense of agency between God and text as manifesting function has attracted Neufeld (1994) to reconceive its text as speech, favouring Derrida, and stressing the importance of restoring creativity to the narrative. Although retaining the expression 'speech act', I do not take metaphor to be merely a category among other speech acts, and concur with her that metaphor can be a function longer than a sentence which may not be a speech act, nor solely limited to a word, since it may be of any finite length – a point significant for later discussion below. But initially, here, we can start with single terms.

Is there a logic of anthropomorphic agency?

Hereafter propositions numbered like (1) will be mentioned by number only after their first use. In primitive form we can represent part of this agency as:

$$\text{'}y = x\text{' respecting a class of properties} \qquad [1]$$

The identity of God with Jesus (John 10: 30) will no doubt occur to readers in [1]. For those worried about the use of a logical schema here, there is some proof of its functional felicity;[12] the 'logic as live metaphor' thesis later in the book (Chapters 3–5) supports and extends this approach. Gibson (forthcoming d) has shown that philosophy of mathematics can be introduced and ironised to provide an abstract arena in which exotic fresh scenarios derived from literature can be depicted.[13]

On one interpretation of the link between the term 'angel' or agency representation and the first person of Yahweh (or the God presupposed to be creator) it might be thought that one is committed to an absolute identity of subjects, not predicates. This ignores the imaging and representation by which [1] can be explained, as the following shows, in an opening attempt to give a logical scenario for some internal biblical uses of revelatory presuppositions.

Simulating subjects

How does an agent refer?

Consider a film, or perhaps better for brevity and simplicity, a television broadcast of, or a recording of, a Prime Minister (PM). Pointing at the screening (Sy) of PM, an observer (O) asks: 'Who is that?' (According to criteria of identifiability on grounds of audio-visual criteria of representation), the answer is, 'The PM' (akin to questions on the identity of Jesus, in John and Luke). That is, where Sy is the screening of the PM, the effective broadcast is y, y is on audio visual criteria a replica of x where x is the PM. Consequently, the question 'Who is that?' dismantles into:

$$\text{What } x \text{ is the referent of } y \text{ in } Sy? \qquad [2]$$

The further referent of x is the object which is broadcast. (Metaphorically parallel with *John* on Christ's origin.) An obvious but significant distinction can be implied by the use of [2], as an observer's presupposition:

$$y \text{ is not the referent of } x, \text{ but the identifiable referent of } y \text{ is } x \qquad [3]$$

And equally clearly has to rest on the premise that:

y is the image of x's referent, while x's absolute identity
(personal identity exhaustively specified) is not y [4]

The conjunction of [3] and [4] yields a concept of reproduction of identities, i.e., replication: the referents of x and y sharing Fs as represented in Sy, but where an ontological asymmetry occurs between them otherwise.

This can be termed 'asymmetrical replication'. Other points are relevant to this state of affairs. First, there is a dependency relation of y on x for the production of sets from the class of Fs comprising Sy. This assumes that communication is a property of revelation, and is not merely a matter of mechanism, but in a complete sense of qualitative content. It may seem invidious and overstrong to parallel television with claims of revelation. But the form is here used as a live metaphor – in terms of its logical syntax, not qualitative identity (this explanation is supplemented in the present book with aesthetic considerations and other aspects of its own semantics).

Second, the media constituting and linking x and y are distinct in x and y (e.g. visionary environment and manifestation in the latter). Third, the visual image of y is discernible from, and recognisably distinct from but identifiable as x. (As with the angel at the bush.) This state generates a fourth aspect: the audio-criterion (or, also a linguistic representation of the situation which satisfies it) may be fulfilled so efficiently as to produce an inability to differentiate x and y at a level – close O's eyes: x is present with O, while also a recording of x as y is being broadcast; Whose voice is it? x's or y's – or, rather, from which immediate source? (A problem posed for Samuel's consciousness in *1 Samuel*.) Even where no evidently discernible difference exists, there is the dependency relation of y on x. So if the replication of x by y is successful, then the reference of y is x, or the derivable referent to be associated with y is x.

Many revelatory contexts of biblical speech acts and other narrative categories deploy visual features transposed to literary form. To the extent to which, on audio-visual criteria, y actually represents x, there is a correspondence of x's actual identity with, what I am terming, his simulated identity y (articulating [1] to [4]). If there is this correspondence and process, the answer to [2] is simply:

The referent of y is the x to which it refers in being y [5]

This is clearly displayed in the use of the *first* person: y manifests x as 'I am the PM', while y relays the unique sign of being (a particular) PM.

How does intentionality degrade reference?

Conversely, to the degree to which the replica y is infected with factors other than the expressions of the conditions which produce the simulation of x's identity on audio-visual criteria, the reference of y becomes indeterminate.

70   *Renaissance in language*

Of course, as Trembath (1991: 39–42) presents it, reflecting Calvin's perspective, a human is not just a port for which revelatory knowledge docks and unloads content. An observer 'O', in so being, has a non-*a priori* relationship with the function of y in y's mediation of knowledge. At a stage of ceasing to simulate what is identifiable as x, y no longer refers, or, never did refer, to x. If there is gross distortion of y intended as x in Sy, the answer to O's question 'Who (or, 'What') is that?' has y in Sy as its referent, and not the referent x as in [5]; for y would not have succeeded in conforming to the audio-visual criteria of identifiability. Therefore, it eventually follows that an observer (prophet, or believer, etc.) O, who is cognisant of x, or wishes to become cognisant of x, and perceive x's revelation about x via Sy by y, is dependent on the following conditions being fulfilled:

> In furnishing a reference to x (a reference to x) y must conform to [1], [3] and [4], which would render Sy an efficient replicator of x as y [6]

It is apparent that, where O is necessarily dependent on Sy and so y for perception or knowledge of x, if [6] is not satisfied, the O cannot have knowledge of x or x's identity or will. In sum, O can recognise y as x where y has the same As x as defined by [1].

For application to any signifying functions (for example: visual, emotional or other qualitative phenomena), [1] and [6] rely on a suppressed premise, namely:

(a) for all visual elements to be represented in y of x there are, or can be, reified or paraphrased linguistic expressions corresponding individually to these elements.

There is a felicity in this since in most of the linguistic states of affairs for which [1] to [6] are the target, the linguistic expressions are said to correspond with an ontological or other state which they mirror.

Reproduction logic

Are there live metaphors in genetics?

Although presuppositions about knowledge of God are centrally expressed in semantics, other subjects can be represented in equivalent semantic form, and yet they also have their own mode of expression (for example, in emotion's aesthetics).

This generalisation also extends to other subjects since (a) above is itself a specific orientation of a principle which can be used to characterise quite different subject matter. For example, its logic occurs in DNA replication, by which hereditary characteristics are reproduced. An aspect of biological reproduction, schematically iterated, is x_1 (male parent), x_2 (female parent) producing y (child, or child's characteristics) which is distinct from x's, but regarding some transmitted features has the same A as some x (or x's). Inherited features have a DNA logic like a telephone conversation: 'Is that y or x (father) speaking?' – 'He has his father's voice (face, disposition, emotion, etc.)!' Here there is a symmetry with the type and application of the audio-visual criteria expressed by the PM as y. With x_1, x_2 and y it is the case that y is not the persons whom y images; however, the level-specific replication is symmetrical with regard to the way the condition is expressed in [1] above – just as many features as are shared is the quantifiable domain for sameness. Of course just because one thing has identical patterns to another, it does not follow that one refers to the other. But some of the above examples in certain contexts do constitute a reference from one to the other counterpart. Jane Heal (1997) has begun work on showing how predicates and non-proper name expressions can function as indexicals to pick out a unique referents. It could be that this approach might be extended to the foregoing types of uses.[14]

So my point is not that internal qualitative properties are shared through these different subjects. Rather, the analysis proposes that the logical semantics in different subjects which share some equivalent simulation patterns. There are explanatory asymmetries between these different and differing subjects. Although the topic will not be pursued here,[15] there is a strong formal basis for investigating the predicates employed of God, the Son of God, the Father to advertise features of their logical relations.

Generally, relations and shared properties between subjects can be the level of discourse for [1] and not only the reproduction of personal identity in communication. This wide role of sharing and its above presuppositions of agency (depicted in [1] to [6]) will have variables and various token values. But basic to many ancient revelatory agency functions are language, a criterion implementing individual identity, as well as other features such as referring emotions. Charles Taylor (1985: 45–76) has explained some of these latter aspects as functions of 'self-interpreting animals'. Fellowship with God, as with relationships with people, is both self-reflecting, self-effacing, enhancing and reciprocal. Ancient biblical exegesis sometimes engages with genres implementing this sort of function. For example, Psalm 119 is treated as a reflexive relationship of reception and expression of communication. This confessional narrative is taken both to express revelation yet speaks in the first person of David, the envisaged writer. Its union with the Other is both experientially isomorphic of man and God interfacing interpretation and is also a mirror and model of the dependency of the 'word' on God.

Does transcendent identity-sharing work?

The question of whether the identity relation between the referent of the name of God ('Yahweh' in the Old Testament) and angels (the latter represented by *'lhym* and/or *ml'k* – literally 'messenger', but usually translated 'angel') is between predicates or subject terms, can now easily be resolved. In the case of PM in *y* as *x*, the referent of *y* is not itself – or is non-referential – but strikes a relation of reference respecting *x*. By analogy, *x* is thereby a sort of antecedent of *y*. The first-person attributions need careful handling in conformity with Anscombe's (1981b: 45–65) and Altham's (1979: 25–53) treatments of the relations. In Altham's use of Geach's expression, *y goes proxy* for *x*, akin to impersonation. This pronominal reference to an *x* by *y* is conditional on S*y*'s production of the simulated identity by which *y* goes proxy for *x* and personifies *x*.

This is rather like an audio-visual 'quotation'. A sentence-quotation, if true, can be treated as a name referring to its source. Contrariwise, gross distortion removes the reference; *y* fails 'to be' '*x*'.

The foregoing characterisation is for biblical phenomena of certain types. 'God' reflects a conformity in use to [3], [4] and [5]. Revelation, however, does not efface the 'receiving' subject's semantics. As Pearson explains it in a Pauline context, revelation is a dialectical function (see Pearson forthcoming). It is important to appreciate that revelatory semantics is often parallel with the semantics of *fellowship* relations (often in the first person of the human).

This does require that the medium by which *y* operates has descriptions which apply to it and not to *x*; it also warrants that those Fs which *x* and *y* share are not criterial for *y*'s personal identity or identity, though union of identity is not excluded. The situation producing *y* – the situation S in S*y* – (e.g. where S is the television or angel) is not itself a replication of *x*. The television is not the PM. It images the PM. In some biblical narratives some angels are given proper names, and other fillers of *y*'s have personal identity attributed to them (e.g. Moses); this concurs with the foregoing scope for *y*.

With PM in S*y*, the latter was the record of an act of the former, whereas with biblical usage it is often that *y* is an expression of *x*'s will; but this is not a counter-example. The asymmetry can be removed by postulating that *y* is a minister *z* who acts on behalf of the PM who is *x*, where *z* reads *x*'s words. In any case, biblical *y*s if fulfilled by 'angels' are always said to exemplify *x*'s will, in relevant uses. God's intending to φ (i.e. where φ is a logic predicate), and *y*'s φing, or relating φ, clearly claims to reproduce *x*'s intention and will. In the presuppositions revelatory agents in biblical contexts are said to mirror Yahweh. The televising of the PM mirrors PM, if [5] is satisfied. And, within the biblical worldview, angels as fillers of *y* are not subject to human limitations in modes of manifestation, which has some analogy with the device of broadcasting audio-visual images, where, in a particular respect, creativity is the criterion of empirical possibility. Creativity also holds a control on television audio-visual production of images at a certain level.

Clearly, there is an immense shift in sensibility when this function is said to manifest revelation. And this function itself also goes qualitatively infinite in the presupposition that its referent is Christ. I later argue that mathematical infinity (cf. Woess 2000) can be used as a model to map the [1] to [6] type of scenario.

Indeterminate theology

Are there divine broadcasting conditions?

As noted earlier, the manifestation of [1] to [6] in typical biblical usage concurs with the presupposition that they are constructs in, and of, revelation from God. If such conditions are not fulfilled in [1] to [6], there is no revelation, and so no support for the conception of God which is said to be a product of [1] to [6]. A facet of this is that x is imaged if, and only if, y has produced a revelation and gone proxy for x and x's will, etc., just as x is broadcast only if y images x. The fulfilment of conditions [1] to [6] leads to a proof that revelation from x via y is a necessary condition for knowledge of the actual identity of x. Knowledge of God (in the relevant revelatory sense) is possible only if there is a y which is an efficient audio-visual or other simulator of x – not least because knowledge of God is not available to unaided sensory perception or for ostensive reference. The same type of constraint would obtain where similar claims to knowledge were made, via a mystical insight, in terms of its structure and causality.

Can transcendence be pragmatic?

An individual's actions and biography are susceptible of representation in propositions. We should also allow for the concept of a counter-intuitive proposition – i.e. one that seems to entail contradictions but does not have to. It follows from such considerations that, if such a person's actions and biography are transcendent by manifesting God, then the propositions [1] to [6], together with the attendant qualifications, will have the capacity to depict that ontological and psychological state of affairs. So the functional scope of [1] to [6] is not merely semantic; it applies to the philosophy of action and event.

Is the universe an intentional object?

An intentional identity (Anscombe 1965) is, roughly, that recipe about an identity which is without a reference; it is an intended reference, but a false one. A mirage is an example of an intentional identity. Proposals about y would merely dismantle into y's being an intentional identity if:

(i) there is not a dependency-relation of y on x, because x *does not exist*;

or,

74 *Renaissance in language*

(ii) x does exist and there has been imaging in y but y is infected with factors other than those which would implement [1] to [6] so as to render y's simulated identity indeterminate;

or,

(iii) y is not intended to image x by x, but O has an illusion that y is x's actual identity.

The y in any of the above types may be made to correspond, in argument or ritual devotion, to an arbitrary referent (e.g. a statue of Baal), but this would be a seeming y or Sy.

In the case of a y of the Prime Minister in Sy, O may test for the veridicality of y as x, by tracing the progress of material causal technological connectives which comprise or produce Sy. However, although this can in principle be done, usually it is very difficult to achieve and exhaustive testing for these phenomena, and one normally accepts the y on the basis of a set of conventions and consistency.

The reproducibility of calculations involving deep mathematical conjectures, and/or attendant problematic astrophysical observations (e.g. black holes) can be deemed to fill y, an x's route to y, yet they not be accessible to veridical testing, while the *coherence* of the y may be measured from criteria of consistency such as [1] to [6]. So the application of the tests for a controlled regress in respect of 'x as Yahweh', for which y goes proxy, for an x, might not be accessible narrowly speaking; but this would not be evidence of incompatibility of biblical phenomena with [1] to [6], however. Technically and narrowly stated, logical proof in science is not always directly achievable; thus its absence in some versions of religious contexts is not self-evidently proof of falsehood.

To where do intentions pave the way?

An intentional identity, on the other hand, due to inconsistency and failure to satisfy [1] to [6] in structural terms, has no reference associated with 'God' by which one refers to an actual referent. This would be parallel with fictional characters. Sometimes perception incorrectly allows the class of the actual to seem to act as host to an intentional identity. Such an intentional non-actual referent fails the extensional test of (i) to (iii); it is an alleged identity to which an O intends to refer but does not succeed. Theologians sometimes obfuscate about this state of affairs. Yet it is not a matter of buying into some questionable formalism in analytical philosophy; it is an entailment of the difference if the contrast between a thing exists, and the use of negation when it does not exist.

To use the term 'God' does not thereby confer a referent on it. The situation in a claim of theistic revelation is constrained by conditions no different, at the appropriate level, from knowledge claimed regarding ordinary communication: where there is no other source than a postulated referent for knowledge of that referent, a criterion of identity for the referent must be supplied by the referent and be understood in use by the set of observers, if they are able to refer to it. Consider the circumstance in which an astronomical object is too far away from us for it yet to have conveyed signals to us. We could not refer to it. There might be conjecture, but not reference satisfying a criterion of identity. So it is with the present conception of the possibility of reference to God, in the absence of some occurrence of communication from, or knowledge gained from outside the world of, such a God. As Wittgenstein argued, 'If there is any sense to the world, then it is outside the world'.

Theological names

Is there a game to being the name?

A criterion of identity is a necessary and sufficient condition for a successful use of a logically proper name n, such that n refers to the required referent (i.e. a singular term). If one follows Wittgenstein, there could be more than one criterion which could enable one to refer by means of a proper name; but some criterion is still needed. There are various ways to formulate such a criterion, or indeed to replace with some other concept, such as Kripke (1980) does.

It could be that more than one such type of concept functions in natural languages, perhaps specific to culture, context or semantic consequence, though these issues have yet to be extensively explored. It could be that a large range of extant logics of proper names could be used, with qualification, as maps for distinct sorts of naming uses in natural languages. Further, it is worth exploring to what degree a certain type of proper name thesis may cut into the scope of use of a proper name less extensively than another thesis. Many of these programmes can be inter-derived from each other, so my canvassed pluralism does not automatically facilitate ontological relativity for proper names.[16]

Are religious names logical?

The criterion of identity in the current examination is furnished from [1] above, where a relevant subset of predicates from the class of A is suitably linked to the identity relation: 'n has the same A as y'. So the biblical usage of 'Yahweh' and *theos* ('God'), on which [1] is based, reflects a correct employment of a criterion of identity structurally speaking. The relation of referent to referring term here is analogous with that of a quoted source to the quotation of it in use. We see in the New Testament (especially in Matthew 1, John's Gospel, Philippians 2 and Hebrews 2) that God's name in the Old Testament form has been erased or transformed from its Hebrew form, as a parallel shift in its transfer to the Son of God. Here, clearly, there is a corresponding, and unique shift of ontology between Father, Son and Holy Spirit. The conditions [1] to [6] above, encapsulated in effect (signified by *a*) can be applied to pick out aspects of that revelatory movement. As a live metaphor in logic, then, [1] to [6] have ontological equivalents. Although we should avoid sloppy uses, for example, of equivocating metaphor which conflates ontology with semantics, there is no reason, as I will argue later, why live metaphor should not occur in an ontological signifier. Namely, (a property of) the referent is itself a semantic ontological identity: a semiotic function in addition to its role in its mode of existence. The presuppositional ontology of Christ is a unique instance, at one level of appreciation, of such ontological live metaphor.

Prior stated (1971: 159): 'the whole contribution which a genuine name makes to the meaning of a sentence is its indication or identification of an individual'; his view was that whatever is a name and actually refers is a logically proper name. Although it may be judged that this thesis is (non-viciously) circular, it is clear. One criticism of it is that natural language proper names have various other semantic features, which someone might judge excludes Prior treatment from the scope of literary usage. Hopefully Prior did not wish to exclude tone, as it seems on a typical reading Frege did (cf. Gibson 1987: 11–14). In a technical sense Prior is correct from within a narrow focus on the logic of proper names.[17]

In a wider perspective, in natural language contractual puns can operate between tonal values frozen in the signs which compose a proper name, and make a contribution to the identification of the individual to which the name refers. Typically, but not exclusively, such allusive uses are secondary in their semantic contribution to identification. On this approach there is a primary function of proper name: that of satisfying a criterion of identity which comprises its reference. But there is also a logic of tone: a term drawn from Frege's *Beleuchtung* and *Färbung* though without his thesis that tone is neither true nor false. Obviously we should avoid equivocation between the semantics of identifying the individual and linguistic depiction of aspects in the person's individuality; yet there are complex relations between a person's identity and the individual's life (as Parfit (1984) has shown) logical representation of which can function as a contribution to criteria of identity. The 'mention' (of a proper name) is itself a subspecies of use. Consequently there can be a logical networking between logical use and tonal mention, given suitable preservation of the differences. Some explanation for this state of affairs has been produced, in which such tonal elements are likened to ossified, sense which is logically mentioned within an idiom, that can be triggered by associative semantics in its context.[18]

Certainly the candidacy of a proper name of God is an exotic and counter-intuitive extreme case to consider when the logic of such matters is not yet a matter of agreement amongst logicians. But this is the present subject, so it is expedient to make some proposals. For instance, [1] above, in which 'x' and 'y' share properties of identity, can be operated as a criterion for identification of, for example, the bearer of '*YHWH*' in use with the proper name making its contribution of reference. But in addition to this function, the proper name is involved in a complex paranomastic theme playing on its presumed future tensed stem ('he shall be' in Exodus 3: 12–14) which both plays on the identity of the reference, relates this to the relation of the referent to the mention of the name of God in temporal contexts, together with articulating the use of the name in the role of in connection with agents (angel and Moses).

On this view, if a (proposed) identity is intentionalistic, then no reference exists. If the identification is not made, then the name serves to falsify the claims made by the predicates which constitute [1]. For the proper name in [1] to be true, in the sense of making a reference to God, (i) to (iii) argues that the set of predicates in use, which yield reference for God's name, presuppose a necessary and sufficient condition by which the bearer has to supply the criterion of identity articulated in [1]. This amounts to a claim of revelation of God in language. Exodus 3, which introduces the explanation of God's name *and* the identity of the bearer, is precisely just such an articulation claiming to be revelation. Linguistically, the items in Exodus 3 ('angel', 'God', etc.) are exact fillers of y, with 'Yahweh' as x. In this manner the possibility of having knowledge of God is bound in with being able to name God.

Of course the foregoing type of scenario would be a retrojective project with an anachronistic message in our contemporary world, for some typical atheists who are philosophers. Yet such philosophers insist that it is only this sort of explicit presentation of beliefs which could occupy the position of claiming to be an account of what it would have to be a philosophy of God, in contrast with, for example, intentionalist models in some theology.[19] This is even the situation concerning an atheist philosopher who considers the first person as the position from which ethics and the limits of philosophy has to be assessed and developed (see Bernard Williams (1985)). Consequently giving prime position to subjectivity is not a correct rubric for an intentionalistic theism, and not even as the basis for an appeal to atheists. Viewed accurately, such intentionalism, on either realist or anti-realist grounds, is a way of conceding that one does not have, and perhaps cannot have, knowledge of God's identity. In my view this would be rather like (pointlessly and needlessly) developing an intentional mythology for the astrophysical cosmology of the universe: criteria can be logically formed to depict what it would be to be the analysis and conceptual construction of the subject. To retreat to intentionalism would be to deny the relation of the external world to conception, and fail to explore our capacity to devise applications of our mental faculties to the subject. One might even utilise Williams's first-person basis for conceptual construction, preserve it for humans, yet thereby propose that any other individual – including God – should be allowed this favoured diectic attention in attempts to construct conceptions of their identity. Accordingly, we should preserve first-person priorities for ourselves and God regarding human and transcendent identities: if we require freedom of will, so should God. Obviously ancient writings present God as supervening authority over human will; but this is different from our failing to craft the logics and criteria of what it is to be a representation of individuality and the explicit separation of the signifying concept from the subject external to such representation.

So it would be mistaken to draw on alleged ascription of non-referring meaning to proper names, as a fragment in a proposal that 'Yahweh' has a meaning which is not decidable by its truth-condition. Wittgenstein's analysis (1995b: sec. 79) of *Philosophical Investigations* does raise acute problems which shows that some proper names in natural languages embrace informal features. In an extensive study of non-formal elements in proper names, Gibson (1981: ch. 3) explains that these sorts of data to which Wittgenstein alludes enjoy logical relations with use of relevant biblical proper names.

Can a name be transcendent?

As Matthew 1 develops the name of 'Jesus', it deploys the statement (so the narrative appears to code it by etymological means, in the above use of 'tonal') 'he shall save his people from their sins'. This satisfies a criterion of identity used in the narrative of Matthew which is composed of predicates that, in part, are applied to God in the Old Testament. The name 'Jesus' reflects the Father: the name of the Father is in him and is Jesus. This theme is asymmetrically extended in John's Gospel, combining the criteria of naming with the 'genetic' transfer of properties between two referents in heaven and on Earth. Thus the matrix in [1] to [6] is enriched and transformed to universal levels of scope by God's own criterion of identity manifested in and to be his Son. This criterion furnishes the semantic content to match the ontological shift in identity. Qualitatively, then, the content of the matrix is unique, reflecting as it does the criterion of identity of the Father and the Christ.

The usage of [1] to [6] of God is an indirect measure of His entry into the categories of our spacetime and intelligibility, since they stipulate the criteria of appearance and communication by revelation. Given this state of affairs, it is important to be able to give an account of the grounds for discriminating between a mere intention to refer to the appearance of God – which does not actually reach the referent because of incoherent specification, and a name which succeeds in referring to God under the descriptions proposed in narratives candidates for revelation. Evidently, this type of transcendent proper name usage fits into the scheme of [1] to [6] above, though there is a heavy-duty literary contribution to its host contexts. This should not necessarily be deemed illogical overkill. We have seen grounds for taking the excess semantics as due to density of sense rather than paucity of logic. Given that philosophical logic has not yet cracked the kernel of what it is to be a definitive theory of meaning, and has entailments of paradox in all such attempts, destructive criticism may backfire. Conversely there is no remit from the above to suggest that the foregoing noted literary uses of divine proper names entail the sort of charge which it has been fashionable to make: that talk of God is of necessity ill-formed.[20]

The variable value of believing

Are we easily bewitched by transcendence?

Surely, statistically, the answer is affirmative. (Conversely, Hume might have considered more seriously the way reductionism may bewitch us to be prejudicial to matters beyond our ken). Christianity is replete with a diet that has led to many deaths down the centuries in the institutional investments of claims to fashions of transcendence, which serve to exemplify the powerful effects of false consciousness. But false consciousness is not an internal property of believing in transcendence since it is a formal property of some scientific concepts (such as the status of some wave-corpuscular equations of light).

Contrariwise, reductionism in some post-structuralism has now been conflated with mentally internalised allegations of transcendence, which the believers claim have no ontology other than their imagination. In some cases atheism could be deemed a tautology of this reductionism. This is inconvenient for the law of the excluded middle. Some philosophers of religion, attracted to such a position, take it as evidence that logic is imperialist and inferior to the form of life which sustains transcendence. The former point is obviously false. For example, Graham Priest's (1995) paraconsistent logic allows that a given expression can be both true and false at the same time, and facilitates some proposals about transcendence. Consequently, paraconsistent logic is true and false. Since this position is supposed to be a biography internal to the reductionist believer, it would follow that his consciousness is both true and false. This unpacks into the inference that it is true that it is false, and that the believer does not know the difference between what is true and what is false. But this falsifies the original belief that he knows paraconsistent reductionism to be true. Nevertheless, such a formalism may itself be helpful as a typology to map such mentalities as exhibit this state of affairs: and this may then be applied to relevant structures of belief are true and false.

It is common for such protagonists of theological reductionism to appeal to Nietzsche. This is a most peculiar resort. As introduced in the Prologue, John Richardson's (1996) specialist research on Nietzsche's 'system' concludes that, as I mentioned earlier, Nietzsche does not reject a correspondence theory of truth, but revolutionises it, and embraces this version.

80 *Renaissance in language*

Richardson (ibid.: 288) observes: for Nietzsche, 'the empirical truth method does apply to the ontological claims as well'. It seems that a false consciousness about Nietzsche pervades some philosophy of religion. We are on more solid ground with Tom Nagel (1997: 71–73) who has argued for the irreducibility of reason, as well as candidly acknowledging his fear of religion: yet he hopes that atheism is true (ibid.: 130). He thinks that there is no available rational explanation to fill the alternative. The present book attempts to prove the opposite, whilst agreeing with Nagel (ibid.: 143) that we should submit to the order of reason rather than creating it.

Can we isolate circular subjectivity?

Anscombe's (1959) pioneering work to open the philosophy of mind exposed a deep similarity between 'intending' and 'believing'. Hacking (1995) has extended this, as well as qualified the distinctions, by showing that such overlaps result in false beliefs in the sphere of memory and false consciousness. Although his topic concerns multiple personality, Hacking warns that the general states of affairs has something to do with a general tendency for us to feed on semantic contagions which breed where intentionality and false consciousness function outside as well as within clinically identified individuals, due to some degree to mass media and cross-fertilisation of culture. Without wishing to develop this in detail, it is worth noting in the present perspective that a book could be written on the applicability of Hacking's analysis to philosophy of religion.

Elements of intentionality are present in some uses of descriptions about an O's relation to a y. For verbs, especially employed in specifying such relations between O and y, O programmes his notion or assumption of ontological status for the seeming object of reference of y. Instances of the use of an intentional identity do not of themselves entail that there is no referent which can be associated with the proposition in which the intentionalistic description occurs, if the description is extirpated of opaque components. For example, in ancient Near East contexts there are no actual ontologies for the purported deities, though there were iconic, cultic and psychological phenomena to uphold and articulate beliefs. These are also the shifting semantics of, for example, 'Satan' with the Essenes; Tom Nagel (1997) exemplifies how the term emerges here as an intended proper name, rather than earlier role term. Intentional identities do not produce a reference. It may be that there is no referent to specify – as with the case of 'the guards' in the Ugaritic Anat myth: 'she plunged up to her knees in the blood of the guard(s)'. When these linguistic phenomena are used in conjunction with a purported name, such as 'Baalzebub', we have what Geach (1980b: 91–92) terms a quasi-name. Here illusions linked to false concepts, or claims of false knowledge (cf. Helm 1994: 18–19), act as a focus to pick out cult or social norms.

Theological verbs, e.g. 'believe', particularly run the gauntlet of being intentionalistic: 'O believes in x'. This schema may, adapting a suggestion of Prior's (1971: 132ff.), expand into 'O believes x F's', where this latter form is a special case of 'O believes that p' where p is a proposition. Of course 'in' is itself often systematically ambiguous and requires analysis. Notice also Helm's (1994: 14) use of Geach's analysis of believing on the analogy of 'saying that', though one may, he comments, express a statement without believing it. Belief (excepting negated subjects, etc.) presupposes an assertion that the object which is believed has ontological status.

What is a proposition? Stage I

In employing the term 'proposition' here, it is quite distinct from the way it is employed by, for example, Trembath (1991: 6) who writes of 'propositionalised' and 'discontinuist theologians'. While recognising the shortcoming of those thus criticised, it is important to allow for the complex and sometimes counter-intuitive forms of statement which 'a logical proposition' can be assigned, and the sort of expressions which are thereby both logical yet not traditionally propositioned. MacKinnon (1979: 82) crisply stated: '(Jesus) must be more than a variable to which we can assign whatever value our devotion prompt us'.

A more modest problem than what it is to be Jesus is antecedent to this query, however; do we know the logic of all propositions? An infinite omniscient mind would know the forms which all propositions could take. In a naïve circular sense, of course, we know what form implication has. But Aristotle did not define implication, and we have yet fully to understand (induction apart) the relation of the relevance of premises and their contents to the identity of implication (logical or otherwise) with which he was concerned. Since there are paradoxes of implication entailed by the predicate calculuses, we are not entirely clear what it is to be the scope of 'proposition', when *content* is a notion that we need to specify of generalisation in relation to the relevance of (presumed) suppressed premises. Given that a logical paraphrase of two or more propositions is a tautology, we need to be careful not to exclude in principle the possibility that we can assign a logical interpretation to a prose expression, especially in view of our need to understand more about what it is to be epistemic distance between premises linked by implication.[21] Paraphrases applying logic could lead to ways in which less than abstract language might, upon deeper scrutiny, satisfy logical criteria (in which an implication is true only if it is impossible for the antecedent to be true and the consequent is false). The suggestion to be developed is that, if we concentrate on the counter-intuitive contingencies which arise in hard cases of logical difficulty, we shall discover not only how proof cannot proceed, but what it is to expose a mimetic propositional bedrock on the deepest outer edge of generalised discourse.[22]

But variables can only receive the values which they represent. If the variable itself stands for a definite identity, then it is only possible to characterise the identity under the predicates which specify the properties which make up the identity. When the relations between premises have to be necessary, true and relevantly related, matters are both clearly focused and yet deep, as with issues of characterising what it is to be God and what it is to be logic. Since in the nature of a concept of the transcendent, God, immortality and other properties are necessary, it is hardly possible for variety in identity, though revelatory depiction of God could deform the intuitive limits of language to create counter-intuitive expressions that mirror the ontologies outside finite sense. We have thankfully lost the medieval past with its tortuous debates, and torture, about the relations between God, doctrine and logic. But as is demonstrated by, for example, Burnyeat (1994) concerning the enthymeme, Smiley (1995) regarding logical form, and Chomsky (2000: 133) arguing about attempts to reconstruct mentality without metaphysical implications (which thereby still seem to pose a complete mystery), we have also failed to maintain a grasp of some true connections between premises and their contents which Aristotle had excavated, though some of these are being retrieved and transformed by scholars such as Lear (1980) and Striker (1998). Nevertheless a core-feature we need is demonstrable: reason and reasons are external to us in their epistemological status, and as such supervene over subjectivity and intentionality as criteria of the ways things are.

Astronomical beliefs and intentions

Do astronomers have artistic disputes?

Problems of intentionality occupy positions within most mental activity and interpretations of the external world. Although there are varieties of identities to such phenomena, they manifest shared internal properties. Even literary interpretation reflects similar problems to astronomy, though there are many uncomparable relations. Certainly, attempts to parallel widely distinct subjects such as religion and astronomy are fraught with so many evident disanalogies that we should proceed with scepticism. But we should not, as a function of this state of affairs, exclude the possibility of counter-intuitive resemblances between features of different subjects. Such possible relations may be invented, be too marginal to be of interest; yet at this stage in history we do not know enough of the identities of religion and astronomy, or indeed of any two or more such widely separated subjects, to decide in principle what criteria to deploy in judgement.

In view of this, not only highly critical assessment, but explicit bold formulations proposing possibilities, are apt for progress. It may be that, for example, Pascal's (1954: 385) interpretative application of a differential calculus, as a model for desire in relation to duration, in such compositions as those that appear in his *Expériences touchant le vide* (1647) seems farfetched by current cultural mores. This viewpoint may presuppose and implement our own improbable presumption about the supervenient superiority of our own culture, however. Alternatively, we might isolate certain recurrent properties in such projects and isolate them from seventeenth-century presuppositions, while using them as a precedent for associating common properties in the sciences and arts. Hockman (1997: 214–17) shows how Pascal's use of calculus to model transcendent functions in a literary narrative, partly by substitution of one function of 'infinite' in a bounded region, can be mapped into a measurable employment of desire and promise concerning the concept of God. I will not here pursue this, but only note it as a precedent for tying at least two modally distinct realms together in an equation of quantitative and qualitative infinities. Clearly this, to some extent, presupposes a sense of relevance about the connection of content to logical form; and this is a question as much to do with our limited understanding of such relations as it is a problem internal to such presupposed equations.

But we also, sometimes unconsciously, engage with identical problems of objectivity in deciding what is intentional in both the arts and sciences. Although failure to agree may only reflect differences about viewpoints, such conflict also presupposes a concurrence of metalanguage communicating functions that constitute the presuppositions of disagreement. This situation itself presupposes the involvement of the requisite functions in philosophy of mind that make contracts with the language we use in such circumstances. Intentionality is one of these sorts of common elements in science and arts. Before proceeding to an astronomical example of intentionality, it is worth noting a case concerning dispute where the actual boundaries between those of authors, their roles as critics, and cases where they are influenced by their own familial presuppositions. These function like quantum indeterminacies in Simone de Beauvoir's (1967) *La femme rompue* story ('The Woman Destroyed').[23] The story attracts conflicting explanations, many of which explicitly conflict with Simone de Beauvoir's view of Monique as a woman consumed by her own delusions, with the reader adopting instead Maurice – the husband – as the rogue type. The dispute displaces certainty about the authorial intention and resists her apparent attempt to transfer elements of her psychobiography to Maurice as a way of marking *the* interpretation of the text. The author's as well as reader's unconscious obtrude in collision over intentionality of the narrative.

Is there astronomical intentionality?

I here push de Beauvoir and astronomy together, in part to embarrass us about our naturally narrow sense of cross-connection between topics, by which we fail to link and identify some common logical issues in disparate subjects. This is reminiscent of two disputing sets of scientific minds attaching themselves to astronomical technology, even allowing for varying belief-policies (cf. Helm 1994: 113–41). Connected with the differences in dispute is the epistemology of observation. For example, intentional verb

84 *Renaissance in language*

uses of 'believe' occur in some astronomical assessments of phenomena (leaving aside the distinct position of irrealism in 'particle' physics).[24] A case in point is:

> O believes in *x*'s existence, where O claims *x* is the set of
> quasars in the galaxy of Boötes   [7]

But it cannot be truly the case that O's object of belief (in the sense of an ontological realism) is the empirical class of referents which, given a proper criterion of application, is the set in the Boötes' galaxy, for O does not believe that:

> The Boötes' quasar observations are effects of subluminally
> moving phenomena at a velocity at most of 90 per cent the
> speed of light.   [8]

Observer O notes that since Wang *et al.* (2000) have demonstrated the occurrence of superluminal velocities in a laboratory context, it is small potatoes to assign this superluminal situation to the Boötes' quasar. Observer O takes support from Martin Rees's (2000) study of the emergence of subgalaxies and pregalactic light from the CDM (cold dark matter) epoch, some 300,000 years after the big bang, when there were redshifts higher than 5 and may be beyond 20. For observer O, the modernist scientific world, in which the velocity of light marks a limit to possibility, is one of imperious myth. O's view is that in the primordial universe – where star formation was efficient – pregalaxies and miniquasars moved at very high redshifts and blur the boundary between. Consequently, O believes in the substitutivity of [7] for the following:

> The Boötes' quasar observations are effects of objects with
> superluminal velocities of ten times the speed of light   [9]

and O builds his criterion of identity from [9], supported by the visual metaphors in Figure 2.2, analogous with *y*'s visual role in [1] to [6] in the foregoing section. In fact O is a rather dated 3C273 observer who, together with some other astronomers at the time, we are told by their colleagues, misinterpreted unresolved observations. We do not require a strong ontological realist theory to sustain such analysis; the present study could be operable with, for example, Tennant's (1997: 365–69) antirealist observation-sentences.

Even some years back, O's position was supportable by observations of phenomena which *appear* to have superluminal velocities. Zensus *et al.* (1987) report observations of superluminal motion in the double-lobed quasar 3C263, and calculate that this is a common relativistic feature among the cores of quasars with extended lobes. Zensus *et al.* observed the quasar

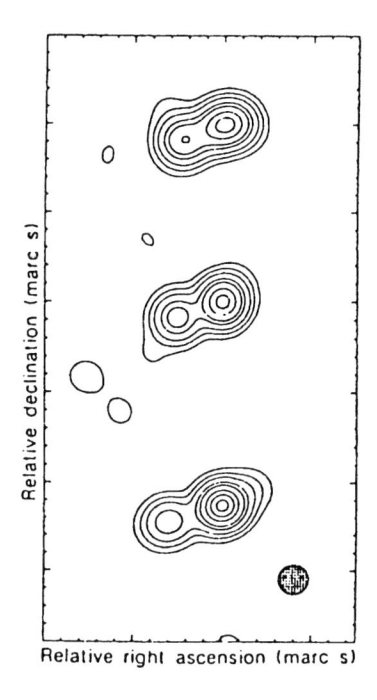

Figure 2.2 Superliminal candidate quasar 3C263
Source: (after Zensus *et al.* 1987)

over three years, and above is the resulting hybrid map which is constructed of the three phases of the (30%) super-resolved images of the core and its extending lobe. The map displays an increased separation between the core and the lobe components.

Since superluminal motion presses the question of whether or not the fundamental constants are indeed fixed, the O observer in [9] above is concerned with how cosmological presuppositions sustain or thwart his objectivity. Clearly, [9] requires a systematic change of identity in contrast with [8] respecting basic constants. Nevertheless O's belief is that:

> The Boötes' quasars are x, and this negates [8]   [10]

How do astronomers fail to refer?

What O claims to believe is [7]; yet he describes [9] as his belief, though [9] cannot consistently replace [8] without falsification and destruction of possible reference to Boötes' quasars.

Here if [8] is true, then the object of belief in [9] is an intended but not actual referent. The conjunction of [7] and [9] produces an intentional identity. So there is no relevant fit of [7] with [9].

The presumed referring from [7] fails, and in this way it has a parallel with incorrect theological propositions when viewed from the standpoint of a correspondence theory of meaning. Part of this failure is because of the internal relation between the structures of *intending* and *believing*. Intention participates in the ontology of extensional belief (though we have to be careful to distinguish such expressions as 'Necessarily n has a property F' from 'n is necessarily F'). Geach (1972: 255–62) argued that *believing* has an element of the logical force of a sign for a theorem's assertion-sign, in Frege's logic. On this view 'Believing p', for example, where 'p' could be [7] and [9], is in this perspective tantamount to 'saying that 'p'. In the above cases, variously of science and of God, knowledge is presupposed, which attracts a state of 'believing', though the modes of discourses are in many ways distinct.

Therefore, intentionality is not itself a property of religious belief statements; scientific beliefs can be of the same family as religion. That there can be arbitrariness in scientific terminology signifying functions in empirical research may seem too obvious to some to need stating. But to others the seeming prescientific status of the nature of religious belief will need adjusting to admit that a scientist's mind can be prescientific.

Can antirealism and irrealism be confused with counter-intuitive realism?

Consequently, we need not conclude that the *asymmetry* between the linguistic sign and its signification, and the *difference* between the domination of the means of representation over what is signified, have to be intentionalistic, though often they are. The concept of live metaphor, which this book suggests, can sometimes be used to transcend and sublime such problems of asymmetry and difference.

We can agree, as an archetypal tendency, with Lacan's thesis on the domination and instability of the signifier over the signified, yet argue that there are semantic possibilities which thwart this impulse. Much structuralist and post-structuralist criticisms inexorably wend their way to the end of realism; and the sort of refined global anti-realism does not invariably oppose the present thesis. Ontological irrealism of the sort which Paul Boghossian (1990a) attacks is quite near some nihilistic philosophy of religion in its absence of commitment to actuality. At the other end of the universes of discourse, traversing through ontological realism and adopting its basic tenets, is what I am designating as counter-intuitive realism. My summary proposal is simply that there is a type of realism(s) whose identity is unexpected, sometimes because it is exotic or remote from typical versions of realism. On the analogy of those who were surprised by the results of

Gödel's incompleteness theorems, so likewise with counter-intuitive realism; it is a conception which, in conjunction with its referents, is a deeply unexpected instance of its type. It might seem to resemble versions of antirealism or irrealism. Or, counter-intuitive realism might incorrectly inadvertently be junked with intractable realisms. We might even discover people unconsciously conflating counter-intuitive realism with anti-realism. Target a crude scenario about realism, and one whose naïve mimetic defence crudely underestimates the subtle contrapuntal twists of supposed 'realist' narratives, and a highly counter-intuitive realism with a revolutionary spacetime ontology could violate one's belief policy. We should thus discriminate in these areas, and be wary of presupposing a universalising recipe that deems narrative generally intentionalistic, concurrently with the above policy that intentionality parading as realism should be isolated and rejected. We should have a strong sense of modesty due to our ignorance of the empirical scopes of our generalisations and the limits of our thought, however; our capacity for surprise and the desire to discover insights of which we are ignorant should not be restricted by conceptual dogma.

Live metaphoric 'revelation'?

Has exotic science a relation to sublime perception?

Obviously we should recognise that literary texts do not have an ontology which is the same as that of science's; we should also be careful to expose the intentional tendencies, mingled with realism, in scientific realisms. But outside of the scope of such confusions literary narratives could contain something like a precise presupposition that warrant health warnings about the differences between science and arts which may be ignored at their peril. At the side of this value-judgement we should allow for counter-intuitive states of consistent sense which may (only) seem to be incoherent.

Sometimes, as Prendergast (1986) demonstrated, for example, with reference to Balzac's realism, texts embody a disturbing mimesis which is at variance with a reader's consciousness of reality, though traditionally mimesis is usually explained as institutional, even crudely representational and realist. In this perspective there is a counter-intuitive analogue of mimesis in some logic – for example, the uses of contingency of the sort explored by Casimer Lewy (1976). He employs the term 'counter-intuitive' to explain some of the unexpected consequences where inference ties together necessity and contingency in unexpected ways. In this type of scenario then, for convenience, and as a first stage in proposing an approach to stretching our grasp of what it is to be a proposition, we can tie Prendergast's thesis of unstable mimesis to Lewy's argument for the counter-intuitive characteristic of some uses of contingency. To some degree this is a strategy for conveying an impressionistic view of fresh elements in what it is to be a proposition. Although this proposal stands independently as an approach to the possibility of structuring new alignments between science and arts, and it is presented as such, it can also be deployed as part of a movement to facilitate a fresh approach to questions of transcendence and what traditionally has been termed 'revelation'. Some readers may wish to take the notion being developed here as a sense of disclosure arising separate from any traditional sense of communication of God, as a transcendent function emerging from within human experience; others may wish to consider the thesis that 'revelation' can be associated with a thesis of disclosure from God nested into natural language or other creative media.

We are all prone to presuppose our modalities of reading as a way of adopting or discarding a narrative's sense. Deconstruction, sometimes rightly, concentrates on the indeterminacy of the narrative to arbitrate on metaphor. As Johnson (1993: 187–200) maps it, infinity is a precondition of Derrida's '*system*', in which semantic determination minimally departs from infinity. But there is a need for a large-scale examination of the indeterminacy of the reader – especially in contexts where the narrative's and the reader's worldviews collide. This is frequently the case with hermeneutic disputes over the sense of 'revelation'. Derrida (1978) says that these sort of terms are ambiguous and so undecidable; others counter that the richness of the determinable sense is the cause of conflict.[25] Derrida argues that a presupposition of infinity is subverted because it is a blind sense, because of its use of metaphor. I shall maintain below that this state of affairs is not true in principle, though it does apply to some narrative.

Riffaterre (1990) contends that undecidable expressions have a type of calculable sense since, he believes, undecidability tags and is a property of difficulty. He proposes that intertextuality (allusive or quoted relations in a narrative to external texts) is a criterion for resolving the measurement of such sense. Bowie (1978: 154), speaking of the difficulty in interpreting Mallarmé's poetry, warns that 'his poems do at moments make rapid thrusts against the reader's sense of his own coherence'. Clearly this does not amount to Bowie maintaining that the demolition of our sense of coherence is itself the state of undecidability within a creative narrative. Derrida (cf. Johnson 1993: 189) upholds the deconstructing force of Mallarmé's (1914) '*Un coup de des jamais n'abolira le hasard*: A throw of the dice can never eliminate chance'. But if throwing the dice is always subject to chance, we should recognise that chance presupposes laws of distributional symmetry. And if artistic creativity employs chance then, for example, musical composition such as Beethoven's late quartets both ironises chance in dissonance while composing a unity that transcends the limits of the *hasard*. It is feasible to suggest this type of transcendence as a property in the logic of cosmological discovery.

Postmodernist worldviews often close themselves off from exposure to claims for any sense of revelation made in narratives, and Derrida's use of 'infinity' is materialist, idealist, and not, say, Cantor's. We might too easily use Derrida as a post-structuralist device in an imperial secular theology, to ward off the metaphysical thrusts of ancient or Classical Christian religious narrative which disturb our coherence.

What is a proposition? Stage II

In particular, this occurs when crude 'propositional' revelatory theology is taken as a normative way to characterise a Christian view, advertising the narrow analytical mould of propositional logic. Propositional theology is at variance with many of the Bible's own narrative presuppositions about revelation and its reality, and much later theological writing; but not for the reason, much canvassed, that a necessary internal property of revelation would have to be non-propositional. Such non-propositionality assumes a superficial division of labour concerning what it is to be the expressibility of thought.

Shoesmith and Smiley (1980) offer a conception of what a 'proposition' is, which is so remote from anything in theology, or indeed much philosophical logic, that we should be fundamentally disturbed and disorientated about what we are to do with the notion of a 'propositional view'. They define one feature of proposition by treating it as a plural relation to multiple consequences. Using a natural logic approach, Shoesmith and Smiley display a strong use of spatial and geometric notions. In a certain sense, reflecting, for example, its ancestry in Gentzen's (1970) calculus of sequents, such an approach is a member of what one may call 'modernist logic'.[26] This sort of conception theorises over the emphasis on logical consequence rather than logical truth (though a bridge from one zone to the other can be mapped), and advances the idea of multiple conclusions as a logical symmetry to multiple antecedent premises. Although such a highly theoretical orientation and viewpoint as those of Shoesmith and Smiley (1980) are distant from the metaphysical priorities of the present book, and their programme will not be adopted in detail here, philosophical theology should nevertheless take account of such theoretical developments which deform and massively extend conceptions which affect what it is to be a proposition. I should like to propose, however, that their work generally can be interpreted as a case of a live metaphoric counterpart to a conventional single-conclusion calculus. So my purpose here is to note that research in the logic of propositions, as functions in the relations of consequence, not only opens up exciting new conceptual territory, but it accelerates beyond the hugely modest use of 'proposition' in much philosophical theology into exotic universes of discourse.

In such a metaphoric spacetime there is a vast amount of work to be done. It may seem audacious to suggest that other subjects require our attention so as to inform on how we may keep open minds to new possible futures; yet it is important in a universe of specialised narrowing of focus, to preserve a grasp of the relations of 'difference' to 'connection'. This partly devolves on the relations between art and science. One borderland task has to do with the gaps between formal and artistic theoretical and creative languages. A feature within this nest of problems is the distance between, and assumptions about the mutual irrelevance of logical languages to aesthetic critical representations of creativity expressions. A common piece of doctrine in such debate is the opinion that post-structuralism has demolished the prospect of using metalanguage in literary analysis. Yet there are dissenting voices, for, as Collier and Geyer-Ryan (1992: 8) state, 'New developments in historical and social theory reopen the whole question of cultural and aesthetic value ... The destabilisation of the critical metalanguages of modernism has, clearly, not been fatal'. Obviously the identity and scope of the metalanguages here are very different from the above logic of propositions. As Stroll (1998) shows, the formulation of differences between direct and indirect representation of external and fictive worlds are extremely complex. Despite this, I wish to argue that the gap between logic and other critical languages can be bridged, though not closed. A property of this bridge will be live metaphor – used to transcend the autonomous limits of each language whose boundaries both craft for the felicity of internal translation yet which thus mask the prospects for external translation between subjects. The enormous projects involved in such a fragmentary sketch, render the current remarks largely impressionistic and individual policies outlining future working spaces.

We can locate a starting-point with one of the versions of Wittgenstein's pivotal notes: 'The epistemological questions concerning the nature of judgement and belief cannot be solved without a correct apprehension of the form of the proposition'.[27] Since we do not have a perfect grasp of what it is to be a logical generalisation over disparate systems, we do not know, in the relevant sense, what it is to be the sense of 'proposition' as a generalised property. I believe that 'proposition' here can be proved to stand for any communicative expression conveying a thought, given a suitable semantics. To this we should adopt as a premise Burnyeat's (1994) research, which identifies the logical identity Aristotle conceived for rhetoric in relation to the explanation of the enthymeme. That is to say, the enthymeme is not a dead metaphor, but a piece of logic terminology which pinpoints deduction of a certain kind, and which has a refined development in modern logic. Gibson (2000c) proposes a conception of the enthymeme derived from philosophical logic to be applied to some religious creative languages. An enthymeme may not only be a missing premise in a piece of object-language deductive inference; it can also be, for example, a premise which needs supplying in the specification of the type of logic one is using. In this sense, enthymeme here indicates the basis for and role of relevance in relation to content, along the lines of Smiley (1998b, 1995) though it will be clear from the current book that this is deployed outside of Smiley's priorities.

Nevertheless, I propose that part of the solution to the collection of problems being addressed in the present context rests on the significance of one's maintaining that content is irrelevant if, and only if, it does not belong to any concise subproof of such content (in the style of Shoesmith and Smiley 1980: 181). This concept of a subproof preserves the features of proof for finite sequences in which abstract irrelevance and redundancy are distinct.[28] Anderson's and Belnap's relevance logic is not right since it presupposes that only if a propositional variable is shared by 'A' and 'B' is 'A → B' valid,[29] especially in view of the incompleteness of relevance proof and semantics for first-order logic. An important feature of their work was conjectured by Lewy:[30] their relation of logical implication forbids suppression of premises and principles; there is no true entailment respecting the law of the disjunctive syllogism. If this is applied to the metalanguage relations of logic to enthymemes, it blocks enthymeme omissions.

In this sense a concern with relevance does not have truth since a prior criterion does not permit enthymemes. So, if one slackens logic for relevance in the Anderson–Belnap mould, it backfires. That is to say, their approach prevents one from applying logical truth to a large class of discourse outside of the propositional calculus. Relative to my concerns stated in the present context, this enables one to insist on truth as a precondition of developing a concept of consequence which treats necessity, formality and relevance. Consequently, a concern with truth is not a doctrinal requirement, but an internal property and precondition of a universalised explanation of inference in language. If the identity and role of such inference is clarified, then it will already have satisfied criteria for being a true concept of relevance conditions. So to isolate relevance as a competitor to Aristotle's own approach to inference splits what is fused in usage.

Can cosmology and art become a singularity?

There are enormous differences between artistic and cosmological subjects; but it is worth proposing constructions to measure the gap subsequent to suggesting scenarios which compose reconfigurations of the borders between each. An upshot of such study will expose overlaps between science and arts. It maybe that, instead of conceiving 'distance' as a metaphor for the gap between cosmology and artistic creativity (or its critical theory), the notion of internal 'relations' shared between two separated subjects is helpful. For example, the Nobel chemist Hoffmann's (1990) research analyses crystal structure's refractions. He concludes that the perception of aesthetic properties within the complex crystallographic state is a physical and mathematical function of their identity. Hoffmann claims that his applied scientific strategy cannot proceed without aesthetic considerations being internal to that analysis and its use of decision theory. This amounts to a form of enthymeme: a conceptual presupposition of a relative basis for generating well-formed implications in crystallographic theory.

In a quite distinct context engagements with entities and functions in spatial relations have been apprehended by Wittgenstein. He later criticised elements of his *Tractatus*'s position of 'proposition' in contrast with his

Investigations. Yet Carruthers (1989) argues that the *Tractatus* contains a set of correct semantic doctrines, including both referential and possible world semantics, which will support my own approaches here to some degree. Wittgenstein (cf. Anscombe 1959: 76–8) transformed a feature of the *Tractatus*, which is heavy with pictorial *and* formal metaphor, into his later work and characterised it thus: 'A description is a representation of a distribution in a space' (Wittgenstein 1997: 187). Mallarmé's *Un coup de dés* is a creative literary work which actually is a description that is a distribution in space. Could we construct some relations with these literary concepts and cosmology? A facet of the possible conjunction of these scientific and artistic domains partly devolves on the functional roles of imagination, in both subjects. Although the identities of such imaginative activity in both scholarly enterprises are distinct, live metaphor parallels between the two can yield instructive points. The uses of spacetime and topologies have complex deep relations whose potential is not yet fully understood. But some unexpected progress can be made. For example, despite severe restrictions on us due to incompleteness and undecidability, Gregory Chaitin (1997) has succeeded in making the stunning connection and parallel between mathematics and statistical mechanics, while linking Gödel's incompleteness theorems to quantum mechanics. With such developments we can have a clearer idea that mathematics parallels aspects of the physical world, and this state of affairs itself mirrors some relations between logic and the actual world. It is interesting in this perspective that the mathematician Hans-Christian Reichel (1997: 11) should conclude his analysis of the influence of mathematics on the philosophy of mathematics with:

> What is the meaning of mathematical propositions? – here we should hold to Wittgenstein's dictum: 'philosophy describes which propositions have a meaning'. With respects to applications, we may ask: what do mathematical sentences say; do mathematical models have any epistemic value? (What we learn from mathematics is just as unanswerable as 'What do we learn from Tolstoy's *War and Peace*.)

This complements and contrasts interestingly with an issue in theism: although we may be unclear and dispute about the specific theoretical sense or status of claims about God and revelation, we should not convert this undecided or undecidable propositional status into an ontological certainty about the vacuity of attempting to frame propositions about divine transcendent phenomena. I wish to draw on Reichel's analogy between the meaning of mathematical propositions and the contents of literary narrative. Taking this sort of view in a different direction, the Nobel physicist John Bell (1987: 194) said of quantum mechanics in physics 'To what extent are these possible worlds fictions? They are like literary fiction in that they are free inventions of the human mind'. Speculation no doubt has its limit, though for someone like Bell to proffer this parallel is worthy of reflection.

We may find the tension between Hawking on baby universes (1993), and the alternative of the probability of an everlasting inflation (Hawking and Turok 1998), puzzling in its contrary directions and see it as a borderland to metaphysics. But it is worth considering how such scenarios can illuminate an empirical basis for, and be philosophically paraphrased by, for example, the work of David Lewis (1986) on the plurality of worlds, or Chihara's (1998) competing anti-realist thesis. Lewis offers us a model of a transworld order modelled on indexicals which could be a backdrop for both cosmology and Wittgenstein's idea of propositions projected in space. My policy proposal is that certain aesthetic phenomena have a place in such a conception alongside science and language. Wittgenstein proposed in the *Tractatus* that 'If there is any sense of the world, then it is beyond the world'. The present book maintains that the interfaces of the foregoing subjects can result in a unified live metaphor conceptions and interrelations of language in those subjects which lay the ground for philosophy of sense that enables us to describe transcendent phenomena beyond the world. Sainsbury (1998) argues that there is a logical reducibility principle for non-indexical expressions to be transformed into indexical language. So there is no insurmountable problem for our extending such talk to the concept of God's indexically using language, and the alleged problems of a limit on a timeless God should consequently be dismissed.

In this state of affairs, the languages of transcendence and the languages of humanity can be represented as forms in a logical space with discontinuous yet connectable topologies. The two languages are separated by a partition, reflecting different ways of relating to ontology. Even so, the two languages have matrices which can be appropriately related by the mapping of the formulae of one onto the other where language about God is transitive with regard to human language in the sense of [1] to [6] above. That is to say, we are dependent on God's semantics for information about his domain, although it is expressible on our languages. We now need to explore the possible relations between these features and the nature of distribution in astronomical space and its cosmological language.

Part II
All in God's space–time

3 Extending scientific languages

Being scientific?

Is science autonomous?

As Worton (1986) seeks to demonstrate for literary narratives, intertextuality denies the fixity, or autonomy of a text, not least because its authors are members of a culturally and causally connected, intermeshed readership. But this does not entail that causal influence is universal nor is it destructive of sense in a narrative. The foregoing suggested – if I may express a general trend of its thesis in another way – that scientific discourses have intertextual relations to the arts.

An oddly untypical, albeit higher level, subset of such intertextuality concerns the possible relations between universalised astrophysical cosmology and the exotic arts' domains in which universalised conceptions are articulated. Within this sphere is the recondite topic of intertextual relations between transcendent discourse in non-veridical physical scientific conjecture and its relation to claims of God as a source for infinity and creativity. This attracts the intertextual question: can scientific languages be extended, and in this way be applied to questions of divine transcendence? Apart from this question resting in some way on the presupposition that God exists – a thesis which is considered below – the question is problematic in many respects, as Clayton (1989) argues, though the current argument will dispute his conclusion. Many of the terms used in the chapters below have a narrowly technical meaning in physics. But we should make explicit that to which, in principle, scientists say they aspire, as opposed to what happens in experimental practice and the veridical explanations derivable from them. If, in practice, a less than the ideal theoretical realisation of what it is to be a science is entrenched in experiment, it is not appropriate to concede that the theoretical model of science as the objective discipline be the criterion of permissible extension of scientific language. Such a partial realisation of scientific idealism could be accounted for in a number of ways, which will not detain us here. Despite such problems, sciences are substantially distinct from the arts, not least because of their (often internally quite disparate) quantitative techniques of measurement in experiments.

Yet in some exotic spheres of terrestrial science, and more particularly in deep areas of cosmology, the concept of 'quantitative measurement' deforms into formal approximations whose status might be classed as a live-metaphorisation of actual quantification. Both science and some arts, ideally including religion, employ inference to achieve the best generalisation with a purpose to explain propositions, and both combine objectivism with concessions to fallibilism. No doubt this sort of use, if correctly assessed, is still very different from live-metaphor in the arts. But, still, there is, I suggest, sufficient grounds for judging that a relation satisfying a criterion of shared identification (rather than identity) could apply, rather than a concept of external distance, shared between some conceptual zones in cosmology and some of the arts.

Is physical theory a defined system?

Some would argue that the above opening questions are of doubtful merit because terminology in physics cannot be used in any permissible way outside the narrow mathematical context in which physics defines theories. Related to this objection is the problem of deciding whether or not such terms can admit of use in a new context which was not part of their intended original scope. On one interpretation of this set of difficulties, one may maintain that:

(P_1) Physical theory is solely a system of mathematically defined material states or objects and relations with rules to operate upon them, from which results can be derived that can then be tested by experiment and observation for their correspondence to the strict domain of the material world thus specified.

This goes against the view held, for example, by the cosmologist Dallaporta (1993), mentioned earlier. Connected with these difficulties is the view that theoretical justification is pragmatic, and hence a physical theory supported by experiment is said to have no significance other than the predictive power of the experiment: here physics is a service industry for the practical world. Consequently, if this were the case, experimentally supported theory carries no implications in spheres, subjects or contexts outside its pragmatic link between theory and experimental explanation.

Frequently, scientists seem to maintain the type of position sketched in (P_1)[1] perhaps in some cases only as a mood or unformulated attitude towards esoteric spheres to which they do not have time to attend in their preoccupation with the practice of experimental science. Yet there are other scientists who take up alternative positions which encourage varying sorts of links between science and theological topics. And there are unexpected admixtures: Polkinghorne (1994) is sympathetic as a scientist to a fairly conservative theology, having later trained as a theologian who has developed a sort of confessional theology. His sort of position manifests, in some perspectives, disapproval of the type of Linde (1990) and Rees's (1997, 1999) multiverse infinite ensemble of universes, since he considers it to be empirically ungrounded speculation. Depending on one's interpretation of the empirically possible range to be derived from the premises supposedly contained in (P_1), one might agree to or demur from a claim that deems Rees's multiverse scenario presentation as a probable inductive consequence of a type of extension of (P_1). So science has internal splits on the identity of relevant prospects that could contribute to the extension of what would count as empirical scientific language in relation to the material quantification of spacetime generalisation. Obviously the absence of agreement among scientists and a philosophy's possible capacity to avoid making mistakes in argument are not sufficient grounds to infer scientific knowledge. Nevertheless, possibly our critical awareness of scientists' own acknowledgement of epistemic fallibilism should provoke us to reflect on whether or not models of scientific empiricism influence too much our picture of what it is to be the present or future scientific range of empirical and mathematical possibilities.

Rorty's (1998: 1–2) claim for pragmatists, that 'if something makes no difference to practice, it should make no difference to philosophy' is false-footed by such considerations. Rorty's (ibid.: 299) claim that, 'contemporary intuitions are to decide the matter, "realism" and representationalism will always win', is certainly not justified by much of the research by cosmological scientists. They often construct astrophysically grounded statements which do not have justification using local physics, in attempts to discover what often are counter-intuitively propositions. In much cosmology, pragmatism implodes. What we are left with is scientific aesthetic and currently un-warranted assertability that contemporary practice relative to present observations do not comply with standard physics audiences, yet a resolution is presupposed for future audiences (*contra* Rorty (ibid.: 282–83)). This is a sort of metaphysical activity, one which presupposes there is a currently non-pragmatic practice in science which is not supported by a notion of correspondence in terms of realism and representation, that has and will yield new predictively tested correspondences between theory and practice. This reverses over and pulps Rorty's mythology of oppositions between pragmatism, justification and truth. In the positive results of cosmological enquiry we sometimes have what is tantamount to the negation of Rorty's (ibid.: 300) assertion of the value of pragmatists, 'pointing to the futility of metaphysical activity, as they pointed to the seeming futility of religious activity'.

Is science complete without aesthetics?

Doubtless, some theologians and philosophers have utilised science with futility. Further, scientists sometimes foreclose discussion on the relevance of some arts to science. But it remains true that there is a genuine issue about the status of scientific language and its possible relations to non-experimental science, as well as to qualitative and non-empirical logical value-judgement criteria whose formulations will or can evoke strong disagreement or uncertainty both within the ranks of scientists, and among philosophers and theologians. A slightly awkwardly framed question illustrates this: since beauty is in a certain sense an empirical property of the physical world (albeit whose aesthetic interpretation – as with quantum physics – evokes disagreement), why do not the physical equations pertaining to the relevant physical state contain aesthetic variables and functions? I have argued that the arts and sciences have intertextual relations, in the specific sense that one is internal, in relevant domains, to the other.

We do not have to have Aquinas's theory of aesthetics to conclude with Eco (1988: 22) about the pervasive relevance of aesthetic functions, even though we may wish to trim 'a transcendental' back to 'transcendent': 'If beauty is to be considered a transcendental, it acquires metaphysical worth, an unchanging objectivity, and an extension which is universal.' Aquinas integrated his aesthetical concepts of form, proportionality and *claritas* into an untenable scheme which collapsed by the time the Italian Renaissance emerged. But we can salvage ideas of proportionality and *claritas* (the latter as the conjunction of the empirical aesthetic feature with the product of the perceiver's recognitional capacity) to structure aesthetic properties of the universe.[2] As suggested earlier, we now have some scientific grounds for concluding that some aesthetic functions have an intertextual relation to empirical properties. Hoffmann (1990), in his researches on molecular aesthetics internal to the geometry and relativity of molecules, suggests that the solutions to fresh puzzles include an aesthetic premise as a function of the empirical decision procedures.

Magnetic poles and monopoles

Can magnetic poles be something else?

What, though, is the internal unity, the 'consistency', which reputedly holds together the science which contrasts with the arts? My strategy is to suggest: (a) that within applied science and theory themselves are metaphoric shifts (as well as other comparable extensions in uses of theoretical and empirical terms), extensions in theory, terms and experiments; (b) that we can employ (a) to infer that its detection of metaphor in some science is metaphor which has a paraphrasing similarity to relevant select use of metaphor in some arts. The content for this inference is the relevant matching between features of metaphoric extension within the relevant scientific discipline's own exploitation of its formal and empirical language to map experimental conjecture and result. For this purpose, as noted earlier, we should recognise that a difference between dead and live-metaphors is that with dead ones the subject shifts, whilst with the live-metaphor in some varying sense the subject (or a subset of it) is preserved or reproduced in the new subject. I emphasise that this programme includes aligning some properties of mathematical and logical language as specialised species of metaphorisation (in the simplest sense, a token value is a live-metaphor of its type or function). Some of these shifts are seminal for generating new theoretical insights.

Consider the bipolar nature of magnetism, and its notion of a magnetic pole. Is a criterion of identity of being a pole for the criterion to presuppose or a suppressed premise, or enthymeme, that there have to be two magnetic poles? Dirac proposed that a monopole could exist: one pole is envisaged as a semi-infinitely long infinitesimally thin solenoid, with no other matching opposite pole. This violates a feature of the, admittedly standardised, notion of scientific language mooted in objections above. We immediately come upon the possibility of equivocation in the science of magnetism here. Is knowledge an approximating concept? How does the relevant theory of bipolar magnetism impinge on monopoles? Monopoles are not experimentally *known* to exist, but theoretically they are sensible, unexpectedly tricky, extensions which originally recombine theories tested in other areas. If they do exist, they would extend and modify the experimental notion of a magnetic pole. The two sets of descriptions – for poles, and for monopoles – overlap; but the sets are partly discontinuous (see Figure 3.1). The theory for this overlaps in certain ways with dipole magnetism, and consequently it illustrates live-metaphor shifts. This could have a tautological relation with a genetic direction either way: monopole first, then metaphorized to two, or vice versa. Obviously, the priority may coincide with a temporal order, though it does not have to do.

This problem is only in its infancy, however. From the resources of local physics of magnetism cosmological occurrences of monopoles should be explained; presumably this involves a further stage in metaphorisation. Turner (1983), as well as Barrow and Tippler (1986), argue that some monopoles were left over from the big bang, and they now occupy the centre of planets and stars, with their large mass and response to gravity pulling them through baryonic material. In this way, the exotic initial state of creation subsumes present-day physical states. If the presupposition that there is a function for continuous creation in the contemporary universe(s), then this could serve as a basis to exemplify a live-metaphor-like reification of origin for exotic physical states in the early universe which have ontological correlates in the present universe. At the juncture where the monopole exhibits experimentally unproved elements, this would be a fecund source for counter-intuitive examples, on the assumption that monopole theory is correct, since the purported empirically comparable environments embodies

102 All in God's space–time?

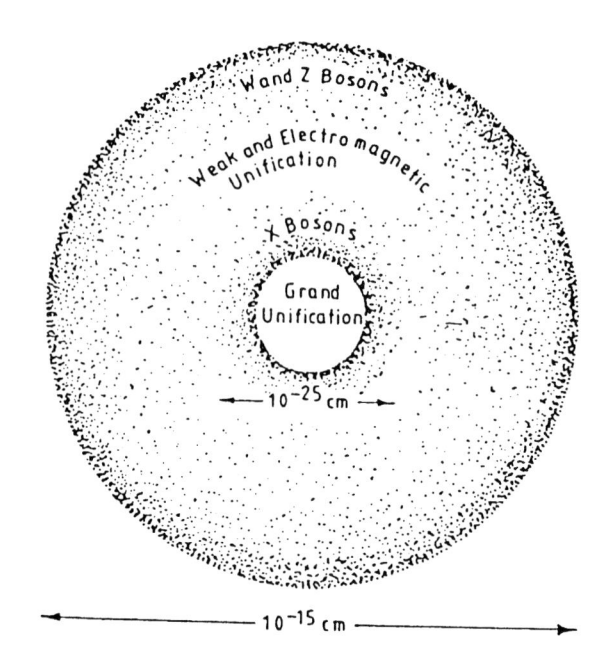

Figure 3.1 A universal monopole

Source: Barrow and Silk (1983)

Note: This is an idealised model of a monopole in grand unified gauge scenarios

physics which are both continuous with, yet partially a departure from, dipole magnetic theory.[3] If monopoles are definitely proved to exist, then this would not falsify the point of the foregoing remark: scientific language has been extended by reference to experimental data which were not included in the scope of the traditional magnetic pole theory.

Is a single pole a metaphor?

Consequently, some metaphoric shift occurs between these magnetic conceptual discontinuities, for which there is a corresponding ontology, if the empirical theory correctly explains the actual physical states. In the magnetic dipoles and monopole theories, the relation between the two concepts is not that of a dead metaphor; nor should we simply say that a single pole *is* a live-metaphor, but that its theoretical representation displays live-metaphor.

The magnetic pole in traditional magnetism is a two-pole concept; the monopole approach does not bar the viability of extending the dipole to construct or envisage a single-pole magnetic field, with the monopole requiring a revision in the idea of what a magnetic field is, and what causes it. In short, this could be viewed as a highly live-metaphoric extension of the concept and ontology of magnetic poles, unsupported by direct experiment. One needs to be wary of conflating ontology with discourse here. Kant's critical special metaphysics could be employed to guard against this,[4] and facilitate relations, especially with its 'interaction' approach. Monopoles are so problematic an extension that some engineering physicists still question the current formulations of monopole theories, without their wanting to rule out their possibly existing.

Monopoles in cosmology

Is a metaphorised live-metaphor empirical?

Preskill (1983) is one of those astrophysicists who has extended the concept of a monopole to the astrophysics of the early universe, to cosmology. He shows that the monopole theory has fundamental importance for understanding particle physics. One reason for this was Guth's (1981, 1997) invention of the inflationary scenario for the universe, in which the universe accelerates its expansion for a period after the big bang, expanding in a flat disc-like shape; in this model the symmetry-breaking generated monopoles are of central importance as ancient building blocks of matter. Rees summarises some aspects of this research as follows:

> There is still no consensus on the link between any specific unified theory and the mechanics of inflation ... It may seem counter-intuitive that an entire universe at least ten billion years across (and probably spreading far beyond our present horizon) can have emerged from an infinitesimal speck. What makes this possible is that, however much inflation occurs, the total net energy is zero. It is as though the universe were making for itself a 'gravitational pit' so deep that everything in it has a negative gravitational energy exactly equal to its rest-mass energy (mc^2). This realisation makes it easier to swallow the concept that our entire universe emerged almost *ex nihilo*.
>
> (Rees 1997: 181)

A backcloth for this sense of the counter-intuitive is the gap between scales in the laboratory and cosmology. Cosmology is a science whose identity is partially a function of exotic extensions from local sciences. A few experimental laboratory physicists, however, carp that the scales of difference between the order of precision in their experiments sharply contrast with weaker control in astronomy and cosmology. There is much to support the cosmologist's possible response to this modish muttering: so when did you try an experiment as big as the universe? The pragmatic scientists who raise this control-freak sort of objection have some common ground with, though dissimilar attitude to, those scientists mooted at the opening of this chapter: scientific language is for a fixed range in a determinate experiment. Stress this sufficiently and you get nothing new from an experiment. We should all become a little edgy with this 'certainty' about security in experimental autonomy and strictly controlled territory. Obviously, the converse is not true: 'anything goes' is false.

One discontinuity between local laboratory physics and astrophysics, is that the universe is not a repeatable experiment on which the scientist can operate; observationally, it is a unique object. This contrasts with a basic aspect of experimental science's techniques of experimental prediction and repetition of tests with which to ensure support for theories. For some restricted classes of objects (eclipses, luminosity of stars, etc.) there are exceptions or ways around the contrasts; but for large scale cosmological enquiry, the contrast becomes a correspondingly greater problem. Nevertheless the differences of scale in laboratory magnetism and in cosmological monopole theory appear to have successful live-metaphoric extensions which show that common processes underpin the association between local dipole and cosmological monopole.

How can *a pole be a particle?*

Dirac's aim was to use the concept of a monopole to unify features of electricity and magnetism, while more recent scenarios place monopoles in the early universe. They are thought to have been large particles generated in the first 10^{-36} seconds of the universe's expansion in which they are often now considered to function in accordance with a form of knot theory. This is itself an extension of the synthesis of knot theory as formulated, for example, by Atiyah (1990). This extends the live metaphoric extension from two magnetic poles temporarily backwards to a monopole. Ontologically, the shifted dipole sense collapses back into a singular entity, the monopole. This sides with Soskice's view (1985: 19–20) that metaphor cannot be defined as 'x is a y'. Yet the relative identity engagement with ontology in the monopole's shifting and sharing identity opposes her almost exclusive stress on the linguistic 'nature' – and not physicalist – domain of metaphor, although linguistic it often and typically is, and though of course she did not include cosmology within the scope of her thesis.

A scientific motivation behind an extension of the idea of a monopole in cosmology is to treat the early universe as a laboratory experiment. The reason for this is that the requisite experiment, by which one could 'test' the theory, cannot be constructed in any extant electron accelerators or conceivable future experimental science on Earth, and experimental physicists might be able to learn about local physics by results derived from theorising about the universe's past.

Accordingly, monopoles in cosmology embody a number of the following live-metaphor shifts. First, the notion of a monopole is now set in an environment for which it was not originally conceived and of which it is partly exclusive in scope. Second, cosmologists ('t Hooft (1974) and Polyakov

(1974)) demonstrated that monopoles exist in all Grand Unified Field theories as a consequence of the quantisation of the field electric charge. Clearly, this does not have to be true of magnetic poles and it was not inherent in Dirac's conception of a monopole.

Third, a cosmological monopole is a massive particle with an internal structure which is strange by comparison with other particles such as quarks. Fourth, it exists when standard laws of magnetism have broken down. Fifth, in the centre of the monopole there is a grand unification of electromagnetic energies which is contrary to any concept in local physics, though a monopole particle may lie at the centre of stars and possibly planets, as Turner (1983) argues.

It is possible to conceive of a thesis, which could be regarded as highly unstable in the present states of monopole theory. The extensive internal structure of the monopole particle might be reinterpreted as two counter-intuitive magnetic dipoles. Here the central core of the particle of about 10^{-25} *cms* would be one pole, and some bosons outside this 'grand unified centre' acting as the other pole, though of course this extension would itself be a substantial departure from the standard idea of magnetic dipoles.

These are types of live-metaphoric shifts which occur within science itself. So it is not simply a case of imposing on science, from outside, linguistic shifts of metaphor which only have parallels outside science in natural languages. We are not playing semantics; we have warrant from within science's functional framework for live-metaphor.

Are beginnings beyond measurement?

An upshot of the development of monopole theory and a range of its possible or probable expected advances, is the appearance of attempts to incorporate monopole theory not only into accounts of the causal structure conjectured for the beginning of the universe(s), but also to the purported future fate of the universe(s).[5] Thus theorisation by live-metaphor in science carries monopole theory far beyond the narrowly defined and tested context of magnetic poles. This type of live-metaphoric extension of the sense, scope and objects of physical theory, in principle, supports extensions of scientific language outside its intended and originally specified scope.

The notion of an experiment at a spacetime point testing a state of affairs at that time furnishes a criterion too strong for an activity to be science, since this would rule out all extrapolations outside of that spacetime-point. This would bar evolution and cosmology as candidates for science in view of their uses of retrojective prediction and attempts to imply physical conditions remote from experiment and one not existing at the time of experiment. If one were to add the property of originality and of origination of a state of affairs as a feature of science to such a criterion, science defined as limited to a contemporary experiment would be seriously incapable of explaining substantial portions of some of its other identities. So much is obvious; but these considerations show that science is a much looser and more conjectural multifarious affair than the account presupposed by some scientists who castigate the apparent contrasting senses of weakened precision in the arts. Rather, the complex indirect routes scientists assume when they articulate statements which are truth-makers using facts and states of affairs when adopting antecedents premises and the partial experimental support are fraught with departure from the foregoing strong formulation of science.[6] My point is simply this: these leaps of faith and complex diachronic gaps between contemporary scientific activity and its remote source, whether in biology or astrophysics, is reminiscent of complex value-judgement in the arts. The absence of 'scientific' experimental testing in the arts is sometimes taken by scientists to be a criterion of demarcation between sciences and arts; yet this test falls apart when applied to some spheres of science.

In the contrast between local physics and cosmology, the known physical content of an experiment usually serves as a major resource for deriving the conceptual content of the new hypotheses, with mathematics formalising these relations. In cosmology, research progress is frequently the other way around: the abstract inventiveness of mathematics is often deployed to produce new physical concepts. These mathematical concepts are used to construct or conjecture the appropriate physical content which would have to have existed for the mathematical scenarios to be true. Obviously, there is an ebb and flow of different combinations of the local physics and cosmological mathematical emphases in astrophysics – the physics of the universe; yet overall, the above contrast holds. When there is a predominance of mathematical invention to produce physical models of physical processes for the universe, live-metaphoric extension will be fruitfully rampant.

The foregoing has been concerned to show that live-metaphoric shifts occur within cosmology, which facilitates a parallel – a semantic spatial domain – from within science by which to situate arts' live-metaphors. We have seen that mathematical and physical explanations of models employ live-metaphorical terms, relations and contexts. To show that this is not in principle entirely distinct in metaphoricity from theology and metaphysics, it is worth noting Popper's (1972) criterion of falsifiability and its relation to observational and mathematical cosmology. Dallaporta (1993: 328) introduces, as a cosmologist, the term 'physico-metaphysics' for the sort of data typified by cosmological monopoles, which foil Popper's test. By Popper's criterion, they are simply not physics. Almost all early cosmology complies with this failure: for example, there is no test for, a time of 10^{-43} secs; nor for temperatures of 10^{32} K; neither for densities of 10^{93} *gr/cm³*. These are also paramorphic models that differ in their identities, yet which fit these data. Given Brummer's (1992) point that the qualitative infinity of God does not prevent qualitative metaphorical comparison and contrast with finite physical qualities, it should be evident from the above sketch that comparison of, and calculable relations between, cosmology and philosophy and the arts are achievable, using their metaphoric relations, interactions and functions, despite vast differences between the various subjects.

Scientific dimensions of live-metaphor

Is history of metaphor relevant to science?

There are many sorts of live-metaphors, and there are many different types of dimensions. These two remarks do not equivocate over the section heading. Just as there are strengths of logical force in sense ranging from 'possible' to 'necessarily', in a similar way there is a variety of classes of live-metaphor.

Consider the photograph as an example of a live-metaphor: we might also take a photograph of the photograph, or produce a rough sketch which is less clear or precise than the initial picture. Conversely, we may beef up our live-metaphors: we may produce a hologram derived from the photograph; and in using this technique we can replay the sequence for film and add dimensions to the live-metaphor. In general relativity there is a live-metaphor trade-off between space and time: within certain specific functions, these two dimensions are treated as having live-metaphor similarities. This starts with the premise that they can both be identified as dimensions. Some people may want to use 'analogy' here. The important aspect presupposed in the use of 'live-metaphor' here, though, is that there is, in principle, a semantic overlap which is quantifiable and not a dead metaphor. In a quite different context of use, Polkinghorne (1986) remarked that a hologram could usefully serve a parabolic purpose. The present live-metaphor explanation is rather narrower: a hologram, and the free-standing three-dimensional projections in virtual reality research yield formalisms of explanatory interest for scientific representation.

Since the live-metaphor satisfies criteria of identity realised in the ontological state of affairs which it represents, I propose that the live-metaphor is a metaphorisation of its *referent* (of course this will also involve issues which require discrimination between use and mention, where a piece of language is a referent). Just as with Aristotle's *Poetics*, a metaphor is a shift between terms, so, I suggest, live-metaphor can exhibit this movement, and also a relation between the ontological state the live-metaphor depicts. The criteria of identity, or relative identity term of 'a = b' respecting a set of properties F, manifested in the relation between a live-metaphor and its referent, correspond to each other. But since it is relative identity, it is not absolute and is revisable. The success of scientific language is centred on its capacity to reproduce the (relevant) feature of its external world. Namely it metaphorises ontology. For example, the geometries of space use live-metaphors, metaphorical complexes or networks *of* space and 'points' in space in some ways as a photograph stands for its referent. A curve in spacetime is a geometrical object,[7] and in the foregoing sense it is a live-metaphor, and this complex metaphor is spatially variable depending upon the functional context.

Derrida (1982: 209–71) suggests that in metaphor there is a sense of infinite reflection and its own ruin in the splitting between the signifier and what is signified. He argues that the self-destruction of metaphor (as a vehicle for the 'generalisation of truth') is within its own identity: an homonymy which simulates identity yet accordingly internalises paradox in metaphor. I have been reasoning that this applies, if at all, when dead metaphor is used in concepts, and not live-metaphor representation, though clearly there will be false uses of live-metaphor. But an objection to Derrida emerges from live-metaphor: if scientific languages use quantifiable, measurable metaphor, this opposes the idea that we cannot, in the relevant senses, get out of language. For example, the use of the names 'Jacques Derrida' refers me to the man who satisfies a criterion of identity, and thereby I have succeeded in transcending language by its use to pick out an empirical existent beyond language. Likewise live-metaphor, correctly deployed in scientific and other languages, have measurable functions which isolate and correctly depict ontological states separate from language.

How are our dimensions?

The notion of dimensions of live-metaphors – of different classes of live-metaphor, is not incompatible with 'paradox' being *in* the ontological states, nor with there being ontological equivalents which can be depicted with causal accuracy, yet allow for a division between signifier and signified.

First, some preliminaries. The ordinary use of 'dimensions' could be characterised as a function governed by a variable which represents something that extends from a point (e.g. a line). Sometimes lost in the history of thought is the extension of 'dimension' to more than one dimension if, in fact, the plural usage of 'dimensions' was subsequent to the singular use of 'dimension'. Barrow and Tippler (1986) offer substantial evidence that the three-dimensional nature of the universe is precisely conducive to the existence of biological life which perceives three dimensionally. Yet how does this pertain to the emergence of thinking in plural dimensions? If this three-dimensional priority applies to the historical development of concepts about dimension, then perhaps three-dimensional awareness would proceed two- and one-dimensional awareness. (In artistic expression two-dimensional pictures were probably prior to three-dimensional art, leaving aside the self-conscious stylised two-dimensional representation of three dimensions in, for example, Middle Kingdom Egyptian art – though, even here, visualisation often satisfies criteria of identity *and* identification.)

As Derrida (1982: 241–42) suggests, Aristotle in the *Poetics* and the *Rhetoric* (III, 11, 1411b21) used the notion of 'liveliness' to characterise a metaphor that both marks an absence and so succeeds in producing a mimesis of the signified, as with a thing cast or 'drawn' in bronze. In a

Kantian framework, we can acknowledge the ambiguities that Derrida emphasises (as delineated by Hobson 1998). Yet this can be complemented by using a process of reduction-realisation to understand ontological states, not least because there is a relation of analogy and live-metaphor between understanding and reason, which also attempts to extirpate the infections of disanalogy (see Hobson ibid.: 227). As Buchdahl observes (1993: 334–37), Kant's application of his topology to the special metaphysics of divinity is similar in some ways to Wittgenstein's (1995) idea of a philosophical game: 'a game meant to bestow fresh significance on the enterprise of ontology and of the associated transcendental framework of the world'.[8] This game is partly composed of the use of live-metaphors representing relations between dimensions. Mellor's (1998: 26, 114–15) research on the causal definition of time and time order shows that Kant's 'the form of inner sense' is the dimension in which our own experiences can be ordered. In a particular sense, then, this inner dimension is a sort of complex live-metaphor of our structuring of dimensions in the external world.

We can regard the three dimensions in space as live-metaphors of a one-dimensional point (without assuming that this represents the historical emergence of geometry). However, I do not want to make much of this comparatively narrow shift of sense. Nevertheless, we should note that Kant raised a number of puzzles about the difficulty of identically reproducing counterparts in space which, employing the foregoing approach, we could interpret as evidence of live-metaphor.

Does the universe know its right hand from its left?

When there is an irreducible difference between counterparts such as a right hand and a left hand, there are also shared similarities. Alexander (1984) notices that if we apply this to rotation in the plane of the two-dimensions, then there is no perfect superimposition, although perfect superimposition can be reproduced in three dimensions. So, although it may superficially seem that three dimensions are merely identical multiplications of one, to two, and to three dimensions, yet conversely the true explanation involves recognising that the concepts of these three dimensions in use display differences between each sense of 'dimension'. These differences (such as the move from one to two and more dimensions) produce a change in kind. This change is evidence of live-metaphor; the switch from one dimension to another articulates a live-metaphor relation; there is an overlap of continuity in the sense of 'dimension', and also discontinuity. Wittgenstein's picture theory of language has rules of projection in space at its centre. The first rule is reference; the second, (a set of) rules for projection on to reality. Perhaps Wittgenstein was thinking of early modernist pictorialist poetics.[9] Wittgenstein parallels the picture with music (*Tractatus* 4.0141). The illusion possible in such a *tableau vivant* is similar to the variables and indeterminacies commented about in the above monopole discussion, rather than and incompatible clash of science and arts. The counter-intuitive relations in monopole cosmology, the puzzles about reproducing counterparts in space, are typical of the many counter-intuitive forms and strategies which serve as precedents to reappraise and transform a picture theory of language and reality. The renaissance of general relativity further stimulates this scenario for a new arts–science live-metaphor *ensemble* of reality depiction, as argued below.[10]

Space–time

How much space has the universe for dimensions?

Einstein added time as a fourth dimension to theories about the universe. Well beyond Einstein's relativity, however, there is superstring M-theory spacetime that yields rips or ruptures (see Polchinski 1998 and Greene 2000), with many other dimensions curled up in clusters deep in the universe's microscopic structure. The time dimension is related to space by use of relativity in which space and time are merged as co-extensive aspects of the universe, resulting in spacetime. The sense of a point in spacetime is an event or state of affairs. Here Einstein's use of time as a dimension both revolutionised the scientific perception of time as well as giving the notion of 'dimension' an original live-metaphoric extension and twist. 'Live', here, has the implication of calculable sense, as with literary metaphors where an aspect of the sense is quantifiable ('stone lion', etc.).

The notion of spacetime is likewise a live-metaphoric extension of relations derived from the other dimensions. This is illustrated by the way in which a cosmologist will take a two-dimensional slice of the four-dimensional world which includes spacetime. Davies (1981) has likened this to taking two-dimensional snapshots of a slice of the world at a given instant. If snapshots are taken in a time sequence through spacetime, then the snapshots would become a movie film. The success of such analogies depends on the live-metaphor relations between these dimensions and the interconnection geometries which are thereby employed to describe the universe.

Does relativity use metaphors?

Relativity makes central use of gravity, by which use gravity was transformed with Einstein's treating it in geometrical terms as a relation, rather than a force. The representation of some relations between gravity and geometry has parallels with the category of live metonymy metaphor. Certain sorts of metonymy metaphor can be classified as types of live-metaphor, though within the category of metonymy metaphor there are many varieties (noted generally by Lakoff and Johnson (1981)). The basic feature of the main metonymy metaphor group is that in which an aspect related to a subject is generalised to represent the subject itself: 'all hands on deck', where 'hands' is the metonymy metaphor for sailors; consider the elliptical: 'drink a bottle'.[11] Here a displacement occurs which condenses the wine to become a bottle because of the close proximity of the wine to the bottle. This is not unlike the contiguity of a line dimension related to the property or point(s) of space which it delineates. An explanatory detour is apt here to assess how identification of a point with its referent presupposes its relevant basis.

Is metonymy a logical enthymeme?

This question is concerned with certain, but not all, uses of metonymy. We might look again at the way Dummett (1981) advances criteria of identity using Frege's notion of name and reference. This matter could be paraphrased in other universes of discourse without discarding its main thesis. We might, perhaps unexpectedly, for example, suggest that the criteria of identity for a proper name are rather like suppressed logical enthymemes similar to Aristotle's *Rhetoric*. This is in the *Rhetoric*'s spirit of finding associations between a formal language of consequence and a logical function within natural language.

The role of mentality for metonymy is a type of enthymeme. For example we could translate in this way Barthes's contributions to metaphor where they identify the Freudian shifts of 'condensation' as 'metaphor' and 'displacement' as 'metonymy', situated in Lacan's portrayal of consciousness as a mirror of a textual unconscious. Moriarty (1991: 85–86) argues from this position that, 'Clearly, these two planes of the syntagmatic and paradigmatic can be discovered in non-linguistic sign-systems'. This clashes with Soskice's (1985) virtual exclusion of the extralinguistic from metaphor. Within this type of French culture theory we have a use of metonymy which bridges the linguistic and the ontological by a live-metaphor displacement. If this conjunction is partially measurable, then we have a guarded parallel with the quite separate formal world of the geometrical dimension. In this light, a geometrical line is a live-metaphor of metonymy for a bit of the universe with an enthymemic basis.

Such a perspective generally complements within a distinct framework Kant's fine insight that we are here concerned with the form of inner sense – with the additional rubric that our form of inner sense is employed for different subjects, and not solely within science, where there is metonymy which is quantifiable. This has a similarity to the role of the logical enthymeme in Aristotle's *Rhetoric* 1 and 2.26–7:[12] a live-metaphor has in principle a measurable function which presupposes a relative basis for a piece of semantics and its deduction. This itself has parallels with Smiley's (1998b) proposals on the notion of consequence relative to a basis, using natural logic, and also Epstein *et al*.'s (1995: 384–88) notion of an enthymeme as a premise for translating between logics in a fashion consistent with the natures of varying logics. I assume this type of basis as a policy, but it needs to be worked out more fully,[13] for the purpose of associating live-metaphors in some uses in natural languages and in formal scientific languages. To this I wish to add the idea that groups of live-metaphor shifts are catalysts for originality in the generation of theories and creativity.

General relativity is not only composed of 'dimensions' that are transformed live-metaphors of earlier formulations of dimension, it also deploys live-metaphors which are metonymy metaphors: gravity is equated with dimensions in geometry. (A thing is treated as a relation.) Just how tightly one can finally interpret this relation is a deep question (see Stewart 1990: 55–58). Obviously, gravity is not geometry. In the relevant geometry, lines are types standing for dimensional relations. Yet the nature of these relations is crucial to analysis of the alleged collapse of spacetime as projections track back to the purported beginning of the universe: does space itself collapse, or is this collapse one feature which does not exhaustively specify what space is? If it does not, then something may be left over after the deformation and implosion of spacetime. Here, the notion of what a scientific live-metaphor extends over when it is a dimension is of particular importance because the live metonymy metaphor, we have seen, can be a measurable function which can be used to assess the degree of overlap and discontinuity between it, its subject (i.e. referent) and the descriptions (i.e. extensions or predicates) of its 'literal' counterparts.

Is 'nothing' a metonymy metaphor?

Related to this is the point (also to be discussed later in the book) that what is left over from this spacetime collapse is not nothing, in the sense of 'creation out of nothing'. The quantum mechanical usage of 'nothing' is applied to a partial 'vacuum' which has a metric structure in which an energy fluctuation can occur and cause the big bang.[14] The adjacent notion of a 'vacuum' in empty space engaged with a black minihole, Rees (1997: 192) delightfully couches its state to be 'seething with activity'.

The existence of live-metaphors is an important phenomenon with which to grade differences between 'creation out of nothing' and the different sense of 'nothing' supposedly correctly applied prior to the big bang: just as we would resist attempts to collapse a person into being his photograph (although we can gauge his identity from it), so these two alleged 'nothings' can be related to the question of the identity of the state prior to, and the relevant logically related aspect of, the universe's origin. But these 'nothings' are not synonymous: I believe that they enjoy relations of live-metaphor, with discontinuities.

Barrow and Tippler (1986: 443–44) review the fact that Hawking's and Hartle's quantum gravity model for creation out of 'nothing' has no functional dependence on time. Hawking (1979) also brings in a Euclidean three-dimensional concept of space, yet he integrates it with four-dimensional geometries which (as Hawking terms it) are complexified.

Here, there is an involuted Euclidean live-metaphoric extension which utilises Einstein's concepts of dimensions; but then the dimensions are profitably re-extended in a quantum view of the early universe by Hawking's use of the complex live-metaphor of a refined, albeit revolutionised, Euclidean view. With this conception, Hawking enveloped the enterprise in groups of equations which amount to a method of simplification of spacetime to enable him to sketch a network for handling the deep structure of spacetime in relation to gravity (a path integral approach to quantum gravity). Such a simplifying group of equations could be depicted as complex live-metaphor of a more complex physical reality, in which a family of equations mirrors a related family group by a live-metaphor resemblance. In a certain respect, as the above *Prologue* argued, this type of use of simplification is contradicted by its presupposition: the premises which are internal properties of it, and its derivation, are complex, and so such simplicity opposes the claim that Ockham's razor is an antecedent property of generalised theory and the universe. Since Ockham's arguments contradictorily vary,[15] the razor is contradictory in any case. The underlying algebraic structures of superstring theory and their geometrical tautologies, nevertheless achieve some unification by mirroring domains of metaphoric extensions (cf. Ross (1989)) in the procedures aimed at unifying strong, electromagnetic, weak and the gravitational interactions.

Could we wrap up quantum gravity?

Quantum gravity is the theoretical unification of subatomic matter and gravity. Although quantum gravity has not been decisively proved to exist, its conjectured structure is that of a symmetry between all matter and energy where the spins of particles are identical. For this state of affairs to be realised, it is usually envisaged that the structure of spacetime itself would deform and perhaps collapse. Yet it is unclear whether or not this state of affairs confuses the theory with that to which it seems to refer: if we construe such a spacetime collapse to be a live-metaphor which is also a metonymy metaphor, we could only erroneously infer from the collapse of the spacetime geometry the annihilation of alternative transcendental modes of spacetime or their underlying metric or manifold. Another way of scheduling this mistake is to present the relevant contents of ontology as a logical enthymeme distinct from merely one (our current spacetime physics) instantiation of a larger ontological, possibly virtually infinite, ensemble. This would concur with Rees's (1997) approach to the scope of the multiverse.

Such a problem (as that which Hawking tackles) is analogous with Einstein's treating of space as a thing. Is such an equation itself a live metonymy metaphor? We shall return to this sort of problem later. The relativistic application of 'dimension' to space itself is a revolutionary shift of perspective, both for space and for what a dimension is. Although there are spheres in which general relativity has some tested observational support, much of it is outside the domain of experiment, and even observation, on the narrow pragmatic view of science sketched at the opening of this chapter; but it is still regarded as a piece of science. Feynman (1985: 151) also emphasised that it is impossible at the present states of conjecture to make any experiment which is sufficiently delicate to measure any effect which requires the precision of a quantum theory of gravitation to explain it: there is no quantum gravity theory which includes all the exotic particles which have been discovered, whilst cosmologists do have to invent alien particles which have not been discovered. As Feynman concluded: 'So not only have we no experiments with which to check a quantum theory of gravitation, we also have no reasonable theory'; but, quite reasonably, cosmology is still called a science.

If a science is allowed such elastic variables in its definition and scope, then there is reason to suppose that it is proper to investigate allowing the possibility that divine cosmology may also be a 'counter-intuitive' extension of science, without satisfactory empirical criteria by which to test such transcendent hypotheses. It would be mischievous to impose some artificial definition of science with which to oppose research into divine cosmology, because (as Dallaporta (1993: 330) argues) this would also prohibit the admissibility of some astrophysics as a science and fail to recognise what ignorance in science is.

Counter-intuition

How surprised can a scientist be?

In this book the expression 'counter-intuitive' is employed to indicate a discovery which is so unexpected as to appear to be at odds which what we know in the immediate sphere of the discovery. If I understand this concept correctly,[16] it has many different, complex and surprising manifestations, as one might expect. Counter-intuition can be associated with a deepening of analysis and understanding, though on occasions it is a reflection of the ignorance under which thinkers labour – where what is known is an initial approximation, or comparatively primitive or superficial formulation, as opposed to a revolutionary advance, which extends beyond normal science. This situation may reflect at least three different sorts of counter-intuition. First, counter-intuition has an internal relation to what is normal science and what is newly discovered: the counter-intuitive element is merely unexpected relative to the approximation or crudity of extant hypotheses in normal science. Second, counter-intuition has a relation between theory and properties in the external world: the physical or other structure of the counter-intuitive thing is unexpected relative to the already determined and definitively formulated nature of other phenomena to which it is in lawlike relation. Third, the newly discovered property stands in contrariety or contradiction to previous treatments, yet these previous approaches were taken to be necessarily true or incapable of being dislodged. There appear to be mergers of these options and other types of cases, and such contrasts seem to occur in all subjects.

Is the universe's depth a virtual infinity?

Exotic physics readily furnishes us with cases of counter-intuitive states: for example, the idea that matter can be both finite and yet contain an infinite series of states. Hawking (1980) has suggested that there may be a virtually infinite number of levels of depth in the atom. Here levels of depth in theories are interpreted as levels of structure in physical stuff in the external world. To be sure, we should avoid confusing the nature of sense in language with assuming that its structure is a mirror of the external world. Structures in languages can sometimes be blind guides about the structure of subjects. The present theme attempts to steer between the extremes of association in form of meaning as though it were a map of the structure of the world. This is developed by using causality and observational tests, among other things, between language and the world to regulate some of the connections between language and the universe.

Does the mind relate to quantum gravity?

In certain contexts, belief, combined with ignorance in our cosmological language, relates to the possibility that true language in philosophical or transcendent cosmology manifests evidence of freedom in our use of mental states. Human indeterminacy in consciousness infects scientists' assessment of empirically quantifiable measurements in physics, and also our estimation of how to construct proofs for deep areas of mathematical logic to do with transfinite set theory. In different ways, this uneasily circumscribes, perhaps over-confident, talk about our knowing the universe. Stephen Hawking stated that:

> the human brain is subject to the Uncertainty Principle. Thus there is an element of the randomness associated with quantum mechanics, in human behaviour. But the energies involved in the human brain, are low. So the quantum mechanical uncertainty, is only a small effect. The real reason why we cannot predict human behaviour, is that it is just too difficult. We already know the basic physical laws … But it is just too hard to solve the equations, when there are more than a few particles involved. Even in the simpler Newtonian theory of gravity, one can solve the equations exactly only in the case of two particles. For three or more particles, one has to resort to approximations, and the difficulty increases rapidly with the number of particles. The human brain contains about ten to the 26th, or a hundred million billion, particles. This is far too many, for us ever to be able to solve the equations, and

predict how the brain would behave, given its initial state, and the nerve data coming into it ... So, although we know the fundamental equations that govern the brain, we are quite unable to use them to predict human behaviour ... One cannot base one's conduct on the idea that everything is determined, because one does not know what has been determined.

(Hawking 1991a: 5)

If we note the successive revolutions from Newton to Einstein to Hawking and others, we can apprehend not only an increasing depth in their conceptions of the physical world, we can also appreciate that with this depth there is often a multiplication in the degree of counter-intuitive structures within the deeper theories. Sometimes the deeper new counter-intuitive theory incorporates aspects of the older hypothesis within it, refining and pitching elements of the earlier view into a fresh unexpected framework.

Can we calculate the future from the past?

Not infrequently in local physics (for example, in the application of equations in solid state physics to polymer physics), the transfer of achievements and their epistemological investments from one subject to another produces more that the sum of each. Astrophysics is a large-scale version of this transfer, from terrestrial physics to the universe. Attending this transfer, of course, is an important change in the basis for adjudication about how to assess the new application: original experiment constructed by scientists is fundamental to physics; yet, strictly speaking, it is non-existent in the astrophysical objects examined. Here, observation displaces experiment. This shift from experiment to observation is productive. However, such a change in the basis for testing evidently fails to comply with the pragmatic definition of science aired at the opening of this chapter.

Parts of geology share parallels here with astrophysics, and they also contrast with normal experimental science. Geologists cannot construct a new experiment to make a new phenomenon, such as occurs in chemistry. So the central predication associated with this type of experiment to test a hypothesis does not happen in geology. Naturally geologists try and circumvent this limitation by predicting the discovery or anticipating the existence of, say, an order of strata in an uninvestigated slice of the Earth, and they attempt to simulate fossil production in laboratory research. Yet, as taphonomists admit (cf. Olson 1980), this procedure is far from perfect. The need for fossil simulation in laboratories is precisely because field investigation and the environments in which fossils are found do not yield ('experimental') results as strong as the secondary simulation approach. Clearly, an astronomer might predict that some new state of affairs will be observed; but this is not identical to the making of a new phenomenon by scientists applying a theoretical prediction to produce an experiment which yields the new phenomenon.

The chapters following will maintain that these considerations support a counter-intuitive realist assessment of these advances that produce fresh phenomena and new theories. I involve the use of shifts of theory and language which extends over the new discoveries in which live-metaphor is employed. In science language is stretched and extended to fresh domains. Cosmology suffers from, or enjoys, massive contrast with local physics. These, as we have seen and will see below, demonstrate that live-metaphor categories are employed in science. It was observed that these live-metaphor uses increase in quantity and quality as more of the counter-intuitive domains are represented. The set of these counter-intuitive elements we can term the counter-intuitive world.

Let us now consider how some aspects of counter-intuition apply to a further extension of the discussions of 'dimension' in the previous section. It was proposed earlier that live-metaphor applies to mathematics in relation to its use of 'dimension'; and it was also noted that cosmology, unlike normal science, often tends to proceed from pure mathematics to physical theory for its results.

Strings of dimensions

Are strings and dimensions metaphorically related?

It was remarked in the last but one section above that the use of 'dimension' in cosmology is already an unusual extension from standard employment of the term. The previous section explained that in cosmology mathematical theories are often used to stimulate the production of new theories about the abnormal physics which might have been connected with the birth of the universe. Just how far one can go in predicting the physical content and nature from pure mathematics is unclear. This difficulty is itself complicated by lack of understanding about what sorts of physics of the many possible theoretical options one should infer from the mathematical framework. Such a problem is heightened by our not knowing precisely what recombinations of constants and/or their values within the physical world are compatible with the identity of the universe's history.

The latter issue is illustrated by Peeble's (1986) discussion about what the universe's average density is. Peebles claimed that astrophysicists might be using the wrong physics to explain the universe, or that a wrong theory of gravity has been assumed in the (as yet unresolved) calculations about the universe's mass. The relevant observational tests cannot now be made on the universe to resolve these sorts of difficulties, so the status of mathematics and the physics produced by such mathematics (as solutions about the universe) is unknown. Nevertheless, tantalising links between esoteric areas in applied mathematics and cosmology have been made and tested regarding some fundamental issues.

This state of affairs has encouraged some cosmologists to look to pure mathematics for new breakthroughs in cosmology. For example, the pure mathematician Boukricha (1985) has shown how Fellers's one-dimensional mathematical theory – basically a conception about a single line – can be applied to quantum mechanics. This one-dimensional model is extended to apply to many dimensions. In achieving this synthesis, Boukricha links the Schrödinger equation of atomic structure to the big bang. He consequently demonstrates a similarity in function between some dimensions in the big bang and in pure mathematics. Here we have a series of live-metaphor extensions of the notion of dimensionality in pure mathematics extended and conjecturally condensed into an ontology. It is as if a form of rhetoric has been practised: the premise leads to a discovery of an enthymeme: the body of proof for a new, hitherto omitted, ontological scheme.

Before 1984 it was customary to envisage a subatomic particle as a point in space. But in the foregoing case, and as exemplified by Green and Schwarz (1984), the esoteric particle called a *superstring* came to be depicted as a line of about 10^{-35} cm long, interpreted as a new dimension (cf. Ross 1989). This has produced a revolution in cosmology whose import is not entirely clear. At such lengths and spacetime, general relativity is already an ontologically impossible physics (which has, as it were, collapsed as we track back in time to the primordial epoch when, or if, such particles were created or had their origins). We could construe this use of a 'superstring' as a live-metaphor sprung (rather than derived) from a mathematical field, a consequence of which is for the superstring metaphor to decompose part of its own mathematical historical context. But as Rees (1997: 173) observes, superstrings pose questions which mathematicians cannot answer. So there are substantial gaps between superstrings and their testbeds: explicit mathematical proof, and empirical justification. Such isolation squares oddly with the fecundity suggested for superstrings. Green (1985) argues that the superstring conception may contribute towards a unified theory about the material universe in which the vibration and rotation properties of superstrings seem to mirror related features in gravity. In such a scenario, superstrings are abstract live-metaphors functioning in ways which have parallels with discontinuities, gaps and contrasts in some musical creativity.

Has the universe strung us along?

Einstein's hope was to offer an overall theory of the material universe; yet he could not effectively link gravity with atomic physics. Green proposes that this link may be achieved if more dimensions are added to the mathematics of the physics we know – because this will produce a new physics which can generate the link for an overall theory of the material universe. Such a programme could be considered a systematic use of live-metaphor applied to standard physics. The dimensions used in standard physics are here not merely multiplied. Their significance is changed, partly by the excision of the standard physical application, and in a sense by the multiplication of dimensions with the hope of generating a new physics whose energy is dissimilar to standard physics.

When the mathematical description of superstrings is set in the needed 10-dimensional space, superstrings appear to overcome a number of problems which have hitherto prevented the combination of gravity theory with the strong and electro-weak forces of atomic structure. Superstrings have also been cast in (a bosonic string of) 26 dimensions, as well as in 496-dimensional space, to facilitate other ways around the problems. But we cannot be even probably certain that the increased dimensions and their relations are token instances of the type of dimensions of which Kant argued that they are the form of our inner sense. This is not to claim that they are not; yet we need to admit the precarious basis of such conjecture, obscured though it is by highly technical justification. Despite this situation, science of the future is sometimes derived from such theorisation. Perhaps someone wants to argue that the link between the four dimensions and the rest are ones in which the latter match hidden variables in the former. But as Mellor (1995: 54–59) argued in causal contexts, if hidden variables cannot be shown to satisfy explanatory need in contexts where standard laws operate, how can they be shown to recur in states of affairs which embody a discontinuity respecting these laws?

Here we have very counter-intuitive live-metaphor hypotheses that transform conceptions and ideas about 'dimension' and which transcend any observable basis relative to content in empirical science: the four dimensions of the relativistic universe are like exploded faces, enlarged and reassembled to produce alien images – superphysics. The concept of 'dimension' associated with Einstein has here accelerated away and been transformed by live-metaphor. Nevertheless, there is an overlap between the four-dimensional world and, say, the 496-dimensional world, where gravity links the edges of each. The attendant notions of 'continuity' and 'discontinuity' presupposed in such research are informally parallel with the overlap between a photograph and its subject. The two-dimensional photograph can act as a calculation for assessing the nature and reality of its three-dimensional subject, to aid identification. Likewise, in some respects, the relativistic and pure mathematical notions of 'dimension' overlap yet contrast with the superstring geometries. And, out of the resulting live-metaphoric dimensions, a new physics is condensed. This new physics results in the smooth unification of energies into one continuum entitled a 'super-symmetry'.

The superstring situation goes well beyond, and in opposition to, the pragmatist sketch of the nature of experimental science at the opening of this chapter. This is well attested by the physicist De Rujula:

> So far, none of these fashionable subjects has proved to have any convincing relationship with physical reality, and yet they have the irresistible power of addiction. Such a gregarious fascination for theories

based almost exclusively on faith has never before charmed natural philosophers [i.e. physicists], by definition. What is the rationale for this seemingly unscientific revolution?

(De Rujula 1986)

Is the mathematical universe metaphysical?

One of Wittgenstein's contributions to the philosophy of mathematics (cf. Diamond 1996) is to represent how relations between the world's range of propositions and realities are uneven, especially in areas where it is problematic to ditch a familiar ontological identity because of an extension of theoretical language. We trade on analogy; yet we misperceive its multifarious identities. Relations we customarily attach to words, he also argued, are fundamentally distinct to the relations between propositions and their referents. In superstring theory such variability returns with a vengeance. Philosophers and mathematicians have some difficulty explaining what it is to grasp a thought expressed in a complex geometrical universe, together with its relation to mental creativity, our objective abilities, and the external world. In the cosmology of superstrings, within the perspectives of conjectured counter-intuitive multiplying dimensions, there is accordingly even less clear a grasp of the solutions to these matters. Consequently, the boundaries between grasping an empirically well-founded geometry of the ancient past, and confused conjecture, are not only unclear, they occupy territory in which counter-intuitive surprise is by definition precisely not where standard mathematics determines a conclusion. Yet to some degree such puzzling identities are prefigured in local physics, as we see below in Figure 3.2.

Schizoid live-metaphor?

Does gravity breed metaphor?

It was acknowledged in Chapter 2 that our own indeterminacy in consciousness infects our talk of truth conditions about general matters in the external world. An analogous state of affairs in observable science obtains at times. Paczynski (1986) conjectured that images of two enormous quasars, observed by radio telescope, might in fact be one object whose imaging was split by massive gravitational distortion. For a while it seemed that Turner *et al.* (1986) appeared to have confirmed that the images were one object, though they ignored differences between the quasars, such the differences in the red wavelengths (cf. Figures 3.3 and 3.4).

They could have been a complex object such as an unusual galaxy; but Turner *et al.* proposed that it could be a single object with a 1000-galaxy mass. If this idea had been correct, then what were thought to be two 19th magnitude quasars (1146+111B and C) might have been one massive problematic object. The unprecedented size of this object, and the double images

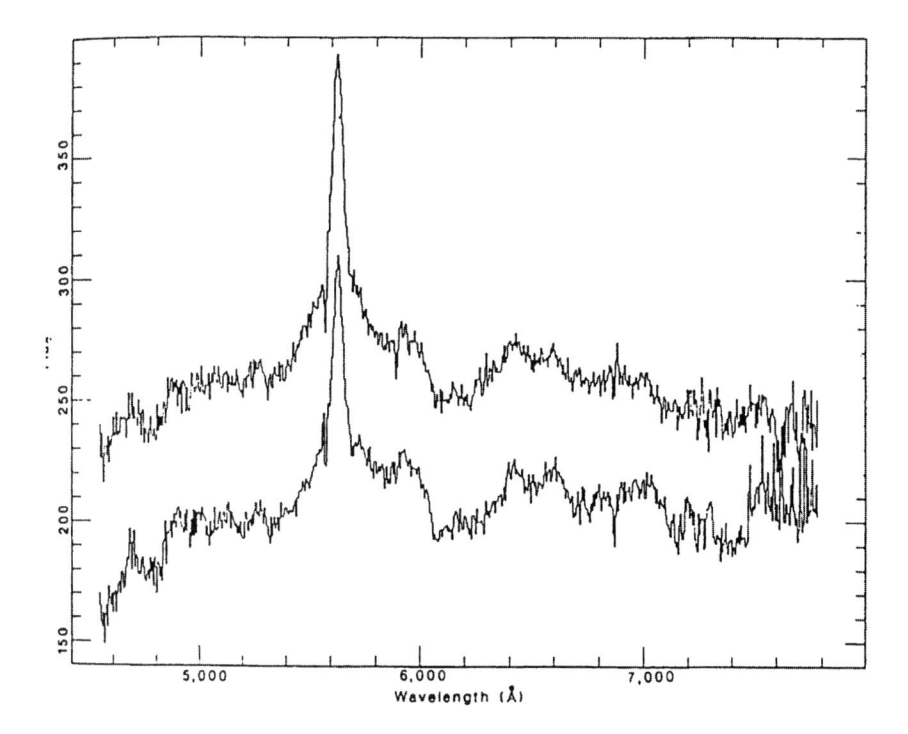

Figure 3.2 Quasars 1146+111B and C

Source: Turner *et al.* (1986)

Note: In retrospect, with this interpretation by Turner *et al.* falsified, one can position the report as an incorrect use of live-metaphor in which an ontology was derived from the multiple imaging. The overlap and discontinuity of observed properties were not evenly either mentioned (e.g. differences in the red wavelengths) or causally connected to their referential environment which would have removed the inferential basis for the gravitational lensing notion.

being separated by the comparatively large 2.6 arc, indicated the possibilities of it being a black hole, or an unclassified object with an unprecedented environment (i.e. a cosmic string in which there is some breakdown of spacetime, see Figure 3.4 and note).

The case of astronomical interpretations for gravitational lensing, from the standpoint of some sceptical observational astronomers assessing Turner *et al.* (1986), should not be overstated, though such individual cases may lead to, or obliquely mirror, unconscious myopia. Should we not allow, however, for the possibility that in Turner *et al.* (ibid.) technological instrumentation confers a higher calculative status on their conception than it warrants in the presentation of their results? Turner *et al.* (ibid.) are not evenly typical of many other scientific enterprises; yet with suitable qualifications, the attendant limitations counsel caution about universalised contrast

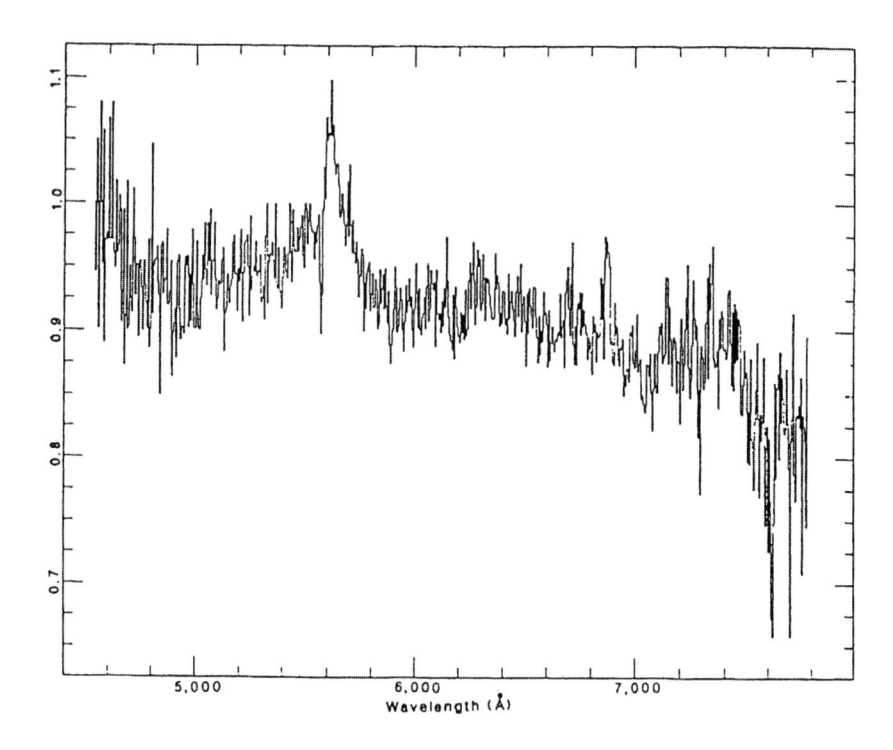

Figure 3.3 Spectra of double quasars

Source: Turner *et al.* (1986)

Note: In this illustration we have the ratio of the spectrum of 1146 + 111B to that of 1146 + 111C. It shows that the line-to-continuum ratio of the two images is somewhat different. Turner *et al.* noted that there is a smooth variation in the ratio from blue to red in which C has a redder detected continuum than B. Had this overlap of match and contrasting hint of asymmetry been pursued, it would have exposed two ontologically distinct quasars or at least placed a ban on inferring that there is one reference from the images.

between cosmology and theology as entirely distinct types of subjects. Ostriker and Vishniac (1986) are among those who have attempted to develop observational criteria to judge the claim by Turner *et al.* (1986) that the double quasars might be reassessed, and converted it into an observational theory identifying not gravitational lensing quasars but a cluster of galaxies of dark matter.

Yet shortly after the publication of the double-lensed quasar report, it was widely recognised that subsequent scrutiny falsified the initial expectations. The phenomena turned out to be two distinct, interesting but not identical, quasars. Nevertheless, from both the standpoints of the sociology of science, and future observations, the interpretation which was falsified reflects intriguing philosophical aspects. Astronomers can, like all of us, fall into generating fallaciously related live-metaphors: incorrectly matched seeming family resemblances. Arp (1986) criticised the publication of the above results, although perhaps drawing questionable general conclusions from the error. He and others had originally discovered the two quasars, without interpreting them in the retrospectivel, (false), exotic context offered by Paczynski (1986). Paczynski had not mentioned, nor accounted for the fact that, Arp's original report which he utilised cited altogether five such tightly related quasars (see Figure 3.3). The two quasars which Paczynski noticed were members of this group of five which were so rare, in their characteristics, size and proximity to one another, that they had less than of the order of 10^{-4} probability of being unrelated.

Arp leaves us with a problem. Given that the gravitational lensing interpretation has been rejected, what do we do to explain this rare group's data? He maintains that the observational data contradict the known physical laws, and notes that the data which Paczynski inaccurately utilised still advertise the problem which he unsuccessfully tried to resolve. Arp observes that this problem is merely one example of the extensive difficulty attending attempts to prove the existence of hidden dark supermasses in the universe, though his view is sharply opposed by a number of astronomers. It is as if one has part of a live-metaphor in the theory, but the ontological source and origin for the live-metaphor is obscured by ignorance. Vilenkin (1986) perhaps returns us to a more central fundamental problem, by noting that in looking for cosmic strings has to recognise that they are often ascribed to large real shifts, and therefore are moving away from us. In the deep structure of the data and interpretation which is selectively addressed and split in terms of surface grammar, there is a deeper identity to be exposed. As with schizophreniform symptoms which are live-metaphor traces of schizophrenia (cf. Hacking 1995: 168, 176), false theories which are intertwined with observational data mimic justified theories.

Paczynski's (1986) work on gravitational lensing attracted international respect; one would not wish to distract from this in citing the above problem. One can use it to illustrate the general point Longair (1994a: 375) makes when reviewing the overall state of affairs in current cosmological research: 'How can we be certain that there are not some subtle correlations between the properties of the objects which render the tests ambiguous?'[17]

Is abstraction a risk?

Faulty abstraction of pure mathematics linked to speculative interpretation of observations can wrongly yield an ontology that contains a bewitched astrophysical mimesis. The foregoing case is an extreme example of the general states of affairs that cosmology is highly provisional, often without definitively formulated tests for falsification. In the above situation there is a link between conjectured knowledge and inability to furnish falsification tests (cf. Popper 1972), yet these emerge in the deepest most fundamental topics in addition to the foregoing case. Surely, it will be an eclectic approach which achieves progress in such a situation, not least when transcendent cosmology is the target of discussion. This not only applies to the protagonist of a thesis for cosmology, it equally applies to those who have a reductive critical interest, since their presuppositions are also subject to similar problems. It could be that this situation reflects a metaphysical problem about logic and scientific statements. We might reflect on Wittgenstein's (1996: 67) early concern to extirpate vague senses from one of his theory of propositions: 'The epistemological questions concerning the nature of judgement and belief cannot be solved without a correct apprehension of the form of the proposition'. Such comprehension would be a conjunction of relevance in content, logic, empirical justification and contextualisation. Cosmology cannot generally furnish these preconditions, just as we have seen that mathematics cannot in domains such as superstrings. Such drawbacks are usually a property of the frontiers of exotic exploration. A problem is that they have mimetic analogues in these sorts of empirical observational associations with less exotic contexts. Sometimes cosmologists are not certain or clear what are the parameters between mistaken mimesis and counter-intuitive accurate departure from known forms of theory and procedure.

Cosmic strings

Can there be unobservable evidence in science?

Cosmic strings are an important instance of conceptual insight. Cosmic strings are hypothetical one-dimensional loops or strands of vacuum defects caused by interactions of quantum energy states made from a space warp. They are microscopic even by subatomic standards, though they can be longer in length than galaxies (cf. Hogan 1986).

Cosmic strings are quite distinct from the superstrings discussed above. McKie (1988) observes that, possibly, the centre of some active galactic could be cosmic strings. Among other options, supermassive black holes have been noted as host for other exotic phenomena. According to D'Auria and Fré (1999), there is a solvable Lie algebra representation for superstrings in blackholes. These researchers add to Hawking's view that black holes evaporate, by proposing that they transform into superstrings or singularities (cf. Thorne 1994: 481–82). If it happens that the above idea of a massive double-lensed phenomenon were to be observed in the form of a single object, it is worth considering that it might afford support, in a given phase, to the identification of a black hole in a terminal state with a superstring, and the association of it with a cosmic string intervening between it and observer or as part of the environment of the black hole. This complex and speculative scenario depends on disputed forms of relations between general relativity and quantum gravity. For example, Hawking and Penrose believe that naked singularities cannot form in our universe, while others dissent.

Should we have a criterion of provisional empiricism?

In Chapter 2 it was argued that even a conjecturally true concept concerning the reproduction of something is an ontological claim. That is to say, the principles about simulating identities in languages are parallel with the objective structure of the external world which they represent. The parallel drawn above, of genetic DNA coding depiction of parental identity with a visual representation of them, is obviously distant from the use of mathematical representation of ontological states; but I argue that there is a relative identity relation between such diverse types of live-metaphor uses.

In contrast, the Paczynski (1986) report, proposing gravitational lensing, is rather like an attempt to reproduce something about an individual without having *a* criterion of identity of what it is to be the subject. This problem also presupposes the absence of a correct criterion of application (cf. Dummett 1981) with which to apply observational descriptions to their ostensible physical referents. Indeed there is progress in cosmology, and errors are often corrected; but, as Thorne's (1994) history of black hole cosmology shows, in the midst of exciting developments there is a basic epistemological instability about the identity of links between theory and observation at many fundamental levels.

Science is rarely speculative in a way reminiscent of some theology. Certainly, the present book does not stand on the claim that because occasionally astrophysical cosmology and divine cosmology have relatable equivocation, theology is linked to or comparable with science. Yet the fashion to contrast science as an empirically justified enterprise as against other subjects in the arts is fraught with confusion and failure to recognise ambiguity and unprovable elements within science. Provisional conjecture is more extensively in evidence within cosmology, while it is also the subject which most naturally explicitly attends to issues of universality at the extremes of scientific generalisation. So, just where one would want science to be clear and decisive – as arbiter filtering gross or coarse-grained claims of universal solutions to the identity of the universe – its scientific testbed cannot itself satisfy all the conditions it requires other subjects to meet to be science. Although this state of affairs is obvious, it is a function of its exotic, counter-intuitive and metaphoric properties that the locus and focus of what the uncertainties are will be goalposts that migrate, depending upon the presuppositions of the referees.

Thus cosmologists sometimes differ over such matters as the existence of God and the relation of this topic to the physical universe. If a given scientific discipline accommodates contrary propositions, we usually interpret this as a property of provisional progress in the routes towards justified claims of knowledge. But it is not evident that this situation is exclusive of the conjectural claims which transcendent propositions make in the arts, and in particular in, say, divinity. My aim is not to conclude that theology is science. Rather, the perennial qualitative and quantitative problems which are internal to the content of many generalised scientific statements and their extension to new empirical domains, involve live-metaphorisation which has some, and only some, relative identity relations to the restrictions in propositional research in some arts, of which certain spheres of divinity are a subset. This circumstance places an elementary limit on the necessary internal capacity we should ascribe to a cosmologist's ability to guide us in matters of the relation between physical generalisation and transcendent inference. Just as philosophy is too important always to be left to philosophers, so science is too important always to be left to scientists. Sure, each has the edge in its respective areas of competence; but each tends to equivocate over inferences when generalising about universal claims where personal epistemology influences judgement. My point is that where the parameters of possibility, originality and future developments are subject to counter-intuition and live-metaphor depiction, we all tend incorrectly to pinpoint and arbitrate over what possibility is. In the state of affairs where the interface of these functions concerns issues of atheism versus divinity, we need to be wary precisely where we see no need to be, to avoid prejudice and to discover new options. 'Eyes wide shut' is not an uncommon demeanour for ourselves to be found in prior to discovery of, for example, Gödel's incompleteness theorems: our surprise is contrary to our comprehension of possibility prior to discovery. So encouragement of studying, for example, the contingencies of impossibility might be encouraged.

Conversely, we should wish to avoid using these cautions and concerns to facilitate vacuity and sophism. For example, we should be uncompromising in our assertion that if something is logically possible it cannot therefore be possibly impossible.[18] If this position is correct, then we can introduce it as a principle of possibility to contribute to the assessment of exotic options. For example, the physicist Gott (1991) constructed a mathematical scenario for a time machine, expressed as a set of closed time-like curves, by postulating the acceleration of two long cosmic strings passing each other. If this seems to entail that there could be time travel, then there must be something false in at least one of the premises. (I refer the reader to a discussion below for other premises being employed here to sustain my criticism.)[19] Consequently the claim that 'this time machine is consistent and could possibly represent a physical possibility' is itself an impossible contention.

Can we distinguish between true and false possibility?

The answer to problems of counter-intuition and narrow-mindedness is not a mediocre mean, but a dynamic explicit research on bold alternatives and the self-critical maintenance of standards of reason as well as creativity. Contrariwise, the view that a specific proposition can be true and false – paraconsistent logic – cannot be allowed to displace the standard grasps of (im)possibility. The work of, for example, Priest (1995) certainly has profound aspects to it, especially when dealing with access to infinity using transfinite set theory. But this can only establish that paraconsistent 'possibility' is contradictory. If possibility is contradictory then it is not a true possibility. So much should be self-evident, because, if the value 'false' is a possible property of true consequence (in paraconsistent logic), then a true proposition cannot be a criterion of true possibility for the reason that internal to its identity is that it is also possibly false. What is possibly false cannot be a premise deployed to discover what cannot be false – namely, what has to be possible; and *vice versa* for impossibility.

How should we classify theory which takes it that a specific proposition can be true and false? It is a counterfeit of the creative crazily original thinking of which Wittgenstein (1980a: 75) spoke, cited at the beginning of Chapter 2, a context to which the reader is referred here as background:

> Even to have expressed a false thought boldly and clearly is already to have gained a great deal. It's only by thinking even more crazily than philosophers do that you can solve their problems. Imagine someone watching a pendulum and thinking: God makes it move like that. Well, isn't God equally free to act in accordance with a calculation?

The sense of 'clearly' is antithetical to a specific proposition in use which is both true and false. Treatments of paraconsistent logic (for example, Epstein and D'Ottaviano 1995: 349) are fond of citing Walt Whitman's:

> Do I contradict myself?
> Very well then … I contradict myself.
> I am large … I contain multitudes.
>   'Song of Myself' (1855: 51)

The similarity of this prose to the mad Legion's speech in Mark 5: 9–10 is evident. This precedent serves to introduce my suggestion that paraconsistent logic is a model which fits the phenomena of multiple personality, especially as explained by Ian Hacking (1995), though he does not draw attention to this connection. Hacking describes the functioning of multiple personalities as a 'semantic contagion', often under duress from and coerced by media influence. I think that these can be modelled by paraconsistent logic, and believe such logic can be employed to map psychosis and some states of schizophrenia. A key feature is a weak (some might argue a homonymic) sense of 'negation' that I used to relate a collection of propositions which are true (and false) to a model of the world but not consistently extensionally to the world, as with Epstein and D'Ottaviano (1995: 360). This is like a psychotic's conflation of an imagined world with the actual world, with recipes to avoid recognising and equivocate over the differences. Epstein and D'Ottaviano (1995: 361) actually state that, 'From their own semantic point of view such theories are consistent, corresponding to a possible description of the world'. But many people will believe that the use of 'possible' here is itself paraconsistent, i.e. only if we are confused about what is true and false is it possible to accept paraconsistent logic as a possible description of the world. Epstein and D'Ottaviano plausibly note that only when the classical true or false logic is applied to the paraconsistent theory is inconsistency detectable. So this really is parallel with a psychiatrist convincing a psychotic that the latter's world is not really the actual world.

Paraconsistent logic, with the interpretation related to mental phenomena proposed above, has of course a different status with regard to psychosis when the relation's intended target is the function of imagination, as with Walt Whitman's creativity. But there is a somewhat counter-intuitive extension of this idea, in a qualified way, to a sort of midpoint between the paraconsistent theoretical position and its application to mental disorders. This is the circumstance in which specialist conjecture at the frontiers of physical and mathematical science is employed to imagine what the solutions to a given large question could be. Complex mathematics are not infrequently deployed to formalise quasi-science-fiction possibilities, since the theoretical insights are considered of value in modelling the universe. There are notorious interfaces here between the imaginative potential of science fiction and futurist writing, which sometimes appear to run in advance of what turn out to be new scientific trends.

Adjacent to this general situation it seems clear or possible that scientists can, within their own research hypotheses, unresolved research proposals and mathematical theories, etc., operate or assume positions and patterns of rationality, as well as fragments of concepts which have at least a suppressed or unmapped paraconsistent status. This status is not usually intended since almost all such scientists hope for consistency and/or realist justification for their research. Yet, in terms of a generalised policy for scientific research, there is a borderland vagueness or conflict, not always recognised or correctly depicted, in what will emerge as the conditions of variance between previous and fresh scientific paradigms or conjectural knowledge. This has an analogue with the above connection between paraconsistent logic, mental disorder and imaginative creativity.

Sure, this is not to deem such scientists ever so slightly mad, but to maintain that there is a live-metaphor relation in rationality between certain types of higher level scientific imagination, mental disorder and artistic creativity with respect to the logical or illogical identity. This rationality, understandably, unevenly merges true and false propositions and/or the states to which scientists refer, including being (often unwittingly) committed to a specific suppressed premise which is treated as true and false. Further, in such a state of affairs the scientist (unaware of which proposition may have this property) handles the paraconsistent facet of the conjectural hypothesis as if it is an internal property of a true hypothesis. This is parallel with paraconsistent attempts to integrate a dialethic propositional system, which has specific propositions that are, or can be, true and false in a particular usage, with standard logical systems. For example, Epstein wishes to produce the paraconsistent semantic system J_3,[20] and place it in some form of conjunction with classical logics.[21] The general situation, sketched in the foregoing, with regard to the anatomy of scientific conjecture and its inconsistent blend of true conceptual fragments with false elements, is a feature of much standard scientific reasoning and construction of hypotheses, as means to stable and justification of empirical theories.

It is not unusual to depict science as an entirely rationally controlled enterprise that is exclusive in contrast with philosophical, theological or other artistic intellectual activities. A purpose in proposing the foregoing model of some scientific conjectural identities is to argue that science, and especially cosmology, has continuities with other subjects in its functional identities, not least in the domain of unstable rationality – i.e. precisely where the realist laboratory scientist may be prone to be imperious about his grasp of explanation. Imagination, incorrect quantification and unstable inference presented with technical excellence can be semantic contagions in scientific theorising, in particular – obviously – where they are not explicitly or accurately recognised. But what is acceptable to the goose is worthy of the gander. It is right for philosophers to respect the demonstrable advantage science has in its success with empirical experiment as the foundation for theory and discovery. But rather too little attention has sometimes been given by scientists to the internal limitations and properties of their own enterprises. Although philosophers would do well to exercise modesty in the context of the emergence of empirical science, yet science would do well to be less defensive and more positive about its own limited capacity to recognise objective limitations in science. Non-empirical and compromised functions contribute to the identity of science in its operations to open up new scientific areas. In short the scientist's ability to think mathematically and experiment empirically does not exclude the hybrid ways humans think, nor does it prevent such admixtures from being engaged (sometimes inadvertently) in multifarious ways as components to produce progress in science. It is not quite right to picture this situation as a mixture of correct pieces of thinking and experiment, into which there are discontinuous confused or false fragments of description and inference,[22] which drop away as a consequence of the scientist's mastery of observation, interpretation and inference. Just because a scientific theory is justified – i.e. it works – does not mean that it is exhaustively true or without prescriptive and inferential dross. Such a picture would be retrospective. It would be more exact to envisage unisolated continuities between true, false and vague as well as ambiguous predicates in some science.[23]

These sorts of qualities draw science closer to some typical characteristics of philosophy and other non-scientifically grounded realms of conceptual construction. It may seem presumptuous, yet true, for philosophers to claim that they are often more careful about inferences than some scientists, though such scientists usually have the edge in empirically grounded experiment. But it is not only the negative sense in which theorising in philosophy has parallels with science. The foregoing suggested that, internal to positive theorising in science, there are unstable metaphoric elements in new justified empirical theories which are used as catalysts for the invention or discovery of creative and empirical features of the universe. One aspect of the derivation of a new conclusion from old premises and new experiment is that there is a mid-ground of speculation in which the quantification of results has not been fully identified or quantified. Rather than this being merely a negative feature of falsehood, this is usually deployed imaginatively to infer a justified empirical discovery. This type of property appears to be an internal sense of creativity which has a relation to subjects outside of science. Another way of approaching the arena for this conclusion is to claim that there are gaps in the empirical scientist's conception and application of realism and experimental generalisation, and at junctures where he perceives continuity.

Why then should not a philosopher, a theologian, an artist proceed in this way when theorising over the external world? Self-evidently, we are not concerned with the differences here, but with selective strands of parallel. Nevertheless, I think that we have general phenomena here satisfying an overlap condition utilising comparable live-metaphor functions and inferential relations. There are at least two different types of feature in this scenario. First, there is a culture theory epistemological connection with empiricism, though I present this only in summary. Although Forster's 'only connect' and Derrida's *différance* are diachronically separated modernist policy fragments of judgement, yet they, suitably transformed for transcendence, should be conjoined strategies. Subjects variously overlap: aims to realise a total work of art will overlap with science in a variety of its properties; and attempts at a total work of science – cosmology – will overlap with other subjects. While we should be careful to preserve the criteria of individuation without equivocation, we should allow for the function of the universe as a single object. If the scientist brings perception of beauty and non-logical value-judgement to empirical assessment, then the philosopher, and others engaged in their uses of judgement about the external world, can bring precision and conjecture to bear on the explanation of the physical universe.

Second, there is an inferential topic, which can be characterised as single and multiple conclusion relations of consequence, using Shoesmith and Smiley's (1980: 247–48) concept of an overlap condition, with a variety of weak and strong senses of relevance (and concerning the latter, see Smiley 1998b). The scope of such relations is of course restricted, and is confined by a criterion of relevance pertinent to the scientific domain where there is a set of functions and the other overlap subjects. Where we need to integrate our ignorance in science or other subjects, we could introduce a partial Kripke model to partition domains of relative ignorance or weak knowledge.[24] In this way we can be aware of the pragmatic role of simulation of indirect knowledge and its generalisation. The point that Thijsse (1996: 224) applies to modal logicians also applies to scientists and others: our standard logics, and scientists' ascription of knowledge to a world community of science, simply go beyond our and any individual's capacity to have cognisance of what is known. Consequently, the interrelations between epistemology and empiricism are not understood. So we need a logic to map this constitutional deficiency, even when partial semantics and logics are available through a vast array of resources.

If a metaphysician is so inclined to develop live-metaphor for transcendental divine entities, some mathematical conventions used in theoretical physics can be employed as the basis for constructing novel exploration. Patient attention to theorising in divine cosmology can consistently be encouraged, not least since opposition to it in principle may here involve over-confidence in an unsupportable contrast between scientific 'realism' and divine cosmologies. Even before Einstein's special relativity is linked to gravity, and quantum mechanics is connected to gravitational collapse, Michael Redhead (1989) has demonstrated what gaps there are in our desire to apply 'realism' to physics. These remarks are intended to be strictly bound in context. Although they may have application at a higher level of generality in other astronomical topics, I appreciate that such criticism needs carefully regulating to allow for the fundamental differences between theology and astronomy.

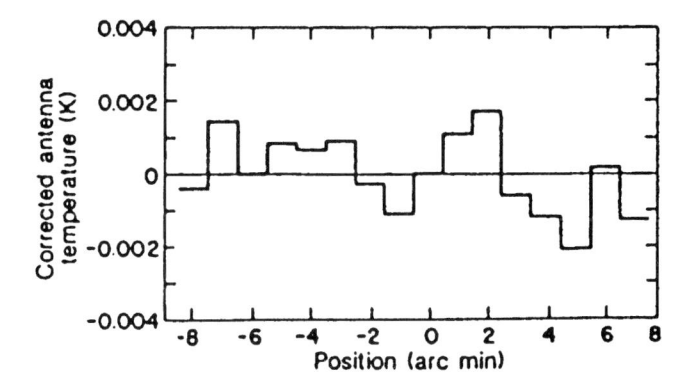

Figure 3.4 Problem chart for a cosmic string

Source: After Stark *et al.* (1986)

Note: Stark *et al.* noticed that the alleged double gravitational lensing quasar of Turner *et al.* (1986) might instead be either a cluster of galaxies or a cosmic string. They suggested that these options could be focused but not proved as certainties by measuring the radiation temperatures in the vicinity of the double quasar 1146-111 BC. At millimetre wavelengths, a galactic cluster would cause a reduction in the background temperature and either side of a cosmic string would have different temperatures. But their calculations did not confirm either possibility, though they did not support the gravitational lensing hypothesis, whilst their work places affords more exact parameters for further work. The above chart offers the corrected antenna temperature at 100GH as a function of position between the two quasars. See pages 120–24 above.

Are there metaphysical elements in cosmology?

These present remarks are not an aside, intent on discrediting provisional and/or pioneering research which involves a risk-factor in judgements. Its aim is to emphasise the speculative factor in scientific cosmology which draws attention to the non-experimental creativity in astronomical interpretations of observations. Sometimes this recognition is obscured by the creative use of technology and mathematics. Such artistic features resist certain of the qualifying assumptions sometimes canvassed to maintain the autonomy of science (in the present context, cosmology and astrophysics), in relation to philosophy, as logically entirely discontinuous domains.

The metaphoric overlaps between philosophy of science, metaphysics, transcendence and astrophysical cosmology are partly empirical; but it is also an impressionistic result of limitations and structural similarities in human experience existing outside both astronomical cosmology and transcendence that intrudes, in the nature of human thought, from the other spheres of life. Nevertheless, I am arguing that there can be a residual sharing of descriptions between some scientific cosmology and other topics which can be generalised to devise a divine cosmology.

Polkinghorne (1991: 15) observes that 'if theology is to maintain cognitive claims it must be an empirical discipline to the extent that its assertions are related to experience'. In developing aspects of this view, the present book is attempting a fine balancing act. Religious experience is not the sole source of analytical perplexity. There are some unexpected complexities in scientific experience. In encapsulating the world as material commodity, science can fall prey to prescribing this commodity with perceptions which externalise an element of fantasy. Technology can become, if applied to underwrite policy, an overly successful corporate process which distorts our ignorance of spacetime relations and hides our subjective limitations.

This book claims that universalised discourse involves counter-intuitive issues. Thorne (1994) typifies the cosmologist who is sharply aware of the speculative nature of study about the early, and the general, structure of the universe. Where science here has quantifying procedures, they implode at these spacetimes, analogous *with* metaphysical qualitative techniques. In this perspective we can sympathise with the tendency to construe the relations between truth and its referents as institutional belief policies, rather than exhaustively veridical science. At the side of this position, we have seen in the foregoing some evidence for the idea that a cosmological live-metaphor 'theory' of meaning confers strength on the support for a counter-intuitive realist view of the universe. Truth is as tricky for the critic as it is for the protagonist.

What is a metal?

Is there live-metaphor in local science?

A general feature of the foregoing is to see that in cosmological science there

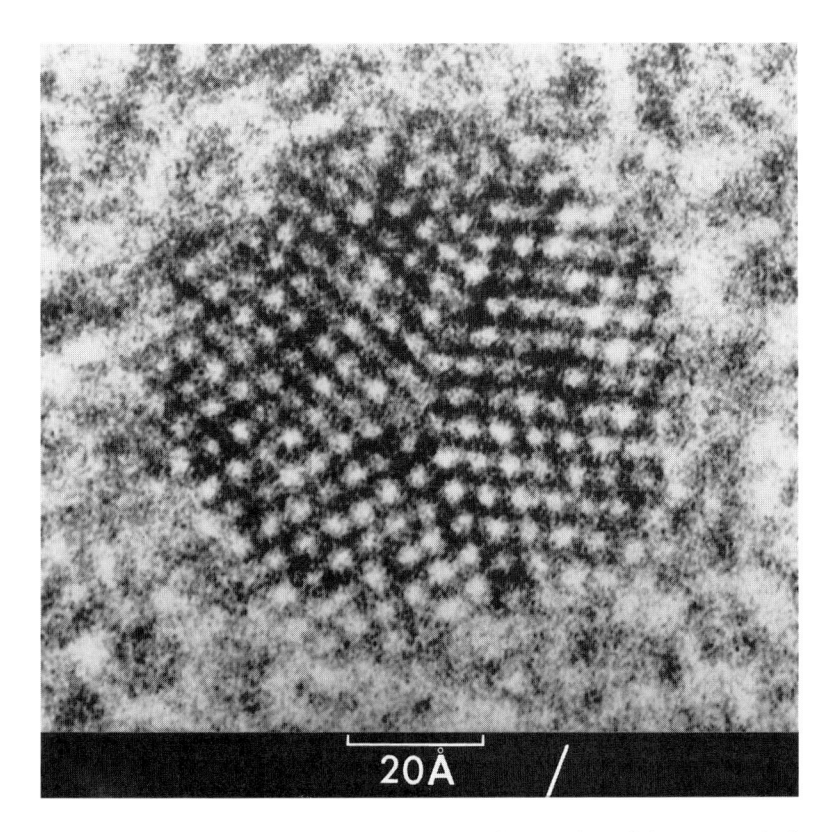

Figure 3.5 An experimental microscope image of a metal particle composed of 1500 atoms

Source: Photography courtesy of Peter Edwards.

Note: This plate was produced by Peter Edwards and his team in Cambridge. The white dots are the atoms. The metal particle represented above is about one millionth of a centimetre in diameter.

are uncertainties as well as justified knowledge claims, often mingled together. We have already seen reasons to suppose that such a state of affairs applies, in various qualified ways, to some local spheres of terrestrial science. It is worth considering an example in such applied science where philosophical problems may only seem to have a remote relation to empirical analysis and its theory.

I have no wish to overload the role of live-metaphor, nor to make it *the* central foundation for the current analysis, while it is a convenient focus for the present purpose. Scientific live-metaphor relations in the material world are not restricted to esoteric matters in cosmology. Live-metaphor occurs in most phenomena at various junctures. Metals are a particularly suitable topic in view of their rich history and applications. Humphry Davy's 1807 identification of sodium and potassium as metals (see Davy 1808) posed a problem which still occupies specialists. These two metals satisfy criteria of standard metal properties, yet they violate the traditional notion of having a very low density. With respect to some criteria of being a metal, sodium and iron are identical.

Ross (1981: 175–76) introduced the notion of 'fact stereotypes' in which cognitive content cannot properly be evacuated of their ontological source. In agreeing with this, we may notice that a type of 'inappropriate form of correspondence' between ontological state and theory can occur not only in spacetime physical frames of reference in language (as Nerlich points out (1994: 106–11; 48–59)) but also in local physics.

Having introduced above the idea of a schizoid live-metaphor in a problematic astronomical context, it is worth weighing the notion more in the light of normal and normative local physics – for example, in metallurgy. The metallurgists Edwards and Sienko (1983) state that a key to the problem about research into metal identity is furnished by Herzfeld's neglected earlier research (see Herzfeld 1927). Herzfeld based his solution to definition on the close link between atomic properties, density and the metallic state. Here, relational properties and contexts are central. Edwards and Sienko demonstrate that the emergence of quantum mechanics contributed towards both the neglect of Herzfeld's seminal work and to distract from its atomistic focus and its attention to the role of density in the formulation of criteria for being metal. They note that research has now revived Herzfeld's type of approach as the basis for solving the definition of metals.

With such variable approaches there is nevertheless a realist commitment to the description of metal; yet the association between criteria of definition, ontology and empirical procedures embody incomplete specification, though different models have value as functional fits to the empirical data. This is like some of the definitional problems associated with observation in large-scale spacetime physics, to which we have and will give attention – for example, as with Einstein's use of Lorenz transforms in space (cf. Nerlich 1994: 112–18), which take the same form under any other suitable basis, but with different set of problems for each form.

How do metals satisfy criteria of identity?

If we consider criteria of identity as logical functions, we can assign a specific metal as a value of that function, and so on, for each metal. There are multiple ways of specifying a criterion of identity. The criteria of identity operate as if they include live-metaphors, with token realisations in different media. (This has some similarity to the use of genetic reproduction of identities in Chapter 2 and evolutionary DNA discussed in Chapter 5: one recognises a subject from a simulation, and if the simulation is attended by a criterion which maps it as a function going proxy for the referent, then the depiction succeeds, whilst it is clear that further analysis is needed to produce a definition of what is to be that referent.) If someone misperceives sodium as a type entirely dissimilar to and exclusive of the type exemplified by iron, he will have presupposed a false surface criterion of identity.

Hoffmann (1990: 199–201) demonstrates that unexplained asymmetry in metal molecular structure (i.e. a feature that is a deviation from extant current quantitative calculation) and aesthetic novelty function together in theoretical reproduction of empirical bonding in the transition metals. In such contexts there are explanatory gaps in the functional setting of a successful applied scientific theory in respect of producing new compounds. These conceptual gaps are to some extent a result of the way any hypothesis privileges representation from its own, and not a universal omniscient standpoint. This is illustrated by some of the geometry for the bonding properties of the molecule $Ca_{0.75}Nb_3O_6$. Hoffmann (1990: 192) explains that this is not a discrete molecule, but one complex extended structure in which sodium, niobium and oxygen atoms run on in a small crystal virtually indefinitely. He states, of the various dimensional models of this phenomenon, that they 'are abstractions of reality. There is no unique, privileged model of a molecule. Instead, there is an infinite variety of representations, each structured to catch some aspect of the essence of the molecule'. In a sense such a focused representation of one feature excludes others and fails to reproduce the density and complex configurations in the ontological state. Of course this need not result in error. Yet such abstraction leaves 'excess space' (along the analogy of Kermode's (1984) literary use of the same expression), and this descriptive gap confers an artificial contextualised focus on the theory present. This situation effectively shifts the function of the geometrical semantics in the explanation to a simplifying position which is not solely a reduction to parsimony of a given physical state, because it does not attempt to represent the multiplicity of its ontological contextual functional contracts. This is tantamount to the use of quantifiable geometrical live-metaphor. The ways the complex abstract predication relates to and abstracts out properties of the ontological states is successful employment of live-metaphor regulated by empirical calculation.

Geach (1980a) wrote of the analogy that holds between representation of a complex molecule, in which a functional 'place' can be occupied by a single atom or a radical (N^{++} or NH^4), and the (Fregean) logic of propositions. This analogy can be paraphrased into support for the above empirically measurable concept of live-metaphor. Geach pointed out that the analogy finally breaks down when substitutions occur within sequences of propositions, yet he considers it a valuable device insofar as the analogy holds, and I wish to argue that the live-metaphor analysis of functions extends further than this analogy, as this book attempts to show. Geach also raises problems about changes in word order which break the analogy. J.A. Hawkins (1983) tackles word order universals related to this problem and some of the changes in truth-value with recombinations of components. If their work is adopted to guard against over-generalisation of the analogy beyond its bounds, and these chemical bonds, the analogy has a relative identity parallel with my use of live-metaphor, in which the analogy can be paraphrased into such metaphor.

It is worth noting the possibility of constructing parallels between metaphor structures in metals and linguistics. It is commonplace to relate the meaning of a word to its use, and this presses the issue of the importance of context in an account of meaning. Change the context, and you change the meaning, in some sense. 'Tune' in music and engine mechanics is a related category involving a live-metaphor shift determined by the contexts. As argued by Ross (1981: 109–10), this type of metaphor involves asymmetrical meaning-related equivocation; and measurability of metaphors will vary with contexts and the capacity to contextualise their senses. Temperature variability composing the environment of a metal is both central and tricky as a feature relation to defining metal. High enough temperature might destroy the metal; low temperature may alter its reaction-relation to its environment. These parameters vary with different metals. In this way, the criteria of identity of a metal impinge on environment, as with the sense of an expression and its relation to its contexts, though we should be very wary of conflating other unrelated albeit contiguous phenomena in these fields.

The sample size of a metal is also important, as is the linguistic length of unit which is abstracted for analysis in a sentence. Inaccurate size-criteria purporting to assess the significance of a property will thwart analysis. Such issues, as those which relate to the identity of a proposition and the length of an expression in relation to the functionally different elements in linguistic usage, are both important and disputed in the perceptions of philosophers down the centuries. In a very different type of context from the present one, Eleonore Stump (1978: 205–14) shows that in *De topicis differentiis* Boethius addressed *words* and *phrases* in the framework of treating Aristotle's *Topics*, yet in the latter the concern is with *proposition*-length expressions. Furthermore, Boethius's emphasis is on syllogisms, whereas Aristotle's is concerned with dialectic and rhetoric. Such slips away from Aristotle's priority results partially from inattention to Aristotle's use of deduction as a presupposition of rhetoric in the enthymeme and not only with the syllogism.[25] Geach (1980a, 1972) has outlined Aristotle's switch from an analysis of propositions which decomposes into the asymmetry of logical subject and predicate, in contrast with his later doctrine of terms in which the proposition is a symmetrical entity; Geach (1991) shows that deontic logic has been attended by the same confusion. So analogies of logical language with other phenomena turns out to be a sensitive disputed affair. A negative reason for mentioning this cluster of issues is that there is the possibility of a range with corresponding confusions in some areas of app-lied science's uses of its empirical language, even when its representation is functionally propitious, for the reason that just because a theory works this is not equivalent to its having a perfect semantic specification without redundancy.

Just as the size of a semantic fragment is a matter of concern for what a minimal semantic unit could be, so with the sample-size of empirical properties in scientific experiment. D.C. Johnson *et al.* (1985) have argued that as few as ten metal atoms (in cluster carbonyl compounds of osmium) are sufficient to allow successful testing to determine magnetic properties which define a thing (e.g. osmium) as metal, arguing that this is the same as the characteristic for testing bulk metal. This might have seemed very little upon which to base an identification of what it is to be a metal, yet I am told by Peter Edwards that the osmium environment facilitates precise measurement.

This oddly relates to analogy between a natural language proper name's criterion of identity for a person and chemical names. A criterion of identity for being a human person *n*, if I may speak somewhat peculiarly, has a minimum sample-size. According to some philosophers, we need a body to be incorporated in the sample-size; yet with Descartes, the body can be disposed of fallaciously,[26] by using the *Cogito*. This has a rather comic uneven parallel with disputes over the sample-size in metal analysis, in which ten metal atoms comprise a criterion of identity for larger molecular clusters. Clearly, once we have a criterion for being human, there are further individuating criteria for each individual, whereas not with a metal. Upon satisfactory scrutiny, however, both chemistry and humanity yield criteria for proper name use variable over the individuals and genus, in which sample-size has a role. Amongst the many differences between metals and humans, there reside elements of logical syntax common to both. Although the ways and extent to which such criteria fit the data are multifarious, it seems that there are grounds, which require further proof than offered here (though to some degree presented elsewhere in this book), to argue that the criteria of identity *for* criteria of identity are invariant over scientific and non-scientific subjects. Should this be the case, if individuation is universal, so is generalisation over its criteria.

Can we generalise beyond our expectations?

It is possible that whenever science or linguistics achieves a fundamental exposure of what it is to be a particular thing, then this logic will match certain corresponding patterns in both these and other subjects. We could extend this to argue that such a logic can be used to map some live-metaphor when such metaphor is deployed in theoretical language for empirical purposes. Hoffmann's (1990: 200–1) study is relevant here; he argues that a pattern underlies and is partially replicated in different molecule bonds, akin to a metaphoric pattern being derived from a shift in sense.

Some new compounds produced in research are violations of what previously classically metallurgists took to be possible. In some cases this is merely a case of a limitation on a scientist's capacity to envisage what might be the next fairly obvious step, evident only in retrospect. Hoffman agrees that certain types of compounds appear to be counter-intuitive violations of empirical possibility when they are discovered, and as such incorporate metaphor that jumps to new semantic field functions to accommodate empirical discovery to new theory. New compounds, which were both thought to be empirically impossible and theoretically incapable of being projected from prior empirical possibilities, are composed in physical research.

Hoffmann (1990: 201) cites the tradition that classically carbon cannot be formed into more than four bonds. He points out that Schmidbaur's team succeeded in making six bonds.[28] A single carbon is at the centre with six bonds, radially from it are six ligands of the $AuPR_3$ groups (see Figure 3.6) It is not that the classical limit was entirely wrong; the extra bonds are somewhat weaker than the usual carbon bonds. Here, the idea of surprise is not only a function of empirical revolution that has been achieved by overriding the natural physical limits and naturally occurring identity of a specific element, the change is a stronger departure from naturally occurring empirical possibility than that. Rather, specialists in the field had not anticipated that the criteria of being carbon, even with a chemist's ingenuity, would provide clear cases of carbon with six bonds. So there is here a sort of complex bunching of considerations concerning empirical (im)possibility, metaphor, limiting theory, transformation and counter-intuitive surprise. The surprise is not solely a psychologically based experience: it paraphrases a change in the empirical scientific physical limits.

If it is right to generalise this sort of account, we can maintain both that in principle logical analysis is predictably applicable to the empirical world, and it incorporates live-metaphoric functions, but that it is also a matter of surprise to specialists. This surprise is partly a function of the scope and fecundity of the logic of live-metaphor potential in empirical theory and how it mirrors empirical states. (On the use of 'mirror', see the next section below.)

To the degree that the universe satisfies criteria of empirical intelligibility, this live-metaphor theory can be generalised to mirror actual states. But even if universal generalisation of it over phenomena were possible, this would not guarantee that scientific or artistic pigeon-holing of phenomena into our extant concepts of classifications or notions of properties would be adequate universally to represent the way things are in, and outside of, the universe.

A difficulty here is that what is newly known is not necessarily a calculable reproduction, or counter-intuitive paraphrase or doubling, of what is known, merely by reformulating what we know as a ladder to the unknown. The foregoing examples of developments in astronomy and local sciences portray related advantages, restrictions and counter-intuitive surprises, many of which violate what were previously thought to be canonical scientific procedures and assumptions. Bechtel and Richardson (1993) question the view that science enjoys one generalisable system in relation to localised, low level science and large-scale science. So we should accept both the internal asymmetries within science's methods and empirical strengths as well as recognise the counter-intuitive symmetries that facilitate generalisation.

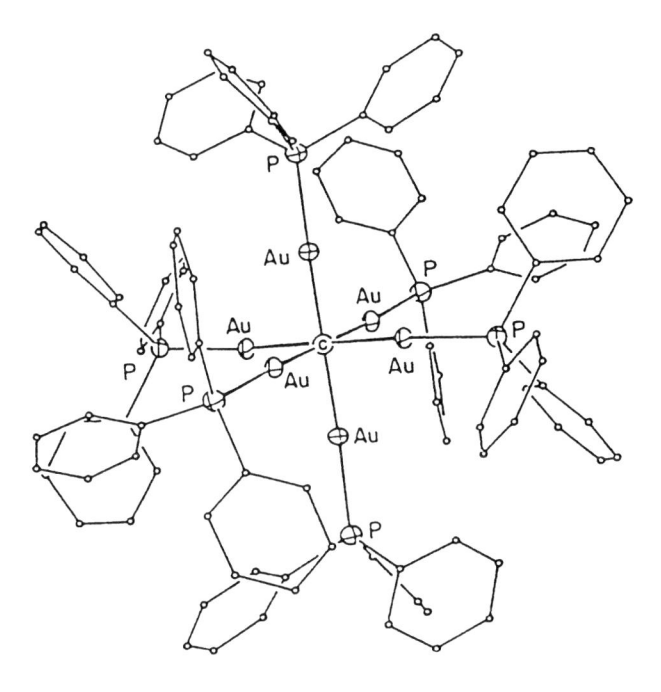

Figure 3.6 A six-bond carbon

Source: Roald Hoffman (1990)

Note: Classically it was judged that four bonds are the limit for carbon; yet depicted here is a single carbon at the centre with six bonds. Extending radially from it are six ligands of the $AuPR_3$ groups, made by Schmidbaur and his team.[27]

Some people try to avoid the force of such conclusions; they have a point. Yet failure to recognise the situation can result in adopting an artificial contrast between science and the arts. True, both subjects are distinctive; but science is reduced to myth if restricted to the pragmatic confident recipes which opened this chapter. This is particularly the case in cosmology. It also holds for deeper areas of fundamental insight in local sciences; in this type of situation, conjecture and revision play roles not entirely dissimilar to some value-judgement procedures in the humanities. Obviously, it is a distinct issue to pose the idea that conjecture and revision might be *relevantly* similar in some zones of cosmology and metaphysical philosophy or philosophical theology. No doubt things in the latter subject are less empirically secure than in science; and subjective novelty can destroy much of the already thin claims to accuracy, as well as credibility in some areas of theology.

Despite this, I argue that there are grounds for revolutionary realignments in the theory of scientific explanation and in the humanities, including philosophy, and philosophical theology. My book furnishes a perspective which questions the assumption of an exclusive type division partitioning science from the humanities, whilst readily embracing the asymmetries between the two. It appears that within the empirical world there are physical characteristics which have not been reduced to what one may term a sort of empirical physicalism alleged to be exclusive of aesthetic and value-laden creative functions. Rather, looking at the foregoing brief résumé of some metal research as one example among many types, we are finding that advanced empirical research in areas of terrestrial, as well as cosmological sciences, while allowing for their internal differences, enfold quantifiable empirical properties with empirical aesthetics, together with features which have traditionally been internal to the humanities, and sometimes used by earlier scientists as points of contrast between science and the arts.

If illusions and false simulations can be avoided, it is not unlikely that, as this book's purpose supposes, astrophysical cosmology and philosophy can be deployed as complex live-metaphors of the universe. In this way, we generalise the above notion of patterns for some domains. For example, philosophy, aesthetics and cosmology could use such similarities and asymmetries from science to relate to one another as different but complementary counter-intuitive doubles of the universe in discrete level-specific topologies.

Although some of these counter-intuitive states may solely occupy communicative media (such as equations, propositions, etc.), it seems clear from some of the examples considered in this book – such as the six-bond carbon case discussed by Hoffmann (1990) and more exotic instances in the early universe to be examined below – that there are counter-intuitive states *in* the empirical world. Some of these appear to be counter-intuitive properties of the physical world, independently of our being surprised by them. Others are formed by our interference with physical conditions. The invention of carbon *six*-bond exemplifies this type. This unexpectedly enfolds empirical possibility with transcendent possibility. That is to say, prior to Schmidbaur's (Scherbaum *et al.* 1988) experimental transformations of naturally occurring physical possibility, in a strict sense a six-bond carbon was a 'natural' impossibility. But there was also a transcendent epistemological possibility which disputed such limits. Derrida (1996) has spoken of the 'possibility of the impossibility of a state', though in connection with problems of transcendence and infinity. Yet we can recognise here in a finite context, a fairly straightforward manner in which restricted empirical sense of 'impossibility' has clearly a contradictory relation to empirical possibility. The possibility of a new physical state changes the status of 'possibility' by a former state of epistemological transcendence becoming a new property of the physical world because of invention, as with the case of a six-bond carbon.

This sort of context is distinct to the case history that Marion Hobson (1998: 59) reports, when she affirms, concerning Derrida's position on the possibility of impossibility that, 'Such paradoxical couplings seem to render doubtful any idea of a transcendentality which would, so to speak, make stable a space for thinking'. Rather, my aim is to claim that the two contexts are separated by extreme degree, and as such we may see, dispute with Derrida's isolation of a problem for speaking of things outside of language, not a ban in principle of transcendence but, a capacity to replicate a new state of affairs in the empirical realm. Now the example of carbon I have given is extremely modest by cosmological scales; it serves as a precedent, however, for constructing a bridge to facilitate the empirical and/or ontological realisation of Derrida's notion of possibility displacing impossibility as a potential internal function of more exotic states. That is to say, eliminable paradox inheres physical phenomena. In a certain respect, Schmidbaur (Scherbaum *et al.* 1988) has introduced transcendence into the chemical world by his experiment that changed the limits of possibility. Clearly, this is not the same as saying that there was a contradiction in an argument and now we have removed it. In the case of the new carbon bond – chosen because it is somewhat obvious and not a deep puzzle – two hitherto distinct and asymmetric world states occur, together.

We should not confer on this situation too great a workload, nor mystify ourselves with obscure prose about ineliminable mystery and eradicable paradox. The migration of transcendent epistemology (for example, a concept of a six-bond carbon atom) into the empirical world produces an obvious enfolding of a possible world into the actual one. But this type of case serves as a precedent for much more counter-intuitive generalised cases – for example, the origin of the universe is just such an occasion: transcendent epistemology becomes ontology. It is wise to ask for a deferral of attention to this more exotic matter until we have considered other adjacent matters.

The double mirror

Can mirrors be misleading metaphors?

Scientific inference depends on dissimilarities within nature's symmetries. Miller (1985) has developed a thesis about the use of doubles in literature and shown how doubling is regulated by cultural assumptions. Eco (1984) has performed a parallel service with the principle of mirroring using some psychoanalysis of semiotics. Hacking (1995) has shown how doubling and multiple personality mirror some aspects of the societies in which they appear, construed as contagious circuits of self-fulfilling imagination. Bowie (1991) shows how Schopenhauer's (1819) visible world is the objectification of the will, taken by Lacan as the ego's mirror, yet this signifier 'opens up furrows in the real world' (Bowie 1991: 198). I propose that these various disparate conceptual fragments associated with the motif of a mirror can be utilised to expand some of the foregoing remarks, and connected to the notion of a window.

Hobson (1998) studies show how rich and elusive are Derrida's views about mirroring. Mirror is not a closed relation; there is a *mise en abîme* of the subject which is open-ended, with an interactive transaction between the referent and the mode of mirroring, influenced by the relation of transcendence and empirical functions. My notion of a live-metaphor has a kinship with this complex pulsating engagement. In a controlled breaking with the exclusive restriction that metaphor is only a linguistic phenomenon, I am arguing that the ontological counterpart mirrored by live-metaphor has a reflexive relation to such metaphor. Evidently, such a claim is partially counter-intuitive and easily prone to misinterpretation, though this latter tendency is no excuse for avoidance of clear treatment of live-metaphor. Nevertheless, at the side of this difficulty is the identity of the complication itself which, if I am right, shows that language and its empirical relations, suffused by transcendence, progress, regression and instability, is an extraordinarily problematic conception to expose and sustain in representative terms, as Derrida has well shown. But this evasive, recondite complexity does not itself show that language is, in principle, unable to communicate or resolve issues in the external world which are either so transcendent as to (merely) seem to escape empirical housing or involve infinity. In other words, there is a possibility of communicating infinity in finite expression (as we already know from set theory), and thus, given the availability of competent creativity or creation, to express possibility in (apparently) impossible circumstances. In an aside which is not intended to be impish or inappropriate, one may conjecture that some such equation will be the formal kernel for showing that from tragedy universal solutions can emerge. This may itself be related to the rebirth of the unconscious as consciousness.

Hobson (1998) has described Derrida's prose transitivity as akin to a cellular telephone network of differential relations that complements Figure 3.7. This interpretation can be used to construct elements representing features of live-metaphor as a complex mirror-relay process. It can be used to explain an aspect of the gaps within some semantics of scientific language by which 'symbols possess room for manoeuvre' (a characterisation used by John Polkinghorne (1991) to pinpoint an aspect of the fertility of metaphor). This has a parallel with what Frank Kermode has called the excess space within a seminal piece of creative literary usage.[29] Of course, this type of remark on the function of live-metaphor has to be a judgement about the scope in use of an expression.

Now it is obvious that tracts of scientific usage are exempt from this parallel. But there are substantial areas of higher mathematics and physics, particularly in cosmology where these analogies have some application. Scientists sometimes associate a less than fully assessable abstract identity with an abstract symbol in families of equations as a presupposition of how it can be used, though the equations (such as some nonlinear Hamiltonians) cannot be numerically integrated and quantified. Some of the equations devised by Stephen Hawking (Hawking and Turok 1998, for example) have this property.

It is a project beyond the scope of the present research to follow up the detailed application of such concepts to scientific language, although it

Extending scientific languages 143

Figure 3.7 The sculpture 'Untitled' (1974) by Ruth Asawa

Source: Ruth Asawa

Note: The idea of a cellular network system can be used as a model for the 'quotation' of one model in another which extends it, whether it be a cosmology scenario applied to a social science model, or a set of literary allusions extending into a group of sources. Ruth Asawa's 'Untitled' (1974) sculpture alternates between natural forms and abstractions in open-work patterns of wire. It can be construed as a figure for such relations, alluding as it seems to neural and tree networks, and Hobson's (1998) model taken from a cellular telephone network (see p. 142).

seems that with success they could apply in a variety of ways to a number of areas in the sciences. The foregoing conceptions of the mirror can be reinterpreted to enlarge the scope of this idea. Where prediction and observation of the external world fit scientific descriptions in the class exemplified by the above metal example, the successful use of live-metaphor exposes the material patterns in the universe in such a way as to show that its physical structure contains mirroring symmetries and asymmetries partially encapsulated by such descriptions. This is obliquely related to the discussion of the logic of agency propositions, listed in [7] to [9] in Chapter 2 above. These initially connect theological with cosmological examples, though they are of more general functional scope,[30] in which the featured patterns (of otherwise disparate subject matter) are common to one other, at the requisite level of live-metaphor, though qualitatively distinct. We here obviously allow for the fact that the medium of representation is distinct to its referent, yet on relative identity criteria of identification and identity there are mirrored measurable patterns. Within this conjunction, then, is an unstable yet objective state of affairs: mirroring of ontological states which are mirrored by live-metaphor. Effectively, the structure of material phenomena resembles live-metaphor relations if a suitably sensitive and often counter-intuitive analysis is implemented.

Hobson's (1998) use of the term 'syntax' to mark Derrida's use of patterns of arguments is a concern with the relation between the empirical and the transcendental, as well as the paradoxes of infinity. This has some parallel with the foregoing study of the ways live-metaphor relates to ontological states. Hobson (ibid.: 3) reserves the expression 'micrologies' for the longer strings of such arguments in relation to syntax. My own aim is to advance the idea that live-metaphor micrologies inhere in empirically based theories, and that transcendental properties are in effect leaked through these patterns and benefit from the logic of justification which such empirical bases enjoy.

Certainly, wrongly generalised or couched, a theory of mirroring could become a travesty of science. Carefully handled, it can be a fruitful way of representing similarities in nature on which new theorising trades and paraphrases into conceptual and abstract live-metaphors to contribute to the birth of new scientific theories. A by-product of this state of affairs is the situation in which patterns of similarity can be constructed and employed to identify and assess qualitatively distinct phenomena.

'Are these possible world fictions?'

Accordingly, live-metaphor accurately deployed to the empirical world is not only a literary pattern, it has ontological equivalents and analogues. Bell (1987: 194), quoted above, dealing with quantum mechanics in physics, asked in respect of interpreting alternative quantum worlds, 'To what extent are these possible worlds fictions? They are like literary fiction in that they are free inventions of the human mind'. It will be clear by now that I am using Bell's remark as a ludic type of literary approach to insist on a concession from within science – a judgement not always shared by some of Bell's colleagues, distinguished though he was. The quotation amounts to a principle underlying inference and generalisation, not only in Bell's sphere of terrestrial physics but also in cosmology. We can introduce this sort of notion into a philosophy of logic that live-metaphor, as explored here, is a logical truth of relative identity ('$x = y$, with respect to property ψ or a set of such properties'). This sort of approach is an extension of the idea developed above in Chapter 2, in which a subject can be reproduced by an expression going proxy for it by satisfying a criterion of identity suited to the depiction of the subject.

When dealing with motion, Nerlich (1994: 138–39) links understanding to the power to visualise. An astronomical object is, as it were, televising a version of its history. In principle, the realist observer can get behind the editing and see the lawlike relations. The laws are subtle, but there is no malicious circle which prevents us from breaking out into cosmology of the actual universe. We can map counter-intuitive use of physical typology (a physical typology which, at its deeper levels, is itself counter-intuitive). This discovery is possible because the physical universe has phenomena parallel with live-metaphor set deep in its causal and random structure. By investigation of live-metaphor relations in the material structure of the universe, we can, in principle, infer what is not apparent in them.

Nerlich (1994: 138) claims that perceptual immediacy and formal systems seem to be contrary to understanding of motion. Although initially we think of 'live-metaphor' applied to a single expression, the present book extends this not only to propositions and formal languages, but also to concepts as well as to whole domains in sciences. The success of this generalisation has to do with the structure of the universe: that the way things are in the physical world is itself an ontological analogue of linguistic live-metaphor. Part of the explanation for this supposes that the linguistic success of live-metaphor has to do with its having a counterpart in the structure of the physical world.

Nevertheless this notion of 'counterpart' will sometimes only succeed counter-intuitively because live metaphor has complex tricky identities; one should not presuppose for them the success of unification or reductionism in formal or natural languages. This approach adapts the idea of language as a natural object in the world, as well as a mysterious one (cf. Chomsky 2000: 107–33, 159–61).The use of experiment to test theory in science enables scientific thought to mirror both its author and its causal relations to the external world about which the scientist theorises. Where this binary juxtaposition holds true it yields a live-metaphor pathway from mind to world.

If, by science, the human mind can be correlated with the world it represents, then questions present themselves for explanation in the perspective of extending scientific language. Humans can produce conceptual counter-intuitive doubling or micrologies of the aspects of the universe; we examine them so as to derive new inferences which identify or propose new empirical states.

If there is a God, is it possible that something resembling this use of human mental activity to infer fresh external knowledge, might also have a distant analogue in the relation of patterned phenomena in the universe to mirror some transcendent properties traceable to God. If God exists, how would God's mind relate to the universe in terms of live-metaphor? Chapter 2 above displayed a logical live-metaphor framework at the theological level for characterisation of God. Chapter 3 proposes that relevantly similar logical live-metaphor manifests itself in scientific explanation and research progress, not only in astrophysical cosmology, but also in local applied sciences in addition to some pure mathematics. The live-metaphor structures generate mirroring principles which reproduce the likeness of the space times they film, so to speak. These live-metaphor languages sufficiently succeed in depicting the universe that they absorb and encode the realist nature of the universe. Roger Penrose (1994a) using Gödel's theorem cautions us that mathematics is incomplete, and that understanding of it is external to it in some senses. We may construe this as a live-metaphor state in mathematics within cosmology. We have seen that, to a substantial extent, this realism has a deeper side which is counter-intuitive with many forms and patterns, in which, so to speak, transcendent functions invade or emerge out of the deeper levels of the external empirical state of the ways things are.

The cosmological constant

Is the cosmological constant a live-metaphor?

Pursuing such priorities could lead to surprising possibilities – unexpected formulations of familiar problems. For example, could the cosmological constant be a live-metaphor for an obscured double? If Hawking (1984) is right to conjecture that the cosmological constant – the repulsive force against cosmic gravitation – is zero, might the 'zero' value be a live-metaphor of a counter-intuitive positive value in the causal state at, or even prior to, the beginning of the universe? Might not the cosmological constant itself be a complex live-metaphor – a counter-intuitive double of an element in a transcendental thought-experiment whose empirical analogue is the universe?

The cosmological constant 'λ' – Einstein's cosmological term – is usually presented as that expression which Einstein later assumed he had been wrong to introduce into relativity, to complete his theory of a static universe, to stop the universe collapsing back into itself. Soon after Einstein developed his theory, Hubble produced evidence that the universe is expanding, and Einstein dismissed the term – assuming it to be a mistake because the expansion explained why the universe was not collapsing, in the sense that expansion repels collapse. If there is a physical state which the cosmological constant represents, then on current estimates it would have to be an enormously small value, less than $10^{-53} m^{-2}$; and there is no observational evidence that this 'bare' cosmological constant has to be more than zero, though precisely what 'zero' amounts to here is problematic, in a manner obliquely reminiscent of the 'vacuum', which (as shown above) is not nothing in cosmology.

Additionally, some theoretical research seems to have isolated a parallel quantum cosmological constant 'λ q' which characterises quantum vacuum field energy states. Davies (1982) supposes that the bare and quantum cosmological constants have opposed negative and positive values which almost, but not quite, cancel each other out (with a quantum vacuum value

Extending scientific languages 147

of about $10^{-2}m^{-2}$), with the quantum contribution to 'λ' conjectured to approximately 50 orders of magnitude greater than the upper limit imposed by observation of the actual value. This figure depends, for example, on the theory presupposed by Barrow and Tipler (1986: 413) who calculate that the minimum value is greater than the limit be a factor of nearly 65 orders of magnitude. Tipler (1995: 149–51) suggests that the cosmological constant counter-balances an energy state permeating the whole of space – the Higgs field; yet he concedes that this field may be incorrectly formulated, so as to affect the concept of the cosmological constant.

In a number of scenarios, this value of the cosmological constant increases in correspondence to the density of the universe as a trajectory is made back to the initial universal epoch. Martin Rees (1983) stressed the importance of the cosmological constant's role in the Grand Unified Field State temperatures, as with the inflationary scenario, and Rees (1997: 158, 267 respectively) suggests that the multiverse may encompass universes with all possible values of λ, or that the purported final theory may offer a deep reason why the value of λ has to be zero. In the former case, we could interpret λ as a type for a live-metaphor of which the various universes λ values were its tokens.

Rees also highlights the unresolved feature that the universe manifests a fine-tuning precision better than one part in 10^{100}, and notes that this relation is unexplained. Those who want to stress the institutional cultural axis of reason over and against nature have a problem in view of this sort of fining tuning. Although we should acknowledge the types of limitation

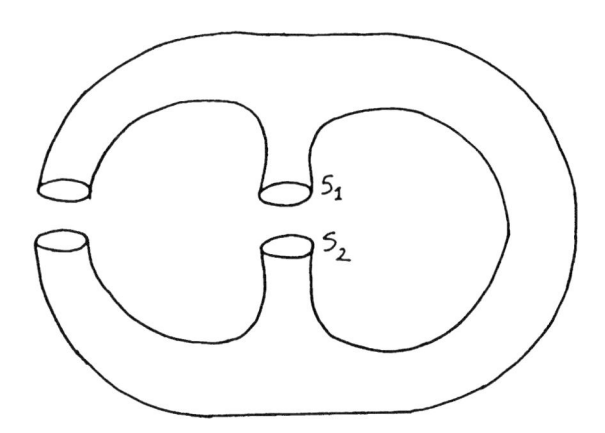

Figure 3.8 A Hawking key for starting the universe

Source: S.W. Hawking

Note: A model of one of the Hawking versions which avoids a complete ontological distinction between the beginning of the universe and its prior origin or form, where universes can be read as cyclic reversions of strings of universes. S_1 and S_2 are respectively end and beginning of universes connectable by a quantum vacuum.

problems under which we labour in developing a general account of reason and causality (such as Hobson 1998, ch. 2 offers), we need to admit the successes of prediction and retrojection which expose such fine tuning to such a degree that it virtually eliminates the probability that our grasp of mathematical reason and its empirical predictive power are accidental or incorrect over large domains of the universe. Certainly this does not entail that our capacity to retrieve the most accurate concept of this concept is correct; but nor can it contribute to the invalid inference that a clear comprehension of the undoubtedly extensive free play of empirical and mathematical signifiers must yield the falsehood of a counter-intuitive correspondence of language to large-scale space times in the universe.

Even so, we should guard against assuming that such a grasp of consequence relations, and their empirical nesting in the universe as we have, do not entail the presupposition that we know what possibility is. As Derrida judged of Foucault,[31] a formulation of a history of the use of reason in relation to its deviant institutional forms is actually only one version or one option among many. This insight is compatible with: (a) the knowledge that such an analysis has identified necessary internal properties (i.e. those that cannot turn out to be false); (b) understanding that the presentation of them will preserve inferential relations, without one having to proceed to the stronger claim that all contents of the concept are true; (c) nor retreating to the weaker position that the internal properties of the concept are composed of falsifying free play of signifiers.

There is an uncertain scope of relations between (a) and (c); yet some of their contingencies can be utilised to construct theories which may result in the identification of true properties. For example, supposedly wormholes in quantum gravity render the cosmological constant zero,[32] but only if a cold universe (as antecedent) is in contact with a warm one (our universe). If other conditions obtain, a warm hole could be a metaphor routing a divine cause. The significance of the fine tuning is heightened by a corollary: in standard cosmological theories, in order for laws to come into existence or start, one has to quantise gravity. So the above close connection between the bare and quantum cosmological constants in their relation to the Unified Field State is a matter of some significance for empirical generalisation over our universe.[33] This asymmetry is an unexpected shift in actual and perceived quantum states, in which observation could be a bewitched mirroring of the referent. Such asymmetry sharply complies with this chapter's description of counter-intuition.

The deeper one goes, the more counter-intuitive the live-metaphor pathway becomes. Penrose (1994b: 400) observes that there is no algorithm for quantum gravity, though creative instinct can in principle furnish a route to estimating the targeted features of the world. Although technically quite distinctive, counter-intuitive states of this problematic last stage in calculation have some similarity to the phenomenon of anamorphism – a notion classically exemplified by the skull in Holbein's painting *The Ambassadors*. The concept of an abstract anamorphism is a fertile idea. Only if the observer surveys the anamorphism from the special correctly interpreting viewpoint does the distorting function not disguise the specification of the referent's identity. This anamorphic visual representation of an asymmetry is a type of live-metaphor of the abstract equivalent: a pure state is characterised as a mixed state, when one is external to the former. This type of pathway itself is parallel with what Hobson (1998: 3, 109, 130–31) has termed a micrology – a series of transitive argument patterns associating empirical and transcendental functions implemented as a syntax in which indeterminacy can obscure anamorphic potential. In the present context this is parallel with the notion of paraphrasing a live-metaphor as an expression which epistemologically interacts with its ontological state.

Is the cosmological constant transcendent?

There are complex micrologies which engage with the live-metaphors in theories surrounding central questions about the identity of λ. Wherever there are informative live-metaphor micrologies, there are underlying asymmetries which can generate consequence relations. Such an asymmetry may obtain for the emergence of the cosmological constant itself: that the magnitude problem converges back on the transcendental origin of the cosmological constant. In a situation in which gravity has to be quantised so that physical laws can be created, with an attended esoteric cosmological constant, it appears that the cosmological constant can be identified as a function which carries over from the causal antecedent which created the universe (for example using a wormhole metaphor as a tunnel exit from this universe).

This would comply with the suggestion, to be developed below, that there is an underlying super-manifold both to the universe's spacetime manifold and to the topology at, or causally prior to, this universe. Talk of this epoch is suffused with unstable, formal, creative anamorphic live-metaphors: the emergence of an *infinite velocity* for *light* in the equations of the early universe brings about the collapse of general relativity into its antecedent *super-physics*, obliquely advertising an extraordinary counter-intuitive phenomenon. Namely, a cosmological constant which switches ontologies through to minus zero *time*, to the first few microseconds, to pass through to the symmetry-breaking conditions in the scenario for the start of the universe. (In these senses, as I argue later, such distinctions of live-metaphor support a concept of transcendent contingent necessity in the universe which can be anamorphically deployed as a trace to properties of God,[34] if interpreted carefully, without involving us in a modal fallacy of inferring necessity from contingency.)

Construed primevally this constant can have a probability of a zero value when it disappears into the first microsecond.[35] Interpreted as a later quantum or large-scale gravitational function, the constant has an inordinately small magnitude which, for example, Dolgov (1983) can only tackle by modifying the expansion scenario itself. As Dolgov (ibid.: 454) affirms: 'At this stage it looks as if fine tuning in the initial value of vacuum energy has been replaced by fine tuning of the parameters of the model itself', though he adverts to the possibility of extenuating symmetry arguments, not yet found, to support a flat spacetime vacuum field to avoid the tuning shift.

There is a circularity in interpretation of the cosmological constant, which becomes a vicious circle if the circle is foreclosed so as to include a course compatible only with the quantum mechanical physics of our universe, where our universe's causal antecedent is thereby excluded. On this approach, we should interpret Hawking and Turok's (1998) view anamorphically. That is to say (if I may summarise my position, which is distributed throughout the present book, towards this type of view), the conception they depict in Figure 3.1 mimics, and/or commits itself to a feature of creation out of nothing, by demanding that the material resources of the universe be the causes of the universe. This is seemingly achieved by moving anamorphically from the equivocal 'vacuum', while yet it is parasitic on a type of scientifically unattested creativity which is suppressed by conflating the initial vacuum state of the very early universe as the source of creation. The logic of agency in Chapter 2 above is that an agency y mediates a consequence of a source x, using a relative identity thesis. If this sort of identity is correct, then it is difficult, in the present context, to see how the commencement of the universe could ever be reducible to its own cause. The same problem applies to the concept of a multiverse with regard to its origin, though obviously some will want to pose its eternal recurrence.

How should we read Kant's science?

To summarise a tendency of the foregoing, one could say that, stripped to a single function, the present book's cosmology takes it that the universe can, in principle, be paraphrased as a complex live-metaphor of its source at various levels. A counter-intuitive extension of this state of affairs is to suggest that within the universe's own structures there are mirroring tautological functions reproducing and reflecting its own shared properties. In a plain sense, this is merely to note that the generalised laws of the universe hold because there are functionally corresponding and calculable empirical states which facilitate stability and lawlike transformation. Digging a bit deeper, we can recognise that this plain situation depends on complex counter-intuitive physical interactions in which symmetry and asymmetry have unexpected relations. Certainly this is true of the universe's later material states which are consequences of the initial state of affairs in the alleged big bang. The universe's start causally coded its future. A possible corollary is the view that the universe, interpreted at the proper set of levels, is a complex live-metaphor of features of the divine source. In this way, material ontology is a live-metaphor of what caused it.

However, if we were to follow Kant's reduction-realisation procedure in which, as Buchdahl (1991: 317–37) observes, such a realisation in its ontology is taken to have a zero-value, cosmological science has an empirical realist position set within a transcendental idealist framework. Buchdahl judges that we should not assign to Kant an objective of deriving deductively the basic laws and concepts of physics, and yet we should estimate highly Kant's metaphysical foundations in the special metaphysics of empirical theoretical science, of general metaphysics. If we leave his problems treating force on one aside, we may identify his various meta-physical scenarios here as live-metaphor's acting as agents from the divine antecedent 'supersensible substratum'. The analogical spaces in cosmology which connive at depicting the cause of the universe – be it to 'nothing' or issues connected to the cosmological constant – on the naked singularity theories, all display a similarity to artistic creativity: they are non-computational or quantifiable in empirical physics.

Counter-intuitive creativity

Is there a new counter-intuitive physics within the current one?

The figure of 'within' in the subsection heading advertises a preference over 'beyond' or, for example, 'under', though either of these other two may be correct. The expression 'within' also tends toward the presupposition that there in the familiar physics we already have are empirical phenomena which are tantamount to answers to unsolved questions at the cosmological level. Sadly, we are not in a position to assess whether or not this figure of our physics, as it were, 'contains' unknown solutions. This is partly to do with the explanatory power of human intelligence to derive new insights from what is known. But the issue also concerns the status of the seemingly simple logical issue of what it is for known premises, in some sense, implicitly to 'contain' an unperceived consequence of them relative to an abstract deductive and presupposition of empirical content.[36] This itself directly connects with the problem: can we only derive from premises what is in them? (And the regress: what does 'in', signify, and so on.) This question, trivially interpreted, attracts the affirmative reply; yet there is something deeper to be tackled in what should be the ensuing interrogation of the identity of this regress.

When we approach deeper areas of cosmology, there is a significant (some physicists of terrestrial phenomena think that there is an alarming degree of) metaphoric extension from empirically measurable mathematical notions, which are suitably guarded by the sort of precisely quantifiable criteria that there are in local physics. On this interpretation there is, therefore, an exponential increase in the instability of the language and its problematic interpretation. First, a caveat against this typical local physics' requirement for precision: the present study documents a number of cases in terrestrial physics where there is a lack of such accuracy, and there are disputes over the interpretation of quantum mechanics. Second, Penrose (1994b: 377) has argued that such cosmological instability betrays the need for a new physics and new scientific worldview. It is worthy of note that this situation is in science, and it is not solely a pejorative prerogative of theology. In fact, the parallels between the two in this perspective are of positive encouragement for establishing a divine cosmology. Penrose maintains that, following Cantor and Gödel, a formal system of axioms and rules must contain propositions which are unprovable (Penrose 1990: 102–48). He suggests that consequently understanding itself is a non-computational function.

Is there a function for musical metaphor in cosmology?

Although we should make a distinction between the theory of a thing and the understanding of it, let us allow some flexibility with respect to their being available in principle (if not at present to us, except in some incomplete but plausible sketch) some form of paraphrase between the understanding of an unfalsifiable scientific empirical theory and an aesthetic theory whose referent is internal to the referent of the scientific theory. For certain cosmological areas of mathematical proof, Penrose (1990: 445) claims that they are reminiscent of the compositional functions and instability in musical transformation. One cannot hope to explore this topic in detail here, but considerations relevant to the present theme as well as priorities developed by other research are appropriate to sketch.[37]

Similarities between cosmology and musical (as well as some literary) aesthetics are obviously limited to certain groups of features. But problems in proposing and assessing such features do not only derive from the issues of unmeasured elements in such aesthetics. The deep issues in theory of the earliest epoch of the universe, with which this book is especially concerned, give rise to the difficulty of judging in what respects treatment of this epoch shares properties with, for example, paradigm experimental laboratory science. The sources of the differences between cosmology and this latter type of science are relevant to the parallels between cosmology and aesthetics. Perhaps some realist scientists believe that there will be no similarities once, if ever, cosmology reaches the state of empirical grounding which terrestrial physics has. This may be the case. Conversely, this, possibly naïve realist stance may be rather like assuming that alchemy will become empirical verified microphysics. In the present state of knowledge, opposed hypotheses should be explored. A presupposition of this present book is that once we enter the areas of the emergence of the empirical universe, we will discover that aesthetics can detect properties of the physical universe which, if correctly characterised, require changes in our understanding of empirical scientific theory. It may be that the use of, and restricting need for, approximation and generalisation over such domains, for which there is no complete causal or empirical exhaustive account, not matters of merely an absent and unobtainable physical theory (narrowly construed), but the functional propriety of some empirical scientific aesthetics as a subset of physical theory.

Such suggestions are unstable, and to some degree foggily based in fully developed systems of assessment; yet so are, for example, the relations of conjectures in monster algebras to experimental physical calculation, though presumably there are links at deep levels, despite limitations in grasp of both subjects. Such comments are not hints in the direction of the possible scientific systematisation of aesthetics. They trade on a presupposition that the more exotic areas of present and future physical cosmology contain signs of a breakdown in some typical modernist scientists' assumption that science is entirely distinct in conceptual identity from aesthetics, particularly in respect of the former's objective descriptive power over the latter's subjective incapability of encompassing physical representation.

Aesthetics is present in the world in ways which Kant's restrictions in the *Critique of Judgement* did not explain. John Milbank's (1997: 19) assessment is pertinent: 'The antinomy between simpleness and compositeness which Kant located "at the margins" of the normal processes of the understanding, in fact runs dialectically throughout our reasonings about the composition of the world.' In cosmology we have the potential to integrate aesthetic and physical functions. Langer's (1967) idea that music shares logical form with some identity could, for example, link up with Kant's view that time, and some related features, have a form of inner sense. Kant's view has been given support by Mellor (1998), especially with regard to causal time and time-order. I have argued in the foregoing that this perspective can be integrated with concepts of features of other dimensions;[38] in this way, properties of music can be explained in terms of live-metaphor relations, suitably qualified, with other dimensions and their contexts.

The function of counter-intuition involves departure from the expected relation, in apparent digression. The present book's attention to live-metaphor as a device by which to characterise language complements some aspects of Susanne Langer's analysis of music as a metaphorical imaging in symbolic virtual form of an ontological domain.[39] Rom Harre's (1993: 208) view of Langer's treatment of 'significance' places her understanding of it in close parallel with Saussure's conception of *valeur*. In this perspective, music expresses knowledge of the emotions in binary senses.

Can literary sensibility be related to cosmology?

Sure, there are many differences between literary usage and cosmological discourse; yet there are connections, even in the terrestrial physics, as Bell (1987: 194), the Nobel physicist quoted above[40] maintained concerning some considerations in quantum mechanics: 'To what extent are these possible worlds fictions? They are like literary fiction in that they are free inventions of the human mind'. Prior to linking up some aesthetics of music with cosmology, it is relevant to detour through how one might provide original literary analysis for development for Bell's perspective applied to cosmology of the early universe

As Malcolm Bowie (1973: 139–41) showed, when applying Langer's view of meaning and rhythm to Michaux's poem 'Iniji', the concept of musical organisation is also particularly appropriate in mapping works of linguistic difficulty, as well as to the few items of propositional sense in 'Iniji', and he suggests that this relation applies (even) more aptly to poetry of a non-discursive kind. Such interplay of qualified disparate considerations form an amalgam which can be used to model some features of cosmological theory in the contexts of which Penrose (1990: 102–48) spoke when maintaining that understanding itself is a noncomputational function. In this context, propositions are expressed, while the propositions which themselves account for the identity of the non-computational function are explicable by use of means other than solely internal formal computation. (This applies, for example, roughly speaking, to those propositions which impart knowledge that 'consequence' is a relation of such and such a property relative to a basis of content ψ, where ψ contains an aesthetic subset and/or certain nonlinear equations which have as yet no numerical expression.) In such a situation, live-metaphors in noncomputational (or aesthetic physically uncomputed) functions assist to explicate the computed explanations.

I have already attempted to make some linkage between live-metaphor and mimesis. This has been complicated and deconstructed by noticing the occurrence of counter-intuition and its impact on some theories of realism. Historically, such a tendency has part of its origin with the *Salon de 1846* in Baudelaire's view of *realisme* in aesthetic correspondence theory,[41] and its general influence, as well as some neglect of its use of the following, in later *modernité* and modernisms. This nineteenth century transformation of perspective, partially initiated by Delacroix, had already shown the realist potential for violation of, or traditional painterly correspondence to, a representation to a referent in the physical world. But this also involved pointing the way to a revolutionary realist preservation of a realist aesthetic. This aesthetic is that of a metaphorised correspondence between aesthetic medium and subject in the physical world, philosophically conceived in terms of the physical world. But this was formulated within a utopian colour harmony, variously further developed – modified by, and for, literary composers such as Baudelaire and Flaubert.

The perspective which can retain correspondence theory realism and counterintuitive visualisation in modernist writing has been somewhat ignored in the use of modernisms to debunk Aristotle's mimesis. I argue that it is possible to combine mimesis with some anti-realist or irrealist conceptions.[42] Aristotle's view that music is an imitation of character is in some ways obscure to us,[43] as is how our listening to performance precisely obtains in this equation. But the picture can be clarified,[44] and extended to some degree, by conceiving of a mimesis of abstract functions and entities.

A precedent for this is a tautological relation between two algebraic propositions – the one is a mimesis or live metaphor of the other, just as arithmetical tautologies map each other. As noted earlier on in the present book.[45] Not dissimilar, but in a quite different linguistic framework Cohen (1993) presents metaphor to be a description of a simulation of the referent *r* matching presuppositions of the referent *r*, with attention to deletion and addition of premises that explain the differences which preserve, as well as contrast with, the two subjects. We can then take these to form a notion of identity relative to a basis assessing similarities and differences as a model for representing some relations between abstract states.

To this suggestion we can now supply an extension to some musical and literary domains. On the basis of such relations, we can articulate the proposal that aesthetic and cosmological properties have counter-intuitive mimetic parallels. Theses parallels are complex and uneven; yet so are many parallels between two or more scientific subjects, and this assertion of similarities can be made allowing for the many differences between cosmology and humanities.

As discussed above,[46] Prendergast's (1986) analysis of mimesis in French modernism argues for a new mimesis whose identity impinges on instability of representation, interfacing successfully with the function of recognition. This complements Terrance Cave's (1988) extensive study sustaining the idea that recognition is composed of unstable elements which perceive a hidden or obscured identity. The Saussurean arbitrariness of sign as a cultural marker for, and yet over and against, nature is an opposition which has been reversed by Derrida. Hobson (1998: 26–29) suggests that the sign is prior to and upstream from this distinction. Indeterminacy is internal to nature, as is our language representing it. Yet, in ways which no doubt contrast with Derrida, I am suggesting that at this juncture we have grounds for accepting in principle that the concept of a bonding of empiricism with transcendence in the physical world can be encapsulated by the semantic interaction of representation and abstraction. We can profit by comparing this to standard accounts of light theory as transcendent explanations because the wave/-corpuscular equations are not, in the required sense, reducible to one consistent account, functional as explanations though they are. Such a situation may well be resolved by future developments. Either way, let us consider that the functional felicity of light theory incorporates transcendence with realist description in abstract terms. This has some analogy with literary representation and Bell's use of it to craft a parallel with possible worlds. (Even if there are no possible worlds, in the technical senses, for example, developed by Lewis (1986), Bell's parallel still fits this pattern of transcendence and abstract functionalism.)

Mathematicians whose work concerns the esoteric epochs of the earliest phase of the universe (see Greene 2000: 366) have fundamental difficulties in developing exact semantically based perceptions of what the formal language's functions are. In such cases they have, so to speak, to construct the key signature in which they are working, so as to devise original solutions and endings. Mathematical cosmologists are not system-free players to compose what they wish, arbitrary, due to the limits of knowledge, though some of their choices have to be. Their job, to uncover the composition and its ontology, is partly a problem of notation and compositional recapitulation which are products not only of astrophysical ignorance and speculation, but a result of the deeply counter-intuitive structure in the universe at recondite levels.

Plainly and crudely expressed from the standpoint of large-scale local physics, if dimensions and scales are so small that Einstein's general relativity and microphysics cannot apply, then there is no matter at such a spacetime. In fact, if this is the case the point cannot consistently be expressed within such physics, since there would be no spacetime for this universe (leaving aside the multiverse, for the moment). This is not only a matter of physics. Proust might have expressed his concern. In his explanation of Wagner's *Tristan* in *La Prisonnière* (V, 178), hinting at the reappearance of a leitmotif from Tristan in the *Ring*'s final act, Proust meditates as a personified Wagner and alludes to what the new era of airflight 'machines' might lead, affirming:

> one of these frankly material vehicles was needed to explore the infinite ... the *Mystère* model – in which nevertheless, however high one flies, one is prevented to some extent from enjoying the silence of space.

Proust is one to elevate the practical artifice, the material, to new heights. But for the narrator, this has a strict finite limit as he enfolds literary creativity into musicality. As Malcolm Bowie (1998: 107–10) argues,[47] here 'There is no such thing as an immaterial art, the narrator proclaims, and the aviation industry provides him with an instructive, up-to-the-minute parable on this theme'. Indeed, it is almost as if Gödel was furnishing him with his calculation, taken as a *reductio ad absurdum*, that one could time-travel if, and only if, one used up all the matter in the universe for fuel to do it – presumably including oneself. We are then left with an apparent paradox: if there is no immaterial art, how is it that the universe came to exist with the trace of art from infinite matter-energy conditions that were not material (in the sense of the physics directly observable to us)? Would not this constitute a counter-example to Proust's finite limit? Eventually, therefore, our backs are against an immaterial wall in the silence of space.[48] We should tune our ears to hear, not the noise of an impossible material engine, but the sounds of infinite music contributing to composing the matter of the universe – or multiverse.

Given the growth of the constructivist and finitist foundations of mathematics since Proust's day (see Marion 1998), we may find that argument committed to the finite backfires if it were to be deployed to exclude the infinite. We cannot generalise beyond finitism to infer that 'what there is' has this intrinsic finitist property. Therefore, finitism should obey its own rubric and keep silence about that of which it cannot speak. But, on the analysis of the present book, since mathematics and equations about the universe are not tautological in identity, finitism, even if it is true of itself, cannot guarantee that it has no consequences to leak out concerning infinity. It may not have a grasp of its own overlap with other domains.

Is there a function for musical metaphor in cosmology? Stage II

For scientists and aesthetes, the criteria of what it is to be the cosmological language accounting for the origin of the universe in physics are, to say the least, unclear. Usually science and aesthetics are taken to be irrelevant to each other in any substantive analysis. In originating cosmology of the universe, they should be partially integrated. Astrophysical cosmology, like most other sciences, trades on generalised policy assumptions which have not themselves, in this exotic domain, been independently explored and subject to empirical confirmation.

A fairly typical case is Hawking and Hayward's (1993) two-dimensional approach to quantum coherence, when four-plus is required. Yet Hawking's overall approach results in an account of pure quantum states, and the dissolution of primordial black holes into the surfaces of a new universe. It may not be impish to hold to the view that this use of high technical precision, to refine what is a fairly obscure empirical state (in terms of observation and number-crunching calculations), contains properties of reason and judgement which have some family resemblance to patterns in the mimesis of music in relation to character. Self-evidently there are vast differences. Taking into account these restrictions and conjectural states in cosmology, it seems appropriate to allow parallels with comparable provisional and formally developed states in other subjects such as music. If the reader is uneasy with this jump, note that it is not a philosopher from outside of cosmological mathematics who has made an apologetic move in aligning these otherwise disparate subjects; it is a distinguished specialist within mathematics (Penrose (1990: 102–48)). This has an analogue in the way, for example, mappings of simulation and inference between subjects can be achieved by projection onto an abstract domain.[49] As Fauconnier (1997: 11–12) shows, such mappings can be extended to treat metonymy to preserve fine-grained partitioning of our mental and epistemological spaces. Such a framework can be lifted, with modification, to musical aesthetics as a live-metaphor for some perception of cosmology.

So, with regard to Aristotle's mimesis of character for music, cannot one permit the technical side of music as a parameter to be associated with, say, the provisional neurophysiology of perception to formalise features of character? Given such a relation, I am arguing, some epistemological patterns in cosmology have some match with Aristotle's musical mimesis; to extend such analysis to expand this type of thesis will have to await another book however. But a direction forward which one could take has its framework in David Mumford (1994) profound mathematical work which shows that Markovian probabilities can be used to structure and facilitate the simulation of perception, visual and auditory. Such a programme could acquire a deductive perspective by transformation into, say, Haack's (1974) treatment of deviant logics, and Smiley's (1995) interpretation of relevance logics. Maybe Mumford's scenario has a structural relation here between style, as a complex of experienced probability relations, and the logic of Hawking's mixed quantum state – mentioned in the foregoing. Here one has a deductive proposal for accounting for the nature of music, on the analogy of Hawking's pure quantum state, integrated with probability.

A reason for the previous remarks is of course the way in which probability has been employed in philosophy of music theory. We need not agree with Meyer's (1956) probability thesis identifying the nature of meaning and emotion in music,[50] whilst appreciating the force of his remarks in a different way from his own conclusion. Budd refines Meyer's thesis by reviewing it as:

> a style is basically a complex system of probability relationships: probabilities as to the occurrence of a sound or group of sounds ... When these probabilities are internalised as learned habits of expectation, the listener is able to experience a work in the style as a complex of felt probabilities.
> (Budd 1985: 162–63)

My own approach is to entertain this perceptual probability as a calculus applying to listener-consciousness, whilst proposing (as above) a deductive live-metaphor framework to represent the relations internal to music. It is with this focus that we could implement Frank Kermode's development (1979, 1986b) of an internal probability hypothesis for literary sensibility, employing the previous subsection as a premise.

Wagner abandons the key signature in Scene 3 of the final act in the *Ring* (see Figure 3.9), as the world he formed decomposes for a counter-intuitive renewal. Hawking has modelled the ending of the universe on the analogy of a black hole, and composed the concept of its time-reverse as a live-metaphor for the beginning of a new universe. Hawking and Turok's (1998) precondition for the start to this universe (see Figure 0.1)[51] is not unlike Wagner's ending of the *Ring*. Rees (1997: 261–63) notes that if stars were formed in a medium of pure hydrogen (and certain processes occur), then the idea of a multiverse with black holes which operate heredity and selection to create new universes could be correct. In all these concepts, the pattern of ending and beginning is central. For all these the property of universal discontinuity involving transformation is fundamental. And for none of these has physics an understanding. Such an unknown comprehension may merely involve an extension of the processes which we now understand. Conversely, many, if not most, of the great discoveries in science have involved fresh concepts which had no linear predictable identity shared with science's past. To neglect the later point commits a quantifier-shift and segmentation fallacy.[52]

Is space a musical silence?

Features of silence in performance could correspond in a live-metaphor way to a region of space, in spacetime, as a functional parallel with a spacetime manifold – the projected ontological bedrock of geometry.[53] Silence and space are elements in creativity. Just as silence in music can be used as a mode to indicate significance, so space is treated as a signifying system of point-functions. One of the paradoxes of cosmology to disturb Euclid is the purported original collapse of space, yet the occurrence of which is tied into the origin of itself and its contents. (Hawking produced a sort of path-integral approach to quantum gravity,[54] but it is uncertain whether or not it would have pleased Euclid.) In a similar way silence is internal to the identity of sound. It is important to consider that such paradoxes or puzzles are constituted by the astrophysics and observations of standard observational cosmology. Consequently, the smoothing out of cosmology into a standard science in parallel with terrestrial physics is not only incomplete, the project collapses because, internal to the identity of cosmology, are currently ineradicable fractures and discontinuities with the presuppositions of terrestrial physics. Even apart from the absence from some cosmology of capacities to observe, predict and repeat experiments, it is not possible that at a future stage all such asymmetries between cosmological and terrestrial sciences can be eliminated.

This has significance for a qualitative parallel between cosmology and

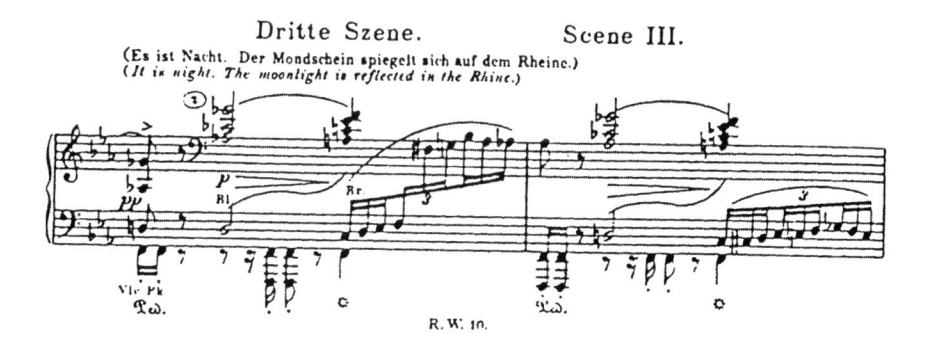

Figure 3.9 A Wagner key for ending the universe

Source: Richard Wagner, *Götterdämmerung*, Final Act, Scene 2

Note: Wagner abandoned the key signature here, a practice which was increasingly to be followed in succeeding generations.

humanities in a counter-intuitive way, which I conjecture will become a more entrenched feature of future sciences, as they dig deeper into the identities of the physical universe, near as well as remote. One can come across a number of scientists who adhere to terrestrial physics, as canonical for hard empirical knowledge claims, who castigate cosmology as a weak(er) science. Although they have some point, it is not uncommon for them to neglect what is at least an equally, and perhaps for the future a more important, implication of cosmology's asymmetry to local physics. It is related to the problem of the ways cosmology is engaged with exotic origins of all physical systems. Terrestrial physics does not have to concern itself with the collapse of spacetime.

The point is that, as a consequence of the origin of the universe being part of cosmology, the qualitative identity of cosmology of the early universe is different from terrestrial physics. Some of the internal properties of such early cosmology are transcendent with respect to the identity of what is physical. And this value of 'transcendent' is a live-metaphor, not having an identical truth-value to the use of 'transcendent' when we speak of the wave-corpuscular equations for light. Although the point is obvious – i.e. in the present state of physics the collapse of spacetime is a violation of demonstrable empirical possibility – a consequence of it is too easily underplayed or underdetermined. That is to say, there is little reason to accept such primordial cosmology as science in the narrow sense of measurable, quantifiable local physics. But it is incorrect to infer from this situation either that the matter of contrast will be resolved by future science, or that such cosmology is 'weak' science. In a sense, the contrast occurs because the cosmology of the earliest phases in the universe tackles empirical states of affairs that are infinitely different in qualitative values from local physics.[55] I submit that this is the nub of why cosmology, more than other sciences, is artistic, in the sense of the origination of a creative pattern. Therefore, even allowing for the exponential advancement of science, cosmology of the early universe is, might one say, more difficult, not weaker, than local physics, irrespective of the proximity of the latter and the distance of the former to laboratory confirmation? The scope of this difference extends further than primordial cosmology because, as subsequent chapters document it, reflecting trends in astrophysical research (cf. Rees 1995), the unique original (supersymmetry) conditions that emerged in the origin of the universe – or its relation to the multiverse – infect and are nested into the early subsequent history of the universe.

Another way we can represent this distinction between the cosmology of the earliest epoch and local physics is to insist on an answer to the question: For a property to be a function in science does it have to have a causal explanation? (Let us leave aside the issue of noncausal quantum mechanics, pertinent though it is.) Even if we represent the universe's initial epoch as a function of probability, we will have to ask what its cause was. The answer will be either that, the universe did not have one, or that its antecedent is a form of causality that is unique (even if, on the latter view, it is composed of quanta allegedly familiar to us). Both answers should produce the reply which will reveal that this cosmology is qualitatively different from terrestrial physics. Causality is of course a function of space as well as time. In a sense, astronomically speaking, radio silence will always be a function of such a time. This was exacerbated originally because, according to standard models, spacetime is said to have collapsed. So, concerning the causality conditions prior to t_1, Wittgenstein's judgement will obtain: whereof an empirical scientist cannot speak, thereof should he remain silent.

Consequently, if the humanities integrate their constructions with the scientists' attempts to gain conjectural knowledge of the origin of the universe, this is not only because empirical science fails to grapple with the absence of observation conditions. Rather, it is because the identity of the subject is not scientifically defined in a restricted manner by the sciences, and changes to an artistic function.

Is there a function for musical metaphor in cosmology? Stage III

So let us presuppose the conclusions drawn in the foregoing section, *Can literary sensibility be related to cosmology?* The expressions implementing conditional probabilities in Mallarmé's *Un coup de dés*, are relevant to isolating an aspect of surprising expansion of sense. This work is almost a poetic paradigm of the counter-intuitive disguised as the self-evident – the use of standard types whose values seem to impart a new typology. Also, as Florence (1986: 42–45) notes, Mallarmé employed Wagnerian vocabulary at times while stretching it into rapid shifts between different levels of (logical) generality. Christopher Wintle states, in relation to Beethoven's piano sonata Opus 10, No. 3:

> The usefulness of formulating empirically-derived principles for music in the harmonic, melodic, formal or whatever sphere is twofold: first (invoking the structuralists' *langue*), to propose models, which through development and variation may generate any number of utterances; second, and reciprocally (the structuralists' *parole*), to show how distinct musical events, within or between pieces, may be interrelated by reference to one or more governing principles, however irreducible the events themselves may seem at first sight.
>
> (Wintle 1985: 147)

Hawking's pure and mixed quantum state thesis is directly connected with conditional probabilities. His style in one version smoothes the singularity that is the big bang into a resolution in which the previous universe is the antecedent value of the underlying function of this universe. In certain respects, this is like the ending of Wagner's *Ring*. The sword motif concerns Wotan's disposition, emerging as a main thematic voice of the *Ring*. The *Ring*'s sword leitmotif is akin to Hawking's use of the cosmological constant. The latter emerges in a fashion in which the path integral method includes all or some range of values of the cosmological constant (Hawking 1984), as with the sword motif for the *Ring*. One chord can evoke a whole tonality in a way which shows that creativity in content, orchestration and harmony constitute the context of musical usage in this work. This involves the sword motif contributing a criterion of thematic identity, parallel with the cosmological function as a chord which self-defines the context. In this way one can strictly speak of a logical conclusion of a piece of music – its resolution, which has a live-metaphor relation to the cosmological constant. The latter is similar to a logical conclusion – the endgame of the universe, concluding in a new beginning.

The cosmological function is a type of universal which encapsulates the values of other universals, as with a leitmotif in music. Lacoue-Labarthe (1994: 38–40) suggests that, in Wagner, music implements *types* which *personify meaning*; and this could apply generally to music, utilising the notion to develop a live-metaphor concept. Introducing the category of live-metaphor to map these relations between cosmology and music, one guards against absolute identification of the two subjects' syntaxes with each other, using a relative identity relation which preserves their own undoubted autonomy at many levels. This project, associating cosmological theory and compositional elements in music, is clearly fraught with problems; but handled sensitively, these are permissible expected difficulties about an unknown highly counter-intuitive set of relations. My aim is to inject aesthetical creativity as ontological features in cosmology.

One such domain backs on to the topic of the relation between the cosmological constant and superstrings. As mentioned in Chapter 4 below, string theory is about vibrational and oscillatory phenomena. It is too much to strike a direct link with the theory of musical sound and string theory, though there is here an acoustic symmetry which is set within the asymmetric properties of music and superstring theory in relation to the cosmological constant's characterisation.

Two further points are of interest. First, the superalgebras on which string theory can draw may be suitable complex formalisms on which to try to model some creative internal relations in music, at a level which is not yet researched but which Penrose (1994a: 377–400) intimates. Second, the tensor calculus which can be developed for supergravity in some cases is relevant here.[56] We have a possible way of gaining access to the link between the cosmological constant and superstring particles, in such a fashion as to expose the way in which the cosmological constant is a live-metaphor of some matter's relation to the point of creation. That is to say, the internal algebraic and geometrical structures of superstrings in relation to the cosmological constant yield deep patterns about original creativity. In this manner, creativity is directly interrelated with the cosmological and other constants. Given the foregoing, this has some parallel with the fashion in which the theory of the leitmotif pertains to its origin and context. Such intricate and subordinate details should not be allowed to suggest a too close alignment between cosmology and music; and using live-metaphor notions one should guard against too strong an identification between the two subjects.

Conversely, there may be a deep discovery-procedure prospect of excavating qualities nested into such empirical and aesthetic relations. Kant's *Critique of Judgement* posits the 'invention' of a rule as a function of genius. Correspondingly, the universe itself has produced relations between differences phenomena that are stunning in their unexpected sharing of qualities. In our explorations we should allow that some forms of surprise have an ontological correlate which our theories mirror.

We might readily rerun the above relations with cosmology and music employing Mozart, particularly as Barth (1986: 48) regarded him. Bowie (1993:103–4) anchors his comparison between the arts, developing a psychoanalytical model. A carefully qualified link of some aesthetic music values with cosmology exposes fresh counter-intuitive possibilities for ontology and epistemology. It is precisely in the marginal and the unstable momentary counter-intuitive states in which cosmology has its origin and generality, amid arrays of other permanent levels of transcendental reality, that the texture of creativity is apprehended. This instability threatens the possibility of adequate analysis, but also it invites contrasting quests and questionings. What is 'beginning' in language and universe? What is 'infinity' in language and universe? To address these issues, we need next to explore notions of cosmological manifolds. Where the foregoing comments to support a highly qualified parallel of some aspects of cosmological theory with compositional theory, this situation would complement the suggestion, made above, that we can view God as a cosmological actor. To do this we add a live-metaphor ascription of composer and conductor to pinpoint an area of creativity in cosmology. This obviously does not require that Wagnerian cosmology be applicable, anymore than Hawking's, though for distinct reasons.

4 The beginning of the matter

Points about manifolds

Can we think of infinity?

How can we truly speak of God? This question presupposes not only that God exists, but also that it is possible for there to be some mode(s) of signification which can carry depiction of God. Such a presupposition is not in itself impossible. The 'thought-experiments' on wormholes concerning, as Thorne states (1994: 493), 'What things do the laws of physics permit an infinitely advanced civilisation to do?' This shows considerable metaphoric as well as anthropomorphised, extension of 'infinity' by cosmologists.

Cantor proved that a formal language can be used to describe infinity in some respects, though the Catholic Church did not respond in a very advanced way to his ideas, as Dauben (1979) explains. One obvious point the church might have noted, however, is that in Cantor's formalism the finite is central. Namely, infinite tableaux are considered to be an infinite series of finite tableaux, as Bostock (1997) develops it. On this view, infinity is the quantitative extension of what we know; but we are not sure that infinity is just the same type of item as what we know. Theory of 'random walks' in pure mathematics (a bridge between algebra, geometry, graph theory, harmonic analysis, potential theory and probability) can take us in the direction of the comprehension of some semantic qualities of infinity: as Woess (2000: 101–23, 283–86) argues, a free product of a graph that can determine singularities leads to proof of a compact boundary involving the set of 'infinite words'.

If this symmetry between finite compact series is the same as infinity, then it might be easier to talk about God. A main problem about attempting to characterise God is that God is entirely Other, not the same as us – a product of negative theology. Contrariwise, if all infinity is more of what we know, then, if God is relevantly associated with such infinity as this, we can in principle readily infer that God is in some respects more than what we know of what we do know. It might be thought that a philosopher would object to this on realist grounds: so how could we verify God? Yet this betrays a naïve realist position; substantive realism is much more subtle than that. In attempting to expound what it is to be a realist logical constant, Christopher Peacocke (1988) argues that a realist is one who allows that a sentence or content can be true though (a subset of which may be) unverifiable by us; certainly, however, there are doubtless many false unverifiable propositions.

Is infinity realistic?

These modest points permit us to have the standpoint that our explanatory capabilities do not in principle fall short of our being able to represent features of infinity and a realist God who is unverifiable. Adjacent to this state of affairs is a group of concepts concerning the presumed beginning of the universe. Infinity conditions seem to have applied to all phenomena which comprise the commencement of this universe, and possibly all others if the Rees (1997) multiverse hypothesis holds true. If Hawking and Turok (1998: 8) are correct, then the multiverse hypothesis gives way to an open universe which is spatially infinite or a closed universe which is finite (and on one interpretation the latter is the only universe). Obviously, since there are different sorts of infinity, it does not follow from whatever the initial infinity conditions were in, say, the big bang, that these are identical to divine transcendent infinities. But given the inter-derivability of mathematical and logic infinities (including transfinite set theory), of which we do have some mastery, together with either their tautological relations and/or live metaphoric relations to other transcendent infinities, it appears that we should be able in principle to use one group of infinities as a thought-bridge to achieve knowledge of other infinities.

If the sort of infinity of which we have some knowledge has a relevant relation to the infinity that is a property of God, if God exists, then we should in principle be able eventually to discover enough about inference of infinities to handle a relevant range of propositions about God. Cantor's less popular contribution to this topic was his view that mathematical infinity is a function of facets of God's mind. It seems presumptuous to adopt this as a mathematical truth, though the mysteries in pure mathematics are not exhausted by an explanation of higher mathematics that is restricted to the construction of mathematical calculus from finite experience.[1]

Was there always infinity?

If God exists, a bedrock block between the universe and God is the structure of finite spacetime. God is said to be infinite, whilst traditionally the universe is finite. But there have been developments in cosmology to enlarge the scope of physical infinity's range of application that either overlaps with traditional notions of God's function or reduces God's functional purview of the material universe, which has its rough counterpart in relations between organic evolution theory and creation at some levels. Deutsch proposes a fresh version of the many-worlds universe in which there is an infinite series of universes with increasing variation.[2] It might be argued that the multiverse option of an infinite group of universes has already undermined a finite beginning to everything physical from other angles. But it does not have to follow from such a scenario that the series always existed, only that it continues, especially if one modifies Hawking and Turok's (1998) thesis where matter-radiation happened at a red shift of 100. So this does not have to be a genuine temporally symmetrical infinity. On this type of interpretation, Deutsch's thesis is a barrier to committing one to the question of: from where did everything come?

Is mystery a feature of our ignorance?

When addressing some issue concerning why the universe displays asymmetries and exploring how this pertains to the notion of an infinite past, Rees (1997: 226–67) explains that some of the universe's current effects are counter-intuitive, choosing the example of gravity (in which certain things accelerate when they might be expected to slow down). He observes that in tracing such states of affairs back to the conjectured ultradense primal beginning, cosmologists are faced with matters that are mysterious. That there are mysterious asymmetries, which question the eternal past regress of the universe, is clear. Some scientists will prefer to assign this asymmetry to a conjectured physical solution that dissolves the mystery; entropy seems to oppose this prospect, though others suggest ways around the difficulty. A response is that since the empirical evidence and proof are not currently available for this dismissal, it could be the case that the proposal is incorrect. There we are faced with a false attempt to derive infinity from finite resources which even when recycled are still finite and entropic – for example, by following possible lines opened up by Hawking and Turok (1998). In this perspective we need an explanation of what the first cause was, despite a willingness to delay it over a regress on a multiverse or many-world universe, which eventually retroject back to a standstill before which there was no prior world. Given the restoration of causality by the universal wavefunction in versions of the many-world thesis, this standstill is an effect for which a universal cause is contingently needed.

Are there foundations to space?

A 'manifold' is the syntax from which geometry or topology is crafted – the bedrock beyond which there is no more fundamental formalism or system of physical relational ontology. The underlying structure of the continuity perceived between space and time is formalised be the concept of manifold, i.e. the bedrock space or surface of the universe and its parts. As Hawking and Ellis (1973) stated: 'a manifold is essentially a space which is locally similar to Euclidean space in that it can be covered by co-ordinate patches'. Hawking points out that the sort of manifold which he is discussing (a Hausdorff space) does not necessarily have to be disjointed. Consider the possibility that there is a universal manifold continuous with this universe and God (in a way which suitably preserves contrasts). In Hawking's interpretation, different co-ordinate systems can exist in the one manifold. As far as we know there is no algorithm for four-dimensional topology equivalence, i.e. no theorem for deciding how all cases of forms deform or blend into other forms.[3] So it is presumptuous to suppose that there is no access point from another *kosmos*; so the co-ordinate systems in God's other 'universe' and this universe, or multiverse, can consistently be different, yet share one underlying counter-intuitive complex manifold.

This brings us to the edges of the fast-moving current development in an exotic branch of pure mathematics concerning manifolds and knot theory, a topic which can only be briefly aired here.[4] Mathematics of manifolds have theorems that imply that new manifolds can be constructed out of prior ones, as Cappell, Ranicki and Rosenberg (2000a: 9–15) explain. This is called surgery theory – largely initiated by Wall (1999). Using a theory about a spherical spaceform problem, a theorem has been devised to link infinite groups with finite quotients using a representation theory (see Stark 2000). A closed finite manifold may be opened up like a book to yield routes to infinite groups, as Winkelnkemper (1998) proves. Now, at least from these standpoints of pure mathematics, we have a complex model for a mathematical rationality that facilitates a connection between finite and infinite domains, with criteria for assessing their borders and mapping the connections between them.

Some people may find this unappealing as a way of assessing talk about routes to God. But for those who allege that there is no logical or scientific support for handling the logic of discourse about a transcendent divinity, because of limits to scientific language, the foregoing is fundamental: they are simply wrong. The higher levels of such pure mathematics are the province of what increasingly physics and astrophysical cosmology takes up as the theoretical basis for modelling the empirical world. Although we may deem these areas speculative, they are mathematics that work, and are an inferentially derived set of theorems that follow from established mathematics, not merely from ungrounded imagination. There are grounds for accepting them as conceptually secure, as are domains of applied mathematics, and some of them are already finding applications in advanced physics. In other words, surgery theory satisfies a number of conditions to be considered formalism that maps empirical possibility, not just speculative probability. I suggest that these developments, though they present major problems of interpretations, can be taken as quantifiable live metaphors to structure a breakthrough in our grasp of spacetimes, and the bedrock manifold of our physical universe, so as to model some conditions for exposing properties of a non-empirical yet ontological infinity. The traditional idea of a mechanistic universe whose theorisation is in principle unable theoretically to move beyond materialism into characterising properties of infinity died with the emergence of such surgery and knot mathematics, as well as empirical concepts of the infinite velocity of light, of energy and matter density, and the like. So what was regarded in Hawking and Ellis's (1973) earlier cosmology as the basic foundation on which spacetime was built – the manifold, now turns out to be only an arbitrary resting-place. Once the knots in it are untied and mathematically mapped, reconstructive surgery can be done to find a route to infinity. Bertrand Russell wanted to reduce mathematics to logic. He got it the wrong way around: logic has to transcend to the level of pure mathematics, aesthetics and cosmology to infinity.

There are also already observational and theoretical conclusions which at least stretch the concept of a fixed manifold to limits which question its empirical limit or basis, and the current versions of its theoretical foundations. The Cavalière *et al.* conception, of black hole remnants that are driven by gravitational power, could be extended and integrated with an eleven-dimensional superstring gravitational coupling in M-theory (cf. Polchinski 1998: 198–99). Cremmer (1982) argues that the supergravity in similar situations has hidden symmetries which indicate a (manifold of) five-dimensional series in its mass parameters; for example, those symmetries which break off unpredictably.

Does space have breakdowns?

Hawking supposes that the breakdown of his manifold formulation would occur if there were a density of 10^{58}gm cm^{-3}. We have no physical or experimental comprehension of what it would be for such a state of affairs to hold – though it is implied by some present theories. Stemming from the research of Edward Witten, and others such as Michael Greene,[5] superstring and M-theory show that spacetime can be torn in 11- (or 11-plus) dimensional supergravity; this amounts to the prospect of a future understanding of how the universe and other spacetimes, as well as (on my interpretation) some other discontinuous domain which has infinity functions could be coupled together through such a tear without physical cataclysm. There is no reason why this could not be used as a metaphor for divine relations. Since such a breakdown of local physics is implied by the astrophysical theories, it eventually follows that this is not a collapse of the manifolds in principle, but solely the manifolds which intuitively account for the universe as it presently seems to manifest itself at empirically observable levels to us. The manifold for this universe cannot be appealed to as *the* fundamental unalterable functional frame, because, in principle for observational cosmology, there is a density at which they collapse. Hence, this universe's manifolds only hold the status of a type of contingent metalanguage for various co-ordinate object-languages, and the situation admits of the possibility that underlying this manifold is a more fundamental transcendental manifold(s) which is not reducible to this universe's manifold.

This backs on to the debate between what philosophers term substantivism and relationism. Do the geometrical points in spacetime theories have referents? Are points ineradicably bits of this physical universe? The foregoing density argument, and related considerations, oppose the notion of spacetime manifolds which are ineradicable. The collapse of classical relativistic spacetime at the projected finite beginning of the universe entails the collapse of the manifold whose frame of reference it is, except otherwise by metaphysical assumption, not only the theoretical cosmology but also the astrophysics of the zero t spacetime commitment for geometric point objects. Yet it should be emphasised that this is *relative to the theory of classical relativity*. Where classical relativity does not hold, neither does the commitment to *this* manifold set. That manifold set is therefore not a universal entailment for all frames of reference. Relativism is the subjectivising view which removes the ontological claim about reference to point-objects in classical relativity. Butterfield's (1984) objects are strong enough for one not to turn to relationism as an alternative; yet even if relationism were true, a manifold more fundamental than the classical relativistic one would be required to account for the above, and following.

The astronomer Bill Saslaw (1985) explains that such theories of point-mass approximations (in sizes from dust grains to galaxies) fail because of catastrophic collisions, tidal gravitational disruption, and angular momentum transfer from the orbit to the spin of an object in the actual universe and its causal description. A root of such failure is inaccurate idealisation. So we are not in a position to guarantee that our formulations of spacetime points are ontologically correct as the definition of manifold spacetime. In other words, we have not isolated the definitive application of this universe's manifold metalanguage.

Can all physical origins be their own physical source?

In view of the foregoing points, the existence of a more fundamental manifold frame of reference behind classical relativity is required if we are to attempt to give the beginning of the universe its own geometry. Tipler (1995) has proposed a programme which illustrates *a* way of doing this. Penrose (1994a) notices that to do this we need a criterion to distinguish between two different spacetime systems, in relation to the energy needed to displace one of the systems.[6] This may or may not be netted by the new physics which he postulates, but we need not agree with Kirkpatrick (1994: 108) that, 'We cannot transcend these models in order to ask intelligibly how the universe came into being in the first place'. Hawking (1993) viably goes outside of these so-called 'models', as does Penrose. No science is in a position to generalise over all models. My model, like theirs, is metaphysical.

This would be a transcendental manifold frame which would be both an empirical contingent necessity (to map the antecedent of this universe's finite beginning and, for example, the associated infinite energy-density and velocity of light). Yet it is a violation of what the constants of the material universe are. The breakdown of spacetime, coincident with the emergence of infinity functions (such as the energy density at the outset of the big bang), is precisely what will serve as a premise of a live metaphor relation between the universe, its cause, and the postulated God who would satisfy the necessary and sufficient conditions seemingly required to originate the first stage from which the multiverse or virtually infinite ensemble of universes could originate. This is partly because the start of the universe is physically at variance with its own future. Just because we track back in time from the later physics to the counter-intuitive earlier cosmological initial physics, this is no ground for assuming the initial physics' origin is explicable in later physics.

The empirical difficulty of starting a universe without a suitably framed concept of God (or an origin transcendent over what it is to be the physics of this universe or a multiverse) should not be underestimated in this context. We have noticed that we do not have algorithms for much cosmology. Given the initial conditions or our views of the origin of the universe, it is relatively easy to envisage, especially if we assume with Hawking and Hartle (1983) and the rather different theory of Hawking and Turok (1998) that the boundary conditions are that the universe has no boundary.

First, matter is finite (GUTs predict that all matter decays, with a half life of 10^{30} years). Second, Penrose (1979) notes that the Hawking postulated end of a previous universe would have an enormous final manifest entropy of per baryon of $\sim 10^{40}$. This is a candidate for being a premise from which nothing emerges, or unusable Hawking radiation, rather than an 'everything' which almost instantly creates using a quantum vacuum. If something did emerge, it would, on entropy grounds, be a permanent quantum cloud of entropy-ruled chaos – not an ordered universe.

Third, if a quantum vacuum is not disposed to behave in accordance with a Hawking scenario, it then conforms to no laws other than Baconian chance (cf. Cohen 1977), and entropy. This would result in an infinite series of random attempted starts to the universe that would produce an even cancellation of all the probabilities that entropy would overcome for it to start. This is especially central because so much of the cosmology of the early universe is a transformation of probability concepts, often with a prediction in observation criteria, an increase in chaos functions, and breakdown of predictability.

Fourth, conversely, if consistency is to be preserved, then Wada's (1986) work on the superspace quantisation of gravity, 'imposes nontrivial constraints for the [universe's] physical state the wavefunction of the universe that severely limits speculation'.[7]

Hawking guardedly imposes a countable basis on his manifold frame; that is to say, there is a countable collection of open sets.[8] This cannot hold as a universally true rule, however, because of Gompf's (1985) unexpected discovery that there is an unaccountable infinity of exotic structures on four-dimensional spacetime universal structure. Stewart (1986) conjectures that Gompf opens the way to showing that inequivalent structures can be on one manifold. Since the foregoing substantivist formalism, which has ontological commitment, attempts to treat points as ineradicable objects, an uncountable infinity of exotic structures on four-dimensional space contravenes substantivism's rigid use of the manifold. This is an extreme form of counter-intuition. To develop this state of affairs further, we should digress to Lewis and Chihara.[9]

David Lewis (1986) has an ontology for the purported plurality of worlds in which he is prepared to actualise subjunctive conditional products of imagination so that they are actual other worlds beyond our ken. Chihara argues against Lewis with an antirealist thesis,[10] targeting Lewis's confusion over what it is to be a set. To get clear on this issue one needs to ensure that we have a distinction between the scope of the actual world and what it is to be the range of possibility internal to the criteria of identity for that world. Depending on how one expounds the nature or identity of the physical world's limits, and the associated success in empirical science's identification of it, one might variously choose realism or anti-realism to connect with a correspondence theory of language for the external world.

If one is disgruntled about science's claims or that its successes are untypical of its overall identity, one might, as a function of modesty and the expectation that the world will hold out more surprises than physical scientific theory can now house, select anti-realism as at least the temporary vehicle for theory. One might tie these considerations to realism, and add the constraint of counter-intuition in its theory of contingency, to restrict generalisation. In these ways, one may argue that many of the formal differences between Lewis (1986) and Chihara (1998) come down to science's internal demeanour towards its referents.

But a significant difference relates to the extent and identity of our actual universe, the prospect of an actual transcendent multiverse and what, if anything, is actual yet outside of the domain of all these. We might be anti-realist, whilst having to concur that there is the possibility of a transcendent counter-intuitive actual states of affairs outside the scope of the correspondence theory supervening over the material universe. Such transcendent states of affairs, partitioned by topologies asymmetric to our local or universe physics, might still be what one could in principle identify as physical (i.e. subject to entropic and/or matter–energy equations characterising causal relation with some form of matter). But they may also be transcendent with respect to not having physical (let us assume, Einsteinian) properties and yet be actual. If this were the case, someone might argue, they would not have a geometry, and so would not exist as a function of what we mean by existence, and we would not be susceptible to the conception of projection by the use of live metaphor to depict topological space presupposed in the present book. Not so. I argue that the Lewis's and Chihara's (and many other) accounts of the universe require integration with exotic researches in pure and applied mathematics in relation to their connections with astrophysics. In the light of these conceptions, it is logically and empirically possible to construct space(s) and physics which do not behave in accordance with even Einsteinian geometries. Therefore, the possibility of a comprehension of space which is counter-intuitively related to our notions of spacetime is consistent with other discoveries. When we wish to model the empirical possibility of transcendent states of affairs (a very different pursuit from producing possible worlds analogous with our own local experience), the collapse of, for example, Einsteinian space does not assess the possibility of the continuation of other discontinuous ones.

For example, counter-intuitive modal realism and its logic can be linked to Gompf's discovery introduced above. Gompf's conception is like Gödel's theorem with a vengeance. Not only do we not have an algorithm to guide us in interpretation of a manifold frame of reference, infinity attends elements of generalisation, thus routing us to a transcendental divine algorithm outside *our* four-dimensional theories and universe. This conjunction could be attached to my own ontological proposal in this book, whereby a counter-intuitive ontology characterises God's domain outside the universe using Lewis's free-range ontologies or Chihara's anti-realism, yet modelled by extension of the foregoing mathematics and cosmology. We might say that Gompf's view of the infinity of exotic structures corresponds in some principal ways to Lewis's plural worlds logic, but we need a transworld identity which Lewis leaves out – which Chihara includes. Chihara (1998: 266) is right to conclude that we need not worry because there is no flock of possible worlds to present us with their problems, so we cannot look into them. But the prospect of there being another counter-intuitive multiverse discontinuous with our own universe, and of a transcendent domain outside of spacetime which is actual, does follow from the complex conjunction of cosmology, mathematics, creativity and logic.

In this situation, we have an explanatory basis for representing how a transcendental manifold might underlie all the worlds (which I take to be universes), yet each universe has a different spacetime from others. We have seen here that the way cosmology counter-intuitively discards some qualifiers and extends scope metaphorically is more than reminiscent of religious metaphor. Clearly, theologically little effort is required to sketch a transcendental universe which satisfies the conditions in that habitation of eternity where God is said to dwell. This would supply a formalism to infer that theistic reality or presence can be a hidden co-ordinate system of this universe and yet is continuous with another super-universe occupying a separate spacetime with a distinct transcendental superphysics (as to be explained in the next chapter).

Language about beginning

If there are infinite possibilities, how can we infer one?

An upshot of the foregoing is that whilst standard versions of the big bang require that the referent of cosmology – the universe – collapses at the beginning, the languages of what it is to be cosmology do not. Some versions of object-languages in observational cosmology do; but in principle, its languages do not. So the manifold frame of reference of this universe is not universally stipulative for what it is to be a manifold, nor all universes or the multiverse. For example, if superstring (M-theory) is going in the right direction, we may have to accept that the currently assumed manifold in cosmology emerged from a function that is not a manifold (see Butterfield and Isham (1998: 132)). Consequently it appears that 'manifold' is a live metaphor of what it represents. So, 'manifold' and pertinent conceptual metaphors should not be construed as a literal account of its referent. While 'manifold' satisfies a spacetime criterion of identity, it is not itself that criterion.

With Gompf's (1985) discovery that there is an uncountable number of exotic structures in four-dimensional spacetime (and in view of the provisional nature of observational cosmology), live metaphors may abound unnoticed, or be only partially exposed. Only the weak observational support is available in cosmology of the early universe, with strong observational confirmation and experiment in applied sciences. Many of those exotic structures mirror one another, obscuring, reifying or twisting important, yet small, differences evident only at the deep structure level. The likelihood of elements from distinct exotic structures being unwittingly merged with each other, hidden in the deep structure of the manifolds, highlights the probability of metaphoric expressions incorrectly interpreted as literal or transparently veridical functions.

For example, in various contexts we could explore alteration of time values, or remove the time value and insert other dimensionless constants. The hot big bang model of the universe's beginning is the appearance of the universe's mass at a point t_1 in history, with an expansion of all length scales to a radius at time t_2 much greater than that at t_1. But imagine that we remove the time function, and postulate that the resultant enlarged radius and the matter instantaneously appeared at t_1. You will recall from the discussion in Chapter 3 that, for example, the Hawking and Hartle (1983) quantum gravity model for creation has no functional dependence on time. So, on this view, time could be reordered in the required metaphoric way to produce instantaneous creation. I do not of course claim that this reification is true, but merely cite it as an illustration, though some other metaphorisation may be true.

Does the multiverse always use big bangs?

If this sort of creation scenario were right, then the hot big bang model would be a somewhat misleading live metaphor of the historical event (in which the temporal element would be one of the metaphoric factors). In fact, here a candidate for being a miracle or a creation would have been incorrectly decomposed into a 'natural' process. If the big bang scenario is correct, and most cosmologists give strong assent to it, its current form may only have a superficial resemblance to the actual historical start of the universe. The hot big bang model may be so unrefined as to be a mimetic cosmetic which could obscure small tuning errors that result in substantive changes. As noticed above, Rees (1995, 1997) suggests that the big bang, on current assessment and support, has about a one-in-ten chance of being accurate as a contender for being the start of our universe. Therefore, if the multiverse scenario were to be correct, it does not follow on present assessment that it is has to be probable that other proposed universes in the multiverse scenario commenced with the big bang origin. On the one hand, if they did, then we can load the problems we assign to the possibility of this universe beginning on its own to other universes in such a symmetrically originated series.

On the other hand, one can argue that at least these problems have to be loaded on to a virtually infinite series of universes with origins asymmetric to our own. Merely one cluster of reasons for this is that since, in a scientific framework in which empirical criteria of theory-construction have to be derived from the conjunction of observation and theory available (even if in other domains), the notion of formulating origins for other universes with origins other than our own has less of an empirical basis than our own. In other words, such theories would be a pluralist metaphysics. Personally, I find such a link, which fixes metaphysics internal to scientific theorisation and empirical grounding, attractive. But for scientists – often those who limit their experiences to laboratories – who tend, often outside the hearing of their astrophysical colleagues, to castigate the looser or less accurate proof-criteria in cosmology as not really empirical science, the idea of formulating notions of origins asymmetric to our own universe's for the multiverse has little credibility. Hawking and Turok (1998) not only question the veracity of the multiverse model, they offer ways of posing the prospect that there could be regions of spacetime that manifest different laws from those of our region of the universe. If they are incorrect to exclude Linde's multiverse idea, their idea of the *a priori* probability of an infinite number of galaxies to the universe (though they regard the implementation of this option as a confused use of their probabilities), leads to the possibility of a prior cause to the universe (even if it were physical, not divine). This reflects a type of puzzling physical infinity situation of which we have almost no way of representing it as a singular quantified physical representation.

Is cosmology poststructuralist?

The point of this question is not to make the tedious move of fitting contemporary cosmology into a fashion. Poststructuralism may be a novelty, yet it may also have arisen at a time because of, and to mirror, puzzling pluralism. This is not to suggest that pluralism is itself true, but that it reflects a stage in conscious awareness of complexity as a deviation from either Enlightenment certainty or modernist nihilism. For example, my use of 'our universe' is intended solely as a convenient means of indexing the present universe. But it could be read as a function of astrophysical anthropology. For some scientists this 'our' could be an autobiographical manifesto for the universe. But for others, such as Rees, its presupposition is a careful estimation of our need for modesty:

> But what we call '*our*' universe may be just one domain, or one phase, of an eternally reproducing cycle of different 'universes', only some ending up (like our own) as propitious locations for complex astrophysical evolution. This scenario, setting out our entire observational universe in a magnificent ensemble, is certainly on the 'way out' fringe of speculation.
>
> (Rees 1995: 118)

(I have suggested that 'eternally' can be interpreted as virtual and not actual infinity.) In this perspective if 'universes' are really subsets of the universe, i.e. variable ontological manifestations of a universal physics of which physicists and astrophysicists have a basic mastery, then an approach which takes from this universe's laws an argument that the proposed initial conditions of the universe are not capable of self-origination is powerful. It can cope with being paraphrased into different versions that allow for the various manifestations of an astrophysical ontology in the multiverse.

It could be that astrophysics has simply exposed that the multiverse scenario is more perplexing and less susceptible to post-Enlightenment modernist scientific presuppositions which are housed in modernist terrestrial and standard astronomical sciences than we have hitherto conceived. In this context one can imagine the cosmologist's retort that the universe is a laboratory so much larger than local experiments that it offers comparable accuracy to local experimental science, given the difference of scale and problems. Beyond such argument there is an overlap between physics and the astrophysics of the early universe, and there is a beneficial exchange of insight and results between the two classes of scientists.

Nevertheless, this process of interaction rests on precision in detail in microphysics and its relevance for the empirical conditions with exotic large-scale phenomena such as primordial blockhouse. Contemporary scientific understanding of some of these areas is cloudy. Since exotic foundations are counter-intuitive, such obscuration is not self-evidently resolvable, and it could deceptively merge or superimpose itself on evaluative description in hypotheses. As the distinguished astronomer Joseph Silk (1986: 505) said: 'In many respects the big bang is to modern cosmology what mythology was to the ancients'; he adds that the big bang hypothesis may turn out to be wrong.

Because of the breakdown of classical relativity, as well as the size of the universe with its outer horizons observable, we cannot content ourselves with the illusion that cosmology can become precise in the sense of local applied science. Consequently, cosmology will not resolve theology's problems. Cosmology has experimentally ruled itself forever incomplete and unable to serve up the full requisite account of the antecedents of the universe. Even so, this circumstance is not contrary to the thesis that some theology or philosophy is the (qualitatively different) content missing from cosmology, which would enable cosmology to complete its foundations. Ancient mythology tried to achieve insights which could only come with other subjects and ways of thinking. Comparable, the hot big bang scenario and the manifold of classical relativity would need true metaphysics to specify the identity of divine cosmological functions beyond the scope of experimental science. Consequently, unexpectedly where cosmology is accurate, some of the subject matter of cosmology is implicitly transcendent in its use of scientific live metaphors. I argue that the foregoing use of cosmology implies elements of an explicit divine cosmology if astrophysical metaphorisation is understood. The idea that God should be postulated as the singularity for the cause of the universe is no doubt naïve. Yet it would be imperious to dismiss a refined replacement for it: the projected superstring (M-theory) and manifold foundations for the universe, or multiverse, regress to a physics of qualitative infinity that is not reducible to self-caused physicalism. And, this leads to the consequence that a particular concept of God is entailed in a complete generalised description of the origins of what there is and the way things are. An implication of this scenario is that the rules of understanding truth change but do not break down for truth.

Observation and infinity

Is the beginning of the multiverse unscientific?

Acceptance of the variety of competing hot big bang models does not render the project describing the point of creation redundant nor contrary, in principle. The limitations under which cosmology labours are severe, however, despite some spectacular successes. Yet on many interpretations, the relativistic language of the early universe breaks down as it approaches zero time t_0. This descriptive collapse is a qualitative dislocation of language from ontology theory. The relativistic theory cannot be *used to 'predict'* (i.e. *retroject*) *what cause created* the singularity. In this sense, general relativity cannot mechanically predict what caused its physical realisation. In this respect, general relativity is incomplete, as Hawking (1979: 746) observed. (We will look at quantum gravity below.)

A nub of the above difficulty is that various senses of infinity loom up in the equations which are aimed at the description of the singularity. This difficulty is entrenched as a physically actual problem because the results of observational cosmology currently confirm that there is a finite age to the universe, and its relativity-violating origin, but in the perspective of infinite antecedents as its cause. The electromagnetic 'blackbody' radiation at 2.7 K has an energy density 5×10^{-13} erg cm^{-3} in the microwave region (cf. Longair 1994a: 1–8) to support only equations that terminate in a past *singularity* or big bang which has an infinite density at t_0 regarding matter (see below). Whether or not the 'infinity' pertains to the physically and mathematically uncountable, *or* limitless number, is an issue for further scrutiny. This need not present problems for the consistency of the, as yet unknown, theorems which might account for the situation prior to t_0. Hawking and Turok (1998) have exemplified, in a controversial scenario, an open inflation model of the universe without false vacua in which the end of the universe has a spatially infinite state. This would be a sort of entropic live metaphor reverse-state to the beginning's infinite energy density state of affairs. On a number of interpretations, this would block the idea of a multiverse, though their proposals are speculative. But as with a series of other alternatives, one upshot of such problems seems to be that the identity of the state at the first instant of the universe, and certainly what preceded it, is almost entirely exotic to such an extent that it does not comply with criteria of being material, when experimental and observational sciences are the suppliers of criteria of assessment. It would be too much to see in this a direct connection to a transcendent power of the sort ascribed to the cause of the universe by theists. But it is state of affairs which could furnish a step that has to go in that direction.

Drawing on suggestions in the previous section, it may be that aesthetical elements exposing physical realist creative processes are required to complete our notions of 'physical law' – not merely to characterise observable beauty, but to encapsulate functional elements. For example, Thorne (1994: 525–25) depicts future gravitational wave detectors as mapping black holes and vibrating spacetimes, terming them 'symphonies'. Obviously, such metaphor is intended as metaphor; yet vibration is an internal function of such physics and of aesthetics, diverse though the respective notions are. Although gravity waves are not sound waves, Thorne (ibid.: 524) speaks of the potential super-computer simulation of these phenomena, and we can thus predict mapping tautologies between the two domains of resonance. The point of this is that Sibley (1993) argues some continuity between music and other sounds and signifiers.

178 *All in God's space–time?*

Is it worth using scientific metaphor to depict God?

Primordial black holes have been used by Hawking (1990b) as models for the end of the universe, and also as the switch-point to generate a new universe (1993). He engaged the Riessner–Nördstrom solution, to describe an energetically charged black hole, and then effectively employed this as a geometric model to speak about spacetime and how another disconnected universe could relate to the world-line of our own universe. In Figure 4.1, Hawking, with his usual sense of parody, has depicted this situation. The diamond-shaped parts stand for flat regions of spacetime.

Hawking suggests that in principle it would be possible for someone or

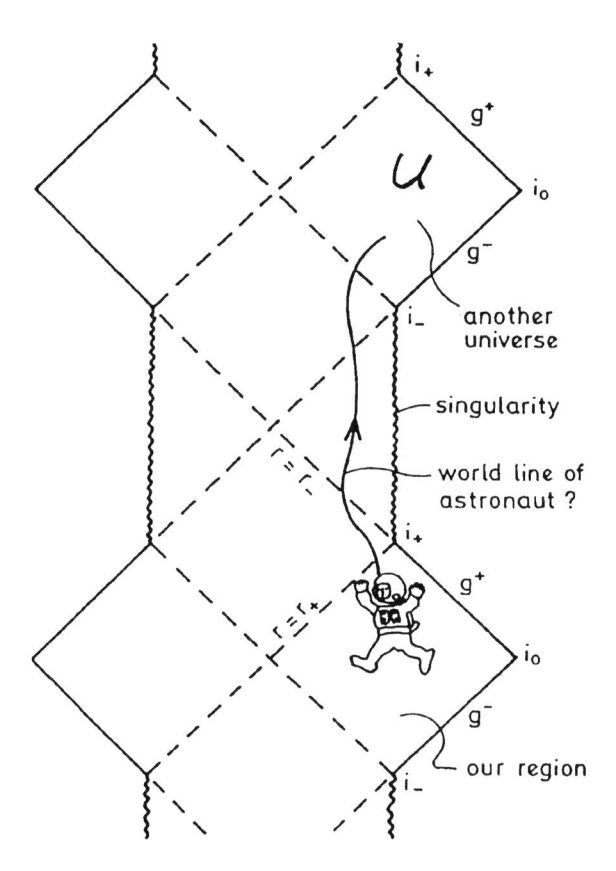

Figure 4.1   Hawking's transcendental astronaut

Source: Hawking (1990c: 454)

Note: This presents Hawking's outline of the Reissner–Nordstrom solution with a discontinuous universe to which an impish transcendental astronaut has access. It appears from the conditions which the astronaut would have to satisfy that this astronaut would be a misnomer for 'God' or his spirit. Therefore, possibly the diamond-shaped space marked 'U' would be all in God's spacetime.

something to fall through the event horizon into the black hole, then pass through a passage and emerge into another region of spacetime. But the conditions for this happening are so delicate that they could trigger off a singularity or a new creation, though classical general relativity has had an *ad hoc* no-go theorem added which arbitrarily blocks this possibility. If general relativity were to collapse, and if the quantum theory of gravity were brought in, this type of objection would not stand. A wormhole is a tunnel from one spacetime or universe into another which on Hawking's, as well as other, models is a bridge between two universes or discontinuous regions of spacetime. There are differing versions of how a wormhole in a singularity or black hole to time-travel or transfer into another universe.[11] The quantum state of the previously mentioned black hole would be formed by particles from the collapsed state of matter, and anti-particles would be evaporated through the wormhole, though there are many variations on this wormhole theme. (Hawking (1990c) argues that two linked black holes can cause a wormhole.)

This collection of ideas, involving the Riessner–Nördstrom solution, black hole, and wormhole, can be used as live metaphors to explore some possibilities concerning what happens when we discuss the scope of the universe and aspects of its relation to transcendence and infinity. If our universe is the only universe in existence (during its astronomical history), and if wormholes are a function for transfer out of, or into, the universe – also, if we assume God can be referred to in a place – then a wormhole can be *a* rough metaphor for a feature of God's relation to the world, and a live metaphor for revelation. This is not to impose a qualitative parallel on what would be God's relation to the universe, however. A reason for suggesting the parallel is to illustrate how a religious feature that sceptics regard as conceptually 'soft' non-science, such as revelation, is in fact susceptible of 'hard' scientific representation, because cosmology itself is having to resort to conceptual functions that are transcendent. That is to say, Hawking's and others' cosmologies are contrary to local physics, and yet are science. We cannot observe infinity directly, so we have to approach aspects associated with it indirectly, using live metaphors. We can attempt to set these distinctions in a framework involving mathematical infinity at the point where general relativity collapses. Various senses of 'infinity' could have transitive live metaphor relations to one another. The formulation of laws is a vexed affair. In mathematical logic, however, 'laws' can be admitted as descriptions of infinite series.[12] The technical aspects of this are far outside the scope of the present discussion, yet some conclusions can be employed – for example, from Quine's (1974: 172–76) research. In this context, an infinite class of truth functional conjunctions (series of propositions in binary relations) is possible. That is to say, roughly, truth can be expressed if there is in principle a series of infinite sentences.[13] We cannot of course handle discussion in terms of an infinite number of sentences, so logicians express the above in terms of a class of schemata. This class of schemata is possible and consistent if each of its finite conjunctions is.

Clearly, however, apart from the quantitative extensions towards infinity, there are the qualitative differences which transcend the bounds of the universe's matter–energy. Some of these 'infinite' qualitative functions can be handled within the framework of refined Einstein field equations (Hawking and Ellis 1973: 117).[14] Hawking notices that (in the foregoing concept of his singularity associated with black holes) the singularity is irremovable and timelike. But theoretically it can be reached by a future directed timelike curve which crosses the singularity. Hawking raises the possibility (Hawking and Ellis 1973: 158–9), discussed above, that this could infer a travel route from one universe to another by passing through a charged 'wormhole'. Thorne (1994) reviews research on whether or not wormholes permit time-travel; he disagrees with Hawking's view that chronology is fixed to eliminate such travel. If our universe and another super universe (the latter where God's 'dwelling' or domain of eternity is) were discontinuously contiguous, then this wormhole could indicate the interface of transfer from one universe to the other universe, or 'absolute mindscape' as Rucker (1982) terms it. A particle, or any other entity such as an immortal person, crossing this singularity in a given situation in the Reissner–Nördstrom solution (Hawking and Ellis 1973: 161) would display an infinite redshift to certain ideal observers. Evidently this would indicate a form of light emission such as that which no observer of finite function could approach, to disrupt lawlike uniformity, not unlike the concept of one 'who lives in light unapproachable'.

Observation and generality

Is the multiverse all that there is?

This sort of infinity and its being derivable from finite elements, provoke the question of how 'what there is' relates to the scope of 'the universe'. Is the synonymy in 'what there is' absolutely equal to 'the universe' – in the sense of absolute identity? Or, is the equation a weaker partial overlap of sense (i.e. theoretical linguistic hyponymy)? Let us use the term 'universe' to include the concept of the multiverse (a virtually infinite ensemble of universes, as with Rees 1997). This way of posing the issue hypostatises the problem of generality: namely, it reduces disparate elements to one identity. For example, a strong claim about:

(a) Knowledge of the universe cannot solely dismantle, in the required sense, into:
(b) Knowing p about some feature of some part of the universe.

But (a) might be transformed into:

(c) Knowing p about some feature of all the universe.

Frege's view, as deployed by Evans (1985), indicates how, on one approach, this relates to time: 'The false appearance that a thought can be true at one time and false at another arises from an incomplete expression. A complete proposition or expression of a thought must also contain the time datum' (as we shall see below). Temporal ignorance entails incomplete grasp of truths. A problem is to know to what extent this partial picture does not anticipate generalisation beyond observation or within incompletely interpreted known observations and times.

All the universe has not been observed, and high redshifts carry parts of it forever beyond our vision. If one follows a standard view, astronomers have observed as far back as roughly well over two-thirds through the universe's history (Rees 2000).[15]

So there is no instance of one's being able to fill p with a (c) category proposition on the basis of observational support for it. This empirically impaired generality restricts the formulation of criteria of identity in, and for criteria of application to, the universe. (This remark is made in the perspective of and presupposes propositions [7] to [10] contained in Chapter 3.) We cannot formally name the universe (i.e. treat 'Universe' as a logical proper name) or name the multiverse, or presuppose for them (Russellian) definite descriptions or the like, because we have no relevantly extensive criteria for universal generalisation or typicality. Certainly we have approximations; but we are still unclear about crucial domains and boundaries. This aspect also blends with uncertainty about the distinctions between an actual and a possible universe, or of two actual asymmetrical universes.

In turn, this perplexity centres on the scope of the universe, and the initial conditions which are assumed to obtain before and after the first microsecond of this big bang. General relativity, we noted above, breaks or broke down at this timescale.[16] So theoretical calculations imply (in conformity with some observational cosmology) that physical laws change, and are the product of states of affairs for which this universe's laws do not hold true. Consequently, the cause of the universe is actual, yet not 'material' (in the physics of Newtonian and relativistic senses of the term), if we adopt material laws as currently formulated in quantum physics, and if we admit their inapplicability, or collapse, in a cosmological singularity. This also pertains to multiverse singularities, and thus raises questions about the transition through each universe throughout a multiverse series, if we admit randomness and entropy of the required level – i.e. as it obtains for our universe. But since chaos is the interface of, and fulcrum for, this universe and its antecedent cause, the rules or patterns depicting our universe metaphorically calibrate, by live metaphor, the relevant causal aspects of its origin (we return below to Hawking's view of this.)

Is the multiverse not its own womb?

Moreover, therefore, the cause of our universe is accordingly ontologically prior to, and qualitatively higher than, the universe since this purported cause created the super-symmetry and infinity conditions causing the universe. It is a possible starting point for a cosmological proof of God's existence that some of the transcendental empirical properties, treated as a complex live metaphor of the universe's cause, can be inferred from the abnormal cosmology of the first few microseconds of this universe. This would be a sort of theological bootstrap theorem. If God exists, non-tautological evidence of God could be, in principle, derived from the identification of the collapse of general relativity (and it precursor states) into infinite magnitudes, without an inference fallacy. This type of transformation of the cosmological proof demolishes, for example, Messer's (1993: 46) type of objection that 'It misconstrues God as ... an all-powerful human being might be'. We might play him at his own game: there is an equivocation over the scope of 'human being' here. If one were to have power sufficient to withstand a cosmic wormhole, a singularity or an infinite density, one would not be a human being jacked up by infinite power. So we have a fallacious equivocation: it is not possible that there might be an all-powerful human being who is not God. Consequently, it at least starts a possibly genuine argument to use 'infinity' in cosmology as a live metaphor basis for estimating the conditions for being a creative power that is immaterial.

It is also an incorrect conjecture, of Messer, to claim that Hume showed how it is impossible to infer God from the world at all. Popper (1972), at least many agree, falsified Hume's attendant induction theory and removed probability as a basis for the sort of objection Messer all too easily assumes. We should, however, be cautious so as not to confuse Hume's careful scepticism with some logical positivists' misrepresentation of him as their champion, as Craig (1987: 129–30) demonstrates.

The point of the sort of cosmological arguments that are being advocated in the present book embraces the conception of an asymmetry between God and humans. It does not presume a sort of analogy between these two subjects that Hume was attacking. The fragments of anthropomorphism presupposed in the book's scenarios pose an infinite difference between God and humans in energetic and qualitative terms. Infinity is a function of this difference, even if it has its physical basis in this universe or the multiverse. Human beings do not have any infinite power nor capacity, and the physicists' uses of 'infinity' as applied to the very earliest phase of the university, conjecture though it may be, is still a conception of scope for which there is no human analogy nor actual capacity. So no analogy here. Nor can it be properly objected that the act of posing a concept of infinity for the universe is itself solely reducible to a function of human imagination, unless, of course, a large part of astrophysical cosmology *and* experimental microphysics are false. If they are false, then one's atheist interlocutor has no basis for relying on scientific induction in any case, so he had better reconstruct his own basis again. But in more refined philosophy of science, Cartwright

(1989) has developed the analysis of 'capacities' in relation to causality and probability which displaces much of Humean induction, and replaces it with a stronger realist version of physical laws. If one were to apply this to the astrophysical cosmology of the earliest universe, we would need a counter-intuitive realist account of the collapse of capacities, whilst developing an explanation of the empirical conditions prior to such a singularity of which it was an effect. If relativistic quantum physics could or did not operate at such levels, we have no grounds for banning causality. The universe would thus be a consequence of the causal antecedent.[17]

Imagine if this situation were reified as a semantic relation, etc., in divine command theory. 'Meaning' is, physically, a dimensionless set of expressions (except when written – even then arbitrarily related as significance to medium of expression). But implementation of its contents produces a situation in which an abstract state-meaning has a physical consequence. It is ironic that semantic expressions in written form are in two dimensions, customarily, and much of the topology of the singularity and quantum gravity is in two dimensions.[18] It may indicate some ideal natural base from which to couch the focus of a theory which in principle can have 26 dimensions, or 10 or more; or it may merely betray the situation that cosmologists are as limited as were physicists prior to the discovery of microphysics. Since supergravity and supersymmetry present unpredicted and unpredictable states and breakdowns of themselves and ordinary space-time which have no empirical proof, use of transcendent language is not unscientific.[19]

How counter-intuitive is the future of original cosmology?

In this respect Addinall (1991: 277) may be too generous in positioning Hawking as an empiricist when contrasting him with Genesis – non-scientific and poetic though Genesis 1 obviously is. Addinall (ibid.: 274–79) has drawn attention to Hawking's recognition of a Kantian antinomy concerning the beginning of the universe, though Hawking, he comments, wrongly assumes Kant claimed that time had no commencement. Addinall notes Kant's general sympathy for analogical use of creation in Genesis. Perhaps a general upshot of such reflection should be expressed in an ironising mood: what warrant do astrophysicists have for ascribing any experimental or observational physics as a model or criterion for what it would have been to be the beginning of the multiverse? Is it not the case that, quite outside any transcendent inclination, we have so little grounds for supposing that we know that any science we have is typical of this origin – other than a non-empirically tested instinct for our present science – that poetry, despite its failure to present any formal theoretical insights, might be in at least the same ball park of relevance for informing us of where the transcendentally receding goalposts might be?

This situation concurs in a pertinent way with the singularity theorem of

Hawking and Penrose (1970). At one level of theorising, if general relativity is correct, then the universe must have begun at and as a singularity – a creation. The recurrent stress here on a finite beginning follows the general state of observational and astrophysical debate (e.g. Rees 1983), and associates with other cosmologists rather than Hawking's views about cyclic universes. Hawking was later to diverge fundamentally from Penrose's approach to cosmology, and Penrose envisages a new physics as the only answer to current problems.

One feature which is a consequence of the states of affairs discussed above is that general relativity might have, or has only, a finite range of applicability.[20] The Hawking and Penrose (1970) theorem above, with its antecedents, appears to require that the physical laws embracing spacetime geometry are self-limiting (cf. Penrose 1979: 581).

This circumstance might unpack into distinct possibilities, of which two are pertinent here. First, creation was produced by some situation analogous with current abnormal phenomena in the universe. For example, a collapsed star such as a black hole, purportedly illustrated by the black hole proposed in regard to Cygnus x-1 (but with the sense of time reversed, so that there is a white hole which explodes into a cloud of matter) could be used to develop a model for the initial singularity.

Zel'dovich and Polnarev (1974) proposed that this explosion would be almost instantaneous. Instantaneous creation is, of course, a defining feature of miracle. Hawking (1976) suggests that it would involve a longer process, albeit in which universals are created – another miracle component. On both accounts, particle creation is involved. There are a number of problems associated with these interpretations and the scenario, which Penrose (1979) has discussed, however. (Hawking and Penrose, who in earlier years collaborated, now firmly disagree about both the need for new physics and the structure of the early universe.)

Penrose offers a second way of treating the singularity. He observes that the universe displays statistical asymmetry. His point is that such things as entropy (high later, low initially) and time exhibit unevenness – if the start and the present times of the universe are contrasted. Penrose (1994a) claims that there is another, asymmetric, physics – an unexpected deeper physics of the universe. All these approaches support Keith Ward's (1994: 291) view: 'If one sees the universe, in the light of modern science ... one need no longer see miracles as arbitrary interruptions into a closed mechanical system'. Counter-intuitive abnormalities in the universe's deep structure mirror and metaphorise its origins in transcendental causes. The large class of laws which account for the normal relativistic structure and behaviour of matter in spacetime, we have seen, have exotic features deep within them. The universe's original asymmetric physics is, Penrose maintains, partially embedded in the universe, but as a recondite feature of its deep structure. The counter-intuitive physics is accessible to observation obliquely by its consequences, either in highly abnormal astrophysical states (e.g. black holes), or more obviously at the time of the singularity – creation. The creation forced out the normal manifold operations, so that the spacetime geometry[21] disappears at the commencement of the first microsecond of the singularity's fireball. Penrose, however, concludes with the generally acknowledged point that we do not know what the formulation of these time-asymmetric laws would be. But this is also a limitation on attempts to understand quantum gravity in the universe.

This situation comprises two distinguishable aspects. First, the counter-intuitive asymmetric physics hovers in the deep structure of our universe, manifesting itself in abnormal situations. This situation supports Kirkpatrick's (1994) idea on immanence. Employment of the signature of astrophysics cannot be applied to formulate what a proper description would be of the physics which caused the state of affairs immediately prior to the creation – the singularity at t_0, because, among other reasons, the reverse primordial black hole model does not correctly fit the requirements at all major points. For example, the nature of classical collapse is not the time-reverse of the quantum Hawking process relating to particle creation, according to Penrose.[22] Furthermore the singularity theorems do not allow that this universe was reproduced by an equivalent previous universe, with a bounce through zero time t_0, because the laws of physics which we know do not hold at and within the minimum radius around t_0 – the point of creation.[23]

Noting superstrings

Is the universe telling us to get knotted?

The superstring research reported here in Chapter 4 renders more extreme the foregoing picture. Tassie (1986) suggests how strings may account for the emergence of the universe, by appeal to an equation which was initially used to classify astronomical objects ranging from planets to superclusters,[24] in which the angular momentum is proportional to the square of the mass, but which has a strong relation to string theories of particles.

These data and their interrelation with 'Grand Universal Theory' and 'Theory of Everything' models, into which superstrings are introduced, support Tassie's (1986) supposition that since strings may originally have comprised most or all mass in the universe, most astronomical objects could derive from superstrings. If this were true, then were we to observe the early epochs in the universe, they would be seen as superstrings. There are many differing preferred approaches superstrings and their projected empirical links to the origin of the universe,[25] but it is not yet understood how to integrate systematically superstring physics with spacetime physics. However, it seems clear that superstrings are violently counter-intuitive and, in extant science, are not empirically veridical. In this situation, then, they satisfy criteria of being metaphysical.

How could universal uniformity have a beginning?

An upshot of the foregoing discussion – to be examined below – is that the postulated deeper laws and states in observational cosmology appear unavoidably to support a transcendental and counter-intuitive explanation of the nature of the universe. Uniformity is the regular recipe on which science advances its understanding. Contrariwise, at one level, the direct product of this uniformity exercise yields states of affairs at variance with its tenets which, by *reductio ad absurdum*, shows that certain standard formulations of uniformity principles are false.

A central violation of uniformity is of course a cosmic singularity or creation itself. So use of uniformity in scientific observation furnishes us with data which suggest and require that the causality of creation is asymmetric to material causality in any extrapolation of experimental physics to cosmology. This type of situation evidently supplies one with a precedent for admitting transcendental violations of material laws as consistent with astrophysical events, not only of initial creativity but of continuous post-creation activity (where phenomena such as black holes offer precedents).

I have suggested that this situation obtains in the event of the multiverse scenario being correct. We may decide to restore a notion of uniformity supervening over a regress of cosmic singularities implemented in each of the multiverse's universes. Clearly this uniformity for singularities stands at odds with the uniformities hypothetical applicability (perhaps in various ways) internal to the multiverse universes. But if we accept that the multiverse has to have a beginning, or had a beginning, the jump-start of the multiverse is itself a creative function for which there is no precedent.

In this perspective, the retreat by some theologians to a defensive position, or one which accepts 'empiricism' as the defining element of science, and as the criterion of possibility, often for denting theological realism, is fundamentally muddled and faulty. To emphasise this point, it is worthwhile exploring further the status of uniformity and its empirical credentials.

Uniformity and matter

Is there a cosmological principle?

The Cosmological Principle (CP), so designated by E.A. Milne incorporates an assumption made by Einstein in an attempt to integrate uniformity into explanation of the universe. Roughly speaking CP is the supposition that the universe is on average homogeneous and isotropic, i.e. evenly distributed. Saunders *et al.* (1991) have mapped the universe out over 74 per cent of the sky to $140h-1$ Mpc. (50 Mpc – i.e. megaparsecs – is 1 parsec; and 1 parsec is approximately 3 light years.) They found that many uniformity assumptions about the density of matter in the universe are incorrect. As noted earlier, Longair (1994a) documents contrary data indicating massive superclusters of galaxies and unpredicted voids which are incompatible with the various standard aspects of uniformity theories.

The survey of Hara *et al.* (1995) also purports to remove the grounds for appealing to cold dark matter (CM) to balance the equations in the universe. There is sustained unevenness (in homogeneity) of CDM. It thus opposes the various alternative forms of cold dark matter theories that have been constructed. The cosmological constant is a singular assumption. Lindley (1991) comments that we have no right to expect that so messy a subject as galaxy formation can be guided by such a single idea. Joseph Silk (1995) offers an attempt to solve an unresolved problem (in the larger unsolved issue of star formation) of the initial mass function, though recognising that two conditions are not satisfied. This general situation leaves us with an uneven skewed lopsided universe in terms of density and relations of galactic sizes. Saunders *et al.*'s (1991) survey involved evidence of the violation of some uniformity assumptions. The Boomerang survey of the universe, reportedly for a time some 14 billion years ago, and a few hundred thousand years subsequent to the big bang, appears observationally to locate, for the first time, an epoch before the formation of galaxies – illustrated by Plate 4. De Bernardis *et al.* (2000) report that aspects of these data are inconsistent with current models based on topological defects, yet are consistent with a subset of cold dark matter models, and they conclude that the Boomerang survey supports a Euclidean geometry of the universe. The Boomerang project and others like it amount to an important new generation for cosmology, and exciting progress. Nevertheless, without, for example, a neutrino survey for earlier periods, and other much more advanced observational analysis, generalised scientific inferences may presuppose metaphysical speculation, even where tied to observations, because theory transcends its empirical support (as shown by Silk 1995: L44), and otherwise incompatible observations can compete with one another. In a similar way – which Hesse (1994) has described a 'transcendentalist' theory — wave theory and particle theory of light contrarily explain what light is. From this and previous considerations, it seems clear that physical theory in cosmology displays even more counter-intuitive uses of terms than local physics. In this general situation there are also potentially exotic problems and issues of unevenness to smooth out in other domains. These are often connected with difficulties of identification in relation to the status of observations.

Are some pulsars spin-doctored?

In the Prologue we saw how some millisecond pulsars are, as it were, disguised transformations of apparently different types of pulsars which have gone through some form of rebirth. The situation is further complicated by the history of mass transfer between such binary stars, with X-ray emissions from gas heated to at least 106 °K. The pulsar PSR 1913+16 has

188 *All in God's space–time?*

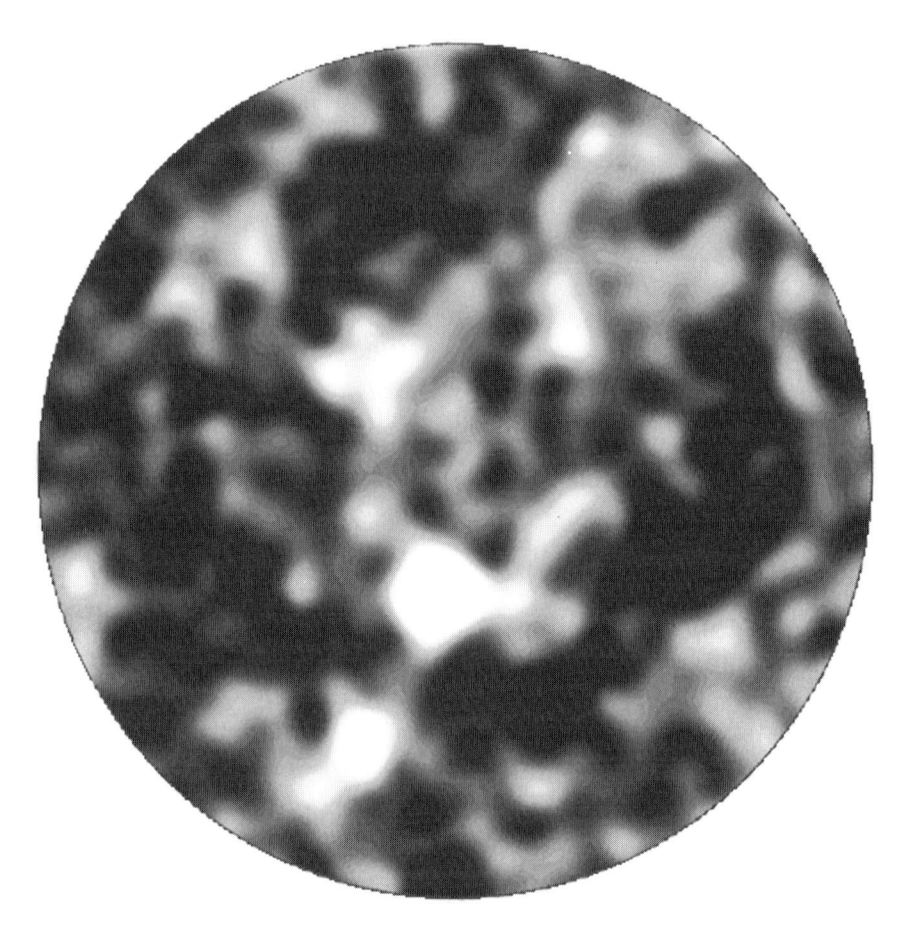

Figure 4.2 An overview of the primeval sky observed by Boomerang

Source: Boomerang, NASA, NSF

Note: This shows the irregular distribution of matter prior to galaxy formation. The data are inconsistent with current models based on topological defects, though they are consistent with a subset of cold dark matter models in a flat Euclidean universe.

an orbit lasting only seven and three-quarter hours, but it has a speed of approximately 10^{-3} of the velocity of light; it also has a very eccentric orbit. The distance between the orbiting binary neutron stars is about the radius of our sun. Smith and Lyne (1987) used this type of pulsar as a test bed for theories of general relativity. In this sort of discussion, the issue of generalisation is problematic, partly because of (isotropic) assumptions in uniformity. There are also peculiar single (10^{-ms}) old pulsars which are in low-density areas of star clusters, for example, the galaxy M13's pulsar 1639+36, which pose problems for assumptions of uniformity. Other extreme cases whose interpretation is unstable await classification; it is not known how these would impinge on assumptions about uniformity.

A most unusual, untypical, and infamous, case is the old pulsar PSR 1958++ in Cygnus, 1000 light years away (see Figure 0.2). Its originally observed orbital speed was once every four-tenths of a second, which on a straightforward calculation, adopting the assumed ratio of rotation velocity to age of pulsar, gave 45 billion years. Clearly, since this is older than the proposed current date of the universe, one either predicts some hitherto unresolved decay rate affecting observations or questions the chronology by which the date is achieved. Although this is a rare case, the complex problems attached to pulsar research resist a global employment of uniformity. The work on spin-histories of binary pulsars may be relevant for modifying this picture, however. For example a study on PSR 1951+32[26] deals with a pulsar which was probably recycled by material from a binary star; but this rebirth, and often other such stars with high velocities of spin, render dating problematic.

Are there miraculous objects?

The enormous difficulties and tantalising opportunities associated with quasars are discussed in various parts of this book. Their very likely location at cosmological distances is itself evidence of ineffable distribution of matter (anisotropy) which may be a key to the early material phase of the universe. The quasars appear to be remote even by traditional norms for uniformity. For the most part, quasars are at much greater distances, at five billion light years away or over. This not inconsiderably questions the assumption of homogeneity with respect to how and at what scale it is applied. The distance itself rests on a disputed means of measurement: Hubble estimated 530 kms per sec per megaparsec as the relation between redshift and distance, from which the above distance is calculated, although some estimates suggest it is too large to be a factor of 5 or 10 with a 15 per cent error factor. This was also assumed to be the error factor of the 530 figure when originally stated. Since these matters of uncertainty directly structure interpretation of the astronomical sources (which need to be fully defined), the sort of expansion of the universe and its associated structure, with logically unstable variables, affect the specification of cosmological hypotheses.

While it is true that the microwave radiation is evenly distributed – isotropic – down to fractions of a percent at all levels, there is also unevenness in a large scale[27] corresponding to a velocity of the Milky Way relative to the microwave background of 603 ± 60 km s^{-1} in a given direction. This also concurs with massive anisotropy of this type elsewhere, indicating substantial inhomogeneities (as McCallum (1979: 533) argues).

Nevertheless, this does not dispute the conclusion that the radiation is a remnant of a hot intensely dense era at the beginning of the universe. Rather, it complicates and disposes of the naïve uniformity predisposition of the past. Conversely, it also replaces the uniformity with specific evidence of design functions in creation. Although there is asymmetry in the universe, its various qualities appear to support, and derive from, a deeply counter-intuitive singular origin. This is even the case with abnormal astronomical phenomena such as black holes which have been used as models to typify the time prior to the 'hot big bang'. The leading black hole authority Chandrasekhar (1979: 370–453) shows that the perturbations associated with a black hole have 'many properties which have the aura of the miraculous about them'.[28] Barrow and Tipler (1986) discuss other cases of 'coincidence'. In addition, these foregoing features have been characterised by Neugebauer and Kramer (1985) in a way which excludes black holes and that applies generally to electrovacuum fields at the beginning of the universe.[29] So, an element of incompleteness pervades these exotic patterns.

These patterns in black holes' function are not only mathematical novelties. Such patterns exhibit parameters of necessary and highly specific conditions which are, it appears, co-extensive with the universe's existence conditions. Hawking notes, for example, that if the proton–neutron mass difference were not approximately twice the mass of the electron, the necessary condition would not have arisen for the possibility of the universe producing the hundreds of stable nucleides that constitute the elements, and which are the foundation of chemistry and biology. Another case of this fine tuning that he cites is the gravitational mass of the proton that, within limits, had to be of that order for the nucleides to have the necessary factory in stars for creation.[30] If the initial expansion of the universe had been of a different scale, it would either have collapsed before stars were produced or expanded in a way that no stars could have formed by gravitational condensation (Hawking 1980: 4). Although, as others have noted,[31] Kant's explanation of 'motion' in the *Metaphysical Foundation of Natural Science* runs into difficulties when linked to Newton's and Einstein's views, yet his sensitivity to the origin and role of motion in relation to matter and energy is profoundly prescient.[32] We may add that the expansion from the big bang circumscribes this in its equations of motion (cf. Kant 1786: 13–18).

Supermassive black hole realism

How far can a sense of realism be stretched?

One problem that needs more attention in philosophy and perhaps in cosmology has to do with the way in which scientific languages are exotically extended on the basis of appeals to local or experimentally grounded laws. A way of expressing one such concern with the problem is to ask: could a concept of realism be stretched so much that it deforms into what a standard view of realism would deem to be anti-realism? By using our own natural languages it could be argued that we cannot thereby express the conditions of what it is to be realist language for the universe. Thus, it is incorrect to infer from our uses of realism that we have exhausted what it is to be realist, though it is not uncommon for some people to draw the conclusion that exotic deviations from our experience are non-realist or just false. Powerful though logic is, it is not a sort of ultraphysics (cf. Wittgenstein 1978) guaranteeing universal truth beyond experience. In contrast, cosmology is a new subject which is plausibly devising unexpected extensions of mathematical and empirical languages for exotic domains. We should allow that a conjunction of logic and cosmology will yield models for fresh virtual inference. As Peacocke (1988: 174) proposes, for certain types of context of realist logic, according to a model of virtual inference, 'a belief is knowledge if there is, for the theorist, a knowledge-yielding abduction from an explicit statement of the subject's reasons for the belief, together with other information available to the subject, to the truth of the belief'. (See Chapter 6 below for an examination of virtual reality and inference.) Although such considerations are in many ways different from matters of divine transcendence, they have a similarity in departure from criteria of local logical realist and empirically testable conditions. There is a partial parallel between talk of exotic deviations from realist experiment in science, together with the crafting of empirical language in the more problematic spheres of astrophysics, and discussion using counter-intuitive realist language applied to divinity.

Is a black hole realistic?

For example, a black hole is already an exotic object, displaying empirical deviance; but this is just the start. Maybe one person's realism is another person's anti-realism, though this does not universalise subjectivity, since this holds for different classes of empirical phenomena. The equivocations would be a function of our ignorance. One of the unexpected developments prompted by black hole research, and especially the Hawking theorems on the black hole, is a central link between quantum mechanics and relativity, although the quantum effects were, in a certain sense, already presupposed in the right-hand side of Einstein's general relativity equations (cf. Zel'dovich 1979: 518). Hawking associates gravity and quantum gravity; the black hole generates a reddening of all radiation, with emission of particles, termed quantum evaporation. Hawking and others propose that there were primordial black holes (PBH) in which particle creation occurred (Hawking 1979: 746–89). Possibly these PBHs had a position which facilitated (by gravitational attraction) galaxy-clustering in the initial stages of the expansion.

Hawking *et al*. (1994: 16) argue that there can be a pair creation of black holes, of two classes: extremal and non-extremal. The latter can, if correctly distanced, annihilate each other, if they are in the same internal state. In the case of extremal black holes, although they can directly annihilate one another, they can create a wormhole in space. On this approach, wormholes were in existence as soon as black holes collapsed. On Hawking's and

Stewart's (1993) view, if a black hole does not settle down as a stable remnant, it would have to be a singularity or thunderbolt.

(As McKie (1988) points out, though, it cannot yet be ruled out that, for example, the label 'supermassive black holes' in relation to active galactic nuclei could be a misnomer for a cluster of collapsed stars or a cosmic string. The presence of a closed trapped surface at the PBH interface (Hawking and Ellis 1973) co-exists with it having boundary generators of infinite length (Carter 1979: 300), which might be evidence of a cosmic string.)

The foregoing might be used to imply that the exact position of a black hole's apparent horizon cannot be assessed (i.e. the Cosmic Censorship Hypothesis), except by possession of exhaustive knowledge of the complete future of spacetime. This puts a severe question mark on those who insist that, in principle, scientific knowledge has to be, and can be, observer-dependent. Such scientific observer limitations contrast with the postulated qualitative competence of an omniscient observer prior to or after, or are temporally related to, creation.

The above situation agrees with Dummett's (1978: 356) belief that a complete description of reality is possible only if it is observer-independent. This additionally serves to emphasise the view that a realist theory of meaning, and not the idealist notion, is correct. Dummett's remark is apt:

> The fundamental difference between the anti-realist and the realist lies in this: that ... the anti-realist interprets 'capable of being known' to mean 'capable of being known by us', whereas the realist interprets it to mean 'capable of being known by some hypothetical being whose intellectual capacities and powers of observation may exceed our own'.
> (Dummett 1978: 24)

It may be thought that the black hole observation situation counters a realist theory of meaning. This is not the case, as Carter explains:

> Hawking's particle-creation mechanism implies the possibility of a fundamental breakdown of classical spacetime in the form of a quantum singularity that would be visible to external observers independently of whether or not Penrose's classical cosmic censorship hypothesis is valid.
> (Carter 1979: 298)

Of course, this presupposes an observer scientist who as yet is not in a position to observe, but one should position an ideal observer who in principle could observe, just as most of Hawking's notions rely on a realist observability in principle, though rarely can this be applied. Barrow and Tipler[33] consider the black hole as a device for the (unlikely) information storage medium in its radiation. Improbable as this is, except for perhaps coding the laws exemplified by a black hole, one can redeploy Barrow and Tipler (1986) to case an unusual angle on realism with observation supporting a realist theory of meaning. In their case, information is coded into physical entities, in the sense that they are live metaphors which signify *in* physical terms.

Blanford and Thorne (1979: 454–503) grade some of the probabilities for black holes to occur in quasars, active galactic nuclei (AGNs) and binary X-ray sources. If these identifications are 'verified', then there would be a generalisation for the foregoing point in an eschatological perspective. Consequently, if the processes associated with black holes are strongly (if only inversely) related to the singularity which commenced the universe, then relevantly characteristic properties of black holes, with appropriate modification, inform us indirectly about lawlike creativity which the singularity at creation programmed into the future history of the universe. Such uses of 'black hole', expanded in primordial, baby massive, and associated with superstrings, all suggest the live metaphorisation shifts developed in Chapter 2 above, which resemble arts metaphor.

The presentation of God as a lawlike creator, for example, in the Bible,[34] is often used as a credential to authorise God's knowledge of the future which parallels the way in which the initial singularity, within seconds, determined the structure and pattern of the future of the universe. Features of this history, going backwards in time, are:

> The lepton era (in which a particle such as an electron does not display strong force). Here the neutron equilibrium is fixed at 15 per cent, proton at 85 per cent.
> The hadron era (a particle exhibiting the strong force) with matter and antimatter in equilibrium possibly with a mixture of fundamental particles, such as quarks (particles with a fractional charge), antiquarks and the gluon. This particle is the carrier for the strong force between quarks.
> And the quantum era.

The quantum era is applied to the stage at which quantum theory is deployed in quantum gravity theories to describe the excitation of a domain by colliding gravitational beams which create particles in virtue of the collision. This type of situation arises in black holes; it has been employed by Hawking to represent an aspect of the initial singularity. A first product of this excitation is usually taken to be photons-light; gravitational waves are also understood to propagate at the speed of light. But it is possible to separate the light-constant from matter (see Chapter 2 above). Here the start to the universe, albeit in disputed senses, is uniquely distinct from its later history. Hawking (Hawking and Ellis 1973) used to believe that this singularity, when associated with the big bang, occurred in real time, and so one would have to seek a prior cause outside general relativity (and its collapse) for the universe. But in 1983 (cf. Hawking 1993: 82) he proposed that the sum of all histories for the universe should not be treated as histories in real time. Hawking and Hartle (1983) suggested an imaginary time dimension, so as to avoid searching for an external cause to the universe's physics and a new physics. Later, however, Hartle (1990) himself revived the opposed 'nucleation from nothing'.

One can anticipate a difficulty with this correlation: if the creation of the universe was itself a quantum object, does not the uncertainty principle eject the need of or propriety for a causal antecedent at all? This is certainly a major philosophical issue that can be thrown into new gear by astrophysics.

A few points suitable to direct discussion are as follows. The Schrödinger equation related to the uncertainty principle is itself deterministic, although current experimental restrictions require the uncertainty as a constraint in physics. So uncertainty is not a quality of the physics in principle. This entails that the origin of the universe was causal.

There is a substantial difference between classical particle mechanics and black hole mechanics (as Hawking and Israel (1979: 19) point out). In classical quantum mechanics, the position or velocity of a particle, but not both, can be predicted. With black holes the situation is more extreme: neither the position nor velocity can be predicted. Only the probabilities that the particles will be emitted in particular modes can be predicted, which is due to the collapse of laws because of this singularity. Also, there certainly is macro-causality attached to the analogous black hole quantum action where radiation is emitted: for the causal antecedents which produce the black hole and its closed surface are causal, in that it is precisely a breakdown of the general relativity which has produced this effect. For example, the gravitational collapse and densities are causal effects which themselves make further effects. 'Causal' here is not literal, but analogical, justly reminiscent of Aquinas (cf. Hesse 1994). This circumstance is a violation of stable causality, but not of causality itself. Even if the initial singularity is one dimensional, e.g. a superstring, we can see from Mellor (1995: 235) that cause would exist in it, and we should treat cause as a fact and not relation.

The cause of the quantum evaporation is the black hole; particles *en bloc* here are not causeless – they are caused by the special effects of the singularity. As Mellor concludes (ibid.), time is the dimension of cause. If one were to take the black hole with the sense of time reversed (metaphorically) as the beginning of creation, this would not dispense with causality even if one were to use the notion of it being a quantum object. A reason for this is that, following the analogical parallel, a relativistic state of affairs exhibited in this universe can 'create' black holes. With the sense of time reversed (i.e. the causal order of the process reorientated a 'world in reverse'), as Luminet (1992: 135) says, some analogue of this universe would have to occupy the position of causal agent for the reversed black hole. Again, a black hole is a well-formed consequence of Einstein's equations, terminating in a singularity. By analogy, we can regard Einstein's equations as descriptive of the causal antecedents of the black hole. Here, in reverse, would be a parallel that showed a quantum object as a singularity which would have to have a causal antecedent. *If* one were to dodge the severe problems with 'bouncing' a cyclic collapsing/expanding universe through t_0 – using it to postulate a regress of universes – this would not succeed in evading the above response. The need for a causal antecedent would merely re-emerge prior to the first quantum-object universe of all the 'universes'.

It is not physically consistent, either, to derive an infinite regress of universes to attempt an avoidance of original causality because of entropy, which perforce requires finitude. Entropy is obviously relatively high now in the universe; and massive *in* black holes. According to a consequence of the second law of black hole mechanics,[35] entropy of a significant sort occurs. Hawking *et al.* (1994) argue that some extreme black holes have zero gravitational entropy and can annihilate when conjoined with other non-external ones.

Causal originality

What is 'beginning'?

One may follow generally Hobbes' (Molesworth 1997) and Anscombe's (1981e) formulation of causality, explaining the beginning of an existent entity. The beginning of the existence of *n* implies the existence of something other than *n*. As Mellor (1995) proves, causally linked facts pick out a single linear dimension of spacetime which cannot loop back. So, the universe cannot be its own cause of existence, as Hawking claims. Indeed, from the foregoing survey, it has been demonstrated that both the asymmetric laws of physics, as well as the nature of the original singularity of creation, require the existence of an antecedent whose criterion of identity is distinct from that which the universe had after t_0, or has in our observations. This position impinges on the question raised in the first section above, and it has provoked the survey of the relation between the universe and its early history. To summarise, *what there is* cannot be a synonym for the *universe*, since if the universe had a beginning, then it had a cause which is *the* or *a* beginning. Because this cause is not itself the beginning, then this cause existed prior to the universe. So *what there is* includes the universe and its cause, whereas the *universe* is not its own cause; in which case, the *universe* is a subset of *what there is*. The postulated physics of this universe, as a consequence of the initial singularity is asymmetric to the superphysics which caused the universe, because general relativity collapses in the Quantum Era's start. Even if Hawking's imaginary time is taken to apply to the beginning of the universe, the 1090 entropy postulated for a primordial black hole would require a discontinuous cause to reverse inertia.

Can we infer outside of the universe?

This itself leads to an entailment the other way: from our universe to infinity conditions. This sidesteps the traditional arguments against a proof which moves from the universe to a transcendental cause. It picks out functional features F, in E (= universe) from which one can entail its cause C. Of course, it does not follow, from the use of the term 'infinity' that such infinity is itself a property of God, but it raises the probability, as we see below. The Quantum Era emerges from infinite effects, and can only thus be inferred from infinite states. Since a finite universe has to have a beginning which is not of itself, the collapse of general relativity into infinite states is itself the entailment which infers an infinity outside our spacetime continuum. Hawking (1990c) wants to distract us from the implications of this by bringing quantum gravity into the equations, though unification has not been achieved. This would be a causeless universe, which opposes the conception of realist science that has been developed in all domains. Prior (1968: 65) has proved that a causeless universe is logically impossible. It is a modal and segmentation fallacy to move from 'quantum indeterminacy of particle behaviour',[36] to infer 'a universal inference that all particle creation is causeless'. We can here use Geach's exposure of some structure in causal propositions (1969: 83), attending also to Prior's (1967: 140) comments on causal logic. If y is God and x is the universe, the bare form of the creation of the universe is:

> (y has brought it about that (for some x (x is the universe)))
> and (it is false that for some x (y has brought it about that
> (x is the universe)))   [I]

The parentheses here isolate the feature that, prior to creation, there was no physical referent of any form in existence which was formed into the universe. But general relativity predicts that there is a stage in its derivation beyond which it will not be able to predict a cause of itself when it ceases to apply to a cosmic singularity. The creation was the formation of a logical referent which had no previous existence. This is contrasted with a proposition which encodes 'making an artefact' from existing material which possesses the reused pre-existing material properties.

What is 'nothing'?

However, one needs to go carefully at this stage. As we saw earlier, the puzzle of 'creation out of nothing' has been used to represent the creation of the universe. Construed narrowly, and with the appropriate ontology bound to x and y above, this expression is true; but it should be noticed that it presupposes or requires other necessary factors. Physical solutions have not yet been mathematically unified with the energy conditions which caused that the universe. At the interface of the universe with its cause, this energy was expressed as created matter. Hawking and Hartle (1983) proposed quantum gravity to avoid the breakdown of physics for largely aesthetic not observational reasons. This was motivated by a desire to avoid disuniformity. This power pre-existed the universe. If 'nothing' in 'created out of nothing' is a universe's topology without physical content, then this is the vacuum which the universe filled. This is not the vacuum prior to Hawking's big bang, in which quantum energy pre-exists. Nevertheless, the causal source, and energy, which comprised the antecedent of created matter was not itself 'nothing'. The creation of the universe accordingly involves a switch over of ontologies. This is consistent with the conception of God's personal ontology, as antecedent, and the universe's ontology. In a Christian theological perspective (e.g. Ward 1994: 295) at the level of intention and causal antecedence, it is logical to position the proposition 'the universe was created out of God' where x in [I] above is the instantiation of a function – a pattern – pre-existing in the mind of God.

Causality and indeterminacy

What chance has cause?

If one were to follow Hawking's (1993) view, arguing quantum indeterminacy and black hole unpredictability, it might be thought that there is no cause of the universe. But does this not wrongly dislocate cause and chance? As Mellor (1995) shows, there is a derivative relation between these functions. But how does original causality relate to indeterminacy? Penrose emphasises the importance of the time-asymmetry in particle physics, as with the decay of the K_0-meson subatomic particles, which conflicts with CP (cf. Penrose 1979: 582). On one interpretation this matches aspects of Everett's global normalisation of quantum mechanics, where quantum phenomena are generalised for the universe as a quantum object. Penrose (1979: 592–4) has conditionally incorporated this into a relativistic scenario termed an Everett-type universe. Hawking (1979: 744) esteems this Everett scenario highly. The notion of possibilities is that of a time-directed tree with trunk and branches, with the branching corresponding to observations along the future, or past, light cones (see Figures 4.3 and 4.4). The branching is associated with a retarded collapse of the wavefunction; namely, a representation of the state of matter in the universe. This preserves possibility and causality for quantum phenomena at the scale of the universe.[37] Some of Everett's (1973) work has increasing support from cosmology. Everett's analysis, as Hartle (1990: 395) points out, is incomplete, since it does not explain the origin of the 'many worlds' nor how to define them, and it might be added that Chihara (1998) has offered grounds to query the empirical possibility of possible worlds, as discussed above.

These problematic features thus need explanation by appeal to the initial conditions of the universe and what caused it. So we are returned to the initial questionable jump-start which quantum gravity was intended to explain, but which regressed to Everett, though unanswered in his work. With either Everett or Hawking's scenarios, the origin of the series on

198 *All in God's space–time?*

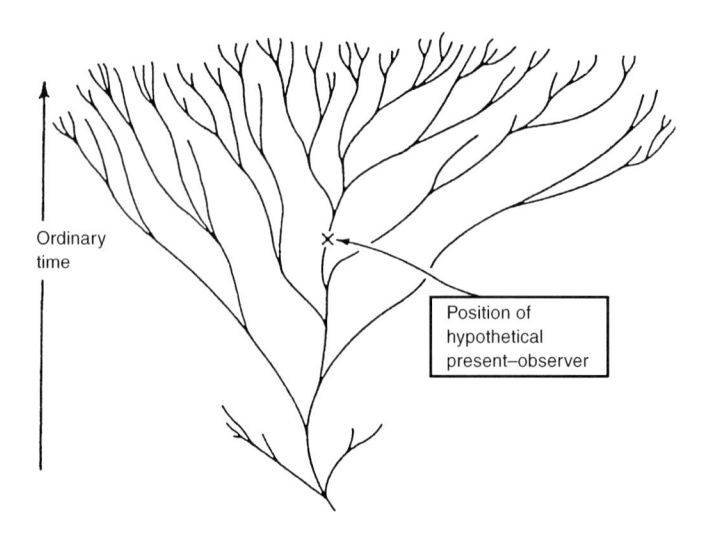

Figure 4.3   An Everett–Penrose model of a universe

Source: After Penrose (1979)

Note: In it there is branching to alternative futures. Penrose suggests that one interpretation of this model can assist in clarifying how, although relativity *seems* to make 'potentialities becoming actualities … highly subjective or meaningless', it can formalise asymmetries between the fixed past and future. This use of 'potentialities' complements Torrance's view in theology, though it is distinct from his formulation.

universes regresses to the familiar problem, disguised in their multiplication of worlds: where entropy and finite energy conditions apply to matter, going backwards in time, there must be a beginning to the series, since infinite series cannot be derived from matter. So Hawking's imaginary time and removal of the boundary conditions are not infinite functions. Hawking has no view of this first cause. The whole arena is vexed with problems and preliminary theories. Yet Everett's work shows how causality can be exposed in a quantum mechanical universe with the time-asymmetry preserved consistent with the evidence for the initial singularity. Of course, research in cosmology might produce a fundamentally different explanation of the possible link between quantum field theory and cosmology, or find no link at all at a substantive level. However, the link is an important issue, not least because it pertains to the alleged need for a revision of two-valued logic due to quantum theory. Haack has argued (1974: 148–67) that local change for quantum mechanical logic cannot justify a change of the laws of logic. The *possibility* of a change of the laws of logic, she observes, could only proceed for candidacy on the basis of a need for global change.

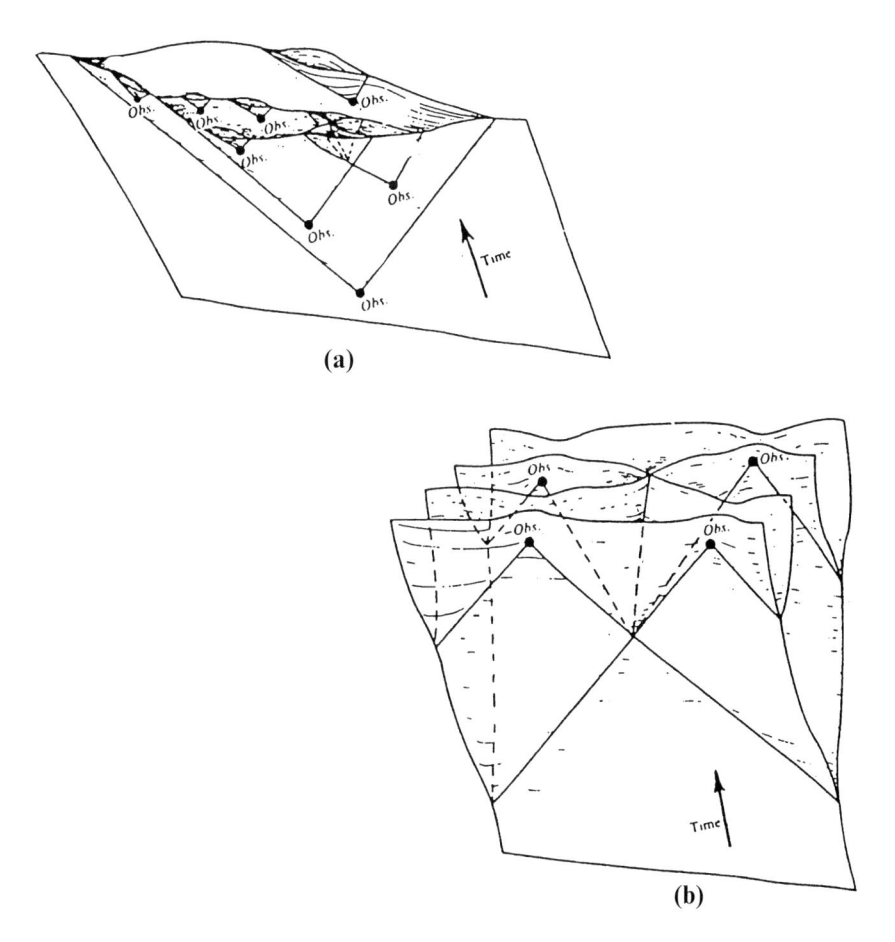

Figure 4.4(a) and (b) Penrose's options for Everett's universe

Source: After Penrose (1979)

Note: Figures (a) and (b) derive from Penrose's options for relativising the Everett model. Penrose regards (a) as more plausible than (b). In (a) branching occurs along the future light cones, whereas in (b) branching is along the past light cones. ('Obs' = observation made at a spacetime point.)

Should cosmology reform logic?

Now it might be proposed by someone that the 'possibility' of the universe as a quantum object furnished a credential for global reform of logic. This could have the novel consequence (if such were the proper term) that religious statements about God associated with such a creation could be neither true nor false (neither probable, nor improbable) on many interpretations of this situation. It may now be rather dated to suggest, with DeWitt and Graham (1973: 744), that the most favourable explanation of a link between quantum mechanics and cosmology is yielded by Everett's work, though DeWitt (1992) has a concept of supermanifolds that offers subtle potential. Hawking and Hartle (e.g. Hartle 1990: 409) proposed a 'no boundary' wave-function defined by a sum over Euclidean geometries, with a wormhole (of a Planck-size tunnel) through to different universes thus eliminating the need for an external cause qualitatively distinct from it. But this is mere conjecture, since infinite density is less than the Planck size. Everett's analysis advances a determinism (not the old-fashioned quantum indeterminacy) thereby removing the thrust for global reform. Further, Penrose's use of Everett's theory is time-asymmetric, with a future branching akin to the logic of possible worlds, and with no return to the past.

This branching is strongly reminiscent, though not presented as, a transitive relation of Prior's branching in time with deterministic features,[38] and his and Fine's calculus of worlds with possible futures.[39] But Everett's ontology is not like Prior's 'possible worlds' theses. It is more akin to David Lewis's (1986) plurality of other worlds, in which multiple inaccessible universes exist, though, as discussed in the foregoing chapters, with a new conception of exotic mathematical structures and astrophysical counter-intuition used to expand realism's scope.[40] It is significant that relevant aspects of Prior's and Fine's work is two-valued.[41] This disposes of the need for global reform regarding the Everett-universe's logic-map. Dummett's (1981: 391–400) research further refined a central feature of Prior's tense considerations developing a two-valued relativization to time.

We can conclude that the universe is not a non-causal quantum. In the light of this situation, then, causality may produce effects (the universe) which contain indeterminacy and causality, yet not resist the claim that the antecedent cause (of the universe) *is* a cause. In the perspective of the philosophy of history and cosmology, these distinctions – branchings with distinct possible futures down a light-cone related to alternative possible futures for history – give formal force to Trevor-Roper's (1981) view, developed in the context of history, that embedded in actual history there are full-bloodied propensities for alternative futures, as Chapter 6 illustrates.

Yet transcendence in cosmology at creation programmed transcendence into the actual universe's future, though leaving open alternative possible futures, while blending this with 'soft' determinism. We are here merely scratching the surface of topology. For example, since light was or went super-luminal in the first microsecond, how would a super-luminal light-cone guide us? This sort of state of affairs is exposed by constructing a logical language whose truth conditions are observer independent of the universe, yet are discovered, not invented – a language of live metaphor which is a mirror of the deep structure which the universe displays.

Does the multiverse dissolve God?

Martin Rees (1997: 184–86) has outlined the prospect of fresh models for the multiverse's identity, which seem to thwart a simple beginning and ending sequence: 'An "eternally inflating" multiverse may sprout separate domains; the laws of physics may vary between one universe and the next', and 'This (literally) enlarged view of the cosmos is crucial for anthropic reasoning'.

If this is the case, Wittgenstein's insistence on shifting away from the question: 'How did the universe come to be?' to 'astonishment *that the universe is*', should be promoted to a confrontation. It is bad enough finding one universe by accident, but how do you explain (away) an infinite number of them? The atheist's unquestioned assumption that the existence of the universe is a matter of chance really does become small potatoes if the problem is that of the existence of a multiverse, an infinite ensemble of universes. This seems to require a theological amount of explanation, though obviously those untouched by a knowledge of the theory of chance will see only more of the same.

Rees (1995: 122–24) has rightly given us two health warnings here. First, avoid claims repeatedly to be pulling the last veil from the face of God. Second, we should be aware that the physics of the first phase of the very early universe is very uncertain and speculative. It is almost an artistic enterprise in which the astrophysical cosmologist and the philosopher are variously and differently involved in conjecturing what the relation of the start of the universe is to its antecedent. Given that much of the multiverse scenario derives from interpretation of this first phase, we do well to ponder on whether or not the status of the question of *what the multiverse is* entails that it may have to have an origin. If it has always existed, it may be that Augustine's concept of a need for a material *cosmos* being sustained by, and derived from, a transcendent God is required; or it may dispense with such an implication. If the latter consequence were to be true, and this universe were merely one local zone of a multiverse, the larger multiverse could be construed to replace the function traditionally ascribed to God. Such a situation would have a parallel with the worship of the heavens castigated in the Hebrew Bible. This might be compared with a neglected medieval strand of theophany: it has the universe to be the body of the deity. Rather, could it be, in that case, that the most unstable of conceptual conjectural speculation – the very earliest phase of the universe – could be misinterpreted?

Could there have been a creation of the multiverse?

Could we devise a super Planckian energy thought-experiment aimed at the creation of the multiverse? The radius of curvature of the universe, or more speculatively the multiverse, would not reduce to zero at the end of time, unlike the beginning of the universe. Gross (1989: 85) encourages the view that approximation will attend a final formulation of string theory where symmetry is achieved at super Planckian energies, and related to a breakdown in our concepts of spacetime at these energies, where the Planck mass is reduced to zero, with a 'large and totally mysterious string theory'.

This seems tantamount to an immaterial superphysics, which perhaps designates the parameters of God's domain outside the universe that would originate the laws which operate in it. In such a scenario the concept of a live metaphor interface between the multiverse and God could relay the superphysics, this insulating against conflation of creator with creation. Material laws would be extirpated, and would be replaced by universals of transcendence. These universals, the foregoing has argued, are obliquely mirrored in a live metaphoric manner by the infinity variables in the physics of the first few microseconds of the universe, as current theories suppose.

In such theories the beginning of the universe violates the causal laws of spacetime manifested in the universe in a way reminiscent of the lording over spacetime by divine foreknowledge. The conditions of fulfilment by such prediction converges with the cosmological conditions which end the material universe and give way to the next universe that would have no entropy.

In Augustine's view our world might be contemporary with, but not temporally co-extensive with, the domain in which God dwells. Transformed into a modified version of the foregoing, this might amount to a transcendent multiverse, discontinuous with the physical multiverse, defined wholly in terms of infinity conditions which were not causally, nor temporally, linked by common physical laws to our universe and multiverse. This would be the ontological correlate of a philosophy of transfinite mathematical infinities, sketched below using Cantor's *Funderungsaxiom*.[42] Certainly, this is metaphysics. And early in the current investigation, the cosmologist Dallaporta (1993) was quoted as characterising the physics of the very earliest phase of the physical universe as metaphysics. So the origin of physics is metaphysics.

Is the independent origin of the universe impossible?

Consequently, if the foregoing considerations are gathered together into premises, atheists are left with the conclusion that there is an insuperable scientific empirical problem in the scenario for the origin of either the universe and/or the multiverse, without a concept traditionally internal. Necessarily, the multiverse and the universe need an external cause for them to exist. There are various technical moves that may be made in an attempt to controvert the following, ones which have largely been examined previously in this book. But it is expedient here to present a bald argument which is all too easily neglected.

The problem is partly that chance cannot yield a multiverse, especially one involved in the sorts of infinity and infinity conditions canvassed in many scientific scenarios. A difficulty in the way of recognising this is that the world's existing empirical patterns, with their causal powers and probabilistic dispositions, are assumed in and are a function of the laws which represent the universe. If we accept the standard arguments for a finite beginning to the universe, and if we adopt this for the multiverse, then the environment out of which the universe came did not have the universe's properties as a subset of its identity. Thus we should strip such properties from our assessment of the possibility of the universe being self-caused. It is possible of course, as we have seen in the foregoing chapters, to presuppose a use of 'nothing' which smuggles quantum properties through the time after, and before, the universe, though this cannot be done without vicious circularity: i.e. assuming what has to be proved. But we still have no theory to account for the actual origin of such phenomena without equivocating over or assuming creation in the big bang scenario.

Even if we – I argue contrarily – assume some such theory of self-origination, almost all astrophysical theories, such as Hawking's (1990c) idea of a model derived from a black hole, speak of an incredible entropy which would block a self-caused origin. Certainly one may invent a mathematical physics to depict this type of origin. But in terms of what physics are known empirically, the state of affairs is impossible. And to extrapolate beyond this boundary is to trade on a physics which cannot function in those exotic states. In short, we have science fiction. So we should not appeal to local physical senses of chance and probability to craft the empirical identity of the probability of the universe being self-caused, since the physics here was not the physics there at or prior to the beginning.

To this the problem of entropy has to be faced. There is the hypothesis, discussed above, of a cosmically sized pre-primordial black hole with an entropic power and concomitant density of 10^{94}gm^{-3} (cf. Hawking and Ellis 1973), and a radius of curvatures is less than 10^{-33} cm, where general relativity cannot function. If this is an origin, or a stage in the origin, of the universe, we have no empirical or logical criteria for demonstrating that it could exist without transcendental external causal interference. That is to say, we have no knowledge of experimental physics or observational astrophysics which could, without speculative metaphysical constructs that contradict empirical science, imply that such a massive entropy could be overcome to produce a universe.

So we should strip our conception of chance to include only chance frequencies combined with 10^{94}gm^{-3} high entropy. It seems fairly obvious that such entropy would obliterate any random effect that might otherwise lead to the creation of the universe.

Conversely, even if we leave high entropy out of the picture (though we cannot do this in any standard scientific cosmological scenario), the absence of our physical universe leaves us with a logic of chance. Chances are probabilities.[43] A problem is that there are very different concepts of chance with correspondingly contrasting varieties of contingency in their applications. A stripped down calculus without application is both plain and of little use in an empirical context which is without parallel in terrestrial macro and microphysical contexts. Insofar as it is worth pursuing this line of argument (in principle and subsequent to the foregoing discussions), there is a self-cancelling termination, I suggest, for an evolution of the universe without some causality fully external to it. That is to say, there is less than a zero probability for the atheist scenario of a self-caused universe on either entropic or theoretical chance grounds. The theoretical chances are what one would have to appeal to in the absence of an empirical interpretation for applying a probability calculus. Crudely put, if one tosses a coin two million times, heads and tails will have one million chances apiece. This state of affairs, if applied to a physical situation without any lawlike order, ends up with that which it started: nothing. If primordial black hole entropy applied to the empirical counterpart of such a conjecture to dictate possibility, there would be no multiverse. Namely, independent physical states manifesting laws asymmetric to uniform massive entropy could not occur.

We cannot here allow complexity theory's prescriptions for order through chaos, because, for example, on this view we have no knowledge of utopian infinite Fibonacci series.[44] Even if there were, the prescriptions would be scrambled by the high entropy and infinite energy-density, and so unknowable to us. Consequently the calculation of what this utopian identity is would be debarred from us because our criterion of a rule for assessing the series would be at variance with the utopian identity. Effectively then, there is a very high negative probability against any deviation from symmetry or zero. This seems to match in some ways Wittgenstein's original finitism in mathematics. It is worth here drawing on and extending the valuable research of Marion (1998). Wittgenstein was concerned that we should not confuse reality with possibility. Yet the assumption that the universe came from an infinite possible sequences of chances does conflate these disparate zones. The story goes: the universe is here, so it must have come about by chance. If we follow Wittgenstein's argument, we will recognise that there is a profound difference between physical, as opposed to mathematical or logical, possibility. For Wittgenstein (*circa* 1931 onwards), infinity is not a number, nor a physical set of states, but a property of a non-empirical logical or mathematical law. As Marion suggests:

> A consequence of the mistaken view that infinity is a number is the illusion that the infinite is to be compared with a finite quantity and then considered as a quantity – an enormous one – while [stated Wittgenstein 1975: sec. 138] 'it isn't itself a quantity'. It is worth noticing that Wittgenstein was certainly aware of the implications of this line of thought, as this remark from 1939 shows: 'If one were to justify a finitist position in mathematics, one should say just that in mathematics "infinite" does not mean anything huge. To say: "There's nothing infinite" is in a sense nonsensical and ridiculous. But it does make sense to say we are not talking of anything huge here' (Wittgenstein 1976: 255).
>
> (Marion 1998: 183–84)

Plate 1 Domenico Veneziano, *The Annunciation* (c. 1445)

Source: The Fitzwilliam Museum, Cambridge

Note: Domenico Veneziano (c.1410–61), who died destitute, is regarded as an early Renaissance realist. He integrated elements of northern Italian painting and Flemish oil technique with his harmonisation of some disparate features in Florentine art. The result was a sense of mystery married to an almost surrealist use of geometry. In this perspective, his deployment of mimesis to represent transcendent reality is a catalyst for reconceiving how we might now quite differently characterise sublime realities beyond, or deeply set within, an eleven-plus dimensional multiverse.

Plate 2 Jean Corbechon, *Des Proprietez des Choses* (*The Marriage of Adam and Eve*) (*c*. 1415)

Source: The Fitzwilliam Museum, Cambridge

Note: Here is a literalist conception for the creation narrative, though such literalism is not one which corresponds to the ancient mind that composed the narrative. It will be argued that the Genesis narrative is not literalist in this manner, but heavily utilised live metaphor. So the present book suggests that such literalism, beautiful though it is, is highly questionable if assumed as a typology for measuring senses in such ancient narrative; it also provokes oppositions between scientific and religious languages which distort the potential for a link at some suitable level between the two domains.

Plate 3 Tibor Csernus, *Untitled* (1987)

Source: Tibor Csernus and the Claude Bernard Gallery, New York.
Note: This painting ironises a painting by Michelangelo Caravaggio.

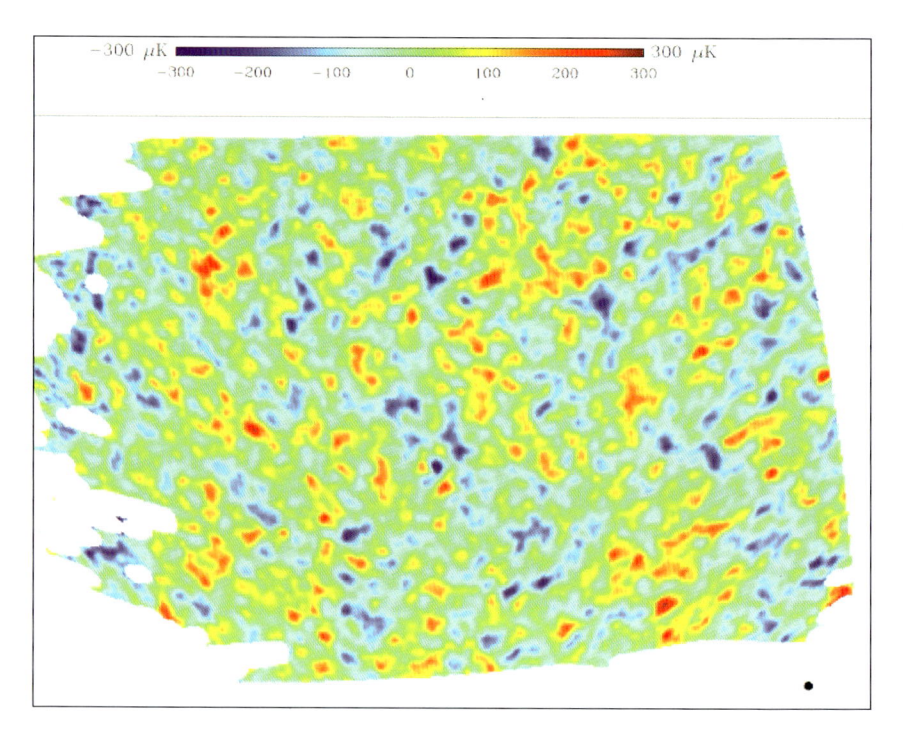

Plate 4 Sample of the new generation cosmology from the Boomerang project

Source: Boomerang Project Team and NASA

Note: From the Boomerang telescope an image of the early universe (allegedly about 14 billion years ago) that remains imprinted in the uneven temperatures in cosmic microwave background. These are dominated by the gravitational redshift of light at that time. The existence of this peak strongly supports inflationary models for the early universe, and is consistent with a flat Euclidean universe.

The beginning of the matter 205

Marion's (ibid.: 187) interpretation identifies Wittgenstein's originality here so as to hinge on his opposing the interpretation of infinity epistemologically.[45] If we take Wittgenstein's line, we cannot derive knowledge of the random finite beginning of the universe from empirical conjecture because it involves generalising over a domain in which scientists mix empirical with mathematical uses of 'infinity'. Here the interpretation of the empirical is incorrectly assigned a probability that has no empirical grounding, even though it is applied so as to 'discover' a potential in physical states. This is not only because we have no physics for it, but due to the point that infinity is not number, and so cannot properly be entered in such an equation.

Conversely, there are the viewpoints of Russell and Ramsey that Wittgenstein was attacking. Marion depicts this situation by noting that Ramsey (1978: 192) insisted that human inability to write propositions of infinite length is 'logically a mere accident', and Marion continues:

> As far as I know, this is the first statement of an argument which has been used over and over by Platonists: the infinite powers of an omniscient being or God are not logically inconceivable. Bertrand Russell used it in a paper published in 1936, 'Limits of empiricism'.
> (Marion 1998: 187–88)

Marion's detective work presents significant background; suffice it to note here that he points out that Russell is having a dogfight with two of Wittgenstein's former students, and he publishes a reply to one of them – Alice Ambrose. Russell retorts:

> She thinks it is *logically* impossible to know that there are not three consecutive 7's in π. But is it logically impossible that there should be an omniscient deity? And if there is such a deity, may he not reveal the answer to a mathematical Moses? And would this be a demonstration? It seems to follow that, if a form of p is syntactically correct, we always 'know what is meant by the statement that p is demonstrated'. If revelation is rejected as a demonstration, it will be found that we do not know of the existence of Cape Horn unless we have seen it.
> (Russell 1936: 143)

Russell is writing as a atheist,[46] though his argument fits into the framework of this book; and his view complements the later use of Cantorian transfinite set theory as a model for the notion of revelation to be developed below. If there is such revelation, so a plausible interpretation of Russell's argument would run, then we can know truths that are consequences of infinity. Wittgenstein's response leads to the objection that if there is no revelation, then we cannot derive epistemological consequences from the idea of 'infinity' because our grasp of rule-following is external to, and thereby different from, the content and logical form of infinity. It should not be concluded that since, on Wittgenstein's approach, infinity is not epistemological, therefore one cannot make positive use, against an atheist position, of the puzzle that the universe (or multiverse) exists. The reason for this amounts to the claim that, in the current state of hypotheses about the state at the beginning universe, the existence of an ordered universe that displays phenomena such as the Fibonacci series is at odds with an extraordinary high entropy and primordial black hole states that would render the emergence of finite physical, and finely tuned, order impossible. Obviously an atheist cosmologist is going to dismiss this view by maintaining that God does not exist, so the universe must have come about by other means. But if we follow the combined implication of the present analysis of the contentions of Wittgenstein and Russell concerning the interpretation of 'infinity', 'empiricism' and what it is to follow the rule for the conjunction of these two domains, we are not in a position to make a symmetry between infinity and empiricism so as to derive a conclusion that the universe does exist. In short, infinity is not a property of empiricism; and universalised entropically enforced randomness does not cause universal law.

One should not be equivocal, as Hacking (1975a: 133) identifies Laplace to be about the probability of a possibility. Rather, the problem is one which has been stranded, not by the above criticisms of attempts to propose that there is a self-caused universe or multiverse, but neglect of how to make explicit the occurrence and explicit representation of a conjectured unknown physical cosmological characteristic – namely, the Leibnitzian equipossibility that, as Hacking (ibid.: 138–40) isolated it, there is a puzzling relation between: (a) probability is a relation between hypothesis and evidence, and (b) a concept of chances should imply that probabilities are matters of physical propensities. The relation between (a) and (b) is still a matter of vexation in terrestrial physics.

How on earth, therefore, can we simply adopt a fixed concept of these relations as a basis for requiring of the origin of the universe that it emerged from quantum gravity subject to entropy of 10^{94}gm^{-3} high entropy, which contravenes pure chance theory, and demands a mystical belief in the miraculous? In contrast, belief in a creation by God seems positively unproblematic. At the very least, there is no equipossibility condition that can be transferred from terrestrial physics to the cause(s) of the big bang. Rather, from the standpoint of satisfying criteria of experimental physics, empirical impossibility seems to attend a contrast between our universe's physics and the possible one(s) which attended our universe's origin. To say the least, the infinity conditions which are supposed to obtain in the state that caused the universe contribute to enlarge this asymmetry and the negative probability. Our hope or expectation that 'somehow' a final definitive account of the physics are invariant with the basic principles of theory and how they are represented, which are experienced now by scientists, should not be confused with either the justification or empirical proof of that equation and the form it would take.

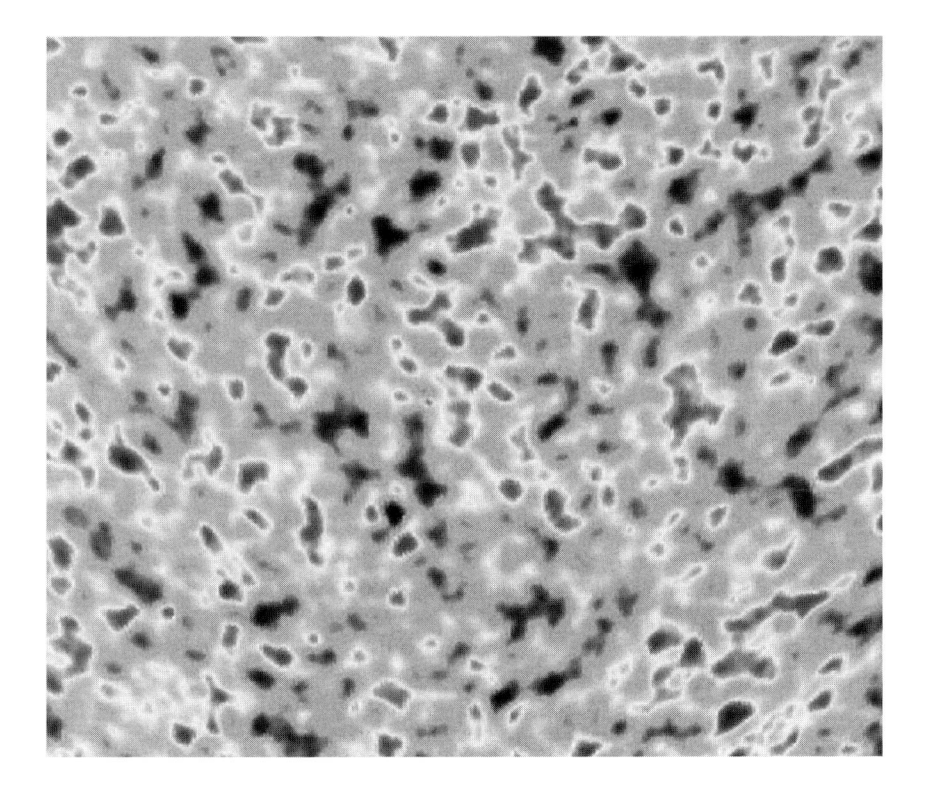

Figure 4.5 Close-up shot of the universe in the microwave background

Source: NASA, NSF, the Italian Space Agency, Italian Antarctic Research Programme.

Note: Apparently some 300,000 years after the big bang prior to galaxy formation. This is immediately after the dark matter phase when light emerges.

The recent history of science and mathematics should teach us that where counter-intuition is a property of conjectural calculation relative to a basis of relevance of which we are ignorant, we do not have the faculties of cosmological retrojection or prediction to infer the exotic unknown from the standardised known. The next two chapters will variously address additional issues involving retrojection and prediction which expose further possibilities in this situation that complicate the matter, but also suggest ways forward.

Part III
The cosmology of life

5 The beginning of life[1]

Biology and entropy

How is evolution subject to entropy?

We have seen that, for the inorganic universe, the end of things is a consequence of their beginning. This could have a peculiar twist in the explanation of the emergence and future for organic life. Increasingly, research on astrophysics and cosmology expose states and links which obtrude on terrestrial issues.

The fundamental problem to be focused on, again, is entropy. If one claims that the Earth is a closed system (which it is not, globally speaking) entropy eventually burns up the possibility, potential, or viability for, or of, life. If one selects a model in which the universe is in direct interface with the Earth, randomness and external entropic factors can create such chaos that no life either ever appeared or could not be uniformly sustained. The trick with evolution theory is to assume a scale on which the exchange rate enables one to bank energy so that the possible emergence of life is not a counterfeit medium of exchange. I wish to argue that, as with the foregoing argument concerning inorganic evolution, we have no empirical or logical grounds for certainty that biological evolution theory can, nor originally did, surmount the problems of entropy and chaos. These problems are internal to the genome (i.e. the genetic identity of a species and genus) and macrobiological systems, as well as the external functions of entropy in the global and larger context of its spacetime physical environments.

Before readers castigate the possibility, or even sanity, of such objections, it is worth asking them to address two types of points: one to do with counter-intuition in other topics, as analogies for the credibility of surprising results; the other, with the counter-intuitive identity which is often a component in original rationalities.

On the first point, briefly: in physical cosmology we have a history of extraordinary discoveries which appeared to violate the canon of the then contemporary astrophysics. The most exotic universal example, still a matter of gross dispute, is the multiverse – discussed in the previous chapter. This conception of an infinite ensemble of universes asymmetric to ours is both incredible as a consequence implied from our knowledge of this universe, and a plausible inference from details little attended to in standard physical cosmology of this universe. So imagine, if there is a comparable type of inferential style in the organic sciences, what could be the unexpected sort of twists to biological evolution theory, even if only to shake up our ability to detect the possibility of being misled. We already have contributions which construct interfaces for inorganic cosmology and the cosmology of life from a perspective within inorganic cosmology. For example, Penrose (1994a) proposes a teleological drive within evolutionary processes to account for consciousness, and calls for a new physics to be devised to structure the resulting subject.

Is Niels Bohr's 'madness' relevant?

Concerning the second point, alluded to in the foregoing, let us consider Niels Bohr on – the live metaphor form of – 'madness'. Chapter 1 considered both the institutional notions of mental disorder, as well as the creative use of madness, on which Wittgenstein and Foucault had written; it noted that both the latter and Derrida (1987) had variously critiqued the crises of madness of institutionalism. To these points it is apt to add the positive counterpoise canvassed by Niels Bohr, speaking to a colleague: 'I know that your theory is mad. But the question is this. Is it really crazy enough to be right?' The Prologue ('Is science Romantic?') documented Ian Hacking's (1995) analysis which demonstrated that clinical metaphors can depict invasion by the mass media of a semantic contagion which regulates and decides upon what is normality and convention. In tension against the idea of an institutional consensus as the creator and censor (which Hacking is concerned to assess) is a complement to Bohr's view, by Wittgenstein – cited in Chapter 1: 'Even to have expressed a false thought boldly and clearly is already to have gained a great deal. It's only by thinking even more crazily than philosophers do that you can solve their problems.'

The geneticist Dover (1990a) cites with approval J.B.S. Haldane's opinion, 'I have no doubt that in reality the future will be vastly more surprising than anything I can imagine. Now my own suspicion is that the universe is not only queerer than we suppose but queerer than we can suppose'. So one does not need to adopt a theistic position to discover aversion to the evangelical claims of some atheist evolutionists. Tom Nagel (1997:131–32), who affirms the hope that atheism is true, asserts in the same context: 'One of the tendencies [of the cosmic authority problem troubling believers and atheists] is the ludicrous overuse of evolutionary biology to explain everything about life, including everything about the human mind.' The cosmic authority problem may be larger for evolutionary biology than it is customary for us to recognise.

What depth is there to evolution?

To this catalogue of views, the reader may like to be reminded of Rorty's (1998: 266) advice that we should encourage people who are tempted to dismiss Aristotle as 'a biologist who got out of his depth'. Dare one consider the possibility that some evolutionists are metaphysicians who are swimming too close to shore to assess the depth of their abstractions? We all know the degree to which some applied scientists scorn a philosopher's approach to their subject, and no doubt they often have good reason; but this is not an unexceptionable reason. My claim here is that a philosopher has warrant for suggesting applied evolutionary possibilities for at least two reasons. First, because evolutionary biology is often unverifiable applied to transcendent metaphysics. Second, because its theories often apply to empirical environments in spacetimes remote from ours, for which there are no observational criteria.

Of course, it may be retorted that evolutionary biology can extrapolate back from our spacetime. Yet is not this precisely the problem? When one infers from the known observation to the spatio-temporally remote unknown state of affairs, which by definition satisfy different criteria of identity (i.e. are a distinct stage in evolution), one cannot imply for sure that the unknown can bear the same interpretation as the known. The result may be a faulty inferential circuit, a vicious circle. One cannot consistently resort to the counter-claim that all the stages in inference are made up of small details, so there is no risk of malfunction in inference. The reason is that it is exactly small detail which, in contingent inferences (we have seen in previous chapters) generate the large changes in the conceptual scheme, especially where original explanation is being constructed.

Is Neo-Darwinism controlled by entropy?

Entropy is usually taken to be a disposition of the universe in relation to time: the universe winds down, with matter's energy less accessible to reuse, rather like the smoke and dust left over from a fire. A variety of ploys are proffered to outwit entropy over the short-term. Black holes have their bright side in seeming to jump-start a universe, but over a finite period even they perish for their entropic sins.

Neo-Darwinian evolutionary models often lock-off the earth system from the short-term entropic effects of the universe so that evolution can occur, though this situation is violated by the astronomical relation which feeds a variety of impulses and radiation, such as gamma rays, into the earth's environment. Features of this thesis depend on, among other things, the contribution made by natural selection and genetic drift. But the Earth still displays properties the early universe had: the weak nuclear force, linked to electromagnetism; left-handed nuclear force; spin of particles and symmetries in the quantum field (cf. Rubbia 1992).

In recent years genetic research has spawned new evolutionary theories whose growing influence competes with standard Neo-Darwinism. A particular feature of these is the allowance for more extensive time periods for evolutionary differentiation than earlier Darwinism had employed. Interpreted in the perspective of the foregoing, this development involves the admission that entropy has a greater operational role than Darwin had anticipated. One such contender is the concept of molecular drive. Molecular drive, principally developed by G.A. Dover, is a process that changes the average genotype or identity of a genetic population, and the mechanism central to this process is the turnover of changes in the copying of DNA.[2] It allows for the survival of inefficient organisms to a greater degree than typical Neo-Darwinist models, partly by documenting the functionally impaired, redundant or disadvantaging secondary features of organisms.

Dover maintains that molecular drive improves Neo-Darwinian theory and offers a new way of constructing evolution theory. Gabriel Dover's (2000: 53–54) assessment of Dawkins's approach seems right, for he maintains that, 'selfish genery is genetically misconceived, operationally incoherent and seductively dangerous'. Dover (ibid.: 198) also argues, however, that we are 'entering a world of understanding in which there are no fixed entities', whilst he is willing to conclude that we can 'derive' generalised relations. Clearly the truth of such a view presupposes problems as to how one proves that one has instances of this truth, if it is accurate. Given this situation, we are free to argue that evolution theory may not yet have mastered the criteria for the origination of life. In evolutionary history the copying of DNA results in errors which, taken up as useful biological novelties, together drive forward at the molecular level to generate new genetic families. This emphasises the processes internal to an organism as the source of new differentiation, in contrast with Neo-Darwinism which associates, for example, genetic drift with the survival of the fittest. According to molecular drive theory the random variation at the DNA molecular level is the source of evolution.

The cosmology of devolution

What if evolution drives in reverse?

Now if the degree or function of entropy has not been accurately gauged, what would be the consequences? I introduce the expression 'devolution' to indicate the idea of backwards evolution; that is to say, regression from and mutation of a state in a genome which is thereby grossly subject to entropy. Teleology is a circular assumption in evolution: if a given theory of evolution is correct, then one adopts it as a premise construed as a teleological direction to suppose that the ends justifies the means.

What if evolution has been going in reverse for millions of years? What if devolution were global. Could it have always gone in reverse? This would raise enormous metaphysical questions. Such a view provokes the question of whether it went forward prior to that. This issue is interwoven with the assumption that amongst the theories of evolution there occurs at least one hypothesis which is not only justified by the evidence but is also true. Yet given the limitations of our occupying one slice of spacetime remote from the first evolutionary phase in biological history, there are a number of other possibilities open to question. For example, let us suppose that there is a true theory of evolution, but it is not yet known to science, though fragments of it have been incorporated into Neo-Darwinism. On this view, Neo-Darwinism might stand in a similar relation to the undiscovered true theory in this hypothesis, just as Newtonian gravitational theory stands in relation to either Einstein's general relativity or to Hawking's quantum gravity. In other words, the errors or limitations in Neo-Darwinism might show up only if exotic questions are pursued, or if they are recontexualised in a new frame of reference.

Could there by a true unknown evolutionary theory?

On this analysis, we might therefore have a peculiar twist in evolutionary possibilities. For example, if evolutionists have not yet exposed the fundamental identity of what evolution is, but only certain properties of it, there could be two discontinuous histories hidden in or obscured by a genome's DNA codes. Let us suppose that biological entropy has typical Newtonian properties – wood is burned, its residue is less accessible to convert to energy, and so forth. Now consider what would have happened if we apply this principle to evolution without evolution countering with a teleology, or to any given epoch when the teleology did not function. The result: extinction. But generalise this state of affairs, diachronically. Namely, let us assume that where no teleology operates, devolutions function. It is plausible to conclude from the sciences that entropy may always have operated to produce a devolution whenever the extant theories of evolution were functional. In short, on this view evolution always went backwards.

This is not to suggest in itself that this excludes the possibility that some other theory of evolution, only fragmentarily grasped by current evolutionary theories, did not operate to produce the organic world. But, perhaps only as an exercise in improbability, it might nevertheless be worth proposing that some mechanism of evolution other than any we have now could be responsible for the emergence of organic life. Ray's (1994) computer program for a self-modifying evolution theory may be such an instance; it incorporates the evolutionary data available, yet is quite different from standard views. So, without teleonomic forward drive, Neo-Darwinism, and perhaps molecular drive, might always have been devolving whilst complying with evolutionary data. This would have the novel consequence that current evolutionary scenarios only describe the processes of life as we know them, and not their origin. In this perspective, there could be another quite different type of evolutionary scenario or some other explanation unknown to us. The effect of this would be to conclude that evolution as we know it is entirely entropy driven. Evidence of this would be the extinction of species and genera. On this analysis, transient property and redundant function are internal to organic types as we know them. If such explanations were to be the case, evolutionists would have conflated devolution with evolution and unsuccessfully treated the former as the latter, thus obscuring another dislocated explanation either hidden in the ghost DNA or an interpretation whose empirical basis is entirely posterior to the functioning of evolution.

Dover's molecular drive thesis about evolution requires a substantially longer period for the development of evolution than its Neo-Darwinian counterpart. This view also internalises the causes which produce forward movement into the evolution of species. There are some genetic grounds for considering that this situation does not entail the consequence that molecular drive has always to generate improvement in the species. Geneticists generally treat this devolving tendency as a side issue, though it has been given distinguished attention, but not in the perspective here being offered. Perhaps we can envisage erratic global changes of direction for evolution rather than merely two long-term alterations in direction. Clearly the extinction of species amounts to a fairly substantial form of devolution for the subject thus selected for a change of gear.

To some degree this argument complements Derrida (1972, 1982), who was influenced by the work of the Nobel biologist François Jacob (1970), when he queries the view that the 'logic of life' is in a 'genetic' script, and concludes that there is indeterminacy in the end for evolution. Although Derrida's use of deconstruction in relation to evolution is not intended to be a biological hypothesis (as Johnson (1994: 170) points out), we could apply his deconstructing scenario to the world. If deconstruction is set into the indeterminacy internal to the teleology of evolution, there is no certainty that it is teleology. It might be deconstructing devolution.

Cancer and evolution

What is cancer of the genome?

Orgel and Crick (1980) have described areas where DNA replication seems to have no function as 'cancer of the genome'. This pioneering idea seems to warrant more development and attention than it is usually given. Cairns (1975) refined the parallel between cancer causation and the emergence of 'immortal' DNA strands. This sort of cancer DNA is similar in its molecular characteristics to DNA mutation in standard evolutionary models. Cairns (1981) argued that prime mutations in cancerous DNA develop increasingly high probabilities for the emergence of deranged DNA programmes of cell renewal. He also showed that this involves transposition of units in the DNA – a changing coding which has parallels with the remapping in evolutionary changes in DNA. Cairns (1978) also showed that mutations in DNA in cancer block gene repair work in a manner which has a parallel with the loss of precision of DNA copying as complex organisms become older.

The role of miscopying and mismatching between two copied sequences of DNA is a central basis for the emergence of new characteristics in DNA theory. These new characteristics do not have to be improvements; indeed as mutants they are not necessarily conducive to the improvement of the host. There are DNA repair genes which rebuild incorrect copying as highlighted in the work by Calderon *et al*. (1983). There are excision enzymes which cut out unwanted or damaged bits of copied DNA. But as Sancar and Rupp (1983) maintain, sometimes the repair functions malfunction and create their own mutations.

Is there a lost evolving past?

It is sometimes said in evolution studies that there are many lost pasts in the genetic pool (cf. Dover 1986, 1990a). Phillips *et al*. (1983), for example, examine the three-dimensional structures of proteins, when very similar structures in molecules have seemingly unrelated amino-acid sequences. They conclude that these structures may provide evidence of now long-absent divergent evolutionary possibilities which have been lost from the functioning DNA. Junk DNA in the present epoch, according to this thesis, might once have had a function some 10^{7+} generations ago. Perhaps another way of expressing this would be to speak of ghost DNA in a state of devolution.

The ghost in the DNA machine could be the hidden past which over large epochs went backwards. A central difficulty in accessing this hypothesis is the timescale which is disputed by molecular drive evolutionists. Clearly we have a problem of observation over the relevant timescale. This is complicated by pinpointing when, or if, there existed an initial primeval environment that was discontinuous with subsequent environments in which another form of evolution developed. There has always been the problem of explaining the difference between an original primeval environment which was immediately antecedent to any evolution but that was the cause of the first stage in evolution. The explanatory assumptions in the two phases would be fundamentally different from each other.

If, to this problem, we add the possibility that our whole evolutionary system changed direction, we have the difficulty of explaining the structure of the environment which would cause such a reversal. The other metaphysical possibility is that if evolution always went backwards, then one would require a qualitatively entirely different previous environment which caused organic life, but which life then drove into reverse. These options need not be implemented as possible worlds which emerge instantly; they could be conceived as having phase-transitions over a finite period.

Was there a global evolutionary catastrophe?

Catastrophe theory[3] can be used to represent an aspect of these states of affairs. We can have an invisible catastrophe set K in an evolutionary framework or manifold m in a vector field X.[4] This X produces a discontinuity which amounts to a terminal retrograde phase for a surviving species, unless a counter-intuitive transformation can be produced in the empirical situation. For example, there is evidence of adaption in chronic circumstances where genes are subject to heat shock.[5] Studies of *Drosophila melanogaster* demonstrate that very ancient genes have survived catastrophic heat conditions. The molecular situation in these genes seems to indicate that they are coded for a lost past which exerted very extreme heat conditions on them. *Drosophila* is, of course, central for much evolution theory. Dover (see, for example, Polanco *et al.* (2000)) are undertaking fundamental research, as are others, on *Drosophila*. Some of their work concerns multiple-copy systems and internal redundancy related to the prospects of molecular coevolution between pairs of interacting genes. If devolutionary entropy operates in the function of redundancy, this will have surprising results.

Miyata and Hayashida (1982) offered the view that the human family evolved between 26 and 12 million years ago. But Wilson *et al.* (1983) reported that a human DNA element existed before the emergence of mammals. The examples in the present and previous paragraphs typify the potential for both reordering evolutionary direction and exposing the hitch-hiker's guide to lost genetic history.

Do solutions cause devolution?

One of the problems in assessing the evolutionary past is to recognise and also measure interference by unexpected forces on the evolutionary process. These forces may come from either inside the molecular structure of the DNA or from the external environment. Solitons readily illustrate some aspects of these problems. The original mathematics of solitons described the lateral pulse going across the top of a sea wave as the wave rolled onto the shore. This pulse of wave across, and on top of, a sea wave is functionally discontinuous in some ways with the sea wave dynamics on which it rides. The mathematics of soliton theory have been variously applied. Some of the less successful applications have been to the spiral structures of galaxies, though the spiral structure of DNA molecules has been more receptive.

Soliton theory[6] has been applied to DNA engaging the idea that there is an electrical pulse and vibration which runs up and down stretches of DNA. This affects the internal structure of the DNA; random properties and Brownian motion (cf. Trullinger *et al.* 1978) are injected into the DNA by these means. This causes an interaction in the DNA which can destabilise aspects of the system. Phenomena such as puckering, stretching and twisting are caused by soliton effects; the electromagnetic fields of RNA may also engage with the soliton process which can interfere with the uniform development of DNA.

A central problem in soliton studies is that the soliton system is discontinuous in its structure from the DNA system on which it operates, and so its random effects can cause a reconfiguration of DNA patterns over a long period. Solitons are just one of the types of effects which can provoke evolutionary changes of an unexpected sort. The mathematics of the soliton are some of the most complex and obscure (a wave-shaped solution involving a nonlinear effect which uses the complex Hamiltonian mathematics; (see Krumhansl and Alexander 1983). This mathematics exposes unusual effects which can cause instabilities as well as copying errors in replication.

If we add the soliton disturbances to the foregoing situation a picture can emerge in which the soliton brings discontinuity, randomness and entropy to the evolutionary hypothesis. Solitons could therefore excite tendencies for evolutionary mutation to go into reverse molecular drive.

On this interpretation, the soliton waves riding on DNA are perturbations invading an alien evolutionary host or, alternatively, are anarchical dispositions within the DNA which dislocate the stable coherence of the forward evolutionary drive. This is not intended to dismiss the undoubtedly true point that solitons could move molecular drive forward in the process of evolutionary differentiation. Rather, my hope is to draw new attention to the role of mathematics, its infinities and complexity that disturb evolutionary theories. Miwa *et al.* (2000) argue that hidden symmetry stands deep within soliton theory (e.g. infinite dimensional Affine Lie algebras). This is not the polemical teleological asymmetry of evolutionary theory, but an enormously complex disruptive set of forces. If we download entropy into such equations, it is not at all clear that evolution in a soliton genetic world can be 'the' origin of, or means to, life. This theoretically complements Stephen Jay Gould's (2000: 86) castigation of what he calls

> a self-styled form of Darwinian fundamentalism ... from the English biological heartland of John Maynard Smith ... Richard Dawkins, ... to the equally narrow ... American philosopher Daniel Dennett.
>
> (Gould 2000: 86)

A reason for introducing the soliton theory here is to add it to other factors, described above, to show that together they constitute grounds for taking seriously the possibility that devolution has had some influence on evolution.

At least three possibilities could arise in this context. Could we position devolution as an overall tendency throughout evolutionary activity, be it in dominant or recessive form? Alternatively, devolution may be characterised as a dislocation operating in the past in some or all epochs. Some people may also wish to consider devolution as a possible world for the future. In these ways devolution theory has parallels with many astrophysical theories about the universe. For example, we have seen that black holes are structural notions which can be used to represent processes in the present, in the past, or at the end of the universe. Devolution in these perspectives is a complex live metaphor mapping the directional identity of life. Just as evolution is a live metaphor for the progress of the world, so devolution would be a live metaphor for the retreat of the world into oblivion.

Is DNA evolution a complex live metaphor?

The concept of live metaphor developed in earlier chapters was applied to the notion of the reproduction of characteristics from one subject(s) to another individual. DNA coding can be construed as a complex case of live metaphor. DNA motifs have many levels of depth and coding capabilities. This is reminiscent of the (contingent) isomorphism thesis in Wittgenstein's *Tractatus* 'picture' theory.[7] In 1985, DNA fingerprinting came into its own as a notion to depict the way DNA represents uniqueness in the individual, as well as its embodying in that DNA a variety of 'frozen accidents' from the genetic past. This, effectively, is fingerprinting which not only photographs the individual's identity, it also captures the mini-satellite arrays of past mutations and copying of patterns. This is as if the DNA is both a photograph of the current identity of an individual, as well as being, in its deep structure, a live metaphor of past maps of chromosomes. As Dover (1990a) concludes, 'the past is still within us'. The postulation of a new 'heavy' photon (Z^0) results in explaining the slight deviation from perfect symmetry and the left-handedness preference of biological molecules, such as the bacteria which uses right-handed D-amino acids and, for example, penicillin. Both exemplify the use of live metaphor imaging.[8]

Is there devolution in genetic drift?

The work on population genetics proposes a genetic drift which presupposes a forward movement in evolution. The work by Ohta (1983a, 1983b) maintains, however, that genetic drift theories are severely limited in their use of probability theory because they cannot prove assumptions about teleonomy, i.e. progressive forward movement. This is not to say, of course, that there is none. The problem is the scope and scale over epochs of forward or backward movement which it is difficult to sustain without metaphysical assumptions. The gap between experimental observation and these assumptions, together with evolutionary data and their alternative explanations, leave space for a devolution concept. This might have the form of a reverse molecular drive using, for example, cancerous DNA as a live metaphor with which generally to model DNA mutation.

Evolution supplies all-too-ready answers to a range of ultimate questions. The foregoing argues that, effectively, we may be at a much earlier stage in grasping the correct identity of the questions that typically stock theories suppose. Consequently, it may be a long way into the future before science can progress to veridical answers which expose the ancient past. Some evolutionary science has made implausible transcendental assumptions, but these may not have always facilitated access to the ancient past.

Does human consciousness devolve?

It remains to apply the foregoing thesis to the human mind. Sure, conceptual, technological and scientific achievements demonstrate that human consciousness has been a substantive party to unparalleled developments. One should not wish to compromise that truth.

There is, however, a quite different problem looming for the third millennium. Once biological evolution has secured itself as the process by which progress is gained at the level of the evolution of consciousness, can it go into reverse? That is to say, is consciousness possibly prone to devolution? Could the states associated with human mentality become so subject to qualitative entropy that they functionally degrade?

One way to encapsulate this idea is to begin with the assumption that human consciousness is (now) non-algorithmic. We then infer that a degradation of functional efficacy could generate a reduction of non-algorithmic states to algorithmic ones: rather like a human being on automatic pilot. Let us appeal to Carruthers's (1992) view that the consciousness of animals is at best rather like someone who is driving correctly along miles of a motorway, in somewhat of a trance of boredom or fatigue, without registering that he is avoiding crashing and is making the right moves to avoid crashing. We adopt and adapt this figure to generate a model of qualitative mental mutations as a live metaphor to qualitative states of consciousness. I suggest that Hacking's (1995) notion of certain mass media operating as a semantic contagion can be introduced to enrich the model.

How does this relate to genetic algorithms? A problem in evolution theory concerns interaction among genetic algorithm parameters. This is discussed, for example, by Deb and Agrawal (1999), and they conclude that when genetic algorithms are applied to more complex problems than a crossover-based approach with optimal solutions, which involve massive multi-modality and misleading functions, mutation based genetic algorithms have failed to solve the requisite problems. This is because even a theoretical population does not exist. If we apply this characterisation to the unexplored arena of the devolution of consciousness, we accept four points. First, the empirical and psychological arenas are so fraught with chaos functions and randomness that ascending evolutionary teleonomic functions have no theoretical or empirical force. Second, the complexity and randomness of the human mind, which is subject to such diverse forces, constitute an instability for which entropy will be a major dynamic in directing the population trends. Third, if there are other human influences which militate against progress that have entropic weight, then there is a proportionately exponential probability of a high order that devolution will be implemented as a major engine drive in population. Fourth, since most genetic algorithm research concentrates on the upwardly mobile evolutionary theory and its innovative prowess related to locality and randomness, – for example, as with Weicker and Weicker (1999) – reverse evolutionary trends are largely unexplored and unmapped, especially as they pertain to mentality.

Since evolution theory is concerned with influence at the generalised level of populations, the occurrence of some non-entropy tendencies of human consciousness is not necessarily evidence that there is no overall devolution of human mentality. A puzzling mixed state could be where technological acumen innovates evolutionary progress for humans generally (say, some mental use akin to global access to e-mail), while yet the qualitative mental states are generally entropically driven by devolution. The former could readily obscure the latter's degrading effect. In this scenario, evolutionary capabilities themselves could be harnessed to cause devolution. An interesting example of this could be the global monopolies that coerce multimedia diets. Evolution is, then, a binary temporal process. Whatever goes forward could go backwards. Degrading commercial and political world views, vying for control of markets and minds, appear to sustain the hypothesis that the devolution of human consciousness is not solely a futurism. Rather, it is a function within the contemporary psychological genome. There is, then, a genuine issue of whether or not the undoubted successes and benefits of technological culture have, in the domain of human consciousness, entropic devolutionary counterparts. The latter may be so subversely embedded in the genetic landscape that they counterfeit progress. In other words, a collective selfish gene that apes humanity – and, in so doing, devolves its capacity for human consciousness. In sum, the ideas that creation originated life, but that devolution – organic and psychological – is the true explanation of evolution, are in urgent need of original research attention. Not least, since gross qualitative entropic forces seem already to have entered the mental world. The imperious confidence that evolution has produced the present maybe sufficiently mythical in its current scientific form to obscure from us the myopic status of the assumption that evolution is in progress.

6 Prediction and the cosmology of God

Live metaphors of transcendence

Is science transcendent?

In the previous chapter, together with a number of contexts earlier in the book, evidence has been offered to suggest that at least some traditional applied science models of empirical science are inadequate to enclose not only exploratory areas of empirical science, but also some of the deeper topics in microphysics and cosmology. In these respects, some science is not a master of facts, but a subtle enquirer after the experimental and theoretical accurate representation of the external world. As science advances, the roles of conjecture, refutation, imagination and counter-intuitive pathways have expanded the criteria of what it is to be such science. Although there is a large amount of invariance in scientific concepts as they are refined and developed, there is a significant proportion, especially in cosmology and microphysics, where the degree of theoretical imagination seems exponentially to develop disproportionately to its past track record. In these perspectives the bold leap forward is not infrequently confirmed by experiment or observation-linked calculations. It appears, in these spheres at least, that the identity of science is increasingly unpredicted or unpredictable.

Is 'God' scientific or philosophical?

Some readers will reply negatively to both possibilities. Chapter 3 attempted to prove that the opposition between philosophy and a religious concept of God, even one derived from ancient usage such as that in parts of the Bible, is incorrect, though doubtless some philosophy and religion are best left out of any reconstruction. Chapter 3 argues that its points [1] to [10] characterise what it would be for language to be used to describe God. Chapter 4 proposed the view that relevant scientific and astronomical languages can be extendible to provide an analogy to furnish a precedent for the religious language characterised in Chapter 3. Chapters 5 and 6 maintained that scientific language about the start of the universe entails transcendental language which is outside the scope of empirical scientific proof criteria. This state of affairs also has parallels with the ascription of properties to God. It does not, of course, follow from such analysis that there is a God; but it does follow that a project examining the question of God's existence has rather different boundaries from those often assigned in the emergence of modernism, and that an enquiry about this could have insights for modernism and science, quite apart from their relevance for religion.

Bernard Williams (1998b) has argued that in respect of the question 'What could philosophy become?', it will have at least two ingredients. First, it will be non-obvious. Second, it should be tested by reference to its history. Accordingly, future philosophy will partly be a conjunction of unpredictability and known patterns from the past. Presumably this will imply an identity which is more than the sum of the parts.

Williams did not apply such remarks to science or religion, though they might be so deployed. The above discussion of cosmology has shown that Williams's two proposals have application to it, not least in the concept of the multiverse. Although the history of recent astrophysics has been fairly well documented, it is not obvious what its controversial future will be. The history of religious ideas (referred to in this book) has well-known scholarly treatments, as well as controversies, and some influential scholars are pushing the putative future of discussion about God in two directions: first, back into the past; second, into an obvious future predetermined by poststructuralist fashions in the present. I am arguing that the future of divine cosmology is less obvious than either of these two options: it will have an identity to come which is counter-intuitive. Perhaps a property of this identity will be that it shares features with, or hitherto unmapped similarities to, new qualities of construction in cosmology and microphysics. And aesthetic and imaginative properties are already being exposed in some scientific researches (as mentioned above, for example, in Hoffmann 1990). A meta-property of such phenomena in relation to their theoretical representation is that they are transcendent and counter-intuitive when contrasted with paradigm instances of what it is to be the science of (even) the recent past.[1] Such a tendency should not be over-stated, but its omission from a somewhat bald realist local experimental scientific position results in excision of a functional zone which is likely to be a guideline for future developments.

Are patterns of the future in the present?

Whether or not we speak of prediction (on which this chapter concentrates) or foreknowledge, it will be argued that this chapter's analysis generates conclusions over both topics (with slight variations in nuance which will not be taken up here because of the priorities of the book). First, discussion will show that linking God and prediction manifests underlying cosmological patterns causally connected with the cosmology discussed in earlier chapters.

Part of the reason for this is that if God can predict the future (even if we do not have knowledge of what he predicts), it entails that God is transcendent in ways which can be theoretically assessed in terms of measurable (live metaphoric) transformation of some current cosmology.

Second, a part of the argument will develop the view that there is a logical relation between cosmological physical prediction and God's knowledge of future events. One might gaze on this connection by appeal to the painting debate on how one looks at a picture: the medium, or the illusion, provoking a vision of a scene? Consider, for example, Monet's *The Seine in Thaw*.[2] The debate over this is one about live metaphor. A cosmology of the world of ideas and social history may possibly be developed by the use of patterns in a cosmology of the physical world. The conception of live metaphor discussed in previous chapters is a fulcrum on which to pivot this idea. Possibly in this perspective some logic of astrophysical prediction could be used to complement many models and historical patterns of social history. If there is such a thing as the God who has foreknowledge, then it might be that such parallels inform discussion of how to interpret and structure transcendent foreknowledge claims.

Is part of transcendence internal to the mind?

An alternative, or perhaps complementary, way of evoking a parallel between a physical world and the social world, may be to think of God's foreknowledge as a complex live metaphor focusing on underlying dynamical patterns in the collective unconscious mind. This is not to presuppose a particular thesis such as that of Jung's archetypes of the unconscious. Malcolm Bowie's discussion of the European unconscious, innovatively using Freud and Lacan to model modernism, is a significant way forward (see Bowie 1993: 117–40), however. We may find Lacan convoluted, terse and bizarre, yet Bowie's own vision transforms psychoanalysis by showing how a scheme of the future can be employed in the present to create a new direction in personal and/or collective history. This invasion of the future by means of creativity not only aptly speaks to society but, as a live metaphor, of God. It might be objected that this would show that God is a live metaphor for the collective unconscious. This would extend Rorty's (1997) argument that philosophy of religion should reduce to philosophy of mind. Readers will take their preference, and such may find the potential for this thesis illuminating in the following. But for those who prefer this position, can one not maintain that it merely delays the emergence, from a study of the collective unconscious, of a conclusion that live metaphor mirrors a transcendental pattern attesting divinity, not only in the fact of the existence of the human mind, but in its functions in historical frameworks which display our internal splits of order versus chaos? (cf. Torrance 1981: 132 and 1999).

Can we quote one model for the future in another?

There is, I suggest, a sort of quantum indeterminacy in society's relation to its possible futures seeking an anchor in teleology. Some of the work of Derrida is a suitable occasion for attempting to extend a metaphoric parallel in narrative. The use of Derrida here and elsewhere adapts individual technical insights of his, rather than by way of appeal to his philosophy generally. Consider the relation between quantum chaos in physical cosmology and the indeterminacy of human social dynamics. Such a parallel would involve a problematic deconstruction of narrative expectations, particularly in the context of attempting to 'quote' one model (of physical cosmology) 'in' another model (of social and political history).

As discussed above, Marian Hobson (1998) shows in her study on Derrida, '"*In*" as a relation between these texts becomes something like a cellular telephone network', in Derrida's view about the reproduction of one representation by its 'citation' in another narrative. (This use of 'in' is not unlike being 'in Christ' or 'Aristotle being in Aquinas'.)

We can fill this out in the following way. In a cellular network there is a telephone relaying system A (representing speaker $A1$) which refers to, and communicates with, the recipient's relaying system B (representing speaker $B1$), and *vice versa* for B. These two systems in turn operate through another, radio, cellular network relation R. In these refined '*A and R and B*' systems, ARB each has coding memory facilities, and extending networks simultaneously to link up with other systems which continue the series A and B.[3] Within the network figuration, we have an infinite capacity for intersecting and modulating possibilities and their contents. Just as light rays pass through a video camera, and are frozen or quoted on film, so one cosmological model may be engaged in teleology.

Can we escape with transcendence?

This relational technological metaphor to some extent is reminiscent of the notion of representation, mediation through an agent, and agencies conceived, in the live metaphor conception presented in the foregoing chapters. That is to say, a literary quotation from one text in another, or an audio-visual reproduction from one source in another film, or the representation of ontological states of affairs in literary media are, in the relevant senses, parallel with the metaphor of a cellular network. (The notion of Cantorian transfinite set theory is applied below to enrich the scope and quality of this relay system motif.)

In some respects the relation of claims of future knowledge to our present empirical experience parallels the attachment of aesthetic predicates to assess the signifiers in an art medium, though this complex projection is not easily measured.[4] In his book *The Truth in Painting* (1987), Derrida develops the analogy of imaging in relation to the quotation of one 'reality' in another. He notices that:

> The principle of analogy is here indeed inseparable from an anthropocentric principle. The human centre also stands *in the middle*, between nature (animate or inanimate) and God. It is only on this condition that we can understand the analogy between determinant judgements and reflexive judgements, an essential part of the matching. Incapable as we are of determining absolutely the particular empirical laws of nature (because the general laws of nature, prescribed in our understanding, leave them undetermined), we must act *as if* an understanding (not our own) *had been able* to give them a unity.
>
> (Derrida 1987: 117)

It is common to add to such a position that we cannot get out of and behind the 'screens' of our hypotheses and language to characterise the significance of the world beyond, though Derrida accepts that we must write as if we can. The present book attempts to remove the force of this objection by arguing that uses of live metaphor in science and theology are media for realistic mirroring of true states of affairs. Some readers may find the adaptation of Derrida to transcendental issues surprising; but we find (even) Rorty (1992: 236) noting that Norris (1987) believes that Derrida should be read as a transcendental philosopher in the Kantian tradition, albeit untypically so.

I suggest that Derrida should take more seriously his belief that we should write as if we can escape from anthropomorphism: anthropomorphism, accompanied by logic, observation and creativity enable us to arrive at a stage beyond the anthropomorphic. It seems to be a modal fallacy to infer from one's using anthropomorphic media the consequence that we cannot reach beyond anthropomorphic domains. For example, our capacity to know that gravity will have a given effect is not in the slightest way restricted by anthropomorphism. The use of 'referring' with a proper name is the most obviously neglected instance of transcending our anthropomorphism in our language usage. Our competence in referring to the city of New York is not in any way anthropomorphically limited. I did actually succeed in referring to New York city. The latter's ontology is entirely other than the former's medium. Our facility to recognise when gravity is working in New York shows that we have the ability to transcend anthropomorphism while inhabiting it. It is a category error to move from observing that it is customary to use a medium of expression to the entailment that one cannot employ the medium to infer something other than the medium. But how do such matters pertain to an attempt to refer to the future?

Prediction

How do we get to the future?

One topic which can be used to strike through and remove our narrative 'screens' that block off scrutiny of the external world is prediction. The idea of 'screen' here is actually a metaphor for a way of looking at a narrative which obscures scrutiny of its references. Derrida resists universalised ('totalized') and global empiricist claims (cf. Hobson 1982a). But if one is seeking an individual, creative, transcendental movement of language which goes beyond these restraints, then prediction is ideal.

Although inductive and probability ideas about prediction predominate the literature, the following exploration discusses the prospect of their being another type of prediction. In respect of tests for divine foreknowledge – for example, a prophecy – it may be incorrect to follow Hume's view assigning diminishing probabilities to rare events. Ian Hacking's (1990) review of chance highlights the way in which the Western world has become 'probabilized'.

Does chance eliminate foreknowledge?

We cannot accurately say things about the future by use of the past *if* the past does not contain like-elements conjectured to be occurring in the postulated future even. Foreknowledge or prescience of a unique event is inexplicable to those who would wish to employ probability theory to explain it. Profound though Mallarmé's poem *Un coup de dés* (*A Throw of the Dice*) is, with its universalising chance – 'A throw of the dice will never eliminate chance', it is unwarranted to apply 'never' to universalise randomness, since chance can produce a result which is qualitatively distinct from the chaos of chance. Can one conclude that a primordial black hole decoheres, all is lost, and yet an ordered universe later emerges? By a throw of the dice? How does the dice get thrown?

Hume regarded prophecy as an hypothetical candidate for being a miracle, in his *Dialogues Concerning Natural Religion*; but also divine foreknowledge would comply with the criteria for a miracle. So we may regard a study of prediction as relevant for exposing some structure in divine foreknowledge. In fact, if there were such a miracle, the prediction and its fulfilment would be miraculous, though the contents of the event fulfilling the prediction need not be. However, we need in the following to be able to isolate guesses from the logic of a unique event.

God's first-person foreknowledge would not be probability, but understanding of a true proposition. A human's first-person attempt to grasp the future would be at best statistical. As Hacking (1990) interprets him, Peirce (1982), advocating absolute chance, believed that probability is nested in metaphysics, that induction is founded in series not individual cases, and so inferences about probability concern, not individual truths, but statistical types, on the basis of repeated precedent. Even so, Nagel (1997: 127–29) argues that Peirce was a pragmatist with a suppressed Platonic platform in his desire that science would, through induction, discover 'eternal forms' in nature (Peirce 1992: 121–22). On a variety of interpretations, such conceptions widely diverge from the proposed identity of the present conception of what it would be to be God's foreknowledge, or indeed a time-transcendent notion of the future.

Non-inductive prediction can be positioned as either a function of God's foreknowledge, or his prophetic knowledge, or both. Such a state of future knowledge need not be known to any person on earth; or it might a function of revelation, for example, as presented by Ward (1994), or by McDonald (1993), in a relativised reading of eschatological narratives in the Bible, initially reflected in the sort of reading tradition provoked by Weiss (1892) or, alternatively, by Rowland (1982). Clearly, the current chapter should be treated as an enquiry into prediction in principle, with the narrative examples as illustrations, rather than as an applied study. For those who do not consider that such prediction can occur in a narrative, they could construe the argument as an attempt to represent conceptual features of foreknowledge depicted by live metaphor of God's mind. In the latter perspective, we could utilise Newlands (1994: 163–65) concept of providence, relating God's knowledge to science and chance. Presumably, the strongest version of God's foreknowledge would be Christ or his resurrection. (Of course, some of these typologies require so much analysis that exegetical and historical discussion is left aside from the present book.)

Is the probability of foreknowledge nil?

How formally *probable* is foreknowledge of the manifestation of Christ, or Christ's resurrection? Employing a variety of inductive scenarios depicting the (secular) past, with or without regard to Humean or ancient reports of revelation as a basis for assigning a conditional probability to the availability of God's foreknowledge of Christ, the probability is *nil*. This is because, in the relevant senses, there had not previously been a relevantly similar son of God to supply a probability–distribution about his future. Alternatively, in principle, an appeal generally to God's foreknowledge or predictions would yield the probability of the next one being infinitely high, since in the hypothesis none is false. On this view, Christ was the unique set. This uniqueness would be qualitatively true of any of God's foreknowledge as a property of divine transcendence, though the ontological instantiation of Christ is more accessible to us. So, if foreknowledge or prophecy is true, it is an altogether more surprising and deep affair than some have supposed. In contrast, probability is intrinsically an averaging process. It takes what is known from the past, and constructs expectations. Scientific experiment adds the twist that it uses recombination and conjectured reification of the patterns of past established distributions to produce a conjectured result.

Would divine foreknowledge be logically unlike probability?

Non-repeating prediction known only by God and candidates for revelatory prediction would, by definition, not be computable from what is known, since such prediction would be the antithesis of inductively averaging over the past. This is articularly the case concerning foreknowledge about a unique future event or humanly inaccessible knowledge, because there would be no probability pattern for its content. The conception of divine prediction is accordingly counter-intuitively non-inductive and non-probabilistic; and the nearest parallel is with deductive logic.

This type of divine foreknowledge or prediction is *a priori*, I suggest, in a number of counter-intuitive senses. That is to say, deduction has a logical status outside, prior to, experience, though this truth does not in itself preclude deduction from predicating truths of experience in referents over which it ranges. This foreknowledge is thus not inductive, *a priori*, yet it speaks of empirical matters, though not a *fortoriori*. If it rains every other day over a period, you get a probability of half by looking at the statistics of the past. With divine prediction, if God is omniscient, all *God's* foreknowledge, all the past prophecies are true, yet distinct as to content. All the future, as yet unfulfilled, instances are unique and not the outcome of past assignments of divided probabilities, nor are they related to choices in which entropy is maximised. So (although it is misleadingly modest to put it like this) prediction by God would have a probability of 1. Namely, it is true. Consequently, there would be no basis for claiming that it could be false.

In this sense, divine foreknowledge would be theoretically and empirically infinitely stronger than scientific inductive prediction, though not by the result of empirical experiment. Experimental approximation and inductive method are interfaces mingling ignorance and knowledge, which regulate experiment and the constructing of accounts of physical law by the scientist. These epistemological limitations would not exist with a God who had foreknowledge, for example, if we adopt Anglin's (1990) thesis on liberty and prescience. A reason for this is that God is not subject to time-bound laws. This God is exempt from the scientist's limitations, not least by being the source of, and satisfying, the infinity-functions discussed in previous chapters. We could draw on the modal realist situation in set theory here: sets, and infinite sets, for example applied to geometry, have been treated as *a priori*, and connected to universals,[5] thus tying together elements of the above issues.

Is the future like a virtual computer program?

Newtonian mechanics adopts a fixed velocity for light though, unlike relativity, its speed is not necessarily restricted. In theory, it allows information to be rushed in from infinity. Conversely, on some standard interpretations, the general relativity of this universe requires the fixed speed of light as a limiting function in which information would travel along time-like curves regulated by the velocity of light. On a basic model of general relativity no information could come in from the future, where the future is a spacetime separated from the present by an earlier spacetime where prediction is expressed.

Geroch (1977) proposed that general relativity be adjusted to allow for astrophysical predictions (with hole-free spacetimes). His theory might be appealed to, if one needed to explain how predictions might be known in this universe, when or while general relativity holds true. Geroch demonstrates that 'direct verification' is possible on his interpretation, with the prerequisite that our universe would have to be a closed universe, which he takes to be observationally probable.

For those who want a more exotic scenario using mathematical cosmology, the superstrings mentioned in Chapter 3 and the manifold of Chapter 4 exhibit a formalism in which (if generalised) the velocity of light is not a necessarily fixed limiting factor on the physics of the universe. Superstrings and the supermanifold exhibit how the structure of space time can be effectively deformed in its material physics. So, using this explanation, and combining with it the increase of the velocity of light beyond its current value towards infinity at the beginning of the universe, we have an account of how prediction in cosmology portrays the intelligibility of divine prediction as it would supervene over time. Tipler (1995: 135–38) argues that infinite information can come from the future. He notes that Penrose, with whom I would agree, faults his appeal to computer theory. One could re-assign this source to the beginning of the universe.

Theoretically (in a way which Augustine would perhaps have liked), we can also consistently posit the initial boundary conditions obtaining at zero time t beginning the universe as criteria for the state at the present boundary of the universe. We could link this to Balthasar's (1992a, 1992b) thesis of transcendence and immanence for God, which would unite the theme of cosmic drama as a functional aesthetic of God's foreknowledge. Malcolm Bowie (1993: 103–4, etc.) outlines a project which could extend this. He writes of how Barth's response to Mozart's music pinpoints the resurgence of the past. If we can generalise these connections, we have some grasp of the discontinuity and access conditions of transcendent knowledge of the future. Although Bernard Williams's (1998a) suggestion – that the past of philosophy is relevant to its future which will be non-obvious – is formed within an atheist perspective, the previous suggestion deploys these two policies. Some Christian theology conceives God as a function derived or manifested from the outside edge of the material universe, in relation to God's revelation to the world. No doubt some will want to adopt a notion of temporal infinity at that point along the lines of: if the heavens declare the glory of God, then it is not unexpected that there is more significance in that glory, as the light to which no man can approach, approaches.

Is foreknowledge a supervenient mirror of cosmology?

This explanation depicts how God can both have access to all time-lines at any point, while yet be distinct from them, in infinity outside the universe. Therefore, in relation to the foregoing examination of creation in Chapter 4, it is logically evident that the cosmological patterns, which would underlie divine foreknowledge and prediction, could manifest conditions tautologous with the beginning of the universe, and later outside the universe, in terms of creativity, as we shall also see below.

This theme relates to the earlier criticism of Aristotle's *Poetics* at the opening of Chapter 3. Mimesis – classical imitation – involves the disclosure of universals in likenesses which manifest their archetypes. Chapter 3's propositions, [1] to [10], laid out the abstract form of some relations in this mimesis, which can be directly applied to represent the mimetic relations in predictions. Divine foreknowledge and prediction could condense God's thought into language in a way that mirror and map – features of the future universe. Correspondingly, the physical universe is in some ways the embodiment of the creative universals which caused it. Both of these transcendental phenomena – cosmological prediction and creation – mirror each other. In Aristotle mimesis is superficial compared with the counter-intuitive complex structures such cosmology requires. We saw in Chapter 3 that one aspect of this limitation is Aristotle's adoption of probability. The foregoing depicts further reasons in addition to Chapter 3 to explain why it is that Aristotle's probability should be replaced with a concept of truth. The movement from ignorance to knowledge is a universal presupposition of knowledge of God, of which foreknowledge or prediction is a subset. Even for those who do not believe that God's predictions or foreknowledge are available to them, the previous points should regulate their regard for 'God', because God's knowledge, on this account, would be infinite in understanding in a manner specifically relatable to the functioning of the universe and would thus compliment God's knowledge in such a fashion so as to expose the deep sense in which God truly knows best. Although this stress on revelation and foreknowledge is unfashionable and taken to be inimical to modernism, we can see with Charles Taylor's *Sources of the Self* (1989), and reaction to it,[6] that there is some poststructuralist precedent for transcendence in the history of ideas and some contemporary philosophy of history.

Must foreknowledge be universally generalised?

If it be objected that a given candidate for being a prediction by God could be solely a good sample from a series of guesses, then this fails to separate out the differences between the two distinct types of prediction. Clearly, some guesses turn out right, and sometimes writers falsely claim that they have predictions or foreknowledge from God. But outside these groupings, if all the predictions by *God* are true, then they can be qualitatively isolated in principle from mere probabilities. Since God always knows what is coming next, and is immortal, God knows an infinite series of predictions. In probability theory, it is not possible that an infinite sequence of probability statements all be true, since this would cause them to cease to be probability. And it goes beyond extant scientific capacity to infer universalised predictive general truths from experimental probabilities, even where there is an empirical premise of uniformity. In this state of affairs, the susceptibility of God's predictions to universal quantification exposes that they are, as it were, deductively true, and not functions of probability. Universal quantification applies because a difference of universal quality inheres in God's foreknowledge which is exclusive of probability. This complies with the cosmology of the matter: the superphysics of the beginning of the universe converges into infinity, and this has an analogy in God's transcendental knowledge as it is qualitatively infinite, admitting neither of ignorance nor probability in prediction. As Coady (1992: 179–98) has demonstrated, Bayesian probability theory, for example, can help us with the consistency of our commitments, but it is ill-placed to help at all with assessing unusual truths.

Social prediction

How could we have foreknowledge of society?

The above sketch did not note that God's foreknowledge falls into the class of prediction which is more difficult than that in the physical sciences. Discussion of God's foreknowledge, if its truth claims were to be true, is not solely a 'thought experiment', though it is helpful to reflect on Sorensen's (1992) revision of the 'thought experiment' and expand it. We can reconfigure empirical borders: you can infer determinate properties from indeterminate ones. Social science is sometimes not recognised as a science, partly because of the problems of formulating social laws and one's inability to construct relevant predictions. For example, it is generally believed by economists that macroeconomic models cannot be used for forecasting. In economic theory, Hall *et al.* (1986) appear to have had some success with mechanical prediction models, whilst further assessment over long periods for distinct sample series of data is needed; but these fall far short in range, quality and quantification of 'deductive' prediction mentioned above, and in foreknowledge of global economic futures.

One way of characterising a contrast between foreknowledge and social 'laws' would be to relate the foregoing to the research of the economic theorist Pesaran. Part of his work has been to develop a computer program for producing prediction models to examine economic time series. Pesaran's theory is probabilistic, yet it incorporates some deterministic explanations and employs algorithms. Pesaran and Slater (1980: 103) comment: 'As is clear from our preceding discussions any satisfactory estimation of dynamic models in small samples requires some knowledge concerning the way the dynamic process is generated.' In contrast, the above studies of God's foreknowledge and prediction have as their sample a unique specific dynamic – their fulfilment of ontological truth conditions. Within the hypothesis, they thus have the property of operating as a universal lawlike dynamic process which is generated by God.

234 *The cosmology of life*

How is divine foreknowledge related to the universe's beginning?

Consequently, a case of divine foreknowledge has a parallel with the beginning of the universe – they have no empirical antecedent or cause in terms of induction. In the contrast of exponentially diverging epistemological contrasts between human dynamic models and God's foreknowledge, Pesaran's algorithms would be replaced by the equations specifying the infinity functions behind the supermanifold and superphysics outlined in Chapter 6 above. (This is supplemented by the account of God's morality which takes up two subsequent chapters later in the book. The question of determinism and free choice in this connection is examined in the next section, and Anglin (1990) relates this question to omniscience.)

Pesaran and Slater (1980: 81) consider the issue of unobserved past history to be of central importance for the subject social prediction. The link between prediction and general relativity in the context of divine foreknowledge, mooted in the previous section, in which God would have access to all spacetime lines and can transfer information between them, shows how God would be, on this theory, in a position to observe all past as well as (in a different sense) all future history.[7]

This, with the presuppositional form of premises above, entails that God has the perfect dynamic conceptual regression to produce a non-probabilistic description of time series and their internal epistemological states. In this perspective God's prediction would be a unique yet logical type lagged with omniscient controls. As Penrose (1994a) argues, such states are not computable by us. Computer models, as it were, are inferior manifestations of a technological mimesis deployed to perform a role which can be perfectly enacted only by God, not by computer algorithms. If God's foreknowledge ranges over this domain, then there is a corresponding promotion for non-algorithmic divine foreknowledge to a status higher than prediction in physical science.

Is scientific social prediction intentional?

Sometimes of course social scientists can predict 'social life'. 'But', Giddens argues,

> [social life's] prediction is in many of its aspects 'made to happen' by social actors; it does not happen in spite of the reasons they have for their conduct. If the study of unintended consequences and unacknowledged conditions of action is a major part of social research, we should none the less stress that such consequences and conditions are always to be interpreted within the flow of intentional conduct.
>
> (Giddens 1984: 285)

Giddens's use of 'always' here is in tension with the problems social theorists have of knowing the intentions of people, when unintended effects emerge from causal motives, and when indeterminacy operates as a cause. Kumar's remarks on the future of industrial progress, in connection with problems of about generalisation, are apt here:

> The future remains open, infinitely variable even though infinitely limited. (Infinite collections contain one another, as Russell showed.) It so happens that all we can know are such persistencies from the past. The future itself, strictly speaking, remains unknown and unknowable. When we attempt to predict the future, on the basis of current trends, we are attempting to dominate the future by the past.
>
> (Kumar 1978: 326)

This clearly embraces a familiar truth of humanity. The econometricist Day (1993) states that a fundamental problem is that the use of quantitative data to explain qualitative phenomena is vexed with chaos and discontinuities with no foundation to determine links between the two. I suggest that the internal logic of God's foreknowledge has a live metaphor relation to our grasp of the past, present and future. This transcendental foreknowledge is counter-intuitive, however; and as such I argue that, in principle, it could avoid the above sorts of anthropocentric limitations and anthropomorphism.

Is being a society a self-fulfilling prophecy?

It is difficult to perceive the past and present in our attempts to comprehend the sense and implications of what it would be to have knowledge of the future, whilst avoiding limiting anthropomorphic ascription to God's foreknowledge. Qualitative issues in history, particularly as depicted by historians, often compose or dispose patterns differently from economists, though there are underlying similarities in relation to all our ignorance and success in envisaging the past and future. We shall see below that Hugh Trevor-Roper (1981) positions the role of imagination in history as a complex function which sometimes can randomly contribute to conceiving aspects of the future. Even here, however, the unpredicted, in random form, can invade our senses of expectation. Simon Schama (1995) portrays the ways collective memory fictionalises and suppresses elements of past world views which hover neglected beneath the surface of standard histories. Schama also presents the historian's imagination as a means to retrieving this obscured past. Sometimes the retrieval of history rests on a dispute of method, in which negative assessment may be too severe.

For example, can we accurately isolate individuality from group identity, be they God or people, in mediaeval European history? The mediaevalist Chinca (1993) notes that this issue clashes with Durkheim's (1912) seminal thesis, sometimes encapsulated by the expression 'God is society'. Hesse

(1994: 247–48) observes that, narrowly construed, this is a misleading summary. But she notes that the phrase 'God is society' is what is entailed by Durkheim's position. Although Durkheim maintains that religion is not reducible to other social forms, since it has its own autonomous existence in the space of sacred symbols, he thereby finds no need for the hypothesis of a transcendent God outside society. Durkheim partially derived his thesis from research on symbolism among Australian aborigines; it is not evident that this is the theistic map stipulating what it is to be Occidental Christianity! No doubt there is some typology which ranges over humanity, but it is far from obvious that this equation exposes it. A reason for this is that Durkheimist reductionist identity (of transcendental divinity to society) snarls up the intricate debate about the human as counter-creator, and divine presence – an arena which George Steiner (1989) has profoundly characterised. Even taken as a metaphor, the equation 'God is society' is a modal fallacy (on this fallacy, see Gibson 1981: 31–2, 83, 88). Durkheim merely paraphrased other people's alleged referential terms as non-onto-logical and, though we will generally concur with this, he presupposes the grounds for this move rather than explicitly demonstrates its correctness.

The influence of Durkheim resulted in an emphasis on collective function and mentality to the exclusion of individuality. This type of equivocation illustrates the difficulty in using extant cultural frameworks to identify historical functions, let alone achieve a characterisation of what it is to be knowledge of the future. When a particular notion or context is central to a correct perception of a part of history, such presuppositions coercing collectivity insulate against direct empirical assessment. For example, Mark Chinca (1993) and Sarah Kay (1989) oppose such uses of sociology by philologists. For example, they maintain that the mediaeval French and German love-lyric is directly based on the individual's biographical experience in courtly love, and they lay stress on the link between 'saying' in the love-lyric and 'doing' in the courtly context, whereas other treatments often assume that there is no individual biography corresponding to the love-lyric content and context. They also highlight, as does Zink (1985), the role of the emerging self-consciousness of the first person in a manner that contributes to a sense of individualism, which complements Nicholas' (1991) argument for a modernist strand of sensibility in this period.

Are we intentional about the past and future?

As noted in the Prologue, Hacking's (1995) pioneering research on the sciences of memory explores ways in which we are extensively prone to intentionality in our attempts to recall the past. Developing Anscombe's (1959) work on intention, and on medical studies of mentality, Hacking develops the thesis that recollection of any particular subject, together with the contribution of its social context, breeds varying and frequently false intentional representations that can trigger deviant mental traits. He explains how in many respects this acts as a semantic contagion, particularly in the sciences of the treatment of memory, but also as a general phenomenon which pervades the present, with influences on future-directed thought and activity.

There is of course a complex elusive connection between individuality and collective identity, and how we are vexed by our inability to formulate objectively a criterion of identity even of our present age that resists our desire to assess the past and project into the future. John Forrester (1990) documents among other things the extent to which Freud was deeply indebted to his own individual unconscious and wish fulfilment as a resource for his theories, with their strong ties to the future (largely unexplicated in Freud). Forrester (1990: 90–96) explains that Freud links 'past' to 'future', as 'wish' to 'fulfilment' by transference and condensation of wish as reality. In this respect, Forrester places 'foreknowledge' as the self-caused fulfilment of 'wish'. He uses the analogy of a diary of schedules announcing future intentions. This expression of a human mental state is thus a mirror of an epistemology in which the statement about the future is not knowledge of the future, but the expression of assent to a description which one hopes to implement as an ontological state.

What is God's intention?

The notion of God's intention, conversely, including when it encompasses conditional statements, is, I shall argue below, qualitatively distinct from the foregoing, and is true cognisance of the future. A presupposition of this thesis is that God's knowledge (as a property internal to God) is not the result of an inference, nor based on a premise of knowledge of the past or present, though it may be related by reason motive or intention to the past or present. Assuming the concept of God presupposed by Geach (1969), God would not have an unconscious since omniscience would guarantee instantaneity of perfect knowledge and understanding. Geach does not address the issue of the unconscious in relation to God, however; but, in the context of human mental acts, he questions Freud's formulation of the unconscious in principle as an inner sense organ.[8] One might also question Freud's view that 'The unconscious is the true psychic reality' (Freud 1938: 542; cf. Geach 1971:110), if by this he was opposing consciousness as the true psychic reality. Since consciousness partially mutes truth, the unconscious retains informative capacities which consciousness does not have. But, on this view, a perfect self-reflexive consciousness, such as that ascribed to God, would have no asymmetry of such functions, even if it possessed multiple levels of perceptual functions. This, then, is another qualitative difference between the epistemology of God and humans.

It is thus, for example, on Abelard's view, reflecting adherence to Boethius,[9] not clear that we even have a clear grasp of the relatively more modest topic of what it is to be human unconsciousness, and so we are limited in our capacity to secure a viable conception of our mental relations to the future, which evidently has a bearing on our attempts to formulate a concept of what is possible for us in connection with the link between imagination and its implementation. John Marenbon shows how,[10] for Peter Abelard, the modalities of what it is 'possible for' humans to do counter-intuitively vary in accordance with a correct, or equivocating, sense of counterfactual alternative possible life stories (not possible worlds). God is presupposed as an omniscient being for whom such equivocation is fully eliminated by terms of knowledge whose contingencies are foreknown but not necessarily causally determined by God.

Are we only virtually conscious?

The more modest scope of one's attempting to index the mentality of a limited group of humans, for example, by marking them with the tag 'European unconscious', often unwittingly presupposes imperious presumption. I may be only slightly over-tuning Malcolm Bowie's (1993: 117–48) fine exposition if I take such a 'European unconscious' to be a fractured serf within Freud's own origins. The localised, yet grandiose, tag 'European unconscious' is valuable only if implemented as an unstable, informative ironic tool which is accurately grounded in the time of its own nineteenth-century *fin-de-siècle* – as so often it has not. In this way, Freud can be measured for the ways he transcended his epoch as a sage for future mental myths. My own account here is ironic, and it has parallels with, for example, Oscar Wilde's inflamatory purpose in the subversive irony in *The Importance of Being Earnest*.[11] As the play is about to climax, Lady Bracknell asserts: 'We live, I regret to say, in an age of surfaces'. While writing this part of *The Importance*, Wilde wrote from Worthing to Lord Alfred Douglas stating that an appeal to 'Chaos' (in relation to the play's manuscript) is 'the stronger evidence for an Intelligent Creator'. The overt over-tidy myth of Lady Bracknell's world, for Wilde, was an irony to mirror the chaos present within society. We may here ponder, however, David Ford's (1992: 21–3) view of the capability of theology to absorb and transform the written past's extraordinary potential for transforming the present and the future, as a voice which dominates the consciousness circumscribed by chaos.

There is a major dispute about whether or not the concept of human consciousness can be captured in a formal theory. Dennett (1991) claims it can, whereas Penrose (1989, 1994a) argues that it cannot. In the present state of theory, anyway, no one has yet presented a formal theory proving that consciousness can by thus represented. So I shall not assume consciousness can be defined. Yet, by-passing this opposition, there is another option.

Igor Aleksander (1997) is one of those considering the proposal of an 'artificial consciousness', produced in theory but not yet in practice by a 'neural state machine'. This, as yet unrealised, theoretical machine is supposed to be the most general model of a finite computing process, which

Penrose (1989, 1994) asserts cannot exist and is logically flawed by Gödels and Turing's work, who claimed that mathematical proofs have no final completed proof. But allow me to sidestep this problem by adopting Aleksander's theory which centres on learning and prediction. He argues that central to consciousness is its capacity for prediction: 'Relationships between world states are mirrored in the same structure of the conscious organism enabling the organism to predict events.' We should demur from the use of the term 'organism' in this quotation, since Aleksander has only succeeded in specifying machine functions, not organic and psychological properties. Consequently, 'artificial' is a premise which betrays the role of (some such phrase as) 'virtual reality individual' as a live metaphor. This is in conformity with the notion of representation developed earlier in Chapter 2, and extends it. My aim is thus to enfold virtual reality as a counter-intuitive strand deployed to complement and extend concepts of mimesis and pictorial poetics, which can be applied both to some issues in the metaphysics of cosmology and to aspects of transcendence concerning divinity.

What are multi-disciplinary relations to the future?

I argue then that proper to a discussion of the possible structure of God's foreknowledge of the world, our use of patterns depicting the past and present heavily obtrude on and influence our projections about the future. We have found that scholarly constructions purporting to identify the past are flawed with contrary assessments and indeterminacy. To the extent that we absorb such obscured visions of the past, we all impose proportionate distortions on to our imagined future(s). In economic theory chaos looms large; this is not unlike the black hole indeterminacy in the early history of the physical universe. But, in contrast, there are examples of creativity and imagination that have been deployed to overcome historical ignorance, usually when such lack of knowledge is amply recognised. I wish to suggest that a live metaphorised notion of virtual reality can be used to reconfigure some of history's relation to the future. That is to say, features of the past's typology metaphorised can be interpreted as a virtual reality mimesis of some senses of a future state of affairs. This projection participates both in the ancient terms of 'there is nothing new under the sun', and attempts to make facets of it explicit in relation to our contemporary cultural theory of the future (see Gibson 2000b).

Malcolm Bowie (1993) has explained how distortions, some of them oddly similar to the foregoing examples, attend our apprehensions of the future. We miss the clues that coerce us to revise the present so as to achieve a future for which we hope; and dreams characteristically displace the optative mood and impose a present tense. Bowie highlights the way in which cultural symbolism constantly, and often invisibly, provokes attempts at the dispersal and deferral of our collective and individual cultural identities as we grapple with our present tense relations to the past and envisaged future.

In other words, the use of the future tense in culture and creativity, as with studies in history and economics, attempts to represent the future by use of the past and present, though of course these subjects are dissimilar in many ways. In certain respects, then, conniving at the future's identity should resort to counter-intuitive simulations of possible futures, as well as utilise recombinations of our presents and pasts, though discontinuities or fractures around our tense-schemes constantly resist our attempts to gain foreknowledge. In contrast, traditional Christian, and some other, metaphysical traditions (cf. Ward 1994) present the God whose foreknowledge has the same degree of knowledge of the future as of past and present.

It is clearly very problematic to attempt any specific structure for knowledge of the future. This counter-intuitively involves and mirrors some relations, which entails the intrusion of transcendence into empiricism, an issue introduced by Donald MacKinnon (1974) when he addressed Cézanne's painting as a token of what it is to be an insight. He proposed that Cézanne's art evokes a presence which goes beyond the sum of its empirical parts. I would like partially to a parallel his enterprise here with attempts to seek the future in our past and present, in which the future is more than the sum of its past and present empirical parts, while the future is analogous with the artistic expression of antecedent projections: metaphoric virtual realities – be they psychological or empirical. George Steiner (1989) extends and complements MacKinnon's thesis. Steiner explores the interaction of Cézanne's own writings in relation to his mental experience and the creative outcome of his paintings Typical of all artists, Cézanne's imagination is fulfilled by manifestation in empirical media. One might conceive of this as a virtual reality transformation from mind to expressive medium, allowing properly for the gap between intention and expression. This virtual reality, parallel with fine art, presupposes a counter-intuitive continuum between transcendent qualities or infinities and quantifiable experience. Freeman Dyson (1985: 55–56) has pointed out that the D function in the equation for metabolism is the same one for the fractional difference in pitch between a perfect fifth and an equi-tempered fifth on a logarithmic scale of pitch (log – log 2), seven semitones or (7/12) log 2. Gibson (forthcoming a) extends this type of relation to compose a live metaphor parallel, a non-algorithmic parallel with only partially understood frontier mathematics (such as M-theory) and qualitative infinities (in say, music and literature). I argue that this will aestheticise formalism, not formalise creativity.

Steiner positions music as the fundamental medium for mirroring the ways in which creativity depicts a sensibility from outside language and empiricism. The role of 'presence' in Barth's positioning of Mozart is obliquely highlighted by Steiner's (1995) view that Barth's negativity has close affinities with Derridean 'absences'. Graham Ward enlarges on such links between Barth and Derrida, concluding that:

> Theological discourse, as a discourse of faith mimes the experience of a

time past and a time postponed; the experience of an ineluctable hope. It generates signs that await a truth to come. Textuality itself incarnates theology's reality; it is a realism in which God's passing resonates in a language which has learned how not to say.

(Ward 1995: 251)

My aim is to suggest that the languages of text and music can be rendered in relevant contexts as virtual reality metaphors of the future in such a way that they will assist to incarnate not only our cosmological scientific perceptions but also our apprehensions of transcendence.

Bowie (1993), as I noted above, circumscribes Barth's use of Mozart, and applies Lacan's (1966) view that the unconscious is textual to interpret Mozart's opera as a metaphor for depicting elements of possible futures. I suggest that such an approach can be incorporated into a virtual reality metaphor of music, in parallel with my foregoing attempts to associate poetry and visual art to virtual reality metaphor. Bowie uses musical and poetic media as devices to explain how visions directed at the future have causal efficacy in displacing the present's consciousness and decomposing the limits of the present tense. We may see in this perspective a live metaphor of music for the pattern of foreknowledge that can be deployed to depict other subjects.

Lacoue-Labarthe writes of Baudelaire's double shock on hearing Wagner:

> because underlying the musical revelation is another revelation, difficult to accept and even scandalous, which is that if Wagner's music attains such power, it does so in the exact measure to which it proceeds with the express and deliberate will to supplant, if not to finish, poetry.
>
> (Lacoue-Labarthe 1994: 6–7)

This is a misleading assertion, though apt in tone. Wagner composed poetry – perhaps sometimes as good as Heine's – as a component in his music, opera, in which he restored the libretto on an equal footing to music. He typifies the marriage of the two sounds – words and music. Here we have the basis for a live metaphor identity relation: the music models and mirrors the identity of the words. Although it is insufficient to suppose that the music paraphrases the words, the relative identity relation which I propose shows some co-extensive properties depicted by the music and words. This relation is uneven and complex and needs developing in relation to music, which is not composed to words (or *vice versa*). Development of this falls outside the scope of the present book, though some note is apt here. In place of the positions occupied by words in Wagner, with respect to, for example, Mozart, one could place emotions (with Budd 1992) and expand this in the perspective of Chapter 1 above. Further, since emotions express disposition towards, and interpret the significance of, the world in their personification of our identities, we may replace words by such elements of the world in the above 'music–words' relative identity equation. Of course, this type of linkage will always be intricate, counter-intuitive and unstable.

Barth's resistance to Kierkegaard's positioning of aesthetics, typified by Mozart, as demoniac, continues this story of resemblance, as does Balthasar's (1992a: 26–9) alignment of some of Barth's with features of Mozart's compositional methods (cf. Oakes 1994b: part II). Consequently, textuality is extended as a basis for a live metaphor of the future by encoding on to it and assessing pictorial poetics and musical aesthetics. In a certain sense, an extension of this live metaphor thread linking music to words to the world employs the past and present to envisage the future.

A series of premises for this live metaphor was formulated in Chapter 2. Filmic realism is utilised there to amplify the live metaphor's representational structure, extending the foregoing groups of relation, enfolding and intercalating properties of music, words, visualisation and movement. In certain ways, such virtual reality mimesis, I have argued, participates in categories parallel with symbolist aesthetics, as, for example, interpreted by Reynolds (1995). Her conclusion draws attention to the role of movement – dance – as a figure and functional variable in representation:

> It has emerged ... that the art of dance, which takes place in real as well as virtual time and space, in many ways provides a paradigm for the kind of spatio-temporal interactions which these poets and painters wished to exploit.

These representational conventions are used to simulate the external world in the filmic domain, in which possible worlds are interwoven by a complex mimesis with actual ontologies. Uses of virtual reality in entertainment technology are, of course, often to the detriment of sensibility. But it is early enough in the development of this medium to draw attention to its more subtle conceptual potential.[12]

Virtual reality and foreknowledge

Could the future be counter-intuitive mimesis?

For some people, the future is virtually a reality, for others it is only possibility composed of (true or false?) worlds; such theses may be combined in a multiplicity of ways together with others. It is worth considering whether or not past approaches to conception of the future may not have an informative interaction with our new contemporary sensibilities based on developments in science – such as 'virtual reality' – and stimulated by critical creativity in the arts.

Central sets of mimesis have a close relation to typical uses of virtual reality. Let us suppose that both notions share the following features. They presuppose the scenario of a world concept and the truth conditions of its referents, in conjunction with, and intersected by, a possible world. This scenario would be fleshed out in various ways, indexing allegiance to a particular version or token instance of mimesis and/or virtual reality. The future can be integrated into this view, in many different ways, as possible worlds, with the past and/or the present as functions both of an actualised or ontological world concept in which originality is a consequence of the conjunction of both actual and possible worlds. Typical instances of art works comply with this sort of outline, with possible worlds being fore-fronted in the aesthetic domain. There are of course complex issues, debates and relations between the empirical and the abstract in art and other domains.

The dispute over Mallarmé's *Un coup de dés* is a case in point.[13] Although this composition is a poem about attempts to outwit randomness in concrete life using abstract reflection, its status regarding surrounding movements (futurism, realism, etc.) is still a matter of conflicting argument. Reynolds (1995, 1992) shows how it links abstraction – not unlike Mondrian's views of painting and poetry – and realism. Mallarmé was both speaking to his absorption with impressionism, in which the subject was reformed and partially dispersed, while he was writing about the structure of the future(s). Reynold's innovative approach to Mallarmé's use of textuality would support this:

> [Mallarmé's writing] invites interrogation of its own ontological status ... it disrupts the '*imaginaire*' as an object of intentional consciousness, ... and opens up an imaginary space which is analogous to textual structures without being reducible to them, thereby making the text ontologically as well as semantically ambiguous ... Imaging activity can be stimulated by the sensory characteristics of language itself.
> (Reynolds 1995: 84)

If we construe 'text' semiotically and allow the visual a role within it, as did Mallarmé in his varying projected illustrations for the poem, as well as permit a transposition between his interest in motion in dance and movement in virtual reality representation, we can see a close parallel here with virtual reality's medium as a resource for new possibilities.

The foregoing is not a commitment to a certain ontology for the future. In the framework of physics, as Polkinghorne (1995a) has pointed out, a correct analysis of relativistic organisations of the past and present, using light cones, preserves temporal distinctions, with no entailment as to the future's 'existence'. Following a strand in David Lewis's (1986) approach to worlds, it may be asked: Is the future a subjunctive conditional set of worlds? Have these constructs the form of possibilities and/or necessities that could be consistent with traditions of insight outlined above in aesthetics? The forms of representation outlined in the foregoing, together with the concept of live metaphor applied to religious and scientific language, are concerned with the media employed to simulate perception of reality. They comprise formal and qualitative devices for depicting a variety of worlds.

Could the future be virtual reality?

The new research done on virtual reality is a domain that can be transformed as a complex live metaphor for depicting the properties of the future. To this bald notion I am suggesting that we add the qualitative insights which cultural mimesis has achieved over the last few centuries. Virtual reality technology is, in qualified respects, an inexorable consequence of earlier cultural developments; so it is worth sketching in summary form some of the close connections between such culture and some virtual reality functions.

'Virtual reality' attempts to represent the conjunction of ideas and their depiction by new technologies – for example, computer simulation and film media to construct models of worlds and their contents. An intriguing facet of this technology is the introduction of actors or actual people into a virtual reality realm so that they blur, and then refocus, the distinction between ideas, virtual reality and actuality. In this way, virtual reality is intended to complete the illusion that simulation of the actual world is virtually identical to the actual world. There is a shortfall in the realisation of this equation, but the consequences of its success are far-reaching. I suggest that this has counter-intuitive and informative relations to a viable conception of the future. It can contribute to a live metaphor structure by which to model features of the way in which people can, to some degree, conceive features of the pattern of God's knowledge of the future. One should not be over enthusiastic about the scope for the use of virtual reality; it is merely one aspect of the concept of representation being presented in this book. Although the technology of virtual reality is new, the categories of illusion it employs are parasitic on, dedicate and modify, previous cultural styles and conventions, many of them struck and honed in the eighteenth and nineteenth centuries. In a sense, virtual reality is a form or mimetic surprise with a live metaphorising of counter-intuitive types, which have relevance for contemporary research about the possibility of representing realities beyond obvious sensory experiment.

This position is not a reactionary yearning for past cultural norms. Baudelaire's (sometimes neglected) attitude to the past is an instructive example here. In 1857 his *Les Fleurs du mal* (1868) was banned in France. The 'offending' poems in the collection were published as *Les Épaves* in 1866. Such innovatory permissiveness is typical of seminal modernism. Yet Baudelaire (as Holland (1993) demonstrates) had, as with many modernists, a strong attachment to the past as a resource for the future. Some postmodernist accounts do not allow for this relation, incorrectly emphasising the role of fracture from the past as a basis for modernist development. The notions associated with 'virtuality' are problematic, yet tantalising. 'Virtuality' seems to rely on the capacity of a set of predicates or proxy properties to produce a simulation that satisfies criteria of identity which are also satisfied by the subject represented. In this sense, 'virtual reality' complies with the logic of live metaphor developed in earlier chapters. Deleuze (1994: 279) argues that 'ideas' are 'pure virtuality'. Such a use of 'idea' evidently participates in history from at least Plato onwards, furnishing us with a tantalising minefield where discussion of ascriptions to God's mind, by analogy, should reconnoitre with care. Our assessment of this depends partly on whether or not we take Descartes to be a pivot from which the modern shifts in the position of God as an external source of 'idea' can be derived. (There is a fruitful discussion on this difference by Charles Taylor (1989, 1994: 241–19) and Susan James (1994).)

So was the Enlightenment an illusion?

Even at the end of the twentieth century David Hume was canonical for many approaches to discussion of divinity, though I believe one can counter the thrust of his main argument against the objectivity of belief, and expose a logically flawed imperialist parochialism in the tenets of his logic. One need not be reactionary, nor yearn romantically for a lost past, in claiming that the dominating strand of interpretation which is now present as the main point of a century's conceptual history is reversible, and by appeal to its own internal discarded or later demoted competing writers. Hume's (1772: secs. 41–43) treatment of 'ideas' internalised and subjectivised 'belief', partly by brief oblique appeal to his contemporary art. Although a widely informed Enlightenment person of letters, Hume narrowly drew on, neglected, and so eclipsed, a (largely Continental) contemporary aesthetic debate, especially influential in France, which was and can be turned against Hume's view of the origin of belief (on the emphasis on 'origin' here, cf. Craig (1987: 90–120)). Hume gave 'illusion' global reductionist scope in his desire to dismiss the transcendental. My point is that the spirit of novelty in the eighteenth century and the winds of change were ripe for the switch we ascribe to Hume. Great though Hume's writings are, they do not analytically achieve a dismissal of the sort he invented for himself. My position does not reflect a reactionary desire to return to the tedious, often analytically bankrupt, Christian theological discourses which he attacked. It is an appeal to get us to recognise how little at least analytical philosophy knows about the Continental culture of Hume's period and its relevance for assessing Hume.

Conversely, Gombrich (1962) and others such as Marian Hobson (1982a) have paved the way to show how illusion can be used to support a deeply realist perception. Hume's thesis on 'belief' stipulated divisions between 'fact' and 'fiction' to the virtual exclusion of 'fact' whose subsequent career, and sometimes its successors' distortion of Hume's complex emphases, ignored his contemporaries' alternative realist aesthetic conceptions. I believe that these can be counter-intuitively transposed in the light of insights already refined in previous centuries, combined with the redeployment of some poststructuralist research.[14] Hume completed his *Treatise* in 1736, publishing it in 1739 and 1740; the first *Enquiry* was published in 1748, and the second in 1751. Rousseau's 1750 essay *Discours qui a remporte la prix a d'Academie de Dijon* and Condillac's *Essai* (1746) intercalate and dispute the presuppositions in Hume's works and their expansions. Hobson advertises how these two French writers functioned as antennae and influences for the topic of illusion in representation. Condillac holds a position close to Rousseau in the 1740s, concerned as he was with the structure of 'attention' in perception of the external world. Condillac was indeed sometimes implausible or uneven in his theories, as Coady notes (1992: 149–51). He and Rousseau were concerned to furnish a framework covering more cultural parameters for the contextualization of belief – for its cultural basis – than Hume. Condillac's *Traite des systèmes* (1749) also agreed with aspects of Newton's concept of relations between science and belief, as against Hume's criticism of Newton. (I return to Newton below.) In some ways similar to the (later) Wittgenstein (1995b), Condillac maintained that language has flaws which radically affect the construction of major metaphysical systems. Yet, unlike Hume, Condillac proposes that one can combine this with composing as 'a Grand Metaphysician', sympathetically teasing out the way in which (if one may take up the (early) Wittgenstein's words in the *Tractatus*) the sense of the world is beyond the world. Language displays and mirrors illusion, but one's taking account of this can lead to redeploying illusion to represent the external world. As shown earlier in Chapter 2, a film recording of a person is tantamount to being that person on grounds of relative identity. The illusion is that the medium conveys the identity of the source of the recording. Virtual reality enfolds this convention and merges it with imagination, as with painting.

Illusion is a function which does not have to fracture the role of consciousness in aesthetic perception, since it is structurally a property of consciousness. Hobson takes this forward and refines Gombrich's (1962) thesis on illusion; and to this we should add the discussion above of Budd's (1992) analysis of an observer's attention to a work of art. The reduction of a three-dimensional world to two dimensions introduces an ambiguity into paintings, and literature. In art, illusion itself is deployed to provoke the simulation of an absent object – the Other. It is in this perspective that George Steiner (1989) has presented the idea of transcendental presence, partly by virtue of an aesthetic artefact successfully standing for what is absent. Frequently the success of this illusion allows a criterion of identity to be derived from the work of art so as to identify the external (empirical) subject of the painting. In this role, illusion is a subset of representation which encapsulates a reality external to the medium it depicts. This state of affairs can be included in a complex live metaphor characterising their transcendental realm of divinity, in which immanent transcendence is a function of creative expression.

Such synthesis runs against Hume's use of a picture and memories to psychologise the status of beliefs based on observing aesthetic illusions of the relevant sort. Thus, it is worth positioning here Hume's distorting neglect of the European and interdisciplinary contexts. In eighteenth-century French writing particularly, art can combine ambiguity with illusion and representation to produce a complex mimesis of the ontological subject. Rousseau was questioning Hume's ownership of talk about probability as a property of atheism. Hobson (1992b: 227–235) allows for the internal shifts and tensions in Rousseau, finding that he used notions of probability which blended with original divine causality and a degree of randomness in human history. Hobson (ibid.: 230) observes that Rousseau, 'was applying to human history modes of argument associated with abstract speculation about the formation of the cosmos, and with concrete evaluation of modes of proof expressed, for instance, in Buffon's *Théorie de la terre* (cf. Buffon 1749). This is not unlike the logic of virtual reality, in which abstract concepts and the implementation of mathematical proofs are applied to human-simulated states of affairs. In virtual reality, chance, causal law, logic and imagination profitably collide to produce an illusion of a world different from our own. This situation has a formal parallel with art in general, in which illusion functions to induce in us an attention to a simulation as if it were a form of life.

The ways in which a possible world, or an actual future world, can be derived through virtual reality representation from ingredients in the present or past world, has particular parallels, for example, with the art of Escher. Of such composition, Escher stated:

> Whoever wants to portray something that does not exist has to obey certain rules. Those rules are more or less the same as for the teller of fairy tales; he has to apply the function of contrasts; he has to shock. The element of mystery to which he wants to call attention must be surrounded and veiled by perfectly ordinary everyday self-evidences that are recognisable to everyone. That environment, which is true to nature and acceptable to every superficial observer, is indispensable for causing the desired shock.
>
> (Escher 1989: 136)

It may be that, in certain respects, Hume did not have the capacity for aesthetic conceptual surprise, such as one finds in some art, and in virtual reality. These aesthetical domains, I argue, have formal and conceptual parallels with the counter-intuitive aspects that comprise scientific cosmology and also transcendence. If this view is correct, it is not surprising that his empiricism eclipsed a continent outside of his purview.

Even so, Hume complimented Newton on his use of imagination in Newton's 'Rules of Reasoning'. Hume admired Newton's 'Rules', though he redeployed aspects of them severely to criticise the argument from design that was associated with Newton, and he also drove a wedge through Newton's synthesis of science and theology (cf. Force and Popkin 1990c). Aspects of Hume's great revolution seem as anachronistic as Newton's association of science with theology did to Hume.

Imagination now has a central role in empirical theorising which, linked to Popper's (1972) falsifiability criterion, faults Hume's inductive empiricism. Hume's supervenience, by which there is no general truth of history, but only individual inductive truths, is at odds with the Big Bang scenario because generalisation for this epoch of the universe is a lawlike consequence of a single initial epoch in the very early universe, whose identity is qualitatively distinct from its consequent effects in the, then, future of the universe. This sort of situation aligns much more with the metaphysical basis of Newton's cosmological empiricism than it does Hume's empirical parochialism.

The foregoing debate impacts on our attempts to grapple with the future. Models of the future can variously construct past and possible life-histories, as well as utilise the present. The above has suggested that a facet of conceiving the future has a structural resemblance in its use of live metaphor to the aesthetics of eighteenth-century illusion. The materials of everyday life, properly simulated and recomposed, produce a sum larger than its material parts. These remarks are cursory, though summarising research, since a lengthy study is not apt here. My purpose is to highlight how one might sketch a structural link with issues in the philosophy of religion, aesthetics and the question of knowledge of an absent subject. This can then be used as elements in constructing a complex live metaphor of transcendental foreknowledge. As such the absent 'other' bifurcates into 'God' and the 'future'. Attempts at representation of the future have parallels with simulation and virtual identity. A variety of examples illustrate these parallels. 'Simulation' and 'virtual reality' are basically complex live metaphor functions. I wish to argue that clusters of distinctions such as these can be harnessed, in suitably tuned forms, to develop further the live metaphor thesis of the representation of God advanced in earlier chapters, as well as link up with the depiction of transcendental functions outlined in astrophysical cosmology. In attempting here to connect the topics of virtual reality and divine foreknowledge, an array of distinctions, debates and relations about human mental reality and prediction need to be presented prior to proceeding directly with their connections.

Can virtual reality falsify knowledge?

One may not agree, as Penrose (1994a) does not, with aspects of Tipler's (1995) programme that stipulates the future of the universe, in which an as yet uninvented super-computer is theoretically formulated and proposed as a metaphor to formalise aspects of transcendence and infinite. But Tipler thereby advertises or betrays to what extent speculative scientific cosmology does at times give itself over to simulation and thought experiment. My own approach inclines to Penrose's assessment, rather than Tipler's, in the use of the computer as a model for mentality. John Polkinghorne's (1995a) criticisms expose a quite unwarranted reductionism in Tipler's formal position; and the latter's appeal to games theory is only one highly improbable interpretation of the data. It is as if Tipler has within him an almost fundamentalist desire to use divine immanent terminology, while converting this into a reductionism which superficially avoids any ascription to that on which his theory would need to depend – God. Tipler (1995) reduces theology to speculative, albeit mechanistic, science. Contrariwise, my hope is to give science and theology their due different emphases, yet support the scientific probity of transcendence, partly by showing that science has hidden transcendental variables in it which resist the reductionist science. Tipler (ibid.: ch. 2) conceives of a super-computer along the lines of a brain, as yet unconstructed, in the way artificial intelligence specialists do, such as the distinguished authority Aleksander (1997). This type of (imaginary theoretical) computing facility is introduced in a virtual reality simulated environment, recombining actual features from our three-dimensional world. Perhaps Tipler is less careful that Aleksander to control the modifying term 'artificial' to 'intelligence'. But as Aleksander's approach shows, one does not have to take on board Tipler's programme reducing qualitative transcendence to the capabilities of computers conceivable in virtual reality.

Theoretical possibilities are deployed to construct virtual reality environments. Novels – for example, Thomas Pynchon's *Vineland* and his novel *V* – amount to literary topologies for a filmic virtual reality fulfilment by composing an artificial world interwoven with our own actual world. At the other end of the spectrum, however, we find virtual reality technology being employed in 'War Games', by military strategists as potential ontological readings of what could happen. This is a subjunctive conditional use of virtual reality to address the future. So here we have both fictional and strategic operational realms employing the same virtual reality principles of simulation. It is worth contrasting this with Tipler's logic:

> Consider the collection of all mathematical concepts. Let us say that a perfect simulation exists if the physical universe can be put into one-to-one correspondence with some mutually consistent subcollection of all mathematical concepts. In this sense of 'simulation' the universe can certainly be simulated, because 'simulation' then amounts to saying that the universe can be exhaustively 'described' in a logically consistent way. Note that 'described' does not require that we or any other finite (or infinite) intelligent being can actually find the description. It may be that the actual universe expands into an infinite hierarchy of levels

whenever one tries to describe it exhaustively. In such a case, it would be impossible to find a Theory of Everything. Nevertheless, it would still be true that a 'simulation' in the more general sense existed if each level were in one-to-one correspondence with some mathematical object, and if all levels were mutually consistent ('consistency' meaning that, in the case of disagreement between levels, there is a rule – itself a mathematical object – for deciding which level is correct). The crucial point of this generalisation is to establish that the actual physical universe is something in the collection of all mathematical concepts. This follows because the universe has a perfect simulation, that is, with its emulation. Thus, at the most basic ontological level, the physical universe is a concept.

(Tipler 1995: 209)

Tipler appeals to 'a logical consistent way'. He is accordingly subject to that to which he appeals, even though we may find it strange that he assumes there to be some self-evident sense of 'logical consistent way' which offers no explicit resolution of interpretative issues. In the above quotation from Tipler, 'described' does not require that an infinite being can find the exhaustive description of the universe. But an infinite being by usual classical Christian definition, has the properties of omniscience and instantaneity. So Tipler's 'being' satisfies a fallacious[15] intentional criterion of identity which is different from God's. Tipler claims that at the most basic level, the physical universe is a concept. This embodies segmentation and quantifier-shift fallacies. If a criterion of identity does not distinguish between itself and a representation of it, it conflates the object-language (such as '3 + 4 = 7') and its meta-language level (i.e. '$x + y = z$'), as well as confusing the three or more dimensions of the external world with the two signifying (notational) dimensions, together with the (possibly 26) dimensions to be depicted in the microphysical world. This sort of muddle is what Russell's theory of types suitably deployed can avoid (cf. Smiley 1982).

Tipler (1995: 210) obviously recognises that there is a difference between the abstract and the physical in representation; but for him, thinking observers entail that thinking is a physically existent concept, since he subsumes such a person in a mathematical concept. But this is simply an abstraction fallacy, by equivocating over the medium as the message, confusing the concept with its empirical reference.[16] Obviously, in a television broadcast (as Chapter 2 showed earlier in this book), the logic of representation has no inference to deem identical the medium that relays an identity with the identity itself since communication facilitates identification, not identity. Tipler, in the above quotation ('we agree to identify the universe with its perfect simulation'), merely conflates, by modal fallacy and category, the relation of 'identify' with 'identity', confuses cosmology with ontology. Even on the hypothesis that the physical universe came from the Word, and that somehow the universe portrays that origin, it does not follow, of course, that the universe is a concept which is physical. Of course this does not oppose the possibility of the universe having an ontology which somehow reflects its transcendental origin.

Tipler (1995) is wide of the mark, though he has (incorrectly) formulated a family resemblance, which on further scrutiny is distinct from his reductionism of God to concept and concept to physical ontology. Perhaps you will excuse my spelling this out in the following way, so as to compose the desired focus on the theme of this chapter in relation to foregoing ones. It is a commonplace to observe that we cannot infer God from the universe. But it seems that the complex mixture of empirical and evaluative (for example, aesthetic) properties in the universe, together with those qualities assigned to its creator, render the relation between the universe and its source on which sidesteps the all-too neat inference block between universe and God.

Does virtual reality merge with the real world?

There are parallels between this inference-block and the collapse of the formulation that one cannot derive an 'ought' from an 'is'. Bernard Williams (1993) argued that actual relation between 'ought' and 'is' is on both sides a complex mixture of empirical and evaluative features, which cannot be dismantled in the required manner into these deontic and empirical states, though both states occur. In earlier chapters we have seen how the physics of the present universe collapses into a super-physics that contravenes the universe's current physics, and shown that transcendental functions are interwoven between, and within, the cross-over point at the pre-Planck time approaching the source of the Big Bang. In this situation, contemporary cosmology amounts to a rather poor virtual reality simulation of the beginning of the universe (see Figure 6.1) which is akin to our attempts to connive at the contents of the future. We saw earlier that according to Rees (1995, 1997) there is a 1-to-10 chance that the Big Bang scenario is right. In the Prologue it was noted that the cosmologist Dallaporta (1993) considers it incoherent not to recognise that astrophysical cosmology uses transcendental equations that are not empirical. In contrast, while agreeing with such views, I have been proposing that aesthetic and transcendental properties occur systematically and often counter-intuitively within and prior to the emergence of the universe. Many of these functions occupy a manifold framework for which there is no empirical classification, save that the physics of the universe seems to derive from them – rather as with the way in which the collapse of the 'ought' versus 'is' contrast is sublimed into the Williams's (1993) inseparable mixture of evaluative and empirical elements.

The traditional use of analogy and metaphor can be counter-intuitively refined and expanded to provide live metaphor and virtual reality worlds, or portions of them, which recombine variables and laws. At one level this gives apparent ontological implementation for functions that were previously thought to be empirically incoherent: it typifies how analogy and live

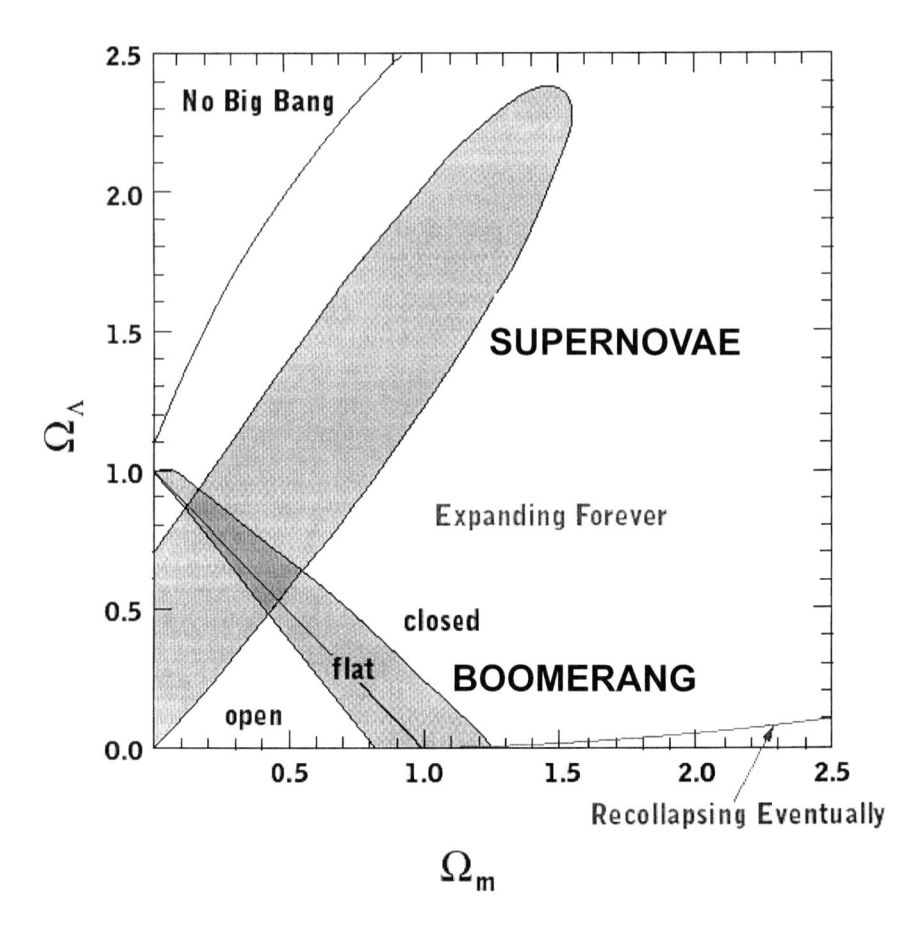

Figure 6.1 History after the big bang à la Boomerang

Source: Boomerang, NASA, NSF

Note: Boomerang cosmological data compared with Type 1a supernovae density of space in matter (OmegaM) that slow down after the expansion from the big bang, and the dark energy of empty space (OmegaLambda) that can cause acceleration. The results here imply that: (a) after the big bang the universe accelerated to velocities much higher than the speed of light; (b) the universe is flat; (c) the universe will not re-collapse.

metaphor for qualitatively transcendent phenomena could be represented by finite material functions in a way empirically inconceivable in the past. A central feature of virtual reality environments is that our own sensory three-dimensional world is interwoven with the virtual reality world to produce cross-over criteria that map the experimental possibilities intrinsic to the virtual reality world. This linkage, I wish to argue, is of assistance in conceiving forms of representation of divinity which are both infinite and immanent.

Prediction and the cosmology of God 253

Can the future be revealed by thought-experiment?

To pursue this notion, we ought first to look critically at refined concepts of 'thought experiment' – a term which, for example, Tipler (1995) takes on board without attention to the relevant philosophical literature. A much more refined use of this topic is Sorensen's (1992: 225–28) study on 'thought experiments' which introduces 'thought simulation' as one of its subsets. He notes that simulations are experiments 'once removed', experimenting on ersatz variables, bridging the gap between it and empirical experiment by analogy. This procedure is typified by Sorensen at lower levels of generality by, for example, using a scale model plane testing for real turbulence in an air tunnel. He also cites Ronald Dworkin's (1978) analogy of jurisprudential and literary scholars (in which David Copperfield is treated as an actual person), and analogy to which I return below. I want to suggest a number of extensions to this notion, so that we might characterise some aspects of what it would be for us to ascribe to God foreknowledge. So far in this book we already have a number of analogies: for example, astronomical prediction, which is an unusual form of retrojection from our contemporary observations to derive knowledge of the early universe. We considered the singular origin of the universe(s) as a unique instance, whose logic could therefore not include an induction from prior precedents. From the standpoint of the ideal observer or creator, prior to this event, the identity of such predictive knowledge would be *a priori*, though empirical. This is thus a partial precedence for an epistemological structure of God's foreknowledge.

Certainly, it is important, however, for us to keep the qualitative distance between our mental states and those ascribable to a creator. As Sorenson points out (1992: 227) in a secular context, we are not actually simulating a (in the present book's perspective, God's) mental process when simulating in a thought experiment. So we can avoid some circular anthropomorphic presumption here. Sorenson draws on Hanson's (1966) illustration to delineate simulation of a mental process by comparing the strain Copernicus put on the imaginations of his contemporaries to imagining oneself on a spinning merry-go-round, and sitting in a revolving chair. You are convinced that you are stationary, and that the world around you is moving, as people perceived it before Copernicus. His contemporaries have to convince themselves that what they see, looking to heaven, is that it is stationary and the Earth is spinning and orbiting. This parallel attempts to recreate for us the mental process of (dis)orientation of those experiencing the Copernican revolution. When we attempt to adumbrate any mental state of God, this simulation of mental process is quite distinct from Hanson's mental simulation. Thought simulation, in the relevant sense, is that in which the conceptual status of God's foreknowledge, and that which is simulated, satisfies the same truth-conditions where a criterion of identity is concerned. And there is an empirically targeted component (such as prediction in cosmology, sociology, psychoanalysis, economics or religious text) which has

254 *The cosmology of life*

a live metaphor relation to the transcendental mental state (foreknowledge) simulated. As observed above, when discussing Sorensen's analysis, parameters and variables can permissibly be reconfigured (as they are in astrophysical cosmology). In the following section I offer a thought experiment using virtual reality as a metaphor to discuss the concept of God's knowledge of the future.

Can we use Newton in a thought-experiment?

In the perspective of philosophy of religion, however, it is worth again drawing attention to Force and Popkin's (1990a) retrieval of the Hume–Newton axis on this matter. Hume was greatly impressed by Newton's scientific methodology and used much of it as a model for his philosophy of science. In contrast, Hume castigated Newton's religious views on God's foreknowledge. In 1703, when Newton became President of the Royal Society (whose 1663 Charter made provision for the providential glory of God in creation), Newton was much concerned with the alleged synthesis between general and special providence, with prophecy figuring centrally in the latter class. Hume classified prophecy as a sub-category of miracle, and Newton, together with Locke (cf. Harris 1994), used biblical prophecies to argue their views on divine foreknowledge. Hume demolished Newton's type of position, and biblical scholars today would give almost no credence to Newton's biblicist methods, just as Newton's alchemy was presented by him as internal to his science.[17] Yet we isolate such mythology from the validity of his gravitational concepts, so we might look afresh at elements in his philosophy of religion. This is not the place to do that, though its position in Hume's polemics and their continuing impact make the issue relevant to science and religion concerning prediction. Newton's views on special providence,[18] were part of complex underground and institutional tradition of biblical interpretation for which there is now no mainstream parallel.[19]

In recognising the incorrectness of this tradition, we should be willing to acknowledge that its passing away has not removed all problematic issues it posed. As a scrutiny of Newton's published and unpublished manuscripts show, his views did anticipate the return of the Jews to Palestine and the Arab renaissance in the twentieth-century Middle East. While it would be foolish to explain this in terms of the biblicist traditions composing Newton's cultural environment, the foregoing study survey[20] of some social prediction theory portrays how little basis there is for a conclusive sociological analysis, since chaos theory and antecedents for possible futures have not yet been susceptible of measurable analysis. For some scholars such as Anglin (1990) patterns of providence could be incorporated into such phenomena, though chance or catastrophe theories could be applied to account for such historical patterns.[21] But let us imagine a thought experiment in virtual reality which accepts Newton's, or anyone else's, knowledge of the future. We then use this as a live metaphor to structure what it would be to assign knowledge of the future to God. How could analytical philosophy handle that?

Logical prediction

What would a logic of the future be?

In the following I am not interested in crafting one narrow interpretation faithful to a particular logician's doctrine of tense. It is hoped the following has some tolerance towards a variety of approaches An opening notation for a prediction: 'Fn p' = 'It will be the case in n years that p'. Here 'Pn' is the past tense, and 'p' signifies a semiotic representation (e.g. a proposition, a picture, a multi-dimensional likeness, etc.) of an event. Similarly, 'Pn p' stands for the past tense state of affairs (cf. Dummett 1981: 391–400). God's foreknowledge at time t_1, roughly, would be: 'If p, then God knows that p, if and only if God exists. In the foregoing, 'p' relates to the theorem:

> At t_1 the one and only x predicts p, and p is fulfilled
> [or comes true] at t_2 if and only if x exists. [11]

Of course the mediation of p from x would be by the instantiation of y in [1] to [6] above. This might help to explain why a person's uttering a prediction had wrongly been identified by exegetes as the person's being the author, whereas y is the agent of x for x's prediction in the relevant biblical uses. (This presupposes no judgement on an exclusion of the agent's personality as *a* factor in the production of p; it only requires at the given level that the predictive content is derived from x.)

The qualitative topology of [11] maps on to the topology between two differential manifolds (as in Thom 1989) where one manifold relates to our universe and the other to that super universe beyond the spacetime boundaries. At appropriate positions these are infinite dimensional manifold vectors. The referent of p is a closed subspace of a finite co-dimension. So p is a subsystem of God's manifold, and comes to be known prior to the occurrence of the target of p by revelation.

The feature of [11] which contrasts with, for example, Swinburne's (1979: 63–8) probability notion of prediction, is that [11] is deductively valid, and valid in an especially strong sense, though of course one allows for the convertibility of probability into deductivist form. Nevertheless, such treatments do not exclude the possibility of contingency and moral choice on the part of agents who fulfil the prediction. Shoesmith and Smiley's (1980: 11–236) fine multiple conclusion logic has features which could be introduced to treat of and preserve choice. They offer a system in which a number of choices are inferred as a block inference, but only one of which may be given uptake in the fulfilment. An omniscient observer could foreknow which choice this would be, and prophesy it. But foreknowledge does not entail causal destruction of the agent's choice in the fulfilment; it merely presupposed knowledge of it in advance.

In terms of Christian theological presuppositions, Christ would be the highest case of this fulfilment who manifested perfect obedience voluntarily, at the same time as being a function of foreknowledge of fulfilling predictions about precisely that mode of person he was. So p above has its ideal case in 'the Word made flesh'. Torrance (1981: 40) states that one cannot reach a final normalisation of such matters. However, even a modest gain in logically representing a strong concept of revelation, which does not distort, will achieve significant results. Torrance states (1969: 280): '[God] nevertheless refuses to be understood merely from within the conceptual framework of our natural thought and language but demands of that framework a logical reconstruction in accordance with His Word.' For example, sensible use of the schema '$Pn\ p$' in tense and predicate logic will prevent 'The Word became flesh' from being equivalent to 'Flesh became the Word'. The same goes for the future-tense schema '$Fn\ p$' by use of temporal token reflexive operators which relativise the expression (cf. Dummett 1981: 389–400).

Behind the schema and [11] is the (Barcan) formula (where ϕ is a function):

'If it could be that something ϕ's, then there is something that could ϕ' [12]

where ϕ stands for the prediction in [11]. Here in the deep structure of the quantifier 'something' in [12], the x corresponds with that x in [11]; x is mediated by the medium specified via [1] to [11], such that $y = x$ where relative identity in revelation conveys the Word. And x is to be filled by the proper name of God or the common noun 'god'. This relies on the Prior–Fine (1977: 60) equation:

'For some x, for all y, y is p if and only if it is identical to x' [13]

which stems from the conjunction:

'Something which is p is q' and 'There is exactly one thing which is p [14]

where p and q are predicate variables typifying the personal identity of God (x) and his foreknowledge such that he is the sole bearer of those properties. Here 'q' stands for the fulfilment in God's foreknowledge. In this way, the class of possible subjects for x in [11] is a one-member 'world' class – God. Within the scope of his presupposition, only God foreknows and predicts the future, excluding chance guesses, and assuming that these two forms of anticipation are qualitatively distinct. It is this which yields the application of the second conjunct in [14] to showing that the bearer is God.

Is a prediction true or false?

In [11] above, the prediction *p* is clearly a controversial affair. Since my concern is not ideological but the nature of prediction, I shall not here defend an expositional framework within which to establish the following projected instances of the predictions which fill the *p* proposition in [11] above. What we need is a proposition which is specific and whose putative referent is recognisable and uncontroversial respecting its representation (i.e. does not encode speculative value-judgements). Let us therefore, within the framework of the thought experiment, enter into the anachronism of Newton's world view. The two alternatives given below, following Newton's actual suggestions are bizarre and eurocentric, but they reflect Newton's own internal choice of presuppositions. Their oddly prescient coincidence with the timescale he envisaged (that such propositions would become true hundreds of years after his demise) is fodder for macroeconomists and historians:

> Arab kingdoms are restored by Arabs in their ancient territorial
> locations in Middle East. [11a]

and:

> Jewish migrants return to the territory named Palestine and
> establish a kingdom.[22] [11b]

Dummett (1981: 395) can be adapted and utilised for a facet of [11]'s use. I modify it as follows: '[11]' uttered at t_1 is true at t_2 (where t_2 implements the possibility which is [11]) under the domain of the actual course of history *C*, if and only if, for every possible above [11] course of history (below termed *C*) which coincides with *C* comprising t_2, [11]' is true at $<t_1C>$, and '*Fn* [11]' revealed at t_1 is true at t_2 under *C* if and only if, for every *C* which coincides with *C* up to t_2, '[11]', uttered at $t_1 + n$ is true at $t_1 + n$ under *C*.

In his exposition, Dummett notices that the law of the excluded middle still applies, and the classical laws hold (where one renders disjunction so that '*Fn*' is distributive into it, in that '*Fn*([11] v −[11])' can be taken to be the equivalent of '(*Fn*[11]) v (*Fn*−[11])'). In this guise, prophecy is either true or false.

How to expand in what respect [11] pertains to [11a, b] and t_1/t_2 needs careful handling as to scope. The early Wittgenstein (1963: 7) can be linked to this programme:

> 'the world is everything that is the case' [15]

This requires that *n* ('the world is the case') is not identical to only the material universe, but to 'what there is'. For it is not evident that the universe

258 *The cosmology of life*

exhausts what there is. And [15] also includes immoral Jewish and Arab acts of free choice which partly led to [11].

History and imagining futures

Is history complex chaos or causal function?

Of course, it could be both. Within this [15]'s specification of a state of affairs, Dummett's C could correspond to Trevor-Roper's (1981) explanation of the potential of freewill and the propensity for multiple future possible courses of history, only one of which is realised, often improbably so. In filling [11] with a reference to the Arabs or Israel, I do not of course display any support for any political stance towards it. One might equally have filled [11] with any grouping as subject. Such historical examples can be viewed as members of a temporal database in artificial intelligence, as well as in the perspective of unique character data (as with Gabbay *et al.* 2000), with the provisos that divine mentality is not artificial and there are nonalgorithmic versions of infinite temporal stress; this thus extends the concept of virtual reality simulation of temporal domains, proposed above. It is interesting to cite Trevor-Roper's observation on the relevant Middle East state of affairs:

> A century ago geopoliticians could have foreseen the continued colonisation by Russia and the United States of the empty lands to the East and to the West; but who could have foreseen that far more astounding colonisation in the Eastern Mediterranean, the creation of the State of Israel? We may like it or not ... we may deplore it as the last Western crusade, the latest venture of Western imperialism, seeking not trade but settlement, *Lebensraum*; and in fact it is surely both of these things. But we cannot deny that it is an extraordinary historical achievement. How little the British statesmen who listened to its early advocates foresaw the present consequences: the replacement of a Jewish 'national home' by a 'national state'; the consequent transformation of the Middle East...
>
> The Islamic Revolution of our day, like the development of the State of Israel, is a phenomenon which could have been predicted – and soon, no doubt, the textbooks will be making it seem the most obvious thing in the world. But it never was predicted by those scientific historians who look too confidently forward into the future because they have looked, with insufficient imagination, on the past.
>
> (Trevor-Roper 1981)

Dummett's 'possibility' and Trevor-Roper's options which I have used for [11] clearly occupy very different roles in their treatment, in contrast with my own formulation here; but we share the sense of possibilities. In the foregoing perspective, they are possibilities which are subject to God's foreknowledge.

Is the future a virtual reality nightmare?

The exegesis of the prophetic framework of [11] is outside the scope of this book. But, while recognising the force of MacKinnon's (1982: 25) criticism of an 'apocalyptic indulgence and a cult of despair' in the twentieth century century, it is also important to position his appeal to the tragic dimension of intractable problems associated with the threat of nuclear warfare. In such scenarios, apocalyptic realism is not fantastic. The resemblance between one facet of a family of prophecies and the modern history of the Middle East, albeit at the secular level, in the form it has taken, both emphasises the tragic domain in the ethics, while yet indicating an historic move in a land. The fulfilment of [11 a, b] is obviously a secular affair; but so was the restoration which preceded the birth of Jesus.

As the ideal prophetic filler for [11], 'the Word became flesh' is a unique qualitative value. Yet at lower levels, this is matched by the unique foreknowledge, exemplified in [11], which true revelation displays. A universal quantification attends prophetic revelation. This contrasts with a mystical guess or a conjecture by historians. These occur in a series of such expectations, which have a probability distribution only at most, a few of which are realised in history. The surface grammar of guess mimics is that of a concept of revelation. But the logic of the former is probability, whereas the logic of the latter presupposes bivalence. The latter is true deduction, the former expectation.

Unique individualism

Is foreknowledge in time?

So, I have argued that the universal quantification of foreknowledge or prediction deriving a concept of God, together with the resulting and related qualitative differences, arise from differences of cosmology.

Dummett's (1981: 394–5) relativisation for future tensed t_1 sentences to be read as true if true at t_2, enables it to be used to support the application of a function (Wp), 'world at time t'. Presupposing Prior's (1967: 80) axioms, 'world at time t' can be defined as':[23]

> The above sense of n is linked to the axiom that p is a truth at
> t_1 from which everything that is true permanently follows.
> This may be expressed as 'if p is the total world-state at t_1,
> and q is true at t_1' then the relation between p and q
> (p contains q) requires that the implication of q by p will
> be true at all times (e.g. t_2)', or introduce Wp as a
> primitive function without propositional quantifiers.   [16]

Rees's (1997) multiverse use of plural universe scenarios could be regarded as an astrophysical corollary and reapplication of Lewis's, Prior's, or

260 *The cosmology of life*

Chihara's (1998) world states. On any of these scenarios, we could interpret them so as to add the following proposition to the present argument:

> There are different ontologies for any world-state in a virtually infinite set of universes, derivable, by an ideal realist observer O, from our present world-state, to facilitate the instantiation of counter-intuitive propositions about other world-states unlike our own. [17]

Could there be transfinite access to this universe from God's domain?

My paraphrase of Rees's 'infinite ensembles of universes' as the multiverse with a virtually infinite regress of universes, is intended to exclude both the claim that universes can be actually infinite, and that if God has a spatial and/or qualitative relation external to the multiverse, God is not merely a functional and qualitative subset of the multiverse.

If one were to regard Priest's (1995) paraconsistent logic as incorrect (with its view that a given proposition can be true *and* false of the same spacetime) as I do, it still might be usable, with modification, to illuminate an issue here. The strategy would be to work a proposal out of the type that some of his conclusions could be preserved for and by a transformed paraphrase into bivalent logics, perhaps using Haack's (1996) analysis of deviant logics, derivable through a Lewis S5 system, to standard logics, or utilising Chihara's (1998) semantics for modal logic as interpreted and extended in the foregoing. I do not suppose that this would salvage Priest's thesis. Priest wants to use a closure less than the set of all propositions as means to infer to a point beyond the limits of thought in classical logic, so that transcendence is achieved though use of transfinite set theory (see below), together with the state of affairs that such logic backs onto the limits outside itself by use of infinities, and universalisation. I suggest that this sort of approach, albeit through counter-intuitive bivalent logical expressions, as well as aesthetic predication, could result in a route to structure relations between this world and God's relation to the world, with some of the deeper areas of cosmology discussed above as a physical analogical precedence for initiating talk of transcendence, distinct though the two spheres are.

What would be an interface from a transcendent universe?

Prior observes (1967: 82):

> 'If p gives the present (t_1) total world state, p permanently implies that q is a future total world-state.' [18]

It should be recalled that C– a possible world course – is a subset of *p* in [18], as are other possible worlds which could become the case, but do not have to, which opposes hard determinism. This type of thesis concurs with aspects of Everett's (1973) scenario, discussed above, though the possible worlds thesis could be replaced with the S5 modal realist approach of Chihara (1998). On this type of interpretation [11] would be a sub-class value of *p*. And importantly, the referent of *x* in [11] would be a member of *n*'s class, which differs from the scope which Wittgenstein gives for 'Welt'. *Wp* would be the total state of knowledge of what there is (which, on Newtonian, general relativistic M-theory grounds, only God could know) including the teleology for the future and predictions respecting it.

Is foreknowledge of the incarnation logical?

Using Prior's formulation (1977: 46–50):

> 'There is some individual who can truly say, "I and I alone satisfy Q", where "*Qx*" is "exactly one thing"' [19]

we can restrict *W* to being an individual, and one who knows *p* in *Wp*. In this way, where [11] and its type fill a subset of *p*, we can align [11]'s credential respecting 'The one and only *x*' as [19]. The predictive element of [11] supports a uniquely knowledgeable individual as sole possessor of predictive subjects of *p*. Using this priority, [19]'s *W* would pick out that *W* which is qualitatively exclusive of the material *W* (i.e. the universe). If one wanted to furnish a topological domain and surface on which to map this [19]*W*, one would draw on the state of affairs obtaining before that causal pathology – the singularity – which is not asymptotic, but satisfies an infinite free product,[24] yet where time is less than t_0, but where there is entailed the existence of an actual situation *W* (either [16] or [19] or both). Let us postulate minus-times here, or regard duration as relativity-independent, such that it extends with a supermanifold before t_0.

It is not inconsistent to view the qualitative existence of both pre-creation or pre-time to conditions of the contemporary universe. Ellis (1978) and Ellis *et al.* (1978) have, for example, advanced a model for the universe where the primeval fireball still exists at the 'top' of the universe, with the Earth at the bottom, rather like a bell and its clangour corresponding to the Earth's position. Matter is transformed at the particle level as it approaches the fireball. Two theoretical weaknesses have been pointed out in this model, to do with the constants and role of gravity. But at least the hypothesis illustrates how one can develop a topology which turns the axes of our time frame and primeval big bang into identical time-points. Davies (1978) has opposed Ellis's view by claiming Ellis does not explain how his static universe could have produced life at one given point in spacetime. Barrow and Tipler (1986) have developed and generalised Davies's thesis.

Of course, in any case general relativity breaks down, or an as yet incompletely specified theory of quantum and spacetime would not hold beyond $t>0$, i.e. in a topology *immediately* before the time of the commencement of this universe's existence.

If this scenario were accurate then Popper's three worlds' thesis would require amending to include a fourth world which would be the world model $W[19]$. This would have at least the ontological status of World I, but without its materialist qualities. We might see this as having a relation of parody or live metaphor irony when contrasted with the poetic and rare formation in Isaiah 57:15, the Lord 'inhabits eternity'.

In relativity all spaces are related, given infinite energy (for example in Gödel's model for the universe). So $W[19]$'s referent would have access to the material universe. But there would be a closure condition of the material universe because of a consequence of Von Neumann's and Mirimanoff's (see Mirimanoff 1917; cf. Von Neumann 1998), which prevents endless descents regarding *Fundierungsaxiom*. Basically, in terms of matter-energy conditions, this axiom points up the universe as a self-contained prison from which energy cannot escape if the available resources are constrained by the physical theories manifested in the universe's structure. (Of course, the way in which this point is put needs complementing by noticing, for example, Popper's avoidance of prescriptive language when characterising the contingencies of physical laws.) This axiom excludes movement outside of a given set (i.e. $W[19]$) regarding inclusion of other members.

It is significant that this restriction also operates, slightly modified, for propositions (cf. Prior 1977: 127–9). If this sort of scenario has any relevance for the theology of revelation or the theology of a revelation based on human creativity, then such conceptions could be treated as tautologous in certain senses with the semantic in proposition [19] above.

Is knowledge of infinity directional?

The foregoing considerations can be positioned so as to have an analogy with Cantor's theory of transfinite well-orderings. It is interesting to note, as Quine (1963: 88) points out, that before Mirimanoff, Cantor in an 1899 letter had anticipated the notion of replacement associated with the *Fundierungsaxiom* (cf. Cantor 1932: 444). Namely, the state of affairs mapped as a series of predications being infinite in one direction and finite in another in a manifold whose scope is co-extensive with this universe and the creator's domain. However, with the closure of the set $W[19]$ at the causal boundary of spacetime, one has to clear delineation between the universe's matter energy system and World IV, i.e. God's matter–energy system, or what Hoyle's (1975) treatment deems 'the other side' of T. In World IV, the universe's decay functions – as values of time – would not exist, having been nested in the universe in primeval time while not being intrinsic in principle for the existence of a universe.

Just as energy was shifted through the interface (the causal boundary of spacetime) from World IV to our universe to produce the creation, so likewise at one level it is the case that for knowledge of and/or from the other side to be accessible to use, revelation or perception of World IV is the prerequisite. This follows on a Minkowski frame of reference, and not the Einstein–de Sitter model. Cantor considered it proved that transfinite numbers are eternally existing realities in the mind of God.

Given this state of affairs, these numbers can be treated as evidence of a qualitative stencil (the theorem for defining a function) in which a feature of the revealed pattern of God's Word is set. On the basis of the foregoing, this manifestation of the Word of God satisfies [1] to [6] and [11] to [19]. To be sure, one must not mechanise or materialise God. But the formal model cannot commit this error because transfinite numbers and their theorems are not material. I do not here subscribe to Cantor's other judgement, however, that the universe is identical to the scope of the infinite in transfinite set theory. Presumably this error was due to the limited way in which he conceived of the universe in ignorance about cosmology and recent developments in the mathematics of infinity. Yet Laplace (1799) had developed part of a mathematics for black holes and related it to physical behaviour in stars (cf. Hawking and Ellis 1973: 364). We have seen above that beyond the causal spacetime boundaries of our universe there is a qualitatively distinct system which explicitly entails that it is surrounded by and is the embodiment of infinity conditions. In this way, Cantor's restriction of infinity to the universe was misconceived, although it does not falsify his mathematics of infinity. Of course, this admission does not entail the exclusion of transfinite series and infinity from this universe because that would not follow from the foregoing analysis, and the above provides grounds for showing that infinite design functions are nested in the laws which are encoded into the universe's ontology.

Resuming the parallel with Cantor's theory, those subject to relativistic matter–energy conditions cannot ascend the scale (series) to move outside and beyond the universe, to World IV. Attempts to counter this would involve us in sideways infinite regresses. But if God exists, then he is at the top of the series and can descend it. Consequently, the foregoing types of distinctions can assist in formulation of relations between transcendence and our world. Concepts of revelation can accordingly benefit from this analysis since revelation can be interpreted as a case of complex, qualitative live metaphors of physical transcendence and transfinite qualities. In perspective, revelation would be descent down the transfinite series (cf. Lear 1980: 16–84). One need not construe this materially of course; the live metaphor can be employed to pick out the metaphoric communication. Matter is a medium for energy; language is a medium for metaphoric energy, represented by its signifying system. On this model, language can be a medium for live metaphoric transcendence. In an attempt to isolate these

264 *The cosmology of life*

sorts of notions more explicitly, it is worth discussing them in relation to knowledge of the future.

Knowledge of the future

What is knowledge of the future?

As Cohen observes (1977: 291) the merit of the explanation of the prediction of an individual event tends to vary inversely with the generality of the covering law(s). A theory's success in explanation is a product of its accounting for uniformities in phenomena. Predictions in natural science are calculations from premises employing uniformities to infer a further occurrence of an event which exhibits uniformity with respect to these laws or a newly assessed causal interrelation of such laws in explanation.

Thus [11] is no known occurrence of such a uniformity, nor of a uniformity known to be calculable from the generality of covering laws, not least since it is not understood that there are any covering laws which are relevantly causally uniform in their antecedents.

Adopting the view that [11] has values which can be filled out with descriptive expansions from prophecies, so as to satisfy being a unique description, provokes a further point. There is no natural law causal precedent by which [11] could be predicted since there are no known covering laws and none formulated at the time of prediction.

Knowledge of the future is usually explained as a consequence of knowledge of causal laws or knowledge of intention which is implemented. Of the former, the above outline excludes an explanation based on knowledge of natural law induction. The latter intention and the future clearly could not reduce to anything but a transcendental non-time-bound origin as an explanation that a given intention is realised in [11]. Of course the possible individual human intentions or other collective political intentions which could lead to the truth of [11a, b] at t_2 could not oppose the foregoing judgement because either (a) it is the intention which produced the specification of [11a, b] at t_1 which would be the relevant intention that, being endorsed at t_2, is the appropriate non-time-bound intention which constitutes knowledge of the future; or, (b) there was no intention external to the actors who comprised the event.[25]

Lyons (1977: 817) has characterised the link between prediction and tense as a modality and the future-oriented logic of directives and imperatives; these points can be adapted to cover promise in foreknowledge and prophecy. Quinn (1978) has developed and account of the logical form around command theory which engages 'promising', that may be helpful in relating these aspects of 'intention' to command theory and 'promise'. Thiemann (1985) has drawn attention to the relational logic of promise between author and recipient. It is clear that my own thesis offers an alternative to

Prediction and the cosmology of God 265

Thiemann's overall approach, while yet his distinction here compliments my view.

Even an hypothesis about some normative anthropological behaviour pattern involving a cycle of dispersion and restoration, resulting in [11a,b] at t_2, is not a valid basis for explaining [11] since this is not an invariable principle, but is exceptional, and offers no explanation of the occurrence of a linguistic expression in [11a, b] at t_1 of that proposed cycle and its realisation at t_2. And if one were to generalise [11] as a type other than over God's foreknowledge predictions, it would present enormous problems to account for their success by this method. A prediction at t_1 which is fulfilled at t_2 is not time-bound, if the foregoing conditions are satisfied and if no materially causal laws produce it, other than mediation of it.

What is the status of time travel?

The true answer, I believe, is that time travel is impossible. This question will only be considered in relation to the immediate context.[26] Scientists, as well as logicians, need to look hard at what they variously intend and are committed to by 'possibility' and its negation. There is a necessary relation between possibility and what is.

The matter is both very technical and can be reduced to a simple issue. Is there such a thing as what is possible? If there is, then it has a negation. If the hypothesis of time travel yields a contradiction to its possibility, then it is impossible. For example, if an individual n had time-travelled back to his birth and killed himself, then he would not have existed to have travelled back to kill himself at birth. Necessarily, consequently, the premise which entails that n did not exist when he actually did, is false. The premise which is necessarily false is that n time-travelled. Within the hard core of what possibility is, this is the foundation for treating all technical examples. Again, imagine that in a sequence of multiverse universes – each antecedent, one of which (except the first) is the cause of the immediate succeeding one – a later universe time-travelled back and destroyed the first one, so that there were never any future universes. Consequently, the initial premise is false, because it entails the falsehood of itself. So time travel did not occur. This is rather like Descartes' confusion that if a thing is expressible, it is possible. Just because we can say 'square circle', it does not follow that there is one; try drawing it on the ground. We are not here adopting an artificial model of 'possibility', by which to outlaw time travel, which is superimposed over a physical solution to constrain its differing actual potential to time travel. Rather, such possibility is internal to what it is to be.

'Time-bound' is employed in the astrophysical sense which is exemplified by being a physical situation in which there is no closed time-like curve. A closed time-like curve is where, given the appropriate theorem and equation, (1) a future directed time-like curve λ exists with past and future terminal points at t_1, with past and future directed time-like curves λ_1 and λ_2 from t_1

to t_2. This has sometimes been taken to be evidence for time travel. Hawking and Ellis (1973: ch. 6) prove, however, that this does not hold in physically realistic solutions to equations for causal structure, proving that the causality and chronology conditions are equivalent. This concurs with the conclusion that time travel entails violating consistency by generating paradoxes (Geach 1972: 302–18).

Nevertheless there has been the proposal that a knowledge of closed sets at t_1 would determine states of affairs at t_2, these being the terms of the future Cauchy developments in which if you know one slice of spacetime, you thereby have enough information to determine other slices of spacetime. Hawking and Ellis (1973: 206) conclude that there does not seem to be any physically strong reasons for believing that the universe admits a Cauchy development, and this view is consistent with Mellor's (1998) quite different philosophical approach. Hawking adds that one would, even on the assumption that Cauchy developments could exist, have to be to the future of the spacetime surface on every count, which is impossible in most cases. Extra information coming in from infinity, or the initial singularity (creation), would upset a prediction made using the closed set.

Does infinity have discontinuities?

It is this discontinuous infinity, and not a Cauchy-type future, which is a feature of the source of the prediction [11]. So the type of prediction represented by [11], whilst not being time-bound, is not a Cauchy domain, by which later times are *physically* determined by earlier ones. The time-bound nature of the universe is expressed in the state of global hyperbolicity: that is to say, the causal conditions shared throughout the universe in principle enables one to generalise over future states. Since there is no material or behavioural causal connection between [11] at t_1 and its coming true at t_2, material physics or global hyperbolicity cannot (nor can anthropology) yield a solution to account for [11], nor provide a probability above zero that [11] is an accidental match for the state of affairs at t_2. Of course, [16] specifies the uniqueness grounds for [11] in two ways. First, it characterises God's knowledge. Second, it displays the logical conditions of uniqueness which foreknowledge would satisfy. The latter aspect implicitly meets the requirement that the specificity of the prediction [11] has been established by descriptions which fill out and thus exclude accidental generalisation or inference on the basis of an accidental fit. The fit has to be such that no probability distribution or failure rate occurs, whereas these two aspects (probability and failure rate) are features of inductive predictive fits.

Divine foreknowledge would possess uniqueness conditions, i.e. singular predictions – in contrast with scientific induction which conjectures by use of repetition of lawlike events. The contrast between revelatory prediction and scientific induction is a matter of distinct logics. Revelation, or the concept of divine foreknowledge, is deductively strong, whilst science is inductively weakened by its inbuilt failure rate. This gap of quantity entails a unique gap of quality. Revelation and divine foreknowledge are the only cases of deductively strong knowledge of the external world. Therefore, on the assumption such a conception is actually true, whatever mode of expression such phenomena occupy, they are logically stronger than claims to 'knowledge' in the physical sciences.

Of course, many will believe that such a claim to divine knowledge is not evidentially supported. But that is a separate issue from establishing philosophically the internal conceptual possibility and logical identity of what it would be to be the God who would satisfy such criteria.

Part IV
Cosmological ethics

7 God and ethical cosmology

Counter-intuitive speculation

Can unlike topics be similar?

This chapter, concerned with ethics, is more provisional than the speculative metaphysics proposed in most previous parts of this book. Such a situation could be because the project is false, or that discussion of it requires more exploration in view of its opaque internal and relational structure, or because it has had less attention than some of the previous subjects.

A parallel between the physical world and signifying medium is notoriously problematic. An attempt to align elements of the physical world and a feature of an ethical language may seem even more obviously discrepant, as well as being held to ransom by coincidental conjunction. Colin McGinn (1997) has developed an approach which differs in many ways from the philosophy of the present book, though his analysis is profound with insights relevant for the present study. McGinn argues that the polymorphous identities of knowledge and the mixed nature of science have not been properly exposed. This, he shows, has an impact on the ways in which, consequent to such neglect, we have an artificial notion of what a paradigm of knowledge is. This inattention has often resulted in a mutant account of the seeming inferiority of the status of ethical knowledge as a shade of knowledge in science.

McGinn (1997: 36) notes a contrast between science and ethics. Science is a sort of firmer knowledge. We should also position Bernard Williams's (1981, 1985, 1993a) attention to the ways in which logical properties in empirical and ethical are intertwined, just as seemingly solely empirical propositions in science actually contain evaluative elements, including projected imagination. He was partly drawing on and expanding distinctions presented by Geach (1969, 1972) concerning attributive and predicative properties. In some ways these parallel Lewy's (1976) internal and external properties of a concept. I believe that this has some unexpected relevance for tying a facet of representation of the physical universe in with what might be termed the ethical universe. Depending on our indexical viewpoint in relation to use of a type, we might position various colours as either the same (i.e. are all coloured), or as different colours (red, blue, etc.). The colours share both identity and have a relation of non-identity. We pick out these differing levels of ascription. We also have a concept of an ideal colour which is presupposed in our matching of colours and theorisation about them. Allowing for many differences, such states of affairs in the empirical and aesthetic universes of discourse are susceptible to parallels with empirical and ethical values.

One distinction between sciences, which is identified by McGinn (1997: 39), is that ethics is not subject to induction nor abduction, whereas science is. The foregoing analysis of divine foreknowledge argued that its identity is not inductive but it has a status strongly related to *a priori* knowledge, and it therefore does not have inductive status. So ethical knowledge shares a property of contrast with divine foreknowledge in relation to the identity of scientific knowledge. The above studies also maintained that the empirical situations at the commencement of the universe, insofar as one can conjecture them, embody a collapsed spacetime continuum from which empirical induction is not a possibility – not only for an observer, but because the ontology does not correspond to any inductive description. (Discussion drew attention to the point that even in respect of non-primordial black holes, Hawking (1993) concludes that neither position nor velocity of particle can be observed.) Such states of affairs have more relation to the non-inductive identity of ethical properties than they have to much non-cosmological empirical science, though clearly there are many differences between ethical and cosmological properties.

Do abstract truths exist?

A variety of Platonist conceptions offer refuge for attempts to develop an account of how physical and ethical properties could mirror each other. But I do not wish to adorn Plato's head with counter-intuitive theses about such a possibility, nor alienate that prospect. Rather, it is worthwhile attending to certain problems which Platonist epistemology attracts, for example, in the differing researches of Hartry Field (1989) and Bob Hale (1994a).

My focus here is not on the identity of mathematics in toto, but to the possibility of partial parallels between some exotic counter-intuitive theory in philosophy of mathematics and formal tendencies in ethical theory. A, no doubt surprising, way of attempting to expose this area here is by routing problems through cosmology. There is, of course, a complex, uneven and problematic though fruitful relation between theoretical cosmology and observational cosmology of the early universe. Such matters in the philosophy of mathematics have not been worked out in relation to the astrophysics and exotic ontology obtaining at the start of our universe, without turning to the more extensive issues of a philosophy of mathematics for the multiverse scenario. There is only space for a hint of a start on the topic here.

The initial conditions at the commencement of the universe allegedly, on most scenarios, involve the collapse of our spacetime. One of the objections to Platonism in the philosophy of mathematics is that, for example, sets and numbers lie outside spacetime and so, the argument runs, they are thus acausal, since they are unconnected to causal conditions in the dislocated general relativity spacetime in which they have instantiation. But since this objection, slightly adjusted, applies to the purported relations between whatever we deem to have been the antecedent condition and its mathematical identity prior to the collapse of spacetime, and yet the universe is said to be a counter-intuitive 'consequence' of that acausal prior condition, the beginning of the universe appears to yield an argument to dismantle the anti-Platonist objection to the existence of mathematical structures beyond our spacetime.

The concept of there being abstract truths outside of our spacetime is accordingly not in competition with their having instantiation or analogues in our spacetime. Just as the physical structures in the universe are, in specially qualified respects, the instantiation of mathematics truths reflected in the equations which express aspects of their characteristic behaviour, so I suggest for consideration the idea that if God exists with certain appropriate ethical qualities, these have their partial mirroring in our universes of consciousness and behaviour. It is not supposed that this has a mechanistic or deterministic realisation. If the truth of general relativity cannot preclude its own collapse, such flexibility should be permitted in an ethical universe in which the negation of its own values are a function of its abstract existence.

Physical and ethical universes

Can generalisation be parallel in different subjects?

Previous chapters have developed aspects of cosmology in relation to God. One unevenly related strand in these concerns, which emerged explicitly at the end of the last chapter, is the interrelation between cosmological structure and prediction in connection with the topics of promise, command-theory and imperatives. In conjunction with the roles and the relations that these have in previous chapters, they were offered prospectively as preparatory premises for this and the following chapter. There are many disanalogies between physical cosmology and ethics (as, for instance, there are between neurophysiology and psychiatry). Yet it will be claimed that there are structural relations between these two classes of affairs in the universe (not quite as close as the brain's and the mind's interfaces, though these enjoy substantial contrasts). There are asymmetries between the two subjects. Since this section is not an exercise in methodology, it attempts to offer a foundation for ethics in a cosmological perspective; a merely descriptive programme of comparison will not be followed. For example, McGinn (1997: 40–41) pinpoints how it is that ethics is causally inert. This has a parallel with the location of mathematical structures or truths outside of spacetime, and their acausal relation to the universe. Although there is no causal relation between the universe and these abstract non-spacetime mathematical and ethical functions, there is a deep and vexing currently undefined group of relations between them and the universe. The relation of the will to ethical value involves functions of the mind of which we are basically ignorant. The same may be said of a theory concerning the logic of God's relation to the world in certain domains. But the conception of an ethics which has invariant value with specific empirical grounding – for example, on the issue of the torture of innocents – is taken to be evident in this book, just as an invariant law mapping an empirical state of affairs is, though as noted above.

Robbie Jennings (1986: 13) states: 'International law is, and must be if it is to fulfil its proper task, a universal system of law. It must not belong to any particular culture or for that matter any particular ideology.' The obvious parallel here with cosmology concerns law and generalisation. His intention is that sufficient generality transcends local culture time-warps so that, although law does not belong to any particular ideology, nevertheless it is applicable to all. Clearly legal systems are not this perfect universal law. Some laws which are national ought, on some views, to be international in scope. For example, legislation makes 'assumptions' which legalise the confiscation of a convicted international drug trafficker's properties (not proved to be a direct result of drug trafficking).[1] In contrast, Jim Bergeron (1998: 39) considers that the European Court of Justice is en route to implementing a modernist mission of state formation. In this sense, the poststructuralist developments in the European humanities have the reactionary corollary at the institutional level – a retreat to nationalist modernism expanded to absorb a group of states. Cosmological ethics should keep an eye to such tensions while attempting to expose general principles and their criteria of application.

Has the anthropic principle a view from somewhere?

Clearly the paralleling of cosmology and ethics involves complex and uneven relations. Anthropic principles in cosmology have an illuminating though not decisive relation to this parallel. Whilst not entirely convincing, the strong anthropic principle (i.e. the parameters of the universe must admit the creation of observers at some point in its history) is an attempt to condense disparate generality into one axiom. Barrow and Tipler (1986: 510) have developed formulations of the anthropic principle, according to which each of its various forms attempts to restrict the structure of the universe by asserting that intelligent life in some way selects out the actual universe from possible ones.

Likewise, I shall argue, right ethical values are the true ones to choose from among other possible (false) ones. Unfortunately, unlike the physical universe (in which the physical cosmology immediately manifests structural consequences of violations, such as supernovae explosions), the moral universe does not neatly encode its true values in the causal framework of the mind or world. So it is possible for a wrong ethical cosmology to seem to be the true one, for a time. The true ethics is antecedent to the universe, like its originating physics, whilst yet (in repeat of some features) counter-intuitively mirrored in it.

Some critics of the anthropic principle have maintained that the universe has served up life only because its initial conditions happen to coincide with life, and so the existence of intelligent life is taken to be a circular feature – not a divine function of cause nor a relation external to the universe. However, Nagel (1986: 82) has objected to this type of view, alluding to the fact that such a predictable situation does not always eliminate the need for explanation; and he quoted Carter's (1974) opinion that: 'even an entirely rigorous prediction based on the *strong* [anthropic] principle will not be completely satisfying from the physicist's point of view since the possibility will remain of finding a deeper underlying theory explaining the relationships that have been predicted'. Consequently the reductive use of the strong anthropic principle (to exclude transcendental explanation about the origins of the universe and life) mimics completeness by obscuring possible (I have argued, actual) deeper counter-intuitive relations between the world and its origin. And I have been attempting to show that remnants of the cause of the universe underlies its contemporary structures in esoteric levels of, for example, atomic structures.

My suggestion is that there is a structural similarity between physics and ethics here. Chapter 3 depicted Hawking's appeal to an almost infinite series of levels of depth in the physical structure of the universe. In comparison, the underlying system of ethics of the universe is recondite and deeper than some thinkers have allowed, while yet manifesting some qualities self-evidently, though the correct ethical 'system' has been disputed. This is at some levels parallel with the notion of a manifold underlying the physical structure of the universe (comparable to that explained by Hawking, utilised and extended to a supermanifold in Chapter 4 above). The life forms of the universe are the media of this mirroring for a system of ethics.

Parfit (1997) has argued that we should agree to an externalist account of normative reasons and motivation. Within a perspective of normative externalism there are aims which rest on internal presuppositions explaining reasons to act in certain ways as reasons for achieving these aims. Parfit (ibid.: 129) believes that such a version of externalism is no less plausible than an internationalist thesis, even though the normative externalism has metaphysical implications that there are irreducibly normative properties or truths. Such a scenario supports the conception of ethical values which are external to us in the sense of being derivable or originating with God occupying this position. Consequently, on this interpretation, reasons for acting, and reasons for acting ethically, are external to each of us. One might fill the metaphysical content of the normative reasons in a variety of ways. For example, Thiemann (1985) has suggested that narrated promise in the Gospel involves revelation, though my own thesis about revelation is here different from his. This thesis concerns not only the role of original authorial creativity in concept of revelation, it involves relating this sphere to ethical theory, as a corollary of cosmological prediction and divine foreknowledge.

The matter of narrative

How do we recognise?

In these perspectives, the source of the true form of ethical values and their relations could be revealed in creative narrative revelation, and only dimly shadowed in what has sometimes misleadingly been called 'natural law': perhaps to humans it is sometimes treated as unnatural law. Roger White (1982), using Wittgenstein's notion that recognition of colour shades presupposes knowledge of the unobserved midpoint ideal colour behind them (for example, perfect white), has argued that in the same way creation variously manifests an archetype which is God. To many unacademic believers, in terms of Psalm 19, the heavens are a printout (*mispar*) of the glory of God, though many dispute that there is such a signifying system. This places the function of perceptual recognition in the place of a proof.

But this displacement is not entire to itself. It is a deeply problematic issue concerning what it would be to be a philosophy of counter-intuitive mathematical perception that could structure foundations or presuppositions of the astrophysics of the original universe. What is it to assess the identity of recognition and instinct in relation to discovery of a proof, as related to or in contrast with the function of calculating in proving? May it not be that the moment of recognition has a live metaphor relation to the calculation itself? A possible approach to this would be to regard the recognition as a logical condensation of a proof in a counter-intuitive use of a conclusion being contained in the premises of an antecedent. If one attempts to apply such considerations to counter-intuitive cases, such as Fermat's Theorem, the complexities are daunting. It may be that ethics engages with comparable complexity at the universal level. The functions of recognition in ethics may have some live metaphor relation to recognition of some significance involved in an cosmic ontological state of affairs. I suggest that the development of the concept of live metaphor in earlier chapters could be brought in here to characterise the idea of a mapping language of recognition and proof which expresses ethical truths.

The adoption of laws in physical cosmology, of universals, it has been argued in the above chapters, rests on assumptions of isotropy and uniformity which are unprovable. They are metaphysical constructs paraded as veridical warrants. Transcendence in the first microseconds is a requisite for a consistent cosmology. Given the foregoing route in analysis, this reflects the principle that theological cosmology can articulate universals without having to concede thereby that theology is structurally or logically weaker than astrophysical science in the relevant respects. Further, the foregoing examinations can be used to infer that the material spacetime topological features portray energetic structures which advertise transcendent design functions. This is especially evident in the proposed preconditions of divine foreknowledge or revelation. Just as one can write out, as it were, a universal from a finite set of conjunctions (namely, the universal), so it is with non-inductive framing of ethical universals.

Is ethics transcendent?

That is to say, in the hypothesis, transcendent ethical abstract value is the empirical seat for an 'ethical universal' – one which is exemplified in a series of finite conjunctions such as moral judgements in, for example, the Sermon on the Mount. This alignment between ethical law and a religious narrative has support from Dworkin's (1985: 146–77), otherwise quite different, conception of law as literature (particularly stressing the aesthetic elements in the latter). This is here consistently construed to be proof of its being a universal – the covering law for a potentially infinite set of conjunctions which instantiate it. Of course, there is a qualitative difference which produces a modal upgrading of the revelatory universal over the status of the astrophysical universal, not least because astrophysics is infected with being partly derived from human contrivance and it is testable, whereas the revelatory universal in the presupposition is an omniscient function obscurely related to veridical confirmation, if at all.

Even so, there is an unstable similarity, since the foundations of the universe are themselves non-veridical. To respond that in each case human interpretation still perverts perfect epistemology, would be to confuse, because the asymmetry of status between revelatory and cosmological universals is that the former is a perfect description of what the universal is, but in the latter astrophysics the imperfect construction of the law is not even certain to have represented what is a universal.

If one were to take seriously a proof in the foregoing of the existence of God from revelation or foreknowledge, this would, if proper bridging proof to the subject matter were forthcoming, show that any revelation endorsed as revelation in this way would yield in pertinent contexts the ethical map of God's mind. These would hold the status of a theorem, not because the germinal feature is solely that God embodies them, but for the reason that God is perfect and can only manifest and propose perfect values. This would be akin to an atheist who held to universalised ethical values in a Platonist mould. Here one might either deem Platonism an aid to theistic ethical ontology, or consider that since God just is the resource for ethical universals, Platonism is a redundant counterfeit of what it is to be God's ethics.

The idea of a transcendent ethical universal would be a live metaphor corollary of the formal typology in application of the transfinite *Fundierungsaxiom* in Chapter 6 above, whereby an entity outside a spacetime continuum could not be infected with the material decay associated with our matter–energy system. Here a finite set of values within spacetime, discloses the identity of the non-spacetime universal on which it is based. In the case of mathematical truths, there would be an acausal relation to the universe. In these respects the ethical values expressed within our spacetime continuum could be regarded as counter-intuitive live metaphors of the ethical universals outside it, rather like mathematical truths.

Is abstract ethics practical?

For those who find this reprehensibly abstract as a basis for practical reason, it should be remembered that even with hard cases in legal practice, such scholars as Dworkin (1985; 1978: 84) advocate that principle, not policy, be the articulate arbiter of values. Dworkin also argues the felicity of abstract rights (1980: 93) and characterises the propriety of an absolute right (ibid.: 92), such as freedom of speech, whereby a political theory should recognise no reason for not securing the liberty it requires for every individual, short of impossibility. Here 'right' has the relation to principle such that the latter is a proposition which describes a right.

Clearly, Dworkin's use of 'describe' at this juncture (Dworkin, 1978: 90; cf. 303–4, 307) is functionally prescriptive not descriptive. Namely 'for all x, x ought to ϕ'. So where does Dworkin procure the deontology for 'right'? By his assumption of the relevant principle as a truth. Indeed 'right' often seems to be articulated in many authors as a self-evident truth; but it is actually an hypostatised sign which presupposes a deontic proposition. (Rather like the prescriptive use of thing's being 'relevant' – where the feature or excluded predicate by which it is, and is shown to be, relevant is not employed by the user.) The hypostatisation masks and ejects the requirement of proof for the right, often because the right is assumed to be a primitive obvious truth for any society. Even if it is, this redress still leaves one without veridical support for being the right, since it is usually assumed that all political rights are universal (Dworkin 1978: 94, n.1). In these respects ethical principles in a revelation with a cosmological basis, and certainly in one which deploys a proof for the status of logical primitives, are superior to a normative rights' thesis which is just assumed.

To respond to the foregoing by asserting that the needs of society are the thesis's basis, generates circularity – because the need to impose the thesis to produce the desired state is evidence that one cannot properly use the desired state as an empirical ground for proof, since it does not yet exist. For example, Marx's 'historical' end is a metaphysical imagination which is programmed back into prior history as normative for the period before the end exists. In differing respects, this seems also to hold for and is illustrative of democratic models. To be sure, one is not here objecting, in principle, to the values presupposed, but solely pointing up the internal analytical status of the assumption, in contrast with a revelatory ethical value. The point of contrast is that one derives a principle 'for all x, x ought to ϕ' from a higher qualitative source than schemata filled by elements featuring human imagination, not by assumption. So where the initial assumption p characterises the adoption of the Dworkin-type principle, in revelatory or theological ethical cosmology that p at that stage in the analysis is marked, not by p's being an assumption but, by p's being a consequence of a set of premises.

The epistemological relations between peace and the Christian means to a peaceful end arise as determined by the logical status which holds for any principle or values of Christ's precepts. Of course, it is notorious to interject that an 'ought' cannot be derived from an 'is', and so to claim that any logic for ethics would be a dubious deviant; but such a response is now misleading and dated. The ought/is objection is usually applied where an ethical theory ought to derive and evaluative consequent from an antecedent which predicates empirical properties. The objection is over-ambitious. Anscombe (1981d) has shown that some of the examples which Hume employed to get the ought/is distinction off the ground are susceptible of a non-evaluative analysis, where a contractual factual obligation is deducible from the antecedent. Bernard Williams (1985, 1993a) decisively showed that descriptive and evaluative properties are inextricably intertwined. Hare (1952) is mistaken, as Geach proves (1972: 270–78), for claiming that special logical principles govern the imperative mood. As Nagel (1986: 163) also points out, Hare does not envisage the prescriptions which require what someone else ought to do, though not committing the legislator to wanting what is prescribed.

At the opposite end of the scale from incorrect abstraction of evaluative ingredients from the external world, is the illicit injection of metaphysical assumptions into the external world. We can easily think of cases of perverse oppression of civilians by a corrupt state. How do we assess and position this sort of deviance? A problem is: to discover how to explain 'value' as exposed, and thereby discovered. Or that 'value' is invented, and thus introduced as possibly damaging fantasy construed as prophetic social realities. Since ethics is often a description of an ideal or projected anticipated reality, the notion of 'discovering' value within the social sphere to which it rightly belongs is, in some cases at least, problematic. In proportion to ethics being counter-intuitive in these situations to the 'natural' norm, ethics will not easily be found to fit that world in which it is needed. Yet, as we have seen from the foregoing discussion on astrophysical science, the employment of evaluative premises is not of itself unhelpful or invalid. So it is a possible starting point to consider such relations as parallels with ethical metaphysics.

Metaphysical premises, paraded as empirical warrants, can render an 'empirical' antecedent evaluative. Foregoing sections illustrate how often transcendental hypotheses (e.g. particle/wave phenomena) are employed as empirical antecedents (cf. Mackie 1974: 216). These states depict a situation in which the gap between evaluative/descriptive is closed and sometimes eclipsed.[2]

The New Testament's use of the Commandments and the Sermon on the Mount's precepts are couched as theorem-like propositions. (This utilises Geach's parallel, and develops it, regarding belief and assertion.)[3] Believing is preceded by an act of judgement resulting in assertion p, since a feature of believing is tantamount to saying 'that-p'. The New Testament proceeds by deploying the stance that illustrations about ethics presuppose, or house, such theorems. The theorems are consequences of and from revelation, where an appropriate formulation of that revelation rehearses a well-formed inference with an empirical set of antecedents based on God's existence. Even if it is held that there is no such proof, the status of these antecedents has a parallel with the adoption of universals in science, although the foregoing attempted proof for God's existence from prophecy, if successful, shows a stronger basis for the equations. In plain language, the above articulates Jesus's own explicit claim: 'the Father which sent me, he gave me a commandment, what I should say, and what I should speak' (John 12:49; cf. v. 50).

The presuppositions of such propositions and, for example, ethics in the Gospel of Matthew appear to be, expressing it anachronistically, that the ethics and ontology of God are implemented in their ethical modalities. I presuppose here, on the basis of other studies[4] that 'should' can be paraphrased into 'ought', i.e. 'deontic' p to q is valid, but relative to the basis developed in earlier chapters. It seems that the typical New Testament writing housing such charters places the deontic operator as a modality sensitive to the internal configuration and variability of propositions, and not as an external constraint on propositions or kinds. Correspondingly, such language is concerned with the deconstruction and asymmetries in the applied context as well as the linguistic expression of value. Although the comparison is somewhat distant, G.H. von Wright's approach has been to treat deontic propositions with the operator external to the whole proposition, which ensures its abstract form in relation to applied contexts. Geach has criticised this, drawing a parallel between Von Wright and Aristotle's original recognition of the asymmetry internal to propositions, and his later assertion of symmetry with the doctrine of terms.[5] Ulanov (1999) develops an algebra of moral judgement, which revives an an interest developed by the thirteenth-century Spanish logician Lullius. Although the present approach differs from Ulanov's, his inclusion of infinity and passing support for an algebraic depiction of 'high moral value' in the Sermon on the Mount, his work complements the present author's link between exotic domains of higher mathematics and ethics.

Transforming the familiar

How can we have some peace?

The present discussion is attempting to break with the conservative or liberal oppositions which usually regulate study of ethics in relation to the New Testament. One facet of this procedure is to notice that the logical structure proposed in Chapter 2, depicting agency relations between God and humanity, also neatly performs the role of agency structure for moral agents. Clearly this emphasis on agency parallels analysis in writers with entirely different views from those in the present book.

Nagel (1986) has proposed the idea of types of agent-relativity, while admitting that there 'is no way of telling what kinds of transcendence of individuality will result over the long term from the combined influence of moral and political progress or decline'. The present book offers a view which agrees with this idea of agency-relativity, whilst offering an explanation by which transcendence has a fixed position over the individual that balances correctly between objective and subjective aspects. (And indeed it is worth weighing Nagel's (ibid.: 165) emphasis on familial typology to advance reasoning for his concept of agency in relation to my book's frequent usage of the same in a logical framework of agency.)

Nagel (1986: 188) insists that: 'There can be no ethics without politics.' In agreeing with this, I shall enfold reflection on ethics into legal politics of peace, and ask: 'Is the conception of peace displayed in the New Testament possibly practicable?' Relevant dilemmas abound. Macquarrie (1973: 59–61) observes that Bonhoeffer played a part in a conspiracy to kill Hitler. Anscombe opposes pacifists, supports 'just war', whilst denouncing Truman's signing of the order to atomic bomb Japan. As a positive move of how to handle such tensions, we need to introduce Martha Nussbaum's (2000) capabilities approach, not only for woman, but all humans, as a function of creating opportunity and choice to resolve dilemmas, rather than solely impose rule of law. This is an unstable counter-intuitive area. Nick Denyer has done much to structure the alternatives. He concludes that:

> The validity that belongs to the law of war is that which belonged to the law of duelling ... For merely forbidding such a conduct of disputes did not and could not achieve anything while there remained an aristocracy with that power. Likewise, it achieves nothing simply to forbid violence between states. Better then that their violence be channelled and limited by the law of war. With duelling, it proved in the end best of all to have none of it, and that meant no aristocracy either. Likewise with war: the best course of all may be to abolish war itself, and therefore abolish with it those institutions whose violence creates the need for a law of war. That would require either one world state, or else no states whatsoever.
>
> (Denyer 2000: 150–51)

Unfortunately the actual 'ethics' of democracy (in contradistinction to its advertised, often misleading, promissory recipes) is made a servant of electability. Such ethics is therefore deformed so as not to threaten the continuation of those employed in the production of war or defence commodities. Such relations between value and employment are in effect firewalls defending against the emergence of peace. Ethical values which are sourced by nation, state or international treaty, are thus subversive, because they are crafted from inside short-term economies which do not allow transcendence to become a source of, or origin for, concern for legal aliens. We may then have to seek for answers outside of political and legal jurisdiction, even if only as a strategic device for convincing a governance and its subjects of the pragmatic need for higher value.

Is there a miraculous ethic?

Such a state of affairs mirrors the traditional picture that no conception is an island entire to its own subject. On occasions, academia and politics, for example, may usurp autonomy as if they shielded human careers from external responsibilities; but a person's or a nation's biography typically displays generalised reliance on things other than itself. The limits of such boundaries may vary, but they yield a precedent for rejecting a person's or a nation's boundaries as the limit of relevance for value. I wish to generalise this to include the pre-existing feature that humans also incorporate external factors and value at almost all levels of experience. For example, in the most familiar way this is true: watching Mozart's *Figaro* on television in the private environment of a home is a function of reliance on an external reality which taps into the mind of some of the most private feelings of an individual – Mozart. Although this obviously does not imply other external realities, it is a precedent for a form of life whose status and identity are both obvious yet quite puzzling. Such experiences include those new ones which bring new knowledge of hitherto unknown or unexperienced societies or individuals. Millions of people have extended this to include claims of at least sharing values with a deity. My concern here is not that of a mystical experience of an external reality. Rather, it is with the common belief that one has values from another domain, of which one has no immediate experience such as when meets friends. Nevertheless, this type of meeting with friends has itself been a basis for models of claims that one knows God. Again, I am not here attending to this situation, but with the different, though related, issue of what it is to use a value which is derived from another domain of which one has no direct experience (in the relevant sense). It is worthwhile isolating this type of precedent to explore the claim that one can, in an as yet unmapped way, happen to have knowledge which is not itself solely a product of one's own experience (say, as with constructivism and strict finitism)? Even for philosophers who seem to have no theological agenda – for example, Wittgenstein[6] – 'God' is taken to be a cipher for this type of claim. So let us pursue the matter in relation to a conception of value that one could introduce from outside of a political economy into it to discover ethics for hard problems. We might term these properties 'universals for peace', presupposing or prefixed by a theistic assertion.

God and ethical cosmology   283

Macquarrie's adoption of theistic universals to promote his discussion of peace is exemplified in his inference:

> if there is the possibility of that radical kind of renewal which is called resurrection, then peace does lie within the range of possibility, and it would seem that only if it lies within this range can it engage men's serious endeavours and call for the sacrifice which the universal law of atonement demands.
>
> (Macquarrie 1973: 73–74)

This statement appears to be important, and yet obscure in a number of respects. Macquarrie positions the statement as a piece of eschatology, yet claims that: 'It [peace] cannot be completely realised in history'. But if this were true, then it would not be a possibility that 'peace does lie within the range of possibility'. So there is a suppressed *reductio ad absurdum* in the structure of his discussion.

Someone might presume that the force of the previous quotation is merely that peace cannot completely be realised in the matter–energy system and societies comprising our cosmos. But this is mistaken, for if 'ϕ's' is a possibility, then it is true in all ontological levels in which a criterion for x's identity is satisfied with a reference, and not just in a materialist situation. (This type of scope confusion is not unique to religion. As Dworkin (1986: 6) says, incredibly American jurisprudence has no plausible theory of theoretical disagreement in law; nor is there thus a social theory of law to measure what is the possibility inherent to the dynamical potential of a society, viewed internally.)

Macquarrie's use of 'resurrection' is, one might assume, that of an actual event happening to Jesus. However, someone might want to claim this linguistic item is a metaphor associated only with behavioural transformation, not the person's resurrection. Contrariwise, Macquarrie's use is based on the Christian 'universal law of atonement' which is housed in a claim about Jesus's actual resurrection. If the term 'resurrection' is merely a metaphor applied to him at his death, then its failure to ascribe or require the continuance of his personal identity after death advertises that there would be no Jesus to experience even a metaphorical application of the term 'resurrection'; in which case, Macquarrie's use would be false. Against this, perhaps, Macquarrie's view holds an element which renders resurrection as an event at the end of history: 'peace in the full sense is an eschatological idea. It cannot be completely realised in history' (1973: 73). Surely this is a peculiar way of speaking? If the *eschaton* is to be an actual event, then it cannot be outside *history* (which is what was *actual*).

On the other hand, if the Macquarrie-type distinction between history and eschatological history is to strike the distinction between the differing qualitative levels of pre-*eschaton* and *eschaton* possibilities with respect to the 'complete' realisation of peace, then this provokes attention to a required difference of teleology. If a given value of peace cannot be achieved in pre-*eschaton* history (or 'cannot be completely realised'), but only implemented in conjunction with and as a consequence of the *eschaton*, then this renders a structural difference in the possible range and domain of possibilities which one can consistently ascribe to pre-*eschaton* history as possibilities to achieve. In this manner, teleology will act as a centralising constraint on the interpretation of what is possible in pre-*eschaton* history. Of course, this will not be because God has arbitrarily snatched peace from our grasp, but that the full range of human free will – democratically or dictatorially followed – will bar full implementation of peace in society.

Is there a transcendent foundation for ethics?

Within the frameworks of much Christian theology the resurrection is an ontologically unique event the language of which is intended to represent it as a sort of theorem of what it is to be the (re)creation of individuality in a transformed ontology but not individual identity. Such language, Chapter 2 reasoned, is a species of live metaphor typology. In the perspective of a number of New Testament contexts, not least Luke 24, the third person indirect reflexives ('he himself') directly associated with bodily relative identity and sensory, while yet transcendent, experience in personal relationships, present a conjunction of creative uniqueness and re-identification of the personal familiar subject. Although, obviously, one should not ascribe to the writers of such documents our metaphysics, yet the central position of creativity, creation and uniqueness all bear the marks of a unique aesthetic ontology.

A formal counterpart to the concept of resurrection here might profitably attend to some of the considerations adduced so far in the foregoing. The following may attract the accusation of science fiction, and this label has been used to castigate some exotic astrophysical cosmology; yet not a little theoretical cosmology has turned out to be prophetic of empirical discovery. Further, although mathematical possibility is only one type of account of what possibility is, given some of the foregoing analyses, the live metaphor as well as a variety of conceptual relations between logic and other subjects such as ethics and aesthetics, a discussion of counter-intuitive structures in the physical universe and their possible informative relations to other qualitative problems is potentially a problem-solving enterprise. First, a live metaphor ethical universal in our language can have an acausal counterpart outside spacetime, along the analogy of mathematical truths in the philosophy of mathematics. Second, it has a defining overlap criterion of definition with an aesthetic function, which (for example, viewed on Mothersill's 1984 approach) is a logical predicate. So, third, in some counter-intuitive way aesthetics can be paraphrased into ethics. Fourth, the language of a requisite set of mathematical truths have instantiations in the ontology of the beginning of the universe. Fifth, this ontology defies general relativity, though at least conjecturally the cosmological language satisfies the envisaged prior conditions for originating the universe or multiverse. Sixth, these parameters generally mirror what it is to be an empirical creation, with a live metaphor extension to be reinterpreted as a model for aesthetic creation. Conjecturally, the empirical and the aesthetic universals have parallels with each other and by extension with ethics on the analogy of mathematical truth. In other words, these factors all point to universals and their interaction being involved in the production of creation or creativity. All of these factors could thus be deployed, together with other apt conceptual elements, into a complex live metaphor by which to model the uniqueness of a theological singularity for which there is no complete precedent: the resurrection. This type's lack of precedence would have a peculiar live metaphoric precedent in its qualitative relation to the formal account given above of divine foreknowledge. But that epistemological state would, in a special sense, already be internal to the notion of this resurrection's purported uniqueness.

The empire of justice

What has philosophy to do with literary narrative?

Bernard Williams (1993), dealing with topics of religious emotion and their logical status, is one of a number of philosophers to reconnect ancient literature with our contemporary moral philosophy. Although the New Testament does not explicitly address philosophical questions in the way Classical Greece did, there are ways in which, for example, according to Betz (1985), the Sermon on the Mount disputes some Greek philosophical views, as I suggest below.

In any case the tendencies to polarise the Sermon's presuppositional backcloth into Hellenistic versus Jewish traditions may well implement an opposition that dissolves into a common, albeit complex, fabric. Hellenised Judaism and the scribal authorities conceived as targets in Matthew and Luke appear to have embraced both Platonic and Aristotelian moral philosophy, intermingled with Romanized perceptions (as heralded in Cicero's *De oratore*), as functions of Jewish tradition by the time the first century commenced. If there was a silent dialectical cultural enemy, other than human nature, presupposed by the Sermon, it seems to be this hybrid conceived by many Jewish leaders, in certain perhaps advantageous contexts, as their unifying tradition. Antecedent to this cultural cauldron, there were other influential features of Jewish inter-ethnic ideological intercourse. Parts of the Sermon's style are not unlike Bion's diatribe of the third century BC (cp. Schenkeveld 1997). But there is no Greek oratory from the last three centuries BC; so we are in difficulty if we wish to estimate Greek relations, and the Sermon covers a period slightly before the full emergence of Roman oratory with Dio Chrysostom (cf. Kennedy 1997b: 17). The identity of reasoning in the Sermon and its relation to philosophy is partly a function of our understanding of relations between a logic of grammar and pragmatics. As Stanley Porter (1989) has shown, the logic of the Sermon's conditional statements embodies extremely technical issues, and scholarly exegesis largely has yet to account for them. At the least, from this research, it follows that we should not classify the Sermon as rhetoric or Jewish *midrash*, and prepare to recognise that there are concerns with modal, propositional reasoning there. In the sphere of history of ideas, a hypothesis worth consideration is that the impact of Semitic Levant mythology, mediated to earlier Greek cultures, is dimly yet tantalisingly mirrored in aspects of the Greek cult phenomena. These were absorbed into Classical Greek literature of which Josephus, and other sources, show that educated first-century Jews were cognisant. There was a sense of reminiscence and perception that these alien literatures obliquely reflected archetypes and values which had partially begun and were coded into the Levant's Semitic literatures. They were still to some degree extant, and remodelled in the first-century Jewish reading of, say, late Phoenician mythology, as Josephus and Philo indicate. All this evidence combines to produce an antagonistic focus for a possible first-century readerly role of the Sermon. My reason, then, for this Diderotesque digression is to query and propel how much more we should be puzzled, than much Sermon scholarship assumes, by what it would be to count as the philosophically interesting facet of the Sermon. And this is quite separable from the additional problem of arguments about the scope of some analytical philosophy in relation to literature which I am implicitly disputing here.

Analytical philosophy has tended to neglect direct engagement with creative literature (whilst McGinn's 1997 study breaks from this mould). Likewise, the source narratives of Christianity tend not to have been given requisite attention by analytical moral philosophers. But the question of the relations between formal metaphysics and creative literature is a deep one.[7] A question of epistemological policy, rather than doctrinal prejudice, should immediately obtrude here: what warrant does a Christian have for deciding to discard a substantive slice as a regulating restriction on his exposition of the Gospels' morality? The excision of the Gospels' teleology from modern theological commentary is exceedingly common, whereby twentieth-century social concerns or Aristotelian ethics perform as values to dress New Testament ethical variables. Robbins' (1997: 42–44) review of rhetorical analysis of the Sermon on the Mount indicates how extensively our competing ideologies deform assessment of this narrative. For some, this will reflect the indeterminacy of narrative. For others, the Sermon has a fecund density susceptible to application to diverse issues because of its addressing general questions. Since diverse traditions are usually concerned with recurrent human problems, the prospect of interfacing disparate cultural worlds and levels of pragmatism and theory is not an exercise in eclectic irrelevance. The information and context of statements ascribed to Jesus should be the context and source for the structure and its parameters, articulating as far as possible the internal viewpoints of Jesus' language to discover how far it carries investigation. A preliminary to this can be how theologians have responded to Jesus' language about peace in relation to the above strictures.

Has the Sermon on the Mount a logical mental causality?

Macquarrie (1973: 20) observes that the Old Testament concept of peace has a fundamental connection with justice; *ṣdq* translated 'justice' is the element of *right*, with this situation tending to be reflected directly in the New Testament use of *dikaios*, the forms of these terms usually being translated by 'righteousness'. He also observes that, if a person lived according to the commandments and precepts, this led to peace.

The Gospels mark Jesus' use of the Commandments with love and mercy as a basis for practice; but this is with the Sabbath law deleted, and yet transformed as typifying an eschatological rest in Hebrews 4. The first two Commandments (love of God, and of people) are substantive members of this paradigm of Commandments. In this way distorting mechanistic application of other principles is excluded by commandment: love is an intrinsic member in what is right, with its being employed in the Gospels, which pervades and centralises other principle commandments in the paradigm of values – there are only just expressions of love.

The Sermon on the Mount gives attention to the mental causality of unjust acts and conceptions of them within a terminology of classifying human nature (e.g. *epthumeo* : 'lust', Matthew 5:28f.). The Sermon incorporates an account of some of the mental elements in the mind's potential criminality here, by reference to fixing the epistemological position of such states as intention and motive in relation to justice, which in type, but not value, is parallel with the Old Testament's Commandments, where the Commandments appear to be used as a set of premises in Jesus's general teaching. The ascription of blame and/or forgiveness in the Sermon has a structural parallel with God's relation to people: God's φ's people; people should φ people.

Criminal mental states are the subject of prohibition, as are unjust actions. This goes beyond, and is distinct from, secular criminal law where (excepting in the case of an attempted execution of an intention, e.g. to murder) mental states are not legislated against. Later the theological themes of atonement and faith also take hold of the associative field of justice. As Hooker (1990: 57–59) shows, the later ethics of Paul are derived from Gospel theology, and are not merely affixed as an adjunct. The extensions of this Gospel ethic matrix are governed by nine theorem-like statements – the Beatitudes, with the corresponding positive and negative responsibilities in tension (but not contrariety): e.g. 'Blessed are the peacemakers' and 'Blessed are they who are persecuted for the sake of justice (*dikaiosunes*)'.

288 *Cosmological ethics*

How does Aristotle contradict Christ?

It is not uncommon to find a theologian applying his interpretation of Aristotle to supplement, paraphrase or displace some of the Gospels' ethics, so it is worth while isolating here and below certain features of Aristotle where he contrasts with the Sermon. It may be thought that Aristotle is the more disinterested party when contrasted with the Jesus of the Gospels. But it is not from the Sermon that we will discover an obsessive Oedipal subversion of the status of women disguised, as Kearns (1997) presents it. Examining Sylvia Plath's (1965) poem 'Daddy', Kearns (1997: 76) shows that it expresses a sense of subversion by the male in the Oedipal dilemma, as: 'virile moderation, a manly Aristotelian balance between desire and control, paternal murder phantasmatically translated into socially, economically, militaristically, politically productive metaphors of itself': the woman as mutilated man. My account here amounts to an extended live metaphor concept ironising history. Against this stark psychohistory, fertilised by Aristotle and entrenched in the medieval Christian theology, we may think of Jesus in contrast as, at worst, a victim feminist, thwarting the dynamics of male control by unmanning a false consciousness. Sylvia Plath's former husband Ted Hughes returns us to the fury caused by Aristotelian subversion of women, counterfeited as a function of transcendent belief:

> Your worship needed a god.
> Where it lacked one, it found one.
> Ordinary jocks became gods –
> Deified by your infatuation
> That seemed to have been designed at birth for a god.
> It was a god-seeker. A god finder.
> Your Daddy had been aiming you at God
> When his death touched the trigger.
>   (Hughes 1998: 16)

We can recover an impression of the force in the psychohistorical momentum in the employment of Aristotle to alienate a women from her equality. We find this pervades the medieval world, through to the Renaissance. And Michelangelo Caravaggio's use of exclusively male-centred sensuality of his Vatican art subjects both embraces and discards this history of alienation.

But let us do this through the post-structuralist photorealism of Tibor Czernus's 1987 'Untitled' painting (see Plate 3). The relation between live-metaphorised mimesis and love already has a deep-seated disputed history even before any attempt to construct a counter-intuitive perspective for the two for our futures. Tibor Czernus's 'Untitled' canvas beautifully, though ironically, circumscribes the loss – yet affects – of aspects left to us by this Renaissance past. The omission of a title marks the absence of a narrative presence in the painting, unlike its oblique exemplar in Caravaggio's religious subjects. The mirrors of sexuality are inverted from homosexual holiness in

Caravaggio to modernist subservient woman. Apparently Csernus here offers us the reverse mirror of what was the Renaissance case. Do the women parody Caravaggio's men in the parallel painting universe? Or have they fallen victim to becoming manned victims? The ambivalence haunts the beauty of the painting.

The switching gender codes some possibilities for a new counter-intuitive realism of emotion and virtue for the future. The anonymity of the painting can symbolise the space for, and need of, a fresh valuation of personal and religious love, using the past, whilst reflecting radically new insights. The painting portrays how similarities may also occupy significant positions of difference. Csernus employs an unstable nervy mimesis punning Caravaggio, yet digressing from him, to heighten the trauma of false memory. In this perspective, their differences illustrate how fundamentally distinct interpretations of meaning can emerge from common handling of signifiers – for example, the use of the same terms in Aristotle and the Sermon on the Mount. Of course, we can circumscribe and circumlocute Aristotle's 'blemish' on women as an apostrophe in psychohistory. Certainly, its direct impact on his other work should not be overstated. Yet there it is: a generalised mirror, not only of his era, but a major authorising influence with the concept of equality at the heart of his ethics, subversive to women's identity.

In the pragmatist theoretical framework of the *Nichomachean Ethics* V, Aristotle's term for *justice* differs in its usage from the New Testament lexical item. Aristotle's *aretê* (rendered 'virtue' or 'excellences') in Aristotle is predicable of men, whereas in, for example, 1 Peter 2:9 (cf. 8, 15) it is linked to God's nature. This 'nature' is projected as a potential property in people. It is not there directly linked with justice, though in other New Testament contexts it has a familiar relation to justice through faith.

Aristotle's justice is a subset of moral virtues, and relates to what is lawful and fair. What is lawful is the law of the state. Law cannot dictate an act of will. Moral virtue is an expression of the will. Hence the state cannot impose a law of being virtuous. How one might be able to interfere with one's own will and mental effects of law in making decisions in relation to Aristotle's view is not properly explored by him.

Conversely, the Sermon on the Mount requires that 'will' conforms to law and ethical theorems, where virtue can be commanded to be voluntarily attempted. Aristotle saw that his one prohibition on a commanding of moral virtue restricted his freedom to construct justice around moral value. He could only command virtue indirectly by linking the values of morality to material actions and consequences. Responding to this difficulty, Aristotle interprets justice as a mean between two extremes: possessing too much, or receiving too little. In one construction, justice is the midpoint between A's having too much, and B's having too little. Aristotle's notion of being just involves assigning *and* receiving a fair (*ison*) portion of material resources.

Christ's position opposes Aristotle here: 'Even sinners lend to sinners, expecting to receive back the fair (*ison*) amount. But love your enemies …

lend without hope of repayment' (cf. Luke 6:34–35). Not only is Jesus's remark on material justice constructed without regard to material civil rights for his follower, the command of love in conjunction with other values displaces a Christian's right to position a material obligation *towards* him or the right to militate for it for *him*.

Aristotle wished to defend the needs of the poor, but by a self-centred structural frame of obligation pitched at a material level (where A defends his rights by ensuring B does not possess more than A). In contrast, the sayings of Jesus yield the paradigm which is selflessly centred on ensuring that other people's needs be satisfied (where A defends B's needs by giving B the product of A's rights). In Christ, material possession is not a goal of justice – as a right, while justice for B's material needs is. Of course Aristotle does not crudely state that materialism is a goal, even though some protagonists of Jesus's values have. One should take care not to dissolve material rights, placed over a pseudo-Aristotelian ethics, into being Jesus's ethics. Material equality, even if it were a goal, would be achieved by just moral principles, not by a material mean. Material distribution is not the ethic, but the implementation of ethics. Assessment of value at the level of the former tends to encourage the submerging of ethics at the cost of a national fiscal differential, while ethics is the level for international law codification of values.

The foregoing outline might be used to exclude Rawls' (1972: 21–51; 1999) notion of equilibrium with his two principles, and construe it to utilise a facet of Dworkin's use of 'natural model' whereby moral value is discovered, not constructed (Dworkin 1978: ch. 6), except that our intuitions about moral value, when true, correspond to revelatory values (cf. Romans 2: 15).

It would be incorrect, I believe, to think that one has to decide whether or not Jesus's ethics are founded on one propositional attitude: e.g. rights-based deep structure of Rawls's theory. Insofar as there may be any parallel with this way of speaking in the New Testament, the previous observations might support the view that Jesus's values are non-self-orientated and love-based. But I think this type of abstraction is a misleading segmentation of an organic whole. It is also important not to make dogmatic assumptions about the separation of various strands in Jesus's ethics. For example, if one severs some aspects of eschatological priority from comments by Jesus on practice, this could damage the characterisation of other matters in the Sermon.

An hypothetical or actual case of this (depending on one's world view) might be that God knows no civilisation will ever implement the Sermon on the Mount as a feature of its society's legal code. So in articulation of a consequence of foreknowledge, the Sermon did not address the question of how it could be applied to municipal, particular and international law, where these will already discount Matthew's ethics in codification. But nevertheless, in eschatological contexts the implementation of the Sermon is universally realised. On one interpretation the absence of penal judgements in the Sermon might not be that for Christ there is none, but that no one should apply, or is incapable of implementing, the proper sentence. So judicial action of a retributive type is a matter of eschatology and not a true function for contemporary society. Again, the absence of judgements on slavery could be that the Sermon is concerned with an individual's obligation to act with faith to ideal principles in a disadvantaged punitive social code in the recognition that slavery is not right, while yet in the knowledge that a desire on the part of the Christian to preoccupy himself with violent political revolution would be built upon a violation of a more primary value to avoid violence and pragmatically to love enemies.

Dworkin (1986) has argued the thesis that law is integrity, and he proposes that Law's Empire is defined by attitude, not territory or power or process (Dworkin ibid.: 413). At least this policy in Dworkin's body of law is comparable with some New Testament ethical principles. In the New Testament the legal ethical individual both loves his neighbour as himself whilst being an alien to the normative society's civil rights by which he privileges selfishness. The thesis I am here developing agrees with Dworkin's, otherwise distinct, philosophy when he states: 'Law's attitude is constructive: it aims, in the interpretative spirit, to lay principle over practice to show the best route to a better future, keeping the right faith with the past'. I am giving these points a twist unexpected to Dworkin by insisting on the right faith to be the one with the religious foundation which has true interpretation.

Contradictory violence

Is the ethical parable a dead metaphor?

Dodd (1951: 51–53) questioned that some of the precepts of Jesus could rationally be taken seriously without ignoring, what Dodd termed, their 'literal' sense. Yet he nevertheless maintained that they are solemn counsels intended to be obeyed. He was careful to emphasise that the difference between the Old and New Testament is not that of 'objective and subjective ethical standards' respectively (ibid.: 71), while yet stating: 'the several precepts cannot ... serve as exact rules of behaviour in particular situations, yet, taken together, they do set before us an ethical task which is obligatory on us' (ibid.: 62). Presumably, despite Dodd's objection to 'literal' reading, he did not wish to claim that these precepts are inexact rules for no particular situation. Conversely Derrett (1994: 51–52), situates the Gospel's non-violence precept with its fellows in other first century AD use: Jewish, Essene and OT usage in the pacific context of Isaiah 50:5–7's blows on the cheek. Dodd's use of 'literal' is puzzling when applied to reading a precept; consider Matthew 5:39:

> But I say unto you, do not resist one who is evil. But if any one strikes you on the right cheek, turn to him the other also.

292 *Cosmological ethics*

How could one non-literally resist evil? Is 'evil' in this precept non-literal? If so, what is metaphoric evil? This questioning and Dodd's assertion presuppose what 'literal' is. The precept is not susceptible of being treated as non-literal language in tests formulated by Cohen (1977: 64–77), for example.

Jeremias (1971: 35–36) has shown that the language of precept, as well as new uses of old terms, can readily be identified owing to the unusually high incidence of terms internal to the New Testament's semantic fields. Individual terms in the above precept, typically, are not semantically opaque, but well known in Semitized *koine* Greek (cf. Mussies 1971: 187). *Rapizei* ('strikes') does not here have a figurative form or use such as its variant has in LXX Hosea, *S.*. 11:4 (*hos rapizon*). The precept, as incorporating a description of and counsel against physical aggression, concurs with Black's (1967: 190) approach as well as with the foregoing data. I conclude from this that the descriptive – crudely speaking, the 'literal' sense – is the precept's functional sense, although this merely orientates and does not exhaust its significance.

Has ethics logical value?

Matthew's use of the precept, and others of this genre, appear to be for illustrative purposes. This articulation of 'precept' is akin to the use of a function F with a value ϕ to highlight the function's contribution to the sense of its context. Of course a function never appears in use as a bare function; it is only calculated with respect to its sense by measuring the set of value(s) which it takes in use. Jesus's use of the precept is parallel with this conjunction of value and function. The value is the use of the precept, whereas the function of the value is the principle thereby enunciated by the precept's use. As a precept, the precept is the value of the function. As a type, the precept displays a universal function. Just as with a function – it typifies any value which falls within its domain – so with the precept, the precept typifies the deontology applicable to any situation which is a member of its class of extensions.

This is analogous to jurisprudence in a number of respects. Jesus has selected a 'hard case' ('hard' with respect to achieving the implementation or peace – which is the principle that provokes the precept's use), as a case which is problematic for a judge attempting to harmonise rights and obligations. In the relevant respect, Jesus's use of the precept emphasises that the function of the precept is the 'statute' which it instantiates. The 'statute' within the precept is the negated theorem: 'do not resist one who is evil'. The inference which this generates is: 'if any one strikes you on the right cheek, turn to him the other also'. This offer of a conditional proposition obliquely exposes the consistency to which Jesus invites the reader to conform in accepting the precept as a law-like function. Such a formulation excludes the ethical propriety of the victim's appealing to the non-Christian action and social policy, if *he* is to apply Jesus's precept. A critic should be careful not to render this a superficial point, for structurally it has forceful parallels with Dworkin's claim about hard cases (Dworkin 1978: 84) in that principle not policy determines the resolution of a hard case. Accordingly, consistent generalisation and application of this type of precept need to keep within the domain of sense which the precept articulates. There are no grounds for turning the precept into a metaphor. One could not consistently apply the precept to a situation involving physical violence (which is its specific domain) and not use it as a prohibition on that physical violence, if the foregoing analysis is correct.

Against this assessment, one might think of Matthew 10: 34: 'I came not to send peace, but a sword' as in conflict with it. However, the Greek for 'send' (*ballō*), as with NEB, imports the sense of 'bring'. This feature does not concur with a proposal that Jesus is advocating his followers to carry swords. This violent action is a consequence of his mission. The point is that others – opposed to Christ – put violence over and above Jesus's teachings.

I suggest that the problems about the identity of 'literalism' in the above cases emerge partly because of neglect to give attention to the live metaphor quality of such ethical expressions. This sort of ethical description can be depicted by seeing the analogy between the function/value and live metaphor relation. 'Turn the other cheek', as indicated above, is akin to the value of a function (as with 32 as a value of the function x). 'Turn the other cheek' is a value of and implements the function about non-use of violence. In a similar way, a photograph is a value of its subject – its function. Of course, a value never exhaustively specifies its subject, yet it preserves its truth-value. So live metaphor meaning can be extended to account for ethical statements of this and other types. This approach to ethics can be generalised to complement the use of 'function' in the employment of the term to characterise an overall ethics and its application. An illustration of this type of use, albeit not explicitly formulated as such, occurs in Eells and Nehemkis (1984).

8 The practice of legal cosmology

The experiment of legal cosmology

Is peace politically feasible?

To the question 'Is Christian peace politically feasible?' one naturally responds with 'Where?', so raising a point of quantification. The Christian's community is, at one level, as large as there are people. Perhaps proportionately few of those people will share a Christian's values and aims. This generates a tension between what can be achieved and what one would like to achieve. An added subsidiary restriction is that the current conflict of laws and values between national groups precludes the contemporary implementation of ethical hopes for unity at the international level.

Quite obviously, to devise civil policy which contradicts the precepts of Christ, in an attempt to circumvent these problems, would leave such an actor no Christian at all. This raises the substantive issue of discarding solutions and means which are infected with functions that are not reducible to Christ's precepts, if one is to sort out what it is to be a practical application of Christ's ethical cosmology. This is not tantamount to polarising, at the relevant level of practice, the Christian from his international or national society, not least because of the causal connection between each and all states of affairs throughout the nonlinear series of the world's national and international communities.

Since the contemporary problems and obligations are at the level of the world community, discussion at the level of national politics would only serve to destroy and localise the scale of problems and possibilities. Hence, international politics is a medium of discourse for attempts to implement peace, although it commences with the individual.

But it is of little transient profit to analyse a balance of opinions from various international politicians since opinion and person frequently change. Generally, their more 'permanent' conclusions, which operate as influential parameters, are found codified in international law. In this perspective, international law is comparative jurisprudence in practice: acting as it does as a mirror of the juridical ethics and teleology of civilisations. It is evolved by democratic consent (or perhaps compromise); and thus might act as, or ape, as consensus of agreement between its actors, which can serve as a projection of possible practice. So, in some respects, international law codes are the public commitment of politicians to a legal morality. Sometimes this coalition is not followed by implementation of its advertisements, and this has been because sometimes the law has been used as a veil rather than a mirror for intentions.

A positive tendency at the structural level is that particular international law – agreement between a few states – inclines in recent history to become universal international law – legation or treaty accepted by many states.[1] Also, as McNair notes (1962: 57), there is an increasing tendency for nations in dispute not to risk conflict on, for example, the issue of borders, but to submit the disagreement to independent arbitration to The Hague, with national courts consequently increasingly applying rules from international courts as precedents to be deployed in national contexts. International terrorism and commercial crime have intensified diplomatic motivation to enlarge such trends.[2]

Until 1989 international law was mainly book law, thus restricting adaptation and requiring application of the book law's political theory; this might be called the Grotius effect. One should recall that Grotius's reputation as a lawyer obscures his prior status as a philosopher and biblical scholar – his only later receiving an honorary law degree. His book-law approach was also particularly centred on his use of the Bible in many controversial topics.[3]

Contrary laws

Is peace negative or positive?

Contrariwise, the position being argued in the present book attacks that strand of self-interest which has as its characteristic in earlier European formulation in Grotius (1625), in which, legally, love for others would have to be centred on self-interest. It is worth contrasting two juridical experts' comprehension of the European Community's self-perceptions of self-interest, composed by Bergeron (1998), in which Fitzpatrick presents the Community law as evoking:

> a unity capable of transcending its diverse and contradictory elements, thus making coherent legal order possible.
>
> (Fitzpatrick 1992: 86)

whilst Bergeron (1998: 14) observes: 'But the myth works because it is based on what it is not'. It is clearly problematic to grasp how a unity is capable of transcending contradictory elements when a principle of coherence is the solution since such a theory allows contradictions – they only have to match within the system to make it cohere. Accordingly, a concept of modernity which preserves such phenomena will encode contrary values of progression in relation to what is the self and how it can be achieved. Such a tendency was already an internal property of Romanticism which bred modernism, and which itself derives from earlier presuppositions of the self generalised to produce a counterfeit of neighbourliness. This view has support from Tuck's judgement that:

> It is important also to stress that according to Grotius this natural sense of society with all other men does not entail any obligation to *help* them ... It merely entails an obligation to refrain from harming them.
>
> (Tuck 1983a)

Self-interest may be conceded as a natural whim; but my points are that one should set the negation of self-interest as an ideal to achieve, and replace self-interest with a function which locates others instead as the object of interest and love. It is surely right seriously to weigh Tuck's (1983a) and also Haggenmacher's (1983) reassignment of Grotius as primarily the founder of modern moral theory rather than the creator of a system of international law: a man principally concerned with specific applied issues and their morality, though international law systems have been conjectured from Grotius.

Associated with Grotius's view is a claim that one has to consent to a minimal set of agreed common values, which concurs with many people's rejection of other values, as a basis for the rational assessment of dissenting alternatives. This is 'secondary' *ius gentium*, in Grotius's analysis, as in Tuck's summary of it:

> consists of parties to their promulgation. They thus correspond to the civil laws of a state to which all citizens have (again, in some sense) consented.
>
> (Tuck 1983b)

To criticise this view is not to oppose Tuck's exposure of the issue. I wish neither to return to the Aristotelian opposition to which Grotius objected, nor admit the minimal basis that he himself advocated or which has been evolved by legal champions thinking to represent Grotius. It does not seem at all logical that an individual moral agent should be coerced into having to accept as the rational basis of his starting point claims about there being universal rules that oblige 'consent' from him. Man is not the *rational* animal he was once thought to be: a democratic pooling of consensus in international or civil morality is not sufficient to prove that legal values procure ethical criteria for inclusion or exclusion of necessary minimal morals.

Some might respond to this by maintaining that, for example, many people would not be convinced that a morality based on aspects of the New

Testament is a rational option. The fact that they remain unconvinced is a collective psychological function of consent, and it is not a property of the logical status of that position. So it would be illogically circular to argue from the desired aim that this is the basis for it. Logic should be internal to rhetoric; and society's consensus should be distinguished from what are the rational starting points of presuppositions. Where they coincide, it is epistemologically accidental and contradictory as an appeal to consensus.

Grotius (1625) himself manifests a consensus which is quite foreign to many of his modern admirers: he made substantial use of the Bible as a structural component of his thesis. Interestingly, a majority of his passages were from the Old Testament – yet used to furnish Christianity with a 'modern' moral framework. King David was unlike Charles I or a current American president, however. Even allowing for fundamental transformation of ways of perceiving the world, Grotius's Old Testament procedure has today a certain contrary anachronistic texture, given his presentation of a morality for his contemporary societies, especially in view of the fact that they were construed by him as needing to admit a minimal theological consensus. What was an admissible appeal to Grotius (1625: ch. 6), to use King David's military prowess against the king of Ammon as a precedent for Christian military conduct, is nowhere present in the New Testament treatment of social action. Grotius proposed such an Old Testament treatment as part of a foundation for his view of Christian society, which is almost the opposite in thematic emphasis to that which the New Testament articulates when it cites the Old Testament in relation to social justice.

Would global financial peace be criminal?

Superpowers, and other seemingly civilised countries in the contemporary world, embody some of these contrary statutory and procedural contradictions. This tension also reflects the duplicitous possibilities of misusing legal structures. A corollary of this is to be found in laws concerning economic order in society. The financial services laws encode obligations and duties of care on institutions with hardly any regard for presenting criteria of implementation. This law is therefore basically a syntax with space for any semantics which one cares to inject.

A typical case in the mid-1980s was the UK self-regulatory authorities. They have, and had, laws supposed to ensure due diligence, often without proper fiscal resources or power to implement them, sometimes even without suitable provisions to ensure co-operation between the self-regulatory authorities.[4] These equivocating modalities appear to be the product of a convenient pragmatism, integrated with the misperceived value of profit over obligation to citizens. The present writer suggests that this goes much deeper than usually reported. For example, it is probable that the international bank BCCI was orchestrated into a position to collapse by its organised crime backers, who appreciated that the 1990 Florida indictment of BCCI and Noriega's arrest would result in critical leaks of criminal information. The removal of the bank would be the 'best' way to dissolve the problems. This took two years because another bank was being penetrated as the new prospective base. This is akin to the advertised major successes in the conviction of Mafia leaders in Italy in the past. It seems evident that these older godfathers were fed to the judiciary by younger elements bent on control. Investigation, with limited resources and talent, is hard put to keep up with basic investigation, let alone expose the underlying political causes of large-scale criminality. The political comedy of fair finance is played in isolation from moral introduction of the true presentation of these dire needs for funding. Illegal agents and politicians therefore cash in on the social and perceptual ambiguities of governance encoded in law. Criminals copy governance and are more able to equivocate at crucial points concerning profitability. With some politicians this demure malaise is a style of compromised thinking, and is partially subconscious. A revolution in training people in the application of idealistic pragmatics is required as a component in the cure for the condition.

Is world peace a tragedy?

Grotius, although firmly against these sorts of connivances, left a heritage whose later devolution was achieved by emphasis on quantity and apparent stability, and not on moral values in implementation. Grotius's literary style, as with politicised discussion about economic policy and morals in the contemporary world, is a collage of non-juridical citations pressed into a myth of unified service. As with the modern world, this is used to support Grotius's morality; their violent conflicting ideologies are suppressed to avoid internal confrontation. Goldhill's (1986) examination of the *Oresteia* is relevant here. He argues that not only do the disparate motives merge to mirror life in this tragedy centring on juridical practice, social self-interest and mythology, but claims that the ambiguities and reversals also reflect the literary method of some juridical thinkers. These ambiguities, of course, format the structure of much diplomatic thinking, where typical political policy supposes that, as Abba Eban (1999) stated, one has to live ambiguously in two different ethical worlds; suffering necessary consequences of individuals (world leaders) who want false choices; and do not expect nations to act outside their nature; and his perspective is analogous with Dworkin's (1986) comparison of legal and literary enterprises. In view of these considerations, we need to reassess Grotius in the perspective of his actual writings, as they operate to disclose functioning suppressed premises in his moral theory about international law.

Despite changes in method and viewpoint, international law still embodies much of what Grotius composed. To be sure, modern international law has shifted from book to case law, though not in conjunction with the injection of an improving public morality to modify the application of the laws.[5] It is clear that there are examples of the reverse of this: the Second World War and various UN decisions illustrate this contention. Despite such a point, however, more recent international law has inclined to practice case and not book law. This has enabled there to be more flexible judgements to embody current circumstances. But this has, in turn, produced acute problems for codification by treaty (cf. McNair 1962: 58). And this can leave law subject to political fashions.

Even when treaties are achieved, their language may permit evasion of obligations or misuse of their provisions. The 1967 Outer Space Treaty might be a case in point. Lovell (1973: 34–38) observed that FOBS (Fractional orbital bombardment satellites) were launched with ambiguous evidence indicating that it is not unlikely that these had megaton nuclear warheads, although the treaty prohibits *armed* FOBS; yet this requirement could be sidestepped by staged remote-control electronic arming. The experimentation with in-orbit laser-beam weapons and other 'Star Wars' technology by USA and USSR were even less clearly regulated by treaty or control. Although the end of the Cold War left such cases on the edge of relevant concern, the possible resurgence of the political conditions which led to these disputes suggests that the problems they embody will be of future concern.

Unsurprisingly, outer space law depicts presuppositions about what occurs in terrestrial law: technological innovation by superpowers, to gain a strategic advantage, outstrips international law codes. Here, political manipulation of law codes and research establishments coincides with political ambition and priority. Ethics is usually servant to politics, if not the serf, although the relation should be inverted if current international problems are to be resolved.

The economic end

What is the cost of selfishness?

The competing ideologies are backed up by economies in the superpowers which are asymmetrical respecting materially deprived nations or societies. A malicious feature built into the superpower or advanced national economies is a set of codes which prevents the fair distribution of basic resources (e.g. meats, fats) to people in other backward economies which are often on the verge of, or suffering from, famine.

This situation is permitted to exist in the EEC codes of practice as a permanent structural feature, not directly to maintain a basic food source for its populations, but to support a maintenance of price-ratios in relation to supplies. If these food mountains are not destroyed, they are usually dumped in such a way and scale that only an advanced nation can respond to purchase. So an advanced economy with an approximate £1,200–£1,800 per capita income in this way maintains its asymmetry regarding backward societies with below £40 per capita income. Prices may change and inflation affects such figures, but the ratio is the same. Viciously uneven distribution of the ratio reflects starvation levels in its main population. Nussbaum (2000) demonstrates that such a situation is far worse for women. And these asymmetries seem to be becoming more extreme.

Hence, a pervasive structural feature of civilisation is a fierce contravention of values concerning love and concern for neighbours. This is not only because of the absent disposition, but in effect by the presence of its opposite – selfish inconsistent concern – militating against any change of structure. Clearly, politicians who depend on a majority, usually for their continuing careers and election, are not going seriously to attempt a fundamental alteration of an economy which reverses the direction of differential, especially when comparatively small alterations of differential within the salaries of advanced economies produces national strikes by the politicians' prospective voters. In this way municipal law indirectly influences international law to ignore and resist Christ's precepts.

To be sure, F.A. Mann observed that it is no longer expedient, commercially or legally, within 'reasonable justice' to maintain that public international law and private law should have separate fields of theory and application.[6] There should be commercialisation of treaties and internationalisation of contracts; but even if this were achieved, and it is unlikely at the relevant level, it would not obviously obviate the foregoing anti-Christian structural state of affairs in international law, including EEC and UN laws.

Is violence an economic function?

Economy has a conceptual relation to violence: the seeds of violent revolution often stem from disunity generated by material inequality. That the foregoing sketch of structural ethical inconsistencies in law occur in 'democratic' as well as totalitarian states, highlights the material problems which usually provoke barriers to peace. Of course, there is a considerable amount of non-official response from voluntary organisations to some needs, with tides of widespread response from the public. However, these are always massively less than quantitatively adequate to meet the requirements of the particular problem, as the 1974–1980 series of famines illustrate; nor was appropriate large-scale action initiated by governments external to the problems. And some governments actively exacerbated difficulties with political pressures and/or military activity. Hardly any of such aid is regular or adequate. Even in this priority, mischief is not beyond the scope of the aid: Gardner (1964: ch. 7) argues that US generosity is for selfish ends. Bowett's (1972: 150) apt judgement: 'contemporary concern … owes much, therefore, to self-interest, in the sense of a wish to avoid a potentially dangerous threat to world peace', epitomises the centre of apprehension which motivates some aid. Nevertheless, it is clear that this concern is not entirely objective: it is bound in with a desire to maintain a given ideology and status quo. This is clear from another area – that of the arbitral process concerning state restrictive immunity from suit in matters which are an implementation or exercise of public authority (see Collier and Lowe 1999: 271–73). Much law is a self-interested amoral safety-net for leaders and executive officers built in just at the point where idealism or corrupt conduct could be made accountable.

The status and disadvantages of backward nations are not allowed to modify this material and ideological priority. That is to say, for example, a UN conference of Trade and Development (1968) advocated that 1 per cent of a national income be given to backward nations. Of course, that amount is meagre compared to the needs of the backward nations, especially contrasted with the relative excess which the advanced nations enjoy in regard to primary and secondary needs having been fulfilled for them. However, not even 1 per cent of aid was furnished by the advanced nations; as the report later stated: 'Plainly, there is not an advance towards, but retrogression from, the terms of recommendation'. If one matches this with the legality of destroying foodstuffs in the EEC to preserve artificially high prices, it is evident that something is fundamentally wrong in the ethical structure of political institutions and attendant opinions. Often aid, slight though it be, is for the military, political or indirect material advantage of the giver, with agreements exacted from the perhaps invisibly controlled receiver on that basis. Rather, what is required is aid sufficient to found a structure that will generate a backward society's own subsistence.

Piero Sraffa (1960) is of help at this juncture. Is it without point that the order of capital required for such a project is dedicated instead to the dominant member state's achievement of further structural advantage, using its surplus-to-needs capital? The disadvantaged areas of the world are thus incapable of reaching the function of an economically self-replacing state precisely because of the external 'assistance' given by the governments and financial aid agencies that are supposedly operating to assist to this end. In Sraffa's conception, one element of the analysis of a market economy has to be external to that economy. For Sraffa, that element is the growth rate; in Kaldor's (1986) view it is the rate of profit. It seems evident, whatever the public visage may advertise, submerged in international superstate fiscal external aid policy for Third World countries, *that* element is invisibly subverted by replacing it with the giver's own exogenous element – therefore ensuring that the recipient of aid will be disarmed as an independent competitor in the world market, and thus be a negation of a self-replacing state.

The world of violence

Is there just violence?

Macquarrie (1973: 48) concludes that: '"Love your enemies and pray for those who persecute you" ... is not only a doctrine of non-violence; it would seem to be a doctrine of non-resistance'. In the New Testament range of principles this judgement is not synonymous with pacifism, though the Sermon on the Mount gives the Christian no warrant for using violence.

The eschatology of the Apocalypse, and earlier prophecies (for example, Matthew 22:13) on many interpretations deploy a counsel of force which appears to be intended literally against those who act against Christ at his return to the Earth. But this is eschatology, not realised, and not a warrant for a pre-eschatological use of violence, and even then it is not couched in terms of a free agent's own decision to implement violence.

There are indeed New Testament references to actions which are so wicked as to be 'worthy of death' (cf. Romans 1:32); yet these uses nowhere attend a hint or instruction that the penalty is to be implemented by Christians, but their fates are left to God's prerogative at the *eschaton*, or 'providence'. The New Testament does not fail to legislate for criminal court procedure. But its court action and penal sentencing are, so to speak, by God at the *eschaton*, and not synchronic with the crime. Failure to appreciate this focus results in incorrect legal consequences being placed on the Sermon.

But is 'just war' a counter-example to the foregoing? Brownlie claims that 'just war' conceptions arose not from the Bible,[7] but originated in Greek practice and came into the Roman law, with Roman writers attempting to inject it with moral content. He maintains that until AD 170 Christians were forbidden to enlist (Brownlie 1963: 5). Augustine defines a just war as a war in which injuries are 'usually' avenged.[8] The New Testament explicitly consigns vengeance to God's prerogative as opposed to his worshippers (Romans 12:19), *and* in a context warning them to endure afflictions (Hebrew 10:30–33). Vengeance is made a matter of eschatology (2 Thess. 1: 7–8), not early Christian history. Aquinas stated that a just war is required if a group deserves punishment because of a fault,[9] and Cajetanus (1515, 1524) classified it as a judicial punishment. Both these options appear to go against the New Testament expressions mentioned above, and conflict with the Sermon's command to love enemies in the situation of the enemy's displaying a fault (i.e. persecution of the innocent: Matthew 5:44). The providential punishment of evil doers is mentioned in 1 Peter 2: 14, but it is not evident from the context that the governors of this punishment are *as a matter of belief* enacting God's will truly. It appears, conversely, that the governors are not believers but unbelievers whose free choice is providentially allowed by God against believers for their chastisement as a consequence of their choices.

Grotius (1625) claimed that laws of war apply to both sides in conflict, since it is in the nature of the polarity for each party to view its role as supporting a just cause. It is often difficult, in any case, to sort out the original actor in causing war because of the complex relation such claims have to the respective ideology and territorial history. Legal specialists such as Schwarzenberger (1968: 37f.), consider 'just war' to be a vague and speculative, subjectively elusive, notion. He records that the substitution of the necessity of self-defence for just war is now the permissible cause of a war (ibid.: 38), and observes: 'If self-defence is right, it necessarily excludes self-defence against self-defence' (ibid.: 38; cf. 28f.). Both the International Military Tribunal of Nuremberg (see UK Command Papers 1946: 28) and the Tokyo Tribunal (1948: 31) conclude that certain impending or actual invasions and/or attacks are the grounds for self-defence.

Is self-defence an unjust plea?

If a society followed the teaching of the Sermon on the Mount concerning non-resistance, there would be no war even in self-defence because it is precisely in this situation that Jesus's words encode objection to violence; and Christian societies have often achieved much by the concerted negation of the Sermon's conception. Very few wars appear to satisfy the requirement of self-defence, except when a particular ideology is presupposed to map the politics of the claims. In principle, of course, if Schwarzenberger's thesis, and the Nuremberg as well as the Tokyo models, were adhered to by all states, there would be no wars. In practice, the massive interaction which opposed these models, and the compromise-permitting legislation with UN democratic procedures permitting consensus, not facts or ethics, to measure what is self-defence, it is evident that no moral criteria act as controls on the inception of war. Self-interest appears to replace justice, and so peace at the world-scale level is remote, if not impossible, in the presence of these legal and political structures.

A case of the unresolved status of a given military action which, from the standpoint of one ideology is self-defence, and from another is invasion or attack, and each a type of 'just war', would be the Israeli military actions in the Lebanon. Here, Arab leaders have termed them acts of war, whereas Israelis allege the actions to be self-defence against acts of war. The political philosophy and history behind each Arab or Israeli position accordingly is embraced by the relevant party and used as a warrant to structure and allegedly to identify its being right. Variously, depending on the ideology prefixed to the relevant accusation, a group involved in military action will be designated as guerrilla, terrorist, or legal liberation army acting on behalf of wrongly displaced persons or invader.

These features delineate a state of affairs which is only ever characterised by political parties through the value-judgements of their ideology and historical conflicts. So, at least in central critical confrontations where self-defence is employed as a justification for war, and where 'just war' is often used by each party, the self-defence claim – as a cause of war – dismantles or is analysable into a judgement about ideology. In sum: in typical modern cases at least, it is overtly simplistic and naïve to consider self-defence as resolving the question of pragmatic moral issues about the proper use of violence. Self-defence unpacks into an item which is not identifiable without redress to questions which just will not find coherent true resolution if one allows political judgement to decide, because answers will be ideological recipes which presuppose, and do not prove, which is the right value to apply to solve the relevant conflict. Of course, this is not to commit one to the view that there is no political examination which will not resolve the cause and identify the guilty party in military action. It is, conversely, a position which is concerned to isolate the pragmatic level at which actual decisions are taken and how self-defence law is used in violent situations.

To be sure, the question of the truth-values of the self-defence and just war principles is distinct from their problems of application; but the two concerns directly interrelate. For example, if it were the case that a given Middle East conflict is not analytically reducible in practice to one of self-defence because of two claims by parties in that each claims self-defence, then an option could be that neither is self-defence. This situation could embody a conflict which is comprised entirely of an arbitrary claim devolving on ideology, but which is stated as self-defence. Here the cause of the conflict on both sides would be that the actors' political philosophy 'verified' the military action: self-defence is claimed because a party's implementation of its territorial ideology is scanned as trespass with intent to invade or attack from the standpoint of the other party's ideology. Of course there are classically evident examples of invasion, such as Hitler's advance into Poland; but even this case was not presented without complicating compromise at the time.

The Middle East category above, however, is not merely unique to that territory or its races. The superpower investment in the polarised Middle East disputes only serves to stress the complex reduction of any violence to ideological commitments, whereby any move by Arab or Israeli group will provoke a corresponding, or at least predictably non-neutral, ideological analysis of fault and its ascription to the alleged aggressor by the relevant superpower bloc. To adopt, for example, the USSR or USA interpretation and measure self-defence from that perspective does not dismantle the opposite viewpoint; and so stalemate often obtains in terms of decisive proof of whether self-defence applies or not. This brief remark has behind it, clearly, a very deep and complex historical and political arena which is so well trodden, with ideology as the language of pragmatism, that much commentary about applying war law is merely ideology. Often this hybrid of ideology as morality is held in genuine sincerity, not least since it is, in various cultures, fed up from earlier historical conflicts. In these cases the regress of 'original' aggressors is an ancestral chain which can only be determined by ideology; where this is the case, it often appears to be true that there can be no proper self-defence plea: for it becomes a matter of implementing a world view.

This is pertinent to crucial pressure-points which are likely to be seminal for future world crises. Those states (such as Iran, Saudi Arabia) are not only agents of their own internal ideology which maps claims for self-defence. The superpowers concerned with them as strategic entities – not to be possessed by the corresponding opposite power bloc – present, for example, Iran as a function of a superpower ideology when disputing self-defence issues. Irrespective of which ideology might be said to hold a true view of a particular issue, it seems obvious that political pressures, in the superpower scrutiny of such possible confrontations, will not yield any completely neutral examination of self-defence claims. In practice, the insulation law received at the hands of operators can make a mockery even where a clear distinction about self-defence is sustained. For example, consider the case of a member of the UN Security Council which initiates an act of aggression and another member responds with self-defence. Under Article 27 of the Charter, the aggressor could apply a veto to exclude any opposing judgement or action the Council might wish to bring against the aggressor: here ideology again falsifies and circumscribes ethics.

Killing logic

Can a violent means be true?

Wortley (1967),[10] who was the first to notice the foregoing possible use of Article 27 of the UN Charter, proposed that it is a paradox that the law permits force without his having given further attention to the nature of the 'paradox'. One of the features usually associated with conditions for 'just war' is that 'the means must be appropriate to the end' (a condition Macquarrie partly criticises: 1973: 55). An early formulation by Anscombe of a related condition stated: 'Only right means must be used in the conduct of the war'. Here 'means' clearly includes use of violence which causes death; but peace is the end, which is the absence of violence of this sort, in the relevant sense. So, interpreted in the evident sense, the conjunction of this facet of the means with the end produces an opposition: violent means; end-peace. Unpacked in an obviously relevant way for the basic ingredients, this reflects a disguised contradiction in such a construction of 'just war'. The means is a contradictory of the end, as 'violence and non-violence', or a contrary as 'by means of death, the end is peace', although other features structure just war as well.

Rawls (1972: 379) renders a detail of this situation explicit in stating: 'The aim of [a just] war is a just peace'. I assume that 'right' and 'just' are used properly in a consistent way only if the values which they contribute to formulate are consistent and true. Rawls (1999: 565) adds to this what he reasonably calls various principles and assumptions. Two of these state that:

1 The aim of a just war waged by a decent democratic society is a just and lasting peace between peoples, especially with its present enemy.
2 A decent democratic society is fighting against a state that is not democratic.

As Rawls notes, (2) assumes that democratic states do not go to war against each other, though they have. It is also worth mentioning that Hitler was democratically elected; so the presence of a democratic process, evidently, does not entail democracy.

Of course, presupposed in general is the point that not only has a cause of a just war to be just, but the principles by which it is enacted need to be just or right. If actions intrinsic to a 'just war' are not right or inconsistent with respect to the values which identify the end, then 'just war' is a contrary expression in use. One might term this state of relations the just war paradox. A central aspect of this opposition in the paradox (to introduce the feature crudely before giving it some examination) is homicide. It is not enough vaguely to say that killing in war is not murder because the war is legal. This type of response would confer anything with morality merely on the whim of a lawmaker, given what laws democracy or dictatorship can sometimes breed. Contrariwise, it would not be correct to depend on a smudging of the distinction between killing and murder to sustain an objection to a just war. An argument to support a criticism of just war theory is required rather to rest on a clear separation between killing and murder, and which does not merely rest on a legal decision but a consistent explanation.

Is war murder?

One feature which is used to isolate murder from killing (e.g. manslaughter) is a particular state of *mens rea* – 'the guilty mind' – the presence of which is a necessary condition for classifying the *actus reus* – 'the guilty act' – as murder. This *mens rea* is intention, usually explained with the ragbag title 'malice aforethought', with a type of manslaughter being identified by, among other things, the absence of such intention. It is customarily taken to be the case that to establish liability in a murder prosecution, unexceptionally, *mens rea* with intention has to be proved. (If A shoots at B, and misses B, but C is killed instead, this is classed as murder of C by A.) Also, an intention to cause grievous bodily harm, which when executed results in the death of the victim, can be categorised as murder, since death of the victim can be categorised as murder as a likely result of the malice could be foreseen to be death. This raises an interesting question of the relation of the actor's mental state in this crime to intention. But it is here left aside, with attention being given to the main and direct sense of intention in the typical murder formulation given first above, and secondarily to the ABC type of case. In sum, it is true to say that in widespread traditions of criminal law the conjunction of (a) *mens rea* intention and (b) *actus reus* state of affairs, appropriately interpreted, is the necessary and sufficient condition for an actor having committed murder. In an area of activity central to being a just war, intentional killing of people occurs. And the conjunction of (a) and (b) applies. So in terms of their being necessary and sufficient conditions for murder, murder is committed in just war, and other wars.

Of course, in criminal law, self-defence allows it that a person does not become convicted of murder if he commits homicide in self-defence to avoid being killed himself. In international law, the self-defence claim as a cause of war has some parallel with this situation.

But what is the status of this exception in criminal law? It is not that (a)–(b) are false, but that they are pushed aside by an *ad hoc* pragmatic requirement. The status of the requirement is survival. However, 'requirement' and 'survival' applied to A do not provide a consistent analysis whereby it is consistent to kill B in terms of avoiding a satisfaction of (a)–(b). So, if the ethics of murder law is not only legally adequate but, more importantly, morally consistent and proper, then it is wrong to scrub that ethics or take it that the ethics is rightly suspended because some issue external to the explanation is presumed to be of higher concern. In this situation, the role of intention is central to my faulting just law defences. And this intention ingredient is the one which some main trends identify as the substantive mental element for definition of murder, including allowing for the distinction between intentional and reckless killing.[11]

Where intention (in conjunction with the *actus reus*) holds a definitional position in respect of formulating what murder is, it is not possible to generalise over these mental and action features as they occur in an alleged just war without thereby being committed to the consequences that this generalisation is quantifying murder over that domain, *if* the formulation in criminal law is true. (I do not hold the position that this recipe in criminal law has to be correct, but merely draw out what is the case if the recipe in criminal law is accepted.)

Hence, whereas it has sometimes been objected that criticisms of just war rest on a lack of discrimination between killing and murder, actually a grasp of the legal positions and standard characterisations of the distinction between killing and murder provokes a strong argument against just war *because* of the distinction. It would be mischievous to dismiss this just war critique (roughly, that just war intentional killing is still criminal murder) by carping that it is an unrealistic luxury about *inconsistency* between legal specifications which gives the objection momentum. The objection is not a narrow issue of logical consistency; it only becomes that because further back in the analysis the mental element and act defined as murder emerge as descriptive of just war. In practice, it appears to me, in any case, that very few military confrontations ever satisfy just war specification – as self-defence, or innocents' avenging a wrong.

If these formulations of the *mens rea* and *actus reus* really do constitute essential features of being a murderer, then one cannot push them aside as not relevant to defining a state of affairs when they comprise that state of affairs in a situation designated a 'just war', especially when (or, because?) it houses a large class of such actors. Surely it has an analogy with someone who insists on defining murder in terms of intentional killing, but fails to recognise that an exception which he permits under the label of 'euthanasia' does not, in virtue of employing that label, cease to be murder? It is, at one level, an awkward issue to determine ethically how the self-defence plea neutralises guilt in a murder. Self-defence clearly does not itself indicate that there is no *mens rea* nor *actus reus* present in the actor who acts in self-defence and intentionally kills. If intention and the *actus reus* form a conjunction which exposes the immoral qualities of the actor, then he is no less guilty of that immoral act by which the conjunction is shown to describe him. So, the addition of another feature – self-defence – to the conjunction does not demonstrate the absence of the conjunction's applicability to the actor thus described.

An upshot of the above sustains the criticism introduced at the beginning of this section, namely, that just war is in opposition to peace in such a way that it cannot be ethically consistent if a standard explanation of murder law be followed. The means is contrary or contradictory of the end, which is peace. Violence is a contradictory means to peace because the ethical values subsuming *means* and *end* are contrary. And this is impossible for a consistent account – that it be true but inconsistent. In some circumstances and analyses, a just war terminates in peace as a secondary – hoped for – end, yet where the main aim is self-defence. But even here the self-defence is itself a mechanism to achieve the peaceful order which has been violated by the aggressor. So my parallel, with this adjustment, holds generally.

There are no such routes as true contradictory means to an end in the relevant ethics. Just as intention picks out a bad feature of a murderer, so, with the foregoing examination, contrariety is comprised of the bad features which produce it. Hence, again, consistency is not a mere formal luxury for ideal situations – for ethical obligations would be ideally satisfied in them, so no argument would be needed. Given this requirement for consistency, and what displaces it as illustrated by just war prescriptions, in principle violence is in conflict with peace. It can be shown to follow from this type of consideration, then, that the Rawlsian 'the aim of a just war is peace' is a stipulation which cannot have law-like status as a principle: for it is untrue unpacked as a principle because it is contrary. So it is in operational and moral conflict with itself. Functionally and ethically, just war is a contrary of peace, so it cannot create in itself a teleological and ethical quality which is aimed at peace (except in the unhelpful and irrelevant sense as an intentionalistic interpretation). To be sure, force might dominate and produce a political 'peace'; but it is the use of 'just' as a means to peace which is the target of this criticism. Just as a liar might sometime tell the truth, this would not imply that one could generalise over his mental states and activities to negate his being a liar, so one cannot rely on war to bring peace. 'War' is not the instantiation of a principle which could guarantee a peace as a consequence of just wars.

In short, liars do not lead to truth. Just wars do not lead to peace. Ethical theory in just war is violated. War is qualitatively in intrinsic ethical opposition to the values embraced in ethical peace, even though some sort of enforced placidity or exhausted warring termination might mimic peace at times. This sort of 'peace' is accidental and is very subject to instability. The fact that no such peace has ever lasted till now, given a reasonable period for the instability to explode into manifesting violence, indicates that qualitatively the 'peaceful' consequence is programmed with the qualitative ethical teleology of the war which preceded it.

If one generalises over the liar–truth/just war–peace oppositions at the practical levels, they cannot yield a correct or consistent quantification over the philosophy of history. Consequently, just war cannot generate a teleology which is ethical. The just war is infected at a deep level with those very values which oppose peace. Who could look at the Second World War and, while admitting that it rid the world of Hitler, yet not acknowledge that the powers which opposed Hitler were not themselves, first in secret then overtly, programming a less than just teleology into current and post-war relations yet future to the Second World War, for which the world is now still suffering, in 'peace'?

Previous just wars have led to the third millenium prospect of thermo-nuclear oblivion. The seeds of opposition which this advertises are at one with the contrary ingredients diabolically set in the world which *Ecclesiastes* tells us are in the heart of man.

The foregoing considerations show grounds for a Christian's not using standard political or legal philosophy and practice as the fount for his ethics. First, they – in some spheres – conflict with central aspects of moral teaching in the Gospels. Second, they exhibit internal inconsistency which appears to be irreducible and opposed in principle to mainstream areas of New Testament ethics. Certainly, this opposes many theological programmes of current interest. But it may be significant that, on the foregoing analysis, people from outside of Christian ethical presuppositions are presenting arguments which are reminiscent of early Christian idealism. It would be a strange situation to discover that theologians had left their origins to accommodate atheists at a time when the latter adopted some of the former's original ethical territory.

9 Eschatological cosmology

Allegorical apocalypse?

Is war the final theatre of the absurd?

Transcendence can emerge from the tragic elements in human action, as MacKinnon (1974: 122–35) argued. Many Middle East crises strangely mimic ancient patterns of conflict albeit in a quite alien guise. In almost a parody of biblical format, the Assyrian (the territory of Iraq), in conflict with one group of Arabs, targets Israel – and vice versa – with Western imperial responses that attract the potential destabilisation of the world. This composite for tragedy should not be cashed as a cheap literal Armageddon. Even where the threats to basic human rights are grave, military action may perpetrate or attract a theatrical absurdity which inadvertently mocks at the moral sanity required to resolve international crisis.

The 'theatre of the absurd' can be used here to reflect on the relation between cataclysm in cosmology as a metaphor which may be applicable to the above type of international arena. Artaud was a central result of the theatre of the absurd. He saw theatre as a double, exposing the world:

> if fundamental theatre is like the plague, this is not because it is contagious, but because like the plague it is a revelation, urging forward the exteriorization of a latent undercurrent of cruelty through which all the perversity of which the mind is capable, whether in a person or a nation, becomes localised.
>
> (Artaud 1968: IV, 19)

Artaud (1947) wrote on Van Gogh and drew parallels between himself and Van Gogh, noting that Van Gogh believed that we have to deduce myth from the most ordinary things in life, and adds the reason that 'reality is terrifyingly superior to any history, any fable, any divinity, any surreality' (Artaud 1961: 29). Artaud's mental illness is something which does not entirely remove his emphasis on the surrealism of 'normal' society. In his view, as David Kelley stated

Eschatological cosmology 311

What passes for madness in a society which is, at the very least, deeply disturbed, is a 'superior lucidity' whose divinatory faculties profoundly disturb the rational structures by which that society attempts to establish norms of behaviour. And, not unnaturally perhaps, given Artaud's recent past experience, his venom is particularly directed towards practitioners of psychiatry as bastions and paradigms of a society which is itself psychologically deranged: 'Set against the lucidity of Van Gogh working, psychiatry is no more than a fortress for gorillas, who are themselves obsessed and persecuted, and who possess only, for the palliation of the most horrifying states of human anxiety and suffocation, a ridiculous terminology' (Artaud 1961: 15).

(Kelley 1990: 243)

We need not accept Artaud's apprehension too literally, while yet implementing it as a live metaphor of some leader mentality in some international crises, to contribute to a perspective which transforms reflection on political and moral cosmology. It may be worthy posing the idea of a counterfeit of sanity and political judgment, as a contrary of true counter-intuitive solution to crises, to depict such leaders.

The apparently sane political absurdity in such situations demands a mythical separation between past and present, between text and interpretation, between humanity and event. But these distinctions cannot be relevantly sustained without treating the individual, or the world, or its cosmology, as a subject suffering from multiple schizophreni form symptoms or those of multiple personality (cf. Hacking 1995).

Is apocalypse deconstruction?

There is indeed a plausible fragmentation, a coherent cosmological breakdown of such a political and moral disarray; but this, to use but one metaphoric mode of exploration, would probably have to go in the direction of deconstruction. Earlier, Chapter 6 discussed Derrida's use of a quotation, an allusion, on the analogy of a cellular telephone network system. To this, with regard to the above suggestions, Derrida's discussion of Van Gogh's painting in relation to Artaud can helpfully be introduced here.

Derrida reflects on Van Gogh's pictures as a mode of autobiography. We can contrast, as well as simulate, Derrida's discussion as a metaphor to assess the role of cosmology, past and present, as figures for present events and their positive transformation.

Van Gogh's paintings are not autobiography. But there again we cannot separate him from them; in an order series of displacements, slips, transformations and recurrences, Van Gogh's paintings cannot be dislodged from their origins. Accordingly, they can be interpreted so as to net a displacement; they evoke his identity.

As Derrida (1987: 381–82), using Artaud, states, there are no past ghosts

312 *Cosmological ethics*

in a recurrence. Yet there is a 'sensation of occult strangeness, of the corpse of a useless hermeticism, its head open, rendering up its secret on the executioner's block'. Derrida replies to Artaud by stating: 'to render this secret yet legible right down on the level of the letter', we have to realise that there is the myth of 'separation' between text and interpretation, between event and interpretation, and between text and event. Derrida insists that

> [S]eparation is in itself already, in the word, in the letter, in the pair, the opening of the secret. Its name indicates this. So one would have to render this secret already legible, like a remainder of a useless cipher. You don't have to render anything. Just bet on the trap as others swear on a Bible. There will have been something to bet. It gives to be rendered.
>
> (ibid.)

Is realised eschatology escapism?

No doubt the multiple personality of Legion might be a model for some latter-day fundamentalists wrongly anticipating 'the end'. But perhaps some who embrace realised eschatology do so to avoid the confrontation with the possibility that our history might be terminal, and thus too mildly prepare for a challenge to judge how to redirect possible future history from apocalypse. Mearns (1981: 157), striking a traditional contrast, argues that the relevance of some New Testament narrative for contemporary Christian belief when he says that a:

> factor in forming the new futurist eschatology was the need Paul felt to counter and correct the radical realised eschatological and charismatic enthusiasm of his converts in Thessalonica. The early dates for the Thessalonian letters obliquely stress the primacy of the eschatological strand in them in relation to elements intrinsic to Christian belief.
>
> (Mearns 1981: 157)

It is improper to dismiss eschatology as either realised or merely obscurant futurist fantasy. Thiselton (1980: 510–26) introduced the idea of a logically clarified description of futurist eschatology as a counter to the excessive claims of Bultmann's realised eschatology, though this can be qualified by Porter's (1996) criticisms. While emphasising the importance of the provenance of apocalyptic for its correct assessment and measurement of its protest, Sweet (1979: 5) has also demonstrated that generalised Christian principles emerge from scrutiny of *The Apocalypse*. Robinson (1976: 252–53) dated *The Apocalypse* to 69 AD. If this is correct, the Middle East is the political origin for eschatology based on the destruction of Jerusalem.

We should not overstate this typological point, though irrelevant fundamentalist misjudgement of it should not detract us from sensitive exploration.

Chapter 1 above speaks of Wittgenstein's advice on calculated madness. Sectarian fundamentalist literalism does not facilitate the rebirth of religious cosmology; Artauld's inversion of sanity and Van Gogh's vision of his future may understate opportunities for renewal; Derrida's deconstruction of imperial rational forms needs hinging to a new door of the future's child. The function of painting as a trace for cosmology is displayed in Deleuze (1985, 1994; see also Deleuze and Guattari 1994). His contribution is to construe Turner's impressionism in the perspective of catastrophe as a positive property of visionary insight (as James Williams (1997) shows). Turner's dissolving of line and form readily attracts a deconstructing treatment. Yet his commitment to a new sort of realism traps the catastrophic function into decomposing conventions while revealing fresh qualitative transformations for realism. Of course, this realism came to be superseded. My point is that Turner exemplifies, within one possible transition of an epoch, a facet of catastrophe stylistics as a means to construction and not destruction. If I may use and vary the way Deleuze and Guattari (1994: 204–5) wrote of Turner: counter-intuitive art can transform chaotic variability and the conflagration of order into new creative birth. This could be typical of what it is to be a counter-intuitive beginning.

Catastrophe mathematics

Can catastrophe cause rebirth?

Stephen Hawking (1990c, 1993) conceived the idea of 'Baby Universes' as an unexpected side-effect of a cosmic black hole. The previous chapters have employed a black hole notion as a qualitative live metaphor for decay as an antecedent for new creativity. These figures evoke poetic sensibility if applied to the above political cosmology and its afterbirth. Hawking's use of quantum gravity involves a central chaos principal which yields foetal universes using the wormhole notion referred to previously.

René Thom (1989) constructed catastrophe mathematics with an eye to the discontinuity and continuity between a foetus and the born child. Thom's theory was devised to range over inorganic and organic systems. Formulating morphogenesis for embryology, Thom commences with the epigram: 'And the word was made flesh' (ibid.). For him 'catastrophe' is a formal term for transformations to birth, and is then a type for other subjects. As live metaphor this blends well with some biblical language on birth and renewal (Isa. 66; Rom. 8:21–3; Rev. 12:5–7). We not only live by metaphor (cf. Lakoff and Johnson 1981: 33), we are born as one, so to speak. I have shown above that [1] to [6] engage not only with audio-visual criteria for communication, but also they characterise some levels of genetic reproduction.

314 *Cosmological ethics*

Is live metaphor pragmatic?

This use of metaphor is an employment of live metaphor. As Caird (1980: 66) noted, live metaphors have double references. The primary functional one is to the metaphor's referent (in the above case to the salvation of those in the *eschaton*), while the second derived reference is the descriptive (sometimes crudely called 'literal') use.

The nature of metaphor itself displays an element of the deep structure of discontinuity, since metaphor is a transformation from one semantic domain to another involving, in the case of dead metaphor, a change of reference. Pun may result in the same reference being used of another thing by live metaphor in which the same reference is retained. Schiffrin (1994: 98–99) delineates the ways in which there can be metaphorical code-switching, so that different levels of discourse or thematic focuses can be stitched together in a semantic transformation. Such potential in metaphor and other devices partially account for the structural position which metaphor holds in the parables of the Kingdom.[1]

It would be wrong to suppose that no phenomena at the semantic and ontological levels are continuous in the metaphoric value of an expression and its descriptive antecedent. If one interprets the two non-metaphoric and metaphoric phases of a lexeme as one lexeme, and not two words, then Cohen's (1993) method of cancellation of literal presuppositions, and addition of new presupposition as a function of the medium of representation, has much to commend it as a critique of metaphor. This is where a set of semantic components in the metaphor is preserved from its non-metaphoric usage, but some of the features of the non-metaphoric value are cancelled upon its usage as a metaphor. So the discontinuity of metaphor is not universalised over all its ingredient features respecting its ancestry. Thus talk of God, the Kingdom, resurrection, and other eschatological phenomena, are not necessarily the expression of complete discontinuity or analogical language.

Will we survive?

That is to say, for example, in 'the end will come', *end* is quantified at two levels. First, it is an end regarding a certain qualitative state of existence. Second, this does not oppose certain properties associated with a thing before 'the end' continuing after the end. 'End' is level-specific. The formal logic distinction between function and value is appropriate here as an illustration: x^2 is a function and 7^2 is a value of that function. If one excises the value 7, one has not thereby destroyed the function x; x is capable of receiving any of a range of values including another 7. So it is with eschatological metaphor. The function is continuous, whereas the value can be discontinuous. If 'mortal life' and 'eternal life' are possible values, then the function *life* performs as a functional pattern for these values. Of course, as with values in formal logic and semantic components in words, a single function is capable of displaying more than one value at a time. However, the nature of the discontinuity manifests the scope of the cancelled or added values and their references. If the discontinuity is described in qualitative functions, then the discontinuity will be qualitative and universally hold for that domain.

The criterion of personal identity would be the same for a person a in all domains, however, where we judge as to whether identity holds by use of a general term 'the same F' which is uniquely satisfied by a. This implements my proposal that logic is a species of live metaphor with similarities to nonalgorithmic, often exotic, mathematics (for which see Gibson (forthcoming d)). So if t_1 is a time prior to the *eschaton*, and t_2 after the *eschaton*, 'a is the same F' for all people at t_2 as at t_1. So personal identity survives the discontinuity, although this does not exclude the application of different predicates before and after t_1 and t_2 respecting qualitative changes associated with the person. This would obtain whether a person existed at the time of the onset of t_2 or had died in the domain of t_1, since reproduction of precisely the person a in t_2 could be achieved by creation of the state of affairs embraced in the realisation of a's under the criterion of identity behind 'a is the same F' in t_1's domain. Biblically, this would correspond to resurrection of the person. This has its parallel with the conditions specified in [1] to [6] in Chapter 3. But, now, where does reproduction of the person replace relative identity representation of the individual on audio-visual criteria? It was seen in that chapter that the criteria also caught the sense of a metaphorised 'genetic' reproduction applied to the Son of God. Appropriately, therefore, resurrection rehearses the same type of stencil which operated in the 'Word made flesh', albeit implemented at a different level. On this view, resurrection in the *eschaton* parallels birth and divine sonship, which themselves are epitomes of the logic of God's mode of revelation in language developed in earlier chapters, which was the reason for the adoption of the birth metaphor above. It is appropriate now to set this in a generalised cosmological framework.

Transforming the universe's end

Is there creation after death?

According to Thom (1989: 7), where M is the space in which observable entities can occur (the universe of part thereof), it contains a given subset K. K is the *catastrophe set*. The evolution of the system – its development historically – is defined by a vector field X on M. A representative state of affairs of the universe of M is depicted by m. If m meets K – i.e. if there is a collision by K on m – then a discontinuity in the system M comes to exist. On a realist theory of meaning, it is possible in principle to predict the occurrence of this catastrophe, given the above parameters. Concerning m, it here indicates the state of continuity prior to the *eschaton*, while K represents its inception. The scope of the catastrophe is not limited to the normal spacetime restrictions (indicated by a light-cone or set of cones), due to the unique boundaries and energy which would attend God's presence and direct intervention, if one follows the idea specified in Part II above. 'K' is a term designating the whole series of Thom's catastrophe models, since the *eschaton* universalises effects typified by *catastrophe mathematics* concerning the qualitative transformation of phenomena.[2]

There are functional constants which, although their values are transformed, remain precisely those constants. For example, time is still time, but its empirical relation to matter is altered. If one imagines that decay in matter is identifiable as a function of a certain application of time to it as a function of matter, then the set K would mark the transformation from mortality to perfection and immortality on the part of all components of the universe embraced by K. This has a parallel with the known variability of other functions in astrophysics such as gravity constants. The parallel has deeper connections: gravity propagates at the velocity of light. Light is an index of the bounds of general relativity which are superseded by any infinity state of affairs which does not decay. Interestingly, this aligns with the situation at the time of creation, where approaching t_0 general relativity breaks down, and, in the language of Revelation 21 and 22, creation motifs recur.

The foregoing scenario has significance for how one classifies the discontinuity which is created by the *eschaton*. History is not suddenly without a future. Time does not unexpectedly end. Resurrection is not thereby non-veridical or not experiential. 'The world' is not turned into an idiom in which poetics replaces existence as a physical reality. In short, catastrophe mathematics exposes a common-sense approach which is part of eschatological description: transformation at the high energy qualitative level with continuity of ontological categories as we know them. This is no less than a supercoordinate transformation in superspace, which is a special generalisation of general relativity's curved spacetime.[3] If this be deemed an analogy, then it should be countered that so is the mathematical transformation. Analogy, relatively speaking, does not relevantly reduce accuracy here.

Is cosmology Pascal's wager or wage?

The cancer that killed Pascal was only the end of a life of great misery which convinced its host that misery was the essence of human nature.[4] He was thoroughly biblicist in much of his prose style. Subsequent to his terminating all scholarly correspondence with such people as Fermat, and ceasing to do further research on mathematics, his philosophical prose, affected by Montaigne's *Esais* with its admonishment of those who took science to be certainty, Pascal used to project his physical condition onto the universe and yet apprehends grounds for waging with the atheist that there he has to accept the probability that God exists, though the universe dies.

Theocritus spoke of the rebirth of stars when their light ceased; 1 Timothy alludes to the light to which no man can approach, with the Apocalypse composing new forms of allegorical light. Perhaps these metaphors are, albeit peripheral, psychological seedbeds for cosmologists composing the end of the universe in terms of changes in, or cessation of, light constants.

Hawking (1991b) regards himself, somewhat impishly, as being in the 'well established tradition of oracle and prophets, of hedging [his] bets, by predicting' two alternative futures for the universe – one based on its eternal expansion, and the other on its recollapse. Hawking (ibid.: 2) describes how, although scientists have a systematic grasp of the general laws which appear to represent the universe's activities in all normal situations, we still do not 'know the exact laws that govern matter under very extreme conditions'. As he explains, this is because the solutions to the equations of physics exhibit the property of chaos, and the equations become unstable to slight changes in the starting conditions of a system. A consequence of this is that the whole system can become unpredictably unstable in its later stages. No known extrapolation of these equations can head off the randomness so that one can forecast the final condition. Hawking (ibid.) argues that there are ways around this for very general solutions, however, if, for example, we adopt the concept of very large black holes or wormholes to fix the constancy of nature.

In the above context of the collapse of a universal physical system time t in the physics should collapse. Nevertheless, I argue that, with time as the property of duration, time does not collapse – only its measurability as a property of the normal physical system dissolves. Duration can be isolated from time-as-property of physical systems. So there can be duration without our having to be committed to our present matter–energy system. Time is often used as *a* way of indirectly describing decay and entropy and the termination of a phase or epoch, and is deployed to depict aspects of matter–energy relations. These functions would no longer be operable in a physical system at terminal time t_2 if we follow some eschatological expressions which involve transformation from a material global system to a discontinuity system manifesting changes described in Chapters 4 and 5 above.

In such a unique and new system there would be change, but it would not be entropic. Such a universe would not be winding down, and may be winding up qualitatively and aesthetically. The temporal function in such a universe would be to mark duration. This duration would perhaps be infinitely multidimensional in ways that we find difficult to conceive. This is a topic for another study, and we should be wary that we can synthesise even the bare outline using metaphysical revisions of current astrophysics to characterise post-historical or post-eschatological time, since the former is not decisively formulated in relation to the relevant issues (but see Thom (1989) for an hypothesis which points out another given type of 'consequence').

The material universe as allegory

How is the universe allegorised?

Deborah Madsen's (1986) study of Pinchon's poststructuralist novels, such as *V* and *Vineland*, demonstrates that they have formal similarities to allegory in medieval literature. Pynchon invented a different set of physical laws from our own world for the *cosmos* of *Vineland*, yet retained our notions of personal identity while employing a set of bridging principles to link the two. Mark Chinca (1997: 58–69) has explored the ways in which Gottfried von Strassburg's medieval *Tristan* combines allegory with personification. The medieval world derived and modified such allegorising from various earlier epochs. For example, as John Jarick (1990) has shown, the third century AD Gregory Thaumaturgos's Greek paraphrase of Ecclesiastes 10 allegorises the theme of death personified as topography. Such allegory implements a set of principles or interpretative conventions to ascribe a fresh meaning to a state of affairs. There is both an overlap and separation between the standard and allegorised accounts of such a subject. The source subject is taken implicitly to house the allegorised sense, which is triggered into recognition by the rules of allegory. Live metaphors, the foregoing chapters have been arguing, perform functions in both philosophical and astronomical contexts. I suggest that, given the ways in which counter-intuitive live metaphors in cosmology can yield fresh senses, these can, if linked to some of the transcendent themes developed in the foregoing, lead to allegory.

Is the universe's death an allegory in mathematical form?

As Hawking and Turok (1998) state (see Figure 0.1), time-like spacetime singularities are not necessarily fatal in semi-classical description of quantum physics. So it is not hopeless to suppose that we could survive the *eschaton*. The more pressing worry for Hawking and Turok's (1998) argumentative preference for our universe's future, however, is that it may infinitely explore the far reaches of entropy: boredom by the death of infinite qualifications. But they allow the possibility of a closed universe that crunches back into itself. On either thesis, there is a problem of explaining what it would be for an individual identity to survive such catastrophic reductionism or inflation.

But out of catastrophe comes rebirth. In René Thom's theory, whole systems are decomposable. This can be connected to some semantics for foreknowledge, providence and immanence. If we adapt the concept of a surface topology to model the past, on this surface there is continuity and homogeneity of material and social phenomena in history. In contrast, Oscar Wilde's 'surface' in the *Importance of Being Earnest* is a chthonic parody of the reordered disruptions betrayed by the false consciousness of social history.[5] One ought to equate the conjunction of these surfaces as a motif to position the idea of God's transcendence breaking through, on certain occasions, and always implicitly impending, in the deep structure of history.

As proposed earlier in Chapter 3, this type of scenario has a counter-intuitive live metaphor parallel with cosmological astrophysics. Continuity and isotropy in the universe are nested into abnormal situations which emerge from time to time (for example, black holes, etc.) which exhibit energy transcendence over other phenomena. In Thom's nomenclature, the Bible offers a deep grammar of providence which, as the spirit of God, regulates the vector field of X on M. In the *eschaton*, the stability of M is decomposed by the deformation of the vector to expose the transcendental powers explicitly.

The astronomer Kopal (1979) explains how the notion of a language applied to describe stars is not an idiomatic way of speaking, drawing attention to a close parallel in the mode of discourse and star-emissions. We do not have to suppose that the same ontologies hold, in astronomy and in ancient eschatology, for us to admit metaphoric parallels between them. The putative coincidence of their symbolic representations is of interest as a function of past memory coded into new sciences. As Hacking (1995, 1998) exposes it, the science of memory has an uncompleted or largely uninitiated task of excavating the depth knowledge underneath this new surface knowledge. We do not yet know what the relations between the two spheres are. Perhaps the current study in the area of creative metaphor offers unexpected ways of configuring elements to discover routes to the past which preserve its asymmetry and continuity with the present and future. Beer (2000) has already well shown, for example, how Darwin's evolutionary creativity nested into scientific discourse many of his childhood memories of fairy-tale language.

Can apocalyptic and catastrophe mathematics be merged?

It is thus worth exploring the features such as the astronomical references in eschatological apocalyptic discourse which present the deformation of star topology: the heavens collapse (Rev. 6:12–14; cf. Isa. 34:4, etc.). This collapse, on actual, symbolic or metaphoric interpretations, corresponds formally to the occurrence of the Thom K set (i.e. the temporal collision of the universe m with the catastrophe set which comprises the *eschaton* in a vector field X). The K set is in ordered conjunction with the consequence of the *eschaton*: 'a new heaven and a new earth' (Rev. 21:1; 2 Pet. 3:13; Isa. 65:17): note that the second half of this verse is also the source for Rev. 21:4 – so the verses Rev. 21:1b to 21:4a are, so to speak, the qualitative fillers – the values of the functions which are the new heavens and earth. Here the bride, the tabernacle of God with humanity, the new Jerusalem, are characterised directly as cosmological functions. So that cosmology is qualitatively

320 *Cosmological ethics*

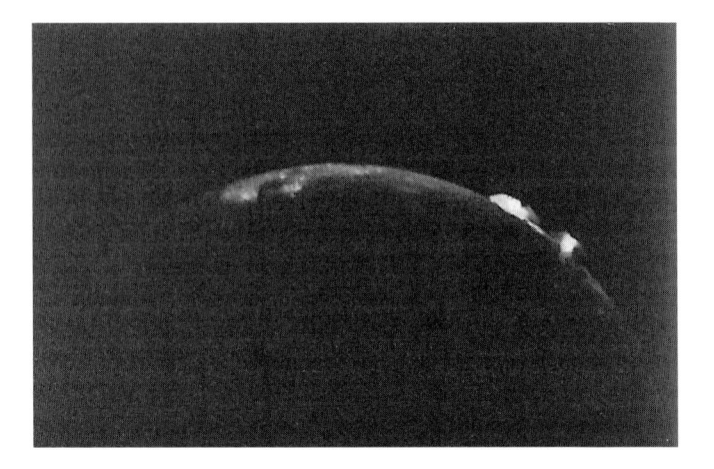

Figure 9.1 Volcanic eruption on an Ionian moon
Source: NASA.
Note: This Voyager II series of photographs shows volcanic eruptions on an Ionian moon. In literary texts the Earth's topography and seismic activity are frequently ascribed to heavenly bodies such as the moon. Coincidentally, space explorations have discovered parallels for some of these ascriptions. There is scope for research exploring how catastrophe mathematics using these seismic phenomena could be redeployed to represent some of the parallel literary images.

condensed into the quality of the life of the saints. Clearly, this mathematics does not exhaust sense.

To employ Thom's expression, the morphogenesis of the universe is the *eschaton*: the transformation by catastrophe (which may be figurative and qualitative, or physical, or both) of one system into another. But the morphogenesis formally shows how an invariant closed set of individuals is preserved. The linguistic level at which one identifies the astronomical references in the Revelation could be construed as a literal representation of physical objects in astronomy. But more likely, if one follows Rowland (1982), the astronomical terminology fits in with a figurative usage, although this does not ban some narrow allusive mixture of both 'literal' and figurative levels of usage. If the language is figurative (although one ought to allow for an intermixing of both levels in allegorical allusion), this does not render obscure the use of the Thom model. At the qualitative level it appears that a use of such language is to stress that, as with the collapse of the universe, so with the entities which are being rehearsed as astronomical motifs. The terminal phase of this absorption seems, in any case, to manifest itself as a claim that the actual properties of (God's) heaven in Rev. 21:1 'invade' the universe's and the Earth's matter–energy system. Using the result reported in Chapters 3 and 4, a number of astrophysical scenarios could be used to estimate the cosmological force of this aspect of apocalyptic language.

Does cosmology expand for ever?

Astrophysical specialists outline two eschatological phases for the cosmology of the universe.[6] One is that, if a given mass is now exceeded for the universe's matter, the universe will collapse back into a singularity akin to a black hole. On this interpretation, one can envisage that all that would be left, in theological terms, would be other universes or God's universe's dwelling outside the causal spacetime boundary of that orb which bounded our universe. So, the spacetime boundary will have retraced its expansion to the singularity and, on the theistic view, God's universal domain would expand over the manifold M – the topology previously occupied by the universe. Even in cosmological astronomy, this way of describing the matter is metaphoric.

On the second model, the universe expands indefinitely, with entropy ever increasing. Hawking and Turok (1998) have given fresh impetus to this option, and in one of their versions they use an anthropic approach, while they insist that we do not know what it would be to know the precise conditions required for the formation of observers. Presumably, the ideal realist observer – God – is also a logical subject of this, our, ignorance. So we should go carefully in fielding this God out of existence at a point at infinity. With the unresolved nature of the redshift, it is not completely certain what is the correct type of physical eschatology. But it may be that some invariant property of what is the true interpretation currently exists partially obscured in contemporary scenarios. At this level, the finitude of the universe appears a basic truth, and this concurs with biblical eschatology. Clearly, we need to be wary of equating the terminus of the astronomical *eschaton* with current knowledge.

10 Creating conclusive beginnings

'Evolution' and 'devolution' can be treated as live metaphors, respectively for life and for death. The twentieth century AD was the first era with a technology sufficient to cause planetary oblivion. This itself is evidence that the human genome has qualitatively gone into reverse: the devolution of consciousness by world leaders and corporate facilities into carnivorous mentality, paraded as the quintessence of achievement, obscured by myths in media hype. It may be claimed that the forces of global society have coerced such leaders into this potential impasse. Such a view requires that there is a devolutionary contagion at work: a counterfeit consciousness that networks leaders into the economics of extinction. Let us hope that humanity is not Othello – 'the victim of long habit, and wanting', as Frank Kermode (2000: 182) circumscribes him.

These destructive modalities in the human mind (which derive from a primordial past, be they manifested by nuclear war, economic terrorism or other symptoms) tend to mobilise against the possibility of a creative future for humanity whilst presuming to insure for the probity of life in the twenty-first century. If probability were applied to this scenario, chaos may ensure the termination of human civilisation. Our uses of the past and present variously contribute to this global mutation.

But the most improbable future can come true. Deriving from the past and present are extraordinary resources that can sublime devolution and yield a creative future. In effect, this book claims that the game of 'throwing the dice' may itself be evolved into a live metaphor by which we can decompose its random deconstructing effects. Surely a work of art such as Mozart's *Requiem* has escaped the dice, even though it engages with death and the dying composer? Malcolm Bowie (1978, 1993) points out that Mallarmé was a poet of terror: he disrupts the composed consciousness at the juncture one least expects it and one is ill-equipped to false-foot randomness. So with the future that he helped spawn. His vision is a mirror of the stage on which, and at which, human consciousness is – consciousness for which evolution has no random explanation. Consequently, the consciousness which has so strongly interrogated the self-consciousness of modernism and its aftermath, is paradoxical in its existence and in qualitative disposition about its existence, if I may thus personify our fragmenting lack of identity. On the one hand, we have no right to a universal explanation of the significance of consciousness and, on the other hand, we have no ground for discarding the possibility of such an explanation.

This book is a preliminary exploration to suggest strategies to discover ways out of this impasse, conceived as the first of a series of books. It displays many limitations: does the book cover too much ground and too many subjects? I do not engage with Hegel, and am content only occasionally to treat Kant. The book addresses Aristotle's *Poetics*, rather than, as one might expect, his *Metaphysics*, and instead attempts to construct metaphysical problems out of our contemporary astrophysics, without introducing the significance of the reception of Aristotle's thinking into Christian theology. But, however one assesses, for example, Kant's contribution to 'faith and reason' and 'God's relation to the world' debates, the effect of systematically commenting upon Kant's great opus, or other seminal authors, is to be regulated by the controlling notions of relevance and commentary to which they subject us, and to which they have been subjected. This is not a whim by which one denounces or discards such authors, but to attempt, however imperfectly, to stand as far as is possible independently of these histories of influence and to think afresh. Yet to ignore them is both impossible and to delight in alienation. I have tried to produce a different sort of use and *this* avoidance of authorities.

The opinion which supports this suture of the disparate is that logic and mathematics are species of live metaphor which, though different from natural language, nevertheless embody criteria of identity that can facilitate the building of a bridge between them. There is, of course, equivocation and incoherence, and one would not wish to warrant those. But the form of logic we have is itself an interpretation, not the final set of laws of reason; the paradoxes of material implication suffice to show that, especially when garnished by Russell's paradox. Just as microphysics was unknown to generations of past physicists, so the future may hold for us worlds of logic that traditional logicians do not now recognise, important though the existing research on logic is. Logic is composed by reference, relation and generalisation. The present book argues that these use live metaphor. An eventual consequence of such analysis is that some poetry is nearer logic in its use of metaphor than many have assumed. The foregoing chapters argue that these points have significance for the discussion of transcendence and cosmology: modernism has tended to foreclose debate on transcendence, and this all too easily attracts a reactionary alternative. I have inclined to avoid both, and sketched a different meeting of pathways.

A feature of this approach is a move towards a counter-intuitive blending of dissimilar matters. This focus also attempts to reinterpret our positioning of subjects themselves, and to reconsider the ways custom and institutions divide them, and questioning which has been pursued elsewhere. The association of physical cosmology with aesthetics, for example, has a parallel with connections utilised between chemistry and aesthetics by Hoffmann (1990), as noted in the foregoing chapters. To some it may seem peculiar to align chromatic harmony in music with mathematical theory in cosmology, though the mathematics of vibration are central to both. Yet surprise is a constant in cosmology.

'Surprise' itself is obviously not worthy to be a legitimising cover for physical law by which to stitch the unexpected and the seeming contrary together. Probability is the philosophy of expectation. Improbability is a function of unfamiliarity. Unfamiliarity is a difficult arena for those who are used to measure things by reference to familiar patterns. Consequently, what is unfamiliar may be misidentified as having no cogent pattern, not least since knowing a concept is not necessarily a recognitional capacity. My aim is not to unseat the notion of recognition, nor champion generalised novel chaos, though some cosmologists, such as Hawking (1993), seem to use this mixture to stir the universe into motion. One strand of this book suggests that counter-intuition underlies the identity of some of transcendence and cosmology, so one would not expect normative criteria to be able to measure that which is contrary to them. This is not designed to secure irrationality as a condition for knowledge, but to question our assumption that uniformity of structure, reason and recognition in surface culture are properties symmetrical to all deeper levels of explanation.

At the deeper level, I have argued, the science and the arts, in certain respects, share a continuum and are only separated by degree. This degree, the foregoing maintains, is often smaller than empirically minded theorists might assume. Much of its mathematics is approximate. Formalisation is not a procedure that ejects imprecision. It sometimes only symbolises it, though to the unwary it removes vagueness. Of course, some of science's knowledge is invariant through generations. But the criterion of identity by which this knowledge is characterised has a coarse graining which fails to encapsulate some of the relevant physical world, or describe it correctly (i.e. for statements to be identical to their 'facts'). I suggest that as current and future science goes deeper it becomes more qualitative and aesthetic, since these are also coextensive properties of the external world at which it connives.

It may be retorted that prediction and repetition in experimental science go far beyond such parallel with the arts. I grant a degree of difference; but science is too full of adjustments to allegedly 'identical' experiments to support a claim that the criterion of identity implemented under the aegis of a scientific law shows we have a perfect match between what the law claims and the identity of the piece of the world it matches for purposes of manufacture, prediction, etc. Imagination is also a function of scientific discovery, as it is in art. Art indeed has its own various precisions. Also science and art are external and internally asymmetric to one another and themselves in many ways.

The live metaphor of portrait of a given person, however, will be just as adequate as a criterion of identity of that person as will be a photograph of him or her. The technology here is continuous with the art in relation to the resulting criterion of identity in producing an image, whilst admitting some bewitched family resemblances between these media, with many differences and similarities to show that this metaphor will not work equally over all art and science. Comparably, local physics has criteria of quantitative proof different from astrophysics. Some physicists are not quite joking when they say cosmology is not an empirically precise laboratory science; and astrophysicists are not joking when they say that their experiment requires a laboratory the size of the universe – of which terrestrial physics is merely a local case. There is a discontinuity between the two, together with an overlap, with loss of precision in astrophysics compared to local physics. Clearly, the parallels between the arts and sciences should be positioned with their many contrasts. But, for example, the philosophy of art has an empirical and generalisable component which is revisable, and so has science. The degree and qualitative forms of the revision in each case will differ, yet these have to be related to internal differences between the sciences, as well as take account of the rather low esteem and knowledge some scientists have of the actually high critical and technical standards in much cultural analysis.

I have proposed that live (not dead) metaphor pervades both science and artistic enterprises, and that visual properties as well as visualisation link metaphor in these two domains. This assertion will need much more development to discover its bite and range. Again, I have not embraced Wittgenstein's (1963) picture theory of language, while modifying details for its technical content. It seems to me that one could produce a picture theory of language which would be both true to the spirit of Wittgenstein (especially if the connections with the *Tractatus* and the *Philosophical Investigations* were dug out more), while being radically dissimilar. Readers may claim that the tendency to compose live metaphor in this book, by pushing scientific and other languages into extended lexical domains, is vexing. But this queries exactly what needs questioning: the limits of language.

Central to this issue is the problem of detail. Infinitesimal differences of detail provoke a new cosmology. Detail is either fundamentally important, or it is a bore not worthy of note. We all can inadvertently privilege or neglect either sort of detail, and figures such as Einstein are no exception. The problem of fashion's influence gives this issue of detail further bite. Postmodernism or retro-chic theology all too easily replace the intolerant institutionalism of the past with themselves. We are not in a position to absorb many of the prevailing era's world-view parameters as regulative presuppositions. Foundation beliefs do correctly change status permanently. The two-dimensional Earth has happily gone forever; but the possibility that, in some spheres of political and cultural influence, the evolution of consciousness may degrade into devolution, should leave us wary of adopting the position of unprecedented observer of a unique epoch, unparalleled though it be.

A new openness for one to be influenced by a future whose antecedents are not composed by such claims will leave a spacetime large enough for original ideas and life. Perhaps a counter-intuitive Renaissance based on a fresh view of the future, rather than a dark age?

Notes

Prologue

1 See Rees (1995: 118–20; 1997: 182–86; 1999: 124–54).
2 See Hacker (1996: 272–73).
3 *atopia*.
4 It is instructive to read Bernard Williams's (1998) *Plato*, since it not only stresses this contrast between academic philosophy and the originality of a philosopher such as Plato, but Williams's own fine literary style exemplifies one way of how depth and simplicity might be combined with technical accuracy.
5 Sen (1995: 27) adds a caveat: 'Despite the bizarreness of the idea of purely internal consistency of choice, the testing of internal consistency can be quite useful as a derivative exercise, *given* an appropriate external reference.'
6 Cf. Singh (1997); also, Gibson (forthcoming b).
7 Robson (1999); Neugebauer (1969).
8 See Hawking (1993); Hawking and Ellis (1973).
9 See John Isbell (1994).
10 See Marenbon (1998a: 5); Gibson (1998a, etc.).
11 See Chinca (1993, 1997); Kay (1989).
12 The contents of (a) to (c) are cited from Kretzmann (1997: 24) where they appear as a continuous statement. I have separated them into (a), (b) and (c) for convenience, and to make them explicitly distinct.
13 Ian Hacking (1995) applies 'schizophreniform' to depict a condition which only partially reflects the more extreme clinical states characteristic of schizophrenia; this could be construed, as I do here, as a live metaphorised use of the former in relation to the latter term.
14 See R.P. Harrison (1992); Gibson and O'Mahony (1995).
15 Cf. Torrance (1990: 147–49).
16 This grafts into science Frank Kermode's (1975) literary conception of the term. See also, Kermode (2000: 15) for the application of Einstein to depict Empson.
17 Cf. Hesse (1994).
18 Cf. Baez (1994).
19 Cf. Plaass (1994).
20 This point has been drawn from a discussion with Jonathan Miller, to whom I am grateful.
21 Malcolm Bowie (1978; 1993); Scott (1988); Dee Reynolds (1995).
22 See Alexander (1984) for an account of this notion.
23 See J.R. Cole (1995: 218–220).
24 Ockham *Reportatio* II, q. 150.

25 This section draws on aspects of, but also develops, Gibson (1998a), while it has entirely new sections on Ockham and cosmology, and so it advances beyond the research results presented there.
26 Ockham *Ordinatio* I, d, 30, q. 1.
27 Ockham *Ordinatio* d.q. 8, 94; see also William of Ockham (1994: 231).
28 See Lynden-Bell (1988).
29 Quoted from Marker and Marker (1982: 2).
30 On 'relative-identity', cf. Geach (1980a), and Chapter 3.
31 Gibson (forthcoming b) offers an analysis of these sorts of situations.
32 See Chaitin (1987); and Stewart (1988).
33 See Barrell (1995).
34 See Polkinghorne (1991).
35 Rees (1997: 83–85) assesses this development.
36 Rorty (1998: 266, 1984: 67).
37 For the development of this see Gibson (forthcoming b).

1 The freedom to question

1 A case in point is the use of the error back-propagation algorithm for mapping and representing for training what are termed feedforward layered neural networks in the human brain (see Sangali's (1998) valuable study). This is supposed to calculate the gradient error in one sequencing throughout the network. This is a resort to the applicability of differential calculus and vector algebra for consciousness; it would be affected if the roles of non-algorithmic functions in consciousness override such neural network theory.
2 See Gibson (forthcoming b) for more detailed analysis.
3 See Marion (1998) for a discussion of this situation.
4 Even the German edition of Wittgenstein's *Remarks on the Foundations of Mathematics* leaves out a number of pages from his manuscripts where they comment on Hardy's approach. It is also worth reading Wittgenstein's (1941) unpublished comments he wrote in the margins of his copy of Hardy's *A Course in Pure Mathematics*. For further detail see Gibson (forthcoming b).
5 See Marion (1998: 195–97).
6 See Woess (2000) and Gibson (forthcoming b).
7 Discussion with the author, winter 1971, and at other times in conversation with David Kelley.
8 See Marion (1998: 178–79), and Sainsbury (1998: 66–69), who notes this point and offers some constructive work on Frege's type of position.
9 I agree with Marion's (1998) analysis, to which the reader is referred, that it is a misreading of Wittgenstein's *Tractatus* to ascribe to him the view that mathematical equations are of a tautological nature.
10 I.e. in the technically required senses of theories leaving nothing out from relevant explanation, and does not include anything that is misleading, redundant or exceeds experimental proof, etc.
11 DeWitt and Graham (1973: 3–83).
12 Hawking and Israel (1979: 744)
13 For example, Lear (1980: 15–33).
14 This type of scenario is further developed in Gibson (1997b, 1998b, 1999, forthcoming b), as well as in the present study.
15 For detailed study of this see Gibson (1997b, forthcoming b).
16 See Bowie (1978); Scott (1988); Gibson (1997b, 2000a).
17 Evans (1996: 76) wrote of 'a photograph model of mental representation'; the live metaphor idea is more aptly illustrated by the example of film, and one which can depict abstract states.

18 Cf. Rees (1999: 150–61).
19 Chihara (1998) expounds modal realism and anti-realism using refinements of the Lewis S5 system, appropriate parts of which may be taken as premises for aspects of the current context.

2 The expression of God in language

1. Cf. Erasumus 1982.
2. For example, Paxson (1994).
3. I.e., the live metaphor concept developed in Gibson (1997b) and (forthcoming b).
4. Eichrodt (1984) considers the temporal sense in ('In beginning' in Genesis 1: 1) as a correct assignment of meaning, though coding a theme of God's relation to people.
5. For some original additions to the above oppositions, see the *Epigraph* in Gibson (1987).
6. Cf. Gibson (1987; 1997b, 1999, forthcoming b).
7. See David Miller (1994).
8. See Levi (1997).
9. This presupposes the researches mentioned above (Gibson 1997b and 2000a, c); and Paxson (1994), together with those cited below.
10. On 'verisimilitude', see Popper (1972).
11. See Gibson (1997a).
12. Gibson (1997b, 1999, forthcoming b).
13. Gibson (1981, 1999), for example, utilised the non-standard Shoesmith and Smiley (1980).
14. See Gibson (1998b, 1999).
15. It has been investigated in Gibson (1997b, 1998b, 1999, forthcoming b).
16. Bob Hale's (1994a, 1996) research refines or makes more explicit Dummett's (1981) development of Fregean criteria. Hale's (1996: 448) idea is that Dummett's criteria should be conjoined with Aristotle's theory for testing namehood, that a primary substance does not have a contrary, whilst a quality has; Gibson (1997b, 1998a, 1999) adds to theses analyses.
17. Karel Lambert (1996) opposes this claim, though see Loptson (1996).
18. See Gibson (1981: 133–39, 1997a, 2000a)
19. Cupitt (1998) is such a case. His reductionism is entirely arbitrary, using it to displace standard conceptions of God and the rejection of logic merely by insisting that the latter two areas are imperialistic and old-fashioned. Cupitt thus seems not to have allowed for, what one might somewhat impishly yet accurately term avant-garde post-structuralist logics (such as those of, say, Smiley (1995)) which are inconsistent with any version of such reductionism. His subject content and basic position change from book to book: note Cupitt's (1998: 114–120) curt dismissal of the basis of his 1980 book, which followers of his views regard as fundamental to his later work.
20. As shown in Gibson (1981, 1997b).
21. See, for example, Smiley (1995), and Fauconnier (1997).
22. See also Gibson (forthcoming b).
23. See, for example, Toril Moi's (1990) and Elaine Marks's (1998) helpful discussions.
24. cf. Tennant (1997; 66–67).
25. Juhl (1980) is an example of this viewpoint, demolished by Kermode (1979).
26. As explained in Gibson (1998b, forthcoming b).
27. L. Wittgenstein (1996) 'Notes on logic', M.A.R. Biggs (ed.), Vol 2: 67 [20].
28. See Shoesmith and Smiley (1980: 182–86, 214).
29. Anderson and Belnap (1992).
30. Lewy (1976: 15–51).

3 Extending scientific languages

1. In fact this position embodies some elements which Professor Alan Cook helpfully outlined to me when depicting aspects which are important to an applied scientist, but which philosophers may not appropriately incorporate in their accounts of what science is.
2. See Gibson (1999).
3. Although Cartwright's (1999: 200–1) study of dipole expectation does not engage with the above sorts of issues, its subtle consideration throws light on of a adjacent issue.
4. As formulated by Buchdahl (1993: 299, etc.); see also the profound book by Langton (1998).
5. See Barrow and Tippler (1986: 657–68).
6. On the terminology of truth-makers, facts and states of affairs, see Mellor (1998: 26–27).
7. See Brown (1999: 58–63)
8. See also, Hobson (1998), Staten (1985: 10–13), on relations between Kant, Wittgenstein and Derrida.
9. See Butler (1994: 25–86).
10. See especially Parts 1 to 3 of the present book.
11. See Eco (1984: 114–17).
12. I am here presupposing the accuracy of Burnyeat's (1994) study as a premise.
13. See Gibson (1997a, 1998a, 1998b, 2000a).
14. For arguments supporting this view see Polkinghorne (1994), and Barrow and Tipler (1986: 438–41)
15. See also Gibson (1998a).
16. Cf. Gibson (2000a).
17. Longair (1994a: 375–76) chooses the redshift problem to illustrate his point about the unusability of tests which favour a given model.
18. See Mellor's (1998: 125–35) application of this principle to the claims for backward time travel.
19. See Chapter 6, section 'What is the status of time travel?'
20. See Epstein and D'Ottaviano (1995: chapter IX), and Gibson (2000b).
21. Concerning the relation of relevance logic to paraconsistent systems, I believe that the latter are incorrect as the basis for logic, while the former is admissible as part of a foundation for logic; roughly, as Smiley (1993) and Read (1988) argue; also see Read (1998).
22. I suggest that this use of 'fragment' can be formulated as an inferential relation by deriving an approach from Shoesmith and Smiley (1980: 248–49), and see the following analysis below concerning overlaps of sense.
23. On the distinction between vagueness and ambiguity, see Williamson (1996).
24. See Jaspers and Thijsse (1996) for one way of presenting partial logics in this perspective.
25. As shown in Burnyeat (1994).
26. See Williams (1978) and Gibson (1998b).
27. See F. Scherbaum *et al.* (1988).
28. Hoffmann refers to this research reported by F. Scherbaum *et al.* (1988)
29. See Kermode (1984, 1986a, b, 1990), and Gibson (forthcoming c).
30. As argued in Gibson (1997a, forthcoming b).
31. cf. Derrida (1998: 44–58).
32. According to Coleman (1993) and Klebanor *et al.* (1993).
33. Although it is generally assumed that this State is exotic. (Greene (2000: 366), while commending Hawking's valiant efforts to bring initial conditions under the umbrella of physical theory, considers this attempt to be inconclusive.)

Employing a framework for density from his (1979) Euclidean path integral approach, Hawking argues that there was a pure quantum state:

(A) $|\lambda> = \lambda a| a <$,

and that factorisation is a hall mark of this pure state. In contrast a mixed quantum state has the profile:

(B) state $p \neq |\lambda> <\lambda|$.

Hawking comments that whilst the physical referential state (A) is pure, from the observer's standpoint it will appear to be mixed, as with (B). This is indirectly reminiscent of the distortion associated with the Heisenberg indeterminacy principle. Basically, if a quantum state does not factorise, then it is a mixed quantum state.

34 See Torrance (1981).
35 Cf. Penrose (1990: 325–26).
36 On the relevance logic pertinent to such a view, see Smiley (1998b).
37 See Gibson (2000a).
38 See Chapter 3.
39 Cf. Ferrara, 1991: 13–18.
40 See pp. 144–45
41 See Kelley (1967). These comments exclude *les soi-disant realistes* painters and theory about them (see Gibson (2000b) for a development of this theme in relation to Baudelaire and Wagner.
42 On the latter terms, see Tennant (1997) and Boghossian (1990 a and b).
43 Aristotle, *Politics* viii, 5, 1340a.
44 Eco's (1988) interpretation of Aquinas's use of *claritas* in aesthetics, including his specification of its limits are valuable for this purpose, in respect of the term's mapping the conjunction of correct perception of an experience with the referent of that experience.
45 See Chapter 1 and also Gibson forthcoming d.
46 See pp. 62–63.
47 I am indebted to Malcolm Bowie for discussion on this topic.
48 Subsequent sections and Chapters 5, 6 and 9 engage with aspects of issues of 'immaterial'.
49 Such as Lakoff's (1987) mapping a spatial source domain which contains modal operators attached to perceptual predicates onto an abstract domain such as Boolean algebra.
50 Cf. Budd's (1985) criticisms.
51 For which, see Greene (2000) for M-theory scenarios that could be used to structure alternatives to Hawking and Turok's idea.
52 For explanation, see Gibson (1981: 10, 13–34); Geach (1972: 56–57). In these fallacies, generalisation is incorrect because it trades by equivocation by not assessing recurrence of variables and predicates in propositions as they recombine in new contexts.
53 See Chapter 4 for discussion of 'manifold'.
54 See Hawking (1979), and cf. Hawking (1983).
55 See Chapter 4 for study of 'infinite' conditions.
56 This is when supergravity is associated with an (N = 2) vector describing the superstring particle in connection with a manifold, a term to be examined the next chapter. The flat potential disappears at the same juncture as that at which the cosmological constant vanishes (cf. Cremmer 1982: 421–25), as the universe

4 The beginning of the matter

1. This discussion is taken up in Gibson (forthcoming b).
2. Cf. Rees (1997): 258–59.
3. Cf. Penrose (1990: 129–30), and Tipler (1995: 161–63).
4. See Gibson (forthcoming b) for some proposals on these issues as they pertain to philosophy of mathematics and infinity.
5. Cf. Witten (1996) and Greene (2000: 266–68).
6. Penrose proposes the equation T~h/E as the basis.
7. at a a = ea = o.
8. Cf. Hawking and Ellis 1973; Hawking 1983, 1984.
9. I leave aside Plantinga's writings on realism because more recent work by, for example, Lewis and Chihara has taken the debate into fresh areas relevant for the present discussion.
10. Chihara (1998: 76–103; 277–86; 313–14).
11. See, for example, Tipler (1995), Penrose (1994a) and Thorne (1994).
12. See Woess (2000) and Gibson (forthcoming b).
13. This employs Konig's infinity lemma and Brouwer's fan theorem.
14. Any spacetime metric in a given interpretation can satisfy them. An example is the Reissner–Nordstrom solution (using a Penrose diagram) where there is an infinite chain of asymptotically flat regions which at the appropriate point is bounded by a time-like singularity.
15. This is illustrated by observation of a radio galaxy in Boötes (mentioned on p. 84) with an 0.461 redshift related to a velocity for the galaxy of 46 per cent the speed of light, giving approximately 0.473 as the value of duration from the first microsecond of the inception of the universe. The largest redshift observed for quasars was 4.01 (as reported by Longair (1994a)), now much higher for miniquasars (Rees 2000).
16. If matters of dimension are adopted as indicative, when the radius of curvatures is less than 10^{-33} cm general relativity does not (yet) apply. As noted previously, Penrose suggests the equation T~h/E to jump-start a criterion to distinguish two spacetime systems. It is *not* a requirement of physics that one of them is not infinite. What the global nature of laws and cosmology would be prior to general relativity's is not known. In particular this is because of ignorance about the concomitant density of 10^{94}gm^{-3} (cf. Hawking and Ellis 1973).
17. This is because the relevant inference-relation is inclusive of an 'overlap-condition' (cf. Shoesmith and Smiley (1980: 14–27, 212–32) for this use of term in mathematical logic): the initial conditions from which the universe emerged (i.e. the first microsecond after t_0) require membership of and dependency on functions of infinity which are not tautologous with this universe's physical specification.
18. For example, Hawking (1993); cp. Witten (1989).
19. Cf. Strathdee (1982: 13–15).
20. As Geroch and Horovitz (1979: 266) note.
21. Weyl curvature.
22. Penrose (1979: 600–11).
23. See Penrose (1979: 616).
24. $J = kM2$ where 'J' is the variation of angular momentum, and 'M' mass.
25. For example, Hawking and Hartle (1983), and Tipler (1994: 180–85).
26. See White and Stello (1988).
27. Anisotropy of a dipole sort.

28 He demonstrates that this is displayed by the mathematics of the black hole's maximal angular momentum described in a Kerr solution and metric, especially due to the way in which the equations can be solved by the separation of variables.
29 But where no current explanation solves the relation between mass, rotation and the hitherto unincorporated static limit.
30 Cf. also the complex sensitivities surrounding the initial mass conditions for the emergence of the stars, in Silk (1995).
31 For example, Buchdahl (1993); Miller and Miller (1994: 157–8).
32 Cf. Miller (1994): 159–62, and Plaass (1994).
33 Barrow and Tipler (1986: 69); cf. Tipler (1995: 135–36).
34 The references above to Barrow and Tipler illustrate how one may use a black hole as a metaphor for information storage.
35 Cf. Gibbons (1979: 675).
36 'Segmentation' and 'modal' fallacies are explained in Gibson (1981).
37 We could link causality and quantum and black hole indeterminacy by interpreting a feature of Mellor's (1995: 56–62) approach. What constitutes a cause C is evidence for an effect E and *vice versa*, where the indeterminate element $ch_C(E) = p$, in which C gives E entails that $P(E,C\ \&\ ch_C(E) = p) = p$.
38 See Prior (1967: 113–36, 190–2; cf. 204).
39 See Prior and Fine (1977: 50–52, etc.).
40 In the perspective of the above discussion of Chihara (1998) and Gompf (1985).
41 It is based on the Lewis S-5 system, and other modal systems, which itself is derivable from the two-valued predicate calculus.
42 See Cantor (1932) and, this book, subsection 'Is knowledge of infinity directional?' in Chapter 6.
43 See Mellor (1995).
44 It is interesting to place medieval research on the Fibonacci series as background not only for the Enlightenment emergence of probability theory which Hacking (1975a) assesses, but also the recurrence of the series in modernist and futurist cultures blended with mysticism (see, for example, Milner (1996, Appendices 1–4)), as a group of influences which may have influenced some edges of complexity theory.
45 According to Marion (1998: 187), Wittgenstein sets himself apart from potentialists such as Hilbertian finitists and the intuitionism advocated by Michael Dummet.
46 Although we could not ascribe a potential for belief that there is a God to Russell, it may be wise not to ascribe a sarcastic mode to his phrasing here. His discussions on revelation and proof with religious people had been a feature of his experience. For example, in his book, *Power* he mentions his World War I experiences with Christadelphian pacifists with whom he was in prison for his pacifist views; they were under threat of the death penalty, and it had already been implemented for some of their number. He affirms in the book that if ever he were to become a Christian, he would hold to their beliefs. It seems that this reflects a close encounter he had with serious reflections on the matter.

5 The beginning of life

1 As a philosopher, of course, I am not equipped to examine applied evolution theory. I do so after working for a period in discussion with and under the guidance of the geneticist G.A. Dover, at his suggestion, in an attempt to measure the logical status of some trends in Neo-Darwinism. This brief contribution, however, is not intended as a study of method, but an attempt offer a fresh hypothesis which meets the data after I had criticised features of the theories, yet which is discontinuous with the general trend of empirical claims concerning the

origin of life. Obviously, the results are intended to provoke debate rather than be offered as the final solution to the problem.
2 See Dover (1986, 1988a, 1988b, 1990b).
3 For a discussion of this topic and its relation to teleology, see Chapter 8.
4 See Thom (1989).
5 See Stephanou (1983).
6 Krumhansl and Alexander (1983) and Sobell *et al.* (1984).
7 Cf. Carruthers (1989: 147–57).
8 Cf. Salam (1992): 23–24.

6 Prediction and the cosmology of God

1 This complements, for example, Hans Urs von Balthasar's study of transcendent beauty; cf. O'Donaghue (1986); Oakes (1994a).
2 Cf. Budd (1992).
3 Hobson (1998) enriches this notion with circuits of argument termed micrologies.
4 Cf. Hobson (1982a); Cavell (1992).
5 See Bigelow and Pargetter (1990: 357–76).
6 See Morgan (1994).
7 This complements the analysis of God's omniscience presented by Anglin (1990: 72–103; 186–99) which links transcendence and God's revelation grounded as communication in creation.
8 Cf. Geach (1971: 110–11).
9 See Marenbon (1998b).
10 See Marenbon (1997, 1991).
11 See Gibson and O'Mahony (1995).
12 As for example Magnenat-Thalmann and Thalmann (1994) have shown.
13 Cf. Reynolds (1995: 201); Millan (1994: 310ff).
14 For research on eighteenth-century history of ideas pertinent to the present concerns, see the study by Hobson (1982a).
15 The fallacies documented here and elsewhere in this criticism are those as described in Gibson (1981): 88–96, 145–46)
16 See Gibson (1981: 70–71, 90–92, 190–99).
17 Cf. Newman (1995).
18 As Force and Popkin (1990a, b, c, d), MacLachlan (1950), and Manuel (1974) demonstrate.
19 For a mid-nineteenth-century parallel, see Thomas (1848).
20 Survey of Pesaran and Slater (1980), Day (1993), together with Giddens (1984),
21 Refined by Castrigiano and Hayes (1993).
22 Of course, termed a 'homeland' in the 1919 Balfour Declaration, but made into a state by arrangement with the UN.
23 We might variously use Chihara's (1998) anti-realist counterpart modal semantics conception of a proposition true at a world under an interpretation Wp.
24 This follows Woess (2000: 284) using infinite graphs.
25 It is worth noticing that, for example, the biblical vocabulary of prediction, while often employing terms which express intention, sometimes employs terms which articulate the feature of promise, where 'promise' is a figurative use of the word for 'speaking' – which links mind and word. Frequently in the Bible and in theology the vocabulary of command is utilised.
26 This context presupposes that the sort of objections to the notion of time travel to be found in Mellor's (1998) analysis are correct.

7 God and ethical cosmology

1 I.e., the *Drug Trafficking Offences Act* 1986.
2 See Hallden (1957) and Prior (1960: 359–61) on the latter case.
3 In Geach (1972: 260–61); and cf. (1971: 96–98).
4 Gibson (forthcoming a, b).
5 See Geach (1991).
6 See Gibson (forthcoming d).
7 Cf. Gibson (1998b, 2000a).

8 The practice of legal cosmology

1 See Oppenheim and Lauterpacht (1955: I 5).
2 In Commonwealth Secretariat (1986).
3 For example, see Grotius (1625, bk 2, ch. V).
4 For example, in 1987 in the UK the SIB had not given the AFBD information which the SIB had about a subsidiary of BCCI (Capcom Services Ltd, London), shortly before the subsidiary was to be named for money laundering with Noriega. I believe that the later collapse of BCCI thus reflected on the inconsistent semantics and misuse of a contradictory duty of care implicit in the semantics.
5 This appears to oppose Oppenheim' and Lauterpacht's (1955: 88) opinion.
6 Mann (1973: 238–39, 241–44).
7 Brownlie (1963: 338f., 4).
8 Augustine (1982); cf. *Questiones in Heptateuchum* vi. 10*b*.
9 See Thomas Aquinas (1948, 1981): II.*ii*).
10 Wortley (1967: 160).
11 For example, see the 14th *Report of the Criminal Law Revision Committee* (see UK Revision Committee 1980: paras 8 and 26).

9 Eschatological cosmology

1 Until their linguistics and rhetoric are integrated this position is unclear.
2 See Thom (1989).
3 See Cole (1995: 189–91).
4 Cf. Gibson and O'Mahony (1995).
5 See Barrow and Tipler (1978), Rees (1995, 1997), etc.

Bibliography

Addinal, P. (1991) *Philosophy and Biblical Interpretation*, Cambridge: Cambridge University Press.
Albright, T. (1985) *Art in the San Francisco Area 1945–1980*, University of California Press, p. 162.
Aleksander, I. (1997) *Impossible Minds*, London: Imperial College Press.
Alexander, P. (1984) 'Incongruent counterparts and absolute space', *Aristotelian Society Proceedings*, Oxford: Aristotelian Society, OUP.
Alferi, P. (1989) *Guillaume d'Ockham le singulier*, Paris: Minuit.
Allott, P. (1990) *Eunomia: a new order for a new world*, Oxford, New York: Oxford University Press.
Altham, J.E.J. (1979) 'The indirect reflexive', in C. Diamond and J. Teichman (eds) *Intention and intentionality*, Brighton: Harvester Press.
Altieri, C. (1995) *Painterly abstraction in modernist American poetry*, University Park, PA: Pennsylvania State University Press; (1st edn 1989), Cambridge: Cambridge University Press).
Anderson, A.R. and Belnap, N.F. (1992) *The Logic of Relevance and Necessity*, 2 vols, Princeton: Princeton University Press.
Anglin, W.S. (1990) *Free Will and the Christian Faith*, Oxford: Oxford University Press.
Anscombe, G.E.M. (1957) *Intention*, Oxford: Blackwell.
—— (1965) 'The intentionality of sensation: a grammatical feature', in R.J. Butler (ed.) *Analytical Philosophy*, Oxford: Basil Blackwell.
—— (1959) *An Introduction to Wittgenstein's Tractatus*, London: Hutchinson.
—— (1981a) *Collected Works*, 3 vols, Oxford: Blackwell.
—— (1981b) 'The first person', in *Collected Works*, 3 vols, Oxford: Blackwell.
—— (1981c) 'The intentionality of sensation', in *Collected Works*, 3 vols, Oxford: Blackwell.
—— (1981d) 'Modern moral philosophy', in *Collected Works*, 3 vols, Oxford: Blackwell.
—— (1981e) 'Times, beginnings and causes', in *Collected Works*, 3 vols, Oxford: Blackwell.
Aquinas, Thomas (1948) *Summa theologiae* (*cura et studio Petri Caramello; cum textu ex recensione Leonina quem*), Turin: Marietti.
—— (1981) *Summa theologica*, Vols 1–5, Westminster, Ma: Christian Classics.
Arecchi, F.T. (1997) 'The limits of mathematical reasoning', in A. Driessen and A. Suarez (eds) (1997) *Mathematical Undecidability, Quantum Nonlocality and the Question of the Existence of God*, Boston, Dordrecht: Reidel, pp. 59–82.
Arom, S. and Khalfa, J. (1998) 'Une raison en acte', *Review de Musicologie* 84(1): 5–17.
Arp, H. (1986) Letter, *Nature* 322(6077): 316.

Artaud, A. (1947) *Van Gogh: le suicide de la societé*, Paris: K editeur.
—— (1961) *Oeuvres complètes*, Paris: Gallimard.
—— (1968) *Collected Works*, trans.V. Corti , London: Calder & Boyars.
Ashby, N.D.F. Bartlett and Wyss, W. (1990) *General Relativity and Gravitation*, Cambridge: Cambridge University Press.
Atiyah, M. (1989) 'Introduction' in Atiyah, M. *et al.* (eds) *Physics and Mathematics of Strings: Proceedings of the Royal Society*, London: Royal Society.
—— 1990) *The Geometry and Physics of Knots*, Cambridge, Cambridge University Press.
Auerbach, E. (1968) [1946] *Mimesis: the Representation of Reality in Western Literature*, trans. W.R. Trask, Princeton: Princeton University Press.
Augustine, Bishop of Hippo (1982) *Eighty-three Different Questions*, trans. D.L. Moser, Washington: Catholic University of America.
Baez, J.C. (1994) *Knots and Quantum Gravity*, Oxford: Oxford University Press.
Balthasar, H.U. von (1992a) *Theo-Drama*, 3 vols, trans. D. Harrison, San Francisco: Ignatius Press.
—— (1992b) *The Theology of Karl Barth*, trans. E.T. Oakes, San Francisco: Communio Books, Ignatius Press.
Banner, M.C. (1990) *The Justification of Science and the Rationality of Religious Belief*, Oxford: Oxford University Press.
Banzhaf, W. and Reeves, C. (eds) (1999) *Foundations of Genetic Algorithms 5*, San Fransisco: Morgan Kaufmann.
Barr, J. (1961) *The Semantics of Biblical Languages*, Oxford: Oxford University Press.
—— (1990) 'Do we perceive the speech of the heavens?', in J.C. Knight and L.A. Sinclair (eds) *The Psalms and Other Studies: Presented to Joseph I. Hunt*, Nashotoh, WI: Nashotoh House Seminary, pp. 11–17.
Barrell, J. (1995) *The Political Theory of Painting from Reynolds to Hazlitt : 'The Body of the Public'*, New Haven: Yale University Press.
Barrow, J.D. and Silk, J. (1983) *The Left Hand of Creation: The Origin and Evolution of the Expanding Universe*, New York: Basic Books .
Barrow, J.D. and Tipler, F.J. (1978) 'Eternity is unstable', *Nature* 276(5600): 453–61.
—— (1986) *The Anthropic Cosmological Principle*, Oxford: Oxford University Press.
Barth, K. (1986) *Wolfgang Amadeus Mozart* (Foreword by John Updike, trans. C.K. Pott), Grand Rapids: W.B. Eerdmans.
Bayley, J. (1961) *Shakespeare and Tragedy*, London: Faber.
Beauvoir, S. de (1967) *La femme rompue*, Paris: Gallimard.
Bechtel, W. and R.C. Richardson (1993) *Discovering Complexity*, Princeton: Princeton University Press.
Beer, G. (2000) *Darwin's plots: Evolutionary Narrative in Darwin, George Eliot and Nineteenth-century Fiction*, 2nd edn, Cambridge: Cambridge University Press.
Bell, J.S. (1987) *Speakable and Unspeakable in Quantum Mechanics*, Cambridge.
—— (1997) 'Indeterminism and nonlocality', in A. Driessen and A. Suarez (eds), *Mathematical Undecidability, Quantum Nonlocality and the Question of the Existence of God*, Boston, Dordrecht: Reidel, pp. 83–100.
Bergeron, J.H. (1998) 'An ever whiter myth: the colonization of modernity in European Community law', P. Fitzpatrick and J. H. Bergeron (eds), *Europe's Other: European Law between Modernity and Postmodernity*, Aldershot: Ashgate, pp. 27–46.
Berlin, I. (1979) *Against the Current*, London: Pimlico.
Betz, H.D. (1985) *Essays on the Sermon on the Mount*, trans. I.I. Welborn, Philadelphia: Fortress.
Bigelow, J. and Pargetter, R. (1990) *Science and Necessity*, Cambridge: Cambridge University Press.

Black, Matthew (1967) *An Aramaic Approach to the Gospels and Acts*, 3rd edn, Oxford: Oxford University Press.
Black, Max (1962) *Models and Metaphors: Studies in Language and Philosophy*, Ithaca: Cornell University Press.
Blandford, R.D. and Thorne, K.S. (1979) 'Black hole astrophysics', in S.W. Hawking and W. Israel (eds) *General Relativity*, Cambridge: Cambridge University Press.
Boghossian, P. (1989) 'The rule-following consideration', *Mind* XCVIII: 507–49.
—— (1990a) 'The status of content', *Philosophical Review* 99: 157–84.
—— (1990b) 'The status of content revisited', *Pacific Philosophical Quarterly* 71: 264–78.
Boretz, B. (1972) 'Meta-variations. Part IV: analytic fallout', *Perspectives on New Music* 10: 146–223.
Bostock, D. (1997) *Intermediate Logic*, Oxford: Oxford University Press.
Boukricha, A. (1985) 'The Schrödinger equation with an isolated singularity', in S. Albervio (ed.) *Infinite Dimensional Analysis and Stochastic Processes*, Research Notes in Mathematics 124, Boston, Mass.: Pitman Advanced.
Bowett, D.W. (1972) *The Search for Peace*, London: Routledge.
Bowie, M. (1973) *Henri Michaux: a Study of his Literary Works*, Oxford: Clarendon.
—— (1978) *Mallarmé and the Art of Being Difficult*, Cambridge: Cambridge University Press.
—— (1991) *Lacan*, Cambridge, Mass.: Harvard University Press.
—— (1993) *Psychoanalysis and the Future of Theory*, Oxford: Blackwell.
—— (1998) *Proust Among the Stars*, London : HarperCollins.
Bowick, M.J., Smolin,L. and Wijewardhana, L.C.R. (1986) 'Role of string excitation in the last stages of black-hole evaporation', *Physical Review of Letters* 56.5: 424–27.
Bradshaw, G. (1993) *Misrepresentations*, Ithaca: Cornell University Press.
Braine, D. (1988) *The Reality of Time and the Existence of God*, Oxford: Oxford University Press.
Broadhurst, T.J.L.*et al* (1995) 'Mapping cluster mass distribution via gravitational lensing of background galaxies', *Astrophysical Journal* 438(1): 49–61.
Brock, S.P. (1985) *The Luminous Eye: The Spiritual World Vision of Saint Ephrem*, Cistercian studies series 124, Rome: Center for Indian and Inter-Religious Studies (rev. edn Kalamazoo: Cistercian Publications).
Brooke, G.J. (1985) *Exegesis at Qumran: 4QFlorilegium in its Jewish context* (JSOT), Sheffield: Sheffield Academic Press.
Brooke-Rose, C. (1981) *A Rhetoric of the Unreal: Studies in Narrative and Structure, Especially of the Fantastic*, Cambridge: Cambridge University Press.
—— (1991) *Stories, Theories and Things*, Cambridge: Cambridge University Press.
Brown, A.J.L. and Ish-Horowicz, D. (1983) 'Evolution of the 87A and 87C heat-shock loci in Drosophilia', *Nature* 290(5806): 677–82.
Brown, H.R. (1999) 'Aspects of objectivity in quantum mechanics', in *From Physics to Philosophy*, J. Butterfield and C. Pagonis (eds), Cambridge: Cambridge University Press, pp. 45–70.
Brownlie, I. (1963) *International Law and the Use of Force*, Oxford: Clarendon (1981 edn, Oxford: Clarendon Press/New York: Oxford University Press).
Brummer, V. (1992) *Speaking of a Personal God*, Cambridge: Cambridge University Press.
Buchdahl, G. (1993) *Kant and the Dynamics of Reason*, Oxford: Blackwell.
Budd, M. (1985) *Music and the Emotions*, London: Routledge.
—— (1992) 'On looking at a picture', in *Psychoanalysis: Mind and Art*, J. Hopkins and A. Saville (eds), Oxford: Oxford University Press.
Buffon, G.L.C., Comte de (1749) 'Théorie de la terre', in *Histoire naturelle generale et particuliere, avec la description du cabinet du Roy*, Paris.

Burnyeat, M.F. (1994) 'Enthymeme: Aristotle on the logic of persuasion', in D.J. Furley and A. Nehamas (eds) *Aristotle's Rhetoric*, Princeton: Princeton University Press, pp. 3–55.
Butler, C. (1994) *Early Modernism*, Oxford: Oxford University Press.
Butterfield, J. (1984) 'Relationism and possible worlds', *British Journal for the Philosophy of Science* 35: 101–13.
Butterfield, J. and Isham, C. (1999) 'On the emergence of time in quantum gravity', in J. Butterfield (ed.) *The Arguments of Time*, Oxford: Oxford University Press/British Academy.
Caird, G.B. (1980) *The Language and Imagery of the Bible*, London: SCM Press.
Cairns, J. (1975) 'Mutation selection and the natural history of cancer', *Nature* 255(550): 197–200.
—— (1978) *Cancer: Science and Society*, San Francisco: Freeman.
—— (1981) 'The origin of human cancers', *Nature* 289(5795): 353–57.
Cajetan, T. de V. (1524) *Summula*.
—— (1515) *Summa Theologiae*.
Calderon, I.L. *et al.* (1983) 'Isolation and characteristics of yeast DNA repair genes', *Current Genetics* 7: 93–100.
Cantor, G. (1932) *Gesammelte Abhanlungen mathematischen und philosophischen Inhals*, E. Zermelo (ed.), Berlin.
Cappell, S., Ranicki, A. and Rosenberg, J. (2000a) 'C.T.C. Wall's contributions to the topology of manifolds' in S. Cappell, A. Ranicki and J. Rosenberg (eds) *Surveys on Surgery Theory 1*, Princeton: Princeton University Press, vol. 1, pp. 3–15.
—— (eds) (2000b) *Surveys on Surgery Theory 1*, Princeton: Princeton University Press.
Carruthers, P. (1989) *Tractarian Semantics*, Oxford: Blackwell.
—— (1992) *The Animals Issue: Moral Theory in Practice*, Cambridge: Cambridge University Press.
Carter, B. (1979) 'The general theory of the mechanical, electromagnetic and thermodynamic properties of black holes', in S.W. Hawking and W. Israel (eds) *General Relativity*, Cambridge: Cambridge University Press.
Carruthers, P. (1992) *The Animals Issue: Moral Theory in Practice*, Cambridge: Cambridge University Press.
Carter, B. (1974) *Confrontation of Cosmological Theories with Observation* (ed. M.S. Longair), Dordrecht: Reidel.
Carter, J. S. and Saito, M. (1994) 'Knotted surfaces, braid movies, and beyond', in J.C. Baez *Knots and Quantum Gravity*, Oxford: Oxford University Press, pp. 191–218.
Cartwright, N. (1989) *Nature's Capacities and their Measurement*, Oxford: Oxford University Press.
—— (1999) *The Dappled World*, Cambridge: Cambridge University Press.
Castrigiano, D.P.L. and Hayes, S.A. (1993) *Catastrophe Theory*, Reading, MA: Addison-Wesley, Advanced Book Program.
Cavalière, L. *et al.* (1982) 'Evolutionary luminosity functions of extragalactic sources driven by gravitational power', *Astronomy and Astrophysics* 114(1): L1–L3.
Cave, T. (1988) *Recognitions: A Study in Poetics*, Oxford: Oxford University Press.
Cavell, S. (1979) *The World Viewed*, Cambridge, Mass.: Harvard University Press.
—— (1992) *The Senses of Walden*, Chicago: University of Chicago Press.
Chaitin, G.J. (1987) *Algorithms and Information Theory*, Cambridge: Cambridge University.
—— (1997) 'Number and randomness: algorithmic information theory – new results on the foundations of mathematics', in A. Driessen and A. Suarez (eds), *Mathematical Undecidability, Quantum Nonlocality and the Question of the Existence of God*, Boston, Dordrecht: Reidel, 15–26.

Chandrasekhar, S. (1979) 'An introduction to the theory of the Kerr metric and its perturbations', in S.W. Hawking and W. Israel (eds) *General Relativity*, Cambridge: Cambridge University Press.
Chihara, C.S. (1998) *The Worlds of Possibility: Modal Realism and the Semantics of Modal Logic*, Oxford: Clarendon Press.
Chinca, M. (1993) *History, Fiction, Verisimilitude: Studies in the Poetics of Gottfried's Tristan*, Bithell series of dissertations: Texts and Dissertations, London: Modern Humanities Research Association for the Institute of Germanic Studies, University of London.
—— (1997) *Gottfried von Strassburg: Tristan*, Cambridge: Cambridge University Press.
Chomsky, N. (2000) *New Horizons in the Study of Language and Mind*, Cambridge: Cambridge University Press.
Clayton, P. (1989) *Explanation from Physics to Theology*, New Haven: Yale University Press.
Coady, C.A.J. (1992) *Testimony*, Oxford: Clarendon.
Cohen, J.L. (1977) *The Provable and the Unprovable*, Oxford: Oxford University Press.
—— (1993) 'The semantics of metaphor', in A. Ortony (ed.) *Metaphor and Thought*, 2nd edn, Cambridge: Cambridge University Press.
Cole, J.R. (1995) *Pascal: the Man and his Two Loves*, New York.
Coleman, S. (1993) 'Why there is nothing rather than something', in G.W. Gibbons and S.W. Hawking (eds) *Euclidean Quantum Gravity*, London, pp. 388–413.
Collier, J. and Lowe, V. (1999) *The Settlement of Disputes in International Law*, Oxford: Oxford University Press.
Collier, P. and H. Geyer-Ryan (1992) 'Introduction: beyond postmodernism', in P. Collier and H. Geyer-Ryan (eds) *Literary Theory Today*, Cambridge: Polity Press, pp. 1–9.
Commonwealth Secretariat (1986) *1986 Meeting of Commonwealth Law Ministers*, London: Commonwealth Secretariat.
Condillac, E.B. de (1746) *Essai sur l'origine des connaissances humaines*, Paris [ed. G. Le Roy, Paris, 1947].
—— (1982) *The Major Philosophical Works of Etienne Bonnot de Condillac*, F. Philip assisted by H. Lane, Hillsdale, NJ: L. Erlbaum Associates.
Copeland, B.J. (ed.) (1996) *Logic and Reality: Essays on the Legacy of Arthur Prior*, Oxford, Clarendon.
Craig, E. (1987) *The Mind of God and the Works of Man*, Oxford: Oxford University Press.
Craig, W.L. and Smith, Q. (1995) *Theism, Atheism and the Big Bang*, Oxford: Oxford University Press.
Cremmer, E. (1982) 'Dimensional reduction in field theory and hidden symmetries in extended supergravity', in S. Ferrara and J.G. Taylor (eds) *Supergravity '81*, Cambridge: Cambridge University Press.
Culler, J. (1994) 'Baudelaire's satanic verses', the Cassal lecture, 6 October 1994, London University.
Cunningham, A. and Jardine, N. (1990) *Romanticism and the Sciences*, Cambridge: Cambridge University Press.
Cupitt, D. (1980) *Taking Leave of God*, London: SCM.
—— (1990) *Creation out of Nothing*, London: SCM.
—— (1998) *Mysticism and Modernity*, Oxford: Blackwell.
Dahlhaus, C. (1983) *Analysis and value judgement*, trans. S. Levarie, Monographs in Musicology 1, New York: Pendragon Press.

Dallaporta, N. (1993) 'The different levels of connection between science and objective reality', in G. Ellis and A. Lanza (eds) *The Renaissance of General Relativity and Cosmology*, Cambridge: Cambridge University Press, pp. 326–31.
Danto, A. (1994) *Embodied Meanings*, New York: Farrar Straus Giroux.
Dauben, J.W. (1979) *George Cantor: His Mathematics and Philosophy of the Infinite*, Cambridge, Mass.: Harvard University Press.
D'Auria, R. and Fré, P. (1999) 'BPS black holes in supergravity', in P. Fré, V. Gorini, G. Magli and U. Moschella (eds) *Classical and Quantum Black Holes*, London/Bristol/Philadelphia: Institute of Physics Publishing, pp. 137–273.
Davidson, D. (1980) *Essays on actions and events*, Oxford: Clarendon Press.
—— (1984) *Inquiries into Truth and Interpretation*, Oxford: Clarendon Press.
Davies, G.I. (1992) *Israel in Egypt*, Sheffield, Sheffield Academic Press.
Davies, M. (1982) 'Idiom and Metaphor', *Proceedings of the Aristotelian Society*: 49–67.
Davies, P.C.W. (1978) 'Cosmic heresy', *Nature* 273(5660): 336–37.
—— (1981) *The Edge of Infinity*, London: Dent (reissued 1994, Oxford: Oxford University Press).
——(1982) *The Accidental Universe*, Cambridge: Cambridge University Press.
Davy, H. (1808) *Philosophical Transactions of the Royal Society* 98, Part 1.
Day, R.H. (1993) 'Complex economic dynamics: from quantitative to qualitative data', in M.H. Pesaran and S.M. Patten (eds) *Nonlinear Dynamics, Chaos and Econometrics*, Cambridge: Cambridge University Press.
Deb, K. and Agrawal, S. (1999) 'Understanding interactions among genetic algorithm parameters', in W. Banzhaf and C. Reeves (eds) *Foundations of Genetic Algorithms 5*, San Fransisco: Morgan Kaufmann' 265–86.
De Bernardis, P., Ade, P.A.R., Bock, J. J. *et al.* (2000) 'A flat universe from high-resolution maps of the cosmic microwave background radiation', *Nature* 404(6781): 955–59.
Deleuze, G. (1985) *Cinema 2: L'image-temps*, Paris. (1983) *Cinema 1: L'image-mouvement*, Paris.
—— (1994) *Difference and Repetition*, trans. P. Patton, London: Athlone Press.
Deleuze, G. and Guattari, F. (1994) *What is Philosophy?*, trans. G. Burchell and H. Tomlinson, London: Verso.
Dennett, D.C. (1991) *Consciousness Explained*, illus. P. Weiner, Boston/London: Little Brown.
Denyer, N. (2000) 'Just war', in R. Teichmann (ed.) *Logic, Cause and Action*, Royal Institute of Philosophy Series: *Philosophy* Supplement 46, Cambridge: Cambridge University Press, pp. 137–51.
De Rujula, A. (1986) 'Superstrings and supersymmetry', *Nature* 320(6064): 678.
Derrett, J.D.M. (1994) *Prophecy in the Cotswolds 1803–1947*, Blockley Occasional Papers, 1, Shipston-on-Stour : Blockley Antiquarian Society.
Derrida, J. (1972) *La dissemination*, Series: Collection Tel quel, Paris: Editions du Seuil.
—— (1978) *Writing and Difference* (trans./ed. A. Bass), London: Routledge.
—— (1982) *Margins of Philosophy* (trans. A. Bass), Chicago: University of Chicago Press.
—— (1987) *The Truth in Painting* (trans. G. Bennington and I. McLeod), Chicago: University of Chicago Press.
—— (1998) *Monolingualism of the Other* (trans. P. Mensah), Stanford: Stanford University Press.
DeWitt, B.S. (1992) *Supermanifolds*, 2nd edn, Cambridge Monographs on Mathematical Physics, Cambridge: Cambridge University Press.
DeWitt, B.S. and Graham, N. (eds) (1973) *The Many-Worlds Interpretation of Quantum Mechanics*, Princeton: Princeton University Press.

Diamond, C. (1996) *Cambridge Companion to Wittgenstein*, Cambridge: Cambridge University Press.
Dodd, C.H. (1951) *Gospel and Law*, Cambridge: Cambridge University Press.
Dolgov, A.D. (1983) 'An attempt to get rid of the cosmological constant', in G.W. Gibbons, S.W. Hawking and S.T.C. Siklos (eds) *The Very Early Universe*, Cambridge: Cambridge University Press.
Dover, G.A. (1986) 'Molecular drive in multigene families: how biological novelties arise, spread and are assimilated', *Trends in Genetics*: 159–65.
—— (1987) 'DNA turnover and the molecular clock', *Journal of Molecular Evolution* 26: 47–58.
—— (1988a) 'Evolving the improbable', *Trends in Ecology and Evolution* 3: 81–84.
—— (1988b) 'The wars of the sons of light against the sons of darkness', *Evolutionary Trends in Plants* 2(1): 61–64.
—— (1989a) 'Slips, strings and species', *Monitor* 5: 100–102.
—— (1989b) 'Victims or perpetrators of DNA turnover?', *Nature* 342: 347–48.
—— (1990a) 'The evolution of tolerance', *Tree* 5: 375–76.
—— (1990b) 'Mapping "frozen accidents"', *Nature* 344: 812–13.
—— (2000) *Dear Mr. Darwin: Letters on the Evolution of Life and Human Nature*, London: Weidenfeld & Nicholson.
Driessen, A. and Suarez, A. (1997) (eds) *Mathematical Undecidability, Quantum Nonlocality and the Question of the Existence of God*, Boston/Dordrecht: Reidel.
Drug Trafficking Offences Act (1986) London: HMSO.
Dummet, M. (1978) *Truth and Other Enigmas*, London: Duckworth.
—— (1981) *Frege: Philosophy of Language*, 2nd edn, London: Duckworth.
—— (1991) *Frege and Other Philosophers*, Oxford: Clarendon.
Durkheim, E. (1912) *Les formes élémentaires de la vie religieuse: le système totemique en Australie*, Paris: Librairie Felix Alcan.
Dworkin, R. (1978) *Taking Human Rights Seriously*, London: Duckworth.
—— (1980) *Political Judges and the Rule of Law*, Proceedings of the British Academy, vol. 64, London: British Academy.
—— (1985) *A Matter of Principle*, Cambridge, Mass.: Harvard University Press.
—— (1986) *Law's Empire*, Cambridge, Mass.: Harvard University Press.
Dyson, F.J. (1985) *Origins of Life*, Cambridge: Cambridge University Press.
Eagleton, T. (1995) *Heathcliff and the Great Hunger: Studies in Irish*, London/New York: Verso.
Eban, A. (1999) *Diplomacy for the Next Century*, New Haven: Yale University Press.
Ebbs, G. (1997) *Rule-following and realism*, Cambridge, Mass.: Harvard University Press.
Eco, U. (1983) [1980] *The Name of the Rose*, London: Secker & Warburg
—— (1984) *Semiotics and the Philosophy of Language*, London: Macmillan.
—— (1988) *The Aesthetics of Thomas Aquinas*, trans. H. Bredin, Cambridge, Mass.: Harvard University Press/London: Radius.
Edwards, P.P. and Rao, C.N.R. (1985) *The Metallic and Nonmetallic States of Matter*, Sevenoaks: Butterworth.
Edwards, P.P. and Sienko, M.J. (1983) *International Reviews in Physical Chemistry* 3: 83–136.
Eells, R. and Nehemkis, P. (1984) *Corporate Intelligence and Espionage*, New York: Macmillan/London: Collier Macmillan.
Eichrodt, W. (1984) 'In the beginning', in B.W. Anderson (ed.) *Creation in the Old Testament*, London: SCM Press.
Ellis, G.F.R. (1978) *General Relativity and Gravitation* 9: 87.
Ellis, G.F.R., Maartens, R. and Nel, S. (1978) *Monthly Notices of the Royal Astronomical Society* 184: 439.

Epstein, R.L. (1995) *The Semantic Foundations of Logic*, 2nd edn, Oxford: Oxford University Press.

Epstein, R. L. and D'Ottaviano, I.M.L. (1995) 'A paraconsistent logic: J_3', in R.L. Epstein *et al. The Semantic Foundations of Logic: Propositional Logics*, 2nd edn, Oxford: Oxford University Press, pp. 349–73.

Epstein, R.L., Carnielli, W.A., D'Ottaviano, M.L., Krajewski, S. and Maddux, R.D. (1995) *The Semantic Foundations of Logic: Propositional Logics*, 2nd edn, Oxford: Oxford University Press.

Erasmus, Desiderius of Rotterdam (1982) *On Copia of Words and Ideas* (*De utraque verborem [sic] ac rerum copia*), trans. and ed. D.B. King and H.D. Rix, Mediaeval Philosophical Texts in Translation 12, Milwaukee: Marquette University Press.

Escher, M.C. (1989) *Escher on Escher: Exploring the Infinite*, contribution by J.W. Vermeulen, trans. K. Ford, New York: H.N. Abrams.

Evans, G. (1985) *Collected Papers*, Oxford: Clarendon.

—— (1996) *Collected Papers*, 2nd edn, Oxford: Clarendon Press.

Everett, H., III (1973) 'The theory of the universal wave function', in B.S. DeWitt and N. Graham (eds) *The Many-Worlds Interpretation of Quantum Mechanics*, Princeton: Princeton University Press.

Fauconnier, G. (1997) *Mappings in Thought and Language*, Cambridge: Cambridge University Press.

Ferrara, L. (1991) *Philosophy and the Analysis of Music*, New York: Greenwood Press.

Feynman, R.P. (1985) *QED*, Princeton, Princeton University Press.

Field, H. (1989) *Realism, Mathematics and Modality*, Oxford: Oxford University Press.

Fishbane, M. (1985) *Biblical Interpretation in Ancient Israel*, Oxford: Oxford University Press.

Fitzpatrick, P. (1992) *The Mythology of Modern Law*, London: Routledge.

Florence, P. (1986) *Mallarmé, Manet and Redon*, Cambridge: Cambridge University Press.

Force, J.E. and R.H. Popkin (1990a) 'The breakdown of the Newtonian synthesis of science and religion: Hume, Newton and the Royal Society', *Essays on the Context, Nature and Influence of Isaac Newton's Theology*, International Archives of the History of Ideas, 129, Boston/Dordrecht: Kluwer.

—— (1990b) 'Hume's interest in Newton and science', *Essays on the Context, Nature and Influence of Isaac Newton's Theology*, International Archives of the History of Ideas, 129, Boston/Dordrecht: Kluwer.

—— (1990c) 'Newton's God of dominion: the unity of Newton's theological, scientific and political thought', *Essays on the Context, Nature and Influence of Isaac Newton's Theology*, International Archives of the History of Ideas, 129, Boston/Dordrecht: Kluwer.

—— (1990d) *Essays on the Context, Nature and Influence of Isaac Newton's Theology*, International Archives of the History of Ideas, 129, Boston/Dordrecht: Kluwer.

Ford, D.F. (1981) *Barth and God's Story*, Studien zur interkulturellen Geschichte des Christentums, Etudes d'histoire interculturelle du Christianisme 27, Frankfurt: Lang.

—— (ed.) (1989) 'Epilogue: postmodernism and postscript', in *The Modern Theologians*, Oxford: Blackwell, pp. 291–97.

—— (1992) *A Long Rumour of Wisdom: Redescribing Theology*, Cambridge: Cambridge University Press.

Forrester, J. (1990) *The Seduction of Psychoanalysis*, Cambridge, Cambridge University Press.

Forrester, J. (1997) *Truth Games*, Cambridge, Mass.: Harvard.

Foucault, M. (1965) *Madness and Civilization: A History of Insanity in the Age of Reason*, trans. R. Howard, London: Routledge.
Frei, H.W. (1992) *Types of Christian Theology*, G. Hunsinger and W.C. Placher (eds), New Haven: Yale University Press.
Freud, S. (1938) *The Basic Writings of Sigmund Freud*, trans. and ed. A.A. Brill, New York: The Modern Library.
Gabbay, D.M., Reynolds, M.A. and Finger, M. (2000) *Temporal Logic*, Oxford: Clarendon Press.
Gale, R.M. (1991) *On the Nature and Existence of God*, Cambridge: Cambridge University Press.
Gardner, R.N. (1964) *In Pursuit of the World Order: US Foreign Policy and International Organizations*, New York: Praeger.
Geach, P.T. (1969) *God and the Soul*, London: Routledge.
—— (1971) *Mental Acts*, rev. edn, London: Routledge.
—— (1972) *Logic Matters*, Oxford: Blackwell.
—— (1977) *Providence and Evil*, Cambridge: Cambridge University Press.
—— (1979) *Truth, Love and Immortality*, London: Hutchinson.
—— (1980a) *Reference and Generality*, 3rd edn, Ithaca: Cornell.
—— (1980b) 'Some problems about the sense and reference of proper names', *Canadian Journal of Philosophy*: 6: 83–96.
—— (1991) 'Whatever happened to deontic logic', in P.T. Geach and J. Holowka (eds) *Logic and Ethics*, Nijhoff International Philosophy series vol. 41, Dordrecht: Kluwer Academic Publishers, pp. 33–48.
Geertz, C. (1994) 'The true estrangement: Taylor and the natural sciences', in J. Tully and D.M. Weinstock (eds) *Philosophy in an Age of Pluralism: The Philosophy of Charles Taylor in Question*, Cambridge: Cambridge University Press.
Gellner, E. (1992) *Postmodernism, Reason and Religion*, London: Faber.
Geller, M. and Huchra, J. (1990) 'The Great Wall', *Science* 246: 897–903.
Gentzen, G. (1970) *The Collected Papers of Gerhard Gentzen*, Studies in Logic and the Foundations of Mathematics (ed. M.E. Szabo), Amsterdam: North-Holland.
Geroch, R. (1977) 'Prediction and general relativity', *Foundations of Space-Time Theories*, Minnesota Studies in the Philosophy of Science 8, Minneapolis.
Geroch, R. and Horovitz, G.T. (1979) 'Global structures of spacetime', in S.W. Hawking and W. Israel (eds) *General Relativity*, Cambridge: Cambridge University Press.
Gibbons, G.W. (1979) 'Quantum field theory in curved spacetime', in S.W. Hawking and W. Israel (eds) *General Relativity*, Cambridge: Cambridge University Press.
Gibbons, G.W., Hawking, S.W. and Siklos, S.T.C. (eds) (1983) *The Very Early Universe*, Cambridge: Cambridge University Press.
Gibson, A. (1974) 'An exhibition of theological fallacies', *Heythrop Journal* 15: 423–40.
—— (1981) *Biblical Semantic Logic*, Oxford: Blackwell/New York: St Martins.
—— (1987) *Boundless Function*, Newcastle: Bloodaxe.
—— (1997a) 'Archetypal site poetry', in J. Milbank, *The Mercurial Wood: Sites, Tales, Qualities*, Salzburg Studies in English Literature, Poetic Drama and Poetic Theory (eds Gortschacher and J. Hogg), Salzburg, Austria: University of Salzburg Press.
—— (1997b) 'The semantics of God: some functions in the Dead Sea Scrolls', in S.E. Porter and C. Evans (eds) *The Scrolls and the Scriptures*, (RILP 3. JSPSup), Sheffield: Sheffield Academic Press.
—— (1998a) 'Modern philosophy and ancient consciousness', in M.A. Hayes, W.J. Porter and D. Tombs (eds) *Religion and Sexuality*, Sheffield: Sheffield Academic Press, pp. 22–48.

—— (1998b) 'Ockham's world and future', in J. Marenbon (ed.) *Routledge History of Philosophy. Vol. II: Medieval Philosophy*, London: Routledge.
—— (1999) 'Logic of the resurrection?', in S.E. Porter, M.A. Hayes and D. Tombs (eds) *Resurrection*, (M. Hayes, W. Porter and D. Tombs (eds), JSNT, Supplementary Series), Sheffield: Sheffield Academic Press): 165–94.
—— (2000a) *Text and Tablet*, Aldershot: Ashgate.
—— (2000b) 'Philosophy of psychotic modernism: Wagner and Hitler', in B. Pearson and S.E. Porter (eds), *Christianity and Judaism in History*, Sheffield: Academic Press.
—— (forthcoming a) *Counter-Intuition*.
—— (forthcoming b) *Beyond Human Meaning*.
—— (forthcoming c) *What is Literature?*
—— (forthcoming d) 'Logic, literary creativity and philosophy of mathematics', in A. Gibson *Biblical Semantic Logic*, 2nd edn, Sheffield: Sheffield Academic Press, pp. 1–113.
Gibson, A. and O'Mahony, N.A. (1995) 'Lamentation sumerienne (vers – 2004)', in *Dedale: Le pardoxe des representations du divin: L' image et l'invisible*, 1 and 2, Paris: Adàle.
Giddens, A. (1984) *The Constitution of Society*, Cambridge: Cambridge University Press.
Goddu, A. (1990) 'William of Ockham's "empiricism" and constructive empiricism', in W. von Vossenkuhl and R. Schonberger (eds) *Die Gegenwart Ockhams*, VCH Acta humaniora, Weinheim.
Goldhill, S. (1986) *Reading Greek Tragedy*, Cambridge: Cambridge University Press.
Gombrich, E.H. (1962) *Art and Illusion*, Oxford: Phaidon.
—— (1993) [1986] *New Light on Old Masters* (orig. *Studies in Renaissance*), 2nd edn, Oxford: Phaidon.
Gompf, R.E. (1985) 'An infinite set of exotic R^4's', *Journal of Differential Geometry* 2: 283–300.
Gott, J.R., III (1991) 'Closed timelike curves produced by pairs of moving cosmic strings: exact solutions', *Physical Review of Letters* 66.9: 1126–29.
Gould, S.J. (2000) 'More things in heaven and earth', in H. Rose and S. Rose (eds) *Alas, Poor Darwin*, London: Cape, pp. 85–105.
Goulder, M.D. (1964) *Type and History in Acts*, London: SPCK.
Green, M.B. (1985) 'Unification of forces and particles in superstring theories', *Nature* 314(6010): 409–14.
Green, M.B. and Schwarz, J.H. (1984) 'Anomaly cancellations in super symmetric gauge theory and superstring theory', *Physics Letters B* 149: 117–22.
Greene, B. (2000) *The Elegant Universe*, London: Vintage.
Gross, D.J. (1989) 'Strings and superplanckian energies: in search of string symmetry', in M. Atiyah *et al.* (eds) *Physics and the Mathematics of Strings: Proceeding of the Royal Society*, London: Royal Society.
Grotius, H. (1625) [1853 edn] *De jure belli et acis, 1625*, trans. W. Whewell, Cambridge: Cambridge University Press.
Guth, A. (1981) *Physics Review* D23: 347.
—— (1997) *Time's Arrow*, London: Jonathan Cape.
—— (1998) *The Inflationary Universe: The Quest for a New Theory of Cosmic Origins*, London: Vintage.
Haack, S.A. (1996) *Deviant Logic*, Cambridge: Cambridge University Press.
Hacker, P.M.S. (1996) *Wittgenstein's Place in Twentieth-Century Analytic Philosophy*, Oxford: Oxford University Press.
Hacking, I. (1975a) *The Emergence of Probability*, Cambridge: Cambridge University Press.

—— (1975b) *Why Does Language Matter to Philosophy?*, Cambridge: Cambridge University Press.
—— (1990) *The Taming of Chance*, Cambridge: Cambridge University Press.
—— (1995) *Rewriting the Soul: Multiple Personality and the Sciences of Memory*, Princeton: Princeton University Press.
—— (1998) *Mad Travelers*, Charlottesville: University of Virginia Press.
Haggenmacher, P. (1983) *Grotius et la doctrine de la guerre juste* (Publications de l'Institut universitaire de hautes études internationales, Geneve), Paris: Presses universitaires de France.
Hale, B. (1994a) 'Singular terms', in B. McGuinness and Oliver (eds) *The Philosophy of Michael Dummett*, Dordrecht: Kluwer, pp. 17–44.
—— (1994b) 'Is Platonism epistemologically bankrupt?', *Philosophical Review* 103 (April 1994) 2: 299–325.
—— (1996) 'Singular Terms (1)', in M. Schirn (ed.) *Frege: Importance and Legacy*, Berlin.
Hall, A.R. (1992) *Isaac Newton: Adventurer in Thought*, Cambridge Science Biographies, Oxford: Blackwell (1996, Cambridge: Cambridge University Press).
Hall, S.G., Henry, S.G.B. and Johns, C.B. (1986) 'Forecasting with an econometric model', *Journal of Applied Econometrics* 1: 163–83.
Hallden, S. (1957) *On the Logic of the 'Better'*, Lund: C.W.K. Gleerup.
Hanson, N.R. (1966) 'Copernicus, Nicolas', in P. Edwards (ed.) *Encyclopaedia of Philosophy*, New York: Macmillan, Free Press/London: Collier Macmillan (repr. edn 1972).
Hara, T., Mahonen, P., Yamamoto, H. and Miyoshi, S.J. (1995) 'Inhomogeneity of cold dark matter due to initial fluctuations in the cosmic string scheme I',*Astrophysical Journal* 438.1:27–39.
Hare, R.M. (1952) *The Language of Morals*, Oxford: Oxford University Press.
Harre, R. (1993) 'Is there a semantics for music?', in M. Krausz (ed.) *The Interpretation of Music*, Oxford: Clarendon Press, pp. 203–14.
Harris, I. (1994) *The Mind of John Locke*, Cambridge: Cambridge University Press.
Harrison, R. P. (1992) *Forests: The Shadow of Civilization*, Chicago: University of Chicago Press.
Hartle, J. (1990) *General relativity and Gravitation*, 1989 Proceedings of 12th International Conference on General Relativity and Gravitation, University of Colorado at Boulder, N. Ashby, D.F. Bartlett and W. Wyss (eds), Cambridge: Cambridge University Press, pp. 391–417.
Hausman, C.R. (1989) *Metaphor and Art*, Cambridge: Cambridge University Press.
Hawking, S.W. (1976) 'Black holes and thermodynamics', *Physics Review D* 13.2:191.14: 191–97.
—— (1979) 'The path-integral approach to quantum gravity', in S.W. Hawking and W. Israel (eds) (1979) *General Relativity*, Cambridge: Cambridge University Press.
—— (1980) *Is the End in Sight for Theoretical Physics?*, Cambridge: Cambridge University Press.
—— (1983) 'Euclidean approach to the inflationary universe', in G.W. Gibbons, S.W. Hawking and S.T.C. Siklos (eds) *The Very Early Universe*, Cambridge: Cambridge University Press, pp. 287–96.
—— (1984) 'The cosmological constant is probably zero', *Physics Letters* B:134: 403.
—— (1990a) 'The effective action for wormholes' (offprint, DAMTP Cambridge).
—— (1990b) 'Spectrum of wormholes', *Physical Review* D:42.8: 2655–63.
—— (1990c) 'Baby universes II', *Modern Physics Letters* A:5.7: 543–66.
—— (1990d) 'Wormholes and non-simply connected manifolds' (offprint, DAMTP, Cambridge).
—— (1991a) 'The future of the universe', *The Darwin Lectures*, Cambridge: University of Cambridge.

—— (1991b) 'Is everything determined?' (offprint: DAMTP, Cambridge).
—— (1993) *Black Holes and Baby Universes*, 2nd edn, London: Bantam.
Hawking, S.W. and Ellis, R. (1973) *The Large Scale Structure of Space-Time*, Cambridge: Cambridge University Press.
Hawking, S.W. and Hartle, J.B. (1983) 'The wave function of the universe', *Physics Review* D:28: 2960–75.
Hawking, S.W. and Hayward, J.D. (1993) 'Quantum coherence in two dimensions' (offprint: DAMTP, Cambridge).
Hawking, S.W., Horowitz, G.T. and Ross, S.F. (1994) 'Entropy, area and black hole pairs' (offprint: DAMTP, Cambridge).
Hawking, S.W. and Israel, W. (eds) (1979) *General Relativity*, Cambridge: Cambridge University Press.
Hawking, S.W., Laflamme and G. W. Lyons (1995) 'The origin of time asymmetry' (forthcoming).
Hawking, S.W. and Penrose, R. (1970) *Proceedings of the Royal Society* A314–529, London: Royal Society.
Hawking, S.W. and Stewart, J.M. (1993) 'Naked thunderbolt similarities in black hole evaporation', *Nuclear Physics* B400: 393–415.
Hawking, S.W. and Turok, N. (1998) 'Open inflation without false vacua', *Physics Letters B* 425: 25–32.
Hawkins, J.A. (1983) *Word Order Universals*, Quantitative Analyses of Linguistic Structure, New York: Academic Press.
Hayman, H. (1980) *Nietzsche*, London: Weidenfeld & Nicholson (republished 1995, London: Phoenix Giants).
Heal, J. (1997) 'Indexical predicates and their uses', *Mind* 102(424): 618–40.
Heath, S. (1986) 'Realism, modernism, and "language-consciousness" ', in N Boyle and M. Swales (eds) *Realism in European Literature*, Cambridge: Cambridge University Press), pp. 103–22.
Hebblethwaite, B.L. (1980) *The Problems of Theology*, Cambridge: Cambridge University Press.
Helm, P. (1994) *Belief Policies*, Cambridge: Cambridge University Press.
Hemion, G. (1992) *The Classification of Knots and 3-Dimensional Spaces*, Oxford: Oxford University Press.
Herzfeld, K.F. (1927) 'On atomic properties which make an element a metal', *Physical Review* 29: 701–705.
Hesse, M. (1983) *Cosmology and Theology*, D. Tracy, N. Lash and M. Lefebure (eds), Concilium 166, Edinburgh: T. & T. Clark/New York : Seabury Press.
—— (1988) 'Physics, philosophy and myth', in R.J. Russell, W.R. Stoeger and G.V. Goyre (eds) *Physics, Philosophy and Theology*, Vatican Observatory, pp. 185–202.
—— (1994) 'The sources of models from God', in J. Hilgevoord (ed.) *Physics and our View of the World*, Cambridge, Cambridge University Press, pp. 239–54, 289–94.
Hiddleston, J.A. (1999) *Baudelaire and the Art of Memory*. Oxford: Clarendon.
Hintikka, J. (1998) *The Principles of Mathematics Revisited*, Cambridge: Cambridge University Press.
Hobson, M. (1982a) 'Deconstruction, empiricism and the postal services', *French Studies* 36.3: 290–314.
—— (1982b) *The Object of Art*, Cambridge: Cambridge University Press.
—— (1987) 'History Traces', in *Poststructuralism and the Question of History: Proceedings of the OLR Conference*, Cambridge, 1985.
—— (1991) 'On the subject of the subject: Derrida on Sollers in *La dissemination*', in *Philosophers' Poets*, London, Routledge, pp. 111–39.
—— (1992a) 'Dans la caverne de platon: Heidegger, Derrida', *Litterature* 85: 44–58.

—— (1992b) '"Nexus effectivus" and "nexus finalis": "causalty" in *Inegalité* and in the *Essai sur l'origine des langues*', in M. Hobson, J.T.A. Leigh and R. Wokler (eds) *Rousseau and the Eighteenth Century*, Oxford: Oxford University Press.

—— (1995) 'What's wrong with Saint Peter's? Or, Diderot, analogy and illusion in architecture', in W. Pape and F. Burwick (eds) *Reflecting Senses: Perception and Appearance in Literature, Culture and the Arts*, Berlin: De Gruyter, pp. 54–74; bibliography: 315–41.

—— (1998) *Jacques Derrida: opening lines*, London: Routledge.

Hockman, K.C. (1997) *The Differential Calculus as the Model of Desire in French Fiction of the Sevententh and Eighteenth Centuries*, The Age of Revolution and Romanticism, vol. 17, New York: P. Lang.

Hoffmann, R. (1990) 'Molecular beauty', *Journal of Aesthetics and Art Criticism* 48(3): 191–204.

Hogan, C. (1986) 'Glaxy superclusters and cosmic strings', *Nature* 320(6063): 572.

Holland, E.W. (1993) *Baudelaire and Schizoanalysis*, Cambridge: Cambridge University Press.

Holquist, M. (1990) *Dialogism*, London: Routledge.

Hooker, M.D. (1990) *From Adam to Christ*, Cambridge: Cambridge University Press.

Horst, S.W. (1996) *Symbols, Computation and Intentionality*, Berkeley: University of California Press.

House of Commons (1946) *Command Paper 6946*, London: HMSO.

House of Commons Revision Committee (1980) *14th Report of the Criminal Law*, London: HMSO.

Hoyle, F. (1975) 'On the origin of the microwave background', *Astrophysical Journal* 196: 661–70.

Hu, W. (2000) 'Ringing in the new cosmology', *Nature* 404(6781): 939–40.

Hughes, T. (1998) *Birthday Letters*, London: Faber.

Hull, C.M. (1987) 'Heterotic sigma models and non-linear strings', *Supersymmetry and its Applications*, Cambridge: Cambridge University Press.

Hume, D. (1975) [1772] *Enquiries Concerning Human Understanding and Concerning the Principles of Morals*, P.H. Nidditch (ed.), Oxford: Oxford University Press.

Huxley, A. (1977) 'Evidence, clues and motive in science', *New Humanist* 93(2): 61–66.

—— (1982) 'Discovery: Accident or design?', *Proceedings of the Royal Society*, London: Royal Society B.216, pp. 253–56.

Isbell, J.C. (1994) *The Birth of European Romanticism*, Cambridge: Cambridge University Press.

Jacob, F. (1970) *La logique du vivant: une histoire de l'heredite*, Paris: Gallimard.

James, S. (1994) 'Internal and external in the work of Descartes', in J. Tully and D.M. Weinstock (eds) *Philosophy in the Age of Pluralism*, Cambridge: Cambridge University Press.

Jameson, F. (1992) *Signatures of the Visible*, London/New York: Routledge.

Jarick, J. (1990) *Gregory Thaumaturgos' Paraphrase of Ecclesiastes*, Septuagint and Cognate Studies 29, Atlanta: Scholars Press.

Jaspars, J. and Thijsse, E. (1996) 'Fundamentals of partial modal logic', in P. Doherty (ed.) *Partiality, Modality, and Nonmonotonicity*, Stanford: CSLI Publications and FoLLI, pp. 111–41.

Jennings, R. (1986) *International Courts and International Politics*, Hull: Hull University Press.

Jeremias, J. (1971) *New Testament Theology*, Vol. 1, London: SCM Press.

John of Reading [unpublished manuscript] *I Sentences*, MS conventi soppressi D.IV.95, Florence: Biblioteca nazionale Centrale.

Johnson, C. (1994) *System and Writing in the Philosophy of Jacques Derrida*, Cambridge: Cambridge University Press.

Johnson, D.C., Benfield, R.E., Edwards, P.P., Nelson, J.H. and Vargas, M.D. (1985) 'Study of magnetism in osmium cluster compunds as molecular models for small metallic particles', *Nature* 314(6008): 231–35.

Juhl, P.D. (1980) *Interpretation: An Essay in the Philosophy of Literary Criticism*, Princeton: Princeton University Press.

Kaldor, N. (1986) 'Piero Sraffa', *Proceedings of the British Academy* LXXI (1985): 615–40.

Kant, E. (1985) [1786] *Metaphysische Anfangsgrunde der Naturwissenschaft* (Riga), J.W. Ellington (ed.) *Metaphysical Foundations of Natural Science*, Indianapolis: University of Indiana Press.

Katz, S.T. (1994) *The Holocaust in Historical Context. Vol. I: The Holocaust and Mass Death Before the Modern Age*, New York: Oxford University Press.

Kay, S. (1989) *Subjectivity in Troubadour Poetry*, Cambridge: Cambridge University Press.

Kearns, K. (1997) *Psychoanalysis, Historiography, and Feminist Theory*, Cambridge: Cambridge University Press.

Kelley, D. (1967) *Baudelaire's Salon de 1846*, Oxford: Clarendon.

—— (1985) in E. Timms and D. Kelley (eds) *Unreal city: urban experience in modern European literature and art*, Manchester: Manchester University Press.

—— (1990) 'Antonin Artaud: "Madness" and "self-expression"', in P. Collier and J. Davies (eds) *Modernism and the European Unconscious*, Cambridge: Cambridge University Press, pp. 230–45.

—— (1994) 'Transpositions', in P. Collier (ed.) *Artistic Relations*, New Haven, CT: Yale.

Kennedy. G.A. (1997a) 'The genres of rhetoric', in S.E. Porter (ed.) *Handbook of Classical Rhetoric in the Hellenistic Period: 330 B.C. – A.D. 400*, Leiden: Brill, pp. 3–42.

—— (1997b) 'Historical survey of rhetoric', in S.E. Porter (ed.) *Handbook of Classical Rhetoric in the Hellenistic Period: 330 B.C. – A.D. 400*, Leiden: Brill, pp. 43–50.

Kermode, F. (1975) *The Classic*, London: Faber.

—— (1979) *The Genesis of Secrecy*, Cambridge, Mass.: Harvard University Press.

—— (1984) *The Bible: Story and Plot*, Ethel M. Wood lectures, 1984, London: University of London.

—— (1986a) 'The plain sense of things', in G.H. Hartman and S. Budick (eds) *Midrash and Literature*, New Haven: Yale University Press.

—— (1986b) *The Uses of Error*, Cambridge: King's College.

—— (1990) *Poetry, Narrative, History*, Oxford: Blackwell.

—— (2000) *Shakespeare's Language*, London: Allen Lane, Penguin.

Khalfa, J. (1998) 'Mathémagie: Sokal, Bricmont et las doctrines informes', *Les Temps Modernes* 53(600): 220–49.

—— (2000) 'Deleuze et Sartre: idée d'une conscience impersonnelle', *Les Temps Modernes*, 55(608):190–222.

Kirkpatrick, F.G. (1994) *Together Bound*, Oxford: Oxford University Press.

Kirsch, G. (1994) 'Unpredictability', in N. Magneat-Thalmann and D. Thalmann (eds) *Artificial Life and Virtual Reality*, Chichester: Wiley.

Kirwan, J. (1990) *Literature, Rhetoric, Metaphysics*, London: Routledge

Klebanov, I., Susskind, L. and Banks, T. (1993) 'Wormholes and the cosmological constant', in G.W. Gibbons and S.W. Hawking (eds) *Euclidean Quantum Gravity*, London: World Scientific Publishing, 414–41.

Kopal, Z. (1979) *Language of the Stars*, Dordrecht: Kluwer.

Krausz, M. (1993) *The Interpretation of Music*, Oxford: Oxford University Press.

Kretzmann, N. (1997) *The Metaphysics of Theism*, Oxford: Clarendon.

—— (1999) *The Metaphysics of Creation*, Oxford: Clarendon.

Kripke, S. (1980) *Naming and Necessity*, Oxford: Oxford University Press.
Krumhansl, J.A. and Alexander, D.M. (1983) in E. Clementi and R.H. Sarma (eds) *Sarma Structures and Dynamics*, New York, pp. 61–80.
Kulkarni, S.R., Anderson, Prince, T.A. and Wolszczan, A. (1991) 'Old pulsars in the low-density globular cluster M13 and M53', *Nature* 349(2312):7–49.
Kumar, K. (1978) *Prophecy and Progress*, Harmondsworth: Penguin.
Lacan, J. (1966) *Ecrits*, Paris Seuil.
—— (1991) *Le Seminaire de Jacques Lacan. Livre VIII: Le transfert*, Paris: Editions de Seuil.
Lacoue-Labarthe, P. (1994) *Musica Ficta: Figures on Wagner*, Stanford: University of California Press.
Lakoff, G. (1987) *Fire, Women, and Dangerous Things*, Chicago: Chicago University Press.
Lakoff, G. and M. Johnson (1981) *The Metaphors We Live By*, Chicago: Chicago University Press.
Lamarque, P. and Olsen, S.H. (1994) *Truth, Fiction and Literature*, Oxford: Oxford University Press.
Lambert, K. (1996) 'Russelian names: notes on a theory of Arthur Prior', in B.J. Copeland (ed.) *Logic and Reality: Essays on the Legacy of Arthur Prior*, Oxford, Clarendon, pp. 411–17.
Langer, S.K. (1967) *Philosophy in a New Key: A Study in the Symbolism of Reason, Rite and Art*, 3rd edn, Cambridge, Mass.: Harvard University Press.
Langton, R. (1998) *Kantian Humility*, Oxford: Clarendon Press.
Laplace, P.S. [1799] *Allgemeine geographische Ephemeriden IV*, reproduced in S.W. Hawking and R. Ellis (1973) *The Large Scale Structure of Space-Time*, Cambridge: Cambridge University Press, Appendix A.
Lear, J. (1980) *Aristotle and Logical Theory*, Cambridge: Cambridge University Press.
Lee, A. (1990) *Realism and Power: Postmodern British Fiction*, London: Routledge.
Leick, G. (1994) *Sex and Eroticism in Mesopotamian Literature*, London: Routledge.
Levi, I. (1991) *The Fixation of Belief and its Undoing*, Cambridge: Cambridge University Press.
—— (1997) *The Covenant of Reason*, Cambridge: Cambridge University Press.
Lewis, D. (1986) *On the Plurality of Worlds*, Oxford: Oxford University Press.
Lewy, C. (1976) *Meaning and Modality*, Cambridge: Cambridge University Press.
Linde, A.D. (1990) *Particle Physics and Inflationary Cosmology*, Contemporary Concepts in Physics 5 (trans. M. Damashek), Reading: Harwood Academic.
Lindley, D. (1991) 'Cold dark matter makes an exit', *Nature* 349(6304): 14.
Lloyd, G. (1999) 'Augustine and the "problem" of time", in G.B. Matthews (ed.) *The Augustinian Tradition*, Berkeley: University of California Press): pp. 39–60.
Longair, M.S. (1994a) *High Energy Astrophysics*, Vol. 2, 2nd edn, Cambridge: Cambridge University Press.
—— (1994b) 'Classical cosmology', in W. Wamsteker, M.S. Longair and Y. Kondo (eds) *Frontier of Space and Ground-based Astronomy*, Astrophysics and Space Science Library 187, Dodrecht/Boston: Kluwer Academic, pp. 369–79.
Loptson, P. (1996) 'Prior, Plantinga, Haecceity, and the possible', in B.J. Copeland (ed.) *Logic and Reality: Essays on the Legacy of Arthur Prior*, Oxford, Clarendon, pp. 419–35.
Lovell, B. (1992) 'Reason and belief in cosmology', in W.R. Shea and A. Spadafora (eds) *Interpreting the World*, Locarno/Canton: Science History Publications, USA.
—— (1973) *The Origins and International Economics of Space Exploration*, Edinburgh: Edinburgh University Press.
Lucas, J.R. (1989) *The Future*, Oxford: Oxford University Press.

Luminet, J.-P. (1992) *Black Holes*, Cambridge: Cambridge University Press.
Lynden-Bell, D. (1988) 'The great attractor', *Astrophysics Journal* 326: 19–49.
Lyons, J. (1977) *Semantics*, 2 vols, Cambridge: Cambridge University Press.
Lyotard, J.-F. (1983) *The Postmodern Condition*, Manchester: Manchester University Press.
McCallum, M.A.H. (1979) 'Anisotropic and inhomogeneous relativistic cosmologies', in S.W. Hawking and W. Israel (eds) (1979) *General Relativity*, Cambridge: Cambridge University Press.
McDonald, J.I.H. (1993) *Biblical Interpretation And Christian Ethics*, Cambridge: Cambridge University Press.
McGinn, C. (1993) *Problems in Philosophy*, Oxford: Oxford University Press.
—— (1997) *Ethics, Evil, and Fiction*, Oxford: Clarendon Press.
McKie, C.F. (1988) 'Supermassive black holes', in M. Kafatos (ed.) *Supermassive Black Holes*, Cambridge: Cambridge University Press.
McNair, Lord (1962) *The Expansion of International Law*, Jerusalem: Magna Press.
Mackie, J.L. (1974) *The Cement of the Universe*, Oxford: Clarendon.
MacKinnon, D.M. (1968) *The Borderlands of Theology*, London: SCM Press.
—— (1974) *The Problem of Metaphysics*, Cambridge: Cambridge University Press.
—— (1979) *Explorations in Theology*, London: SCM Press.
—— (1982) *Creone and Antigone*, London: SCM Press.
—— (1987) *Themes in Theology*, Edinburgh: T. & T. Clark.
MacLachlan, H. (1950) *Sir Isaac Newton: The Theological Manuscripts*, Liverpool: Liverpool University Press.
Macquarrie, J. (1973) *The Concept of Peace*, London: SCM Press.
Macé, G. (1993) *La mémoire aime chasser dans le noir*, Paris: Gallimard.
Madsen, D. (1986) *Postmodern Allegory in the Novels of Thomas A. Pinchon*, Leicester: Leicester University Press.
Magnenat-Thalmann, N. and Thalmann, D. (eds) (1994) *Artificial Life and Virtual Reality*, Chichester: Wiley.
Mallarmé, S. (1996) [1897 *Un coup de dés* (la premiere edition présentée par David Mus. Ulysse, fin de siècle 37), facsimile reprint of text originally published in *Cosmopolis*, May 1897, Editions du Tiroir (1996) Plombières-les-Dijon: Diffusion.
—— (1914) *Un coup de des jamais n'abolira le hasard*, Paris: Librairie Gallimard.
Mann, F.A. (1973) *Studies in International Law*, Oxford: Oxford University Press.
Manuel, F.E. (1974) *The Religion of Isaac Newton*, Oxford: Oxford University Press.
Marcet, A. (1994) 'Simulation analysis of dynamic stochastic models', in C.A. Sims (ed.) *Advances in Econometrics: Sixth World Congress*, Vol. II, Cambridge: Cambridge University Press, pp. 83–118.
Marenbon, J. (1991) 'Abelard's concept of possibility', in B. Mojsisch and O. Pluta (es) *Historia philosophiae medii aevi*, Amsterdam/Philadelphia, pp. 595–609.
—— (1997) *The Philosophy of Peter Abelard*, Cambridge: Cambridge University Press.
—— (1998a) 'Introduction' in J. Marenbon (ed.) *Routledge History of Philosophy*, Vol. III, London: Routledge, pp. 1–10.
—— (1998b) 'Boethius: from antiquity to the middles ages', in J. Marenbon (ed.) *Routledge History of Philosophy*, Vol. III, London: Routledge, 11–28.
Marion, M. (1998) *Wittgenstein, Finitism, and the Foundations of Mathematics*, Oxford: Clarendon Press.
Marker, L.-L. and Marker, F. J. (1982) *Ingmar Bergman*, Cambridge: Cambridge University Press.
Marks, E. (1998) 'Encounter with death in *A Very Easy Death* and the body in decline in *Adieux: A Farewell to Sartre*', in E. Fallaize (ed.) *Simone de Beauvoir: a Critical Reader*, London: Routledge, pp. 132–54.

Maurer, A. (1984) 'Ockham's razor and Chatton's anti-razor', *Medieval Studies* 46: 463–75.
Mearns, C.L. (1981) *New Testament Studies* 27: 2.
Mellor, D.H. (1981) *Real Time*, Cambridge: Cambridge University Press.
—— (1998) *Real Time II*, London: Routledge.
—— (1995) *The Facts of Causation*, London: Routledge.
Messer, R. (1993) *Does God's Existence Need Proof?*, Oxford: Oxford University Press.
Meyer, L.B. (1956) *Emotion, Meaning and Music*, Chicago: Chicago University Press.
Michalowski, P. (1989) *The Lamentation over the Destruction of Sumer and Ur*, Mesopotamian Civilizations 1, Winona Lake: Eisenbrauns.
Milbank, J. (1990) *Theology and Social Theory*, Oxford: Blackwell.
—— (1997) *The Word Made Strange*, Oxford: Blackwell.
Millan, G. (1994) *Mallarmé: A Throw of the Dice*, London: Secker & Warburg.
Miller, A.E. and Miller, M.G. (1994) 'Translators' Introduction and Commentary', in O. Plaass, *Kant's Theory of Natural Science: Translation, Analytic Introduction and Commentary*, Dordrecht/Boston: Kluwer, pp. 7–162.
Miller, D, (1994) *Critical Rationalism*, Chicago.
Miller, K. (1985) *Doubles*, Oxford: Oxford University Press.
Milner, J. (1996) *Kazimer Malevich and the Art of Geometry*, New Haven: Yale University Press.
Milstein, S. (1992) *Arnold Schoenberg: Notes, Sets, Forms*, Cambridge: Cambridge University Press.
Mirimanoff, D. (1917) *L'Enseignement Mathématique* 19: 37–52.
Misner, C.W. (1977) 'Cosmology and theology', in W. Yourgrau and A.D. Breck (eds) *Cosmology, History and Theology*, New York: Plenum Press.
Miwa, T., Jimbo, M. and Date, E. (2000) *Solitons: Differential Equations, Symmetries and Infinite Dimentional Algebras*, Cambridge: Cambridge University Press.
Miyata, T. and Hayashida, H. (1982) 'Recent divergence from a common ancestor of human IFN-a genes', *Nature* 295.5845: 165–68.
Moi, T. (1990) *Feminist Theory and Simone de Beauvoir*, Oxford: Oxford University Press.
Molesworth, W. (1997) *Elements of Philosophy: The collected English works of Thomas Hobbes* Vol. 1 (intro. G.A.J. Rogers), London: Routledge, Thoemmes Press.
Moonan, L. (1994) *Divine Power*, Oxford: Clarendon Press.
Morgan, M.L. (1994) 'Religion History and Moral Discourse', in *Philosophy in an Age of Pluralism: The Philosophy of Charles Taylor in Question*, Cambridge, Cambridge University Press, pp. 49–66.
Moore, A.W. (1990) *The Infinite*, London: Routledge.
Moriarty, M. (1991) *Roland Barthes*, Cambridge: Polity.
Mothersill, M. (1984) *Beauty Restored*, Oxford: Oxford University Press.
Mottron, L. (1989) 'René Thom's semiotics: An application to the pathological limits of semiosis', in T.A. Sebeok, J. Umiker-Sebeok and E.P. Young (eds) *The Semiotic Web*, Berlin: de Gruyter, pp. 91–127.
Mumford, D. (1994) 'The mathematics of perception', lecture delivered at Princeton Institute for Advanced Study, Colloquium honoring Freeman Dyson, April 1994.
Munitz, M.K. (1990) *The Question of Reality*, Princeton: Princeton University Press.
Murdoch, I. (1992) *Metaphysics as a Guide to Morals*, London: Chatto & Windus.
Mussies, G. (1971) *The Morphology of New Testament Greek*, Novum Testamentum Supplements 27, Leiden: Brill.
Nagel, T. (1986) *The View from Nowhere*, Oxford: Oxford University Press.
—— (1997) *The Last Word*, Oxford: Oxford University Press.

Nerlich, G. (1994) *What Spacetime Explains*, Cambridge: Cambridge University Press.
Neufeld, D. (1994) *Reconceiving Texts as Speech Acts: An Analysis of 1 John*, Leiden: Brill.
Neugebauer, G. and Kramer, D. (1985) 'Stationary axisymmetric electrovacuum fields in General Relativity', in M.A.H. MacCallum (ed.) *Galaxies, Axisymmetric Systems and Relativity*, Cambridge: Cambridge University Press, pp. 149–65.
Neugebauer, O. (1969) *The Exact Sciences in Antiquity*, 2nd ed, New York: Dover.
Newlands, G. (1994) *God in Christian Perspective*, Edinburgh: T. & T. Clark.
Newman, W.R. (1995) *Gehenical Fire: The Lives of George Starkey, an American Alchemist*, Cambridge, Mass.: Harvard University Press.
Newton, I. (1754) *Prophecies Fulfilling*, London.
—— (1974) 'Of the day of judgement', Yahuda MS 6, in the Hebrew University, Jerusalem (cf. Manuel (1974), Appendix B).
Nichols, S.G. (1991) *The New Medievalism*, New Haven: Yale University Press, ch. 1.
Norris, C. (1987) *Derrida*, Cambridge, Mass.: Harvard University Press.
Nozick, R. (1997) *Socratic Puzzles*, Cambridge, Mass.: Harvard University Press.
Nussbaum, M. (2000) *Women and Human Development*, Cambridge: Cambridge University Press.
Oakes, E.T. (1994a) *Patterns of Redemption: The Theology of Hans Urs von Balthasar*, New York: Continuum.
Oakes, E.T. (ed.) (1994b) *German Essays on Religion*, New York: Continuum.
Offler, H.S. (1990) 'The "influence" of Ockham's political thinking', in W. von Vossenkuhl and R. Schonberger (eds) *Die Gegenwart Ockhams*, Weinheim: VCH Acta humaniora.
Ohta, T. (1983a) *Genetic Research* 41: 47–55.
—— (1983b) *Theoretical Population Biology* 23: 216–40.
O'Hanlan, G.F. (1990) *The Immutability of God in the Theology of Hans Urs von Balthasar*, Cambridge: Cambridge University Press.
Olson, E.C. (1980) 'Taphonomy: Its history and role in community evolution', in A.K. Behrensmeyer and A.P. Hill (eds) *Fossils in the Making*, Chicago: Chicago University Press.
Oppenheim, L. and Lauterpacht, H. (1955) *A Treatise, Volume 1: Peace*, 8th edn, London/New York: Longmans, Green.
Orgel, L.E. and Crick, F.H.C. (1980) 'Selfish DNA: the ultimate parasite', *Nature* 284(5757): 604–607.
Ostriker, J.P. and Vishniac, E.T. (1986) 'Effect of gravitational lenses on the microwave background, and 11 and 46+111B,C', *Nature* 322(6082): 804.
Paczynski, B. (1986) 'Will cosmic strings be discovered using the space telescope?' *Nature* 319(6054): 567–68.
Pagels, E. (1991) 'The social history of Satan, the "intimate enemy"', *Harvard Theological Review* 84: 105–28.
Panofsky, E. (1934) 'Style and medium in the motion picture', *Bulletin of Department of Art and Archaeology*, Princeton: Princeton University Press.
Parfit, D. (1997) 'Reason and motivation', *Aristotelian Society, Supplementary Volume* LXXI: 99–130.
—— (1984) *Reasons and Persons* (repr. with corr.), Oxford: Oxford University Press.
Pascal, B. (1647) *Expériences touchant le vide* (cf. Pascal 1954).
—— (1954) *Oeuvres Complètes*, Paris: Gallimard.
Pasnau, J. (1997) *Theories of Cognition in the Later Middle Ages*, Cambridge: Cambridge University Press.
Paxson, J.J. (1994) *The Poetics of Personification*, Cambridge: Cambridge University Press.

Peacocke, C. (1988) 'Understanding logical constants: a realist's account', *Proceedings of the British Academy* LXXIII (1987): 153–99.
Pearson, B.W.R. (1998) 'Dry bones in the Judean desert', *Journal for the Study of Judaism* 29(2): 192–201.
—— (forthcoming) *Paul, Dialectic and Gadamer*.
Peebles, P.J.E. (1986) 'The mean mass density of the universe', *Nature* 321(6065): 27–32.
—— (1993) *Principles of Physical Cosmology*, Princeton: Princeton University Press.
Peirce, C.S. (1982) *The Writings of C.S. Peirce*, Bloomington: University of Indiana Press.
—— (1992) *Reasoning and the Logic of Things* (ed. K.L. Ketner), Cambridge, Mass: Harvard University Press.
Penrose, R. (1979) 'Singularities and time-asymmetry', in S.W. Hawking and W. Israel (eds) (1979) *General Relativity*, Cambridge: Cambridge University Press.
—— (1990) *The Emperor's New Mind*, Oxford: Oxford University Press.
—— (1994a) 'Mathematical intelligence?', in J. Khalfa (ed.) *What is Intelligence?*, Cambridge: Cambridge University Press.
—— (1994b) *Shadows of the Mind*, Oxford: Oxford University Press.
Pepper, S.C. (1961) *World Hypotheses*, Berkeley: University of California Press.
Perloff, M. (1996) *Wittgenstein's Ladder*, Chicago: Chicago University Press.
Perrin, N. (1978) *Jesus and the Language of the Kingdom*, Philadelphia: Fortress.
Pesaran, M.J. and Slater, L.J. (1980) *Dynamic Regressions*, Chichester: Wiley.
Phillips, D. C. *et al.* (1983) in D.S. Bendall (ed.) *Evolution from Molecules to Men*, Cambridge: Cambridge University Press, pp. 145–73.
Pickstock, C. (1997) *After Writing*, Oxford: Blackwell.
Pippin, R. B. (1991) *Modernism as a Philosophical Problem: On the Dissatisfactions of European High Culture*, Oxford: Basil Blackwell.
Plaass, P. (1994) *Kant's Theory of Natural Science*, Boston Studies in the Philosophy of Science 159, Dordrecht/Boston: Kluwer.
Plath, S. (1965) *Ariel*, London: Faber.
Polanco, C., González, A.I. and Dover, G.A. (2000) 'Patterns of variation in the intergenic spacers of ribosomal DNA in Drosophila melanogaster support a model for genetic exchanges during X–Y pairing', *Genetics* 155: 1221–29.
Polchinski, J. (1998) *String Theory II: Superstring Theory and Beyond*, Cambridge: Cambridge University Press.
Polkinghorne, J. (1986) *The Quantum World*, London: Pelican.
—— (1990) *The quantum world*, Harmondsworth: Penguin.
—— (1991) *Reason and Reality*, London: SPCK.
—— (1994) *Science and Christian Belief*, Gifford Lectures 1993–1994, London: SPCK.
—— (1995a) '"The Physics of Immortality" F. J. Tippler', review, *New Scientist* 14 February.
—— (1995b) 'Temporality in relation to divine action', unpublished Princeton Research Paper.
—— (1998) *Belief in God in an age of science: The Terry Lectures*, New Haven: University Press.
Polyakov, A.M. (1974) 'Particle spectrum in quantum field theory', *JETP* (formerly *Soviet Journal*) 20: 194–95.
Popper, K.R. (1972) *Objective Knowledge*, Oxford: Oxford University Press.
—— (1982) *Unended Quest: An Intellectual Autobiography*, rev. edn, La Salle: Open Court.
Porter. S.E. (1989) *Verbal Aspect in the Greek of the New Testament, with Reference to Tense and Mood*, New York: Peter Lang.

—— (1996) 'Wittgenstein's classes of utterances and Pauline ethical texts', *Studies in the Greek New Testament*, New York: Peter Lang.
—— (ed.) (1997) *Handbook of Classical Rhetoric in the Hellenistic Period: 330 B.C. – A.D. 400*, Leiden: Brill.
Potter, D. (1994) *Prophets and Emperors*, Cambridge, Mass.: Harvard.
Prendergast, C. (1986) *The Order of Mimesis*, Cambridge: Cambridge University Press.
Preskill, J. (1983) 'Monopoles in the very early universe', in G.W. Gibbons, S.W. Hawking and S.T.C. Siklos (eds) *The Very Early Universe*, Cambridge: Cambridge University Press, pp. 193–246.
Prevost, R. (1990) *Probability and Theistic Explanation*, Oxford: Oxford University Press.
Priest, G. (1995) *Beyond the Limits of Thought*, Cambridge: Cambridge University Press.
Prior, A.N. (1960) 'S. Hallden's *On the Logic of the "Better"* ' (review), Copenhagen, 1957.
—— (1967) *Past, Present and Future*, Oxford: Oxford University Press.
—— (1968) *Papers on Times and Tense*, Oxford: Oxford University Press.
—— (1971) *Objects of Thought*, Oxford: Clarendon Press.
—— (1977) *Worlds, Times and Selves* (with K. Fine), London: Duckworth.
Prior, A.N. and Fine, K. (1977) *Worlds, Times and Selves*, Oxford: Clarendon Press.
Quine, W.V.O. (1963) *Set Theory and its Logic*, Cambridge, Mass.: Harvard University Press.
—— (1974) *Methods of Logic*, 2nd edn, Cambridge, Mass.: Harvard University Press.
Pynchon, T. (1973) *Gravity's Rainbow*, New York: Viking Press/London: Cape.
—— (1990) *Vineland*, London: Secker & Warburg.
Quinn, P.L. (1978) *Divine Command Theory*, Oxford: Oxford University Press.
Ramsey, F.P. (1978) [1931] *Foundations: Essays in Philosophy, Logic, Mathematics and Economics*, fully rev. edn incorporating new material, D.H. Mellor (ed.), London: Routledge & Kegan Paul (1931 edn published as *The Foundations of Mathematics and other Logical Essays*, R.B. Braithwaite (ed.) London: K. Paul, Trench, Trubner).
—— (1990) *Philosophical Papers*, Cambridge: Cambridge University Press.
Ranicki, R. (1998) *High-Dimensional Knot Theory: Algebraic Surgery in Codimension 2*, Springer Monographs in Mathematics, Berlin/New York: Springer.
Rawls, J. (1972) *A Theory of Justice*, Oxford: Oxford University Press.
—— (1993) *Political Liberalism*, New York: Columbia University Press.
—— (1999) *Collected Papers* (ed. S. Freeman), Cambridge, Mass.: Harvard University Press.
Ray, C. (1991) *Time, Space and Philosophy*, London: Routledge.
Ray, T. (1994) 'Evolution and complexity', in G. Cowan, D. Pines and D. Meltzer (eds) *Complexity: Metaphors, Models, and Reality*, Santa Fe Institute Studies in the Sciences of Complexity, Vol. 19, Reading, Mass.: Addison-Wesley. pp. 161–76.
Read, S. (1988) *Relevant Logic*, Oxford: Blackwell.
—— (1998) 'Relevance logic and entailment', in E.J. Craig (ed.) *Routledge Encyclopaedia of Philosophy*, London: Routledge, pp. 200–204.
Recanti, F. (1993) *Indirect Reference*, Oxford: Blackwell.
Redhead, M. (1989) *Incompleteness, Nonlocality and Realism*, Oxford: Oxford University Press.
Rees, M.J. (1983) 'What the astrophysicist wants from the very early universe', in G.W. Gibbons, S.W. Hawking and S.T.C. Siklos (eds) *The Very Early Universe*, Cambridge: Cambridge University Press.

356 Bibliography

—— (1995) *Perspectives in Astrophysical Cosmology* (Lezioni Lincee), Cambridge: Cambridge University Press.
—— (1997) *Before the Beginning*, London: Simon & Schuster.
—— (1999) *Just Six Numbers*, London: Weidenfeld & Nicholson.
—— (2000) 'The "first light"', in C.S. Frank and S.D.M. White (eds) *The Formation of Galaxies*, Philosophical Transactions of the Royal Society of London, A 2000 358: 1989–99.
Reichel, H.-C. (1997) 'How can or should the recent developments in mathematics influence the philosophy of mathematics?', in A. Driessen and A. Suarez (eds), *Mathematical Undecidability, Quantum Nonlocality and the Question of the Existence of God*, Boston, Dordrecht: Reidel, pp. 3–14.
Reynolds, D. (1992) 'Mallarmé as "Maitre": the (en)gendering of genre', *Journal of the Institute of Romance Studies* 1: 439–52.
—— (1995) *Symbolist Aesthetics and Early Abstract Art: Sites of Imaginary Space*, Cambridge: Cambridge University Press.
Richards, I.A. (1936) *The Philosophy of Rhetoric*, Oxford: Oxford University Press.
Richardson, J. (1996): *Nietzsche's System*, New York: Oxford University Press.
Ricoeur, P. (1977) *The rule of metaphor: multi-disciplinary studies of the creation of meaning in language*, trans. R. Czerny with K. McLaughlin and J. Costello, Toronto: University of Toronto Press.
Riffaterre, M. (1990) 'Undecidability as hermeneutic constraint', in P. Collier and H. Geyer-Ryan (eds) *Literary Theory Today*, Cambridge: Polity Press, pp. 109–24.
Robbins, V.K. (1997) 'The present and future of rhetorical analysis', in S.E. Porter and T.H. Olbricht (eds) *The Rhetorical Analysis of Scripture*, Sheffield: Sheffield Academic Press, pp. 24–52.
Robinson, J.A.T. (1976) *Redating the New Testament*, London: SCM Press.
Robson, E. (1999) *Mesopotamian Mathematics, 2100–1600 B.C.*, Oxford: Clarendon Press.
Rogerson, J.W. (1984) *Anthropology and the Old Testament*, JSOT series, Sheffield: Academic Press [1978, Oxford: Blackwell].
Rorty, R. (1980) *Philosophy and the Mirror of Nature*, Oxford: Oxford University Press.
—— (1984) 'The historiography of philosophy', in R. Rorty, J.B. Schneewind and Q. Skinner (eds) *Philosophy in History*, Cambridge: Cambridge University Press.
—— (1989) *Contingency, Irony and Solidarity*, Cambridge: Cambridge University Press.
—— (1992) 'Is Derrida a transcendental philosopher?', in D. Wood (ed.) *Derrida: A Critical Reader*, Oxford: Oxford University Press, pp. 235–46.
—— (1997) 'Religious faith, intellectual responsibility, and romance', in R.A. Putnam (ed.) *The Cambridge Companion to William James*, Cambridge: Cambridge University Press, pp. 84–102.
—— (1998) *Truth and Progress*, Philosophical Papers 3, Cambridge: Cambridge University Press.
Ross, G.G. (1989) 'The (low-energy) physics of the superstring', in M. Atiyah *et al.* (eds) *Physics and the Mathematics of Strings: Proceedings of the Royal Society*, London: Royal Society.
Ross, J.F. (1981) *Portraying Analogy*, Cambridge: Cambridge University Press.
Rousseau, J.J. (1750) *Discours qui à remporte la prix à d'Academie de Dijon* (subsequently: *Discours sur les sciences et les arts*, reprint Modern Language Association of America, Monograph Series) New York: Kraus Reprint Corporation/Oxford University Press.
Rowland, C.C. (1982) *The Open Heaven*, London: SPCK.

Rubbia, C. (1992) 'The role of symmetries in the infinitesimally small', in W.R. Shea and A. Spadafora (eds) *Interpreting the World*, Canton, MA: Science History Publications.
Rucker, R. (1982) *Infinity and the Mind*, Brighton: Harvester.
Ruse, M. (1989) *The Darwinian Paradigm*, London: Routledge.
Rushdie, S. (1988) *The Satanic Verses*, London: Viking.
Russell, B. (1936) 'The limits of empiricism', *Proceedings of the Aristotelian Society* n.s. 36: 131–50.
Sahlin, N.-H. (1990) *The Philosophy of F.P. Ramsey*, Cambridge: Cambridge University Press.
Sainsbury, R.M. (1998) 'Indexicals and reported speech', in T.J. Smiley (ed.) *Philosophical Logic*, Oxford: British Academy, pp. 45–70.
Salam, A. (1992) 'The unification of fundamental forces', in W.R. Shea and A. Spadafora (eds) *Interpreting the World*, Canton: MA: Science History Publications.
Sancar, A. and Rupp, W.D. (1983) 'A novel repair enzyme: UVRABC excision nuclease of escherichia-coli cuts a DNA strand of both sides of the damaged region', *Cell* 33(1): 249–60.
Sangalli, A. (1998) *The Importance of Being Fuzzy*, Princeton: Princeton University Press.
Saslaw, W.C. (1985) *Gravitational Physics of Stellar and Galactic Systems*, Cambridge: Cambridge University Press.
Saunders, W., Frenck, C., Rowan-Robinson, G. *et al.* (1991) 'The density field of the local Universe', *Nature* 349: 32–38.
Schama, S. (1995) *Landscape and Memory*, London: HarperCollins (1996 Fontana).
Schenkeveld, D.M. (1997) 'Philosophical prose', in S.E. Porter (ed.) *Handbook of Classical Rhetoric in the Hellenistic Period: 330 B.C. – A.D. 400*, Leiden: Brill, pp. 195–64.
Scherbaum, F., Grohmann, A., Hilber, B., Kruger, C. and Schmidbaur, H. (1988) '"Aurophilie" als konsequenz Relativisticher Effekte', *Angewandte Chemie* 100: 1602–04.
Schiffrin, D. (1994) *Approaches to Discourse*, Oxford: Oxford University Press.
Schopenhauer, A. (1819) *Die Welt als Wille und Vorstellung*, Frankfurt am Main: Insel (1987 facsimile reprint, Leipzig: Brockhaus, 1819, vols. 1 and 2).
Schulte-Sasse, J. (1987) 'On the difference between a mimetic and a semiotic theory of the modern drama', in Peter P. Szondi *Theory of the Modern Drama* (ed. and trans. M. Hays), Cambridge: Polity, pp. vii–xviii.
Schwarzenberger, G. (1968) *International Law as Applied by International Courts and Tribunals. Vol. 2: The Law of Armed Conflict*, London: Stevens.
Scott, D. (1988) *Pictorialist Poetics*, Cambridge: Cambridge University Press.
Segelstein, D.J., Rawley, L.A., Stinebring, Fruchter, A.S. and Taylor, J.H. (1986) 'New millisecond pulsar in a binary system', *Nature* 322(6081): 714–17.
Sen, A. (1995) 'Is the idea of purely internal consistency of choice bizarre?', in J.E.J. Altham and R. Harrison (eds) *Making Sense of Humanity: Essays on the Ethical Philosophy of Bernard Williams*, Cambridge, Cambridge University Press, pp. 19–31.
—— (1997) *On Economic Inequality*, Oxford: Clarendon Press.
Shea, W.R. and Spadafora, A. (eds) (1992) *Interpreting the World: Science and Society*, Canton, MA: Science History Publications.
Sherry, R. (1550) *A Treatise of Schemes and Tropes*, London.
Shoesmith, D.J. and Smiley, T.J. (1980) *Multiple Conclusion Logic* (cor. ed.), Cambridge: Cambridge University Press.
Shohat, E. and Stam, R. (1994) *Unthinking Eurocentrism*, London: Routledge.

Sibley, F. (1993) 'Making music our own', in M. Krausz (ed.) *The Interpretation of Music*, Oxford: OUP, pp. 165–76.
Silk, J. (1986) 'Faith in the physicists', *Nature* 322(6079): 505.
—— (1989) *The Big Bang*, rev. edn, New York: W.H. Freeman.
—— (1995) 'A theory for the initial mass function', *Astrophysical Journal* 439: L41–L44.
—— (2000) 'An empirical approach to galaxy formation', in C.S. Frank and S.D.M. White (eds) *Philosophical Transactions of the Royal Society of London*, A 2000 (358): 2153–57).
Singh, S. (1997) *Fermat's Last Theorem*, London: Fourth Estate.
Smiley, T.J. (1982) 'Theory of descriptions', *Proceedings of British Academy* 97 (1981): 321–37.
—— (1993) 'Can contradictions be true?', *Proceedings of the Aristotelian Society* 67: 17–33.
—— (1995) 'A tale of two tortoises', *Mind* 104(416): 725–736.
—— (1998a) (ed.) *Philosophical Logic*, Oxford: British Academy.
—— (1998b) 'Conceptions of consequence', in E.J. Craig (ed.) *Routledge Encyclopaedia of Philosophy*, London: Routledge, pp. 599–602.
Smith, G. and Lyne, A.G. (1987) *Pulsar Astronomy*, Cambridge: Cambridge University Press.
Sobell, H.M. *et al.* (1984) 'The structure of DNA', presented at Cold Spring Harbor Symposium in Quantitative Biology.
Sorensen, R.A. (1992) *Thought Experiments*, Oxford: Oxford University Press.
—— (1998) 'Logical luck', *Philosophical Quarterly* 48(192): 319–31.
Soskice, J.M. (1985) *Metaphor and Religious Language*, Oxford: Oxford University Press.
Sraffa, P. (1960) *Production of Commodities by Means of Commodities*, Cambridge: Cambridge University Press.
Stark, A.A., Dragovan, M., Wilson, R.W. and Gott, J.R., III, (1986) 'Observations of the cosmic background radiation near the double quasar 1146+111B,C', *Nature* 322(6082): 805.
Stark, C.W. (2000) 'Surgery theory and infinite fundamental groups', S. Cappell, A. Ranicki and J. Rosenberg (eds) *Surveys on Surgery Theory 1*, Princeton: Princeton University Press, pp. 275–305.
Staten, H. (1985) *Wittgenstein and Derrida*, Oxford: Oxford University Press.
Steiner, G. (1978) *On Difficulty*, London: Faber.
—— (1984) *Antigones*, Oxford: Oxford University Press.
—— (1989) *Real Presences*, London: Faber.
—— (1995) 'To speak to God', review of B.L. McCormack, *Karl Barth's Critically Realistic Dialectical Theology*, Oxford, *Times Literary Supplement* 19 May 1995: 47–8.
Steinkraus, W.E. (1984) *Philosophy of Art*, rev. edn, Langham/London: University Press of America.
Stephanou, G. (1983) *Developmental Genetics* 3: 299–308.
Sternberg, M. (1985) *The Poetics of Biblical Narrative*, Bloomington: University of Indiana Press.
Stewart, I. (1986) 'Exotic structures on four-space', *Nature* 322(6077): 310–11.
—— (1988) 'The ultimate in decidability', *Nature* 332(6160): 115–16.
Stewart, J. (1990) *Advanced General Relativity*, Cambridge: Cambridge University Press.
Strathdee, J. (1982) 'Introduction to supersymmetry', in S. Ferrarar and J.G. Taylor (eds) *Supersymmetry '81*, Cambridge: Cambridge University Press.
Striker, G. (1998) 'Aristotle and the uses of logic', in J. Gentzler (ed.) *Method in Ancient Philosophy*, Oxford: Oxford University Press.

Stroll, A. (1998) *Sketches of Landscapes: Philosophy by Example*, Cambridge, Mass.: MIT Press.
Stump, E. (1978) *Boethius's De topicis differentiis*, Ithaca: Cornell University Press.
Sweet, J. (1979) *Revelation*, London: SCM Press.
Swinburne, R. (1979) *The Existence of God*, Oxford: Oxford University Press.
—— (1992) *Revelation* Oxford: Oxford University Press.
—— (1994) *The Christian God*, Oxford: Oxford University Press.
Szondi, Peter P. (1987) *Theory of the Modern Drama* (ed. and trans. M. Hays), Cambridge: Polity.
Tachau, K. H. (1988) *Vision and Certitude in the Age of Ockham*, Leiden: E. J. Brill.
Tassie, L.J. (1986) 'Cosmic strings, superstrings and the evolution of the universe', *Nature* 323(6083): 40–42.
Taylor, C. (1985) *Human Agency and Language: Philosophical Papers I*, Cambridge: Cambridge University Press.
—— (1989) *Sources of the Self*, Cambridge, Mass.: Harvard University Press.
—— (1994) '"Reply and re-articulation": "Foundations: Susan James"', in J. Tully and D.M. Weinstock (eds) *Philosophy in an Age of Pluralism*, Cambridge: Cambridge University Press, pp. 214–19.
Tennant, N. (1997) *The Taming of the True*, Oxford: Clarendon Press.
Thiemann, R.F. (1985) *Revelation and Theology*, Notre Dame: University of Notre Dame Press.
Thijsse, E. (1996) 'Fundamentals of partial modal logic', in P. Doherty (ed.) *Partiality, Modality and Nonmonotonicity*, Stanford: CSLI Publications and FoLLI, pp. 223–49.
Thiselton, A.C. (1980) *The Two Horizons*, London: SCM Press.
Thom, R. (1989) *Structural Stability and Morphogenesis: An Outline of a General Theory of Models*, 2nd edn (trans. D.H. Fowler of French 1st edn, updated by R. Thom), Reading, Mass.: Benjamin/Cummings Advanced Book Program).
Thomas Aquinas *see under* Aquinas, Thomas
Thomas, J.T. (1848) *Elpis Israel*, London.
't Hooft, G. (1974) 'Magnetic monopoles in unified gauge theories', *Nuclear Physics B* 79: 276–84.
Thorne, K.S. (1994) *Black Holes and Time Warps*, London: Macmillan (1995 edn London: Papermac).
Tiles, M. (1989) *The Philosophy of Set Theory*, Oxford: Oxford University Press.
Tipler, F.J. (1995) *The Physics of Immortality*, London: Macmillan.
Tokyo International Military Tribunal (1948) *Tokyo International Military Tribunal: Judgements* (English Transcript), Part A, ch. 3.
Torrance, T.F. (1969) *Theological Science*, Oxford: Oxford University Press.
—— (1981) *Divine and Contingent Order*, Oxford: Oxford University Press.
—— (1990) *Karl Barth, Biblical and Evangelical Theologian*, Edinburgh: T. & T. Clark.
—— (1999) 'Creation: contigent world-order, and time', in M. Wegener (ed.) *Time Creation and World-Order*, Acta Jutlandica 74.1, Aaarhus: Aarhus University Press, pp. 206–36.
Trembath, K.R. (1991) *Divine Revelation*, Oxford: Oxford University Press.
Trevor-Roper, H. (1981) *History and Imagination*, Oxford: Oxford University Press.
Trullinger, S.E., Miller, M.D., Guyer, R.A. and Bishop, A.R. (1978) 'Brownian motion of coupled nonlinear oscillators: thermalised solitons and nonlinear response to external forces', *Physical Review of Letters* 40(4): 206–10.
Trusted, J. (1991) *Physics and Metaphysics*, London: Routledge.
Tuck, R. (1983a) 'Grotius, Carneades and Hobbes', *Grotiana* New Series 4: 43–62.
—— (1983b) 'P. Haggenmacher's *Grotius et la doctrine de la guerre juste* (Paris, 1983),' review, *Grotiana* New Series 5.

Turner, E.L., Schneider, D.P., Burke, B.F. et al. (1986) 'An apparent gravitational lens with an image separation of 2.6 arc min', *Nature* 321(6066): 142–44.
Turner, M.S. (1983) 'The end may be hastened by magnetic monopoles', *Nature* 306(5939): 161–62.
Ulanov, O.N. (1999) *Introduction to Mathematical Ethics* (trans. M.A. Shelehovskaya), St Petersburg: Text/Roscon.
Ulmer, G. (1989) *Teletheory*, New York/London: Routledge.
United Nations Conference on Trade and Development (1968), *Report, February–March 1968. I: Report and Annexes*, Part 1, Doc. Sec. 32.
Vilenkin, A. (1986) 'Looking for cosmic strings', *Nature* 322 (6080): 613–14.
Vitz, P.C. (1988) *Sigmund Freud's Christian Unconscious*, New York: New York University Press.
Vlastos, G. (1991) *Socrates*, Cambridge: Cambridge University Press.
Von Neumann, John J. (1998) *Continuous Geometry*, Princeton Landmarks in Mathematics and Physics (Princeton: Princeton University Press/Oxford: Oxford University Press.
Wada, S. (1986) 'Consistency of canonical quantization of gravity and boundary conditions for the wave function of the universe', *Physical Review* D34: 8.
Wall, C.T.C. (1999) *Surgery on Compact Manifolds*, Mathematical Surveys and Monographs 69 (ed. A.A. Ranicki), 2nd edn, Providence: American Mathematical Society.
Wang, L.J., Kuzmich A. and Dogariu, A. 'Gain-assisted superluminal light propagation', *Nature* 406 (6784): 277–79.
Ward, G. (1995) *Barth, Derrida and the Language of Theology*, Cambridge: Cambridge University Press.
Ward, K. (1994) *Religion and Revelation*, Oxford: Oxford University Press.
Weeks, J.R. (1985) *The Shape of Space: How to Visualize Surfaces and Three-dimensional Space*, Monographs and Textbooks in Pure and Applied Mathematics 96, New York: Dekker.
Weicker, K. and Weicker, N. (1999) 'Locality vs. randomness', in W. Banzhaf and C. Reeves (eds) *Foundations of Genetic Algorithms 5*, San Fransisco: Morgan Kaufmann, pp. 147–63.
Weiss, J. (1971) [1892] *Die Predigt Jesu vom Reiche Gottes*, Göttingen (*Jesus Proclamation of the Kingdom of God*), London: SCM Press.
Wesson, P.S. and Ponce de Leon, J. (1995) 'The equation of motion in Kaluza–Klein cosmology and its implications for astrophysics', *Astronomy and Astrophysics* 294: 1–7.
White, N.E. and Stello, L. (1988) 'Spin histories of PSR 1841–24 in M28 and PSR 1951–32 in CTB80', *Nature* 332: 416–18.
White, R. (1982) 'Notes on analogical predication and speaking about God', in B. Hebblethwaite and Sutherland (eds) *The Philosophical Frontiers of Christian Theology*, Cambridge: Cambridge University Press.
Whitman, Walt (1959) [1855] *Leaves of Grass*, ed. M. Cowley, New York: Viking Press.
Wilder, A.N. (1971) *Early Christian Rhetoric*, rev. edn, Cambridge, Mass.: Harvard University Press.
William of Ockham (1967–68) *Opera philosophica et theologica*, 17 vols., St Bonaventure: Franciscan Institute.
—— (1983) *Predestination, God's Foreknowledge and the Future Contingents* (trans, intro., notes and appendices M.M. Adams and N. Krezmann), Indianapolis: Hackett.
—— (1991) *Quodlibetal Questions*, 2 vols, (trans. A.J. Freddoso and F.E. Kelley), New Haven: Yale University Press.

—— (1994) 'Five questions on universals' from the *Ordinatio* in P.V. Spade (ed. and trans) *Five Texts on the Medieval Problem of Universals*, Indianapolis: Hackett, pp. 114–231.
Williams, B.A.O. (1978) *Descartes*, Harmondsworth: Penguin.
—— (1985) *Ethics and the Limits of Philosophy*, London: Collins.
—— (1981) *Moral Luck*, Cambridge: Cambridge University Press.
—— (1985) *Ethics and the Limits of Philosophy*, London: Fontana.
—— (1993a) *Morality*, Cambridge: Cambridge University Press.
—— (1993b) *Shame and Necessity*, Berkeley: University of California Press.
—— (1995) 'Replies' in J.E.J. Altham and R. Harrison (eds) *Making Sense of Humanity: Essays on the Ethical Philosophy of Bernard Williams*, Cambridge: Cambridge University Press, pp. 185–224.
—— (1998a) *Plato: the Invention of Philosophy*, London: Phoenix.
—— (1998b) 'What Could Philosophy Become?' (forthcoming).
Williams, J. (1997) 'Deleuze on Turner: Catastrophism in Philosophy?', in K. Ansell-Pearson (ed.) *Deleuze and Philosophy: the Difference Engineer*, Warwick Studies in European Philosophy, London/New York: Routledge.
Williams, R. (1992) 'Hegel and the gods of postmodernity', in P. Berry and A. Wernick (eds) *Shadow of Spirit*, London: Routledge.
Williamson, T. (1996) *Vagueness*, London: Routledge.
—— (1998) 'Iterated attitudes', in T.J. Smiley (ed.) *Philosophical Logic*, Oxford: British Academy, pp. 85–134.
Wilson, V., Jeffreys, A. J., Barrie, P.A. *et al* (1983) 'A comparison of vertebrate interferon genes families detected by bybridization with human interferon', *Journal of Molecular Biology* 166(4): 457–75.
Winkelnkemper, E. (1988) 'The history and applications of open books', in A. Ranicki *High-Dimensional Knot Theory*, Berlin: Springer, pp. 615–26.
Wintle, C. (1985) 'Kontra Schenker: *largo e mesto* from Beethoven's op. No.3', in *Music Analysis* 4 nos 1/2: 145–182.
Witten, E. (1989) 'The search for higher symmetry in string theory', in M. Atiyah *et al.* (eds) *Physics and the Mathematics of Strings: Proceedings of the Royal Society*, London: Royal Society, pp. 349–57.
—— (1996) 'Strong coupling expansion of Calabi-Yau compactification', *Nuclear Physics* B471: 135.
Wittgenstein, L. (1941) [Wittgenstein's handwritten notes in the margins of his copy of G. Hardy, *A Course of Pure Mathematics*, 8th edn, Cambridge: Cambridge University Press, 1941, archives of the Wren Library, Trinity College.].
—— (1963) *Tractatus Logico-Philosophicus*, trans. D.F. Pears and B.F. McGuiness, 2nd cor. impr., London: Routledge.
—— (1974) *On Certainty*, G.E.M. Anscombe and G.H. von Wright (eds), trans. D. Paul and G.E.M. Anscombe, Oxford: Blackwell.
—— (1976) *Wittgenstein's Lectures on the Foundations of Mathematics, Cambridge 1939*, from the notes of R. Bosanquet, N. Malcolm, R. Rhees, and Y. Smythie, Ithaca: Cornell University Press.
—— (1977) *Remarks on Colour*, G.E.M. Anscombe (ed.), trans. L.L. McAlister and M. Schattle, Oxford: Blackwell.
—— (1978) *Remarks on the Foundations of Mathematics*, 3rd edn, G.H. von Wright, R. Rhees, and G.E.M. Anscombe (eds), trans. G.E.M. Anscombe, Oxford, Blackwell.
—— (1980a) *Vermischte Bermerkungen*, Frankfurt-am-Main, (Hereausgeben von G.H. von Wright and M. von H. Nyman, trans. P. Winch, Oxford: Blackwell.
—— (1980b) *Culture and Value*, G.H. von Wright (ed.), trans. P. Winch, Oxford: Blackwell.
—— (1993) *Philosophical Occasions: 1912–1951*, J.C. Klagge and A. Nordmann (eds), Indianapolis/Cambridge: Hackett Publishing.

—— (1995a) *Philosophical Investigations*, trans. G.E.M. Anscombe, Oxford: Blackwell.
—— (1995b) *Philosophical Occasions: 1912–1951* J.C. Klagge and A. Nordmann (eds), Indianapolis/Cambridge: Hackett Publishing.
—— (1996) 'Notes on logic', M.A.R. Biggs (ed.) *Editing Wittgenstein's 'Notes on Logic'*, vols 1 and 2, Working Papers from the Wittgenstein Archives at the University of Bergen, No. 11.
—— (1997) *Philosophical Investigations* (trans. G.E.M. Anscombe), 2nd edn (1998 printing), Oxford: Blackwell.
—— (1998) *The Collected Manuscripts of Ludwig Wittgenstein on Facsimile CD-ROM*, ed. Wittgenstein Archives at the University of Bergen, Oxford: Oxford University Press.
Wodeham, A. (1973) 'Sentences 1, I, I in G. Gal, "Adam of Wodeham's question on the 'complexe significabile' " ', *Franciscan Studies* 37: 66–102.
Woess, W. (2000) *Random Walks on Infinite Graphs and Groups*, Cambridge Tracts in Mathematics 138, B. Bollobas, F. Kirwan, P. Sarnak and C.T.C. Wall (eds), Cambridge: Cambridge University Press.
Wollheim, R. (1993) *The Mind and its Depths*, Cambridge, Mass.: Harvard University Press.
—— (1999) *On the Emotions*, Cambridge, Mass.: Harvard University Press.
Woods, J. (1974) *The Logic of Fiction*, The Hague: Mouton.
Wortley, B.A. (1967) *Jurisprudence*, Manchester: Manchester University Press.
Worton, M. (1986) 'Intertextuality', in D. Kelley and I. Llasera (eds) *Cross-References*, Society for French Studies, Supplementary Publications 8.
Young, F. M. (1994) *The Theology of the Pastoral Letters*. Cambridge University Press.
Yourgrau, W. and Breck, A.D. (eds) (1976) *Cosmology, History and Theology*, New York: Plenum.
Zel'dovich, Ya B. (1979) 'Cosmology and the very early universe', in S.W. Hawking and W. Israel (eds) (1979) *General Relativity*, Cambridge: Cambridge University Press.
Zel'dovich, Ya B. and A.G. Polnarev (1974) 'Radiation of gravitational waves by a cluster of superdense stars', *Soviet Astronomy* 18: 17–23.
Zensus, J.A., Hough, D.H. and Porcast, P.R. (1987) 'Superluminal motion in the double-lobed quasar 3C263', *Nature* 325: 36–38.
Zink, M. (1985) *La subjectivité littéreraire autour du siàcle de Saint Louis*, Paris: Presses Universitaires de France.

Name index

Abelard, Peter 237–38
Addinall, P. 183
Agrawal, S. 221
Aleksander, Igor 238–39, 249
Alexander, D.M. 219
Alexander, P. 109
Altieri, C. 63
Ambrose, Alice 205
Anderson, A.R. 91
Anglin, W.S. 230, 254
Anscombe, G.E.M. 40, 72, 73, 80, 195, 236, 279, 281, 305
Aquinas, Thomas 15, 17, 194
Arecchi, F.T. 26
Aristotle 15, 45–46, 55, 62–65, 81, 90–91, 108, 136, 155, 213, 280, 289, 323
Arp, H. 122
Artaud, A. 310, 311–12, 313
Atiyah, Michael 5, 21, 104
Auerbach, E. 35
Augustine, Saint 5–6, 201, 231

Baez, J.C. 5
Balthasar, H.U. von 231, 242
Balzac, Honoré de 87
Barrow, J.D. 58, 101, 102, 108, 112, 147, 190, 192, 262, 274
Barth, Karl 19, 111, 163, 231, 240, 241, 242
Baudelaire, C.P. 14, 18, 154, 155, 241, 244
Bechtel, W. 138
Beer, G. 319
Bell, J.S. 26, 27, 144, 144–45, 154, 156
Belnap, N.F. 91
Bergeron, J.H. 274, 295
Bergman, Ingmar 34
Berkeley, George 45
Berlin, Isaiah 3
Black, Matthew 292
Black, Max 52, 53
Blandford, R.D. 193
Bohn, Niels 212
Bonhoeffer, Dietrich 281
Boretz, B. 36

Boghossian, Paul 86
Bostock, D. 164
Boukricha, A. 37, 118
Bowett, D.W. 300
Bowie, Malcolm 18, 35, 36, 88, 141, 154, 156, 163, 225, 231, 238, 239, 241, 322
Brock, S.P. 64
Brooke, G.J. 60
Brooke-Rose, Christine 33, 34
Brouwer, Luitzen 48, 49
Brownlie, I. 302
Brummer, V. 106
Buchdahl, G. 109, 151
Budd, M. 158, 241, 246
Buffon, G.L.C.: Comte de 247
Burnyeat, M.F. 45, 90
Butterfield, J. 54, 169

Caird, G.B. 314
Cairns, J. 216–17
Cajetanus 302
Calderon, I.L. 217
Calvin, John 70
Cantor, G. 88, 152, 164, 263
Cappell, S. 167
Caravaggio, Michelangelo 288–89
Carruthers, P. 221
Carter, B. 275
Carter, J.S. 22, 192
Cartwright, N. 182–83
Cavalière, L. 168
Cave, Terence 46, 155
Chandraskhar, S. 190
Chateaubriand, F.R. 14
Chihara, C.S. 57, 171, 172, 197, 260, 261
Chinca, M. 235, 236, 318
Chomsky, N. 145
Clayton, P. 97
Coady, C.A.J. 233, 246
Cohen, L.J. 56, 155, 170, 264, 292, 314
Collier, J. 90, 301
Condillac, E.B. de 246
Copernicus 253

Name index

Corbechon, Jean 60
Craig, E. 182, 245
Crathorn, William of 26
Cremmer, E. 168
Crick, F.H.C. 216
Csernus, Tibor 288–89
Culler, Jonathan 14
Cunningham, A. 11

Dahlhaus, C. 33
Dallaporta, N. 19, 20, 27, 28, 98, 106, 114, 202, 251
Dalton, John 37
Dante, Alighieri 18
Darwin: Charles 214, 319
Dauben, J.W. 164
D'Auria, R. 124
Davidson, D. 51, 57
Davies, G.I. 66
Davies, M. 57, 147
Davies, P.C.W. 110, 261, 262
Davy, Sir Humphrey 133
Dawkins, Richard 214, 219
Day, R.H. 235
De Beauvoir, Simone 83
De Bernardis, P. 30, 187
De Rujula, A. 119–20
Deb, K. 221
Delacroix, Ferdinand 154
Deleuze, G. 245, 313
Dennett, Daniel 219, 238
Denyer, N. 281
Derrida, Jacques 18, 47, 67, 88–89, 130, 140–42, 148, 155, 216, 226–27, 240, 311–12, 313; and metaphor 108, 226, 228
Descartes, René 15, 137, 245, 265
DeWitt, B.S. 199, 200
Diderot, Denis 5
Dirac, Paul 104, 105
Dodd, C.H. 291–92
Dolgov, A.D. 150
D'Ottaviano, I.M.C. 127–8
Dover, G.A. 212, 214, 216, 217, 218, 220
Dummett, M. 111, 125, 192, 200, 255, 256, 257, 259
Duns Scotus, John 25–26
Durkheim, Émile 52, 236
Dworkin, Ronald 253, 277, 278, 283, 290–91, 293, 298
Dyson, F.J. 240

Eban, A. 298
Ebbs, G. 37
Eco, U. 141
Edwards, P.P. 134, 137
Eells, R. 293
Einstein, Albert 20–21, 110, 113, 116, 118, 119, 131, 134, 190, 325; and cosmological constant 146
Eliot, T.S. 43
Ellis, R. 12, 166, 168, 180, 192, 193, 203, 261, 263, 266
Epstein, P.L. 111, 127–28
Erasmus 61
Escher, M.C. 247
Euclid 160
Evans, G. 181
Everett, H.: III 20, 55, 197, 198, 199, 200, 261

Fauconnier, G. 158
Fellers, William 118
Fermat, Pierre de 23, 316
Feynman, R.P. 114
Field, Hartry 17, 272
Fitzpatrick, P. 295
Flaubert, Gustave 155
Florence, P. 161
Force, J.E. 248, 254
Ford, David 238
Forrester, John 237
Foucault, M. 47, 148, 212
Fré, P. 124
Frege, Friedrich 45, 50, 55, 76, 86, 111, 181
Freud, Sigmund 225, 236

Galileo 21
Gardner, R.N. 300
Geach, P.T. 15, 72, 80–81, 135, 136, 196, 236, 266, 271, 279, 280
Geroch, R. 231
Geyer-Ryan, H. 90
Gibson, A. 15, 18, 25, 45, 65, 66, 68, 76, 90, 236, 240, 315
Giddens, A. 44, 234
Goddu, A. 26
Gödel, Kurt 152, 239, 262
Goldhill, S. 298
Gombrich, E.H. 37, 245, 246
Gompf, R.E. 170–71, 172
Goncharov 53
Gott, J.R.: III 126
Gould, Stephen Jay 219
Goulder, M.D. 64
Graham, N. 199
Green, M.B. 118, 156
Greene, Brian 21
Greene, J. 110
Greene, Michael 168
Gross, D.J. 201
Grotius, Hugo 295–99, 302
Guattari, F. 313
Guth, A. 54, 103

Haack, S.A. 158, 198

Hacking, Ian 15, 47, 80, 122, 127, 141, 206, 221, 311; and chance 228; and memory 11, 236, 319
Haggenmacher, P. 296
Haldane, J.B.S. 212
Hale, B. 17, 272
Hall, S.G. 55, 233
Hanson, N.R. 253
Hara, T. 187
Hardy, G.H. 48
Hare, R.M. 279
Harre, Rom 153–54
Hartle, J.D. 112, 170, 193–94, 196, 197, 200
Hawking, Stephen 20, 112–13, 142, 147, 150, 157, 162, 163, 170, 183, 195, 196, 200, 266, 275, 318, 324; and black hole mechanics 12, 180, 191, 192, 194, 195, 197, 203, 263, 272, 313; and cosmological constant 146; and end of the universe 158–59, 317; and expansion of universe 17, 190, 321; and the human brain 115–16; and inflationary universe model 54, 177; and manifolds 167; and multiverse hypothesis 6, 165–66, 178–79; singularity theorem 124, 183–84, 193; and spacetime 168, 169
Hawkins, J.A. 134
Hayashida, H. 218
Hayward, J.D. 157
Hazlitt, W. 39
Heal, Jane 71
Heisenberg, Werner 20
Helm, P. 64, 80–81, 83
Herzfeld, K.F. 134
Hesse, M. 42, 52, 187, 194, 235–36
Hitler, Adolf 281, 304, 306, 309
Hobson, M. 5, 109, 140, 141, 142, 144, 148, 149, 155, 226, 245, 247
Hockman, K.C. 83
Hoffmann, R. 36, 91, 135, 137, 138, 224, 324
Hogan, C. 124
Holland, E.W. 18, 244
Hooker, M.D. 287
Horst, S.W. 25
Hoyle, F. 262
Hu, W. 30
Hubble, Edwin 146, 189
Hughes, Ted 288
Hume, David 79, 182, 228, 245, 246, 247, 248, 254, 279
Huxley, Sir Andrew 33

Isham, C. 54
Israel, W. 194

Jacob, F. 216
James, William 23
Jameson, F. 66
Jardine, N. 11

Jarick, John 318
Jennings, R. 274
Jeremias, J. 292
Jodrell Bank Radio-Astronomy Laboratories 41
John on the Cross 18
Johnson, C. 88, 216
Johnson, D.C. 137
Johnson, M. 110, 313
Josephus, Flavius 286
Jung, Carl Gustav 225

Kaldor, N. 301
Kaluza, 21
Kant, Immanuel 14, 24, 38, 103, 109, 111, 119, 151, 183, 323
Kay, Sarah 236
Kearns, K. 288
Kelley, David 43, 45, 310–11
Kennedy, G.A. 285
Kermode, J.F. 20, 62, 135, 142, 158, 322
Kierkegaard, S.A. 65, 242
Kirkpatrick, F.G. 169, 185
Kopal, Z. 319
Kramer, D. 190
Kretzmann, Norman 15–16, 17
Kripke, S. 60, 75, 130
Krumsansl, J.A. 219
Kumar, K. 235

Lacan, J. 35, 111, 225, 241
Lacoue-Labarthe, P. 162, 241
Lakoff, G. 110, 313
Langer, S.K. 153–54
Laplace, Abbé 12, 206, 263
Lear, J. 263
Levi, I. 23
Lewis, D. 156, 171, 200, 243, 259
Lewy, Casimer 87, 91, 271
Linde, A.D. 6, 53, 99
Lindley, D. 187
Longair, M.S. 30, 122, 177, 186
Lovell, Sir Bernard 21, 299
Lowe, V. 301
Lukács, Georg 35
Lullius 280
Luminet, J.-P. 194
Lyne, A.G. 188
Lyne, Andrew 41
Lyons, J. 264

MacCallum, M.A.H. 189
McDonald, J.I.H. 229
McGinn, Colin 271, 272, 273, 286
McKie, C.F. 124, 192
Mackie, J.L. 279
MacKinnon, D.M. 81, 240, 310

366 *Name index*

McNair, Lord 295, 299
Macquarrie, J. 281, 283, 287, 301, 305
Madsen, Deborah 318
Mallarmé, S. 22, 35, 36, 45, 52, 57, 88, 161, 243, 322
Mann, F.A. 300
Marenbon, John 238
Marion, M. 50, 157, 204–05
Mearns, C.L. 312
Mellor, D.H. 109, 119, 153, 194, 195, 197, 266
Messer, R. 182
Meyer, L.B. 158
Milbank, John 153
Miller, K. 141
Milstein, S. 36
Mirimanoff, D. 262
Miwa, T. 219
Miyata, T. 218
Molesworth, W. 195
Mondrian, Piet 243
Moriarty, M. 111
Moses 72
Mothersill, M. 38, 284
Mozart, Wolfgang Amadeus 163, 240, 241, 282, 322
Mumford, David 158
Mussies, G. 292

Nagel, T. 80, 275, 279, 281
Nehemkis, P. 293
Nerlich, G. 134, 145
Neufeld, D. 66
Neugebauer, G. 190
Newlands, G. 61, 229
Newton, Sir Isaac 116, 190, 246, 248, 254, 257
Nichols, S.G. 15, 17, 236
Nietzsche, Friedrich 10, 79–80
Norris, C. 227
Nussbaum, Martha 281, 300

Oakes, E.T. 242
Ockham, William of 25–29, 113
Ohta, D. 220
Olson, E.C. 116
Orgel, L.E. 216
Ostricker, J.P. 122

Paczynski, B. 120, 122, 125
Parfit, D. 275
Pascal, Blaise 23, 82–83, 316
Pasnau, J. 15, 26
Paxson, J.J. 34
Peacocke, Christopher 165
Pearson, B.W.R. 72
Peebles, P.J.E. 117
Peirce, C.S. 228
Penrose, R. 37, 146, 149, 154, 157, 163, 169, 170, 231, 234, 248–49; and consciousness 238–39; Everett-type universe 197–200; and new physics 152, 184; and singularity 124, 184–85
Pesaran, M.J. 233
Phillips, D.C. 217
Philo 286
Pickstock, Catherine 24–25
Pippin, R.B. 24
Planck, Max 22
Plath, Sylvia 288
Plato 7, 8, 65, 272
Polanco, C. 218
Polchinski, J. 110, 168
Polkinghorne, J. 30, 36, 52, 99, 107, 132, 142, 243, 249
Polnarev, A.G. 184
Polyakov, A.M. 104, 104–05
Popkin, R.H. 248, 254
Popper, K.R. 29, 63, 106, 123, 182, 248, 262
Porter, S.E. 286, 312
Prendergast, C. 62, 63, 87, 155
Preskill, J. 103
Priest, G. 79, 126, 260
Prior, A.N. 76, 80, 196, 200, 259, 260, 262
Proust, Marcel 156, 157

Quine, W.V.O. 179, 262
Quinn, P.L. 264

Ramsey, F.P. 205
Ranicki, A. 167
Rawls, J. 290, 305–06
Ray, T. 215
Redhead, Michael 131
Rees, Sir Martin 21, 22, 84, 103, 112, 147, 166, 184, 251; and metaphysics 19, 20; multiverse hypothesis 6, 53, 99, 113, 148, 159, 165, 180, 200–01, 259, 260; and superstrings 118
Reynolds, D. 35, 242, 243
Reynolds, Sir Joshua 39
Richards, I.A. 53
Richardson, John 10, 30, 79–80
Richardson, R.C. 138
Ricoeur, P. 56
Riffaterre, M. 88
Robbins, V.K. 286
Robinson, J.A.T 312
Rogerson, J.W. 60
Rorty, R. 5, 13, 14, 23, 24, 25, 30, 54, 225, 227; and Aristotle 15, 45, 55, 213; and pragmatism 56, 99
Rosenberg, J. 167
Ross, G.G. 113
Ross, J.F. 118, 134, 136
Rousseau, P.E.T. 246, 247
Rowland, C.C. 229, 320

Rubbia, C. 213
Rucker, R. 180
Rupp, W.D. 217
Russell, Bertrand 168, 206, 250

Saito, M. 22
Salam, A. 20
Sancar, A. 217
Saslaw, W.C. 53, 169
Saunders, W. 29, 187
Schama, Simon 235
Schenkeveld, D.M. 285
Scherbaum, F. 139, 140, 141
Schiffrin, D. 314
Schmidbaur, H. 139, 140, 141
Schopenhauer, A. 141
Schulte-Sasse, J. 35
Schwarz, J.H. 118
Schwarzenberger, G. 302–03
Scott, D. 36
Shakespeare, W. 33
Sherry, R. 61
Shoesmith, D.J. 91, 130, 255
Shohat, E. 54
Sibley, F. 177
Sienko, M.J. 134
Silk, J. 102, 187
Slater, L.J. 233
Smiley, T.J. 45, 90, 91, 111, 130, 158, 250, 255
Smith, John Maynard 219
Smith, G. 41, 188
Socrates 7, 65
Sorensen, R.A. 55, 233, 252, 254
Soskice, J.M. 53, 104, 111
Sraffa, Piero 49, 301
Staël, Mme de 14
Stam, R. 54
Stark, A.A. 131
Stark, C.W. 167
Steiner, George 236, 240, 246
Sternberg, M. 63
Stewart, I. 171
Stewart, J. 112, 192
Strassburg, Gottfried von 318
Stump, Eleonore 136
Swinburne, R. 19, 255
Szondi, P.P. 35

Tachau, K.H. 26
Tassie, L.J. 185
Taylor, Charles 71, 245
Tennant, N. 84
Thaumaturgos, Gregory 318
Thiemann, R.F. 264, 276
Thijsse, E. 130
Thiselton, A.C. 312
Thom, R. 255, 313, 315, 317, 318, 319, 320

t'Hooft, G. 104–05
Thorne, K.S. 124, 125, 132, 164, 177, 193
Tipler, F.J. 108, 112, 169, 190, 192, 231, 248–50, 251, 253, 262; and anthropic principle 58, 274; and cosmological constant 147; and monopoles 101
Torrance, T.F. 51, 225, 256
Trembath, K.R. 65, 70, 81
Trevor-Roper, H. 200, 235
Trullinger, S.E. 218
Truman, H.S. 281
Tuck, R. 296
Turing, A.M. 239
Turner, J.M.W. 313
Turner, M.S. 101, 105, 120, 121, 123
Turok, Neil 6, 142, 150, 159, 165–66, 170, 177, 318, 321

Ulanov, O.N. 280

Van Gogh, Vincent 310–11, 313
Vilenkin, A. 122
Vishniac, E.T. 122
Vlastos, Gregory 8
Von Neumann, J.J. 262

Wada, S. 37, 170
Wagner, Richard 156, 159, 241
Wall, C.T.C. 167
Wang 84
Ward, G. 240–41
Ward, K. 184, 197, 229, 240
Weeks, Jeffrey 22
Weiker, K. 222
Weiker, N. 222
White, R. 276
Whitman, Walt 127, 128
Wilde, Oscar 12, 238, 318
Williams, B.A.O. 4, 12, 77, 224, 231, 251, 271, 279
Williams, J. 313
Williams, R. 18
Williamson, T. 51
Wilson, V. 218
Winkelnkemper, E. 167
Wintle, C. 161–62
Witten, E. 21, 168
Wittgenstein, Ludwig 7, 8, 15, 40, 50, 75, 201, 206, 246, 257, 276, 282; on madness 47–48, 212, 313; and mathematics 48–49, 120, 204–05; and picture theory of language 109–10, 325; theory of propositions 90, 91–92, 124, 127
Woess, W. 72, 164
Wollheim, R. 10
Wolzyzan 42
Wortley, B.A. 305

Worton, M. 97
Wright, G.H. von 280

Young, 60

Zel'dovich, Ya B. 184, 191
Zensus, I.A. 84
Zink, M. 236

Subject index

Note: Italicised page numbers indicate figures

abstraction 8, 63, 123–24, 155, 243, 250; and metaphor 56–57
active galactic nuclei (AGNs) 193
aesthetics 152, 152–53, 154–55, 168, 242, 245, 248, 323–24; and ethics 284; in science 100, 130, 157–58
agencies 281
aid: international 300–01
algorithms 37, 172, 233; genetic 221, 222; Pesaran's 234
Ambassadors, The (Holbein) 149
analogies 22–23, 227, 251–52, 253, 293, 316; in science and linguistics 135–36
analyses 49–50; cultural 325; and sample sizes 135–37
analytical philosophy 3–4, 286
anamorphism 149–50
ancient Greeks: and modernity 12; philosophy and literature 285–87
angels: as agents of God 65–68, 71–73, 77
anthropic principle 6, 58, 274–76, 321
anthropomorphism 58–59, 182, 227, 235, 253; evolutionary 59; propositions 68–70; rebirth 60–62
anti-realism 25–26, 52, 171; and Ockham's razor 28–29; and ontology 29; and parsimony 26–27; and realism 86–87, 192
Apocalypse 302, 310–13, 317, 319–21
Apocalypse, The 312
Aristotelian mimesis 62–65, 155, 157
Aristotelian philosophy 285, 289–90, 296, 323
Aristotle's theory of implication 45
art 108, 154, 157, 226, 240, 243, 246, 288–89, 324; counter-intuitive 313; and live metaphor(s) 225
arts: and cosmology 58, 91–93, 154–55, 193; and sciences 5, 11–12, 19, 23, 89–90, 97–98, 139–41, 324–25; and theology 19
arts—sciences reciprocity 33–37, 87–88
astronomy 319; beliefs and intentions 82–87; and metaphoric language 40, 42
astrophysics 19–20, 34, 58, 97, 106, 116, 125, 175, 185, 200, 224, 284, 319; and local

physics 104; and mathematics 172; as metaphysics 27; research 211; as a science 114; theories of 203; and uncertainty principle 194
asymmetrical replication 69
asymmetry: in early universe 30; and live metaphor 86; and semantics 71
atheism 13, 77, 126, 201, 202, 205, 212, 231, 309; and reductionism 79–80
atoms 115

Beatitudes, the 287
beauty: in mathematics and music 36–37
belief(s) 79–82, 245, 247, 312
Bell's theorem 26
Bible, the 45, 61, 89, 201, 297, 315, 319; and God's identity 65–68, 223
big bang 101, 173–76, 248, 251, *252*; and eternal universe conception 5–6; hot big bang models 174, 176; hypothesis 27; and infinity 165; and Schrödinger's equation 37, 118; and string theory 23
binary pulsars 42
biology 58, 106, 190; and entropy 211–14
bizarreness 8, 9
black holes 55, 125, 157, 159, 168, 178–80, 184–85, 203, 220, 313, 317; creation and reversal 194; extremal and non-extremal 191–92; and mathematics 12, 263; as miraculous objects 190; primordial (PBH) 191–92, 195, 203, 206; supermassive 124, 190–95
Boomerang project 30, 187, 188, 252
Boötes galaxy 84–85
borders *see* boundaries
boundaries: cosmological 231, 263, 316, 321; personal and national 282, 295
brain: human 115–16
Brouwer's pendulum 48–49

calculus 82–83, 89, 91, 163, 203
capacities 183

carbon bonding 138–40
Cartesian dualism 15
catastrophe 313, 315–16, 318; mathematics 55, 313–16, 319–21; models 316; theory 218, 254
Cauchy developments 266
causality 161, 166, 183, 186, 194; and indeterminacy 197–207; of the universe 195–97
CDM *see* cold dark matter
chance 202–04, 206, 228, 247, 254; and foreknowledge 228–29
chaos 58–59, 181, 204, 211, 221, 225, 226, 239, 317, 322, 324; theory 33
chemistry 190, 324
Christ *see* Jesus Christ
Christianity 37, 231, 236, 240, 250, 297, 312; and creation 197; and ethics 279, 286, 290, 309; and international peace 294–95; in modern society 43–44; theology of 284, 288, 323; and transcendence 79; and use of violence 297, 302
Christology: and identity 66
cold dark matter (CDM) 84, 122, 187, 188
communication 35
complexity theory 30, 175, 204
compounds: new 137–38
comprehension: and rules 49–50
computer programs 215, 230, 233
concepts: and understanding 50–51
Confessions (Augustine) 61
connections: interdisciplinary 22, 38–39; and logic 16
consciousness 59, 111, 115, 120, 238–39, 246, 322, 323; and Cartesian dualism 15; and devolution 221; and evolution 32; false 79, 80; and language 50–51; and scientific metaphors 33; shifts 47
consequence 89, 91, 130, 154, 317
constant: cosmological 146–52
constructivism 49
continuities: between past and future 18; in history 14–15
correspondence theory 10, 30–31, 79–80, 171
'Correspondences' (Baudelaire) 18
Cosmic Censorship Hypothesis 192
cosmic strings 124–32, *131*
cosmology 124, 175, 198, 211–12, 277, 311–12, 316–17, 319–21, 323; and arts 58, 91–93; astrophysical 19–20, 34, 125, 140, 157, 167, 251, 284; black hole 125; and counter-intuition 183–85; and cultural history 11; definition 3; and devolution 214–16; divine 114, 125, 131, 224; and foreknowledge 231–32; legal 294–309; and literature 154–57; as a live metaphor 53; and local physics 40; and logic 191, 199–200; mathematical 117–18, 231; metaphorical 39–42; metaphysical elements 20, 132; and music 152–63, 324; observational 31, 272; and Ockham's razor 25–28; philosophical 33; and proper/improper suppositions 28; and quantum mechanics 199–200; research 211; as a science 105–07, 114; scientific 52, 249; and transcendence 35, 324
Cosmology Principle (in reference to Cold Dark Matter) 186–87, 197
counter-intuition 38–39, 87, 126, 171, 185, 207, 323, 324; and cosmology 103–04, 183–85; and creativity 151–63; and foreknowledge 230; and strangeness 8–9
Coup de dés, Un (Mallarmé) 22, 45, 52, 57, 66, 92, 161, 228, 243
CP *see* Cosmology Principle
creation 101, 142, 166, 173, 184–85, 194; after death 315–16; and God 199, 276; and uniformity 186, 189–90
creative language 13
creative literature: and logic 57
creativity 10, 128, 130, 142, 239, 319; counter-intuitive 39, 151–63
Critique of Judgement (Kant) 153, 163
cross-connections between disciplines 10, 12
crystallographic theory 91
cultural history: and cosmology 11
cultural patterns: and switches 6–7
cultural philosophy 4
cultural symbolism 239
culture 44–45, 245; technological 222
Cygnus *x*–1 184, 189

'Daddy' (Plath) 288
Darwinism 214
De l'Allemagne (de Staël) 14
De oratore (Cicero) 285
De topicis differentiis (Boethius) 136
Dead Sea Scrolls 66
deconstruction 88, 311–12, 313; and evolution 216; and reductionism 18
definitions 56
democracy 281–82; and warfare 305–06
density 194, 203; infinite 200
determinism 26, 234, 261
devolution 218–20, 322; and consciousness 221; and cosmology 214–16; and entropy 215; and genetic drift 220–21
Dialogues Concerning Natural Religion (Hume) 228
dimensions 21–22, 108–09, 110–11, 113–14, 183; and strings 117–20
dipole magnetic theory 102, 104
Discours qui a remporté la prix a d'Academie de Dijon (Rousseau) 246
discourse 51; and international peace 294–95; religious 52, 240, 245; scientific 97
divinity 109, 125–26, 245, 247, 252
DNA 70–71, 125, 214, 215, 216, 220;

cancerous 216–17, 220; fingerprinting 220; ghost 217; and soliton theory 218–19
dramatic representation 65
Drosophila melanogaster 218
dynamic models 234

Earth 211, 213, 253, 261
Ecclesiastes 309, 318
economics/economies 233, 239, 240, 282, 299–301; and violence 300–01
EEC (European Economic Community) 299, 300, 301
Einstein field equations 180, 194
electricity: and monopoles 104
electromagnetic energies 105
emotions 10, 241–42
empiricism 131, 186; provisional 125–26; and transcendence 3
energy 263, 316; and entropy 211, 213; finite 198; as matter 196–97, 263
energy-density 169–70, 204
Enquiry (Hume) 246
enthymemes 82, 90–91, 101, 113, 136
entropy 166, 170, 181, 184, 195, 198, 206, 214, 219, 318, 321; biological 211–14, 215; devolutionary 218; and Neo-Darwinism 213–14; of primordial black holes 195, 204, 206
Épaves, Les (Baudelaire) 244
Epic of Gilgamesh 18
epistemology 59, 131, 141, 163; and Ockham 25
equations 49, 113, 142, 177, 185, 234, 317; Prior-Fine 256
eras: of the universe 193
Esais (Montaigne) 316
eschatology 55, 283, 312, 319, 321; and values 57–59
eschaton 283–84, 302, 314, 315, 316, 318, 319, 320, 321
Essenes 80
ethical theory 4
ethics 271–72, 278–80, 292–93; and material distribution 290, 299–300; and New Testament 285–91; transcendent 282–85; and warfare 280–82, 307–09
Euclidean geometry 187, 200
Euclidean space 112–13, 159, 167
Everett-type universe 197–98, 200
evil 291–93
evolution 216–22, 322; biological 211–12, 213, 221; catastrophe in 218; and deconstruction 216; and entropy 211–12, 216; inorganic 211–12; in reverse 214–15, 217, 220; theories of 58, 105, 166, 211, 214–16, 218, 219, 222
Exodus 66, 77
Experiences touchant le vide (Pascal) 82
experiments 106–07, 115, 116, 137, 145

externalism 275–76
extinction: of species and genera 216

'fact stereotypes' 134
fallibilism: of science 99
falsehoods: and truths 47–48
falsification 106, 121–3
famine 299, 300
Fellers' one-dimensional theory 118
Fermat's last theorem 9
Fibonacci series 204, 206
film(s)as live metaphor 56, 107, 110, 242; philosophy of 35; and realism 66; and relative identity 246; and simulation 68, 244
finances: international 297–98
finitism 157, 167, 195, 204
flat earth concept 21
Fleurs du mal, Les (Baudelaire) 14, 18, 244
foreknowledge 232–33, 237, 256; and chance 228–29; and cosmology 231–32; divine 266–67, 276, 277; and the incarnation 261–62; and probability 229–30; and time 259–60; and virtual reality 242–55
fractional orbit bombardment satellites (FOBS) 299
free will 234, 284
Funderungsaxiom 202, 278
future (the) 226, 227–28, 239–42, 264–67; as counter-intuitive mimesis 242–44; and the past 18, 57–58, 116–17, 236–37; relationship with past and present 10–11, 224–25, 240, 322; as a virtual computer program 230–31; and virtual reality 244–45

galaxies 30, 122, 191, 218; Boötes 84–85; formation 187
gender: codes 289–90; typology 61
general relativity 118, 124, 146, 156, 176–77, 179, 181, 191, 215, 316; breakdown 194; and creation 184; and the future 230–31; and live metaphors 112; and prediction 234; and pulsars 188; renaissance 20, 110
generalisation 137–41, 171, 172, 235, 273, 323
generality 161; and observation 180–85; and singularity 32–33
Genesis: and creation 60–61, 183
genetic drift 213, 214; and devolution 220–21
genetics: algorithms 221, 222; lost history 218; reproductive 70–73, 313; research 214
genomes 211, 214, 215, 216–17
genotypes 214
geology 116
geometry 52, 109, 110, 112, 120, 159, 171; Einsteinian 172; Euclidean 187; and manifolds 166; in molecular structure 135; spacetime 185

Subject index

global hyperbolicity 266
God: and creation 23, 197, 199; in early Christianity 58; existence of 13, 59, 125, 164, 165, 182, 206, 224, 263, 277, 280; and foreknowledge 224–25, 228–30, 234, 239, 244, 253, 254; and humanity 182–83; identity of 60–65, 256; and intentionality 237–38; knowledge of 73–75, 146; as a live metaphor 225, 248; manifestation of 65–68; and mathematical functions 49; and multiverse hypothesis 200–01; nature of 223–24; proper name of 76–77; and Romanticism 14; routes to 167; and science 61–62, 178–80; and society 235–36; and the universe 38, 176; Word of 263
Gödel's incompleteness theorems 38, 87, 92, 126, 146, 156, 172
Gospels, the 286, 287, 288, 291, 309; *see also* John; Luke; Mark; Matthew; New Testament
Grand Unified Theories (GUT) 15–16, 54, 105, 148–49, 185
gravitational lensing 121–22, 124
gravity 110, 113, 131, 148–49, 166, 170, 191, 316; *see also* quantum gravity
Gravity's Rainbow (Pynchon) 33

hadron era 193
Hebrews (NT) 75, 287
history 59, 240, 312, 316, 318–19; and continuities 14–15; and poetry 61; and social prediction 234–35
holism 25
holograms 107
humanities: and live metaphor 20; and science 19, 32–33, 52
humanity 58–59, 93, 235–36, 322; evolution of 218
hypotheses 128

ideas 15, 245
identity 81–82, 125, 250, 323, 324, 325; collective 235, 237; counter-intuitive 211; and DNA 220; and gender codes 289–90; in genetic reproduction 70–73, 134–35; and history 14; individual 284, 318; intentional 80, 86; and live metaphor 107; of metals 132–41; and personification 65–68, 72; and proper names 75–79, 111, 137; shared 71–73, 272; transworld 57, 172
ideology 59, 304–05
idioms 54–55
illusion 245, 246, 248
imagination 235, 239, 246, 247, 248, 324
imaging 220, 226, 243
imitation: and meaning 60–65; *see also* mimesis

Importance of Being Earnest, The (Wilde) 238, 318
incarnation: and foreknowledge 261–62
indeterminacy: and causality 197–207
indeterminate theology 73–75
individualism/individuality 235, 237, 259–64, 281, 284
inferences 213
Inferno (Dante) 18
infinity 126–27, 142, 163, 164–66, 174, 179–80, 182, 195–96, 204–06, 240, 262–63; mathematical 73, 204; and observation 176–80; virtual 115–16
inflationary universe model 54
intelligibility: universal 37–38, 42
intentionality 69–70, 73–74, 73–75, 77–78, 235, 264; astronomical 83–85; problems of 80–83; and religious belief statements 86
International Military Tribunal of Nuremberg 303
Investigations (Wittgenstein) 40, 91–92
iron 134, 135
irrealism 86–87
isomorphism of man and God 71

Jesus Christ 256, 279, 280, 283; and Aristotelian ethics 288, 289–90; and foreknowledge 229; and God's identity 65; identity of 68; name of 78; precepts of 291–93, 294–95, 300; and Sermon on the Mount 286–88
John, Gospel of 36, 66, 78, 280
Judaism 285–87
just wars 281, 301–09
justice 285–91

Kant's science 150–51
killing: and war 305–09
knot theory 104, 167–68
knowledge 50–51, 248, 267, 271–72, 319; of the future 264–67; and virtual reality 248–51; without experience 282–83

La femme rompue (de Beauvoir) 83
language-consciousness 33–34, 35–36, 39
language(s) 23, 50, 59, 61–62, 82, 91, 93, 115, 246; biblical 61, 313; and cosmology 61, 173–76; creative 13, 43, 45; interrelation between arts and sciences 11–12, 141–46; mathematical 50, 156, 191; of music 22, 36–37, 241–42; religious 34–35; scientific 13, 23, 28–29, 97–163, 142–64, 190–91; theory of 109, 110, 325; transcendent 93, 183
law(s) 276–77, 289–90, 324; causal 202, 247, 264; collapse of 194; criminal 287, 307; economic 297–98; EEC codes of practice 299–300; formulation of 179, 192–93, 202;

international 274, 281, 290, 295, 295–300, 307; of logic 198; material/physical 177, 181, 184, 186, 201, 202–03; of nature 227; scientific 190, 317; social theory of 283; universal 202, 203, 206, 263; and warfare 302–09
leitmotifs 162, 163
lepton era 193
Lie algebra 124, 219
life: biological 108; identity of 220; organic 211; origins of 33, 214, 215; and survival 314–15
light 160, 180, 200, 226, 316, 317; theories of 42, 155–56, 187; velocity of 41, 84, 149, 168, 170, 230
light cones 200, 243, 316
linguistics: and terminologies 56
literalism 60–61
literature: ancient 286; French 246, 247; medieval 318
live metaphor(s) 56–58, 57, 86, 101, 313–14, 319; in art and music 225, 241–42; in cosmology 103–04, 146–49, 146–52; in genetics 70–71, 220; and language-consciousness 33–34; and logic 68; and mimesis 62–65, 154–56; and mirroring 141–46; and narratives 63; schizoid 120–24, 134; scientific 52–53, 105–06, 107–10, 112, 132–34, 227, 243; shifts 104–05, 106–07, 136, 193; in theology 227, 243; of transcendence 223–27
live metaphor(s) in philosophy 13, 65, 140
live metaphor(s) in theology 248
logic 16, 124, 158, 247, 249–50, 260, 264–65, 297, 315; causal 196; and cosmology 191, 199–200; and creativity 45, 57, 90; and enthymemes 90; of the future 255–56; and language 57, 136; laws of 198; as live metaphor 56, 68, 145, 323; and mathematics 50–51, 168; and music theory 36; philosophical 79, 89; and pragmatism 55–56; and Sermon on the Mount 286
logico-linguistics 66
love: and conflict 302; and mimesis 288
Luke: Gospel of 284, 285, 290

M-theory 110, 168, 173, 176, 240; *see also* superstrings, theory
madness 47–52, 212, 311, 313
magnetism 100–5
manifolds 113, 163, 164–72, 173, 251, 255, 275, 321
Mark: Gospel of 127
mathematics 49, 73, 92, 128, 272, 280, 324; applied 172; and black holes 12, 263; catastrophe 55, 313–16, 319–21; Hamiltonian 219; of knots and strings 21; and language(s) 50; and live metaphor 27, 117, 146, 323; and logic 50–51, 168; and

music 36–37; philosophy of 17, 92, 120, 272, 273; pure 49, 123, 164, 165, 167, 168, 172
matter 197, 261; and energy 2, 196–97, 263, 317, 320; and uniformity 186–90
Matthew: Gospel of 75, 78, 285, 287, 290, 291, 292, 293, 302
medievalism 12, 14–15, 17, 18, 235–36
Melchizedez Scroll 66
memory 80, 236–37, 319
mental states/disorders 127–28, 212, 236–37, 310–11
metalanguages 90, 168, 250
metals: identity 132–41
metaphor(s) 53, 104, 108, 155, 251–52, 314, 319; artistic 40; and astronomical hypothesis 42; clinical 47, 212; in cosmology 20; dead 53, 56, 101, 102; literary 33, 110; mathematical 27; metonymy 110–11, 112–13; and realism 52–54; scientific 33, 100–01; and symbolism 57; *see also* live metaphor(s)
metaphoric shifts 21, 42, 100–01, 102, 106–07
metaphorisation 101
metaphysical cosmology 20
Metaphysical Foundation of Natural Science (Kant) 190
metaphysics 59, 63, 103, 120, 185, 202, 279; and astrophysics 27; and creative literature 286; and evolutionary biology 213; and probability 228
Metaphysics (Aristotle) 323
metonymy 110–12
microphysics 27, 31
Middle East 254, 257, 258; conflicts 304–05, 310
Milky Way 189
mimesis 87, 232; counter-intuitive 242–44; and live metaphor 62–65, 154–55; and love 288; status of 63–65
mind: God's 245; human 212, 221, 322; philosophy of 23, 83, 225; and quantum gravity 115–16; and transcendence 225
miracles 184, 206, 228
miraculous objects 189–90
Mirror of Nature (Rorty) 31
mirroring 113, 138, 141–46, 150–51, 227; interdisciplinary 34–35; music and words 241–42
models: catastrophe 316; dynamic 234; of the future 233, 244, 248
modernism 37, 155, 225, 244–45, 296, 322–23; and arts and sciences 19; and Christianity 43–44; and medievalism 14–15, 17, 18; in physics 26; and religion 44; and the Renaissance 18
molecular drive 214, 215–16, 217, 219; in reverse 220
molecular structures 135–36, 217

Subject index

monopoles 100–07, *102*, 104–05
morality 289–90, 296; and ideology 304–05; and warfare 308–09
morphogenesis 313, 320
motion 190
multi-disciplinary collaboration 239–42
multidimensions 118–20
multiple personalities 47, 80, 127, 141, 311, 312
multiverse 5–7, 53, 99, 113, 148, 165, 166, 180–81, 186, 201, 211–12, 259, 265, 272; and big bangs 174; and black holes 159; and God 200–01, 224; origins 29, 170, 176–77, 181–83; transcendent 171, 202
murder: and warfare 306–09
music: aesthetics 33; and cosmology 177, 324; language of 22, 36, 37; and mathematics 36–37; Mozart's 231, 241–42; theory of 36; and transcendence 88
mystery 166

Name of the Rose (Eco) 33, 34
names: and identity 71–73, 108, 111, 181; origins 60; proper 75–79, 111, 137, 227; quasi- 80; theological 75–79; transcendency 78–79
narratives 62–63, 276–80; biblical 66; literary 87, 92; and live metaphor 63; and logic 57; and philosophy 285–87
natural science 264
natural selection 213
natural theology 19
Neo-Darwinism 213–14, 215, 216
networks 142, *143*, 226, 311
neutron star pulses 40–42, *41*
New Testament 66, 75, 280, 281, 284, 285, 289, 290, 291–92, 312, 313; and use of violence 296–97, 302, 303, 309
Newtonian theory of gravity 32, 115, 215
Nichomachean Ethics (Aristotle) 289
Nietzsche's system 79
non-realism 52, 53
non-resistance doctrine 302–03
nothingness 112–13, 196–97
novels: palimpsest 33–34
nucleides 190
numbers: and randomness 52

observation(s) 83–85, 114, 116, 123, 180–85, 192; and infinity 176–80
'Obsession' (Baudelaire) 18
Ockham's philosophy 28–29
Ockham's razor 25–28, 29, 113
Old Testament 18, 72, 75–76, 78, 287, 291, 297, 313
omniscience 234, 237, 250
ontology(ies) 25, 163, 251, 260, 314; and anti-realism 29; counter-intuitive 172; and creation 197; and scientific language 107; and semantic theory 28–9
Ordinatio (Ockham) 27
originality 47–52
origins: physical 169, 169–72
Other, the 71, 164
Outer Space Treaty (1967) 299
overlaps between disciplines 130–32

pacificism 302
paintings 39, 225, 240, 242, 246, 288–89, 311, 313; abstract 63, 243; *see also* art
paraconsistent logic 127–29
paraphrases 55–56, 81
parsimony: and anti-realism 26–27
particle mechanics 194
particle physics 197
particle theory of light 187
particles 104–05, 185
past (the) 32, 54–56, 244; and the future 10–11, 18, 57–58, 230, 236–37, 240; lost 217; reinterpretation 45–46
patterns: cosmological 190, 224–25, 232; and creation 197; historical 254; in literature and science 144–46; of past, present and future 224–25, 239
peace: and ethics 279, 280–85; international 294–97, 298–99; and warfare 305–09
Pensée (Pascal) 23
perception: and exotic science 87–89
personification: and representation 65–68
phenomena: exotic 124
Philippians 75
Philosophical Investigations (Wittgenstein) 78, 325
philosophy 3–5, 7–10, 35, 50, 140, 286; future 14–17, 224; and literary narrative 285–87; of mathematics 17, 92, 120, 272, 273; medieval 14–15; of mind 23, 83, 225; religious 17, 19, 23, 80, 225, 248, 254; and theology 15–17
photographs: as metaphors 53, 57, 107, 324–25
photons 220
physical science 19
physico-metaphysics 106
physics 98, 164, 167, 243; counter-intuitive 151–52, 184–85; and ethics 275; laws of 201; local 20, 40, 104, 160, 325; mathematical 203; and modernism 26; new 118, 169, 184, 194, 212; spacetime 185; superstring 185
Piano Sonata Op. 10: No. 3 (Beethoven) 161
Planck mass/energy 19, 27–28, 201
planets 42, 101
Platonism 17, 273, 277, 285
Poetics (Aristotle) 45, 61, 62, 107, 108, 232, 323

Subject index

poetry 17, 43, 61, 63, 154, 242, 322; French 18, 22, 35, 44–45, 88, 243
poles: magnetic 100–03; monopoles 100–07
politics/politicians 278, 281, 282, 294–5, 298–300, 311
possibilities 64, 126, 173, 197, 204, 206, 265, 284; empirical and transcendent 140, 140–01; true and false 126–32
post-structuralism: and arts and sciences 19; and cosmology 175–76; ending of 30–34; and imperialism 13–14; and metalanguages 90; renaissance of 17; replacement 38–39
postmodernism 88–89, 244–45, 325
potassium 133–34
pragmatism 23, 99; and live metaphor 314; and logic 55–56
precepts 291–93, 294–95, 300
prediction 227–33, 255–58, 264, 273, 276, 324; and general relativity 234; logical 255; social 233–42
premises 82, 90, 101, 287
primordial black holes (PBH) 191, 195, 203, 206
Prior Analytics (Aristotle) 45
Prisonnière, La (Proust) 156
probability 64, 158, 183, 206, 324; and foreknowledge 229–30, 232; and metaphysic 228; and Pascal 23; pattern of 63
properties: classification of 138; as a function 161; shared 71
propositions 68–70, 84–85, 87, 91, 124, 136, 144, 181, 255–57, 259–61, 280; definitions (Stage I) 81–82; definitions (Stage II) 89–91; incorrect 84–86, 86; mathematical 92; true and false 125–28
prosopopeia 61
proteins 217
protons 190
Psalms 66, 71, 276
psychoanalysis 35, 225
psychohistory 288
pulsars 40–42, 187–89
puns: contractual 76

quantum energy 197
quantum era 193, 195, 196
quantum field theory 33, 179, 198
quantum gravity 21, 22, 112, 113–14, 124, 149, 159, 215, 313; and creation 173, 183, 196, 197, 206; and gravity 191; and mind 115–16
quantum mechanics 19, 20, 42, 92, 115, 131, 144, 150, 152; and cosmology 199–200; and particles 194, 197; and relativity 191
quantum physics 181, 183
quantum vacuum 147, 170
quasars 120–24, *121*, 189, 193; Boötes 84–85

radiation 189, 191, 192, 213
'random walks' theory 164
randomness 52, 58–59, 181, 211, 219, 221
rationality 128–29
realism 131, 165, 171, 243; counter-intuitive 5, 86–87, 154; and epistemology 25; filmic 66; future 34–36; and language 190–91; of metaphor 52–54; and non-realism 53; and theory of truth 10
reality 204, 237, 310; external 282; and virtual reality 35, 239, 240, 251
recognition 46, 155, 276–77, 324
redshifts 29, 30, 122, 181, 189, 321
reductionism 13, 18, 25, 26, 29, 79
Reissner-Nördstrom solution 178, 179, 180
relationism 169
relative-identity 36, 125–26, 246
relativism 169, 176
relativity 110–11, 146, 176, 191; cultural 17, *see also* general relativity
relevance 42–44; and irrelevance 7
religion 4, 65; language of 34–35; and modernism 44; philosophy of 17, 19, 23, 80, 225, 254
renaissance: future 14–15, 17, 38–39, 325
Renaissance of General Relativity, The (Dallaporta) 19
Renaissance, the 17, 18, 44–45, 100, 288–89
Requiem (Mozart) 322
resurrection 283, 284, 315, 316
revelation 72–73, 179, 229, 262, 263, 266–67, 276, 277, 315; live metaphoric 87–93; properties of 69–70; and transcendence 88
Revelation (NT) 316, 319, 320
Rhetoric (Aristotle) 45, 108, 111
rights: civil/human 278, 290, 291, 292, 310
Ring, The (Wagner) 159, 162
RNA 219
Romanticism 14, 296
'Rules of Reasoning' (Newton) 248

Satanic Verses, The (Rushdie) 34
Schrödinger's equation 37, 118, 194
science fiction 128, 203
science(s) 19, 23–24, 128–29, 192, 223; and aesthetics 100, 130, 157; and arts 5, 11–12, 19, 23, 87, 89–90, 97–98, 139–41, 324–25; and ethics 271–72; and humanities 19, 32–33, 52; language of 13, 28–29, 97–163; and live metaphors 39–42, 52–53, 98, 100–01, 105, 132–34; reciprocity with arts and humanities 32–35, 87–88; and theology 19, 248
Second World War 304, 309
Seine in Thaw, The (Monet) 225
self-consciousness 236, 322
self-defence 303–5, 307–08
self-interest 295–96, 299–301
semantics 54–55, 71, 76, 80, 260, 292, 314–15,

Subject index

318; and multiple personalities 47; theory of 28–29
Sermon on the Mount 277, 280, 285–91, 302, 303
shifts: of theory and language 80, 117; *see also* metaphoric shifts
silence: and space 159–61
simplicity 25–26, 29
simulation 68–70, 248, 249
singularity 27–28, 124, 164, 177, 183, 184–85, 318; and generality 32–33; and particles 194; theological 285; theorem 183–84
social science 233–35
society 233–42, 322
Socrates (Vlastos) 8
sodium 133–34, 135
soliton theory 218–19
'Song of Myself' (Whitman) 127
sound 160, 177
Sources of the Self (Taylor) 232
space 107, 110, 112, 166–69; and silence 159–61
space warps 124
spacetime 57–58, 61, 92, 110–14, 156, 160, 165, 167, 168, 230, 316; breakdown of 202, 273; and evolutionary biology 213; metaphoric 89; multidimensional 21, 173; quantification of 99; theories 169–70
speculation: counter-intuitive 271–73
speech acts 66, 69
stars 12, 101, 104, 159, 317, 319; binary 187–9
Stoic logic 52
strings: and big bang 23; cosmic 124–32; and dimensions 117–20; theory 21, 22, 120, 162, 201
structures: agency 281; exotic 173, 200; mathematical 273–74; spiral 218
subatomic particles 118
subjectivity 80–81, 82
substantivism 169
Summa (Aquinas) 36
Summa contra gentiles (Aquinas) 15
Summa theologiae (Aquinas) 15
superalgebras 162–63
supergravity 53, 163, 168, 183
superluminal motion 84–85
supermanifolds 149, 200, 234
supermasses 122
superphysics 149, 202, 233, 234, 251
superspace 170, 316
superstrings 40, 42, 118–20, 163, 185–86; and black holes 193; theory 21, 110, 120, 168, 173, 176
supersymmetry 119, 161, 182, 183
surgery theory 167–68
survival 314–15
switches: and cultural patterns 6–7
syllogisms 136
symbolism 52, 57, 236, 239

symmetry 71, 201
Symposium (Plato) 8
systems 4, 317; and complexity 30; Derrida's 88; macrobiological 211; medieval 8; multiple-copy 218; Nietzsche's 10, 79–80; organic and inorganic 313; in science and philosophy 10; spacetime 169

teleology 214–16, 226, 284, 285
teleonomy 220, 221
television: and identity 68, 250
theatre 310
theism 92
theological reductionism 79–80
Theological Science (Torrance) 35
theology 132, 198, 248, 309, 325; and arts and sciences 19, 125–26; Christian 284, 323; indeterminate 73–75; natural 17, 19, 36–37; philosophical 89; and philosophy links 15–17; post-modern 18; post-structuralist 15; traditional 17
theophany 201
Théorie de la terre (Buffon) 247
theories 7, 10, 17, 21, 29, 30–31, 35, 36, 98–99, 100, 264
Theory of Everything (TOE) 20, 21, 27, 29, 185, 250
thought 8, 34, 59, 181, 237
thought-bridges 20, 49, 165
thought-experiments 164, 201, 233, 249, 253–55
time 107, 112, 153, 166, 181, 194, 200, 316, 317; asymmetry 198, 200; and big bang 173, 195, 198; emergence of 54; and entropy 213; and foreknowledge 259–60; reversal of 184, 194; in spacetime 61, 110; zero (t_0) 150, 185, 195, 231
time-geography 44
time machines 126
time travel 156, 179, 180, 265–66
Tokyo Tribunal 303
Topics (Aristotle) 45, 136
topologies 92, 166, 171, 183, 197, 255, 318
Tractatus (Wittgenstein) 91–92, 109, 246, 325
tradition: and originality 51–52
Traite des systèmes (Condillac) 246
transcendence 73, 93, 156, 179, 226–27, 247, 249, 264, 276, 319, 324; and cosmology 35, 149–50, 200; definition of 3; divine 191; and the mind 225; and modern society 44–45; of names 78–79; realist 23; and revelation 88; and traditional theology 17
transcendentalism 5, 187
treaties: international 299
Treatise (Hume) 246
truth 13, 32, 91, 179, 181, 191, 214, 232, 278; abstract 272–73; correspondence theory

79–80; and cultural relativity 17; and falsehood 47–48
Truth in Painting, The (Derrida) 226
typology 161, 236, 277

UN Conference of Trade and Development (1968) 301
UN Security Council 305
uncertainty principle 115, 194
unconsciousness 225, 237–38
understanding 50–51, 152
uniformity 186–90, 264
universality 32–33
universals: theistic 282–83
universe(s) 186, 195–97, 204, 273–76, 317; as allegory 318–21; as an intentional object 73–74; asymmetries of 166, 190; baby 93, 313; boundaries of 170, 231, 263, 316, 321; creation 101, 105, 183–84, 189–90, 193, 194, 234; density of 117–20; early 27, 29–30, 37–38, 101, 184, 185, 201, 213; ending of 158–59, 315–17, 318–19; expansion 17, 103, 146, 190; and God 38, 165; histories 193–94; origins 6, 22, 28–29, 54, 55, 150–51, 157, 159, 160, 165, 170, 181–83, 202–07, 233, 250–51; transcendent 260–61; and virtual infinity 115–16, 180–1
'Untitled' (Csernus) 288–89

V (Pynchon) 249, 318
vacuums 112, 147, 150, 197
Vineland (Pynchon) 33, 34, 249, 318
violence 291–93, 301–05
virtual reality 35, 239, 240; and foreknowledge 242–55

war 310–11; justification for 281, 301–05; and killing 305–09
'War Games' 249
Waste Land, The (Eliot) 43
wave-particle theories of light 42
wave theory 187
wavefunction 197, 200
white dwarfs 41–42
white holes 184
Word, the 51, 250, 256, 315
worlds: many 262–63
worldviews 18, 46, 88–89
wormholes 148, 149, 164, 179, 180, 191–92, 200, 313, 317

Yahweh (YHWH): as proxy for God 65–68, 72, 74, 75–78

Zeitgeist 7
Zone (Apollinaire) 43